English Language Education

Volume 33

This series publishes research on the development, implementation and evaluation of educational programs for school-aged and adult learners for whom English is a second or additional language, including those who are learning academic content through the medium of English. The series has a dual focus on learners' language development and broader societal and policy-related issues, including the implications for teachers' professional development and policy support at the institutional and system level. The series seeks to engage with current issues in English language teaching (ELT) in educational institutions from a highly situated standpoint, examining theories, practices and policies with a conscious regard for historical lineages of development and local (re)contextualisation. By focusing on multiple educational contexts and adopting a comparative perspective, the series will transcend traditional geographical boundaries, thus will be relevant to both English-speaking countries and countries where English is a very much an additional, but important language for learning other content. This series will also cross disciplinary and methodological boundaries by integrating sociocultural and critical approaches with second language acquisition perspectives and drawing on both applied linguistics and educational research. In drawing together basic and applied policy-related research concerns, the series will contribute towards developing a more comprehensive, innovative and contextualized view of English language education internationally. Authors are invited to approach the Series Editor with ideas and plans for books.

Ahmed Sahlane • Rosalind Pritchard
Editors

English as an International Language Education

Critical Intercultural Literacy Perspectives

 Springer

Editors
Ahmed Sahlane (iD)
English Language Institute
University of Jeddah
Jeddah, Saudi Arabia

Rosalind Pritchard
Faculty of Arts, Humanities & Social
Sciences
Ulster University
Coleraine, UK

ISSN 2213-6967   ISSN 2213-6975   (electronic)
English Language Education
ISBN 978-3-031-34701-6   ISBN 978-3-031-34702-3   (eBook)
https://doi.org/10.1007/978-3-031-34702-3

This Springer imprint is published by the registered company Springer Nature Switzerland AG
The registered company address is: Gewerbestrasse 11, 6330 Cham, Switzerland

This book is dedicated to all educators who aim to decolonize minds and promote inclusive pedagogy by resisting hegemonic discourses, narratives, and practices. We hope that the voices of marginalized and minoritized teachers and students will be clearly heard in this collection of chapters.

Foreword

Teachers, researchers, administrators, and policymakers in the field of English as an International Language are frequently confronted with an uncomfortable dilemma: on the one hand, are we complicit in promoting an imperialist language in a world that is characterized by global inequity and the loss of linguistic diversity? On the other hand, if people are denied access to this powerful international language, does this perpetuate their marginalization? This dilemma is sometimes called the "access paradox" by scholars such as Janks (2009), a leading literacy scholar from the Global South. As Janks notes, "The access paradox recognizes that domination without access excludes students from the language or the language variety that would afford them the most linguistic capital, thereby limiting their life chances" (2009, p. 140). At the same time, Janks notes of the South African context, "access without a theory of domination naturalizes the power of the dominant language, English, and devalues students' own languages."

The edited collection by Ahmed Sahlane and Rosalind Pritchard, on "English as an International Language Education: Critical Intercultural Literacy Perspectives," serves as a compelling and innovative response to the access paradox. While recognizing the centrality of English in our global culture, the diverse authors in this comprehensive collection seek to challenge the delegitimation of minority languages, including Indigenous languages, and foreground issues of race, gender, class, sexual orientation, and religion in efforts to promote multilingualism and reimagine a more equitable world. In doing so, the authors address, collectively, the way power operates at local and global levels and highlights challenges associated with providing access to English while simultaneously valuing and leveraging students' own linguistic and cultural capital.

The authors in the collection take the reader to English as an International Language initiatives across the globe, including Iran, Morocco, Vietnam, Saudi Arabia, and Sri Lanka. We learn about Chinese students in Anglophone countries, pre-service English teachers in Japan, and Indigenous perspectives in Canada and Norway. In making a powerful case for a decolonial, anti-racist, and anti-sexist approach to English as an International Language, the authors are advancing contemporary ideas on language and power aligned, for example, with the work of

Pennycook and Makoni (2019, p. 100), who note the "many potential paradoxes, disagreements, diverse images of decolonial futures, and possible strategies for arriving at these different futures." Of particular relevance is the work of Makoe (2022) who seeks to problematize the privileging of European knowledge and language, while challenging the "invisibilization of non-European forms of knowing" (Makoe, 2022, p. 49).

As noted by many authors in this collection, the conceptualization of language as both a linguistic system and a social practice, inscribed by relations of power, has been convincingly articulated by Bourdieu, the French social theorist. Bourdieu's constructs of "legitimate language" and the "legitimate speaker" provide important insights into debates on language, power, and identity (Norton, 2013). What and who is considered "legitimate" must be understood with respect to a given "field" or social context that is often characterized by unequal struggles for meaning, access, and power. As authors in this collection note, issues of legitimacy are relevant to both learners and teachers of English, and are indexical of prevailing ideologies on language, culture, and identity. What identities are made available to those who teach English, whether native or non-native speaker, white or racialized, gay or straight, male or female? Indeed, many authors would claim that the very existence of such binaries needs to be challenged and dismantled.

English as an International Language Education: Critical Intercultural Literacy Perspectives makes an important contribution to contemporary debates on English, literacy, power, and possibility. I look forward to engaging in the debates which arise on the access paradox, decolonialism, and the future of English as an International Language.

Vancouver, Canada   Bonny Norton
December 30, 2022

References

Janks, H. (2009). *Literacy and power*. Routledge.
Makoe, P. (2022). Navigating hegemonic knowledge and ideologies at school. In C. McKinney & P. Christie (Eds.), *Decoloniality, language and literacy* (pp. 46–62). Multilingual Matters.
Norton, B. (2013). *Identity and language learning: Extending the conversation* (2nd ed.). Multilingual Matters.
Pennycook, A., & Makoni, S. (2019). *Innovations and challenges in applied linguistics from the Global South*. Routledge.

Acknowledgements

First and foremost, we would like to thank all contributors for taking part in this exciting project. We are indebted to them for their enthusiastic support and their unfaltering collaboration.

We are grateful to Springer Nature for contributing their time, expertise, and support in making this book possible. We are deeply appreciative of Natalie Rieborn and Karthika Menon (Springer), whose patience and support during the first stages of this work were very helpful. Our thanks go to the general editors of this series, Chris Davison and Xuesong Gao, and to Immaculate Jayanthi (Production Editor, Springer) for their professionalism. Likewise, we are grateful to the anonymous reviewers of the whole manuscript for their thorough and very useful comments.

We are also very thankful to Zia Tajeddin, Ruanni Tupas, Roby Marlina, and Helen Murray for reviewing the first drafts of a chapter each in this volume; they contributed constructive suggestions.

Ahmed Sahlane is indebted to Rosalind Pritchard for her work on this project and for her continuous and unswerving support as a former supervisor of his PhD thesis (which he completed in 2009) and a great friend since then; her editorial rigor and partnership have been instrumental in making preparation of this volume a very interesting and enjoyable research experience. As we committed ourselves to include diverse voices and perspectives from international scholars at various stages of their academic careers, we were faced with much editing labor.

We are delighted to bring together researchers based in nineteen geographical locales: Australia, Canada, China, Costa Rica, Germany, Iran, Italy, Japan, Morocco, Norway, Qatar, Saudi Arabia, Singapore, Spain, Sri Lanka, the UAE, the UK, the USA, Vietnam.

This project would have been far more difficult without your help.

Jeddah, Saudi Arabia   Ahmed Sahlane

Coleraine, UK   Rosalind Pritchard

Contents

About the Editors

Ahmed Sahlane (PhD, Ulster University, Belfast) is Senior Lecturer in English at University of Jeddah (English Language Institute). He coordinated several EAP/ESP programs at Saudi universities, where he served in a variety of leadership roles such as business English program academic advisor and curriculum designer. He has taught English at all levels (K-12 and tertiary) in Morocco, Oman, Saudi Arabia, and Canada. He was the winner of Top Gun Master Teacher's Award, CDIS, Burnaby, Canada, 2001. His publications focus on the critical analysis of mediated political discourse from the perspective of argumentation theory and critical linguistics. He has published several articles and book chapters about the coverage of the 2003 Iraq War in Western opinion-editorial press. Sahlane's current research interests revolve around the rhetorics of populist discourse and media (mis)representation of cultural otherness. His research interests also include intersectionality and decoloniality studies, social semiotics, and critical pedagogy. Email: asahlan1@uj.edu.sa

Rosalind Pritchard is Emeritus Professor of Education and Senior Distinguished Research Fellow at Ulster University, where she was Head of the School of Education and Coordinator of Research. Her research interests include higher education and TESOL (especially cross-cultural adaptation and teaching strategies). She is a member of the British Academy of Social Sciences, an honorary member of the British Association for International and Comparative Education, secretary of the European Association for Institutional Research, and a member of the Royal Irish Academy, of which membership is considered the highest academic honour in Ireland. She has held grants from the Leverhulme Trust, the Economic and Social Research Council, the UK Council for International Education, the German Academic Exchange Service, and the Higher Education Innovation Fund. Email: R.Pritchard@ulster.ac.uk

Abbreviations

AA	Academic Adaptation
ACE	Asian Corpus of English
ACTFL	American Council on the Teaching of Foreign Languages
ASEAN	The Association of Southeast Asian Nations
AVE	Average Variance Extracted
BCQ	Behavioural Cultural Intelligence
CALD	Culturally and Linguistically Diverse
CALL	Computer-Assisted Language Learning
CC	Communicative Competence
CCGM	Cultural Competence and Global Mindset
CCQ	Cognitive Cultural Intelligence
CDA	Critical Discourse Analysis
CEDAW	The Convention on the Elimination of all Forms of Discrimination against Women
CEFR	Common European Framework of Reference for Languages
CICLT	Critical Intercultural Language Teaching
CIP	Critical Intercultural Pedagogy
CLIL	Content and Language Integrated Learning
COIL	Collaborative Online International Learning
CQ	Cultural Intelligence
CQS	Cultural Intelligence Scale
CR	Composite Reliability
CWR	Corona Warriors Recovered
DEI	Diversity, Equity, and Inclusion
DMIS	Developmental Model of Intercultural Sensitivity
ECE	Early Childhood Education
EFL	English as a Foreign Language
EI	Emotional Intelligence
EIL	English as an International Language
ELF	English as a Lingua Franca
ELFA	English as a Lingua Franca in Academic Settings

ELT	English Language Teaching
EMF	English as a Multilingua Franca
EMI	English as a Medium of Instruction
ENL	English as a Native Language
EP	English Proficiency
ERPP	English for Research Publication Purposes
ESL	English as a Second Language
FREPA	Framework of Reference for Pluralistic Approaches to Languages and Cultures
GCLC	Global Cultural Leadership Competency
GE	Global Englishes
HE	Higher Education
IC	Intercultural Competence
ICC	Intercultural Communicative Competence
IETs	Internationally Educated Teachers
IQ	General Intelligence
IRSs	Indian Residential Schools
L1	First Language
L2	Second Language
LGBTIQ+	Lesbian, gay, bisexual, transgender, intersex, queer, and more
MCCQ	Meta-Cognitive Cultural Intelligence
MCQ	Motivational Cultural Intelligence
MTB-MLE	Mother Tongue-Based Multilingual Education
NCOC	National Command & Operation Centre
NES	Native English Speaker
NESs	Native English Speakers
NNESs	Non-Native English Speakers
NNS	Non-Native Speaker
NNSTs	Non-Native Speaker Teachers
NS	Native Speaker
OECD	Organisation for Economic Cooperation and Development
RCAP	Royal Commission on Aboriginal Peoples
SBA	Standards-based Approach
SCA	Sociocultural Adaptation
SES	Socioeconomic Status
TBL	Task-Based Learning
TEACUP	Teacher–Culture–Pluri
TEIL	Teaching English as an International Language
TESL	Teaching English as a Second Language
TESOL	Teaching English to Speakers of Other Languages
TOEIC	Test of English for International Communication
TRC	Truth and Reconciliation Commission
UNCEDAW	The United Nations Committee on the Elimination of Discrimination against Women
VOICE	Vienna-Oxford International Corpus of English
WE	World Englishes

List of Boxes

List of Figures

The Impact of English Proficiency on the Sociocultural
and Academic Adaptation of Chinese Students in Short-term
Exchange Programs: The Mediating Effects of Cultural Intelligence

"She Is Not a Normal Teacher of English":
Photovoice as a Decolonial Method to Study Queer Teacher
Identity in Vietnam's English Language Teaching

Intercultural Competence – A Never-Ending Journey

List of Tables

(De)Coloniality, Indigeneity and the Cultural Politics of English as an International Language: A Quest for the 'Third Space'

Ahmed Sahlane ⓘD and Rosalind Pritchard

Abstract The forces of globalisation and empire are inexorably interconnected with English as a global language. English has been de-territorialised and indigenised in a way that has considerably transformed Southern local identities. First, theoretical constructs related to English as an international language and the concept of (de)coloniality are defined. Then, decolonial projects associated with the need to regenerate Indigenous knowledges and the pluriversal modes of thinking are briefly outlined in relation to educational and academic spaces. Finally, it is argued that hegemonic Eurocentric knowledge systems have always been inextricably linked to colonialist thinking in the ways they have misrepresented, demonised, problematised, and pathologised cultural others.

Keywords Coloniality · Epistemicide · Eurocentric · Hegemony · Genocide · Globalisation · Indigenous · Interculturality · Muslim · Orientalism · Whiteness · World Englishes

1 The De-territorialisation of English as an International Language

English as a "global" language refers to the US/Anglophone dominance over the global flows of technology, the media, and finance (i.e., 'technoscapes,' 'mediascapes,' and 'financescapes,' respectively) (Block, 2010, p. 300). In other words, English has acquired the vital role it enjoys today because of the

A. Sahlane (✉)
English Language Institute, University of Jeddah, Jeddah, Saudi Arabia
e-mail: asahlan1@uj.edu.sa

R. Pritchard
Faculty of Arts, Humanities & Social Sciences, Ulster University, Coleraine, UK
e-mail: R.Pritchard@ulster.ac.uk

A. Sahlane, R. Pritchard (eds.), *English as an International Language Education*, English Language Education 33,
https://doi.org/10.1007/978-3-031-34702-3_1

"Americanisation expanding through economic, financial, military, and media influence" (Phillipson, 2023, p. 144). Besides, English has a hegemonic status in several international institutions (e.g., the World Trade Organisation, the World Bank, the International Monetary Fund), as well as in major inter-governmental associations which are of global impact (e.g., the North Atlantic Treaty Organisation, the Association of Southeast Asian Nations, the European Union).

On the other hand, *English as an International Language* (EIL) refers to the wide expansion of the language and its adaptation to the local cultures of "outer" and "expanding" circles (i.e., World Englishes) (Kachru, 1985); hence, it serves both local, regional, and global communication needs. The main implication for materials development is the need to adopt an EIL-aware approach by including diverse languacultures in ELT textbooks. While World Englishes (WE) draw on local realities within national boundaries, *English as a lingua franca* (ELF) covers interactions between speakers of English in regional and/or global contexts. The rise of WE has challenged the relevance of 'inner circle' countries (e.g., Australia, Britain, Canada, Ireland, New Zealand, and the United States) as "norm-providers" of native-speaker "models" of ELT pedagogy.

In "outer circle" postcolonial settings (e.g., India, Nigeria, and the Philippines) English continues to play an associate institutionalised official role, and consequently it has been indigenised to reflect the local cultural/linguistic realities. For example, "English has become a language of the Philippines which has been adapted by Filipinos to mirror and reflect their own lived experiences" (Kirkpatrick, 2018, p. 26). Hence, ideally the ELT curriculum should be localised by providing culturally relevant content, as well as making use of the multilingual and translingual resources that well-trained Filipino teachers could bring to the classroom, using lingua franca approaches (Tupas, 2018, p. 94). The use of the mother tongue as a medium of instruction in the elementary levels of education should be prioritised (Kirkpatrick, 2018, p. 26). Such reclaiming of marginalised languages in institutional spaces entails the need to counterbalance the colonialist hegemony of English by implementing multilingual education. EIL-aware approaches dictate that the West-centric English-only monolingualist ideology (embedded in research methods, thinking modes, teaching methods and pedagogical approaches) should cease to be the norm in post-colonial societies.

In "expanding circle" contexts (e.g., Morocco, Saudi Arabia, and Japan) English remains a native-speaker-norm dependent foreign language (mainly encountered in the classroom or in other academic or social media spaces). However, there is a tendency for mainly the elite to gain access to private English-medium education. As a result, the gaps deepen between the world's haves and have-nots; and the growing symbolic power of English grows together with its widespread role in sustaining unequal power relations. For example, while one of the authors (AS) was teaching French in high school in Canada, he noticed that Asian international students from affluent families migrate to Anglophone countries before college as a strategy to acquire English immersion education; this becomes symbolic capital which maintains their social prestige and upward mobility. Therefore, access to English is associated with social stratification. The sociopolitical and historical context of learning

English as a foreign language is different from that of the former colonial (outer circle) contexts, wherein English has displaced mother tongues and retained its role as the 'legitimate' language of instruction and economic development. However, the dominance of English over global media spaces (movies, music, Internet content, etc.) has also reduced the space available for indigenous cultural expression in 'expanding circle' contexts.

In the European Union countries, a diglossic situation has obtained, where using English for instrumental purposes has resulted in English as a *lingua franca* (ELF). ELF communication can be conceived in terms of 'communities of practice' in that interactants are actively engaged in collaborative meaning negotiation, based on their repertoires of linguistic and cultural resources. Since ELF theorists advocate a pluricentric model of English, there is no need to prescribe the codification of a single English variety, and users are encouraged to adapt their linguacultural resources to effectively accommodate the communicative needs of their interlocutors (Jenkins, 2006, p. 161). Hence, in an ever more integrated Europe, English has become a "transactional language" par excellence, with a vast cross-border communication potential. While ELF is functionally used as "a medium for border-crossing", national languages have maintained their privileged position as the symbol of identification and the preservation of sociolinguistic and cultural-historical roots (House, 2003, p. 563). In addition, "Euro-English" provided a more convenient medium for effective intercultural communication.[1]

The Association of Southeast Asian Nations (ASEAN) adopted English as its sole official lingua franca. Therefore, English has become a compulsory subject in primary school (except in Indonesia).[2] Singapore is "the only former British colony that made English the sole medium of instruction for all levels of education" (Phillipson, 2023, p. 151). However, "English is being used as an Asian language by Asian multilinguals within an Asia-centric cultural milieu" (Kirkpatrick, 2018, p. 22). Decolonial scholars continue to press for English language curricula that promote regional "intercultural sensitivity" (e.g., by teaching Asian literature written in English). Students should be trained (and assessed) in developing multilingual "functional proficiency" by equipping them with effective communicative strategies required for meaning negotiation. Besides, as the goal is not to conform to "native speaker" norms, the local teachers of English are encouraged to make use of their shared multilingual resources to provide the "most appropriate linguistic models for their students" (p. 29). Continuing to "judge speaker performance against monolingual native speaker norms" is "not only unjust"; it is also "plainly wrong" (Kirkpatrick, 2018, p. 21).

---

[1] The BRICS group (Brazil, Russia, India, China, and South Africa) is another lingua franca situation, in which English is learned as an additional language.

[2] There are more than 718 languages in Indonesia. Javanese is the most frequently used at home (32% of the national population), followed by Bahasa Indonesia (mother tongue of 20% of Indonesians), which is the official national language; it is spoken by 92 % of the population; and it is used for all official purposes (e.g., K-12 and higher education); and thus, it serves as a kind of "national lingua franca" (Coleman & Fero, 2023, p. 73).

As Jenkins (2006, p. 167) rightly puts it, "attempts to label the English of whole speech communities as deficient and fossilized are thus unjustifiable because these labels ignore the local Englishes' sociohistorical development and socio-cultural context." ELF varieties should not be regarded as instances of "interlanguage", and consequently as inferior to the standardised Anglocentric English varieties. Besides, claiming the ownership of English based on the notion of "nativeness" that excludes speakers of non-standard varieties of English and other indigenised international versions in postcolonial non-Anglophone countries is fallacious because "[English] is only international to the extent that it is not their [native speakers'] language. It is not a possession which they lease to others, while still retaining the freehold. Other people actually own it" (Widdowson, 1994, p. 385). In other words, given that English "serves the communicative and communal needs of different communities, it follows logically that it must be diverse" (p. 385). Moreover, "the standard language is no one's native language insofar as it is a set of cultural practices that cannot be learned until after the period of normal first language acquisition" (Train, 2009, p. 47).

2   Global Coloniality and the Colonial Power Matrix

"Coloniality" refers to the more subtle and pervasive forms of radically asymmetrical power relations in contemporary societies that continue to shape the (re)production of Northern colonial patterns of domination by normalising the persistent hierarchisation of racial identities ("coloniality of being") (e.g., 'whites', 'Indians', 'Mestizos'/ 'Métis', 'negroes', 'Arabs') and privileging Western people over racialised others; this ontological dimension of a global hegemonic model of power is also based on racist social classification ("coloniality of power") and the subalternisation and marginalisation of Southern peoples' epistemological knowledges ("coloniality of knowledge"). Hence, the multiple entangled constellations of a "colonial power matrix" (Quijano, 2000) involve different levels of hierarchisation that are "not just social and political but also epistemic in nature" (Walsh, 2007, p. 230). In other words, as Maldonado-Torres (2010, p. 96) puts it,

> while the coloniality of power referred to the interrelation among modern forms of exploitation and domination (power), and the coloniality of knowledge had to do with impact of colonization on the different areas of knowledge production, coloniality of being would make primary reference to the lived experience of colonization and its impact on language.

The global multifaceted system of control, domination and exploitation has helped to perpetuate the long-standing ideological blueprints, structural conditions, and frameworks of colonial orders conspicuously visible in the (neo)colonial situations and discourses that are entrenched in the way the ex-colonisers' hegemonic narratives help in the shaping of historical memories of the ex-colonised peoples through an imperial lens. These persisting structures of power relations have enduring injurious impact on the ex-colonised subjects' minds. As Said (1994) eloquently argues, coloniality is not equivalent to colonialism; "direct colonialism has largely ended; imperialism … lingers where it has always been, in a kind of general cultural sphere as well as in specific political, ideological, economic, and social practices" (p. 9). Therefore,

> Though for the most part the colonies have won their independence, many of the imperial attitudes underlying colonial conquest continue… the old divisions between colonizer and colonized have re-emerged in what is often referred to as the North-South relationship, which entailed defensiveness, various kinds of rhetorical and ideological combat and a simmering hostility. (Said, 1994, pp. 16–17)

Southern theory challenges 'coloniality of power' that is shaped by a history of colonialism and the ongoing regimes of oppression that perpetuate North-South global inequalities and injustices, deriving from the detrimental effects of transnational capitalism on uneven distribution of global wealth and resources.

3 Decoloniality as Epistemic Interculturality

Decolonial approaches, methods, and intellectual projects (grounded in the continuous lived experiences of coloniality) seek to delink from colonial attitudes, rationalities and discourses that position Eurocentric episteme and logic as 'universal' while "localizing other forms of thought as at best folkloric" (Walsh, 2007, p. 225). For example, "[t]he cultural repression and the massive genocide together turned the previous high cultures of America into illiterate, peasant subcultures condemned to orality; that is, deprived of their own patterns of formalized, objectivised, intellectual, and plastic or visual expression" (Quijano, 2010, p. 24). Southern theory seeks to "liberate the production of knowledge, reflection, and communication from the pitfalls of European rationality/modernity" (Quijano, 2007, p. 177). Quijano argues that

> the intersubjective universe produced by the entire Eurocentered capitalist colonial power was elaborated and formalized by the Europeans and established in the world as an exclusively European product and as a universal paradigm of knowledge and of the relation between humanity and the rest of the world. (pp. 171–172)

The European colonial cognitive paradigm of 'rationality' fails to acknowledge the importance of "intersubjective dimension of social relationship" in that it conceives the role of the "subject" as the "bearer of 'reason'", while the "object" is constructed as "not only external" to knowledge production, but it is of a "different nature. In fact, it is 'nature'" (Quijano, 2007, pp. 172–173). Here the state of 'nature' constructs Indigenous communities as outside the state of 'civil society' and 'political modernity'. The erasure of the objectified cultural other helps to hierarchise the relationship between the West and the rest, and consequently normalise the inferiorisation of racialised bodies and subalternised knowledges. In other words, "the other cultures are different in the sense that they are unequal, in fact inferior, by nature" (p. 174).

Postcolonial theory is built in large part around the concepts of otherness and cultural identity. Postcolonial scholars criticise the binary colonialist representations of otherness and believe that hybridity is central to cultural identity formations (e.g., Said, 1978). Said argues that "Far from being unitary or monolithic or autonomous things, cultures actually assume more 'foreign' elements, alterities, differences, than they consciously exclude" (1994, p. 15). He also contests the racist sentiments propagated in European Orientalist discourse. Likewise, decolonial academics problematise the "centeredness in western paradigms, frameworks, and theory" (Walsh, 2007, p. 225) by interrogating the ongoing Eurocentrification process and call for an epistemic and ontological delinking from Western hegemonic frameworks of reference by recalibrating the unbalanced flow of knowledge between the Northern 'Centre' and the Southern 'Periphery.'

The decolonial projects, which have been initiated in the Global South,[3] have been based on the Southern scholars' argument that writing from a Southern perspective allows for a regeneration of Indigenous knowledge and thinking and a continued growth within an Indigenous research paradigm. As Quijano (2010) puts it, "epistemological decolonization, as decoloniality, is needed to clear the way for new intercultural communication, for an interchange of experiences and meanings, as the basis of another rationality which may legitimately pretend to some universality" (p. 31). In this sense, decolonial thought requires not only changing perceptions by critically addressing issues related to ethnicity, social inequities, and race, but it should also offer a roadmap to better knowledge production and praxis by opening up new avenues for change in research methods, perspectives, and epistemologies to promote other knowledges and alternative ways of categorising the world.

This 'epistemic resistance' calls for a repositioning of education and research in a way that valorises local languages, knowledges, and voices, and this might necessarily engender significant systemic reforms in the realms of education policymaking (i.e., curriculum design, pedagogy, etc.), learning theory, and research methodology (Heugh et al., 2021). For example, educational research "must centre local knowledges, realities, and voices in power-sensitive dialogue" (Osborne, 2021, p. 243) and resist Northern claim assumptions about the Indigenous peoples' epistemological and methodological 'ineptitude'. Such a position questions the universality of knowledge produced in the Global Northern Metropolis. 'Decoloniality,' hence, seeks to advance alternative perspectives and positionalities that resist 'epistemic violence' ('epistemicide') by contesting Northern perspectives and epistemologies.

For example, African feminist studies' methods are criticised for lacking analytical rigour and 'objectivity.' Western feminist paradigms, which are embedded in colonialist manipulation, ultimately lead to a systematic process of cultural ethnocentrism (Pindi, 2021). The decolonisation of the Eurocentric stereotypical

---

[3] 'Global South' is not a geographic entity. Hence, the term 'South/southern' refers to social inequities, subjugation and historical oppression and other types of injustices that are also part of the realities of many minoritised groups in affluent Northern societies (Heugh et al., 2021).

portrayal of African women (e.g., 'primitive,' 'uncivilised', 'savage', "ignorant') calls for rethinking the role of Western feminist scholarship in the validation of such ethnocentric and racist representations (p. 333). Viewing African sexuality from a Western epistemic lens merely imposes Eurocentric categories on African cultures. Research on/about African people should be grounded in Afrocentric perspectives. African women's lived experiences should not be assimilated to those of their African American sisters, solely based on the colour of their skin. The homogenisation of blackness and the dehistorisation of Black African women's lived experiences is instrumental in the validation of Western epistemic hegemony and the systemic erasure of "African epistemologies and bodies" (p. 237).

Therefore, there is an urgent need to "(re)theorize intersectionality from African perspectives" (Pindi, 2021, p. 238). The questioning of western "master universal narratives" (Ellis et al., 2011, 274) by proposing alternative pluriversal modes of thinking, knowledge frameworks and methods of research (e.g., 'de-whitening' intersectional feminist research) does not entail de-Westernisation. Rather, decolonial theory tries to promote a dialogue that acknowledges the co-existence of diverse knowledge systems and mobilise for a cooperative ethos essential for epistemic justice in a way that transforms individuals and communities and promotes social change. Southerners should stop being presented as mere 'objects' of research rather than 'agents' of research and knowledge production.

4   Decoloniality, Interculturality and Teacher Education

The recolonising of the global Southern mind is enacted through Northern academic industry that (re)circulates refined (decontextualised) "raw materials of southern thought" in "packaged, regurgitated form for further consumption by Indigenous intellectuals" (Heugh et al. 2021, p. 12). Decolonial scholars call for an epistemic break by discontinuing the adaptation of decontextualised Eurocentric pedagogies and research perspectives within Southern local realities. Decolonising research methodology is very fundamental in granting Indigenous and marginalised communities voice and epistemological agency. For example, the revitalisation of Aboriginal languages is an essential condition for "participatory engagement in both education and research methodologies that can gauge authentic views of communities about the appropriacy, effectiveness, and relevance of education provision for Aboriginal children and youth" (Osborne, 2021, p. 232). Dialogic engagement as a collaborative ethnographic approach that involves whole communities of stakeholders in a process of unpacking the underlying ideologies of English-only policy in Nepal (Phyak et al., 2021, p. 158) is an example of how decolonial projects should rethink Anglocentric methods of inquiry, processes of data collection, and representation of findings.

This decolonial thinking has led several educational institutions to embark on a broader range of initiatives to diversify their teaching curricula to promote a more culturally responsive and equity-oriented learning and training in an attempt to redress the detrimental effects of coloniality on education. However, the diversification of the curriculum poses considerable challenges due to limited expertise and relevant resources, and the conspicuous marginalisation of racialised academics. Racialised scholars who are invited to inhabit pre-established white research spaces as nonwhite bodies are denied any epistemological agency and their alternative decolonial research perspectives are muted because 'whiteness[4]' yields enormous power over the generation and validation of knowledge (Johnson & Howsam, 2020, p. 678). For example, in Canada "half of the country's public universities have a leadership team composed of all white administrators" (Cukier et al., 2021, p. 575). Likewise, in American universities "tenure denials" are part of "a systemic pattern of exclusion" of racialised academics (Monture, 2009, p. 94). Hence, to "inhabit whiteness as a nonwhite body can be uncomfortable" (Ahmed, 2012, p. 40) because it is like "walking into a sea of whiteness" (p. 35).

In a context where neoliberalist colonialingual ideologies and whiteness structure the articulation and validation of knowledge, racialised and Indigenous academics experience institutional barriers and discriminatory practices that limit their scholarly potential and challenge their professional legitimacy and entitlements. In their questionnaire survey of eight universities in English Canada, Henry et al. (2016, p. 8) found that racialised academics are underrepresented in the Social Sciences and Humanities, but they outperform their white colleagues in winning research grants and publishing articles. However, their scholarly research is devalued by claiming that it is too "ideological" and "rhetorical". The surveyed racialised academics also revealed that research publication and winning grants (hard metrics) tend to be undervalued in comparison to soft metrics (i.e., 'collegiality', 'personality', and 'civility'), which are very crucial for tenure and promotion processes. Similarly, "intellectual agendas" in British universities "operate to maintain a narrow, inward-looking perspective that reinforces Orientalism and whiteness/Europeanness" (Sian, 2019, p. 103). Hence, to navigate institutional racism, racialised academics need to perform 'whiteness' roles by "cracking white hidden codes and infiltrating white networks where mysterious opportunities and breaks seem to happen time and time again for white members of staff" (p. 133).

More telling, whiteness 'normativity' tends to equate the role of professor with white academics to the extent that some racialised and Indigenous faculty are mistaken for students (Mohamed & Beagan, 2019, p. 345). It seems that "[b]eing asked whether you are the professor is a way of being made into a stranger, of not being at home in a category that gives residence to others" (Ahmed, 2012, p. 177). This "intellectual homelessness" (Monture, 2009, p. 93) is debilitating because while white bodies can move around institutional academic spaces with ease, racialised faculty may sometimes be treated as trespassers by security guards. Hence, racialised and Indigenous faculty are regarded as "tokenistic," and get higher visibility than "dominants" (Kanter, 1993) because they are constructed as undeserving

---

[4]"Whiteness refers to a system of beliefs, practices, and assumptions that constantly centre the interests of White people, especially White elites" (Gillborn, 2021, p. 102).

'occupants' of the academic space, even by colleagues who believe that racialised and Indigenous faculty are hired only for fulfilling 'employment equity' requirement (the affirmative action/ 'token' hires). More seriously, non-native accented academics are blamed for students' poor achievement. Racialised and Indigenous academics remember instances when overachieving (as students) was penalised as it was presumably associated with 'cheating'. Hence, such toxic environments only breed structural racism, epistemological injustice, culture-bound elitism, neoliberal assimilationist managerialism, power hierarchies, and tokenism (Mohamed & Beagan, 2019, pp. 346–351).

The promotion of decolonial perspectives has significant implications for teacher education. Due to the massive displacement of populations and the issues associated with mobility and migration, 'intercultural literacy' has become a central concern of most teacher education programs today. Because there is a greater likelihood that teachers will be working with diverse student populations from various multicultural backgrounds, there is a greater need for teachers and students alike to develop 'intercultural competence' to be able to interact in an effective and appropriate way in multicultural situations, based on acquired assumptions related to attitudes, intercultural knowledge, skills, and critical self-reflection (Byram, 1997).

However, educational policies intended to advance cultural diversity fail to go beyond the usual generic statements of 'valuing difference' and 'advancing equity and diversity'. It seems that "white privilege remains unchallenged within the hallowed halls of academia in particular and the wider public arena" (Henry, 2021, p. 310). Despite the continuous claims for embracing diversity, the monolingual 'native-speakerism' and the standard English ideologies (concurrent with the increasing homogenisation of world cultures and the continuing global internationalisation of higher education) have led to the "coloniality of language", which engendered "brutal erasures of other forms of knowledge and modes of being" (Stroud, 2021, p. 23). For example, in Morocco, 'linguistic coloniality' manifests itself in the fact that the political elite maintain their powerful status through access to French. As Kabel (2023, p. 388) points out,

> Neoliberal multilingualism rests on the naturalization of a hierarchical patterning between Amazigh[5] and Arabic, and French and English where the former are encased in a primordialist straitjacket as languages of identity while the latter are promoted as idioms of modernity, the knowledge economy and progress.

"Cultural coloniality" (Quijano, 2010), thus, remains the most prominent form of domination in the Global South today in that the coerced linguistic hierarchy has become a constitutive part of the conditions of a system of sociocultural and political control that sustains the perpetuation of legacies of colonialism.

---

[5] After Morocco gained its independence from the French colonisation in 1956, it adopted Arabic-French bilingualism in the key domains of education and media and banned Tamazight language and culture from public domains. Tamazight (Amazigh language) was initially granted an official status in 2011 after a long battle by Amazigh activists. Now Tamazight (Berber) is taught in primary education in over 5000 schools (Sadiqi, 2014).

5   Barriers to Intercultural Dialogue: Essentialism, Othering & Eurocentrism

By linking "coloniality of power" to dehumanisation, the (ex)coloniser imposes the Eurocentric idea of 'modernity'/'coloniality' on the post-colonial Global Southern peoples, through ideological manipulation by misrepresenting their 'local' histories ("coloniality of being"). Colonial thinking has moulded and distorted cultural others' collective sense of self-worth and excluded 'them' from 'our' realm of shared humanity (Quijano, 2007). For example, a single (mis)representation that has wide currency is the portrayal of Africa as the bastion of 'darkness', 'backwardness', 'irrationality' tribal 'feuds', (motivated by Africans' 'irrational' instinctive propensity to fight), 'corruption', 'superstition', and diseases (Brookes, 1995; Crawford, 1996).

However, the real causes of African problems are muted in media frames (i.e., Western arms sales in support for local dictatorships, foreign intervention dressed as 'liberation', the Cold War, etc.). These imaginings of Africa reflect a Western desire to justify their alleged 'benevolent' interventions in Africa to loot, (re)colonise, and (re)enslave African people. For example, the CIA-assisted overthrow of democratically elected leaders in African and Muslim countries is well corroborated (e.g., Marxist Patrice Lumumba in Zaire & Mohammad Mossadegh in Iran) (Nutt, 2005). Hence, as Nutt argues, rich Western countries must take their fair share of responsibility in the very genesis of the African plight because when European colonialist rulers pulled out of Africa, they left behind a disreputable legacy of colonialist government systems based on "elitism, patronage and power – a fertile ground for the seeds of corruption". As Phillipson (2023, p. 2) eloquently puts it, "[t]he 1884 Berlin share-out of Africa between competing European empires, without any African people being consulted, cut across African geographical, cultural, and linguistic realities and thereby sowed the seeds for conflicts and unstable national units".

It is also worth noting that the persisting injurious colonial effects in post-colonial Africa are still prominent. For example, economic dominance of whites in post-apartheid South Africa is unfavourable for the majority of black communities. In other words, "the levels of poverty and inequality in South Africa continue to bear a persistent racial character" (Phaswana, 2021, p. 202); race, gender, and spatial divide (rural vs urban) remain key markers of an individual's human development (p. 204). Besides, while white South Africans are more likely to find well-paid jobs or create their own entrepreneurships, unemployment rate is largely high among blacks, and it remains "gendered and racially hierarchized" (pp. 205–206).

Likewise, media construction of the "Mexican peon draws on racial assumptions about differences between primitive and civilized peoples and, in so doing, it precludes Mexican access to American-ness" (Flores, 2003, p. 381). Besides, "English-only as the medium of instruction" in the US schools' "racist and sexist curricula and materials," as well as "discriminatory treatments" all serve as a "coercive pedagogical tool for submission" (Macías, 2021, p. 77). As Tupas (2018) puts it, speaking the mother tongues is equated with "littering and other instances of 'misbehavior'"

(p. 89). Hence, our role as critical pedagogues is to reconceptualise English language education by creating open educational spaces for critical engagement with linguicist policies and subtractive monolingual language ideologies.

Similarly, representations of Aboriginality have been shaped by racist discourses that serve to normalise social control, marginalisation, and exclusion of Indigenous communities from the state of what it is to be 'human.' For example, the Aboriginal Australian woman was portrayed as "dirty, unintelligent, lazy, prone to alcoholism, sexually promiscuous, and uncaring for her children" (Synott, 2003, p. 205). Such sexist/racist narratives of Indigenous women are merely deployed to construct them as unfit mothers. The Aboriginal Australian was referred to as "myall" and "boong", the equivalent of American "coon" and "nigger" (p. 207). "The Indian was depicted as a cannibal, an idolater, and someone with highly deviant sexual behaviour" (Blommaert & Verschueren, 1998, p. 19). The Spaniards legitimated their conquest of the New World by accusing the Indians of practising "abominable lewdness even with beasts" and eating "human flesh, slaying men for that purpose" (Krisch, 2002, p. 324). This racist categorisation of Aborigines served to 'legitimise' the 'terra nullius' ('empty land') colonialist myth. Hence, "[t]he earliest phase of genocide and land theft was accompanied by sets of ideas that sanctioned the dispossession, particularly the European basis of scientific racism embedded in the theories of social evolution" (Synott, 2003, p. 206).

The 'assimilationist' policies of successive Australian governments vis-à-vis Aboriginal people portrayed them as "a form of nonhuman native pests to be dispersed, shot out, and carelessly, violently, and utterly destroyed" (Synott, 2003, p. 207). Former Prime Minister, John Howard, characterised the violence perpetuated against Australian Indigens ('timber niggers') as a "heroic triumph over hardship and adversity that is to be celebrated in the present" rather than "a tragedy of invasion, conquest and violent destruction of Indigenous communities" (Augoustinos et al., 2002, p. 112) that has transgenerational traumatic effects. Likewise, the colonialist "educational regimes" in modern Australia "encourage epistemic violence and the invisibilization of minority languages" (Osborne 2021, p. 232). Thus, the on-going struggle for recognition and social justice prioritises the need to decolonise knowledge, minds, and research epistemologies by promoting "active engagement in Alter-Native pathways in understanding and (re-)shaping our world" (Macías, 2021, p. 93). Lisa Poupart (2003, p. 87) states that,

> As American Indians participate in, create, and reproduce Western cultural forms, we internalize Western meanings of difference and abject Otherness, viewing ourselves within and through the constructs that defined us as racially and culturally subhuman, deficient, and vile.

In a similar vein, former Prime Minister Stephen Harper framed residential schooling as "a matter of individual past suffering" (James, 2018, p. 835) in his 2008 'apology'. He blatantly declared that Canada had "no history of colonialism" (Nagy, 2020, p. 225). The gap between his robust apologetic narrative and the practices of engagement with Indigenous alterity (e.g., the absence of appropriate restitution, the overincarceration of Indigenous offenders, accelerated pipeline expansions, the scandalous problem of unsafe drinking water on First Nation reserves, and the exacerbation of the quotidian intersectional violence against Indigenous women) revealed the Prime Minister's hypocritical 'double-speak' logic (James, 2018, p. 836). The representation of Indigenous trauma today within a transitional justice discourse is a mere rhetorical manoeuvre to redefine settler colonialism as part of a "closed dark chapter" (reconciliation-as-closure) and maintain the status quo (Grey & James, 2016, p. 316).

Similarly, Muslims are depicted in Western media within an "Orientalist discourse relating to sexual deviance, primitivism, gender, generation, illegality, immorality and perfidy (fraudulent faith), which formulate a meta-discourse of cultural incompatibility" (Poole, 2002, p. 110). Therefore, "[c]overing Islam is a one-sided activity that obscures what 'we' do, and highlights instead what Muslims and Arabs by their very flawed nature are" (Said, 1997, p. xxii). There has been a systemic portrayal of Muslims as a homogeneous collective threat to the Western Judaeo-Christian belief and value systems. The image of terrorism "has been so completely enmeshed with Islam in the dominant Northern discourses that even Christian Middle Easterners involved in violent confrontations are presented as being Muslim" (Karim, 2003, p. 80). Besides, as Said (1997, pp. 6–7) argues,

> The academic experts whose speciality is Islam have generally treated the religion and its various cultures within an invented or culturally determined ideological framework filled with passion, defensive prejudice, sometimes even revulsion; because of this framework, *understanding* of Islam has been a very difficult thing to achieve. (Emphasis original)

This stereotypical image of Muslims is more salient in the way the U.S. 'silver screen' represents Arabs and Muslims as threatening cultural 'Others'. Islam is "often equated with holy war and hatred, fanaticism and violence, intolerance and the oppression of women" (Shaheen, 2000, p. 23). The Hollywood film industry has always depicted Muslims as "billionaires", "bombers" or "belly dancers" (p. 25). Hollywood has created "myths" about the Muslim Arab as the "villain", the "unkempt", the "uncivilized", the "brutal", the "promiscuous" "bedouin bandit", and the "fundamentalist bomber who prays before killing innocents" (pp. 25–26). Hence, Western children have been socialised into a cultural reconstruction of Arabs and Muslims as the villainous 'Others'.

Next to the topos of violence, Islam is most frequently associated with unrestrained sexuality. This imagined 'Islamic' sexual 'depravity' is cited as evidence of lack of religious piety. Such imagery of Muslim exotic sensuality has turned the "Islamic Paradise" into a mere "tavern of unwearied gorging and a brothel of perpetual turpitude" (Norman, 1993, p. 173). Therefore, "Muslims are uniformly represented as evil, violent, and, above all, killable" (Said, 1997, p. xxvii). This monolithic Islam reflects "the bias of Western reporters and image-makers" (Shaheen, 2000, p. 23) and fails to capture the complex realities of Muslims in modern societies.

The Muslim woman provided "a useful image in the armoury of western justifications for war rather than the occasion for demonstrating any real concern with her plight" (Khiabany & Williamson, 2008, p. 83). The Islamic Hijab (headscarf) became a symbol of victimhood that justified the U.S. bombing of Iraq and Afghanistan. The Islamic Hijab has also been constructed as a metonym for Islamic 'fundamentalism', gender oppression, and an ethnic marker that has invaded Western public space. These media and political representations, however, have silenced the voices of Muslim women in the West for whom the Islamic Hijab is "an expression of identity politics, used to deliver a message in the public sphere: a message that is not about religion per se, but about difference and a right for public recognition" (Ismail, 2004, p. 614). Besides, the U.S. mainstream media use Islam as a "device to racialize Arabs as being distinct from and inferior to white Americans" (Naber, 2000, p. 53). As Blommaert and Verschueren (1998, p. 21) succinctly put it,

> [Muslim] Migrants are our Indians, no longer a Plinian race, but at least 'pagans' (of the expansionist and fanatical Islamic type) and 'savages' (barbarians who chop off hands, imprison their circumcised wives, and allow polygamy). In contrast to the Indians of old, they do not only *symbolize* the intra-European enemy. They *are* the enemy. (Emphasis original)

This image of the West as 'civiliser' was also mobilised in the 2003 'humanitarian' invasion of Iraq, and the U.S. mainstream media played a crucial role in the propagation of Bush's 'mission civilisatrice' (see Sahlane, 2012). After the 9/11 attacks, the globalisation of fear through routinised mediated discourses of securitisation has led to the problematisation of Muslim cultural 'penetration'. As border restrictions become tighter, we have seen the re-emergence of populist movements in Western countries reflecting Eurocentric notions of the Fortress West. Thus, the images of (North) African bodies washing up on the Mediterranean shore evoke the persisting insidious economic, political and cultural legacies of the colonial past. The *harragas* (undocumented immigrants) are portrayed as invading Europe. Hence, it is important to notice the place of race in the current world order. As Turner (2018) argues,

> Deaths of migrants in the Mediterranean, expanding networks of detention, deportation, prison systems, police violence, experiments in aerial bombardment, walls and enclosures, and surveillance and counterterrorism tactics call upon us to examine the circulations of practices of violence that render certain populations as suspect, abject and 'unworthy' (p. 766).

The 'Islamic-ness' of Western Muslims is what motivates their representation as the cultural out-group, and thus, a threat to 'our' 'Judo-Christian-ness', "through either [media's] wilful manipulation of evidence, generalisation or ignorance" (Richardson, 2004, p. 114). An uncritical alignment between media actors and Western institutions of power has always helped to reproduce neo-imperialist propaganda that reframes international relations in ways that resonate with official colonial agendas (see Sahlane, 2022). Social work has become another site for "internal colonial management" in Western societies, "where colonising and racialising tactics of empire are relocated and remobilised" (Turner, 2018, p. 782). For example, holding 'fundamentalist' values has increasingly been regarded as a form of 'child abuse' that might necessitate forced removal of children from their Muslim families. The (re)positioning of Muslim communities as the 'breeding ground' of terrorism in

Islamophobic discourse is essentially a "discursive form of elite power reproduction that is against the best interests of dominated groups and (re)produces social inequality" (van Dijk, 2006, p. 364).

As Said (1994) puts it,

> While it is certainly true that the media is far better equipped to deal with caricature and sensation than with the slower processes of *culture and society*, the deeper reason for these misconceptions is the imperial dynamic and above all its separating, essentializing, dominating, and reactive tendencies (p. 37; italics added).

Therefore, there is an urgent need for the promotion of a non-Eurocentric and critical dialogue with the subalternised cultural others. Integral to this decolonial effort is the de-linking from hegemonic and Orientalist discourses and the de-essentialisation of identity by fostering intercultural dialogue in a way that grants legitimacy to coexisting pluriversal knowledges and epistemic pluralism.

6 The Scope of the Present Volume

By integrating various critical theoretical threads such as critical gender theory, critical discourse studies, intersectionality theory, and critical pedagogy, *English as an International Language Education: Critical Intercultural Literacy Perspectives* is an attempt to offer a multidisciplinary analysis of epistemic injustice and the institutionalisation of domination and inequity in academic and institutional spaces. Providing both contextual background and curriculum specific subject coverage ranging from English as a lingua franca and educational management to argumentation theory and health care, each chapter provides a clear picture of how critical intercultural literacy and the internationalisation of education relate to neoliberal performativity and global colonial power. It is argued that a shift in the mission of higher education institutions from being knowledge-oriented to having a mere entrepreneurial, 'utilitarian' and business-oriented function (corporate ethos) has negatively impacted their academic intellectual preoccupation (promotion of critical thinking).

Studies presented in this volume help cover the need for establishing variable pedagogical norms in teaching EIL. EIL-oriented approaches are championed by educationists and researchers in the field of World Englishes and critical pedagogy; they attempt to develop a comprehensive framework for the teaching of English as a tool for international communication in a globalised world. Within an EIL-based teaching framework, focus has been on issues such as different global varieties of English, target proficiency, intercultural sensitivity, and the role of students' own languages and cultures. EIL-focused teaching sees English as a global language whose goal is to develop students' interaction strategies in a way that caters for intercultural diversity and epistemological pluralism.

The present volume also brings together a host of international scholars from different parts of the world who propose pedagogies and alternative perspectives to counter the assimilationist policies and language fallacies that pervade the English language teaching (ELT) profession. In this sense, it creates intercultural spaces for dialogue amongst education scholars, language specialists and young researchers from the field of ELT education and other diverse disciplines; it offers a good opportunity to cater for 'epistemic diversity' in ELT teaching, pedagogy, and research in that the chapters promote the creation of a reasoned discussion forum, wherein contributors collaborate beyond cultural borders, theoretical perspectives, research agendas, and/or research paradigms. The different chapters are inspired by 'critical interculturality' as a decolonial project that seeks to interrogate the structures, conditions, and mechanisms of colonial power relations that still pervade our increasingly globalising postcolonial societies and perpetuate discrimination (e.g., sexism, racism, classism, heterosexism, linguicism, etc.). Therefore, this book provides a fresh breath of air amidst the polarising world of essentialising divisions in the mainstream ELT education. Each chapter, while focusing principally on the national context, makes connections across global educational settings.

References

Ahmed, S. (2012). *On being included: Racism and diversity in institutional life*. Duke University Press. https://doi.org/10.2307/j.ctv1131d2g

Augoustinos, M., Lecouteur, A., & Soyland, J. (2002). Self-sufficient arguments in political rhetoric: Constructing reconciliation and apologizing to the stolen generations. *Discourse & Society, 13*(1), 105–142. https://doi.org/10.1177/0957926502013001005

Block, D. (2010). Globalization and language teaching. In N. Coupland (Ed.), *The handbook of language and globalization* (pp. 287–304). Blackwell. https://doi.org/10.1002/9781444324068.ch12

Blommaert, J., & Verschueren, J. (1998). *Debating diversity: Analysing the discourse of tolerance*. Routledge. https://doi.org/10.4324/9780203029275

Brookes, H. J. (1995). "Suit, tie and a touch of juju"– The ideological construction of Africa: A critical discourse analysis of news on Africa in the British press. *Discourse & Society, 6*(4), 461–494. https://doi.org/10.1177/0957926595006004002

Byram, M. (1997). *Teaching and assessing intercultural communicative competence*. Multilingual Matters.

Coleman, H., & Fero, D. (2023). Struggling to access health information in the midst of a pandemic: Linguistic human rights in Indonesia. In T. Skutnabb-Kangas & R. Phillipson (Eds.), *The handbook of linguistic human rights* (pp. 71–93). Wiley Blackwell). https://doi.org/10.1002/9781119753926.ch5

Crawford, N. C. (1996). Imag(in)ing Africa. *Press/Politics, 1*(2), 30–44. https://doi.org/10.1177/1081180X960010020

Cukier, W., Adamu, P., Wall-Andrews, C., & Elmi, M. (2021). Racialized leaders leading Canadian universities. *Educational Management Administration & Leadership, 49*(4), 565–583. https://doi.org/10.1177/17411432211001363

Ellis, C., Adams, T. E., & Bochner, A. P. (2011). Autoethnography: An overview. *Historical Social Research, 36*(4), 273–290. https://doi.org/10.17169/fqs-12.1.1589

Flores, L. A. (2003). Constructing rhetorical borders: Peons, illegal aliens, and competing narratives of immigration. *Critical Studies in Media Communication, 20*(4), 362–387.

Gillborn, D. (2021). The colour of schooling: Whiteness and the mainstreaming of racism. In L. Heidrich, Y. Karakaşoğlu, P. Mecheril, & S. Shure (Eds.), *Regimes of belonging –schools –*

Migrations. Teaching in (trans)national constellations (pp. 97–110). Springer. https://doi.org/10.1007/978-3-658-29189-1_6

Grey, S., & James, A. (2016). Truth, reconciliation, and "double settler denial": Gendering the Canada-South Africa analogy. *Human Rights Review, 17*, 303–328. https://doi.org/10.1007/s12142-016-0412-8

Henry, W. L. (2021). Who feels it knows it! Alterity, identity and 'epistemological privilege': Challenging white privilege from a black perspective within the academy. In D. S. P. Thomas & J. Arday (Eds.), *Doing equity and diversity for success in higher education: Redressing structural inequalities in the academy* (pp. 299–312). Palgrave/Macmillan. https://doi.org/10.1007/978-3-030-65668-3_22

Henry, F., Dua, E., Kobayashi, A., James, C., Li, P., Ramos, H., & Smith, M. S. (2016). Race, racialization and indigeneity in Canadian universities. *Race Ethnicity and Education, 20*, 1–15. https://doi.org/10.1080/13613324.2016.1260226

Heugh, K., Stroud, K., & Taylor-Leech, K. (2021). In P. I. De Costa (Ed.), *A Sociolinguistics of the south*. Routledge/Taylor & Francis. https://doi.org/10.4324/9781315208916

House, J. (2003). English as a lingua franca: A threat to multilingualism? *Journal of SocioLinguistics, 7*(4), 556–578. https://doi.org/10.1111/j.1467-9841.2003.00242.x

Ismail, S. (2004). Being Muslim: Islam, Islamism and identity politics. *Government & Opposition, 4*, 614–631. https://doi.org/10.1111/j.1477-7053.2004.00138.x

James, M. (2018). Narrative robustness, post-apology conduct, and Canada's 1998 and 2008 residential schools' apologies. In B. Bevernage & N. Wouters (Eds.), *The Palgrave handbook of state-sponsored history after 1945* (pp. 831–847). Palgrave Macmillan. https://doi.org/10.1057/978-1-349-95306-6_45

Jenkins, J. (2006). Current perspectives on teaching world Englishes and English as a lingua franca. *TESOL Quarterly, 40*(1), 157–181. https://doi.org/10.2307/40264515

Johnson, G. F., & Howsam, R. (2020). Whiteness, power and the politics of demographics in the governance of the Canadian academy. *Canadian Journal of Political Science, 53*(3), 676–694. https://doi.org/10.1017/S0008423920000207

Kabel, A. (2023). A tale of two springs and an impending winter: Linguistic human rights and the politics of dignity in North Africa. In T. Skutnabb-Kangas & R. Phillipson (Eds.), *The handbook of linguistic human rights* (pp. 383–391). Wiley Blackwell. https://doi.org/10.1002/9781119753926.ch27

Kachru, B. (1985). Standards, codification and sociolinguistic realism: English language in the outer circle. In R. Quirk, & H. Widdowson (Eds.), *English in the world: Teaching and learning the language and literatures* (pp. 11–36). Cambridge University Press.

Kanter, R. M. (1993). *Men and women of the corporation*. Basic Books.

Karim, H. K. (2003). *Islamic peril: Media and global violence*. Black Rose Books.

Khiabany, G., & Williamson, M. (2008). Veiled bodies – Naked racism: Culture, politics and race in the sun. *Race & Class, 50*(2), 69–88. https://doi.org/10.1177/0306396808096394

Kirkpatrick, A. (2018). English in multilingual settings: Features, roles and implications. In I. P. Martin (Ed.), *Reconceptualizing English education in a multilingual society: English in The Philippines* (pp. 15–28). Springer. https://doi.org/10.1007/978-981-10-7528-5_2

Krisch, N. (2002). Legality, morality, and the dilemma of humanitarian intervention after Kosovo. Review essay. *European Journal of International Law, 13*(1), 323–335. https://doi.org/10.1093/ejil/13.1.323

Macías, R. F. (2021). Chican@ Studies, Chican@ Sociolinguistics: Dialogues on decolonizing linguistic studies and Southern multilingualisms. In K. Heugh, C. Stroud, K. Taylor-Leech, & P. I. De Costa (Eds.), *A Sociolinguistics of the South* (pp. 77–97). Routledge/Taylor & Francis. https://doi.org/10.4324/9781315208916

Maldonado-Torres, N. (2010). On the decoloniality of being: Contributions to the development of a concept. In W. D. Mignolo & A. Escobar (Eds.), *Globalization and the decolonial option* (pp. 95–124). Routledge. https://doi.org/10.4324/9781315868448

Mohamed, T., & Beagan, B. L. (2019). 'Strange faces' in the academy: Experiences of racialized and Indigenous faculty in Canadian universities. *Race Ethnicity and Education, 22*(3), 338–354. https://doi.org/10.1080/13613324.2018.1511532

Monture, P. (2009). 'Doing academia differently': Confronting 'Whiteness' in the university. In H. Francis & C. Tator (Eds.), *Racism in the Canadian university: Demanding social justice, inclusion, and equity* (pp. 76–105). University of Toronto Press. https://doi.org/10.313 8/9781442688926-004

Naber, N. (2000). Ambiguous insiders: An investigation of Arab American invisibility. *Ethnic and Racial Studies, 23*(1), 37–61. https://doi.org/10.1080/014198700329123

Nagy, R. (2020). Settler witnessing at the truth and reconciliation Commission of Canada. *Human Rights Review, 21*, 219–241. https://doi.org/10.1007/s12142-020-00595-w

Norman, D. (1993) *Islam and the West: The making of an image*. One World Publications.

Nutt, D. (2005, July 5). Who pays Africa's bribes? *The Guardian*. https://www.theguardian.com/world/2005/jul/05/g8.development. Accessed 14 Dec 2022.

Osborne, S. (2021). Aboriginal agency, knowledge, and voice: Centring Kulintja Southern methodologies. In K. Heugh, C. Stroud, K. Taylor-Leech, & P. I. De Costa (Eds.), *A Sociolinguistics of the South* (pp. 232–247). Routledge/ Taylor & Francis. https://doi.org/10.4324/9781315208916

Phaswana, E. D. (2021). Women, gender, and race in post-apartheid South Africa. In O. Yacob-Haliso & T. Falola (Eds.), *The Palgrave handbook of African women's studies* (pp. 197–215). Palgrave/Macmillan. https://doi.org/10.1007/978-3-030-28099-4_141

Phillipson, R. (2023). Language policy implications of 'global' English for linguistic human rights. In T. Skutnabb-Kangas & R. Phillipson (Eds.), *The handbook of linguistic human rights* (pp. 143–157). Wiley Blackwell. https://doi.org/10.1002/9781119753926.ch9

Phyak, P., Rawal, H., & De Costa, P. I. (2021). Dialogue as a decolonial effort: Nepali youth transforming monolingual ideologies and reclaiming multilingual citizenship. In K. Heugh, C. Stroud, K. Taylor-Leech, & P. I. De Costa (Eds.), *A Sociolinguistics of the south* (pp. 154–170). Routledge/ Taylor & Francis. https://doi.org/10.4324/9781315208916

Pindi, G. N. (2021). Promoting African knowledge in communication studies: African feminisms as critical decolonial praxis. *Review of Communication, 21*(4), 327–344. https://doi.org/10.108 0/15358593.2021.2001843

Poole, E. (2002). *Reporting Islam: Media representations of British Muslims*. I. B. Tauris. https://doi.org/10.5040/9780755604579

Poupart, L. M. (2003). The familiar face of genocide: Internalized oppression among American Indians. *Hypatia, 18*(2), 86–100.

Quijano, A. (2000). Coloniality of power, ethnocentrism, and Latin America. *NEPANTLA: Views from South, 1*(3), 533–580. https://doi.org/10.1177/0268580900015002005. Duke University Press.

Quijano, A. (2007). Coloniality and modernity/rationality. *Cultural Studies, 21*(2–3), 168–178. https://doi.org/10.1080/09502380601164353

Quijano, A. (2010). Coloniality and modernity/rationality. In W. D. Mignolo & A. Escobar (Eds.), *Globalization and the decolonial option* (pp. 22–32). Routledge.

Richardson, J. E. (2004). *(Mis)representing Islam: The racism and rhetoric of British broadsheet newspapers*. John Benjamins. https://doi.org/10.1075/dapsac.9

Sadiqi, F. (2014). *Moroccan feminist discourses*. Palgrave Macmillan. https://doi.org/10.1057/9781137455093

Sahlane, A. (2012). Argumentation and fallacy in the justification of the 2003 war on Iraq. *Argumentation, 26*(4), 459–488. https://doi.org/10.1007/s10503-012-9265-8

Sahlane, A. (2022). Covering the war on Iraq: The pragmatics of framing and visual rhetoric. In I. Chiluwa (Ed.), *Discourse, media, and conflict: Examining war and resolution in the news* (pp. 93–116). Cambridge University Press. https://doi.org/10.1017/9781009064057.006

Said, E. W. (1978). *Orientalism: Western conceptions of the orient*. Vintage Books.

Said, E. (1994). *Culture and imperialism*. Vintage Books.

Said, E. W. (1997). *Covering Islam: How the media & the experts determine how we see the rest of the world*. Vintage Books.

Shaheen, J. G. (2000). Hollywood's Muslim Arabs. *The Muslim World, 90*(1/2), 22–42. https://doi.org/10.1111/j.1478-1913.2000.tb03680.x

Sian, K. P. (2019). *Navigating institutional racism in British universities*. Palgrave Macmillan. https://www.palgrave.com/gp/book/9783030142834

Stroud, C. (2021). Framing stories of the south and their storytellers. In K. Heugh, C. Stroud, K. Taylor-Leech, & P. I. De Costa (Eds.), *A Sociolinguistics of the south* (pp. 23–30). Routledge/Taylor & Francis. https://doi.org/10.4324/9781315208916

Synott, J. (2003). Discourse resistance and negotiation by indigenous Australians. *Peace & Change, 28*(2), 202–220. https://doi.org/10.1111/1468-0130.00259

Train, R. (2009). Toward a "natural" history of the native (standard) speaker. In N. M. Doerr (Ed.), *The native speaker concept: Ethnographic investigations of native speaker effects* (pp. 47–80). Mouton de Gruyter. https://doi.org/10.1515/9783110220957.47

Tupas, R. (2018). Teacher ideology in English language education. In I. P. Martin (Ed.), *Reconceptualizing English education in a multilingual society: English in The Philippines* (pp. 85–98). Springer. https://doi.org/10.1007/978-981-10-7528-5_6

Turner, J. (2018). Internal colonisation: The intimate circulations of empire, race and liberal government. *European Journal of International Relations, 24*(4), 765–790. https://doi.org/10.1177/1354066117734904

Van Dijk, T. A. (2006). Discourse and manipulation. *Discourse & Society, 17*(3), 359–383. https://doi.org/10.1177/0957926506060250

Walsh, C. (2007). Shifting the geopolitics of critical knowledge: Decolonial thought and cultural studies 'others' in the Andes. *Cultural Studies, 21*(2/3), 224–239.

Widdowson, H. G. (1994). The ownership of English. *TESOL Quarterly, 28*(2), 377–389. https://doi.org/10.2307/3587438

Ahmed Sahlane (PhD, University of Ulster, Belfast) is Senior Lecturer in English at University of Jeddah (English Language Institute). He coordinated several EAP/ESP programs at Saudi universities, where he served in a variety of leadership roles such as business English program academic advisor and curriculum designer. He has taught English at all levels (K-12 and tertiary) in Morocco, Oman, Saudi Arabia, and Canada. He was the winner of Top Gun Master Teacher's Award, CDIS, Burnaby, Canada, 2001. His publications focus on the critical analysis of mediated political discourse from the perspective of argumentation theory and critical linguistics. He has published several articles and book chapters about the coverage of the 2003 Iraq War in Western opinion-editorial press. Sahlane's current research interests revolve around the rhetorics of populist discourse and media (mis)representation of cultural otherness. His research interests also include intersectionality and decoloniality studies, social semiotics, and critical pedagogy. Email: asahlan1@uj.edu.sa

Rosalind Pritchard is Emeritus Professor of Education and Senior Distinguished Research Fellow at Ulster University, where she was Head of the School of Education and Coordinator of Research. Her research interests include higher education and TESOL (especially cross-cultural adaptation and teaching strategies). She is a member of the British Academy of Social Sciences, an Honorary Member of the British Association for International and Comparative Education, Secretary of the European Association for Institutional Research and a Member of the Royal Irish Academy, of which membership is considered the highest academic honour in Ireland. She has held grants from the Leverhulme Trust, the Economic and Social Research Council, the UK Council for International Education, the German Academic Exchange Service and the Higher Education Innovation Fund. Email: R.Pritchard@ulster.ac.uk

Part I
Intercultural Literacy in EIL Education: Towards a Post-Native-Speakerist Approach

In Part I Tajeddin and Rezajejad investigate the Iranian EFL teachers' perceptions of critical intercultural language teaching and their actual classroom practices. The study concludes that most teachers believe that intercultural sensitivity (involving the learner's need to express their own and recognise others' cultural identities) is crucial in EFL education. Besides, teachers contend that students should be encouraged to look at their own culture and other cultures from an objective critical perspective and reflect upon their shifting and hybrid cultural identities. However, the study reveals that not many teachers (45%) tend to integrate culture tasks into their language instruction. It seems that critical discussion of cultural content in textbook materials is strategically avoided. Hence, a clear mismatch between teachers' beliefs and actual classroom practices is exposed. This is partly due to lack of appropriate training in integrating intercultural teaching in foreign language instruction.

The creation of engaging online collaborative communities of learning can help to promote students' critical intercultural awareness and expand the availability of active learning opportunities in synchronous authentic communication environments. One goal of such technology-supported collaborative intercultural/educational encounters is to enhance learner autonomy by encouraging students to engage in critical co-construction of knowledge across cultural boundaries. EL Boubekri's qualitative study is a good step in that direction. He explores networked collaborative learning in the context of an online media course, delineating how computer-supported collaborative task-based learning proceeds through criticism of advertisement production and discussion within an US-Moroccan community of university learners. The illustrative deconstruction activity of a Febreze advert is a very interesting technology-mediated, task-based and group project-oriented assignment that trains students to collaboratively be engaged in the development of their critical media literacy by engaging in 'authentic' intercultural interaction. Virtual intercultural collaboration gives learners some agency as to the need to express a difference of opinion in the form of reasoned dialogue. US and Moroccan media students have the opportunity to nurture a decentred approach to diversity and difference while they interact, observe, compare, reflect on, and negotiate intercultural differences through the created closed Facebook group.

In our globalising world, students need to understand different worldviews to be able to interact successfully beyond cultural borders. In current consumerist-driven global English language teaching (ELT) textbooks adopted in Saudi university foundation year courses, "[t]he value systems conveyed are eminently capitalist, consumerist, and ultimately conformist" (Block, 2010, pp. 298-299), which necessitates that teachers have to resort to adapting strategies that help reshape these published 'global' materials to fit the cultural realities and the actual needs of their students. Resistance to the homogenising globalisation of ELT education ranges from superficial substitution (e.g., replacement of global celebrities with local ones) or replacement of international malls with local markets or 'souks.' Hence, to question such a homogenisation of ELT textbooks, Aleisa's chapter is about promoting the Saudi EFL learners' critical intercultural awareness in a Saudi university's Foundation Year Program's curriculum. It describes how to empower local teachers by assigning them the responsibility of being more independent in choosing their own teaching materials and approaches, based on prescribed learning objectives by proposing an EFL intercultural teaching syllabus which offers a more comprehensive roadmap to developing critical thinking skills and critical intercultural literacy in the English Language Program (ELP) classroom. The proposed ELP (which originates from a partnership between a Saudi and a US university) aims at training students to navigate interculturality by introducing various global sociocultural topics, designed to develop language proficiency and critical intercultural communication skills. However, such a curriculum has actually encountered several institutional and professional constraints related partly to lack of proper teacher training and the inadequacy of the research infrastructure within the Saudi educational institution. In addition, native-speakerist ideologies continue to devalue glocalised attempts to replace commercialised Western textbooks.

Reference

Block, D. (2010). Globalization and language teaching. In Nikolas Coupland (Ed.), *The handbook of language and globalization* (pp. 287–304). Blackwell. https://doi.org/10.1002/97814443 24068.ch12

Critical Intercultural Language Teaching: Moving from Beliefs to Instructional Practices in EFL Classrooms

Zia Tajeddin and Atefeh Rezanejad

Abstract Although several studies have addressed intercultural language teaching, there seems to be a dearth of research in English as a foreign language (EFL) contexts, specifically focusing on its critical aspects. To address this gap, this chapter reports on a study investigating the non-native language teachers' beliefs about critical intercultural language teaching (CICLT) and their actual critical intercultural practices in their language classrooms. Data collection was done in two phases, through questionnaire administration and class observations. To explore the language teachers' perceptions of CICLT, 219 teachers participated in the first phase by filling out a 20-item CICLT questionnaire. In the second phase, 40 class sessions from 20 teachers were randomly observed using an observation checklist to obtain a clearer picture of the teachers' practices of CICLT. The findings indicated a mismatch between the teachers' beliefs and pedagogical practices. Although the majority of teachers were favourably disposed toward CICLT in their responses to the questionnaire items, class observations revealed that this positivity was not necessarily manifested in their instruction. The findings of this study have implications for educators, policy makers, and practitioners regarding the significance of CICLT. As such, they call for more attention to the content of teacher education programs to raise teachers' awareness and enhance their ability to adopt a more critical perspective.

Keywords English as a foreign language · Teacher beliefs · Instructional practices · Critical intercultural competence · Language teaching

Z. Tajeddin (✉)
Tarbiat Modares University, Tehran, Iran
e-mail: tajeddinz@modares.ac.ir

A. Rezanejad
Allameh Tabataba'i University, Tehran, Iran

© The Author(s), under exclusive license to Springer Nature
Switzerland AG 2023
A. Sahlane, R. Pritchard (eds.), *English as an International Language Education*, English Language Education 33,
https://doi.org/10.1007/978-3-031-34702-3_2

1 Introduction

In the contemporary globalized and "media-saturated" world (Halualani, 2019, p. 20), intercultural communicative competence (ICC) is acknowledged to be one of the most critical aims of language teaching. Globalization has resulted in an increasing emphasis on learning English as an international lingua franca used ubiquitously by non-native English speakers (NNESs) around the globe (Genç, 2018). This has led to transformations in the general goals of English language teaching (Byram & Wagner, 2018; Hong & Cheon, 2017; Kohler, 2020; Zhang & Zhou, 2019). Though it is valuable for NNESs to hold a critical stance while learning English, the majority of them assume that they need to adopt new L2-driven cultural ideologies when learning the language. They may overlook the point that NNESs have the right to "claim ownership of English" (Chamberlin-Quinlisk & Senyshyn, 2012, p. 20) on a par with native English speakers (NESs) and can challenge the idea of superiority of native speakers (Porto, 2020). In this regard, non-native language teachers, constituting the majority of English teachers around the world (Braine, 2010; Tajeddin et al., 2018), are the main agents for educating NNESs for a decolonial option in which they are not "uncritical victims of the global hegemony of NS-based pedagogic model" (Li, 2009, p. 82). In the same vein, Nault (2006) argued that "the globalization of English complicates the issue of how to teach culture" (p. 324). Non-native language teachers may get confused in answering the question of "whose culture must be taught?" as most of them feel a need to teach native-based cultural norms while teaching English to learners of English as an additional language. In undertaking this responsibility, language teachers' own intercultural beliefs exert a great impact on their pedagogical practices and their acceptance of new instructive approaches and activities. Despite the importance attributed to critical intercultural language teaching (CICLT), it has received scant attention in EFL contexts.

Against this backdrop, this chapter commences with a review of the current theories of ICC and the necessity of adopting a CICLT approach. Next, it reports on an empirical study of non-native EFL teachers' beliefs and practices in the Iranian context. The (mis)matches between beliefs and practices are investigated through a survey questionnaire and classroom observation. The chapter continues with a discussion of the findings, and implications for teachers and policy makers to bring to the fore the significance of heightening teachers' critical intercultural awareness. It ends with concluding remarks and directions for further research in teacher education for intercultural language teaching. This section consists of two parts. First, the notion of critical intercultural competence is described. Next, critical intercultural pedagogy and research on it are reviewed.

1.1 Critical Intercultural Competence

In the early 1970s, Hymes (1972) introduced the term communicative competence (CC). It was concerned with social interaction and communication largely within a monolingual and perhaps monocultural community. In 1980 in North America, Canale and Swain further developed the idea of CC, which included grammatical, sociolinguistic, and strategic competences. Later, in Europe, the theory was further elaborated by van Ek (1986). He put forward the concept of sociocultural competence, in addition to linguistic, strategic, sociolinguistic, and discourse competence introduced by different scholars during the previous years (Canale, 1983; Canale & Swain, 1980; Hymes, 1972). The notion of CC was then integrated into foreign language instruction and turned into one of the most important concepts in communicative language teaching. However, the main shortcoming was taking the native speaker as a model for foreign language learners to follow (Byram & Guilherme, 2000). That is why Byram and Zarate (1994) proposed the idea of 'intercultural speaker' as the main goal for foreign language education.

During the coming years, Byram (1997) proposed his theory of intercultural communicative competence (ICC), a framework that insisted on preparing foreign language learners for appropriate, effective, and meaningful interactions with people from other cultures by focusing on the five knowledge types: (1) knowledge (*savoirs*): knowledge of self and other, of how interaction occurs, and of the relationship of the individual to society; (2) skills of interpreting and relating (*savoir etre*): knowing how to interpret and relate information; (3) attitudes (*savoir comprendre*): knowing how to engage with the political consequences of education and being critically aware of cultural behaviours; (4) skills of discovery and interaction (*savoir apprendre/faire*): knowing how to discover cultural information; and (5) critical cultural awareness (*savoir s'engager*): knowing how to be; how to relativize oneself and value the attitudes and beliefs of the other.

In today's world, which is characterized by globalization and transformation in communication tools, we are facing a constant interrelationship of language and culture. As Liu and Nelson (2018) state, one of the most notable features of second language instruction in today's world is the diversity of contexts. The global spread and use of English around the world have resulted in a "kaleidoscopic plurality of the language in terms of use, users, cultures, and linguistic forms" (Marlina, 2021, p. 73). It seems that the most significant factor within the framework of ICC would be critical cultural awareness defined by Byram (1997) as the ability "to evaluate critically and on the basis of explicit criteria, perspectives, practices and products in one's own and other cultures and countries" (p. 53), at the heart of which lies the concept of "evaluation" (Houghton, 2008, p. 222). Halualani and Nakayama (2010) also argued that the most significant and rapidly growing addition to the debates on intercultural communication is the critical approach to it. As Nakayama and Martin (2018) maintain, "critical intercultural communication is not a unified, singular paradigm, nor theory; instead, it is a perspective, a lens for viewing the relationship between culture and communication, and intercultural encounters" (p. 1).

Through intercultural dialogues and interactions, criticality in ICC prompts the ability to cope with both personal and social transformation. Porto et al. (2018) view this transformation as "conscious and deliberate," flowing from "the critical exploration, analysis and evaluation of self and other" (p. 3). Likewise, Liddicoat et al. (2003) assert that a fundamental element of CICLT is gaining knowledge of one's own culture prior to learning about the foreign language culture. In this regard, the "post-native-speakerist approach" (Porto et al., 2018, p. 4) has challenged using native speakers as a model for learners. As English is a widely used international language, it is argued that it also reflects multifaceted beliefs, identities, cultures, and values (Pennycook, 2017). As such, Porto et al. (2018, p. 4) call for "an informed rejection" of the native-speaker as either a socio-cultural or linguistic model.

According to Nakayama and Martin (2018), critical studies in intercultural communication were mainly influenced by three scholarly movements, namely (1) the Frankfurt School, (2) cultural studies in the UK, and (3) the postcolonial movement. In fact, critical researchers believed that some very important facets of intercultural communication were overlooked. Nakayama and Martin (2018) rightly summarized some key elements of the traditional and critical intercultural approaches and enumerated a list of some key ideas and features of the latter approach (see Table 1; based on Nakayama & Martin, 2018), the first of which is "elimination of oppression." Put differently, this approach strives for the elimination of unequal power relationships and tries to "create more just and equitable human relations" (p. 3). Likewise, Halualani (2019) stressed the need to adopt this approach as it will sensitize interactants to the issue of power in intercultural relations, "embedded in many visible and invisible aspects of [their] lives" (p. 23).

Table 1 A comparison of the features of traditional and critical intercultural approach

Traditional intercultural approach	Critical intercultural approach
aims at the understanding and the prediction of communication practices of diverse cultural communities	proposes a more complex notion of culture and cultural identity to include groups/communities within a nation
compares and contrasts communication patterns of different national cultures	identifies unequal power relations and oppression in intercultural encounters
ignores complex cultural variations	creates more just and equitable human relations
considers culture as stable and static	views culture as more fluid, dynamic, & changeable (cultures change and are changed)
focuses on the interpersonal micro level of interaction	focuses on hybridity (no discrete cultures in the era of globalization)
equates a nation with culture	regards power, social justice, and equality as central concerns
references to US Americans actually mean white US Americans and/or often white male Americans	is concerned with hegemony (how and why people consent to domination)
peoples of other nation-states (e.g., French) are considered a homogeneous group	regards history as an integral macro context for understanding intercultural relations

1.2 Critical Intercultural Pedagogy (CIP)

Language is regarded as the realization of a society with its own specific cultural norms (Canagarajah, 2014). Thus, it is not a "stable and neutral system of communication, but (…) a dynamic and value-laden activity" (Chamberlin-Quinlisk & Senyshyn, 2012, p. 15). A fairly commonplace supposition would be that learning a language is "naturally intertwined" with knowledge about the culture of that language (Merse, 2021, p. 92). In fact, due to globalization, more and more opportunities for intercultural encounters and experiences are introduced in diverse educational contexts around the world (LaScotte & Peters, 2021). To integrate linguistic and cultural diversity into English language classrooms, there has been a shift from teaching English as a second or foreign language to teaching English as an international language (Marlina, 2021; Matsuda, 2012; McKay, 2012). The main premise from this paradigm shift, opposing the "practices that glorify lingua-cultural norms and practices of a particular speech community" (Marlina, 2021, p. 75), seems to be challenging the old pedagogical principles and practices of idolizing native English speakers and paying more attention to the learners' own linguistic and cultural norms as an asset in language instruction (Marlina, 2018).

Efficacious and successful ESL/EFL (English as a second or foreign language) learners are considered to be those who are not only competent in technical and linguistic aspects of language but also able to handle intercultural interaction (LaScotte & Peters, 2021). However, the development of ICC has not been a priority in many English language classrooms (Liddicoat & Scarino, 2013). According to Byram and Wagner (2018), a common fallacy held by some language teachers is that there is no extra need to teach culture, as language and culture are really interrelated. In fact, they assume that they would ineluctably teach culture while teaching the language.

However, according to CIP, it is necessary to understand the "variations in interactional norms between speech communities" (Hismanoglu, 2011, p. 805) and the ability to discover the norms of other cultures. According to Byram (2000), language learners specifically need the ability to interact effectively with people of cultures different from their own. Likewise, Hismanoglu (2011) stressed the need to acknowledge the diverse values and behaviours of others by developing appropriate skills and attitudes to deal with differences in a "non-judgmental way" (p. 805). This is mainly because, in the past two decades, the concept of effective language pedagogy has greatly changed. As Byram and Wagner (2018) maintained, a successful language teaching system will no longer rely on an absolute provision of grammatical or lexical information, but aims to prepare the learners for communication and interaction with people of diverse cultural backgrounds. When teaching a language, the intercultural dimensions cannot be neglected. Similarly, attention needs to be paid to both local and global representations of culture.

The main argument underpinning CIP is that English language learners do not need to clone or strive too hard to emulate native English speakers (Alsagoff, 2012), but could be "competent users of English" (Matsuda, 2018, p. 25) in a world in which English language users encounter many more varieties of English speakers and cultures than the American or British ones. In fact, "such a change of minds and practices seems urgent if the global ELT sector as a whole wishes to stay in sync with today's cultural and intersectional realities so as not to lose its credibility for cultural learning" (Merse, 2021, p. 95). Also, according to Atay and Toyosaki (2018), the main goal in CIP is to "understand, critique, transform, and intervene upon the dynamics of power and domination embedded inside and outside classroom walls" (p. ix). Likewise, Halualani (2018) asserted that CICLT "is a central vehicle that shapes critical intercultural communication studies and makes it accountable in terms of its larger goals, commitments, theorisings, concepts, and actions" (pp. 4–5).

As to CICLT, it should be noted that language teachers are the most important agents who play a crucial role in equipping the learners with necessary skills. Also, teachers' beliefs inform their pedagogical practices and manifest their conceptions of teaching (Mori, 2011). Breen et al. (2001) argued for the importance of researching teachers' beliefs and perceptions and asserted that it can assist researchers in the description and explanation of teacher actions in the classroom by promoting reflective practices. It can indeed play a role complementary to observational studies. Reviewing the literature shows that several studies have explored teachers' perceptions of CICLT (e.g., Gu, 2015; Nguyen, 2014; Oranje & Smith, 2017; Young & Sachdev, 2011). Nevertheless, research on teachers' perceptions indicates that they are not a "straightforward construct" (Feryok, 2008, p. 228) and many factors may affect their variability in different sociocultural contexts. For instance, Freeman (1991) reminded scholars of the implicit nature of perceptions, which needs to be made explicit in order for it to be comprehensively examined. However, understanding teachers' classroom practices entails listening to their voices and exploring their thoughts, as minds and attitudes have a significant role in shaping their performance. In response to a seemingly small body of research on teachers' perceptions and practices with regard to CICLT in the EFL context, the present study set out to demonstrate the perceptions-practices (mis)match through observations of language classes. In view of this, the main objective of this chapter is to explore the EFL teachers' practices of CICLT and to inspect how their perceptions inform their practices. Hence, the following research questions were put forward:

1. What are English language teachers' beliefs about CICLT?
2. How is CICLT practised in language classrooms by English language teachers?

2 An Empirical Study

In view of the two research questions on CICLT raised in this study, this section describes the method of data collection and the findings of the study.

2.1 Method

2.1.1 Participants and Setting

A total of 219 nonnative Iranian EFL teachers (110 males and 109 females, with an average age of 32) teaching at private language institutes were recruited through convenience sampling. These institutes offer multi-level courses in general English from basic to advanced levels. The textbooks used are global English textbook series published by international publishers such as Cambridge University Press, Oxford University Press, and Pearson Education. In one of the institutes taking part in this study, global textbooks are modified for localisation purposes. Teachers' recruitment was through direct contact or email communication with teachers and institute managers. Based on the snowball sampling, those teachers who accepted to participate in the study were asked to encourage other teachers to participate. The participating teachers taught English in three nationwide language institutes with many branches as well as other local language institutes. Their L1 was Persian, and they had an average teaching experience of eight years.

2.1.2 Data Collection and Analysis

The research instruments comprised a newly developed survey questionnaire and an observation checklist to collect data on the teachers' perceptions and practices of CICLT. The questionnaire contained 20 items and was based on a five-point Likert scale (1 = strongly disagree, 2 = disagree, 3 = neither agree nor disagree, 4 = agree, 5 = strongly agree). To make sure of its reliability, it was piloted with 60 EFL teachers similar to the main participants of the study (with Cronbach's alpha of .80, which according to Pallant (2010) indicates an acceptable reliability coefficient). Also, to gain a clear picture of the teachers' critical intercultural language teaching in language classrooms, an observation checklist was prepared. The checklist included 14 items (see Table 3) whose development was based on the current relevant literature. It mainly revolved around the issues of the general class atmosphere, class activities and instruments, and assignments and projects.

The questionnaire was administered in different ways in order to access more teachers and collect the data in a shorter span of time. As a priority, the questionnaire was handed to the EFL teachers along with some explanation of the nature of the study and the importance of the issue. The electronic version of the questionnaire was sent through email to teachers who had accepted to participate in the study. They filled out the questionnaire and returned it to the second author. Also, the observation data were collected by visiting different language classes in an unobtrusive way so that both teachers and students would feel free to act as naturally as possible. In addition, class observation checklists were filled out immediately after each class session, not during it, to avoid distracting class members. Observations were also recorded and later transcribed to assist data analysis. Finally, the questionnaire items and the different episodes on the observation checklist were analysed with descriptive statistics (frequencies and percentages) to discover the prevalent types of activities.

2.2 Findings

The findings are organized in two parts: teachers' beliefs about CICLT and teachers' practices of CICLT.

2.2.1 Teachers' Beliefs Regarding CICLT

The first research question in this study probed the teachers' perceptions of CICLT. To address this question, the EFL teachers' responses to the different questionnaire items were analysed. The results provided the data displayed in Table 2. As illustrated in the table, item 1 had the highest rate of agreement as 93.1% of the teachers agreed or strongly agreed with the statement that "When teaching cultural issues, a language teacher should remind the students to respect and value all cultures around the world, irrespective of its being L1, L2, or global". Interestingly, not even one teacher strongly disagreed with this assumption. Likewise, item 18 was the second agreed-upon statement in which over 86% of the teachers concurred with the statement that "Through critical discussions on intercultural issues, the students will have a better understanding of their own culture and its values". Similarly, item 20 received the third highest approval with 84.5% of the teachers believing that "Teaching about cultures will increase the language learners' willingness to communicate". These last two favoured statements pertained to some of the outcomes of critical intercultural pedagogy (CIP). On the other hand, the lowest consensus was observed in item 13 in which 43.4% disagreed or strongly disagreed with the statement that "Learning a new language requires the acceptance of its cultural norms". Also, the second lowest agreement was found in item 11 and with regard to the statement "Learning a new language should increase the students' awareness of their own L1 cultural identity" in which 29.2% disagreed.

2.2.2 Teachers' Practices of CICLT

To inspect the current status of CICLT in EFL classes, 40 different class sessions from 20 different EFL teachers were observed using an observation checklist. The detailed results pertaining to each item are summarized in Table 3. As illustrated, the highest observed practice was related to the general class atmosphere. In nearly half of the observed cases (F = 18, P = 45%), the teachers were inclined to teach culture in support of the unit topic (Item 1), i.e., they viewed it as a compulsory part of the book to be taught, in a very limited form. Similarly, item 9 received the next

Table 2 Descriptive statistics for teachers' beliefs about intercultural language teaching

		1 (%)	2 (%)	3 (%)	4 (%)	5 (%)	M	SD
1	When teaching cultural issues, a language teacher should remind the students to respect and value all cultures around the world, irrespective of their being L1, L2, or global.	0	4.1	2.7	39.7	53.4	4.42	.74
2	A language teacher should present a realistic image of the L2 culture by touching upon both the positive and negative sides of the foreign culture and society.	0	8.2	15.5	52.5	23.7	3.92	.84
3	A language teacher should make the students aware of the similarities and differences between cultures.	0	1	18.7	56.2	24.7	4.05	.67
4	A language teacher should remember that the cultural values of non-native speakers of English are as legitimate and valuable as those of native English speakers.	3.7	0	26.9	41.6	27.9	3.92	.93
5	A language teacher should ask the students to critically compare an aspect of their L1 culture with that aspect in the L2 culture and cultures of other non-English speaking countries.	0	1	35.6	50.2	13.7	3.77	.67
6	A language teacher should foster their own cultural awareness in order to be able to help the students improve their intercultural knowledge.	1	4.6	17.8	63.5	14.2	3.87	.69
7	A language teacher should try not to consider American/British culture as representative of global culture.	5.5	10	35.6	26.5	22.4	3.56	1.11
8	A language teacher should encourage the students to culturally behave like people in English-speaking countries.	3.7	19.6	30.1	27.9	18.7	3.38	1.10
9	Intercultural language teaching will enhance students' self-esteem and strengthen their cultural identity.	0	2.3	29.7	60.7	7.3	3.73	.62
10	By teaching the cultural values of other nations to the students and helping them respect all of them, they will develop a global cultural identity.	2.7	0	17.4	67.6	12.3	3.87	.72
11	Learning a new language should increase the students' awareness of their own L1 cultural identity.	0	29.2	22.8	34.2	13.7	3.32	1.04
12	A language teacher should enhance the students' understanding of their own national cultural identity.	0	19.2	21	33.3	26.5	3.67	1.06
13	Learning a new language requires the acceptance of its cultural norms.	14.2	29.2	10.5	41.6	4.6	3.07	1.20
14	Teaching and learning critically about cultures will stimulate the students' intercultural curiosity and motivate them to learn more.	1	4.1	23.7	54.8	17.4	3.85	.74

(continued)

Table 2 (continued)

		1 (%)	2 (%)	3 (%)	4 (%)	5 (%)	M	SD
15	Through intercultural awareness-raising in language classes, the students will be able to discover the relationship between language and culture.	0	5.5	26	54.8	13.7	3.77	.75
16	A language teacher should help the students notice and critically evaluate the hidden cultural elements in textbooks.	0	9.6	44.7	37.9	7.8	3.44	.77
17	A language teacher should encourage the students to value their own L1 culture along with other cultures.	0	4.1	16	52.5	27.4	4.03	.77
18	Through critical discussions of intercultural issues, the students will have a better understanding of their own culture and its values.	0	2.7	10.5	76.7	10	3.94	.55
19	Making the students aware of the significance of their own L1 culture in addition to L2 culture will enhance their L1 cultural self-esteem.	0	2.7	29.2	52.1	16	3.81	.72
20	Teaching about cultures will increase the language learners' willingness to communicate.	1.8	1	12.8	68.5	16	3.96	.69

[a]1 = strongly disagree, 2 = disagree, 3 = neither agree nor disagree, 4 = agree, 5 = strongly agree
[b](N = 219)

highest frequency of occurrence. As depicted, in 37.5% of observed classes, the teacher asked the students to participate in role-play situations in which people from different cultures met. Moreover, in 32.5% of classes, the teacher asked the students about their experiences in a foreign country. This made item 2 the next most frequent one. By contrast, item 8 on the checklist was the least important event in observed classes. Observations indicated that literally no teacher tried to critically discuss a text's meaning with the students while teaching linguistic skills. In addition, the second lowest practised activity was found in item 14. Only 2.5% of the teachers required the students to prepare a short lecture on an aspect of culture.

2.3 Discussion

The main objective of this chapter was to explore the interplay between language teachers' perceptions of CICLT and their actual practices in their language classes. The overall findings indicated that a clear incongruity could be observed between the teachers' beliefs and practices. Whereas the questionnaire results documented that almost all teachers concurred on the merits of incorporating a critical stance toward teaching culture in language courses, very few of them followed this belief in practice. The results corroborate the findings by Cheng (2012), who reported on

Table 3 Descriptive statistics for teachers' instructional practices of CICLT in their classrooms

	Statements	*F	**P
1	The teacher teaches culture in support of the unit topics, e.g., discussions on clothing habits and fashion in a unit on clothes.	18	45%
9	The teacher asks the students to participate in role play situations in which people from different cultures meet.	15	37.5%
2	The teacher asks the students about their experiences in a foreign country.	13	32.5%
3	The teacher could overcome his/her own stereotypes (e.g., not try to show any positive or negative attitude regarding the country the L2 is spoken on to their students).	11	27.5%
4	The teacher focuses on an aspect of the foreign culture regarding which he/she feels positive.	9	22.5%
10	The teacher asks the students to compare an aspect of their own culture with that aspect in a foreign culture.	9	22.5%
13	Students are told to write a conversation between interlocutors of different cultural backgrounds.	8	20%
5	The teacher teaches the students to understand and respect people from other cultures.	5	12.5%
11	The teacher asks the students to talk about both positive and negative aspects of L2 culture.	3	7.5%
12	Students were invited to talk about different aspects of a topic presented in their textbook, e.g., compare and contrast different aspects of it in different cultures.	3	7.5%
6	The teacher encourages the students to take risks, analyse, and reflect on their own experiences and learning.	2	5%
7	The class is decorated with posters illustrating some different aspects of world cultures.	2	5%
14	Students are required to prepare a short lecture on an aspect of culture.	1	2.5%
8	The teacher tries to critically discuss a text's meaning with the students even when teaching linguistic skills.	0	0%

*F = Frequency, ** P = Percentage

some discrepancies between EFL teachers' understandings of intercultural competence and their self-reported instructional practices. A comparable incongruity could also be observed between the beliefs and practices in Tian's (2013) research on 96 EFL teachers. Fung and Chow's (2002) study also revealed the very limited relationship between the teachers' favoured teaching procedure and their real pedagogical practices in classrooms. Likewise, Kohler (2015) reported on some language teachers from Australia who showed awareness of the real need to integrate language and culture but faced some challenges in doing so in class.

In the current study, more than half of the teachers agreed on reaching a mutual understanding by focusing on all cultures, irrespective of being L1, L2, or global culture. This was, to some extent, anticipated in the multicultural society of Iran, where people of different ethnic varieties have long lived together peacefully. However, the point is that this was not observed in practice. Despite this stated belief, only a small number of the teachers endeavoured to teach multicultural values directly to their students. In the same way, the majority of the teachers thought that a language teacher must encourage the students to value their own L1 culture.

However, this was witnessed in only a few language classes where the teachers, for instance, asked the students to write a conversation between a native and a non-native English speaker as an assignment. This substantial beliefs-practices mismatch seems to be rooted in the teachers' poor understanding of CIP and the need for reflection on it as a means of developing "a meta-level understanding of oneself and one's own culture" (Moeller & Osborn, 2014, p. 681). This might also be the direct result of a lack of continuous professional development programs for in-service teachers to enrich their ICC-oriented teaching skills and to enhance their knowledge about CIP approaches and teaching materials conducive to the integration of teaching culture in foreign language classes. As Oranje (2016) argued, the absence of this reflection can best designate whether a teacher's approach is intercultural or not. According to some scholars (e.g., Han & Song, 2011; Sercu et al., 2005), what really prevents teachers from being completely intercultural, in spite of having perceptions favouring CIP, is the absence of this reflection. The answer is simple: "as the EFL curriculum does not prescribe specific intercultural teaching strategies, teachers need to make independent efforts to provide learners with opportunities to translate the stated cultural objectives into practice" (Sahlane & Pritchard, this volume, Chap. 17).

What is more, while the integration of language and culture is emphasized at all levels of language learning, the teachers in the present study did not link language and culture to any appreciable extent; they demonstrated a mere passive understanding. This echoes Liddicoat's (2011) differentiation between *static* and *dynamic* views on the nature of culture. Whereas considering culture as static means viewing it as facts, information, and things to be learned separate from language, the dynamic view entails promoting skills of comparison, reflection, and discovery, and is more in line with the fundamental principles of CICLT. As our observations revealed, the language teachers were more attached to the traditional static view, largely neglecting the integration of language and culture and primarily viewing it as "supplementary and optional" (Byram et al., 1991, p. 17) or even as fun activities. The findings are, likewise, in tandem with those reported by Sercu et al. (2005) and Oranje and Smith (2017), who also reported that the majority of the teachers correspondingly favoured teaching language over teaching culture. Similarly, a number of other research studies reported an analogous mismatch between cultural beliefs and instructional practices (e.g., Conway et al., 2010; Han & Song, 2011).

3 Implications for Interculturally Oriented Teacher Education

The current study mainly brings to the fore the significance of fostering critical intercultural competence among second/foreign language teachers. In the current "era of globalization, transnationalism, and multilingual/multiculturalism" (Shin & Jeon, 2018, p. 125), teacher education needs to be envisaged differently if we plan to realize the goals of CIP. What teachers really need is an education program focused on critical intercultural teaching so that they would clearly know what to do in their classes. Language teachers need to be educated on how to give voice to the local cultures of the learners and create spaces for their active participation in shaping CIP in language classrooms. They should provide the language learners with "multicultural tasks and materials in a balanced context along with the English materials" (Tajeddin & Ghaffaryan, 2020, p. 15). What cannot be denied is that teacher quality and student success are intricately interrelated and teacher education programs play an important role in teacher quality (Rivkin et al., 2005).

Notwithstanding the widespread agreement among language educators on the necessity of intercultural language teaching and its important role in language classrooms, the intercultural dimension is still largely neglected in language pedagogy. This might stem from teachers' lack of confidence and knowledge in dealing with intercultural topics. It is thus suggested that teachers be aided through the incorporation of cultural pedagogical content in teacher education programs; this may help them to grow into teachers who are more conscious and aware of the critical aspects of intercultural language teaching. Teachers need to be assisted in developing critical awareness of pedagogical knowledge to overcome the uncertainty they may experience with regard to culture teaching tasks and activities (Baker, 2015; Byrd et al., 2011). It follows that the beliefs-practices gap can be largely filled through some education sessions in which teachers are made aware of the different procedures to translate beliefs into practices.

As many teacher educators have high university degrees related to the field of applied linguistics, it is assumed that they possess the basic theoretical knowledge of CICLT. Teacher educators may be aware of the basic principles of CICLT, but not conscious of the significance of adding it to teacher education courses, which brings to the fore the importance of noticing. Also, the literature indicates that explicit attention to intercultural language education is often neglected in teacher education courses (Ngai & Janusch, 2015). Hence, there is a big gap in the ESL/EFL education system which can only be filled with more explicit attention to intercultural language teaching. Enhancing the intercultural knowledge of language learners can assist them in becoming more proficient users of English in multicultural contexts.

In this regard, teacher educators may benefit from the results of the study, as the findings revealed that Iranian language teachers are not adequately aware of the theoretical and practical foundations of critical intercultural language teaching. Teacher educators may want to dedicate more time to practical ways of integrating culture into the language course. They also need to further stress the necessity of observing CICLT in classrooms as many teachers are not even aware of CICLT. Therefore, through critical intercultural teacher education courses and workshops, the teachers would appreciate that "learning the English language is learning a way of thinking, perceiving, and acting" and therefore they can "explore ways to guide their students to experience the language in context" (Ngai & Janusch, 2015, p. 366).

The results of this study could also be useful to policy makers and language institute principals around the world. Our findings indicate that language teachers are ready in principle to critically integrate culture into their teaching courses. However, it seems that they face various challenges and problems that prevent them from practising it in classrooms. This calls for more attention to the intercultural principles of language centres. On a larger scale, of course, materials developers and international publishers need to produce materials that are rich and balanced in intercultural content and keep an eye on the significance of CICLT.

4 Conclusion and Directions for Further Research

This chapter sought to shed light on the current status of CICLT in English language classrooms. The findings indicate a clear gap between the teachers' beliefs about CICLT and their pedagogical practices. From the findings, it can be concluded that although the teachers' beliefs generally align with the tenets of CICLT, they do not have knowledge-in-practice to incorporate it into their language classrooms. This manifests itself in language teachers' poor understanding of CICLT and its foundational principles. To have open-minded, tolerant language learners, teachers need to develop critical intercultural competence in their learners by engaging them not only with the language but also with its culture. Teachers need to remind the learners that the language learning experience cannot in any way be isolated from its culture and that the two are closely intertwined. In the global world of today, language learners need to be provided with ample opportunities to reflect upon their own culture and compare it with the foreign culture through openness to otherness, acceptance of differences, stimulation of tolerance, and exclusion of prejudice and prejudgment (Sobkowiak, 2014).

Overall, if we are about to see some real transformations in language classrooms and in teachers' pedagogical practices, some key steps need to be taken beforehand to alter the language teachers' mindset regarding CICLT. As Fullan (1991) stated, educational changes hinge upon "what teachers do and think" (p. 117). In fact, mere awareness-raising might not lead to a real transformation in the teachers' beliefs and instructional practices (Dogancay-Aktuna & Hardman, 2017; Suzuki, 2011). As Dogancay-Aktuna and Hardman (2018) argued, awareness-raising needs to be accompanied by real practical work so that the desired pedagogy will emerge. We advocate that teacher educators equip language teachers with a clear theoretical understanding and aid them in making appropriate instructional decisions while teaching intercultural issues in their own specific sociocultural context.

It needs to be noted that the present study was limited to EFL teachers; therefore, future studies may explore critical reflections of the EFL learners on their intercultural language learning beside the impact of critical intercultural education on their attitudes, which is of significant value and seems to be an underexplored area. Moreover, future studies may take a more in-depth approach by investigating numerous variables such as age, gender, education level, ethnicity, and the whole educational and political environment and their impact on the language teachers' CICLT adoption. Also, further research is needed to explore the impact of critical intercultural teacher education courses and workshops on teachers' critical intercultural understanding in general and their practices of CIP in particular. In addition, the current study used questionnaires and observations as data collection instruments. Future studies may explore the topic with other research instruments such as interviews.

References

Alsagoff, L. (2012). Identity and the EIL learner. In L. Alsagoff, S. L. McKay, G. Hu, & W. A. Renandya (Eds.), *Principles and practices for teaching English as an international language* (pp. 104–122). Routledge.

Atay, A., & Toyosaki, S. (Eds.). (2018). *Critical intercultural communication pedagogy.* Lexington Books.

Baker, W. (2015). Research into practice: Cultural and intercultural awareness. *Language Teaching, 48*(1), 130–141. https://doi.org/10.1017/S0261444814000287

Braine, G. (2010). *Nonnative speaker English teachers: Research, pedagogy, and professional growth.* Routledge.

Breen, M. P., Hird, B., Milton, M., Oliver, R., & Thwaite, A. (2001). Making sense of language teaching: Teachers' principles and classroom practices. *Applied Linguistics, 22*(4), 470–501. https://doi.org/10.1093/applin/22.4.470

Byram, M. (1997). *Teaching and assessing intercultural communicative competence.* Multilingual Matters.

Byram, M. (Ed.). (2000). *Routledge encyclopedia of language teaching and learning.* Routledge.

Byram, M., & Guilherme, M. (2000). Human rights, cultures and language teaching. In A. Osler (Ed.), *Citizenship and democracy in schools: Diversity, identity, equality* (pp. 63–78). Trentham Books.

Byram, M., & Wagner, M. (2018). Making a difference: Language teaching for intercultural and international dialogue. *Foreign Language Annals, 51*(1), 140–151. https://doi.org/10.1111/flan.12319

Byram, M., & Zarate, G. (1994). *Definitions, objectives and assessment of socio-cultural competence.* Council of Europe.

Byram, M., Esarte-Sarries, V., Taylor, S., & Allatt, P. (1991). Young people's perceptions of other cultures: The role of foreign language teaching. In D. Buttjes & M. Byram (Eds.), *Mediating languages and cultures: Towards an intercultural theory of foreign language education* (pp. 103–119). Multilingual Matters.

Byrd, D. R., Hlas, A. C., Watzke, J., & Valencia, M. F. (2011). An examination of culture knowledge: A study of L2 teachers' and teacher educators' beliefs and practices. *Foreign Language Annals, 44*(1), 4–39. https://doi.org/10.1111/j.1944-9720.2011.01117.x

Canagarajah, S. (2014). In search of a new paradigm for teaching English as an international language. *TESOL Journal, 5*(4), 767–785. https://doi.org/10.1002/tesj.166

Canale, M. (1983). From communicative competence to communicative language pedagogy. In J. C. Richards & R. W. Schmidt (Eds.), *Language and communication* (pp. 2–27). Longman. https://doi.org/10.4324/9781315836027

Canale, M., & Swain, M. (1980). Theoretical bases of communicative approaches to second language teaching and testing. *Applied Linguistics, 1*(1), 1–47. https://doi.org/10.1093/applin/I.1.1

Chamberlin-Quinlisk, C., & Senyshyn, R. M. (2012). Language teaching and intercultural education: Making critical connections. *Intercultural Education, 23*(1), 15–23. https://doi.org/10.1080/14675986.2012.664750

Cheng, C. M. (2012). The influence of college EFL teachers' understandings of intercultural competence on their self-reported pedagogical practices in Taiwan. *English Teaching: Practice and Critique, 11*(1), 164–182. http://education.waikato.ac.nz/research/files/etpc/files/2012v11n1dial2.pdf

Conway, C., Richards, H., Harvey, S., & Roskvist, A. (2010). Teacher provision of opportunities for learners to develop language knowledge and cultural knowledge. *Asia Pacific Journal of Education, 30*(4), 449–462. https://doi.org/10.1080/02188791.2010.519545

Dogancay-Aktuna, S., & Hardman, J. (2017). A framework for incorporating an EIL perspective into TESOL teacher education. In A. Matsuda (Ed.), *Preparing teachers to teach English as an international language* (pp. 19–31). Multilingual Matters. https://doi.org/10.21832/9781783097036

Dogancay-Aktuna, S., & Hardman, J. (2018). Teaching of English as an international language in various contexts: Nothing is as practical as good theory. *RELC Journal, 49*(1), 74–87. https://doi.org/10.1177/0033688217750642

Feryok, A. (2008). An Armenian English language teacher's practical theory of communicative language teaching. *System, 36*(2), 227–240. https://doi.org/10.1016/j.system.2007.09.004

Freeman, D. (1991). To make the tacit explicit: Teacher education, emerging discourse, and conceptions of teaching. *Teaching and Teacher Education, 7*(5/6), 439–454. https://doi.org/10.1016/0742-051X(91)90040-V

Fullan, M. (1991). *The new meaning of educational change*. Cassell.

Fung, L., & Chow, L. P. Y. (2002). Congruence of student teachers' pedagogical images and actual classroom practices. *Educational Research, 44*(3), 313–322. https://doi.org/10.1080/0013188022000031605

Genç, G. (2018). Are Turkish EFL pre-service teachers ready to manage intercultural challenges? *Intercultural Education, 29*(2), 185–202. https://doi.org/10.1080/14675986.2018.1429790

Gu, X. (2015). Assessment of intercultural communicative competence in FL education: A survey on EFL teachers' perception and practice in China. *Language and Intercultural Communication, 16*(2), 254–273. https://doi.org/10.1080/14708477.2015.1083575

Halualani, R. T. (2018). Demarcating the "critical" in critical intercultural communication studies. In A. Atay & S. Toyosaki (Eds.), *Critical intercultural communication pedagogy* (pp. 3–9). Lexington Books.

Halualani, R. T. (2019). *Intercultural communication: A critical perspective*. Cognella.

Halualani, R. T., & Nakayama, T. K. (2010). Critical intercultural communication studies: At a crossroads. In T. K. Nakayama & R. T. Halualani (Eds.), *The handbook of critical intercultural communication* (pp. 1–16). Wiley Blackwell. https://doi.org/10.1002/9781444390681

Han, X., & Song, L. (2011). Teacher cognition of intercultural communicative competence in Chinese ELT context. *Intercultural Communication Studies, 20*(1), 175–192. https://www-s3-live.kent.edu/s3fs-root/s3fs-public/file/13XiaohuiHanLiSong.pdf

Hismanoglu, M. (2011). An investigation of ELT students' intercultural communicative competence in relation to linguistic proficiency, overseas experience and formal instruction. *International Journal of Intercultural Relations, 35*(6), 805–817. https://doi.org/10.1016/j.ijintrel.2011.09.001

Hong, Y. Y., & Cheon, B. K. (2017). How does culture matter in the face of globalization? *Perspectives on Psychological Science, 12*(5), 810–823. https://doi.org/10.1177/1745691617700496

Houghton, S. (2008). Harmony versus critical cultural awareness: A case study of intercultural language education in Japan. *Intercultural Communication Studies, 17*(2), 222–235. https://web.uri.edu/iaics/files/19-Stephanie-Houghton.pdf

Hymes, D. (1972). On communicative competence. In J. B. Pride & J. Holmes (Eds.), *Sociolinguistics: Selected readings* (pp. 269–293). Penguin.

Kohler, M. (2015). *Teachers as mediators in the foreign language classroom*. Multilingual Matters.

Kohler, M. (2020). Intercultural language teaching and learning in classroom practice. In J. Jackson (Ed.), *The Routledge handbook of language and intercultural communication* (pp. 413–426). Routledge.

LaScotte, D. K., & Peters, B. D. (2021). Fostering intercultural learning experiences in the ESL/EFL classroom. In S. Garton & F. Copland (Eds.), *International perspectives on diversity in ELT* (pp. 55–71). Palgrave Macmillan.

Li, D. C. S. (2009). Researching non-native speakers' views toward intelligibility and identity: Bridging the gap between moral high grounds and down-to-earth concerns. In F. Sharifian (Ed.), *English as an international language: Perspectives and pedagogical issues* (pp. 81–118). Multilingual Matters.

Liddicoat, A. J. (2011). Language teaching and learning from an intercultural perspective. In E. Hinkel (Ed.), *Handbook of research in second language teaching and learning* (Vol. II, pp. 837–855). Routledge.

Liddicoat, A. J., & Scarino, A. (2013). *Intercultural language teaching and learning*. Wiley-Blackwell.

Liddicoat, A. J., Papademetre, L., Scarino, A., & Kohler, M. (2003). *Report on intercultural language learning*. Commonwealth of Australia.

Liu, D., & Nelson, R. (2018). Diversity in the classroom. In J. Liontas (Ed.), *TESOL encyclopedia of English language teaching* (pp. 585–590). Wiley-Blackwell.

Marlina, R. (2018). Revisiting the pedagogy of English as an international language. *RELC Journal, 49*(1), 3–8. https://doi.org/10.1177/0033688218765831

Marlina, R. (2021). "Let's play 'Sok says', not 'Simon says'": Evaluating the international and intercultural orientation of ELT materials for Cambodian secondary schools. In S. Garton & F. Copland (Eds.), *International perspectives on diversity in ELT* (pp. 73–90). Palgrave Macmillan.

Matsuda, A. (2012). Teaching materials in EIL. In L. Alsagoff, S. L. McKay, G. Hu, & W. A. Renandya (Eds.), *Principles and practices for teaching English as an international language* (pp. 168–185). Routledge.

Matsuda, A. (2018). Is teaching English as an international language all about being politically correct? *RELC Journal, 49*(1), 24–35. https://doi.org/10.1177/0033688217753489

McKay, S. L. (2012). Teaching materials for English as an international language. In A. Matsuda (Ed.), *Teaching English as an international language: Principles and practices* (pp. 70–83). Multilingual Matters.

Merse, T. (2021). Task typologies for engaging with cultural diversity: The queer case of LGBTIQ* issues in English language teaching. In S. Garton & F. Copland (Eds.), *International perspectives on diversity in ELT* (pp. 91–109). Palgrave Macmillan.

Moeller, A. J., & Osborn, S. R. (2014). A pragmatist perspective on building intercultural communicative competency: From theory to classroom practice. *Foreign Language Annals, 47*(4), 669–683. https://doi.org/10.1111/flan.12115

Mori, R. (2011). Teacher cognition in corrective feedback in Japan. *System, 39*(4), 451–467. https://doi.org/10.1016/j.system.2011.10.014

Nakayama, T. K., & Martin, J. N. (2018). Critical intercultural communication: Overview. In Y. Y. Kim (Ed.), *The international encyclopedia of intercultural communication* (pp. 1–15). Wiley-Blackwell.

Nault, D. (2006). Going global: Rethinking culture teaching in ELT contexts. *Language, Culture and Curriculum, 19*(3), 314–328. https://doi.org/10.1080/07908310608668770

Ngai, P., & Janusch, S. (2015). Intercultural communication training for English language teachers: A case study of an immersion program for south Korean teachers. *Journal of Intercultural Communication Research, 44*(4), 345–368. https://doi.org/10.1080/17475759.2015.1081853

Nguyen, L. (2014). Integrating pedagogy into intercultural teaching in a Vietnamese setting: From policy to the classroom. *International Journal of Pedagogies and Learning, 9*(2), 171–182. https://doi.org/10.1080/18334105.2014.11082030

Oranje, J. M. (2016). *Intercultural communicative language teaching: Enhancing awareness and practice through cultural portfolio projects* (unpublished doctoral dissertation). University of Otago.

Oranje, J. M., & Smith, L. F. (2017). Language teacher cognitions and intercultural language teaching: The New Zealand perspective. *Language Teaching Research, 22*(3), 310–329. https://doi.org/10.1177/1362168817691319

Pallant, J. (2010). *SPSS survival manual: A step by step guide to data analysis using SPSS* (4th ed.). McGraw-Hill.

Pennycook, A. (2017). Translanguaging and semiotic assemblages. *International Journal of Multilingualism, 14*(3), 269–282. https://doi.org/10.1080/14790718.2017.1315810

Porto, M. (2020). English as a foreign language teachers' understandings of the native/non-native dichotomy: An Argentine perspective. In S. A. Houghton & J. Bouchard (Eds.), *Native-speakerism: Intercultural communication and language education* (pp. 69–88). Springer.

Porto, M., Houghton, S. A., & Byram, M. (2018). Intercultural citizenship in the (foreign) language classroom. *Language Teaching Research, 22*, 484–497. https://doi.org/10.1177/1362168817718580

Rivkin, S., Hanushek, E. A., & Kain, J. F. (2005). Teachers, schools, and academic achievement. *Econometrica, 73*(2), 417–458. https://doi.org/10.1111/j.1468-0262.2005.00584.x

Sercu, L., Bandura, E., Castro, P., Davcheva, L., Laskaridou, C., Lundgren, U., Méndez García, M., & Ryan, P. (2005). *Foreign language teachers and intercultural competence: An international investigation.* Multilingual Matters.

Shin, H., & Jeon, M. (2018). Intercultural competence and critical English language teacher education. *English Teaching, 73*(4), 125–147. https://doi.org/10.15858/engtea.73.4.201812.125

Sobkowiak, P. (2014). Intercultural teaching in the polish context. In M. Pawlak, J. Bielak, & A. Mystkowska-Wiertelak (Eds.), *Classroom-oriented research: Achievements and challenges* (pp. 185–202). Springer.

Suzuki, A. (2011). Introducing diversity of English into ELT: Student teachers' responses. *ELT Journal, 65*(2), 145–153. https://doi.org/10.1093/elt/ccq024

Tajeddin, Z., & Ghaffaryan, S. (2020). Language teachers' intercultural identity in the critical context of cultural globalization and its metaphoric realization. *Journal of Intercultural Communication Research, 49*(3), 263–281. https://doi.org/10.1080/17475759.2020.1754884

Tajeddin, Z., Alemi, M., & Pashmforoosh, R. (2018). Idealized native-speaker linguistic and pragmatic norms in English as an international language: Exploring the perceptions of nonnative English teachers. *Language and Intercultural Communication, 18*(3), 300–314. https://doi.org/10.1080/14708477.2017.1413105

Tian. J. (2013). *Beliefs and practices regarding intercultural competence among Chinese teachers of English at a Chinese University* (unpublished doctoral dissertation). George Mason University.

van Ek, J. A. (1986). *Objectives for foreign language learning* (Vol. 1: Scope). Council of Europe.

Young, T. J., & Sachdev, I. (2011). Intercultural communicative competence: Exploring English language teachers' beliefs and practices. *Language Awareness, 20*(2), 81–98. https://doi.org/10.1080/09658416.2010.540328

Zhang, X., & Zhou, M. (2019). Interventions to promote learners' intercultural competence: A meta-analysis. *International Journal of Intercultural Relations, 71*, 31–47. https://doi.org/10.1016/j.ijintrel.2019.04.006

Zia Tajeddin is Professor of Applied Linguistics at Tarbiat Modares University, Iran. His main areas of research include language teacher education, EIL/ELF pedagogy, and second language pragmatics. He is the co-editor of the book series *Studies in Language Teacher Education* (Springer) and co-edits two international journals titled *Applied Pragmatics* (John Benjamins) and *Second Language Teacher Education* (Equinox). He is the co-editor (with Carol Griffiths) of *Lessons from Good Language Teachers* (Cambridge University Press, 2020) and the co-editor (with Minoo Alemi) of *Pragmatics Pedagogy in English as an International Language* (Routledge, 2021). In 2022, his co-edited book (with Atsuko Watanabe) titled *Teacher Reflection: Policies, Practices and Impacts* was published by Multilingual Matters. Email: tajeddinz@modares.ac.ir

Atefeh Rezanejad obtained her Ph.D. in Applied Linguistics from Allameh Tabataba'i University, Iran. She teaches various university courses in applied linguistics. Her main areas of research include intercultural language learning, pragmatics, language teacher education, and sociolinguistics. She has published papers in numerous language teaching journals. Email: rezanejad_a85@yahoo.com

Promoting Intercultural Critical Literacy among Moroccan University Students Through Online International Collaborative Education

Abdellah El Boubekri

Abstract The present chapter aims to explore technology-mediated Task-Based Learning (TBL) as a stepping stone towards intercultural and internationalized learning. It starts by reviewing the research done on implementing TBL in technology-based learning and teaching. It revisits some crucial contributions related to the theory and practice of intercultural communication education. To illustrate this approach, the chapter re-examines and reviews the methodological organization of a Collaborative Online International Learning course (COIL), a program that aims at connecting classrooms, students, and faculties across the world. It discusses the end outcome of students' collaboration; a sample COIL project of teachers and students from Morocco and the US is analysed and discussed in the light of such a synergistic approach. Cooperating students are reported to have bolstered their cross-cultural critical competence.

Keywords COIL · TBL · Technology · Intercultural competence · Internationalised learning · Morocco · The US

1 Introduction

Critical intercultural literacy refers to the development of certain competencies and attitudes needed for successful involvement in cross-cultural communication which has become a required skill for an empowered global economy. This literacy is closely related to the contemporary internationalization of higher education which focuses on the integration of technology into learning and teaching. Among the rationales for advocating internationalized learning is the growing need for intercultural skills and enhanced cultural understanding within the global economy. Escrigas (2016) envisages an urgent transformation in human concept of progress which

A. El Boubekri (✉)
Faculty of Letters and Human Sciences, Mohamed I University, Morocco, Oujda

© The Author(s), under exclusive license to Springer Nature
Switzerland AG 2023
A. Sahlane, R. Pritchard (eds.), *English as an International Language Education*, English Language Education 33,
https://doi.org/10.1007/978-3-031-34702-3_3

reconsiders "the interdependence of the economic, social, political, and environmental spheres. The international community of students now needs to comprehend the diverse instructional contexts and approaches through which knowledge is mediated and meaning is created" (para 35). The celebrated initiative of Collaborative Online International Learning (COIL) embodies a viable opportunity for international students to engage with cross-cultural differences and fully connect with a global education that is free from cultural biases. It is run and sponsored by the State University of New York in the context of its drive to promote a global community of practice that is based on students' and teachers' mobility, ideas exchange, resource sharing, contextualized decision-making, critical digital literacy, professional support, leadership and cooperative problem-solving (for further information, see this website https://coil.suny.edu/about-suny-coil/).

Due to the difficulty of attending educational programs abroad, the celebrated initiative of Collaborative Online International Learning COIL (see this website https://coil.suny.edu/about-suny-coil/) customizes cost-effective partnerships and projects to connect faculty and students from varied cultures drawing on the existing resources of technology. The ubiquity of internet-assisted communication tools allows for networked classrooms through which the partners exchange innovative learning and teaching styles. According to Fowler (2014), the assistant director of SUNY COIL Center, "the courses are team-taught with professors working closely with international peers to generate a shared syllabus based on solid academic coursework emphasizing experiential and collaborative student learning" (para 4).

To explore the COIL initiative, the present study revisits a partnership experience of a COIL course in which the researcher's class collaborated with an American class on *Media Studies and Society.* The aim of the COIL program is to initiate and facilitate global academic partnerships through COIL-enhanced modules for both international partners. The COIL example boosts the spirit of collaboration and team-working through the task and project-based approaches. The ultimate goal is to enhance cross-cultural and multidisciplinary learning environments which would serve the professional development of the partners. Through the use of synchronous and asynchronous digital tasks, the collaborating students developed their intercultural competence; Moroccan students in particular had the opportunity to learn how to switch between their native language and English. The assigned tasks were often seeded with cultural information gaps involving stereotypical situations from both cultures; they paved the way for the negotiation of intercultural content and triggered critical consciousness of cultures. Even with the less culturally-oriented tasks, students demonstrated a capacity to decentre themselves and act as global citizens who are more concerned with diversifying their learning resources and strengthening their global insight awareness.

Theoretically, such collaborative learning is informed by a symbiosis of three fundamental research methodologies, namely technology-assisted instruction, task-based learning, and intercultural learning. Technology-assisted instruction works effectively through Task-Based Learning (TBL) which can be defined as the principled adoption of teaching activities that have "the potential to involve learners in meaningful language use." (Müller-Hartmann & Ditfurth, 2011, p. 22). TBL is known for its usefulness in the teaching of languages, but it can also be used to teach humanities and social sciences in English as a foreign language (Purdam, 2016; Khatib et al., 2011), as the case in Morocco. Technology-mediated TBL is supposed to enhance intercultural learning which is promoted by the increasing calls for internationalized education. Such intercultural communicative competence is grounded on critical pedagogy that feeds on comparative and reflective practices fostering cross-cultural sensitivity and the promotion of global citizenship.

The present chapter seeks to investigate the feasibility of the approach of technology-mediated TBL to foster critical intercultural learning. After reviewing the literature related to the suitability of applying TBL methodology to technology-based learning and teaching, it sets out to explore some important academic works pertinent to the theory and practice of intercultural communication education. Eventually, it proposes coupling the three pedagogical frameworks into one working approach instrumental for internationalized paradigms of learning. To illustrate this mixed approach, the chapter re-visits the methodological organization of the previously mentioned COIL course. It discusses the implications of a collaborative project undertaken by COIL students.

2 A Theoretical Framework

This section aims at shedding light at the three methodological frameworks which guide the present case study of a COIL project. It argues that technology-mediated learning is less effective in the absence of a principled methodology. Therefore, it lists some theoretical rationales for implementing the methodology of Task-Based Learning. The resultant Technology-mediated TBL is supposed to facilitate the critical intercultural learning goals underlined by the COIL initiative.

2.1 Background of Technology-Mediated TBL

TBL is one popular trend which accompanied the flourishing of the Communicative Approach in the late 1970s. Its principal objective is to train students for genuine use of language in life-like communicative situations. The application of modern educational technologies has likewise been motivated by language teachers' emphasis on the pedagogic gains from enhancing learners' engagement (Mofareh, 2019) and immersion in virtual interactive activities that are closer to reality. Apparently, although both TBL and technology appear to serve the same communicative purpose, attempts at combining their strengths remain unexplored.

Definitions of task-based learning are abundant in language learning literature. For the sake of simplicity, the current study will content itself with Jane Willis's understanding which is in harmony with the present communicative conception of English as a Foreign Language (EFL) learning and teaching. For one thing, TBL is compared to adventure-like learning whereby activities and content should not be determined a priori (Willis, 1998). This unpredictability reinforces the authenticity of learning, the creativity of learners, and reflects their real learning needs. It addresses their whole person learning requirements (socio-affective, cognitive and linguistic). In TBL, the purposeful use of target language is preferred to the structural rehearsal of grammatical forms; it is a "Goal-oriented communicative activity with a specific outcome, where the emphasis is on exchanging meaning, not producing specific language forms" (Willis, 1996, p. 36). As such, task designs are to observe Skehan's (1998) communicative criteria of the primacy of meaningfulness, purposefulness, innovation, authenticity, and the priority of the end product in assessment. Pedagogically, Willis' (1996) and Ellis' (2013) methodology is relevant to the present discussion. This methodology comprises three main steps. In the pre-task phase, the teacher brainstorms a certain topic with the students (the constructive nature of ads, for instance). As for the second phase (task cycle), the students are required to work in groups to plan, draft and report a certain task (analysing and deconstructing certain ads from two different contexts, say the US and Morocco). Finally, the post-task cycle is devoted to the language focus (analysis and practice).

Ellis (2019) addresses the need for teachers to understand exactly what is meant by TBL. As one example, he notes that tasks encourage "incidental learning [which] occurs when we pick up things without making a special effort to learn them" (p. 16). In a book offering practical pieces of advice to language teachers, Ur (2016) reminds us that students need to understand why they are being asked to do a particular task, not just how. By this, she means not only the surface learning goal but also the underlying one. For instance, she points out that through a discussion task students may have the aim of "reaching consensus on the solution of a problem" (p. 62) but, more deeply, the discussion is intended to improve fluency and skills, such as turn-taking.

The rationales for integrating technology in foreign language teaching are diverse and interlocking. To begin with, digital technologies have now become embedded in our life and learning/thinking processes. They have given rise to new tasks in real life; thus, they are transforming language needs. If the pedagogy does not match such changes, students are likely to be disengaged and become disaffected by school (Zyngier, 2008). Language teachers need to bear in mind that "today's language learners are expected to be able to develop multimodal communicative and task competencies above and beyond the reading and writing skills required by previous generations" (Thomas & Reinders, 2010, p. 6). In addition, instructional technologies are supposed to respond to diverse needs (Wahl & Duffield, 2005). Using cell phones, for instance, can secure full involvement of learners in class and outside school, which can culminate in increasing language retention and student engagement (Godwin-Jones, 2018).

Technology provides multimedia learning materials in the curriculum at any location in the world. It helps to link learners and teachers in geographically distinct locations and allows for flexible scheduling and interaction, which are supported by the multimodality options of networked computers which easily afford for online and offline communication resources (Evans, 2009). In addition, technology-enhanced language learning softens the affective filter in that it reduces anxiety and the fear of making mistakes (Krashen, 1982) Arnold (2007) uncovers more anxiety among students from the traditional classroom setting than among the ones in computer-assisted classes. Kung & Eslami (2019, p. 1533) corroborate Arnold's findings by arguing that synchronous computer mediated communication reduces the anxiety of learners.

The need for a kind of symbiosis between technology and TBL is articulated by several researchers (Thomas & Reinders, 2010; Lai & Li, 2011; González-Lloret & Ortega, 2014; Chen, 2019; Norris, 2009; Samuda & Bygate, 2008; Branden, 2006). They all seem to agree that in the absence of the methodological guidance of TBL, technology may turn into a means of entertainment rather than instruction. TBL can maximize the potential of technological innovations for EFL education. Computer-assisted language learning (CALL), for example, is congruent with active learning. González-Lloret & Ortega (2014, p. 3) argue that

> Web 2.0 technologies create unprecedented environments in which students can engage in "doing things" through technology-mediated transformation and creation processes, rather than just reading about language and culture in textbooks or hearing about them from teachers. It is this potential of new technologies to engage students in active learning and holistic tasks that makes them excellent candidates for their integration in TBLT.

Hence, TBL is a natural choice for E-learning since both are based on experiential instruction and learning by doing. The use of technology can engagingly facilitate the accomplishment of various learning tasks: playing interactive games, exchanging information with native speakers and doing group work projects.

Another reason for basing technology-enhanced education on the methodology of TBL is provided in Lev Vygotsky's sociocultural theory which posits that human mental and physical activities are always mediated by tools. It is considered as "a theory of mind that recognizes the central role that social relationships and culturally constructed artefacts play in organizing uniquely human forms of thinking" (Lantolf, 2004, pp.30–31). Such a sociocultural argument is endorsed by language scholars. Qin (2017), for instance, supports research concentration on the influence and function of sociocultural theory in the social formation of the mind and enmeshment of learning in socially and culturally mediated activities. In the same vein, Chen (2018, p. 95) asserts that these activities can be facilitated through the use of blended learning (the mix of online and offline learning). According to Bellefeuille (2006), social constructivism encourages the learner to actively craft ideas from prior experiences, shared information, and collaborative undertakings. Language classroom is seen as a space which provides for collaboration, discussion, authentic learning, scaffolding, reflection, self-directed learning and learner autonomy. Closely related to social constructivism is the theory of connectivism, which also sees learning as a function of forming networks, sharing networked content and connecting with people either in reality or virtually through technological tools (Siemens, 2005).

It is important to highlight that technology alone is insufficient in maintaining online classes. The role of pedagogical methodology in using digital tools is crucial.

For example, in the contemporary context of Morocco, with the social and physical distancing and lockdown brought about by the outbreak of COVID-19, the Ministry of Education declared closure of public schools and universities; resort to online learning was the only viable solution to keep students engaged in their classes. With a particular focus on higher education, the availability of electronic platforms on the universities' websites was not as helpful as the Ministry ambitiously claimed. In spite of the affordable technological tools at their disposal, both students and professors seem not quite confident and well-informed enough to use these platforms effectively. They lack educational procedures to invest in technology-based learning.

In spite of the crucial role of blended learning as "one of the most significant developments of the 21st century" (Thorne, 2003, p. 18), the feasibility of technology-based TBL is not without challenges. Salient among these challenges is teachers' resistance (see Howard & Mozejko, 2015; Howard, 2013; Gläsel, 2018), which is attributed to several factors that range from their lack of digital skills, misconception of technology as fad or sometimes as an authority that dictates what and how to do things, doubt about their ability to control the class, and affordance of internet connection facility. The other serious challenge is the lack of teachers' preparedness to methodologically integrate technology in foreign language classes. In order to support teachers in their use of technology, some researchers have emphasized the need to include this topic in language teacher education programs. Another important challenge for this instructional symbiosis is how it can be systematically customized to incorporate intercultural pedagogy that has recently received monumental hype in the field of language teaching and internationalized learning (Mezger-Wedlandt, 2010, p.1). A preliminary question that can be asked here is how technology-mediated tasks can sustain chances for learners to compare their cultural knowledge with other cultural backgrounds to boost their spirit of openness and value cultural difference.

2.2   Technology-Mediated TBL and Intercultural Learning

Intercultural education features as one of the most enquired-about topics in recent ELT scholarship. It has been recommended by international organizations such as the United Nations and UNESCO, as well as international and national educational documents, including the Common European Framework of Reference for Languages (Alderson, 2002), and UNESCO Guidelines on Intercultural Education (UNESCO, 2006). Fantini (2005, p. 1) defines intercultural competence as "the complex of abilities needed to perform effectively and appropriately when interacting with others who are linguistically and culturally different from oneself." Similarly, Schenker (2012, p. 450) draws on Byram's (1997) famous *savoirs* (knowledge-abilities) to illustrate his definition of intercultural communicative competence. He summarizes these *savoirs* as follows: "knowledge of self and other, attitudes of openness and curiosity, skills of interpreting and relating, skills of discovery and interaction, and critical cultural awareness."

Research on the development of intercultural communicative competence (ICC) through the integration of technology has recently gained much pedagogical credence. The accumulating research probes different dimensions of this integration. Lawrence (2013) discusses the challenges that limit the pedagogical incorporation of online intercultural collaboration into classroom language teaching. He insists on involving the learners in the design and organization of these collaborations by investing in their sense of identity and community to maximize intercultural language learning procedures. In another context, El Boubekri (2017) advocates blended modes of instruction in Moroccan higher education to promote intercultural awareness; the study reveals that technology and intercultural learning rank at the top of students' curriculum expectations and needs. Likewise, Perren (2018) researches the effect of practical technology applications such as CALL and telecollaboration on intercultural communication. He looks into the pedagogical possibilities of reflective blogging, graphics and mobile devices. (See also Marczak, 2013; Uzun, 2014; Hoat, 2016; O'Toole, 2018; Taskiran, 2020). The application of technologies in intercultural language teaching and learning has been extensively tackled. For instance, Liddicoat and Scarino (2013, p. 107) claim that the spread of technology has contributed to the teaching of culture in contextual situations. The advent of the Web 2.0 instils an internet participatory culture which blurs the previous distinction between information technologies and social technologies such as e-mails or chats that facilitate social interaction across cultures (see also Kiswaga & Triastuti, 2019; Chen & Yang, 2014; Custer, 2016; Saba, 2016).

The implementation of TBL in intercultural learning is not uncommon (see East, 2012; Yi Ji, 2018; Lingling & Lv, 2019). In his study of intercultural tasks, Corbett (2003) capitalizes on Nunan's (1998) TBL framework in designing tasks for intercultural classroom. Nunan's framework consists of deciding on (1) the goal (a combination of intercultural and linguistic exploration); (2) the input (comparing L1 and L2 cultural constructs); (3) the activities (observing and discussing the input); (4) the learner's role (analyser, negotiator and reflector of cultural behaviours); (5) the teacher' role (adviser and guide of cultural behaviours); (6) the setting (individual, pair and group work). Liddicoat and Scarino (2013) suggest a circular intercultural classroom language methodology which starts with the process of (1) noticing two cultural constructs, then (2) comparing them, (3) reflecting on their similarities and differences and eventually (4) interacting and exchanging opinions. The authors think that well-designed pedagogic intercultural tasks involve EFL learners into reflective exchanges which might signal "the beginning of a process of decentering from their own cultural assumptions and beginning to think about their culture from other perspectives" (p.112). Intercultural tasks that require students to contrast and compare beliefs and views about certain everyday cultural constructs (e.g., family, youth, gender, authority, values, media, education...) to fill a cultural information gap can elevate their negotiating skills vis-à-vis the cultural content (Crookes & Gass, 1993). Equally, Mezger-Wedlandt (2013, p. 2) states that "with their focus on meaning, interaction, sharing and negotiating, tasks create an effective and motivating learning environment for intercultural learning". In addition, Müller-Hartmann (2000) advocates the use of TBL in intercultural learning as its interactive nature helps learners unpack freely their personal as well as cultural views. He states that "task-based approach develops its fullest potential by allowing learners to develop and express their views, thus making real communication possible and consequently setting the stage to initiate processes of intercultural learning" (p. 145).

Apparently, the previous research tackled different manifestations of either the technology usefulness in boosting ICC in classroom or the effectiveness of TBL approach in intercultural learning. However, the customization of TBL approach to optimize such technology-based intercultural learning is poorly studied; intercultural learning through technology-assisted TBL is a timely and intriguing subject that has not carefully been attended to. E-learning materials enable intercultural interaction and collaboration with the target language native speakers in both synchronous and asynchronous ways. They provide opportunities for authentic language use and rich input. To optimize E-learning resources and activities for a meaningful intercultural instruction, E-learning materials should be handled in the light of TBL approach.

The very little research (e.g., Canto et al., 2014) that has touched upon the issue of intercultural learning through technology-mediated TBL has not drawn on a clear methodological organization of tasks like the ones suggested above by Willis (1996) and Ellis (2013). Practically, it is not enough to argue that tasks involve learners in discovery, challenge, reflection and co-operation and overcoming cross-cultural conflict. Instead, it is significant to evince how to design and organize tasks electronically for the sake of managing interculturally-oriented language classroom. In this regard, O'Dowd and Ware (2009) affirm that

> [T]elecollaborative tasks generally involve different linguistic and cultural communities and thereby have a strong possibility of producing negotiation of meaning and providing opportunities for the exploration of different cultural perspectives. This makes them particularly suited to recent approaches to task-based learning which include a focus on issues related to intercultural communication…and…a focus on the skills of electronic literacy. (p. 175)

However, their concern was mainly on experimenting with the communicative task types as advanced by Nunan (1998) and Pica (2005). The focus of this chapter is, however, on implementing the methodological framework developed by Willis (1996) and Ellis (2013), which allows a concrete assessment of the learning outcomes in intercultural collaborative projects.

To sum up, this literature review section has attempted to suggest a methodological framework that can guide collaborative online international initiatives targeting the enhancement of university students' intercultural communicative competence. The feasibility of this framework will be verified through exploring a sample collaborative project. The major research question that informs this exploratory endeavour is the extent to which online internationalized educational projects can sustain opening up students' perspectives to unbiased ways of being, thinking and learning in a globalized age.

3   Method

This section provides details about the methods adopted to address the research's major problem. It aims particularly at highlighting the context of where, when and how the research was conducted, information about the methods of sampling, collecting and analysing data, and finally sketching out an example of an ad deconstructed and reconstructed into a counter-ad by a group of collaborating students.

3.1   The Research Context

The present chapter draws on a descriptive exploration of a Collaborative Online International Learning experience in which two teachers from Morocco and the US collaborate in the form of blended learning. Collaborating teachers participated in Stevens Initiative Workshop at the American University of Cairo, Egypt (October 30 to November 3, 2016). They received instructive sessions on how to design tasks that respond to the requirements of their current courses and open opportunities for intercultural learning through educational technologies.

In collaboration with Professor Marcia Blackburn, a SUNY college partner from New York, the researcher taught a joint-module on *Media and Society*. It was part of his semester 4 class: *Media Studies*. Starting in March 2017, he selected twenty interested students to collaborate with Blackburn's students (20 in total as well). This collaboration gave them the unique opportunity to explore topics in mass media with students from another country and culture. Before starting the collaboration and as icebreakers to test for technological equipment, the collaborators launched a mini-COIL unit at the end of fall semester 2016; they created a closed Facebook group and students were assigned to record personal videos about the places where they lived and some details about their daily routines. Students were prompted to comment on the things that seemed new to them.

During the spring term 2017, the collaborating students had a blended class on *Media Studies and Society*. In the offline classes, students received the same syllabus, which was centred on media literacy, the language of persuasion, deconstruction of print ads and reconstruction of counter-ads. Following Willis (1998) and Ellis (2013)'s models, the teachers structured online classes as follows:

Pre-task
Paired students choose print ads (from a given list) from either Morocco or the US. They discuss, describe, compare and analyse the contents of the ads. Drawing on their cultural knowledge, students interpret the meaning expressed in the ads. Teachers post some media literacy concepts and examples of deconstructed ads through some guided questions and assignments. Teachers encourage students to reread the ads based on their new acquired knowledge.

Task-cycle
Task:

In group of four (2 Americans and 2 Moroccans), students choose print ads of their
own choice. Students discuss, compare and analyse the topic, language, audience, form, text and subtext of the selected ads.

Planning:

Drawing on the feedbacks of the other groups and the teachers, students create their
own counter-ads in writing or speaking using pictures in which they demonstrate
a grasp of the intended message.

Report:

Presenting and comparing the ads and whole class check if the deconstructed meaning is countered.

Post-task

The teachers provide some commentaries on the language used and concepts
employed, along with some suggestions for improvements. Students provide
debriefings about the challenges and the new learned knowledge. Students are
encouraged to re-create their counter-ads based on the received feedback.

3.2   Sampling Technique

The collaborating students were required to create counter-ads as the end-products
of their COIL session; the researcher selects randomly and anonymously one example of these counter-ads from the platform to elucidate the intercultural dimension
of such collaboration.

3.3   Data Gathering and Analysis Method

The following data were posted in the SUNY Blackboard platform that the cooperating students used to interact and accomplish their collaborative work. Besides,
drawing on some of their displayed comments and feedbacks, the researcher reports
the selected ad as it is, how the partnering students deconstruct it in the light of the
techniques discussed in offline classes, and how they manage to create counter-ads
that translate their awareness of common global issues. This is followed by a general discussion of how this collaborative initiative, which was sustained by a
technology-mediated TBL, contributes to the development of students' intercultural
cognizance.

Fig. 1 Deconstructing an Ad (a reported example)

3.3.1 The Sampled Data

The following data consist of a sample ad that a group of collaborating students choose to deconstruct and turn into a counter-ad. Their analytical and deconstructive texts are reported as they appear in the platform (see Fig. 1). In deconstructing ads, students are taught to focus on identifying the source of the ad, its audience, its text and subtext, the techniques of persuasion it utilizes, and finally the points of view it reflects.

Source In 1998, Procter and Gamble P&G came up with the idea of *Febreze*. In 2008, it got upgraded to what we know today.

Audience Women, wives, and moms: middle class, working class; car and pet owners.

Text & Subtext
Text: "We're out to make the world breathe happy": The text claims that the company is working closely for consumer satisfaction by providing a fresh odour. This is further depicted through the images which show women of different ages who seem to be from the middle class based on their clothing, and are exposed to a dirty area, but clueless to the fact thanks to Febreze.

Subtext: The sentence (we are out to make the world breathe happy) itself is not only vague but grammatically incorrect. However, in most cases with product promotion, the expression has been used as a catchphrase indicating that Febreze will provide a likeable odour that would enhance the consumer's happiness. Nonetheless, Febreze seems to have neglected the negativity behind the message it conveys through the images. The fact that the images depict the previously mentioned concept of negativity makes the consumer think: "Is Febreze really cleaning the odour, or simply masking it and exposing me to even more germs?"

Persuasion techniques   The methods of persuasion used are simple, and effective:

Plain Folks – The ad uses everyday Americans, average working-class people, to authenticate **P&G's claim**. It also allows the audience to associate with people using the product in the ads.

Scientific Evidence – They use experts and test to prove that Febreze cleans the air; they also use a fake study, with a test to show it.

Association – The ad links Febreze to a clean, odour- free home that many people strive to have.

Explicit Claims – Although the ad doesn't mention the dangerous aspects of Febreze, it does present the claim that Febreze totally cleans the air.

False Claims – The first issue with these commercials is that their claims are untenable. Febreze barely masks the odours, let alone destroys them. Consumer Reports actually did an experiment of their own, using the exact same situation. They used 2 groups of test subjects, both blindfolded. First was the smelly room without Febreze (the room was full of day-old sardines, a used cat litter box... etc). The test group found the room absolutely intolerable. The second group was sent into the room immediately after it had been sprayed with two types of Febreze, odour eater, and pet odour eliminator. Although the stench had improved slightly, it was still intolerable to the second group of test subjects.

The Hidden Secret – Procter and Gamble has hidden a dark secret from the public. A few of the active ingredients in Febreze have been linked to health complications. These issues run across a wide, varying spectrum ranging from skin irritation, to cancer, and even death.

Points of view   The points of view reflected in this ad are simple. The first point of view is of an outside viewer watching the above-mentioned experiment and the outcome: this makes us feel like it is true and scientifically proven. The second point of view is of the people who own homes or cars. The reason they do this is to invite us to feel like we are the owner of the property, and have empathy for the fact that their car or home smells like dogs, or football equipment, or garbage (see Fig. 2).

4   Discussion

The ice breakers session on a closed Facebook group (available on the following link https://www.facebook.com/groups/1741673092824469/) constitutes a significant platform for collaborating students to gain first-hand understandings of one another's lifestyle, cultural identities and worldviews, which are essential prerequisites for the development of intercultural skills and mutual acceptance. Students appreciate their differences and the particularity of each culture. They exchange information about the posted videos and pictures of current political

Fig. 2 Reconstructing counter-ads (reported examples)

events and cultural ceremonies. Through the use of diverse forms of technology (social networks, videos, pictures, and Blackboard platform) Moroccan students have the chances to listen, observe, watch and know about the nuances in verbal and non-verbal communication styles which help them express appropriately their views and stories both in English writing and speaking. Students from both cultures come to notice different cultural practices, interact, compare and reflect on their specificities without being biased to their own cultural mindsets. Such cultural interchanges make the students less intimidated by the difference of their peers and prepare them for collaboration in task-based assignments related to the subject of *Media Studies and Society*.

The technology-assisted task-based teamwork reflects a process of intercultural collaboration in which students from different cultural and geographical backgrounds are trained to deconstruct a print ad and create a counter-ad that is possibly free from cultural stereotypes. In so doing, students demonstrate a critical awareness of an issue that is germane to their human existence and commonality. They expose the health damage that Febreze and other similar chemical products might cause while giving the illusion of catering for the wellbeing of the customers. They contest the producer's marketing claim of masking the odour and warn against the insidious effects of the product. The use of air freshener products is not perceived through the prism of cultural stereotypes. For instance, during the deconstruction stage, it is easy to notice that the partnering students display respect for each other's views and eschew some clichéd presumptions related to the hygienic states in their cultures. They do not perceive the use of these products in terms of the cleanliness habits in their corresponding cultures. Similarly, they do not interpret the ad along the gender-based line of thought which would underline women's obsession with cleanliness and household distribution of roles. During this group's discussion of the poster, a Moroccan female student reported that the focus of the deconstruction should be on gender-based employment of women in issues related to household chores. She said, "…is it a normal thing to see only women dealing with bad odour in different parts of the house? Why not men? Are not they concerned with the sanitation of their homes?" The different group members started commenting on the validity of this remark and its relevance to both their cultures only to eventually agree on concentrating on what is more harmful for both men and women. They cast away these controversial issues and grappled with what is commonly hazardous to all humans. In circumventing the specificities of cultural settings and dwelling on the mutual threat, the collaborating students displayed an intercultural consciousness based on self-decentring and negotiation of what was taken for granted. They developed a kind of international citizenship and literacy with regard to the consumption of media and shared sense of humanity. In this connection, Ramirez (2019, p. 1) finds that "COIL project students demonstrated global citizenship skills such as the ability to analyse international relationships, critically consume media, and make them identify points of global interconnectedness."

TBL guides the use of online synchronous and asynchronous interaction which is entailed in COIL projects. TBL provides a more structured and organized framework whereby students get involved in a sequence of meaningful, authentic, purposeful, and situated communicative tasks. Ziegler (2016, p. 137) explains that the interplay of TBL and technology "can enhance or facilitate the benefits of task-based language teaching as well as addressing how TBL can serve as a framework in which to ground research conducted in CALL contexts." Technology-mediated tasks allow for genuine opportunities of cultural interaction between the collaborating students who scaffold one another. They are also encouraged to confidently communicate with their teachers and receive continuous support and feedback during the completion of the tasks.

In using technology-assisted TBL, this study argues that the COIL initiative has to some extent achieved its intercultural agenda. Given the centrality of the latter to the increasing interconnectedness of students' cultural backgrounds and educational systems, developing intercultural skills and competence has become a priority for universities. The omnipresence of technological tools and students' positive attitudes to them can substitute for the dire unaffordability of physical mobility in trying to attain intercultural skills. Situating this study within similar quantitative and qualitative research context, it is easy to notice that previous research on COIL internationalized partnerships has often touched on the significance and achievability of intercultural awareness among students who are experientially involved in COIL-mediated instruction. Asojo et al. (2019, p. 15), for instance, confirmed that "COIL can be one of the best tools for bridging the gaps between different parts of the world and improving understanding of cultural differences, developing cultural sensitivity, and ensuring cultural transmission and exchange." Likewise, Hildeblando and Finardi (2017, p. 30) concluded their investigation of the impact of COIL experience on their collaborating students by stating that "COIL may foster more balanced and sustainable internationalization processes as well as the development of intercultural competence and the preservation of multilingualism."

5   Conclusion

This chapter has aimed to bring together both the theory and practice of technology-assisted TBL geared towards boosting intercultural responsiveness. In the researcher's experience of observing and monitoring the COIL interaction of students at different stages during the completion of their joint tasks, he has become convinced that the traditional mode of teaching about global cultural awareness and the functioning of media-generated content seem to lack the authenticity required by the teaching pedagogy of these scholarly areas. When students look at these global cultural subjects through their localized perspectives, an aura of ethnocentrism and bias pervades their critical assessment of how knowledge and cultural discourses create meaning. They tend to either posit the unconditional validity of their mindsets in understanding global issues of media-oriented worldviews and other various cultural forms, or occasionally become alienated from their cultural standpoints on the assumption that they are unsuited to modern universal notions of progress. Either consequence is at loggerheads with the latest view of education as breeding a paradigm that looks at knowledge as product and reflection of intertwined sources and contexts. Escrigas (2016) corroborates such a new and vital trend in education. She believes that this view of higher education can help graduates promote an inclusive, just, and fair social systems, cultivating in them a critical consciousness of the interconnected world they inhabit and preparing them to act in a framework and spirit of trust and collaboration. Such a mindset is essential to articulating processes for building societies attuned to the interdependence of the Planetary Phase of Civilization (para. 26).

Based on this miniature analysis of COIL project, it can be implied that the collaboration had positive impacts on students. First, they had a genuine chance to activate their academic knowledge of critical abilities in authentic situations. Most of them had been introduced to critical thinking skills in secondary schools and early years of university. However, this theoretical acquaintance was sharpened by their actual and experiential real-life tasks of presenting local cultural spaces, responding to others, and demonstrating critical media literacy not only about how global and local media shape people's mind, but also about how to react in reducing its damaging effects. Second, unlike the offline classes which are very limited in time, the partnering students displayed a rich liveliness and a continuous real engagement during their COIL exchanges. Their favourable attitudes to these online interchanges and the cultural nature of the subject matter were conducive to actual intercultural interaction and hence to the promotion of their intercultural sensitivity. Third, another outcome of such intercultural sensitivity is the possible enhancement of students' communicative language use in English. Moroccan students had a chance to enrich their linguistic and cultural fluency. Mulling over their participations in the closed Facebook group and in the Blackboard platform, one can see the sense of linguistic appropriateness and cultural adequacy they had developed over the course of joint class. Generally, the significance of COIL initiative has become clearer when students had to deal with the physical confinement imposed by COVID-19 government quarantine. Online learning skills emerged as a prerequisite for schooling in general, and instrumental tools for developing intercultural competence when international mobility had been restricted.

This chapter has tried to illustrate the feasibility of intercultural learning through technology-mediated TBL. This approach proves very useful in structuring the class content and organizing students' activities. Yet, more research is needed in the field of technology-assisted TBL to optimize effective instructional procedures of combining pedagogy and technology and customize their implications to include all subjects in the university English studies. Indeed, humanities today need digitisation to achieve a kind of connectivity with students' technological needs and the requirement of the international education and global economic markets.

However, one of the perceived limitations of the present study is its retrospective nature. It took the author about three years to come up with a theoretical synergy that allows for reflecting on the COIL experience of his class. More effective undertaking is provided by action research which would diagnose the involved students' intercultural skills before the start of the program; then a follow up examination of the same targeted skills after the end of program to measure their progress. A pre-planned variety of this research permits administering questionnaires, surveys and interviews whose triangulation may augment the validity of the findings. Besides, investigating and comparing a good number of COIL projects can yield more comprehensive results. Moreover, exploring COIL's impacts on the involved teachers is under-researched. It is not discerned yet if students can reach COIL's goals if the involved teachers lack intercultural critical competence and online collaborative skills.

References

Alderson, J. C. (Ed.). (2002). *Common European framework of reference for languages: Learning, teaching, assessment – Case studies*. Council of Europe.

Arnold, N. (2007). Reducing foreign language communication apprehension with computer-mediated communication: A preliminary study. *System, 35*, 469–486. https://doi.org/10.1016/j.system.2007.07.002

Asojo, A., Jaiyeoba, B., & Amole, D. (2019). Multicultural learning and experiences in design through the collaborative online international learning (COIL) framework. *Journal of Teaching and Learning with Technology, 8*(1), 5–16. https://scholarworks.iu.edu/journals/index.php/jotlt/article/view/26748

Bellefeuille, G. L. (2006). Rethinking reflective practice education in social work education: A blended constructivist and objectivist instructional design strategy for web-based child welfare practice course. *Journal of Social Work Education, 42*(1), 85–103.

Branden, V. (Ed.). (2006). *Task-based language education: From theory to practice*. Cambridge University Press.

Byram, M. (1997). *Teaching and assessing intercultural communicative competence*. Multilingual Matters. https://doi.org/10.21832/9781800410251

Canto, S., Graaff, R., & Kristi, J. (2014). Collaborative tasks for negotiation of intercultural meaning in virtual worlds and video-web communication. In M. González-Lloret & O. Lourdes (Eds.), *Technology-mediated TBLT: Researching technology and tasks* (pp. 183–212). John Benjamins.

Chen, X. (2018). A literature review of task-based language teaching in college reading comprehension – Exploration of tasks design to foster reading strategies. *International Journal of English Language Teaching, 5*(3), 90–106.

Chen, K. (2019). The effects of technology-mediated TBLT on enhancing the speaking abilities of university students in a collaborative EFL learning environment. *Applied Linguistics Review, 12*(2), 1–26. https://doi.org/10.1515/applirev-2018-0126

Chen, J. J., & Yang, S. C. (2014). Fostering foreign language learning through technology-enhanced intercultural projects. *Language Learning & Technology, 18*(1), 57–75. Retrieved from http://llt.msu.edu/issues/february2014/chenyang.pdf

Corbett, J. (2003). *An intercultural approach to English language teaching*. Multilingual Matters.

Crookes, G., & Gass, S. M. (Eds.). (1993). *Tasks in a pedagogical context*. Multilingual Matters.

Custer, L. (2016). Using technology to promote intercultural competence. An exchange between Japanese and U.S. college students. *Journal of studies in English and American Literature, 51*, 49–67.

East, M. (2012). Addressing the intercultural via task-based language teaching: Possibility or problem? *Language and Intercultural Communication, 12*(1), 56–73. https://doi.org/10.1080/14708477.2011.626861

El Boubekri, A. (2017). The intercultural communicative competence and digital education: The case of Moroccan university students of English in Oujda. *Journal of Educational Technology Systems, 45*(4), 520–545. https://doi.org/10.1177/0047239516670994

Ellis, R. (2013). *Task-based language learning and teaching*. Oxford Applied Linguistics.

Ellis, R. (2019). *Introducing task-based language teaching*. Shanghai Foreign Language Education Press.

Escrigas, C. (2016). *A higher calling for higher education*. The Great Transition Initiative forum. https://greattransition.org/publication/a-higher-calling-for-higher-education.

Evans, M. (Ed.). (2009). *Foreign language learning with digital technology*. Continuum.

Fantini, A. (2005). *About intercultural communicative competence: A construct*. Retrieved April 17, 2022, from http://www.sit.edu/SITOccasionalPapers/feil_appendix_e.pdf

Fowler, J. (2014). Connecting classrooms across the border with technology. *Profweb*. Nov 2. Retrieved March 30, 2022, from https://www.profweb.ca/en/publications/articles/connecting-classrooms-across-the-border-with-technology

Gläsel, A. (2018). *6 reasons why teachers don't use technology in the classroom – What can EdTech companies learn? The EdTech World*. Retrieved October 17, 2021, from. https://medium.com/the-edtech-world/resistance-tech-classrooms-981b86d862fc.

Godwin-Jones, R. (2018). *Using mobile devices in the language classroom: Part of the Cambridge papers in ELT series*. Cambridge University Press.

González-Lloret, M., & Ortega, L. (Eds.). (2014). *Technology-mediated TBLT: Researching technology and tasks*. John Benjamins.

Hildeblando, C, & Finardi, K. (2017). *Internationalization and virtual collaboration: Insights from coil experiences*. Retrieved December 10, 2021, from https://www.academia.edu/Documents/in/Coil

Hoat, T. (2016). *Developing intercultural competence with web 2.0 technologies in an EFL context*. The University of Queensland.

Howard, S. K. (2013). Risk-aversion: Understanding teachers' resistance to technology integration. *Technology, Pedagogy and Education, 22*(3), 357–372. https://doi.org/10.1080/1475939X.2013.802995

Howard, S. K., & Mozejko, A. (2015). Teachers: Technology, change and resistance. In M. Henderson & G. Romeo (Eds.), *Teaching and digital technologies: Big issues and critical questions* (pp. 307–317). Cambridge University Press.

Ji, Y. (2018). Task-based language teaching (TBLT) in Asian EFL classes: Challenges and strategies. *Advances in Social Science, Education and Humanities Research, 120*, 152–164.

Khatib, M., Derakhshan, A., & Rezaei, S. (2011). Why and why not literature: A task-based approach to teaching literature. *International Journal of English Linguistics., 1*(1), 213–218. https://doi.org/10.5539/ijel.v1n1p213

Kiswaga, G., & Triastuti, A. (2019). *The application of technology in intercultural language learning: International students program at a University in Yogyakarta* (pp. 121–125). Atlantis Press. https://doi.org/10.2991/icille-18.2019.26

Krashen, S. D. (1982). *Principles and practice in second language acquisition*. Pergamon Press.

Kung, T., & Eslami, Z. (2019). Learners of different language proficiency levels and incidentals focus on form in synchronous text-based discussion. In *Computer-assisted language learning: Concepts, methodologies, tools, and applications* (pp. 1521–1539). Edited by Information Resources Management Association. https://doi.org/10.4018/IJCALLT.2015070103.

Lai, C., & Li, G. (2011). Technology and task-based language teaching: A critical review. *CALICO Journal, 28*(2), 498–521.

Lantolf, P. (2004). Sociocultural theory and second and foreign language learning: An overview of sociocultural theory. In K. van Esch & S. Oliver (Eds.), *New insights into foreign language learning and teaching* (pp. 13–84). Peter Lang.

Lawrence, G. (2013). A working model for intercultural learning and engagement in collaborative online language learning environments. *Intercultural Education, 24*(4), 303–304. https://doi.org/10.1080/14675986.2013.809247

Liddicoat, A., & Scarino, A. (2013). *Intercultural language teaching and learning*. Blackwell Publishing.

Lingling, C., & Lv, J. (2019). Task-based approach to develop intercultural communicative competence in college English education. *Journal of Language Teaching and Research, 10*(6), 1279–1287. https://doi.org/10.17507/jltr.1006.17

Marczak, M. (2013). *Communication and information technology in (intercultural) language teaching*. Cambridge Scholars Publishing.

Mezger-Wedlandt, G. (2010). Developing intercultural competence: Task based learning. *StudyLib*. Retrieved April 21, 2022, from https://studylib.net/doc/7465058/developing-intercultural-competence%2D%2Dtask-based-learning

Mezger-Wedlandt, G. (2013). Developing intercultural competence: Task based learning. *Arts & Humanities Communications*. Retrieved September 30, 2022, from https://studylib.net/doc/7465058/developing-intercultural-competence%2D%2Dtask-based-learning

Mofareh, A. (2019). The use of technology in English language teaching. *Frontiers in Education Technology, 2*(3), 168–180. https://doi.org/10.22158/fet.v2n3p168

Müller-Hartmann, A. (2000). The role of tasks in promoting intercultural learning in electronic learning networks. *Language Learning & Technology, 2*, 129–147.

Müller-Hartmann, A., & Ditfurth, S. (2011). *Teaching English: Task-supported language learning*. Schöningh UTB.

Norris, M. (2009). Task-based teaching and testing. In M. H. Long & C. J. Doughty (Eds.), *The handbook of language teaching* (pp. 578–594). Blackwell.

Nunan, D. (1998). *Designing tasks, for the communicative classroom*. Cambridge University Press.

O'Dowd, R., & Ware, P. (2009). Critical issues in telecollaborative task design. *Computer Assisted Language Learning, 22*(2), 173–188.

O'Toole, C. (2018). Technology enhanced learning (TEL) intercultural competence: A phenomenological exploration of trainees' experiences within global virtual training environments. *Irish Journal of Technology Enhanced Learning, 3*(1), 12–29. https://doi.org/10.22554/ijtel.v3i1.23

Perren, M. (2018). Intercultural communication through technology. *Teaching and Technology*. Retrieved December 14, 2021, from https://doi.org/10.1002/9781118784235.eelt0415

Pica, T. (2005). Classroom learning, teaching, and research: A task-based perspective. *Modern Language Journal, 89*(3), 339–352.

Purdam, K. (2016). Task-based learning approaches for supporting the development of social science researchers' critical data skills. *International Journal of Social Research Methodology, 19*(2), 257–267. https://doi.org/10.1080/13645579.2015.1102453

Qin, J. (2017). *Introduction to sociocultural theory in second language acquisition*. Peking University Press.

Ramirez, C. (2019). Global citizenship education through collaborative online international learning in the borderlands: A case of the Arizona–Sonora megaregion. *Journal of Studies in International Education, 25*(1), 83–99. https://doi.org/10.1177/1028315319888886

Saba, N. (2016). Telecollaboration and intercultural competence. *International journal of language and applied linguistics, 2*(special issue intercultural and 21st school), 96–122.

Samuda, V., & Bygate, M. (2008). *Tasks in second language learning*. Palgrave Macmillan.

Schenker, T. (2012). Intercultural competence and cultural learning through telecollaboration. *CALICO Journal, 29*(3), 449–470.

Siemens, G. (2005). Connectivism: A learning theory for the digital age. *International Journal of Instructional Technology and Distance Learning, 2*(1), 3–10. http://www.itdl.org/Journal/Jan_05/Jan_05.pdf

Skehan, P. (1998). *A cognitive approach to language learning*. Oxford University Press.

Taskiran, A. (2020). Telecollaboration: Fostering foreign language learning at a distance. *European Journal of Open, Distance and E-Learning, 22*(2), 87–97.

Thomas, M., & Reinders, H. (Eds.). (2010). *Task-based language learning and teaching with technology*. Continuum International.

Thorne, K. (2003). *Blended learning. How to integrate online and traditional learning*. Kogan Page.

UNESCO Guidelines on Intercultural Education. (2006). Retrieved March 5, 2021, from http://www.ugr.es/~javera/pdf/DB2.pdf

Ur, P. (2016). *100 teaching tips*. Cambridge University Press.

Uzun, L. (2014). Utilizing technology for intercultural communication in virtual environments and the role of English. *Procedia – Social and Behavioral Sciences, 116*, 2407–2411.

Wahl, L., & Duffield, J. (2005). *Using flexible technology to meet the needs of diverse learners: What teachers can do*. Wested. Retrieved July 12, 2022, from https://www.wested.org/online_pubs/kn-05-01.pdf

Willis, J. (1996). *A framework for task-based learning*. Longman Limited.

Willis, J. (1998). Task-based learning: What kind of adventure? *The Language Teacher, 22*(7). Retrieved December 23, 2021, from https://jalt-publications.org/tlt/issues/1998-07_22.7

Ziegler, N. (2016). Taking technology to task: Technology-mediated TBLT, performance, and production. *Annual Review of Applied Linguistics, 36*, 136–163. https://doi.org/10.1017/s0267190516000039

Zyngier, D. (2008). (Re)conceptualising student engagement: Doing education not doing time. *Teaching and Teacher Education, 24*(7), 1765–1776.

Abdellah El Boubekri is an Associate Professor of Cultural Studies at Mohamed First University, Faculty of Humanities, Department of English Studies, where he is the leader of a research group (Cross Cultural Communication Studies). He is a member of an MA program in Communication and Translation. He is also a Board member of a research unit in Cultural Studies (CERHSO). He is a former teacher trainer at the Education Centre (CRMEF) Oujda. He is a former Fulbright scholar (Missouri State 2007/2008). Currently, he is a coordinator and trainer in a national educational program (English Teaching Internship Initiative). He has published several books and articles in national and international journals. Email: aelboubekri@hotmail.com

The Transformation of an English User into an Intercultural English User

Tahany Abdulaziz Aleisa

Abstract In our globalized world, intercultural competence has increasingly become an essential skill for foreign language (university) students. Literature relating interculturalism to linguistic and cultural competence is expanding; the findings suggest that the most common problem among learners in multicultural contexts is that they hold an ethnocentric attitude, as they tend to idealize their own cultures and ignore cultural diversity. This intercultural trend has motivated a new language institute at a Saudi public university to develop its curriculum based on an intercultural learning approach that aims at promoting cross-cultural sensitivity within the educational spaces by preparing EFL learners to become responsible global citizens. This chapter investigates how the English program offered for Foundation Year students integrated an intercultural syllabus, with sociocultural topics, designed to develop students' linguistic abilities and their critical thinking and intercultural skills. The chapter is based on reviewing a curriculum launched during the years of 2016–2018.

Keywords Interculturalism · EFL · Curriculum · Intercultural competence · Culture · Saudi Arabia · Communication · Language learning · Foreign language education

1 Introduction

Modern realities require knowledge of English in many jobs around the world due to constantly accelerating technological development and globalization with rapid dynamics which require education to keep up with these processes. In addition to the essential functions of mastering grammatical rules, reproducing phonetic

T. A. Aleisa (✉)
College of Education, University of Jeddah, Jeddah, Saudi Arabia
e-mail: talbeiz@uj.edu.sa

© The Author(s), under exclusive license to Springer Nature
Switzerland AG 2023
A. Sahlane, R. Pritchard (eds.), *English as an International Language Education*, English Language Education 33,
https://doi.org/10.1007/978-3-031-34702-3_4

sounds, and developing communication skills, many additional components can be incorporated within the learning process and culture is one of them. Naturally, students get acquainted with the culture of many countries where the studied language is not their native language. Modern trends in building an intercultural society meet the requirements of social responsibility, and it becomes necessary to expand the cultural function throughout the learning processes. This chapter assesses an English as a Foreign Language (EFL) curriculum precisely in terms of culturalism and the intercultural aspects of this curriculum. This critical analysis will reveal the positive aspects of this curriculum, which in the future can help in the design of intercultural education.

2   Theoretical Framework

The issues and terms of culturalism and interculturality in education have recently assumed greater prominence. The concept of interculturalism was born in response to the concept of multiculturalism, which believes that each diaspora should preserve its own culture and language (Wang, 2017). Interculturalism reflects a model of integration in contexts of diversity, a way of thinking about globalized reality and intercultural dialogue, or an instrument of "positive interaction" (Catarci et al., 2020). This concept considers the multiplicity of identities and differences, but the focus is on the ways of coexistence of different cultures in the context of globalization. Thus, it turns out that interculturalism is at the equator between the concepts of multiculturalism and the theory of the "melting pot," which implies the fusion of cultures into one new one (Elias & Mansouri, 2020). Echoing modern trends in the formation of new approaches at the intersection of disciplines, interculturalism has sought to make the best of the modern teaching methods.

The study of foreign languages, always at its core, contains communication, regardless of the approach. Vocabulary-based techniques provide sufficient rapid impact but not deep understanding (Itmeizeh & Hassan, 2020). Grammar-focused approaches are designed for more reliable and long-lasting results (Moradkhani, 2019). However, reading, listening, and communication combine approaches to teaching a foreign language. Communication, moreover, indirectly and explicitly develops several other functions and capabilities of the student: thinking skills, adaptation, flexibility, critical thinking, and pragmatic (e.g., politeness) communication skills (Khan & Alasmari, 2018). As a result, a particular type of thinking is formed from these skills, including cultural aspects. The study of a foreign language can be built on creating intercultural situations, within which the student will conduct a dialogue, be immersed in another culture, interact with it, and exchange experiences.

Nevertheless, this approach, focused on maximizing the potential for developing communication skills while considering cultural implications, is quite challenging to implement. It requires a sufficiently high teaching competence, the appropriate training of students, the correct teaching model, and the relevance of the application (Park, 2020). The process of globalization, on the one hand, dramatically simplifies the establishment of intercultural contacts, and at the same time, creates the need to interpret socio-cultural events for a coordinated and respectful coexistence in the modern world (Yueqin, 2013). Therefore, several different techniques have already been successfully used.

First, intercultural learning is about creating an authentic atmosphere, using posters, maps, and other interactive material. The presence of another culture in the form of such artifacts within the educational process motivates students and engage them in the learning process (Makhmudov, 2020). Exposing students to the foreign culture is especially relevant in countries far from where the target language is native. Secondly, there are teaching techniques that can promote self-awareness, which are aimed at a deeper analysis of students' values and beliefs. These techniques promote cultural learning as a multi-level concept, where behaviour is only the tip of the iceberg, and values and thinking patterns are laid down at a deeper level (Toliboboeva, 2020), where understanding and recognition of differences serve as guides in communication. Third, the quiz technique in the study of new materials invites students to test their intuition and anticipate various cultural aspects in the educational process of learning a foreign language (Cinkara, 2020). Increased interest and involvement in the process are the strengths of this technique.

The fourth technique can be called drama – the straightforward process of staging intercultural scenes. Students experiment with different roles and can put themselves in the shoes of a different cultural 'other'. With the correct presentation by the teacher, while practising the language, such an interaction can engrave itself in the students' memory and, as a result, improve their intercultural sensitivity (Wuryandari, 2021). However, this technique requires a relatively long preparation period and the necessary will to participate, which not every teacher can demonstrate. Some other techniques are highly developed in universities such as project work. Students seek new information, present it in class, answer questions, and immerse themselves in the discussion. Project-based learning demonstrates highly positive results since students are encouraged to choose a topic of interest to them, which they should openly present to an audience and defend (Alavinia & Rahimi, 2019). However, traditionally training students in research skills only contributes to the grasp of the theoretical material without giving students ample time to try it in practice or to tackle the cultural aspects.

It is also worth considering the vast variability of views on the culture of a particular country. There are many of them: attitude towards foreigners, political system, public transport, geographical history, demographic situation, behaviour in restaurants, attitude towards the elderly, and much more (Çetin et al., 2017). The student should understand the phrases accepted by the etiquette of a given culture and beware of taboo expressions and actions to be able to perform appropriately in intercultural encounters. Unravelling the tangle of specific causes and effects leads to a much deeper understanding of culture and promotes student involvement in the learning process (Kostikova et al., 2018). In informal communication situations, grammatical incompetence cannot be a serious barrier to effective communication as it can be easily compensated for by developing a sociocultural know-how that promotes a respectful and polite attitude towards the interlocutors.

Nowadays, intercultural interaction is becoming more and more relevant. Firstly, social networks are now connecting many people worldwide, and technology allows communicating via video link with any person on Earth who has the Internet. Moreover, students' communication on social media with people from different cultures helps improve their skills of learning English as a foreign language (Özdemir, 2017). Secondly, a global disaster in the form of a pandemic has rallied representatives of different states to fight against a common enemy. Distance education was forcibly worked out, which opened up opportunities for interactivity without being tied to one place. Of course, it is challenging to replace face-to-face communication with video communication since a specific part of non-verbal signs is lost, voice intonation is distorted, and much more (Sutiyatno, 2018). Nevertheless, in the process of distance learning, various advantages of this approach have been identified, which can be applied together with conventional classroom teaching. Technologies can and do contribute to the development of intercultural relations, in connection with which one should always consider the possibility of their implementation in the educational process.

Nevertheless, implementing culture in the educational process of learning a foreign language is not without specific problems. The interpretation of certain linguistic expressions in the English language requires a reflection of the cultural context they originate from. Lack of such intercultural knowledge can lead to misunderstandings or more severe consequences (Vetrinskaya & Dmitrenko, 2017). Moreover, the cultural aspects of language are not limited to patterns of behaviour and the context of phrases; non-verbal sign language also plays an important role. For example, in some cultures, it is customary to express interest in the interlocutor's speech with a continuous gaze directed at him, while this gesture is impolite in other cultures (Wahyuni, 2018). In this regard, the models for the integration of culture in the foreign language learning process should be implemented very carefully in a way that prudently attends to the complexity of the issue, as described above. Given all of the above, the EFL curriculum intended in this chapter will be critically described and assessed for unlocking the potential of intercultural interaction among students.

3   Critical Analysis

An analysis of the language curriculum of the English language institute (ELI) at a public Saudi university begins with the principles and vision that guided its founders. First of all, it should be noted that a relatively large amount of attention is paid to the development of thinking and communication skills. By involving students in critical dialogue, they can develop research and critical thinking skills necessary to perform as responsible global citizens. Such a diverse approach can consider almost all the critical roles of a student for the development of cultural interaction in the framework of language learning. The ELI launched its newly structured EFL curriculum serving Foundation Year students. The two suggested levels target a blended framework composed of the Common European Framework of Reference for Languages (CEFR) levels (B1-B2-C1) and the Canadian Language Benchmarks (CLB 4-5-6-7-8). The ELI has a vision of serving the wider community. It is committed to providing the students with a progressive language curriculum infused with thinking and communication skills. This mission is pursued through uniquely contextualized research and professional staff development which also extends to corporate business (Aburizaizah, 2021). Student engagement is a significant part of the curriculum as students will be engaged through the following components which lead to three significant categories of students' behaviour (intellectual work, engagement activities, student talk) as described below:

3.1 Intellectual Work

- Students' classroom work embodies substantive intellectual engagement (reading, thinking, writing, problem-solving and meaning-making).
- Students take ownership of their learning to develop, assess and refine their thinking.

3.2 Engagement Strategies

- Engagement strategies capitalize on and build upon student's academic background, life experience, culture, and language to support rigorous and culturally relevant learning.
- Engagement strategies encourage equitable and purposeful student participation and ensure that all students have access to and are expected to participate in learning.

3.3 Student Talk

- Students learn best by actively using the language they are learning.
- Student talk reflects genre-specific conventions of thinking and ways of communication.
- Student talk involves substantive intellectual work.

Students who take English as a mandatory subject are enrolled in the Foundation Year Program as a requirement before transiting to their subsequent academic specializations within the various university disciplines. The syllabus in its semi-decentralized mode is organized at two English levels (levels 110 & 120) and around three overarching themes- Community, Academics, and Employment. These themes are developed in depth during the academic year through the study of related topics. These are explored in correlation with vocabulary development, as it is an essential component of the English program and a key factor in receptive and productive language development. A comprehensive and extensive list of vocabulary words has been designed for each level. The syllabus goes beyond the four core language learning abilities (i.e., writing, reading, speaking, and listening) and promotes presentation and thinking skills. Since one of the main goals of English curriculum is to develop students' communicative skills in relation to their future careers, many themes focus on business, society, and employment.

For a detailed analysis, it is necessary to disassemble the topics of the lessons and each aspect that they relate to. Students at the 110 level are expected to have a B1 level of English already and, as a result, be able to navigate the most common travel situations. This fact means that the program provides a deeper understanding of culture and intercultural relations that go beyond meeting simple travel needs, such as situations in restaurants, shops, and hotels. By involving students in role-play activities, they are trained to develop a clear idea about intercultural exigencies that transcend mere teaching about surface-level cultural features, such as tourist destinations and cultural traditions (Carbone, 2017). Therefore, a critical review of the language program will take this detail into account. Table 1 below provides an overview of some topics that students were encouraged to explore at both levels.

At level 110, the first topic of the lesson is about society, and "rules around the world" (see Tables 2 and 3) is chosen as the topic of discussion. The topic is quite extensive, but it is generally suitable for a good start and for involving students in the intercultural learning process. The interculturalisation process is raised immediately in the first lesson by allowing students to explore different "rules around the world", without trying to cover the third-party vocabulary of emerging sub-topics. The vocabulary sheet provided can be significantly expanded through student research, such as the names of gestures or descriptions of mannerisms. In addition, the lesson must devote time to tone control and attitude involved. For the development of polite intercultural relations, this is one of the main aspects that allow a person to show their good side at once (Estévez-Saá, 2017).

It is noteworthy that the ELI English language program not only works with classical texts, dialogues, and other traditional forms of presenting information; it also includes tasks that require making a mind-map, working with lists, interviews, and presentations. Moreover, many of these assignments require some degree of critical media literacy, which is most important in our interconnected modern world (Shmakova et al., 2021). Involving students in project-based group presentations promotes students' public speaking skills, trains them in effective learning and promotes awareness of audience-oriented perspectives in public dialogue.

In the second week of this program, issues of the ecology of the planet are raised in terms of garbage handling and healthy eating (see Tables 4 and 5). Environmental responsibility in our time is put on a par with social responsibility, the requirements

Table 1 Culture-based topics and learning outcomes for levels 110 & 120

Topic	Summary of student learning outcomes (SLOs)
Rules around the world	Make predictions and identify key information related to "rules around the world" based on prior knowledge and through skimming and scanning relevant texts and other educational materials. Map a visual outline of home/family rules and write an outline of home/family rules. Give short presentations to introduce some rules.
The other face of trash	Make predictions about a content related to "trash in community and how recycling makes a difference". Connect prior knowledge to their predictions and identify and analyse key information from info-graphs. Brainstorm environmental problems related to trash and identify (causes and effects) and write sentences that include giving advice and making suggestions to the brainstormed problems. Present a list of recyclable materials and provide suggestions on how to reutilize them.
We serve more than food!	Make predictions, identify and analyse key information related to "Uncommon restaurants and supermarkets around the world". Write a list of requests that can be emailed to any unusual restaurant and/or food market, asking for more information on their products and services and providing reasons for these requests. Present a list of requests which includes different orders and requests when dining or visiting an uncommon restaurant or supermarket.
Tough jobs	Make predictions and find key information related to tough jobs. Write a job description "as an employer/company owner" of the roles and responsibilities in that job. Present a specific TOUGH job of your preference to the class.
Most expensive laptops in the world	Make predictions, identify and analyse key information related to "the most expensive laptops in the world". Write a summary on features of laptops over desktops. Present mind-maps or clusters where a comparison between two laptops is displayed.
How photographers make Connections	Make predictions and identify and analyse key information related to "the industry of photography and how photographers create unique moments", including the language of images, photography quality, inferring emotions and moods within photographs, uncommon and most astonishing photographs taken around the world. Write an essay describing selected photography. Present descriptions of a picture indicating possible implied meanings.
Global university education	Make predictions, identify and analyse key information related to "global university education". Information includes global trends in university education around the world, greatest development in universities, remarkable ranking of programs, colleges and academic fields. Write an essay comparing/contrasting two universities, colleges, programs using patterns of exemplifications. Design and present an info-graph which compares two universities, colleges, programs, fields of study based on specific categories.

(continued)

Table 1 (continued)

Topic	Summary of student learning outcomes (SLOs)
Food as communication	Make predictions and find key information related to "food as communication around the world". Write a descriptive summary of a popular dish in a selected region and/or country. Give short presentations of a popular dish in a restaurant.
Future living	Make predictions and find key information related to "future living". Write sentences about future predictions (students give their opinions). Present future technologies of their preference.
Recruitment-the gold of business	Make predictions and find key information from a specific content related to "recruitment and hiring human resources". Write a job description. Present a summary of a selected job description in a form of a visual presentation including different required skills and qualifications.
E-business revolution	Make predictions, identify and analyse key information related to "E-business revolution and the internet shopping". Write a summary interpreting a visual graphic or a chart on E-business. Deliver presentations using data from visual graphics.
Social responsibility	Make predictions and find key information related to "social responsibility". Write a summary about a selected corporate initiative that promotes "social responsibility". Brainstorm and present a social responsibility initiative that promotes "local social responsibility".
Take a selfie	Make predictions and find key information related to "the modern face of taking selfies (self-portrait photographs)". Describe in writing "injuries while taking a selfie". Deliver a short presentation "describing the worst/best selfie you have ever taken".
Saudi Vision 2030	Make predictions and find key information from a specific content related to "Saudi Vision 2030". Write an essay on personal goals that fit into the Saudi Vision 2030. Present a mind map on individual contributions to participate in the Saudi Vision 2030.
Second language learning	Make predictions and find key information from a specific content related to (second language learning). Write a descriptive summary of a selected foreign language. Interview a classmate on the difficulties of learning a second language.
Personality	Make predictions and find key information from a specific content related to personalities through skimming and scanning. Write 2–3 paragraphs on describing a feature of personal character that a learner finds important. Design a presentation on how to describe one's personality.
International tests of English	Make predictions and find key information from a specific content related to "the different proficiency tests of English" through skimming and scanning. Write a 2–3 paragraph composition on "how to improve language proficiency and increase test score". Present a summary of language proficiency requirements in local and international universities.

(continued)

Table 1 (continued)

Topic	Summary of student learning outcomes (SLOs)
The culture of coffee	Make predictions and find key information from a specific content related to coffee as a global phenomenon and its traditions around the world through skimming and scanning. Write a paragraph summary of a 2-page article on pros and cons of coffee. Present a short description of a favourite coffee.
Best business leaders ever	Make predictions and find key information from a specific content related to "best business leaders ever" through skimming and scanning. Write a 2-paragraph narrative about a selected business leader.
Reading for quality minds	Make predictions and find key information from a specific content related to reading for quality minds through skimming and scanning. Write a paragraph summary of a 3-pages article/research on "what reading does to our minds/how reading affects our brains."
Problem- solving	Make predictions and find key information from a specific content related to problem solving through skimming and scanning. Write 2–3 paragraphs solving a problem, following problem solving steps as guided by the instructor. Give presentations identifying a problem and make suggestions based on a written or audio scenario.

of which must be met by both large companies and educational institutions (Aarnio-Linnanvuori, 2019). Naturally, garbage is a hot issue of etiquette in many cultures and countries, so tackling such a global issue will sensitise students to the need to be responsible global citizens by doing their parts in the protection of our endangered planet. Brainstorming technique can be used to fill gaps in students' knowledge in relation to vocabulary development and 'factual' matters. The development of intercultural communication skills is nurtured by addressing the issue from a global perspective.

In the weeks that follow, students also deal with business and study topics. At these stages, their ability to express their own opinions is developed and evaluated. The students are trained to be able to maintain a reasoned dialogue with their interlocutors while defending their arguments in a rational way. The intercultural approach also includes adjusting one's own speech following the possibility of showing respect for the interlocutor's views (perspective shifting) and avoiding cultural conflicts (Steinfatt & Millette, 2019). This section also develops critical thinking skills by training students to be more open to cultural diversity by reading texts about people from different cultural and national backgrounds. Academic topics alternate with business and employment topics so that the cultural aspects discussed during classes are associated with all spheres of human life where contact with strangers is required. This program also progressively develops verbal skills of description, storytelling, and reasoning. Group work fosters the team orientation and collective reasoning often required in the workplace (Bravo et al., 2019; Feldman, 2017).

The theme of education is also presented in this program, with reference to cross-cultural diversities in global contexts. As a result, education and the specific features of its process form a significant part of a person's sociocultural identity. By understanding this socialising aspect of education, students can look at language learning

Table 2 Main learning outcomes and vocabulary (rules around the world)

Pacing guide – week 1	
Level	ELI_110
Total class hours	18
Total ONLINE enriching hours	4
Target levels	CEFR (B1-B2) – CLB (6) – IELTS (4.5)
Essential thinking skill	Making predictions Activating prior knowledge
Essential study skill	Skimming and scanning Mind-mapping Note-taking
Essential presentation skill	Using proper voice tone Using proper posture
Theme	Community
	Topic: Rules around the world
Material	Available on ELI E-inventory & extra materials as provided by instructor
Vocabulary list	Relax (relax the rules) Compulsory Recommend Especially Competent Appropriately / Respect Awkward Elderly Rude Rule(s) (n.) Civilized Thorough / Convert Implement Trial Manners Behaviour Etiquette / Actually Dangerous Enough License Gestures Block (v.)

Main SLOs
By the end of this week, students can: Make predictions about content related to "rules around the world". Connect prior knowledge to their predictions. Find key information from a specific content (recording, passage) related to "rules around the world". Use modal verbs of prohibition in meaningful contexts. Ask wh-questions in meaningful contexts. Use suffixes that change verbs into nouns in meaningful contexts. Use listed vocabulary in meaningful contexts and sentences. Write an outline of home/family rules. Interview a classmate and present home/family rules to the class.

from a multi-perspective relativist stance. By realising how languages display huge diversity, students learn to respect the idiolect and sociolect particularities of each language variety and its native speakers. However, various aspects of linguistic manifestations must be explored explicitly (Shaules, 2019). In addition, this section provides an opportunity to sharpen critical thinking when comparing the two universities in the writing part of the week.

Table 3 Specific learning outcomes (rules around the world)

Weekly plan – 1	
Skill/language	Specific SLOs
 IT'S Sunday What Are You Learning?	Use modal verbs of prohibition in meaningful contexts: Make-stop-keep-prevent-encourage-discourage-expect. Ask wh-questions in meaningful contexts: Who, what, when, where, why Use suffixes that change verbs into nouns in meaningful contexts. Use listed vocabulary for the week in meaningful sentences and contexts. Identify parts of speech.
 IT'S Monday What Are You Listening to?	Make predictions about a listening text related to "rules around the world" based on prior knowledge, supporting visuals and other cues. Identify key information through skimming & scanning. Identify the basic genre or type of a listening text.
IT'S Tuesday What Are You Reading?	Make predictions about a reading text on "rules around the world" based on prior knowledge, supporting visuals and other cues. Find key information using skimming and scanning.

IT'S Wednesday What Are You Writing?
	Map a visual outline of home/family rules.
	Write an outline of home/family rules, using modal verbs of prohibition and proper nouns. (6 rules only)
	Use grammatical patterns for this week and necessary vocabulary.
	Employ proper rules related to spelling, capitalization, and punctuation.
	Guidelines for instructors:
	  Instructor provides a model outline/mind-map.
	  Students brainstorm ideas on mind map.
	  Main task: Students produce the first draft of writing an "outline" of own home/family rules.
	  At home, students edit and rewrite their work based on instructor's feedback and upload/send their final drafts to the instructor.
	  Instructor scores students' written pieces and hands to students next class.
	  Students compile their work in their portfolios.

IT'S Thursday What Are You Speaking About?	In pairs, interview a classmate to find out key information about home/family rules through using wh-questions (3 questions only per student).
	Take notes on classmates' answers.
	Give a short presentation to introduce a classmate's home/family rules.
	Use proper tone and posture during presentation.
	Guidelines for instructors:
	  Instructor divides students in pairs.
	  Instructor provides sample interview questions.
	  Students brainstorm interview questions on worksheets.
	  Main task: Students present their classmates' answers and instructor scores their presentations using a scaled checklist.
	  Scored sheets are kept with the instructor till the following week.
	  Students compile their work in their portfolios.

Table 4 Main learning outcomes and vocabulary (the other face of trash)

Pacing guide – week 2	
Level	ELI_110
Total class hours	18
Total ONLINE enriching hours	4
Target levels	CEFR (B1-B2) – CLB (6) – IELTS (4.5)
Essential thinking skill	Making predictions Activating prior knowledge Identifying causes and effects
Essential study skill	Skimming and scanning Graph analysis
Essential presentation skill	Using proper voice tone. Using proper posture.
Theme	Community
	Topic: The other face of trash
Material	Available on ELI E-inventory & extra materials as provided by instructor
Vocabulary list	Guaranteed Incineration Properly Nutrients Outcome Equal Global / Pressing Bacteria Disease Disgusting Forest Dump Ever / Ocean (Un)Treated Contaminate Acid rain Cause Community / Garbage Environment Recycling Energy Disposal

MAIN SLOs

By the end of this week, students can:

Make predictions about a content related to "trash in community and how recycling makes a difference".

Connect prior knowledge to their predictions.

Identify and analyse key information related to "trash in community" from an info-graph.

Identify and use language patterns of giving advice and making suggestions.

Use listed vocabulary in meaningful sentences and contexts.

Brainstorm environmental problems related to trash, and identify causes and effects.

Write sentences that include giving advice and making suggestions to the brainstormed problems.

Present a list of recyclable materials and provide suggestions on how to reutilize them.

Given the reciprocity of globalization and technological development processes, many employers in the modern world target specialists remotely. This fact is facilitated by the pandemic, which led to forced self-isolation. During this time, various means of communication have developed, making it possible to work comfortably from anywhere in the world, conduct video conferences, and exchange instant messages and information. In this regard, intercultural learning has become a necessary component of foreign language learning as employment situations have increasingly become a global institutional space. If the earlier cultural dialogue was

Table 5 Specific learning outcomes (the other face of trash)

Weekly plan – 2	
Skill/language	Specific SLOs
IT'S Sunday What Are You Learning? (Grammar & Vocabulary)	Identify and use patterns of giving advice and making suggestions in meaningful sentences and contexts as: *Should, shouldn't, ought to, could*
	Use listed vocabulary for the week in meaningful sentences and contexts.
	Identify parts of speech.
IT'S Monday What Are You Listening to?	Make predictions about a listening text related to "trash in community" based on prior knowledge, supporting visuals and other cues.
	Identify purpose, main ideas, specific details through skimming & scanning.
	Identify the basic genre or type of a listening text.
IT'S Tuesday What Are You Reading?	Make predictions related to "trash in community" from related info-graphs and based on prior knowledge & supporting visuals.
	Identify and analyse key information from info-graphs.
	Identify causes and effects.
IT'S Wednesday What Are You Writing? (Think, Write, Edit)	In pairs, brainstorm a list of 2 environmental problems related to trash.
	In pairs, brainstorm their causes and effects.
	In pairs, write a list of 5 sentences that include giving advice and making suggestions to the brainstormed problems.
	Use grammatical patterns for this week and necessary vocabulary.
	Notice proper rules related to spelling, capitalization, and punctuation.
	Guidelines for instructors:
	Instructor divides students into pairs.
	Instructor provides a model answer.
	Students brainstorm ideas on worksheets.
	Main task: Students produce 'first draft' of their writing.
	At home, students edit and rewrite their work based on the instructor's feedback and upload/send their final drafts to the instructor.
	Instructor scores students' written pieces and hands to students the following class.
	Students compile their work in their portfolios.
IT'S Thursday What Are You Speaking About?	In groups, brainstorm a list of 2 recyclable materials in environment/community.
	In groups, present 3 suggestions on how to reutilize each recycled item.
	Use language patterns of giving advice and making suggestions and necessary vocabulary.
	Use proper tone and posture during presentation.
	Guidelines for instructors:
	Instructor divides students in groups.
	Instructor provides model brainstorming techniques/shapes.
	Students brainstorm ideas on worksheets. Instructor gives instant feedback.
	Main task: Students present their brainstorming output and the instructor scores their presentations using a scaled checklist.
	Scored brainstorming sheets are kept with the instructor till the following week.
	Students compile their work in their portfolios.

possible only in companies of the scale of the international market or while travelling, now it is available to almost everyone (Dauletbekova et al., 2020). In this regard, the importance of intercultural communicative skills needed to appropriately interact with other co-workers should be prioritised.

This program also touches upon issues of the future, telemedicine, and technologies of the future. Given that it was difficult to imagine the current progress even twenty years ago, the questions are relevant. Considering them in the context of intercultural relations, new, rarely discussed aspects arise. Many educational materials are devoted to the development of technology and the works of science fiction (Gravemeijer et al., 2017). However sociocultural issues of the future are rarely raised. In this program, it is necessary to pay more attention to this topic to promote students' prediction and problem-solving skills.

In the third week of the 120 English language program, discussion of previously tackled issues deepens by encouraging students to think about corporate responsibility in the workplace, using the brainstorming technique. Corporate responsibility includes social and environmental issues, etiquette, and respect for the multicultural and pluriversal worldviews workers may bring to the workplace. Developing the topic of intercultural relations in the fourth week, students raise the topic of selfies. It would seem that the once-popular trend has become entrenched in the culture of most of the people active on the Internet. Students are invited to conduct a more thorough and detailed analysis of this cellphone craze phenomenon from a cross-cultural perspective by unwinding its history, and understanding the possible views about selfie-taking across global contexts. This topic presents the teacher with an ample opportunity to sensitise students to the cultural implications of globalization. Moreover, students will learn to distinguish between global trends that may be unacceptable for a particular culture. In order to avoid unpleasant situations during intercultural dialogue, the study of this aspect can lead a group of students to a deeper analysis of such global trends. In this sense, the issue of globalisation is explored in relation to cultural diversity to help students to decentre and relativise the soundness of culture-based attitudinal behaviours.

In the sixth week, students discuss the Saudi Vision 2030 program, which addresses many environmental and social issues (Thompson, 2017). Here students tackle several issues pertaining to areas such as education, ecology, Saudi dependence on oil to generate income, the creation of more jobs for women, the advancing of the tourism sector in Saudi Arabia, and healthcare. This course unit contains a set of reforms that promise to 'modernise' the country and improve the wellbeing of Saudi citizens. Here, cultural dialogue has several dimensions that are worth considering. First, it is a dialogue between the state and the people: how much will the new changes affect the established conservative traditions? Secondly, this is an invitation to explore how such ambitious plans can be achieved and in what way they might set a model to emulate for other neighbouring or foreign countries. The ability to meta-analyse is essential for students to develop critical thinking.

Another topic addressed in the 120 course is the importance of studying a foreign language. Developing skills in describing a foreign language contributes to a deeper understanding of its structure. However, often in the language itself, many cultural aspects are accessible only to those who understand this language at a high level. We are talking about the etymology of words or contextual expressions and the assumptions that can be concluded based on the material studied.

In this program, the gradual transition from global issues to more local ones, up to the study of personality, is implemented. Students are encouraged to express their views about different contemporary societal issues from a cultural and personal perspective. Self-awareness is a life-long critical skill as it is grounded in an intuitive sense of emotional intelligence. A high indicator of this skill is appreciated in many professions and among leaders. Moreover, leadership qualities are discussed further in the training plan as a separate topic.

Human resource management is a responsible task. The student should be prepared not only for stressful situations but for possible situations of disagreement in which they will have to make difficult decisions. Conflicts can arise due to misunderstanding or failure to appropriately understand cross-cultural conventions and rules. Hence, students are prepared not only for ordinary situations of reasoning and communication in which cultural issues are embedded. As future leaders, they need to be able to act as cultural mediators and help resolve such conflicts, taking into account each party's diverse interests.

Finally, the program moves from leadership skills to a concluding discussion of the cognitive skills that develop with reading. Here, the topic of self-awareness continues; students explore themselves under challenging situations and look for ways to become effective readers. Completing the course with a discussion of further development can contribute to students' continuous learning and involvement in the intercultural learning process. After defending the final group projects, a test is carried out according to the program to determine the new level of students' knowledge. With proper teaching and support of teaching materials, the results of the program would be satisfactory.

4   Discussion

The program is relatively well structured and affects the main aspects of teaching a foreign English language. The program covers all general and more advanced grammar topics. The vocabulary is represented by a somewhat limited number of words for each unit; however, constant tasks with in-depth research of the topic imply a more significant expansion of the students' vocabulary. Each unit includes reading, listening, writing, and speaking on a chosen topic. Expanded use of brainstorming, mind-map, presentations, and infographics brings additional interactivity and allows better understanding of the language and the skills necessary for professional aptitude.

On the development of intercultural competence and intercultural relations, in general, the course meets the requirements of effective intercultural learning, touching on the most pressing issues. Extensive topics are covered in curriculum 110; critical discussions of controversial topics are encouraged as the level of students advances in curriculum 120. The structure is consistent; however, the disclosure of some topics may be criticized. First, the topic of culture, as such, is not touched upon when discussing the future. Topics such as advertising, restaurants, coffee and much else illuminate the types of the culture of many countries and peoples. However, the future is being discussed in terms of technology. As labour automation and other technological issues are inevitable processes of globalisation, the social and cultural aspects need to be discussed by students in class Socratic circles.

Secondly, although the course is focused on developing the future career of students and is more focused on issues of employment and professional skills, there are no explicit topics with a discussion of culture. Cultures such as cuisine, travel, attitude to the environment, and many other things are touched upon in the program to varying degrees. However, no study time is allocated to define the category or concept of culture itself. Since the program should be focused on the development of interculturalism, students need to be trained in becoming cultural mediators. In this vein, the curriculum addresses international education, culture-sensitive leadership, self-awareness and empathy towards cultural others. The definition of culture should also be included in discussion topics to highlight better the themes of religion and art, values, and traditions, which also have a significant impact on the formation of an individual's personality and are the regulator for many of their attitudes and behaviours. Students should be trained to develop effective critical thinking skills to advance their views in a rational way in environments of conflict of opinion.

5   Conclusion

Studying English at the university is not devoid of specific problems, but every year the development of pedagogical methods, including those oriented towards the promotion of intercultural competence might facilitate learners' overall competence. The EFL program delineated in this chapter aims at transforming students into intercultural mediators and contributes to the development of their sociolinguistic skills necessary for easy performance in workplace environments. Students are trained to be fluent in the foreign language, improve their meaning negotiation skills while interacting with their interlocutors, and develop emotional intelligence, critical thinking, and leadership skills. While an implicit promotion of native-speakerism is challenged in most lingua franca teaching contexts and EFL textbooks, Saudi English curriculum developers tend to adopt a more English as an International Language-informed pedagogy to prepare learners to become successful intercultural mediators.

References

Aarnio-Linnanvuori, E. (2019). How do teachers perceive environmental responsibility? *Environmental Education Research, 25*(1), 46–61. https://doi.org/10.1080/1350462 2.2018.1506910

Aburizaizah, S. (2021). Higher education in Saudi Arabia: Rooted in bureaucracy, inspired by an EFL semi-decentralization model. *International Journal of English Language Education, 9*(1), 1–25. https://doi.org/10.5296/ijele.v9i1.17941

Alavinia, P., & Rahimi, H. (2019). Task types effects and task involvement load on vocabulary learning of EFL learners. *International Journal of Instruction, 12*(1), 1501–1516.

Bravo, R., Catalán, S., & Pina, J. M. (2019). Analysing teamwork in higher education: An empirical study on the antecedents and consequences of team cohesiveness. *Studies in Higher Education, 44*(7), 1153–1165. https://doi.org/10.1080/03075079.2017.1420049

Carbone, F. (2017). International tourism and cultural diplomacy: A new conceptual approach towards global mutual understanding and peace through tourism. *Tourism: An International Interdisciplinary Journal, 65*(1), 61–74.

Catarci, M., Gomes, M. P., & Siqueira, S. (Eds.). (2020). *Refugees, interculturalism and education.* Routledge.

Çetin, Y., Bahar, M., & Griffiths, C. (2017). International students' views on local culture: Turkish experience. *Journal of International Students, 7*(3), 467–485. https://doi.org/10.32674/jis.v7i3.204

Cinkara, E. (2020). Quiz study as a professional development activity for tertiary-level EFL test writers. *The Electronic Journal for English as a Second Language, 24*(3), n3.

Dauletbekova, Z., Berkinbayeva, G., Meirbekova, G., Yelubayeva, P., & Shalabayeva, Z. (2020). Experimental system of learning the culture of dialogue speech through 4C modeling skills in education. *Journal of Talent Development and Excellence, 12*(2s), 3051–3060.

Elias, A., & Mansouri, F. (2020). A systematic review of studies on interculturalism and intercultural dialogue. *Journal of Intercultural Studies, 41*(4), 490–523. https://doi.org/10.108 0/07256868.2020.1782861

Estévez-Saá, J. M. (2017). Multiculturalism, interculturalism, transculturalism and the reluctant fundamentalist. *SARE: Southeast Asian Review of English, 53*(1), 1–11. https://doi.org/10.22452/sare.vol53no1.2

Feldman, K. A. (Ed.). (2017). *College and student: Selected readings in the social psychology of higher education* (Vol. 28). Elsevier.

Gravemeijer, K., Stephan, M., Julie, C., Lin, F. L., & Ohtani, M. (2017). What mathematics education may prepare students for the society of the future? *International Journal of Science and Mathematics Education, 15*(1), 105–123. https://doi.org/10.1007/s10763-017-9814-6

Itmeizeh, M., & Hassan, A. (2020). New approaches to teaching critical thinking skills through a new EFL curriculum. *International Journal of Psychosocial Rehabilitation, 24*(07), 8864–8880.

Khan, M. S. R., & Alasmari, A. M. (2018). Literary texts in the EFL classrooms: Applications, benefits and approaches. *International Journal of Applied Linguistics and English Literature, 7*(5), 167–179.

Kostikova, L. P., Prishvina, V. V., Ilyushina, A. V., Fedotova, O. S., & Belogurov, A. Y. (2018, March). Culture in teaching English as a foreign language. In *2nd International conference on culture, education and economic development of modern society* (ICCESE 2018) (pp. 13–17). Atlantis Press.

Makhmudov, K. (2020). Ways of forming intercultural communication in foreign language teaching. *Science and Education, 1*(4), 84–89.

Moradkhani, S. (2019). EFL teachers' perceptions of two reflection approaches. *English Language Teaching Journal, 73*(1), 61–71. https://doi.org/10.1093/elt/ccy030

Özdemir, E. (2017). Promoting EFL learners' intercultural communication effectiveness: A focus on Facebook. *Computer Assisted Language Learning, 30*(6), 510–528. https://doi.org/10.108 0/09588221.2017.1325907

Park, A. Y. (2020). A comparison of the impact of extensive and intensive reading approaches on the reading attitudes of secondary EFL learners. *Studies in Second Language Learning and Teaching, 10*(2), 337–358.

Shaules, J. (2019). *Language, culture, and the embodied mind: A developmental model of Linguaculture learning*. Springer.

Shmakova, A., Ryzhova, Y., & Suhorukhih, A. (2021). The impact of ICT education on humanistic innovative potential. In *Education and information technologies* (pp. 1–16).

Steinfatt, T. M., & Millette, D. M. (2019). Intercultural communication. In D. W. Stacks, M. B. Salwen, & K. C. Eichhorn (Eds.), *An integrated approach to communication theory and research* (pp. 307–320). Routledge. https://doi.org/10.4324/9780203710753

Sutiyatno, S. (2018). The effect of teacher's verbal communication and non-verbal communication on students' English achievement. *Journal of Language Teaching and Research, 9*(2), 430–437. https://doi.org/10.17507/jltr.0902.28

Thompson, M. C. (2017). 'Saudi vision 2030': A viable response to youth aspirations and concerns? *Asian Affairs, 48*(2), 205–221. https://doi.org/10.1080/03068374.2017.1313598

Toliboboeva, S. J. (2020). Teaching intercultural communication in English. *Science and Education, 1*(Special Issue 2), 152–156.

Vetrinskaya, V. V., & Dmitrenko, T. A. (2017). Developing students' socio-cultural competence in foreign language classes. *Training Language and Culture, 1*(2), 23–41.

Wahyuni, A. (2018, January). The power of verbal and nonverbal communication in learning. In *1st International conference on intellectuals' global responsibility (ICIGR)*. Atlantis Press.

Wang, Q. (2017). Interculturalism, intercultural education, and Chinese society. *Frontiers of Education in China, 12*(3), 309–331.

Wuryandari, D. A. (2021). Teaching media in studying collocation for increasing students' language intuition. *LADU: Journal of Languages and Education, 1*(4), 171–177. https://doi.org/10.56724/ladu.v1i4.62

Yueqin, H. A. N. (2013). Research on fostering intercultural communication competence of foreign language learners. *Cross-Cultural Communication, 9*(1), 5–12.

Tahany Abdulaziz Aleisa (Ed D, the University of Pittsburgh, USA) currently works as Professor in EFL Education at the Faculty of Education, University of Jeddah. Her recent research is a co-authored paper published at *Comparative Education Review*. Her research interests include EFL literacy, cultural awareness, and educational policies. Email: talbeiz@uj.edu.sa

Part II
Fostering a Culturally Responsive Pedagogy in Teacher Education

Part II addresses how the multilingual/multicultural and pedagogical capitals of non-native English-speaking teachers (NNESTs) are not recognised as valuable assets in Western neoliberal educational systems. It also argues for the crucial role teacher educators have to play in the promotion of intercultural learning in contemporary diverse educational settings. Sahlane's chapter addresses the need to infuse teaching English curricula with Aboriginal perspectives. He also objects to the persisting discrimination against educators who have been labelled 'non-native speakers' in the Canadian teacher education system. The study gives a personal account of being Othered and professionally marginalised because he was foreign educated; it also demonstrates how dealing with associate teachers in curriculum placement has not always been an easy experience because divisive native-speakerist discourses surround everyday teaching practices and create the coercive need to fit within the Eurocentric normative models of 'good' teaching. Racialised and minoritised teacher candidates have to cope with all forms of systemic racism and individual microaggressions in a way that devalues their worth as potential professionals and detrimentally impacts their psychological well-being along the road. Hence, NNESTs need to delink from the 'native-speakerist' agenda by seeking to advance alternative perspectives and positionalities that resist 'epistemic injustice' and contest white domination and deficit thinking.

In the same vein, Marom's chapter argues about how race is a crucial mechanism of oppression in that teacher education programs in Canada run counter to the heterogeneous linguistic realities of racialised student and staff populations. She discusses barriers to the diversification of teacher education in Canada via three interconnected case studies. She investigates the different hurdles internationally educated teachers (IETs) must surmount to be able to get recertified in the BC teacher education system. Instead of assigning them to a teacher education program that is tailored to their unique needs as experienced immigrant (and thus older) teachers, IETs have to 'fit in' within the mainstream program designed for domestic preservice teachers (who are mainly monolingual, white and in their twenties). Marom also addresses the challenges racialised Canada-born teacher candidates face and how they are often represented as 'outsiders' to the profession. Lastly, she describes the case of Punjabi international students in Canada and highlights how teaching is constructed as 'one size fits all.' The author concludes that to diversify the teaching body, there is a need for the questioning of the underlying structures of teacher education.

Hence, both Sahlane and Marom point to the need to dismantle regimes of oppression that still pervade societal and educational spaces, wherein marginalised, minoritised and racialised teacher candidates/learners are denied voice and the co-construction of knowledge by reframing them within the deficit discourses that devalue the pluricultural and plurilinguistic capitals they bring into Canadian inter-cultural encounters and educational spaces. Adopting new inclusive pedagogies in teacher training programs is a prerequisite for the empowerment of teacher candidates to develop a critical intercultural pedagogy in their teaching. In Canadian context, the K-12 curriculum instructional methodologies, documents and assessment mandates fail to be culturally appropriate in that they ignore local ethnolinguistic and sociocultural realities and target the exclusive needs of white, middle-class, monolingual, and monocultural learners.

Eurocentric discourse in academic spaces reflects power relations in society, and by naturalising ways of speaking about cultural others, it helps maintain the patterns of white domination and power abuse by normalising social inequality. Murray's chapter investigates the portrayal of Indigenous peoples in EFL textbooks at Norwegian secondary schools. The author addresses the discursive strategies that serve to conceal the identities of the perpetrators of negative actions. Besides, in-group/outgroup categorisation (us vs. them) serve to include white groups and exclude Aboriginal communities (e.g., in the 2008 national reconciliation apology address of Former Australian PM, Kevin Rudd). However, unlike in mediated political discourse, textbook narratives tend to grant a speaking role to the (Australian) Aboriginals, and thus enabling them to contest official mainstream definition of relations between First Nations and their white settler compatriots.

Learning is a dynamic, historically situated and socioculturally mediated process that shapes the languages and literacies of young children. Diaz's chapter is about the roles that early childhood educators and superdiverse communities might play in preparing multilingual Aboriginal and immigrant children for effective learning and socialisation in mainstream Australian society. Inspired by insights from critical intercultural theory and cultural literacy, the study draws on interview, participant observation and field notes data from two empirical studies to investigate the quality of multilingual support provided for the children attending early childhood education (ECE) settings. The study reveals that inclusive and culturally appropriate discourses reframe families as 'experts' in the lives of their multilingual children, by valuing the maintenance of linguistically and culturally diverse literacies children bring into the classrooms (case study 1). However, such maintenance of home languages is problematised by assimilationist monolingual/monocultural counter-narratives and deficit discourses that perceive multilingual/ multicultural capitals from a cultural deficit point of view (case study 2). The study shows the critical role of multilingual early childhood educators who engage in reciprocal partnerships with families. The distance between Indigenous cultural ways of knowing/being and those of the mainstream white settler educational environments is perpetuated by a persistent power imbalance in which Eurocentric norms dominate within Australian ECE system. By pathologising Indigenous and immigrant family cultural-linguistic practices, assimilationist assumptions about English as the standard to measure children's competencies perpetuate enduring neocolonial monocultural and monolingual views of language and literacy.

Likewise, Dobinson's study investigates how international students (and heritage language students) in Australian university settings have to adapt to the mainstream Eurocentric pedagogical models and assimilationist frames of knowledge production that perpetuate deficit assumptions and devalue Indigenous and international students' knowledges and diverse cultural and linguistic capitals brought into the classroom. This hegemonic epistemological dominance of West-centric modes of knowing, being and seeing the world is detrimental for the promotion of inclusive and culturally responsive pedagogies that acknowledge the value of alternative pluriversal worldviews and perspectives. To enact such culturally responsive pedagogies, the author proposes an alternative approach to teaching university students, which draws on the valuable resources and cultural/linguistic funds of knowledge that both students and teachers use when navigating the intercultural/educational encounters on the university campus and beyond, both in Australia and in Vietnam. Hence, the author wants them to progress towards 'interculturality' (the promotion of learners' intercultural competence in a way that enhances their ability to circumvent intercultural barriers and sustain their plurilingual repertoires); to develop their diverse knowledge systems, and their hybrid identities; to move in the direction of 'linguistic inclusion' (the fostering of a pedagogy of translanguaging as an emancipatory and counter-hegemonic approach to language teaching); and towards 'linguistic diversity' (the internationalisation of higher education and the relevance of global Englishes in teaching academic skills). The study also shows how mediated cultural diversity manifests itself in 'bottom-up' film production practices such as the Arab Film festival project that serves to contribute to wider cultural diversity debates beyond culturalist and monolithic stereotypical images. Such a participatory community media approach is instrumental in promoting cultural diversity in that 'communities of identity' use cultural spaces to contest dominant cultural representations or provide alternative self-portrayals.

Hence, in our increasingly globalising modern societies, we need to prepare language teachers to be able to bridge the language and cultural worlds they will encounter with the increasingly diverse student populations. The TEACUP Project proposed by Parra & Pfingsthorn (consisting of modules developed by over 30 language education professionals from five different countries) is a good European intercultural learning project that aims at delivering teaching materials and professional development theoretical modules that highlight the importance of integrating multicultural/multilingual approaches into EFL education in different transnational settings (especially, within the EU context). The chapter particularly addresses the pre/in-service teacher candidates' responses to the Project's Key Concepts in an attempt to evaluate the relevance and 'applicability' of multicultural/ multilingual theoretical constructs in foreign language teacher education context. Hence, the assimilationist educational ethos that pervades ELT theory and pedagogy is interrogated by advocating the need to make preservice teachers aware of and encourage them to adopt a more multilingual/multicultural approach to foreign language education to accommodate a rich repertoire of intercultural experience. The definition of plurilingual competence in the Common European Framework of Reference for Languages (CEFR) is revisited to validate the need to 'decompartimentalise' the learners' linguistic and cultural multicompetencies (translanguaging/ transculturality) by encouraging teacher educators to make their students more independent L2 users who could navigate across languages with a flexible cognitive dexterity.

In the same vein, Suzuki's chapter demonstrates how Japanese preservice English teachers can be trained to develop intercultural sensitivity in their teaching. The study reveals that short-term educational training can promote the student teachers' awareness of the diverse needs of Japanese EFL learners. The study shows that teacher trainees are ready to adopt inclusive attitudes towards different varieties of World Englishes. Hence, in the Asian lingua franca situations, effective multilingual/multicultural communication requires a socioculturally informed and inclusive pedagogy that can prepare pre/in-service teachers to develop a pluralistic approach to foreign language/culture learning.

Similarly, Tennekoon's chapter delineates the various educational challenges that persist in the Sri Lankan teacher education system. The author argues that ELT pedagogy in Sri Lanka has failed to satisfactorily train preservice teachers to become intercultural 'mediators' so that they can effectively attend to the students' diverse ethnic, religious and linguistic needs. Tennekoon's study is an attempt to train language professionals to educate for peace in a society that is ravaged by ethnoreligious conflicts. Its aim is to develop an inclusive and critical pedagogy that equips student teachers with the appropriate intercultural knowledge, skills, and attitudes to nurture an ethnorelative attitude and intercultural empathy in Sri Lankan students.

As Marlina rightly argues, because in an English as an International Language (EIL) setting learners display a great diversity of linguistic and sociocultural profiles, any sound EIL curriculum development for TESOL teacher education should be appropriately informed by a theory of language learning and teaching that sufficiently reflect complex diversity within multilingual communities. In this chapter, the author describes the various planning and implementation processes involved in an EIL-oriented TESOL teacher education program. These processes constitute a network of interacting systems in a way that any modification in one part of the system has an important impact on other parts of the system.

The author also delineates the major assumptions that need to inform EIL-based TESOL curriculum development. First, he argues that the nature of English in our globalised world today reveals that most English users have acquired English as an additional language, which results in large-scale multilingualism. Consequently, English has become a language of global communication (i.e., a global lingua franca). As English is mostly used in 'outer circle' and 'expanding circle' contexts to interact with other L2 speakers rather than with native speakers, deficit and assimilationist monolingual theories that serve to maintain colonialist ideologies and cultural/epistemological dominance of English over other alternative Global

South pluriversal worldviews have become irrelevant in the design of EIL-informed TESOL curriculum.

The second major assumption is that as the ownership of EIL has become 'de-territorialised' and 'de-nationalised', learners of EIL do not need to internalise the native speaker linguistic and cultural norms to communicate in English in cross-cultural encounters; and since English is no longer linked to a particular nation or culture, native speaker models can no longer appropriately inform effective TESOL curriculum development or teaching pedagogies. Curriculum objectives and approaches should be designed to meet the learners' sociocultural and cross-cultural communicative needs (i.e., abiding by the motto: "think global, act local"). The learning needs and goals of bilingual speakers of English in multilingual contexts are different from those of monolingual speakers. Hence, a 'native-like competence' concept cannot constitute the basis for EIL curriculum development. Teaching EIL requires that curriculum developers thoroughly examine individual learners' specific uses of English within their particular speech communities.

The third main assumption is that in TESOL teacher education, student teachers should be sensitised to the importance of promoting critical intercultural competence in the design and teaching of EIL instructional materials. The fourth key assumption is that EIL-informed TESOL curriculum should encourage the repoliticisation of pedagogy. After all, pedagogy cannot be divorced from its political context because it is intimately connected to the struggle over epistemic agency. Hence, English teaching in post-colonial contexts should be conducted in a socioculturally and politically sensitive manner by encouraging the local educational practitioners to design and implement indigenised curricula using multicultural/ multilingual pedagogical approaches.

(En)Countering the 'White' Gaze: Native-Speakerist Rhetorics and the Raciolinguistics of Hegemony

Ahmed Sahlane (iD)

Abstract The present autoethnographic account challenges the 'myth' that we live in a 'post-racial' multicultural Canadian society; it provides an insider's perspective on the researcher's embodied experience of being socialised into the role of a non-native English-speaking teacher while striving for integration into K-12 public education in British Columbia, Canada. Taking a critical race theoretical perspective, informed by an intersectional discourse analysis of the (re)construction of professional identity as linked to the hierarchisation of power relations within academic spaces, this chapter investigates how the dominant Eurocentric academic discourses and practices tend to impose their ideological frameworks and rationalities on non-native educators by promoting a neo-racist narrative which serves to delegitimise the multilingual/multicultural capitals and the pedagogical skills internationally educated teachers bring to the Canadian teaching profession.

Keywords Critical race theory · Bearing witness · Indigenous peoples · Truth and reconciliation · Highway of Tears · White privilege · Intersectionality · Teacher education · Residential schools

1 Introduction

The present study explores the researcher's lived experience of (re)certification as an English language teacher in mainstream public K-12 education in British Columbia (BC) "not in terms of progress, development and reproduction, but in terms of being out of step, out of place and, possibly, productive of alternatives" (Weatherall &

A. Sahlane (✉)
English Language Institute, University of Jeddah, Jeddah, Saudi Arabia
e-mail: asahlan1@uj.edu.sa

© The Author(s), under exclusive license to Springer Nature Switzerland AG 2023
A. Sahlane, R. Pritchard (eds.), *English as an International Language Education*, English Language Education 33,
https://doi.org/10.1007/978-3-031-34702-3_5

Ahuja, 2020, p. 406). My re-credentialisation trajectory took about one-year full-time campus-based coursework in curriculum methods and educational studies (coupled with an extensive 12-weeks practicum) at the Faculty of Education in a Canadian university. After my foreign credentials had been evaluated by BC College of Teachers, I was required to update my pedagogical skills to match Canadian 'standards'.

I successfully completed my BEd updating studies in June 2010 and was awarded a Teacher's Certificate of Qualification. As my practicum reports were excellent, I was very optimistic about getting hired as a teacher of English. However, after sitting for several interviews (mostly for French teaching positions), I realised that raciolinguistic ideologies naturalise hegemonic structures of power in a way that adversely impacts the career trajectories of non-native English-speaking teachers (NNESTs) who choose to work in different sociocultural environments from the ones in which they were initially socialised.

Although speaking a language involves much more than just "accent," the status given to "native-speaker" English has consequential sociopolitical, linguistic, cultural, and professional implications. Whiteness trumps nativeness as a hiring benchmark (Holliday, 2014; Sian, 2019; Rivers, 2019; Moosavi, 2022). For example, in non-Anglophone countries it is "possible for native speakers of English to be employed as English teachers solely on the grounds that they are native speakers" (Kirkpatrick, 2016, p. 241). Likewise, about 60% of Intensive English Programs' administrators asserted that the "native-speaker" criterion is very crucial in hiring ESL teachers in Anglophone contexts (Mahboob, 2004), despite the fact that not all international students buy into the "native speaker fallacy" (Phillipson, 1992). Besides, the effectiveness of "pedagogical skills" of non-native English-speaking teachers (NNESTs), their higher level of "language awareness", "dedication", "strong collegiality", "creativity in the classroom" and "'curricular flexibility" is well attested in the literature (Moussu, 2010, p. 408; Murtiana, 2013). Hence, "racialized peoples are often disadvantaged, marginalized, and excluded because of their skin colour and its associated stereotypic beliefs" (Henry & Tator, 2009, p. 25).

This chapter is divided into three main parts. Following a brief introduction to critical autoethnographic narrative as a decolonial research method, the first section discusses the need to decentre 'whiteness' in teacher education curriculum as a crucial step in the transitional process of reconciliation and healing in Canada. The second section is an account of the researcher's personal practicum experience as a racialised professionally experienced foreign-educated teacher. The third section delineates how the practicum teaching experience could be transformed into a good opportunity to create educational spaces for equity and social justice. Finally, the study concludes with relevant pedagogical implications.

The present study addresses the following questions:

(a) Are student teachers trained to teach for equity, social justice, and reconciliation in the face of enduring manifestations and impacts of structural inequalities and conflicted narratives of Canadian colonialist history?

(b) How is the 'native speaker'/'non-native speaker' divide negotiated in a racially conscious Canadian teacher education context? And in what ways are linguistic variation and phenotypic traits co-naturalised in institutionally consequential

ways to the effect of (re)positioning teacher subjectivities according to a naturalised internalisation of hegemonic Centre-Periphery power hierarchies?

(c) How is the increasing diversity of student body in K-12 classrooms reflected in
BC pre-service teacher education programs? And how can we, as educators,
create spaces for intercultural dialogue in our classrooms, with explicit commitments to critical, antiracist, and inclusive pedagogies?

2   Critical Autoethnographic Narrative as a Decolonial Research Method

The present study adopts an analytic autoethnographic method that builds upon
critical race theory and critical pedagogy as tools to interrogate 'whiteness' in
Canadian teacher education context. By engaging in "self-conscious introspection
guided by a desire to better understand both self and others through examining one's
actions and perceptions in reference to and dialogue with those of others" (Anderson,
2006, p. 382), autoethnography addresses the importance that "affect" and "emotion" play in the construction of "individual identity" and "social agency" (Giroux,
2016, p. 67). Identity is regarded as the core locus of "writing the self and others
into social and cultural contexts" (Weatherall & Ahuja, 2020, p. 410). Therefore,
"autoethnographies could uncover contextualized knowledges and experiences,
articulate individual privileges, elucidate discursive praxis, reveal intersectional
identities, and validate affective experiences" (Swearingen, 2019, p. 11). In this
sense, analytic ethnography seeks to generalise from self-experience by blending
introspective 'counter-storytelling' with rigorous academic inquiry (Anderson,
2006, p. 388). Moreover, autoethnographic research methods are decolonial in that
they problematise the presumptive universality of Eurocentric research perspectives
contending that knowledge production should be 'neutral', 'objective', 'rational',
and 'impersonal'. Dutta (2018, p. 95) notes that,

> As a storied form of voicing knowledge claims that works through/on the location of the
> scholar, autoethnography offers possibilities for making visible the contours of the per-
> sonal, the political, and the professional, inviting us as participants to critically examine the
> terrains of power that disenfranchise the postcolonial voice, and the many possibilities of
> resistance that are opened up through our participation in the *telling of stories* (emphasis
> added).

Autoethnography is criticised for being 'subjective' and 'cathartic' ('epistemic therapy'), and thus "based on nonempirical think-pieces" and this "poses a clear danger
to the [ELT] field" (Moussu & Llurda, 2008, pp. 333–334). The argument is that
authorial bias may discount the autoethnographer's 'reliability.' In addition, the
'generalisability' test (i.e., how the autoethnographic account speaks to readers
about their lived experiences) might also be contested. However, most of this criticism revolves around the need to differentiate between art and science, a dichotomy
from which evocative autoethnography seeks to delink. "Autoethnographers view
research and writing as socially-just acts; rather than a preoccupation with accuracy,

the goal is to produce analytical, accessible texts that change us and the world we live in for the better" (Ellis et al., 2011, p. 184).

3   Teacher Education in a Post-truth and Reconciliation Canada

Teacher training curriculum reforms are crucial as pathways to any healing and reconciliation effort, transitional justice, and the redressing of Canada's historical wrongs of which more will be reported below. Teacher education in British Columbia (BC) requires teacher candidates to "recognize and respect the diversity of students in schools to create safe, anti-racist, and socially just learning spaces that invite critical reflection on contemporary issues in society" (BC Teachers' Council, 2022, p. 5). BC professional standards also stress that "educators [should] contribute towards truth, reconciliation, and healing" by creating a "safe and inclusive learning environment that reflects the diversity of all students" (BC Teachers' Council, 2019, p. 2).

The purpose of this section is to reflect on BC teacher education's disengagement with knowledge and perspectives that interrogate Canada's residential school system and the continuous gender-based violence inflicted upon Indigenous women. The historical context of white settler domination is outlined. A "process of structural genocide is … visible in the historical narratives that either sanitise history or give the appearance of a temporal rupture where there is a past, present or future break from a colonial genocidal history" (Willsher & Oldfield, 2020, p. 204).

3.1   White Settler Colonialism and the Legacy of Residential Schooling

Canada's notorious Indian residential schools (IRSs) should be recognised as state-inflicted tools of "colonialism and genocide" (James, 2018, p. 840) in that they were "mandated, funded, and regulated by the Canadian federal government" (p. 832). They were run by the state and the church from 1883 to 1996 (Starblanket, 2018, p. 89), outlawing all Indigenous linguistic, cultural, and spiritual practices. More than 150,000 First Nations, Inuit, and Métis children as young as 3 years old were abducted and forcibly placed in 139 IRSs throughout Canada. The explicit goal was to "kill the Indian in the child" (TRC, 2015, p. 130), that is, "education for extinction" (Starblanket, 2018, p. 94).

From 2010 to 2015, Canada's Truth and Reconciliation Commission (TRC) hosted 7 national (and 17 community or regional) truth and reconciliation hearings and collected testimony from over 6750 residential schooling survivors (Nagy,

2020, p. 219).[1] Some former IRS students testified before TRC that "priests at the schools had fathered infants with Indigenous students, that the babies had been taken away from their young mothers and killed, and that in some cases their bodies were thrown into furnaces" (Austen, 2021). According to Murray Sinclair, a former judge who headed the TRC commission, it is estimated that students who died or went missing from IRSs were "well beyond 10,000" (Austen, 2021). Therefore, in its six-volume final report of December 2015, TRC concluded its 7-year investigation by qualifying residential schooling as a form of "cultural genocide" (p. 133).

The recent discovery of the remains of 751 Indigenous children in unmarked graves on the grounds of former residential schools in southern Saskatchewan has rekindled debate over Canada's sinister colonial legacies of mass atrocity and provoked a general anti-Catholic sentiment amongst the Indigenous peoples. This came weeks after the discovery of 215 body remains in British Columbia, near Kamloops Indian Residential School (which was run by the Catholic Church from 1890 to 1969). Prime Minister Justin Trudeau described the tragic event as "a shameful reminder of the systemic racism, discrimination, and injustice that Indigenous peoples have faced" (BBC News, 2021).

TRC called for an apology from Pope Francis for the Roman Catholic church's grim role in running about 70% of IRSs. Therefore, on 25 July 2022, Pope Francis in his 6-day "penitential pilgrimage" of healing and reconciliation to Canada finally apologised to the Indigenous survivors of IRSs for the Roman Catholic church's prominent role in wrongs committed against Indigenous peoples, which he later described as 'genocidal' (White et al., 2022). In the same vein, a motion from Leah Gazan (a Member of Parliament for Winnipeg Centre, New Democratic Party) calling on the Canadian federal government to recognise residential schooling as genocide[2] was passed with unanimous consent in October 2022 (Raycraft, 2022).

The Canadian federal government has made significant efforts to settle the historical injustices inflicted upon the Indigenous peoples through commemorative initiatives, official apologies (e.g., Stephen Harper's 2008 'weak' parliamentary apology), inquiries and financial reparations to survivors and families of the victims. For example, in 1998, a $350 million "healing fund" was offered by Jean Chrétien's Liberal government after a brief "quasi-apology" by the Minister of Indian and Northern Affairs (Jane Stewart) for the horrific sexual and physical abuse endured by residential school students. In 2007, the Indian Residential Schools Settlement Agreement provided $2.1 billion as reparation for past harms. This came as a direct result of the residential schooling survivors' tough struggle for justice

---

[1] It is important to note that TRC was a victim/survivor-centred independent truth commission, convened as part of a court-ordered class-action settlement involving tens of thousands of Indigenous plaintiffs, the churches, and the Canadian federal government (James, 2018, p. 832). It lacked any judicial powers as it did not seek perpetrator accountability.

[2] Article II of the UN Convention on the Prevention and Punishment of the Crime of Genocide defines genocide as an intention to "destroy in whole or in part, a national, ethnical, racial or religious group." Genocidal acts include "[f]orcibly transferring children of the group to another group" (United Nations, 9 Dec. 1948).

extending over 20 years and their ability to get their class action suit about "loss of culture" certified by the Canadian courts. Hence, "the decision was significantly due to looming liabilities rather than a desire to see justice done" (Nagy, 2020, p. 223).

It is argued that "the goal of Indigenous residential schooling was to seed patriarchy and displace [Indigenous] women" (Grey & James, 2016, p. 314) as they represent "the agents of the intergenerational transmission of a powerful claim of settler illegitimacy" (p. 312) and the bearers of Indigenous counter-imperial order (Lavell-Harvard & Brant, 2016, pp. 2–4), as I will delineate in the following section.

3.2   Highway of Tears: Missing and Murdered Indigenous Women and Girls

In Northwestern British Columbia, Indigenous women continue to disappear while hitchhiking along the remote and underserviced Highway 16 ('the Highway of Tears') since 1950s. The former Prime Minister Stephen Harper's deprioritisation of the issue was motivated by the need to invisibilise the intersectional violence Indigenous women suffered (Grey & James, 2016, p. 305). In its March 2015 report, the United Nations Committee on the Elimination of Discrimination against Women (UNCEDAW) condemned the ongoing failure of Canada to effectively address the widespread disproportionate rates of sexualised and racialised violence against Indigenous women and girls. A 2017 report released by Firelight Group (an Indigenous-owned consulting group) revealed a strong correlation between Coastal GasLink pipeline's workforce accommodation sites and increased rates of sexual assault against Indigenous women (Morin, 2021). Hence, the intersection of race, gender, (auto)mobility and violence is crucial to the understanding of the continuities of such disproportionate number of femicide acts against Indigenous women and girls (Morton, 2016, p. 300).[3] Their poverty is a major factor of their vulnerability to male violence.[4] They have been "forced" and "trapped" into "extreme poverty", "homelessness", and "street-level prostitution"[5] (Bentham et al., 2016, p. 241). Calls to decriminalise prostitution in Canada will further increase the racialised sexual violence that has led to the killing and disappearance of over 1200 Indigenous women and girls across Canada (Kappo, 2014).

---

[3] Over a quarter of the missing and murdered Indigenous women disappeared in Vancouver's Downtown Eastside and the Highway of Tears, British Columbia (Razack, 2015, p. 54).

[4] One highly publicised case of white men perpetration of egregious violence against Indigenous women is the notorious case of Canada's worst serial killer Robert ("Willy") Pickton. When he was arrested in February 2002, the DNA of 33 missing women was found on his Port Coquitlam pig farm (Culbert, 2022).

[5] In Vancouver, where Indigenous peoples make up about 2% of the city's population, studies estimate that about one third of women in street prostitution are Indigenous (Bentham et al., 2016, p. 241).

However, the Canadian criminal justice system consistently fails Indigenous women because they are framed as "willing victims" who bring violence upon themselves (blaming the victim strategy) because of their precarious lifestyles. The conflation of hitchhiking with immorality positioned Indigenous women "outside of the conventional boundaries of privileged femininity" (Morton, 2016, p. 303). The colonial context of violence against Indigenous women can be traced back to the Indian Act of 1876, which, in addition to confining First Nations peoples to reserves, helped to disempower Indigenous women by stripping those who married non-Indigenous men (or Indigenous men from other nations) of their Indian status, and thus this "sexist policy" contributed to the "uprooting and displacement of thousands of Indigenous women and damaged the ties to their families by denying Indian status to their children and grandchildren" (Bentham et al., 2016, p. 232). Besides, Christian charity and Victorian racist and sexist ideas provided the ethical-ideological foundation for such assimilationist attitudes (Grey & James, 2016, pp. 311–312).

Settler colonialism in Canada is an ongoing structural process which is aimed at "control over indigenous bodies, resources, and territories" (James, 2018, p. 837). It is also a deculturation process. For example, dysfunctional parenting is invoked to justify the ongoing systematic forcible transferring of Indigenous children into white foster care homes. Although Indigenous children make only 7.7% of the Canadian child population, they represent 52.2% of children in foster care. In 2018, the chairman of the TRC on residential schools (Senator Murray Sinclair) said, "The monster that was created in the residential schools moved into a new house [...] and that monster now lives in the child welfare system" (Morin, 2021). State-sponsored removal of Indigenous children from their homes and communities has detrimental health impact on Indigenous mothers (e.g., depression, social isolation, displacement, and 'survival' prostitution) (see Caplan et al., 2020).

Hence, transitional justice and reconciliation should start with "settler decolonial learning" (Nagy, 2020, p. 235) by encouraging teacher educators to "reach beyond ourselves through affective learning and responsiveness to the agency and self-determination of the [Indigenous] other" (Nagy, 2020, pp. 237–238). They should interrogate the ontoepistemological and axiological racism in Canadian teacher education and promote a (re)politisation of pedagogical spaces to encourage decolonial learning.

3.3   (Re)politicising Pedagogy and Decolonial Learning

The fact that Alexie Sherman's *The Absolutely True Diary of a Part-Time Indian* featured among the required reading list entries in one of my teacher education courses ("Teaching Adolescents' Literature") was a good step towards the adoption of a decolonial learning approach. Alexie fictionally re-explores his precarious Indian childhood and revisits the intergenerational traumas being suffered through the painful memories of his character (Junior), who has experienced many disheartening losses in his family. Junior's sense of estrangement and the desire to find a place to belong describes the plight of Aboriginal youth in a very satirical way. Alexie's use of multi-layered dark humour addresses absurdity predicated upon such adverse conditions as unemployment, poverty, alcoholism, mental illness and eroded cultural traditions. His goal is to point out the connections between historical and contemporary conditions of inequality generated by white hegemony and persistent assimilationist practices.

However, I noticed that the "Teaching Adolescents' Literature" course deployed categorising appellations (e.g., 'First Nations literature' vs. 'Holocaust literature') to mitigate the devastating loss and grief of 'non-deserving' Indigenous others. "Colonial horrors perpetrated in the Americas" (MacDonald, 2020, p. 582) were massive acts of a government-sanctioned history of unspeakable atrocities. Hence, the concept of "Holocaust" as a "unique" traumatic experience (i.e., "judeocide"[6]) is deployed to deflect attention away from "the reality of Indigenous genocide", and thus help to "erase the memory" of "extermination" of "between ninety and one hundred million Indigenous people over five centuries" (MacDonald, 2020, p. 582).

When I raised the issue of double standard and the "power exercised over the production and control of knowledge" (Giroux, 2016, p. 59), I sensed a strange insensitivity from both the students and the instructor to the issue. I felt that "diversity is outwardly championed albeit on the internal condition that it aligns with the approval of those in positions of power" (Rivers, 2019, p. 382). It seems that "critical modes of agency" (Giroux, 2016, p. 59), which advocate the rational management of difference, are silenced because challenging deep-seated racialised Euro-Canadian "regimes of truth" (Foucault, 1980) is unwelcome. Though my argument was legitimate, it was too hard to sustain when my body was too exposed to be subsumed into mainstream 'white normativity'. So, I felt 'out of place'. Racialised students who dare to speak openly about white domination in the curriculum "often face denial or backlash in doing so, usually in subtle forms" (Henry & Tator, 2009, p. 48).[7]

Dominant discourses are articulated through Canadian universities' Eurocentric curricula, pedagogy, research priorities, methods, and recruitment gatekeeping (Tator & Henry, 2010, p. 376). For example, "current mainstream teacher education programs do not typically introduce the importance of Indigenous language education to teacher candidates, who are the next generation of K-12 teachers" (Jacob et al., 2019, p. 126). Though the federal Parliament of Canada adopted the *Indigenous Languages Act* in June 2019 (which recognises Indigenous language rights), it failed to provide effective implementation procedures (Nicholas et al., 2023, p. 235). Moreover, "the structure of many Native studies departments' curriculum reflects non-Indigenous ideologies and ideas about people (and even a variety of colonial biases)" (Monture, 2009, p. 82).

---

[6]The use of the term implies that "Jews were by no means the only 'human group' upon whom genocide was inflicted by the Nazis" (Starblanket, 2018, p. 36).

[7]The grade I got in the course was below 'average' (82%).

Hence, as "education and pedagogy do not exist outside of relations of power, values, and politics" (Giroux, 2016, p. 66), racialised student teachers should critically engage with texts, images, and all other forms of meaning-making as they are transformed into pedagogical practices by openly registering their own 'subjective' involvement in how and what they are supposed to 'learn' (and later teach to their students). They should resist "all calls to depoliticize pedagogy through appeals to either scientific objectivity or ideological dogmatism" (Giroux, 2016, p. 66).

Diversity initiatives need to be reflected in curricular and staffing policies. As BC schools have become more ethnically diverse so have concerns that the teacher corps and the teacher education curricula should reflect the communities they serve. Although many Canadian universities have an increasingly diverse array of student population that spans a variety of demographics and identities, such diversity is poorly matched with research perspectives and pedagogical methodologies as racialised academics are noticeably underrepresented (especially within the senior ranks and in the social sciences and humanities) (Henry & Tator, 2009, p. 42). Besides, there is a strong lingering "tendency to make appointments based on the perceived capacity of the candidate to 'fit' into the existing [white] culture of the faculty" (James, 2009, p. 132). Qualified racialised faculty members "continue to be underrepresented in the senior ranks of university governance" (Johnson & Howsam, 2020, p. 687). For example, a recent study, which investigated 324 listed senior administrators across all publicly funded Canadian universities, corroborated the dominance of whiteness in academia. It revealed that even though racialised people constitute 22.3% of Canada's population (Statistics Canada, 2017), racialised senior university leaders (mainly from STEM disciplines) only represented 13.3% (2.2% of whom were women, and only one was a university president) (Cukier et al., 2021, p. 569).

4   Racialisation and Hierarchical Positioning of Foreign-Trained Educators

Stories of "practicums gone wrong" abound among racialised adult male African teachers of French and their associate teachers, which sometimes necessitates the interference of the Professional Ethics Committee to take disciplinary action or mediate a reasonable resolution of the problem (Dalley, 2020, pp. 151–152). Issues raised mainly relate to African teachers' heavy French 'accents' (different from 'Anglicised' Ontarian French) and their alleged "arrogant" and "sexist" attitudes (framing gender violence as an immigration problem). It is claimed that African immigrant teachers tend to "lecture rather than teach" and "they discipline rather than manage the classroom" (pp. 152–153). Therefore, the pedagogical skills and teaching experiences of teacher candidates of colour are represented as "problematic", "foreign", "invisible", and "invalid"[8] in an educational space predominantly inhabited by white, female, middle-class, monolingual, Canadian-born practising teachers (Schmidt, 2021, p. 441). Any failure to meet the expectations of whiteness is penalised with "derision and the threat of exclusion and punishment" (p. 444).

My experience of the practicum placement in a British Columbia (BC) secondary school was not different from the situation described above (see also Cushing (2023) for similar issues of "language oppression" in the British teacher education context). The first hurdle I encountered was the need to ape the 'native speaker' model. In his 'progress report', my associate teacher didn't cease to draw attention to my 'accented' English. As a 'professional improvement plan', he proposed that I should take an 'accent reduction' course at University of British Columbia to develop a native-like 'pronunciation' (a Pygmalion-like 'accent shift' dressage). Therefore, as a racialised and 'accented' teacher, I was relegated to the status of a "culturally deficient 'non-native speaker' subaltern" (Holliday, 2015, p. 20), and thus, a forever foreigner to the teaching profession (perpetual invisibilisation strategy). Ironically, these 'accent policing' courses "target students who have already successfully completed advanced-level English courses" (Saarinen & Ensser-Kananen, 2020, p. 120). Hence, it seems that "what stands [in] the way of non-white students' success [is], in fact, deficit perspectives on racialized students' linguistic practices, in other words, racism inherent in the [Eurocentric] higher education system" (p. 120). As Ahmed (2012) pointed out, "if whiteness is what the institution is oriented around, then even bodies that do not appear white still have to inhabit whiteness" (p. 41).

My associate teacher considered me as a disentitled newcomer to the ELT profession by including a specific accent-based assessment in my practicum report, suggesting that "Ahmed should take a methods course in French[9] … to make himself more employable as a *French* language teacher" (emphasis added). It seems that I simply don't fit into his ideal 'white nativeness' realm to qualify as being a 'good' teacher of English in an Anglophone context ('gatekeeping' role). His judgement was mainly premised on my 'foreign' accent. However, as pedagogical skills and language proficiency are both crucial in language teaching, ethnolinguistic background should be regarded as inconsequential. My associate teacher's presumed role as "modeler of teaching" and "advocate of the practical" discounted other more important responsibilities, such as "supporter of reflection", "purveyor of context" and "convenor of relation" (Clarke et al., 2014, p. 163); this demonstrates his underpreparedness to engage in a more inquiry-based and "developmentally appropriate" support for pre-service teachers (p. 191). Effective mentorship is more than mere matching of willing school-based instructors to student teachers; there is a

---

[8] Such a deficient view is extended to international students, who are constructed as "incapable" of rational reasoning (e.g., sustaining an argument) and critical thinking because they are "passive," "uncreative" and "rote" learners. This is an instance of "cultural determinism that reproduces colonial relations of Self and Other" (Pennycook, 2007, p. 21).

[9] I successfully completed a three-credit course, "Teaching & Learning French as a Second Language: Elementary & Middle Years" (LLEE 324), at UBC.

conspicuous lack of intercultural awareness amongst some 'cooperating' teachers who tend to homogenise racialised teacher candidates based on preconceived essentialist stereotypes (Schmidt & Schneider, 2016).

However, it seems that making appropriate school placements of student teachers is strategically challenging because associate teachers are basically volunteers. Hence, some school principals may even object to accepting "immigrant or new Canadian teacher candidates" (Dalley, 2020, p. 156) because some white teachers may be unwilling to help a student teacher "who does not correspond to their image of a good teacher" (p. 161). In this sense, evaluation tended to be based on "individual" and "social acceptability" criteria rather than on teaching ability. Besides, ineffective mentors create an "ethos of subservience in their working relations with preservice teachers by not attempting to balance the asymmetrical power relations in their roles" (Cherian, 2008, p. 95).

The subtle (usually well-intentioned and gentle) silencing of non-native English-speaking teachers (NNESTs) is a clear manifestation of the racialisation of the teaching profession under the mask of 'accent' ('accentism'). Such discrimination is a clear instance of ethnocentrism as "there is no 'scientific' evidence to support any notion of an inherent superiority or inferiority, premised on phenotypic difference between the so-called races" (Henry, 2021, p. 308). Raciolinguistic and ethnocultural stereotypes co-articulate with diverse forms of racialised othering in ways that are intersectionally constitutive of persistent 'white' privilege. These oppressive societal dynamics merely serve to uphold 'normative whiteness,' which is inherent in colonialist language ideologies that reinforce a chauvinistic view of an imagined ideal monolingual linguistic order through the 'native speakerist' 'deficit' discourses that serve the interests of "colonial and/or nation-building and neoliberal processes of governmentality" (Saarinen & Ennser-Kananen, 2020, p. 121).

Such Orientalist thinking is deeply rooted and sustained within the fabric of mainstream ELT professionalism which associates 'nativeness' with 'whiteness.' For example, "many self-identified monolingual white teachers in a Chicago high school viewed their bilingual Puerto Rican principal, who held a doctorate in education, as intellectually and linguistically inferior" (Rosa & Flores, 2017, p. 629). Likewise, even non-white native speakers of English who were born and raised in Anglophone countries are not considered as 'legitimate' language models. ESL students also believe that "only White people can be native speakers of English and that only native speakers know 'real' English" (Norton, 1997, p. 423). Similarly, "any Caucasian speaker of English (even Eastern Europeans who speak it as a second or foreign language) are automatically considered to be native speakers of English" (Braine, 2010, p. 74).

In today's globalised world, multilingual teachers are driving forces in implementing a culturally sustainable pedagogy into their teaching, and thus are key educational stakeholders (Kirkpatrick, 2016, p. 241). Therefore, a paradigm shift away from the 'native/non-native speaker divide should be promoted by delinking from the fallacious attitudes that "English is best taught monolingually; the ideal teacher of English is a native speaker; the earlier English is taught, the better the results; the more English is taught the better the results; and if other languages are used much, standards of English will drop" (Phillipson, 1992, p. 185). A "non-native speaker-ist" curriculum would be necessary to empower ELT educators to focus on "an English that expresses the cultural realities of their students" while preparing them to engage creatively with the world "on their own terms" (Holliday, 2014, p. 3). As Jenkins (2006) eloquently puts it, native speakerist deficit ideologies are the result of a "monolingual bias" that is "unable to comprehend" the multilingual experience (p. 167).

5 Discursive (Re)Construction of Self Through Storied Transformative Agency

In this section, I will delineate how I tried to encourage my students to view language as a vital medium for the creation of modes of being and belonging and a crucial tool for social struggle over competing meaning constructions in dialogue (Fairclough, 1995). In the first part, I will outline my endeavour to decentre Eurocentric media narratives by proposing a counter-hegemonic account of the Israeli-Palestinian conflict (micro-teaching project). In the second part, my attempt to adopt a resource-based instruction approach that helps to meet the specific needs of my students during my practicum is outlined.

5.1 Critical Media Pedagogy and Decolonial Learning

During my teacher education program, I noticed that very little effort had been made to invite discussions on the social dimensions of education and the importance of situated critical pedagogy-oriented practices. Hence, an opportunity to bridge such a gap was seized in "Curriculum and Instruction in English" course. I prepared a micro-teaching project about "teaching editorial political cartoons in Canadian high school" and my case study was Naji Al-Ali (1937–1987), the Palestinian Cartoonist, who transformed the victimhood discourse of Palestinians into a narrative of graphic remembering of the *Nakba* (Catastrophe) and resistance to the dominating Zionist narrative. As texts are becoming increasingly multimodal, and students are being more exposed to an abundance of visual images that dominate their daily lives, my goal was to promote students' (in this case my colleagues') critical visual literacy skills by fostering a decolonial critical media pedagogy curriculum that aims at providing some "spaces of relief from whiteness" (Ahmed, 2012, p. 37) and 'edutainment'.

Al-Ali's child-character graffiti became the national/global symbol that bears witness to the injustices inflicted on the Palestinians by the Israeli occupation. *Handala* (a 10-year-old barefooted, raggedly dressed Palestinian refugee camp child) epitomises Palestinian national consciousness and struggle for self-determination. *Handala*'s hands are always clasped behind his back as a sign of defiance and the just struggle for the right of return (Barnes, 2019, p. 234). Al-Ali's cartoons evoke nostalgic themes that solidify national narratives of a sense of state-lessness, uprootedness, as well as resistance and steadfastness. These visual discourses of endurance and defiance are instrumental in the memorialisation of the Palestinian plight. They also display several layers of meaning, targeting global audiences. The use of Christological images (the crucifix symbol) is meant to mediate the Palestinian experience and evoke global empathy with the Palestinian cause. As Barnes pointed out, "Al-Ali's art – banned by the Israeli state – represented a reclamation of the Palestinian past, a reversal of the discourse of Orientalism through a colonised population asserting its own narrative, rather than being written (or, in this case, drawn) into history by the coloniser" (p. 233).

Such counter-narratives can create intercultural encounter spaces in class in a way that promotes a critical self-reflection by interrogating 'our' roles in the structures of domination. They can also encourage students to engage critically with visual discourses of social experiences of Palestinians against all forms of 'memoricide', 'epistemicide', and mystification of history (e.g., 'ethnic cleansing' is reframed in Western media discourse as 'voluntary exodus' and 'occupation' as 'settlement') by promoting transitions from cultures of impunity and human rights abuse. Preservice teachers should be encouraged to engage in a process of "decentring dominant narratives with the stories and experiences of the oppressed" (James, 2017, p. 364) by striving to "achieve a deep understanding of the colonial forces which continue to reproduce structural racism, territorial invasion and structural genocide" (Willsher & Oldfield, 2020, p. 208). This process of de-linking from the colonial episteme will help student teachers to "rethink the cultural and ideological baggage they bring to each educational encounter" (Giroux, 2016, p. 66). It equally will sensitise educators to the need to be ethically and politically responsible and self-reflective for the "stories they produce, the claims they make upon public memory, and the images of the future they deem legitimate" (p. 66).

Implementing a curriculum grounded in decolonial critical media pedagogy is empowering for students as such multimodal approaches can help them to develop a critical lens and analytic skills required to deconstruct images in the media (see Sahlane, 2022). Likewise, conventional educational spaces could be transformed into humane sites of 'struggle' over pedagogical content for educational equity. Critical media pedagogy can also encourage educators and students to critically discuss contentious topics around cultural otherness to learn to "move beyond their traditional roles as mere consumers of policy and media discourses" (Schmidt, 2021, p. 441).[10] For example, as British Columbia has recently welcomed many refugee families from the Middle East, engaging with multimedia accounts of their lived experiences can help teachers to "honour different backgrounds and realities

---

[10] "[I]n the US, faculty in Texas were prohibited from criticizing the Israeli government's oppression of the Palestinians and were prohibited from advocating for the boycott of Israel" (Waite & Waite, 2021, p. 172).

and most appropriately meet the needs of the students and families they serve" (p. 442). These refugee children had experienced traumatic events, compounded with the precarity engendered by interrupted or no schooling because of continuous displacement. Hence, a "transformative intellectual" is the "one whose intellectual practices are necessarily grounded in forms of moral and ethical discourse exhibiting a preferential concern for the suffering and struggles of the disadvantaged and oppressed" (Giroux, 1988, pp. 174–175).

However, my project about "teaching political cartoons" drew some criticism from a few ('white') colleagues. It is not uncommon that racialised student teachers feel that their knowledge could be easily "discounted and devalued by their peers" (Guo & Guo, 2020, p. 16) simply because the decentring of the dominant whiteness most often translates as a vulgar promotion of particular forms of 'anti-Western' agendas. Should not teachers avoid "pushing [their] political views down [their] students' throats?" (Pennycook, 2017, p. 301). However, if all educational spaces are potential sites of cultural politics, then it is fallacious to suggest that Eurocentric forms of knowledge formation are neutral. Adopting a critical pedagogy approach invites educators to contest the "inclusion/exclusion divide in the global knowledge pool, where only certain knowledge is legitimated and codified to be seen, used, trusted, and valued" (Xu, 2022, p. 37). Critical educators should maintain their roles as agents of 'reform' through the 'social justice' topics they address, as well as the decolonial pedagogical perspectives they tend to support. For example, neo-colonialist 'epistemic violence' in discourses of 'enlightenment' and 'emancipation' (e.g., in Bushspeak rhetoric during the lead to war on Iraqi in 2003; see Sahlane, 2012, 2013, 2019) should be challenged by contesting the "Western ways of knowing and the Western ways of *languaging*" (Kumaravadivelu, 2016, p. 78; italics added).

5.2   Creating Educational Spaces for Inclusive Pedagogy

As I got to know my students well over the 12 weeks of my practicum, I tried to incorporate a more relationship-centred teacher identity in my teaching approach. For example, when I was teaching English literature (e.g., Shakespeare's *The Taming of the Shrew*), I invited students to reflect upon how marriage has become a transaction involving the transfer of money. I encouraged them to examine gender roles across historical and cultural boundaries (group project). I also included world 'literatures in English' from non-Anglophone linguacultures to balance the hegemony of the traditional ELT curriculum. I introduced students to *Pretty Flowers*, which is part of Deborah Ellis's book, *Lunch with Lenin*. The book contains a variety of short stories about how drugs affect the youth in modern societies. The story was about a 12-year-old Afghani girl, whose father had defaulted on his debts to a rich old man. His opium fields were bulldozed by the Afghani government, and he had no money to pay his loan back. As a consequence, the father had no choice except to marry his daughter to the creditor or go to jail ('child brides' issue). After exploring the plot development and the themes of the story, students were invited to engage in a role play activity to decide how to reach a reasoned ethical solution to the problem.

My faculty advisor and associate teacher were very impressed with students' construction of social difference and the struggle for voice. However, in the beginning my host teacher expressed some reservation vis-à-vis what he called teaching with an "agenda." Hence, I had to manage the debilitating task of coping with this 'intersectionality identity space' (speaking English [linguistic border crossing] with a 'foreign' accent [false documents], having a Middle Eastern appearance [cultural otherness], being a newcomer to Canada ['outsider' and 'not like us'] and my status as veteran recertifying teacher [trespassing my mentor's territory/'domain of authority']).

'White privilege' erodes any possible sense of academic belonging and eventually personal wellbeing as 'tokenised' bodies are required to make greater efforts to 'fit in'. As a racialised teacher, I felt disempowered by being stigmatised as a 'non-native' speaker of English despite being highly qualified (a holder of Masters and Ph D degrees from well-ranked British universities). Linguistic imperialism "serves to establish inequalities between native speakers of English and speakers of other languages, and teachers from different backgrounds, irrespective of their qualifications" and this is a "clear evidence of linguicism structurally and ideologically" (Phillipson, 2016, p. 86).

My attempt to reshape curriculum and pedagogy in a way that meets the needs of diverse students turned the classroom into an inclusive and supportive community of learners and created rewarding learning opportunities as students were engaged in 'authentic' self-expression often experienced beyond the classroom walls. My faculty advisor acknowledged that I "respected the multicultural nature of the classroom and aimed for students to see themselves and their heritage reflected in the lessons. Ahmed has a strong commitment to social justice" (Practicum report, 2010). As educational resources that reflect Indigenous perspectives are essential to advancing an inclusive curriculum, I tried to embed Indigenous pedagogy in teaching Ben Mikaelsen's *Spirit Bear* in grade 9. I used 'circle of justice' as a role-play activity. The 'healing circle' starts with assigning roles (Elders, keeper, judge, culprit, victim, parents, etc.) and explaining rules (Indigenous justice protocols). Then, in 'circle hearings' community members (students) voice their 'feelings' about the committed offence (Cole's smashing of Peter's skull into the sidewalk, which resulted in a serious head trauma) and how to reach a just resolution to the conflict. 'Focus questions' (that were 'social justice'-oriented) served to guide students' discussions. The act of 'yarning' (respectful listening to community members) proved to be an engaging activity because it encouraged students to respectfully relate to other members of their community (of learners) in a more authentic and empathetic way. My associate teacher was very impressed by this role-play activity and characterised it in my practicum report as "a particularly successful event" (Practicum report, 2010).

I equally introduced Grade 12 students to critical race theory by teaching Alice Walker's 'Flowers' (a short story) to invite them to reflect upon the racialised processes of discrimination in the U.S. I used this short story to teach plot development in narrative writing. I also invited students to read Holocaust literature by teaching Innocenti's *Rose Blanche*. Then, I scheduled a session to watch David Heyman's film, *The Boy in the Striped Pyjamas,* as a follow-up activity. One of the goals of showing this video was to engage students in discussing the intersectional experiences of oppressed others in late modern societies. Likewise, I introduced my students to Albert Camus's *The Guest*, one of six stories in the collection *Exile and the Kingdom*. The story focuses on the ethical dilemmas faced by Daru (an instructor and a native of the French-occupied Algeria), and the two visitors he receives one day: Balducci (a 'gendarme', who arrives on horseback), and an unnamed Arab prisoner (who has his hands bound and is on foot). Balducci informs Daru that he has to deliver the prisoner to police headquarters. Daru treats the Arab very respectfully by providing food, bed, and a chance to escape. The following morning, Daru and his prisoner set off on their journey. When they reach an intersection, Daru gives him the choice (he refuses to hand him over) either to take the path that leads to the prison (captivity) or walk towards a local nomadic tribe that will protect him (freedom). The prisoner chooses the first (a fatal decision). After Daru returns to the schoolhouse, he finds a note on the blackboard left by tribesmen, threatening to revenge their handed-over 'brother.' What is appealing about the story is that it is pregnant with multiple reading possibilities.

As my intercultural perspective conflicted with my host teacher's, I had no reservation questioning his 'native speakerist' mindset manifested in his "cultural disbelief" and "deficit" discourses (Holliday, 2015) and I refused to play "subservient and enslaved roles to [his] idiosyncratic demands" (Cherian, 2008, p. 101), an attitude he ultimately penalised me for by qualifying my "response to criticism" as "can sometimes be stubborn" (in contrast to my faculty advisor's description of my collaboration as "reflective of his practice" and "open to suggestions and advice") (Practicum report, 2010). The way my associate teacher conceived of his role was very traditional: either as a "placeholder" (no co-teaching or co-planning assumed) or as a "supervisor" (overseeing my performance with a dominating stance). Both conceptions expect the student teacher to assume a 'compliant' role to be able to navigate the racialised practicum successfully. Post-lesson feedback tended to be "more confirmatory (positive) than investigative (reflective) in nature" (Clarke et al., 2014, p. 175). However, the presence of a NNEST who is ready to return the gaze and talk back contests the authority of a NEST as the sole legitimate 'knower.' Reflective teaching practice dictates that native speakers should cast the analytic gaze on themselves first by recognising their biases and being ready to unlearn their prejudices.

During my practicum, I participated in teacher-parent conferences and acted as liaison with parents. I also managed to motivate disengaged students by inviting them to work on group projects with serious classmates. Some parents had some concerns about my NNS professional 'competence', only to support me later after realising the great progress that had been achieved by providing extra help to the struggling students in the school's Learning Centre. Similarly, some reticence was initially experienced from a few students who were worried about getting proper preparation for upcoming provincial and university entrance exams. This challenge was partially alleviated by assigning graded project-based group activities (e.g., researching stereotyping in relation to their ethnic communities in BC). This project-oriented learning encouraged students to bring their lived experiences as complex people into the classroom, by capturing moments of community hardship and growth, and thus offering their classmates a glimpse into their lifeworlds. Therefore, teaching in Canadian K-12 context offered me ample opportunities for identity negotiation in that the effort to adjust my pedagogical skills and theoretical knowledge to the potential institutional constraints (while also incorporating my values and teaching ideals in my daily teaching practice) constituted a dynamic part of my professional identity development. This autoethnographic account, thus, reflects on how the friction I experienced from being 'out of place' opened up new opportunities for me to learn how to become an ELT professional on my own terms.

6 Conclusion

My experience of teaching mentorship—though partial in its truth and incomplete in its telling of critical moments—provides a snapshot in time of my journey as a process of peril, hope, and potential in the struggle for authentic voice, professional legitimacy, and pedagogical agency. It is pregnant with moments of tension and good collegiality. It also provides a cautionary example of how colonialist white supremacist language ideologies continue to mould and shape teaching practices and educational policies that serve to devalue the linguistic and cultural capitals that both multilingual students and racialised language educators bring into classrooms.

The present study has also made the case that teacher education programs should refrain from training student teachers solely for jobs through the reproduction of a meritocratic system of competitive, disempowered, ethnocentric and deskilled educational technicians and clerks (Giroux, 2016). Prospective teachers should be encouraged to develop their own teaching approaches around themes that align with students' own lived experiences and that serve to counter all forms of discriminatory and exclusionary views and practices in educational spaces. More importantly, teacher preparation programs need to be (re)structured around the foreign-educated teachers' realistic needs by designing training courses that accommodate and recognise their prior skills and professional expertise; they should not be treated the same as the novice domestic pre-service teacher students ('one-size-fits-all' approach).

Besides, as school-based master educators play a very influential role in training (re)certifying practised internationally-educated teachers (IETs), they need to develop theoretically informed and interculturally sensitive mentoring strategies to be able to assist prospective teachers to recontextualise and put into practice their accumulated theoretical and practical knowledge. Mentoring programs premised on monolingualist ideologies and a deficit view of racialised teachers fail to encourage re-certifying IETs to reflect critically on their own transcultural experiences and multilingual/multicultural perspectives and fail to recognise social constructions of white privilege and inequality. Failure to contest the structured racial hierarchisation prevalent in educational spaces and beyond is "tantamount to committing 'mentacide'" (Henry, 2021, p. 305).

References

Ahmed, S. (2012). *On being included: Racism and diversity in institutional life*. Duke University Press.. https://doi.org/10.2307/j.ctv1131d2g

Anderson, L. (2006). Analytic autoethnography. *Journal of Contemporary Ethnography, 35*(4), 373–395. https://doi.org/10.1177/0891241605280449

Austen, I. (2021, June 7). How thousands of Indigenous children vanished in Canada. *New York Times*. https://www.nytimes.com/2021/06/07/world/canada/mass-graves-residential-schools.html. Accessed 9 Nov 2022.

Barnes, J. (2019). Handala and the Messiah: Christological representation in the cartoons of Naji Al-Ali. *Culture and Religion, 20*(3), 231–247. https://doi.org/10.1080/14755610.2019.1684331

BBC News (2021, June 24). *Canada: 751 unmarked graves found at residential school*. https://www.bbc.com/news/world-us-canada-57592243. Accessed 13 Nov 2022.

BC Teachers' Council. (2019, June 19). *Professional standards for BC educators*. https://www2.gov.bc.ca/assets/gov/education/kindergarten-to-grade-12/teach/teacher-regulation/standards-for-educators/edu_standards.pdf. Accessed 11 Nov 2022.

BC Teachers' Council. (2022, March 29). *Teacher education program approval standards*. https://www2.gov.bc.ca/gov/content/education-training/k-12/administration/legislation-policy/public-schools/bc-teacher-education-program-standards. Accessed 11 Nov 2022.

Bentham, S. R., Kerner, H., Steacy, L., et al. (2016). Sisterhood on the frontlines: The truth as we hear it from Indigenous women. In D. M. Lavell-Harvard & J. Brant (Eds.), *Forever loved: Exposing the hidden crisis of missing and murdered Indigenous women and girls in Canada* (pp. 231–246). Demeter Press. http://www.jstor.org/stable/j.ctt1rrd8g6

Braine, G. (2010). *Nonnative speaker English teachers: Research, pedagogy, and professional growth* (1st ed.). Routledge.

Caplan, R., Nelson, J., Distasio, J., Isaak, C., Edel, B., Piat, M., Macnaughton, E., Kirst, M., Patterson, M., Aubry, T., Mulligan, S., & Goering, P. (2020). Indigenous and non-Indigenous parents separated from their children and experiencing homelessness and mental illness in Canada. *Journal of Community Psychology, 48*, 2753–2772. https://doi.org/10.1002/jcop.22455

Cherian, F. (2008). Placing and mentoring student teachers: Issues, challenges, and new possibilities. In C. A. Lassonde, R. J. Michael, & J. Rivera-Wilson (Eds.), *Current issues in teacher education: History, perspectives, and implications* (pp. 88–102). Charles C. Thomas Publisher.

Clarke, A., Triggs, V., & Nielsen, W. (2014). Cooperating teacher participation in teacher education: A review of the literature. *Review of Educational Research, 84*(2), 163–202. https://doi.org/10.3102/0034654313499618

Cukier, W., Adamu, P., Wall-Andrews, C., & Elmi, M. (2021). Racialized leaders leading Canadian universities. *Educational Management Administration & Leadership, 49*(4), 565–583. https://doi.org/10.1177/17411432211001363

Culbert, L. (2022, June 24). True crime byline: Families knew 'horrible creature' was taking Vancouver women long before police did. *Vancouver Sun*. https://vancouversun.com/news/true-crime/true-crime-byline-families-knew-horrible-creature-was-taking-vancouver-women-long-before-police-did. Accessed 19 Nov 2022.

Cushing, I. (2023). "Miss, can you speak English?": raciolinguistic ideologies and language oppression in initial teacher education. *British Journal of Sociology of Education*, 1–16. https://doi.org/10.1080/01425692.2023.2206006

Dalley, P. (2020). From Africa to teacher education in Ontario. In A. M. Phelan, W. F. Pinar, N. Ng-A-Fook, & R. Kane (Eds.), *Reconceptualizing teacher education: A Canadian contribution to a global challenge* (pp. 141–168). University of Ottawa Press. https://doi.org/10.2307/j.ctvxcr8wz

Dutta, M. J. (2018). Autoethnography as decolonization, decolonizing autoethnography: Resisting to build our homes. *Cultural Studies ↔ Critical Methodologies, 18*(1), 94–96. https://doi.org/10.1177/1532708617735637

Ellis, C., Adams, T. E., & Bochner, A. P. (2011). Autoethnography: An overview. *Historical Social Research, 36*(4), 273–290. https://doi.org/10.17169/fqs-12.1.1589

Fairclough, N. (1995). *Media discourse.* Edward Arnold.

Foucault, M. (1980). *Power/knowledge: Selected interviews and other writings, 1971–1977.* Pantheon Books.

Giroux, H. A. (1988). *Schooling and the struggle for public life: critical pedagogy in the modern Age.* University of Minnesota Press.

Giroux, H. A. (2016). Beyond pedagogies of repression. *Monthly Review, 67*(10), 57–71. https://doi.org/10.14452/MR-067-10-2016-03_6

Grey, S., & James, A. (2016). Truth, reconciliation, and "double settler denial": Gendering the Canada-South Africa analogy. *Human Rights Review, 17*, 303–328. https://doi.org/10.1007/s12142-016-0412-8

Guo, Y., & Guo, S. (2020). Internationalization of Canadian Teacher Education: Teacher Candidates' experiences and perspectives. *ECNU Review of Education*, 1–25. https://doi.org/10.1177/2096531120946045

Henry, W. L. (2021). Who feels it knows it! Alterity, identity and 'epistemological privilege': Challenging White privilege from a black perspective within the academy. In D. S. P. Thomas & J. Arday (Eds.), *Doing equity and diversity for success in higher education* (pp. 299–312). Palgrave Macmillan. https://doi.org/10.1007/978-3-030-65668-3

Henry, F., & Tator, C. (2009). *Racism in the Canadian university: Demanding social justice, inclusion, and equity.* University of Toronto Press. https://www.jstor.org/stable/10.3138/9781442688926

Holliday, A. (2014). *Native-speakerism.* https://adrianholliday.com/wp-content/uploads/2014/01/nism-encyc16plain-submitted.pdf. Accessed 2 Jan 2022.

Holliday, A. (2015). Native-speakerism: Taking the concept forward and achieving cultural belief. In A. Swan, P. Aboshiha, & A. Holliday (Eds.), *(En)Countering native-speakerism: Global perspectives* (pp. 11–25). Palgrave Macmillan. https://doi.org/10.1057/9781137463500_2

Jacob, M. M., Leilani, S., Johnson, S. R. H., Jansen, J., & Morse, G. S. N. (2019). 'We need to make action now, to help keep the language alive': Navigating tensions of engaging Indigenous educational values in university education. *American Journal of Community Psychology, 64*, 126–136. https://doi.org/10.1002/ajcp.12374

James, C. E. (2009). 'It will happen without putting in place special measures': Racially diversifying universities. In H. Francis & C. Tator (Eds.), *Racism in the Canadian university: Demanding social justice, inclusion, and equity* (pp. 128–159). University of Toronto Press. https://doi.org/10.3138/9781442688926-006

James, M. (2017). Changing the subject: The TRC, its national events, and the displacement of substantive reconciliation in Canadian media representations. *Journal of Canadian Studies, 51*(2), 362–397. https://doi.org/10.3138/jcs.2016-0011.r1

James, M. (2018). Narrative robustness, post-apology conduct, and Canada's 1998 and 2008 residential schools' apologies. In B. Bevernage & N. Wouters (Eds.), *The palgrave handbook of state-sponsored history after 1945* (pp. 831–847). Palgrave Macmillan. https://doi.org/10.1057/978-1-349-95306-6_45

Jenkins, J. (2006). Current perspectives on teaching world Englishes and English as a lingua franca. *TESOL Quarterly, 40*(1), 157–181. https://doi.org/10.2307/40264515

Johnson, G. F., & Howsam, R. (2020). Whiteness, power and the politics of demographics in the governance of the Canadian Academy. *Canadian Journal of Political Science, 53*(3), 676–694. https://doi.org/10.1017/S0008423920000207

Kappo, T. (2014, December 19). Stephen Harper's comments on missing, murdered aboriginal women show 'lack of respect'. *CBC, Indigenous-Opinion.* https://www.cbc.ca/news/indigenous/stephen-harper-s-comments-on-missing-murdered-aboriginal-women-show-lack-of-respect-1.2879154. Accessed 21 Nov 2022.

Kirkpatrick, A. (2016). Just because I'm a native speaker. In F. Copland, S. Garton, & S. Mann (Eds.), *LETs and NESTs: Voices, views and vignettes* (pp. 241–242). British Council. https://publications.aston.ac.uk/id/eprint/28660/1/pub_BC_Book_VVV_online_screen_res_FINAL.pdf

Kumaravadivelu, B. (2016). The decolonial option in English teaching: Can the subaltern act? *TESOL Quarterly, 50*(1), 66–85. https://doi.org/10.1002/tesq.202

Lavell-Harvard, D. M., & Brant, J. (Eds.). (2016). *Forever loved: Exposing the hidden crisis of missing and murdered Indigenous women and girls in Canada.* Demeter Press.

MacDonald, D. B. (2020). Indigenous genocide and perceptions of the Holocaust in Canada. In S. Gigliotti & H. Earl (Eds.), *A companion to the Holocaust* (pp. 577–597). Wiley Blackwell. https://doi.org/10.1002/9781118970492.ch32

Mahboob, A. (2004). Native or nonnative: What do students enrolled in an intensive English program think? In L. D. Kamhi-Stein (Ed.), *Learning and teaching from experience* (pp. 121–148). University of Michigan Press.

Monture, P. (2009). 'Doing Academia Differently': Confronting 'Whiteness' in the university. In H. Francis & C. Tator (Eds.), *Racism in the Canadian university: Demanding social justice, inclusion, and equity* (pp. 76–105). University of Toronto Press, 10.3138/9781442688926-004.

Morin, B. (2021). *The stench of death: On Canada's highway of tears.* Aljazeera. https://www.aljazeera.com/features/longform/2021/11/8/the-stench-of-death-life-along-canadas-highway-of-tears. Accessed 27 Nov 2022.

Moosavi, L. (2022). 'But you're white': An autoethnography of whiteness and white privilege in East Asian universities. *Research in Comparative & International Education, 17*, 1–17. https://doi.org/10.1177/17454999211067123

Morton, K. (2016). Hitchhiking and missing and murdered Indigenous women: A critical discourse analysis of billboards on the Highway of Tears. *Canadian Journal of Sociology, 41*(3), 299–325.

Moussu, L. (2010). Toward a conversation between ESL teachers and intensive English program administrators. *TESOL Journal, 1*(4), 400–426. https://doi.org/10.5054/tj.2010.234767

Moussu, L., & Llurda, E. (2008). Non-native English-speaking English language teachers: History and research. *Language Teaching, 41*, 315–348. https://doi.org/10.1017/S0261444808005028

Murtiana, R. (2013). NESTs and NNESTs at an Islamic Higher Institution in Indonesia: Is the Former better than the Latter? In N. T. Zacharias & C. Manara (Eds.), *Contextualizing the pedagogy of English as an international language: Issues and tensions* (pp. 99–118). Cambridge Scholars. https://www.cambridgescholars.com/resources/pdfs/978-1-4438-5125-1-sample.pdf

Nagy, R. (2020). Settler witnessing at the Truth and Reconciliation Commission of Canada. *Human Rights Review, 21*, 219–241. https://doi.org/10.1007/s12142-020-00595-w

Nicholas, A. B., Fontaine, L., Key, A., Jr., & Thomson, K. T. (2023). Using the UN human Rights treaty system to defend LHRs. In T. Skutnabb-Kangas & R. Phillipson (Eds.), *The handbook of linguistic human rights* (pp. 235–250). Wiley Blackwell.

Norton, B. (1997). Language, identity, and the ownership of English. *TESOL Quarterly, 31*(3), 409–429. https://doi.org/10.2307/3587831

Pennycook, A. (2007). ELT and Colonialism. In J. Cummins & C. Davison (Eds.), *International handbook of English language teaching* (pp. 13–24). Springer. https://doi.org/10.1007/978-0-387-46301-8

Pennycook, A. (2017). *The cultural politics of English as an international language.* Routledge.

Phillipson, R. (1992). *Linguistic imperialism.* Oxford University Press.

Phillipson, R. (2016). Native speakers in linguistic imperialism. *Journal for Critical Education Policy Studies, 14*, 80–96. http://www.jceps.com/wp-content/uploads/2016/12/14-3-4.pdf

Raycraft, R. (2022, October 27). *MPs back motion calling on government to recognize residential schools program as genocide.* CBC News. https://www.cbc.ca/news/politics/house-motion-recognize-genocide-1.6632450. Accessed 5 Nov 2022.

Razack, S. (2015). *Dying from improvement: Inquests and inquiries into Indigenous deaths in custody.* University of Toronto Press.

Rivers, D. J. (2019). Walking on glass: Reconciling experience and expectation within Japan. *Journal of Language, Identity & Education, 18*, 377–388. https://doi.org/10.1080/1534845 8.2019.1674149

Rosa, J., & Flores, N. (2017). Unsettling race and language: Toward a raciolinguistic perspective. *Language in Society, 46*, 621–647. https://doi.org/10.1017/S0047404517000562

Saarinen, T., & Ennser-Kananen, J. (2020). Ambivalent English: What we talk about when we think we talk about language. *Nordic Journal of English Studies, 19*(3), 115–129. https://doi.org/10.35360/njes.581

Sahlane, A. (2012). Argumentation and fallacy in the justification of the 2003 war on Iraq. *Argumentation, 26*(4), 459–488. https://doi.org/10.1075/jlp.11.1.01wil

Sahlane, A. (2013). Metaphor as Rhetoric in Newspaper Op/Ed Debate of the Prelude to the 2003 Iraq War. *Critical Discourse Studies, 10*(2), 154–171. https://doi.org/10.1080/1740590 4.2012.736397

Sahlane, A. (2019). Discursive (re)construction of the prelude to the 2003 Iraq War in op/ ed press: dialectics of argument and rhetoric. In L. Jeffries, J. O'Driscoll, & M. Evans (Eds.), *The Routledge handbook of language in conflict* (pp. 13–43). Routledge. https://doi.org/10.4324/9780429058011

Sahlane, A. (2022). Covering Iraq: The pragmatics of framing and visual rhetoric. In I. Chiluwa (Ed.), *Discourse, media & conflict: Examining war and resolution in the news* (pp. 93–116). Cambridge University Press. https://doi.org/10.1017/9781009064057.006

Schmidt, C. (2021). Teacher education for social justice in the Canadian context. In L. Heidrich, Y. Karakaşoğlu, P. Mecheril, & S. Shure (Eds.), *Regimes of belonging – Schools – Migrations: Teaching in (trans)National constellations* (pp. 437–447). Springer. https://doi.org/10.1007/978-3-658-29189-1

Schmidt, C., & Schneider, J. (Eds.). (2016). *Diversifying the teaching force transnational contexts: Critical perspectives*. Sense Publishers. https://doi.org/10.1007/978-94-6300-663-7

Sian, K. P. (2019). *Navigating institutional racism in British universities*. Palgrave Macmillan. https://doi.org/10.1007/978-3-030-14284-1

Starblanket, T. (2018). *Suffer the little children: Genocide, Indigenous Nations and the Canadian State*. Clarity Press.

Statistics Canada. (2017, 25 November). *Ethnic and cultural origins of Canadians: Portrait of a rich heritage*. https://www12.statcan.gc.ca/census-recensement/2016/as-sa/98-200-x/2016016/98-200-x2016016-eng.cfm. Accessed 14 Nov 2022.

Swearingen, A. J. (2019). Nonnative-English-speaking teacher candidates' language teacher identity development in graduate TESOL preparation programs: A review of the literature. *TESOL Journal, 10*(4), 1–15. https://doi.org/10.1002/tesj.494

Tator, C., & Henry, F. (2010). The Struggle for anti-racism, inclusion, and equity in the Canadian academy: Representation is not enough. *Our Schools, Our Selves, 19*(3), 369–398.

TRC Canada. (2015). Honouring the truth, reconciling for the future. *Summary of the final report of the truth and reconciliation commission of Canada*. TRCC. Winnipeg. https://ehprnh2mwo3.exactdn.com/wp-content/uploads/2021/01/ Executive _ Summary_ English_Web.pdf. Accessed 18 Nov 2022.

United Nations. (1948, December 9). *The genocide convention*. https://www.un.org/en/genocideprevention/genocide-convention.shtml. Accessed 28 Dec 2022.

Waite, D., & Waite, S. F. (2021). The work of the neoliberal university: A critique. In J. Zajda (Ed.), *Third international handbook of globalisation, education, and policy research* (pp. 170–191). Springer.

Weatherall, R., & Ahuja, S. (2020). Learning as moments of friction and opportunity: an autoethnography of ECR identities in queer time. *Management Learning, 52*(4), 404–423. https://doi.org/10.1177/1350507620970335

White, P., Fiddler, P., & Grant, T. (2022, July 25). Pope Francis begs forgiveness for abuses at residential schools: A close look at the papal apology. *The Globe and Mail*. https://www.theglobeandmail.com/canada/article-pope-francis-apology-residential-schoolscanada/. Accessed 9 Nov 2022.

Willsher, M., & Oldfield, J. (2020). History in the now: Asserting Indigenous difference in "top end" higher education using culturally responsive pedagogy. In J. Frawley, G. Russell, & J. Sherwood (Eds.), *Cultural competence and the higher education sector Australian perspectives, policies and practice* (pp. 197–212). Springer. https://doi.org/10.1007/978-981-15-5362-2_11

Xu, X. (2022). Epistemic diversity and cross-cultural comparative research: Ontology, challenges, and outcomes. *Globalisation, Societies and Education, 20*(1), 36–48. https://doi.org/10.1080/14767724.2021.1932438

Ahmed Sahlane (PhD, University of Ulster, Belfast) is Senior Lecturer in English at University of Jeddah (English Language Institute). He coordinated several EAP/ESP programs at Saudi universities, where he served in a variety of leadership roles such as business English program academic advisor and curriculum designer. He has taught English at all levels (K-12 and tertiary) in Morocco, Oman, Saudi Arabia, and Canada. He was the winner of Top Gun Master Teacher's Award, CDIS, Burnaby, Canada, 2001. His publications focus on the critical analysis of mediated political discourse from the perspective of argumentation theory and critical linguistics. He has published several articles and book chapters about the coverage of the 2003 Iraq War in Western opinion-editorial press. Sahlane's current research interests revolve around the rhetorics of populist discourse and media (mis)representation of cultural otherness. His research interests also include intersectionality and decoloniality studies, social semiotics, and critical pedagogy. Email: asahlan1@uj.edu.sa

"I Wasn't Good Enough Through Their Eyes": White Dominance and Conceptions of the "Good Teacher" in Teacher Education in Canada

Lilach Marom

Abstract To diversify the teaching force, there is a need for profound change in the underlying structures of teacher education, the gatekeeper to the profession. This chapter discusses barriers to the diversification of teacher education via three interconnected case studies. The first involves the re-certification trajectory of internationally educated teachers (IETs). While IETs mostly belong to racialized groups and bring diverse cultural, linguistic, and international experiences that have the potential to enhance the teaching profession and support diverse students, they face numerous barriers when attempting to re-enter their profession in Canada. The second case is that of racialized teacher candidates who, although born and raised in Canada, are still often constructed as "outsiders" to the profession. Lastly, the case of Punjabi international students in Canada highlights how teaching is context dependent and there is no "one size fits all." This chapter analyses these cases as located at the intersection of Western colonial structures of educational institutions and neoliberal trends impacting teacher and higher education.

Keywords Internationally educated teachers · Teacher education · Canada · International students · Anti-racism · Intersectionality · Critical race theory · Equity · Inequality

1 Introduction

The discourse on diversity in the teaching force in Western countries has a long history and is invoked repeatedly in the face of changing social forces such as globalization and immigration. Studies have highlighted the discrepancy between the diversity of the student population and the relatively homogenous composition

L. Marom (✉)
Faculty of Education, Simon Fraser University, Burnaby, BC, Canada
e-mail: lmarom@sfu.ca

A. Sahlane, R. Pritchard (eds.), *English as an International Language Education*, English Language Education 33, https://doi.org/10.1007/978-3-031-34702-3_6

105

of the teaching force. This discrepancy underscores the need for the teaching force to more accurately reflect the diverse backgrounds, cultures, and languages of the students it serves. There is a growing understanding that a more diverse teaching force can better address the needs of an increasingly diverse student population (Li et al., 2021). Yet in many Western countries, including Canada, the teaching force remains highly homogenous, composed primarily of White, middle-class women who speak English (or the respective national language) as a first language (K. D. Brown, 2014; Sleeter & Milner, 2011). In Canadian higher education, despite a range of equity-based educational initiatives, full professor and senior leadership positions are still male dominated (Statistics Canada, 2019). The gender gap is rooted in the conceptualization of primary education as "maternal" (S. D. M. Moore & Janzen, 2020); yet Whiteness is predominant across the board (Statistics Canada, 2020). Western education institutions are also criticized for privileging and universalizing Western knowledge while marginalizing other, diverse forms of knowledge (Henry et al., 2017; Simpson et al., 2011).

This chapter draws on critical social theories, particularly critical race theory (CRT), critical Whiteness studies (Picower, 2009; Solórzano et al., 2000; Solórzano & Yosso, 2002), and the Bourdieusian concept of capital (Bourdieu, 1997). It shares meta-analysis of three research projects to highlight marginalization processes in teacher education. This is of particular relevance in the Canadian context, where discourses on the importance of diversity are prevalent, yet systemic marginalization of people of colour still underlies educational institutions (Henry et al., 2017; Henry & Tator, 2009).

Internationally educated teachers (IETs) are certified teachers in their home countries who, post immigration, wish to teach in Canada. In order to do so, they must go through a credentials evaluation process and are often required to take a re-certification program that, in British Columbia (BC), is modelled on pre-service teacher education (Marom, 2017a). There are no data available regarding the numbers of IETs applying annually for re-certification, but with growing immigration and refugee cases, there is consistent demand for re-certification programs in the province. Because immigration to Canada is mainly from non-Western countries, IETs often belong to racialized and minoritized groups. As such, they can bring diverse cultural, linguistic, and international experiences that have the potential to enhance the teaching profession and support diverse students.

Problematically, studies identify numerous challenges that IETs face when attempting to re-enter the teaching profession (Deters, 2011; Marom, 2017a, 2019a; Schmidt, 2010). Some of these challenges emerge from prevalent conceptions of the "good teacher," which IETs often do not meet. While it is tempting to see the "good teacher" as capturing teacher professionalism, such definitions often contain biases and cultural specificity that stand in the way of diversifying the teaching profession.

With the increasing diversification of Canadian society and the declared commitment toward reconciliation, more first and second-generation immigrants as well as Indigenous teacher candidates (TCs) attend teacher education programs. Yet minoritized TCs must also adapt to a certain model of the "good teacher." Studies show that racialized[1] TCs, just like IETs, are often constructed as deficient and face barriers during teacher education (K. D. Brown, 2014; Li et al., 2021; Marom, 2019b).

While it is important to acknowledge skills and competencies that contribute to effective teaching in a certain context, teaching an increasingly diverse student body in many Western countries has brought new challenges for teachers. Teachers need to navigate classrooms with students from diverse backgrounds who speak numerous languages and belong to multiple ethnic communities. In an era of superdiversity (Li et al., 2021; Vertovec, 2019), teachers must go beyond Eurocentric models of teaching to more intercultural and inclusive pedagogies.

Findings from a study on Punjabi international students (PS) further demonstrate the need for enhanced intercultural pedagogies. With increased international competition, Canadian universities have expanded their markets to untapped areas in order to attract more international students (Brunner, 2022). PS have become a main recruitment target among teaching universities and colleges in Canada. PS are often from farming families, a sector that experiences economic and social instability. For them, international education is a potential route toward immigration (Marom, 2021, 2022a). Canadian education institutions take pride in being inclusive and student-centred, yet PS face multiple barriers in their academic trajectory. Although universities claim that international students create diversity that enriches their institutions, in reality, these institutions do not adjust their practices, which leads to Othering and deficit thinking toward international students (Tran & Vu, 2016).

The barriers that PS face (Marom, 2021, 2022a, b) have intensified in the current neoliberal context in which international students' tuition has become a main source of revenue for Canadian universities (Beech, 2018; Brunner, 2022; Scott et al., 2015). Universities gladly collect high tuition fees from international students, but they do not always commit to providing inclusive education and student support.

In all three cases, IETs, minoritized TCs and PSs, teacher education programs and post-secondary institutions expected TCs and students to adapt to the system, rather than challenge the system to expand its knowledge base, curriculum, and pedagogy in order to relate to the changing student body it serves.

2   Methodological Note

The excerpts below are taken from multiple research projects. The first was centred on the experiences of IETs and explored conceptions of the "good teacher" as a form of professional capital promoted in Canadian teacher education. It looked at the barriers these conceptions create in the re-certification process of IETs (Marom, 2017a, b, 2019a). A second study explored the experiences of racialized TCs and

---

[1]This chapter uses the terms "racialized" and "minoritized" rather than the Statistics Canada (2021) term "visible minority" to imply that race is a social construct identifying someone in relation to Whiteness.

schoolteachers who, while born and raised in Canada, did not fit the prototypical image of teachers (typically, White, middle-class women who speak English with a Canadian/American accent; [Marom, 2019a]). The third study was focused on the experiences of Punjabi international students (PS). PS faced numerous barriers in Canadian higher education, often due to their background in a non-Western educational system (Marom, 2021, 2022a, b). Each research project was conducted independently, and the findings were published, including an in-depth methodology explanation. This chapter draws on the main findings from these previous projects, to provide a meta-analysis of Whiteness in teacher education.

The focus on the voices of people from marginalized groups is central in frames such as critical race theory (CRT). CRT often uses counter-stories to share voices that are less heard in public discourses. The importance of counter-stories is that they can highlight institutional mechanisms that are easily overlooked by people who identify with the normative group but that are experienced by those on the margins. Using counter-stories, studies demonstrate that exposure to daily forms of subtle manifestation of racism (or other forms of discrimination) has a cumulative and long-lasting impact on both the academic success and the well-being of members of minoritized groups (Solórzano & Yosso, 2002).

The main source of data in these projects was semi-structured interviews. Interviews were supplemented by observations, policy analysis, and publicly available data. The diverse forms of data acted as a means of triangulation (Kvale, 1996; Maxwell, 2013; Seidman, 2006). All the interviewees were students (at the time of the study) or graduates of either teacher education programs or higher education in British Columbia[2]: IETs; racialized, second-generation immigrants; Indigenous students; and Punjabi international students.

3   Findings

A meta-analysis of the findings of the project discussed above revealed four main categories. These categories weave together dominant discourses and external influences on education and demonstrate how they contribute to the marginalization of teachers and learners from equity seeking groups. The first section demonstrates the cultural specificity of teaching dispositions and how conceptions of the "good teacher," are located in a specific context. The second section focuses on neoliberal influences on education and the barriers they pose to the inclusion of diverse learners and teachers. The third section focuses on the devaluation of international and intercultural experiences in education programs that are still underlined by Whiteness and colonial structures. Lastly, the fourth section demonstrates institutional barriers that teachers and students from equity seeking groups need to overcome in order to gain access to professional fields.

---

[2] Please read Marom, 2019a/2021/2022a for a detailed discussion of data sources and methodology.

3.1 *"You Have to be More Enthusiastic": The Cultural Specificity of Teaching Dispositions*

To teach in Canada, many IETs have to go through a re-certification process that lasts between eight months and one year of full-time study in British Columbia (BC). This is a demanding and costly process that involves multiple barriers, during which it is difficult for IETs to work and provide for their families (Deters, 2011; Faez, 2010; Frank, 2013; Pollock, 2010; Schmidt, 2010, 2016).

While being interviewed about her experiences in a re-certification program for IETs at the University of British Columbia, Miruna, an immigrant teacher from Eastern Europe, shared the following:

> I was given the feedback that I have to be a lot more enthusiastic ... My faculty advisor pointed out that [Canadian teachers] tend to be more enthusiastic ... I did feel a little uncomfortable with that comment ... Thinking back on that, it made me feel a little bit of an outsider ... I mean, I think I'm a very enthusiastic person ... but I can't be like that the whole time. That's where a lot of the feedback was coming from. That's what the faculty advisor wanted from me. That is why I felt that I do need to change. I do need to blend in more because I wanted to do well.

Miruna's experience demonstrates that notions of enthusiasm may reflect cultural and context specific preferences. It may be that in the Canadian teaching context, enthusiasm is more highly regarded than, say, in China. After all, while there is nothing wrong with enthusiasm per se, there is no indication that enthusiastic teachers are inherently better or more effective than teachers who are engaged, provoke critical thinking, or are experts in their fields.

Furthermore, the ways in which teachers embody enthusiasm is not universal. For example, expectations about the formality and approachability of teachers differ between contexts. Gomez et al. (2004) provide similar arguments regarding the concept of "care" in teacher education. They explain that alternative ways of caring enacted in marginalized groups "do not necessarily fit the hegemonic model of what caring is 'supposed' to feel and look like" (p. 476).

Nasjeh (meaning "to heal, to make better"), a Dakelh First Nation from Northern BC, shared a similar example in relation to one's "teaching voice":

> I remember that after being observed in my practicum, they wanted me to have more "crispness," and I didn't really know what they meant. After watching many teachers, I now understand what it is ... but I still struggle with this. Because of the natural tone of voice, my word usage, I have a hard time being crisp .... This is not just about voice or accent: if you talk too slow, or if you have too many pauses, it is deemed not smart and not fast .... But if I'm not crisp enough to be a good teacher, then it means that there has to be another definition of what it means to be a good teacher.

This example demonstrates deficit assumptions associated with patterns of speech (Rosa, 2019). Indigenous teachers can be judged as not speaking "proper English" if they talk in a way that is associated with Native dialects. However, this is an arbitrary distinction that prioritizes the colonizer's dialect as the universal "teaching voice."

Similar observations about the cultural specificity of teaching ideals were shared by PS when discussing their experiences and challenges in a Western university. For example, comparing the school system in India and Canada, Arshdeep shared, "[In India] the thing that is tested is your memory. You are just given lots of notes. You have to just memorize them and then copy. But here … teachers are looking for your knowledge, rather than your memory." While there are good reasons to support deep understanding rather than memorization in the classroom (Harpaz, 2005), students from non-Western educational backgrounds may need scaffolding to adjust to a different classroom culture. Jasandeep explained how the smaller classrooms and focus on discussions could be overwhelming for students coming from India: "[In Canada, there are] just 35 students in a class. [There are] more activities, projects, like practical things. In India, we don't do that much. … It's like a fear for students. We can't pass this because we haven't done this before".

Similarly, Shereen shared,

> Students face problems because the teaching style here is different: In India we only copy and paste, and we get full marks, but here you must think by yourself and then paraphrase, and then cite … . [In India] you have … final exams after 4–5 months, or even after a year, here you have assignments and midterms, and students are not prepared for that.

Even where the content of teachers' professional capital is non-arbitrary, it is important to keep in mind that in international and diverse school systems, students come from different educational contexts and, thus, need support to adjust to new expectations. Skills related to reflexivity and dialogue, for instance, do not develop overnight and, without proper mentorship and guidance, students can feel othered and alienated for not already possessing them.

The quotes above demonstrate the blended nature of teachers' professional capital which contains both arbitrary and non-arbitrary components (Marom, 2019a). Some teaching ideals are arbitrary, as in the above examples of enthusiasm or a "teaching voice," in which a certain overt display of enthusiasm or "crispness" in one's voice was promoted as superior. Other elements of teachers' professional capital are non-arbitrary in the sense that they have been proven useful for enhancing understanding and deep learning (e.g., inquiry, dialogue). However, since pedagogy is always located within a specific context of teaching (Gomez et al., 2004; A. Moore, 2004; Pratt, 2002), teachers who embody preferred dispositions in different ways may be regarded as lacking in their teaching ability. Canadian education needs to extend its definition of what good teaching looks like through an intercultural frame in ways that acknowledge and appreciate the diversity of both teachers and students.

3.2 *"Parents Sacrifice … for Their Kids so They can get a Good Life": Neoliberal Influences on Education*

When analyzing IETs' re-certification, one must consider the "big picture," that is, the impact of neoliberal trends on international education (S. L. Robertson, 2012; Sleeter, 2008; Walsh et al., 2011). While reasons for internationalization vary from the academic, social, political, and economic, a main driver appears to be the neoliberal shift of the 1970s toward a global knowledge economy (Weis & Dolby, 2012). In this regime, education was reconstructed as a prime driver for economic advancement and the catalyst for knowledge-based economies (Grubb & Lazerson, 2007). Neoliberal influences on education shrank government funding and constructed global universities as competitors, with an eye to increasing revenues through expansion of international markets (Harvey, 2005; Olssen & Peters, 2005). International students were increasingly seen as a revenue stream (Connell, 2013; Mazzarol & Soutar, 2001).

This global shift from education as a human right toward education as human capital manifests in the field of teacher education. It is reflected in the "formation of institutions and processes at a global scale, to frame, measure, and sell a particular brand of teacher; one who is flexible, privileges constructivism as a pedagogical approach, and who use[s] 'evidence' to make teaching and learning decisions" (Sorensen & Robertson, 2018, p. 120). This neoliberal promotion of the "one size fits all" teaching model decreases the importance of diversity and intercultural competencies (Fenwick, 2003).

In theory, following the neoliberal logic of market exchange, global teachers such as IETs would be valued; in reality, the diverse and cosmopolitan skills and experiences IETs possess are often devalued (Collins & Reid, 2012). While Western teacher education programs construct teaching as a "reflective profession" and promote constructivist pedagogies as the mark of good teaching, similar terminology is used by forces that aim "to reduce teachers to the status of clerks, technicians, or 'entrepreneurs,' a subaltern class of deskilled workers with little power, few benefits, and excessive teaching loads" (Giroux, 2016, p. 64). IET re-certification is at the centre of these axes: on the one hand, they are susceptible to the decrease in teachers' autonomy by the standardization and deregulation of the profession (Grimmett & Young, 2012); on the other hand, they are subjected to Westernized models of teaching that construct them as deficient. IETs are doubly at risk of being marked as "outsiders."

Similar forces operate in the case of PS and other international students. The reconfiguration of international higher education as a revenue source for universities has led to growing access for students from groups who historically did not attend universities. Many more students from racialized and lower socioeconomic classes have gained admission to higher education institutions (Brunner, 2022; Sidhu, 2006; Trilokekar & El Masri, 2019). As Rajiv shared,

> We can see these success stories, right? We can think that maybe we can go to these countries too and get a better life or something … . When so many people came to these other countries, and we saw them, and we can relate … . That's what I thought, too … . Maybe I can study, and I'll get a better job.

On the surface this may look like a favourable process that increases both the accessibility of higher education and the diversity of the student body. However, it has a "darker side" that emerges because of the intertwining of educational processes with the neoliberal business model (S. Robertson, 2013). In the case of PS, families often sell land or take loans to afford international education, assuming students will be able to access a better career trajectory and gain permanent residency post-graduation. Yet, universities are not committed to providing the support that would allow students to succeed in a highly competitive job market in Canada. On the contrary, "Academic teaching staff regularly complain about poor language skills, improper learning styles and poor motivation. Committees, sub-committees and inquiries are increasingly established to explore 'the international student problem'" (Caluya et al., 2011, p. 85). What these deficit perceptions do not consider are the barriers facing international students both inside and outside the university. As Gunkar described:

> Working 20 hours [the limitation on a student visa] legally can hardly get through tuition, and day-to-day expenses. This is how the trap is laid and now that student is getting into that trap. They cannot discuss this with family back home, so PS start working illegally.

Many PS end up graduating from Canadian postsecondary education with a non-competitive diploma that leads to low-skilled jobs (Marom, 2021, 2022a).

The neoliberal reframing of higher education positions international students, many of whom belong to racialized groups, at the intersection of education and migration discourses, seen simultaneously as "outsiders" and "newcomers." While education-migration (Brunner, 2022) is built around the assumption that international education provides both a valuable education leading to skilled jobs and migration (McCartney, 2020), in reality, it mostly provides the latter. This system prevails because of the assumed superiority of Western education that leads parents to entrust their kids to it (P. Brown et al., 2011). Yet, when education is subjected to the market, it keeps many international students on the margins, providing education paths that lead to low-skilled jobs (Marom, 2022a).

3.3 *"There's no Place to Share": The Devaluation of International and Intercultural Experience*

IETs are not typical TCs—the students in their twenties who were born and raised in Canada. Meeting the requirements needed to enter a re-certification program (such as prerequisite courses and volunteer hours) is already a demanding and time-consuming process, and the construction of the program (full time, 8 months) makes it extremely hard for those re-certifying to work or attend to family needs.

For example, Peter, who was a head teacher in China, shared, "I had to take the full program, which is 30 credits, so of course I feel not good about it because I had to waste my time and I need to waste more money." Similarly, Sophia, who was a teacher in South America, explained, "I started in 2011. All year I studied English, and then in 2012 I took six credits of English, and this year it is the re-certification program. It has been three years of school."

Instead of a program designed to meet the unique needs of immigrant and refugee teachers, IETs had to take a program designed with local, young, domestic, pre-service teachers in mind. While the interviewed IETs entered the re-certification program as experienced teachers, the program was not established as a professional development program, but rather, as a form of training for novice teachers. As a result, IETs were seen more as newcomers to the profession than as experienced teachers who are newcomers to Canada (Marom, 2017a, 2019a).

For many IETs, the construction of the re-certification process resulted in feelings of frustration. While they needed to repeat parts of their teacher education, their previous experiences and knowledge were not recognized in the program and were not deemed valuable enrichment of the local context of teaching. Ewa argued, "In BC, you don't value and appreciate people from the outside: 'if you have it from outside, we don't need it because we know better.'" Peter also spoke of the lack of interest in his previous experience: "Nobody asked me about the Eastern Asian system. Nobody asked me to open up and share which system is different, which system is not so good. I didn't have this opportunity."

The theme of "fitting in" emerged also in interviews with racialized TCs. In this case, interviewees were not newcomers and yet were still seen as "outsiders." Both terms carry similar implications that one's knowledge and experiences are of lesser value. Tamam, a Middle Eastern, Muslim TC, shared,

> I have not even thought about connecting my teaching to my heritage and culture because where is the place for it in the system? There is no place, even if I wanted to. I feel like everything is so predominantly based on the White population. Even if I want to bring something from my culture, will it be welcomed? Even if they say it will be, in reality, I don't think so.

Tamam felt that there were limited spaces within the school system to deeply explore diverse content, which made her feel less valuable as a teacher. Racialized TCs shared how they had to solely conform to a certain model of teaching rather than draw on their own experiences and knowledge. The White, Eurocentric underpinnings of teacher education can lead to a disconnect because teaching is a personal profession that relates to one's identity. Ying, a Chinese Canadian TC, shared her experiences as a racialized body in a teacher education program:

> I felt very disadvantaged by having the FA [Faculty Advisor] I had … . She was a White female teacher and had not only cultural norms but also a set of rigid teaching methods that did not give me the opportunity to figure out my teaching style. Having to fulfil this image of the White female teacher, I felt that … I was going to fail because I am simply not her … . I, as a racialized body, was incompatible with this image and social construct of the White female teacher.

Similarly, Simran, an Indo-Canadian TC, felt that her positionality impacted how she was judged as a teacher:

> It feels like it is a little bit about who you are perceived to be rather than about where you are at in your career—more about my race or gender or age rather than about my capabilities as a teacher. I struggled with that, with my school advisor. There were other TCs who were White, and it felt like they had this positive connection [that I didn't have].

Both Ying and Simran described a feeling of being outsiders to the professional field although they were born and raised in Canada. It seems that Whiteness was embodied in the gatekeepers of the field (faculty and practicum supervisors) and played a part in their mentorship and supervisory roles. This led to a sense of "sharedness" that both interviewees felt othered by.

IETs were expected to morph into "good Canadian teachers," yet prevalent conceptions of the "good teacher" were grounded in a Canadian White normativity. White normativity also underlies the experiences of racialized TCs who were positioned as "outsiders within," resulting in feelings that their knowledge and experiences were not welcome in the school system. Both cases demonstrate that Whiteness still yields "enormous power over the generation and validation of knowledge" (Johnson & Howsam, 2020, p. 12) in teacher education. Whiteness operates both through the gatekeepers of the field (e.g., advisors, supervisors, and administrators), and the Eurocentric design of the curriculum.

3.4 "How Many Hoops do I Have to Jump Through?" Barriers to the Diversification of the Teaching Profession

Returning to Miruna's observation about enthusiasm, it is not surprising that IETs were less likely to display excitement and enthusiasm in a re-certification process that did not acknowledge their knowledge, value, or experiences. It is much easier for young, White, monolingual TCs to express enthusiasm than it is for experienced immigrant teachers for whom the re-certification trajectory is another hurdle among many in the immigration process. Furthermore, while identifying different stages in the careers of teachers, Hargreaves and Fullan (2012) explain that new teachers are generally more enthusiastic but less competent, and that teachers reach their professional peak mid-career (between 10 to 20 years in the profession).

Hargreaves and Fullan (2012) describe a prevalent stereotype in schools where older, experienced teachers are seen as "burned out," and new teachers as enthusiastic "new blood." However, they argue that this conception takes the focus off the societal construction of the teaching profession and the lack of support and professional development offered to teachers. Instead, it puts the blame on individual teachers. The authors wonder, "Is it possible that [these teachers] were once as enthusiastic and idealistic as many of their young colleagues are now? And if they were, what happened to them in the meantime?" (p. 65).

Hargreaves and Fullan's (2012) argument is pertinent to this case since IETs are not only experienced (and thus older) teachers, but also immigrants, which puts them in even stronger contrast to the Westernized image of the young, enthusiastic teacher. However, this image as less enthusiastic is misleading since, as the participant IETs shared, they needed to be highly motivated and committed in order to succeed in the re-certification process since the barriers they faced far exceeded those faced by "mainstream" TCs. Nehlia, an IET from an island nation, explained,

> You just need to have devotion. I set up my mind; I wanted to be certified, and I did it … . I had the guts to do it, but it was difficult. Now that I'm thinking of it, I don't know how I did it … . I know so many immigrant teachers who work as teacher assistants. They don't want to go through the process. They're terrified. They say, "this is too difficult. Canada asks for too much."

Ewa summed up her frustration in facing numerous barriers in the re-certification trajectory and when searching for a teaching position:

> How many hoops do I have to jump through? Everybody is telling me, "Be patient, you're almost there." But when I'm thinking, I'm almost there, there is another hoop, and another one, and another one … . I've worked already for ten years below my qualification. How [much] longer can I do it? I'm not 20 years old anymore … . Our life here, it's a struggle. And to get re-certified, it's a struggle on top of that.

Similar experiences in the re-certification process are repeated in the scholarly literature on IETs in Canada and elsewhere (e.g., Janusch, 2015; Pollock, 2010; Reid et al., 2014; Schmidt, 2016). They explain why IETs are at a disadvantage when superficially compared to "mainstream" TCs. When put into context, the ability of IETs to take the re-certification program and succeed in it requires high levels of motivation, resilience, and enthusiasm.

Like IETs, racialized TCs faced adversity during teacher education in ways that impacted their well-being and confidence. They had to be resilient in order to succeed in a system that conveyed a message of their deficiency. This message was embedded in the colonial and Eurocentric structures of the program and manifested in subtle ways that may be invisible to those who fit in but that are felt by those on the margins (Levine-Rasky, 2000; Picower, 2009). Celeste, a second generation Asian-Canadian, described the pressure to adjust to the unspoken norms of the institution:

> The goal for me and for my minority friends was always to be as Whitewashed as we can and to prove that we are not different. It was always a bad thing to be part of your own culture. If you are very, very Whitewashed, you could bring a little bit of your culture in, and people would say, "cool." But if you were deep in your culture, people would think, "[T]his is too much. This is too different."

Educational institutions adopt some elements of multicultural education into their programs, but these act as "add-ons" rather than challenge the existing curriculum (Arshad-Ayaz, 2011; St. Denis, 2011). The "add-on" approach was also apparent in the spatial dimensions of the institutions as Imran, a PS who volunteered at international students' services, shared:

A lot of people came to the office and … they were like, "Why are there only Christmas decorations here? We really feel bad." … When I told it to my immediate boss, they were just like, "Okay, you can take a printout from the laptop of those candles and just put them up. They'll be happy." But that's just doing it for the show and then, there's no respect for other cultures. If they're actually trying to be diverse, they need to take care of other people.

It is important to note that representation of diverse cultures does not equate to a disregard of Christian traditions as some might worry. The Canadian public school system claims to be separated from religion. At the same time, many of its cultural traditions (as well as its calendar) are grounded in Christianity. This affiliation is neutralized and universalized, rather than seen for what it is: one option among many.

CRT scholars claim that education programs are still grounded in White normativity while often including discussions of racial issues and social justice as "add-ons" without deep commitment to change (Ahmed, 2007; Ladson-Billings, 1998; Solórzano et al., 2000). Curtis, a First Nation student from Vancouver Island, shared a metaphor that captures the reproduction of White normativity:

If you look at education as a type of food, I would say it's an English crumpet. We're just adding a little bit of fish and deer meat on top and saying it's Indigenous Education … . Inclusivity is tokenized. So, we're using diverse names of kids for math problems, but it's not really inclusive; it includes the names but not the concepts of different cultures. A coffee is still a coffee if you put cinnamon in it. An English crumpet is still an English crumpet if you put smoked fish on top.

Curtis articulates the difference between "tokenized inclusivity," which helps people feel good while making little structural change, and "real inclusivity," which demands shifts in power and structures. Daria, a First Nation from Northern BC, shared the impact of White normativity on her experiences in the teacher education program:

I really feel that when people bring down the importance of Indigenous education, they were bringing down me as a whole, as a person, my identity … . I remember just going home and crying after every school day in the practicum, [feeling] that I wasn't good enough. But actually, I wasn't good enough through their eyes, and I had to remind myself of that. Today I still feel surprised by how well I'm doing in my career because I was so convinced that I was going to be a bad teacher.

The example above demonstrates that marginalization took place in the form of microaggressions (Sue, 2010), subtle and consistent manifestations of racism that operated via relations and pedagogy, in institutional spaces that claimed to be diverse and multicultural. Facing microaggressions can lead to what looks like the burnout and exhaustion experienced by IETs and racialized domestic TCs. It can further lead to higher drop-out rates and a lack of success in teacher education programs. While dropping out can be mistaken as a sign of the deficiency of racialized TCs, it is actually a mark of the deficiency of Western teacher education in its mission to diversify the teaching force.

4 Concluding Thoughts

One of the concerns that emerged from the interviews with IETs is that teacher education in North America, in spite of its claim to foster diversity, often becomes a site for social reproduction (Fleras & Elliott, 2002). As a result of recent immigration waves to Canada, most IETs belong to racialized groups. Comparing their experiences to those of racialized domestic TCs, it seems that IETs' position as "outsiders" to the profession had to do not only with their status as immigrants, but also with constructs such as race and ethnicity.

Critics argue that while Canadian universities mention diversity as a value, there is a gap between the rhetoric and the practice of diversity. Diversity is prevalent on paper yet, in reality, programs (e.g., admission policies, structures, and pedagogies) often privilege White, Eurocentric, middle-class norms and values, and are designed with "mainstream" students as the mould. Hence, critical analyses of education should focus not solely on terminology, but rather, raise questions regarding the implications of factors such as race, ethnicity, gender, class, and nationality as they pertain to accessibility and success in teacher education.

Superficial changes can, in fact, contribute to maintaining White normativity because they convey an image of inclusivity under which it is easier to overlook how powers and privileges are still distributed unevenly at the institutional level. For example, many educational institutions hold events to celebrate diversity; although such events can be enjoyable and open learning opportunities, typically, they are not geared to critically examine racial relations in Western societies. Another popular route taken by institutions is "diversity workshops" and "diversity training"; these are also criticized (from both the left and the right) as acting more as training in "virtue signalling" rather than triggering deep commitment to change (Abrams et al., 2020; Newkirk, 2019). In other words, the language of diversity can be co-opted, allowing for the appearance of progressiveness without the hard work of dismantling the uneven accumulation of power.

This chapter argues that "good teaching" is not universal. While neoliberal trends aim to quantify teaching and break it into measurable parts, teaching is always context dependent, and diverse teachers may have diverse yet similarly effective ways of teaching. Western ideas about teaching, whether important or harmful, are not neutral. The idea of a "good student" is similarly complex. As the case of PS demonstrates, students from diverse backgrounds who lack familiarity with Western school systems are often constructed as deficient while their knowledge and experiences are disregarded. In highly diverse Western societies within the global context, what constitutes "good teaching" is elusive if definable at all. Ongoing discussions about pedagogy and curriculum are important in all teaching contexts and must contain self-critique aimed at unpacking biases. Conceptions of the "good teacher" in teacher education can promote an arbitrary distinction between what is "from here" and what is "not from here." Such distinctions negatively impact not only IETs but also teachers from marginalized groups (Marom, 2019a).

Holding unexamined conceptions of the "good teacher" as based on individuals' characteristics can lead teacher educators and policy makers to favour and create teachers who are "like us," and discourage different forms and models of teaching (A. Moore, 2004; Pratt, 2002) and of being (Pinto et al., 2012). Definitions of "good teaching" tend to formalize the ideas and conventions of current members of the profession; as a result, teaching can become less open to diversity. Meanwhile, teachers like IETs are the ones who can meaningfully contribute to diversification of the teaching field, a field that is still overwhelmingly White and monolingual (Marom, 2019a).

One direction to take in answering the urgent need to diversify the teaching force is to design flexible and more reciprocal teacher education programs to increase accessibility for and the success of IETs and TCs from marginalized groups. It is important to learn from the experiences and knowledge of diverse TCs and experienced teachers such as IETs, especially during teacher education. Teacher educators, administrators, and policymakers alike must regularly reflect on what lies beneath models of "good teaching," looking for blind spots and hidden cultural assumptions.

References

Abrams, S., Campbell, B., Haidt, J., Manji, I., Martin, C., Pinker, S., Quirk, P., Strossen, N., & Zimmerman, J. (2020, December 24). *Five years of challenging orthodoxies: Reflections on challenges and opportunities ahead*. The Blog. https://heterodoxacademy.org/blog/five-years-of-challenging-orthodoxies-reflections-on-challenges-and-opportunities-ahead/

Ahmed, S. (2007). The language of diversity. *Ethnic and Racial Studies, 30*(2), 235–256. https://doi.org/10.1080/01419870601143927

Arshad-Ayaz, A. (2011). Making multicultural education work: A proposal for a transnational multicultural education. *Canadian Issues*, 71–74.

Beech, S. E. (2018). Adapting to change in the higher education system: International student mobility as a migration industry. *Journal of Ethnic and Migration Studies, 44*(4), 610–625. https://doi.org/10.1080/1369183X.2017.1315515

Bourdieu, P. (1997). The forms of capital. In A. H. Halsey, H. Lauder, P. Brown, & A. S. Wells (Eds.), *Education: Culture, economy, and society* (pp. 46–58). Oxford University Press.

Brown, K. D. (2014). Teaching in color: A critical race theory in education analysis of the literature on preservice teachers of color and teacher education in the US. *Race Ethnicity and Education, 17*(3), 326–345. https://doi.org/10.1080/13613324.2013.832921

Brown, P., Lauder, H., & Ashton, D. (2011). *The global auction: The broken promises of education, jobs, and incomes*. Oxford University Press.

Brunner, L. R. (2022). Towards a more just Canadian education-migration system: International student mobility in crisis. *Studies in Social Justice, 16*(1), 78–102. https://journals.library.brocku.ca/index.php/SSJ/article/view/2685

Caluya, G., Probyn, E., & Vyas, S. (2011). 'Affective eduscapes': The case of Indian students within Australian international higher education. *Cambridge Journal of Education, 41*(1), 85–99. https://doi.org/10.1080/0305764X.2010.549455

Collins, J., & Reid, C. (2012). Immigrant teachers in Australia. *Cosmopolitan Civil Societies: An Interdisciplinary Journal, 4*(2), 38–61. https://doi.org/10.5130/ccs.v4i2.2553

Connell, R. (2013). The neoliberal cascade and education: An essay on the market agenda and its consequences. *Critical Studies in Education, 54*(2), 99–112. https://doi.org/10.1080/17508487.2013.776990

Deters, P. (2011). *Identity, agency and the acquisition of professional language and culture.* Continuum.

Faez, F. (2010). Linguistic and cultural adaptation of internationally educated teacher candidates. *Canadian Journal of Education Administration and Policy, 100*, 1–20.

Fenwick, T. J. (2003). The 'good' teacher in a neo-liberal risk society: A Foucaultian analysis of professional growth plans. *Journal of Curriculum Studies, 35*(3), 335–354. https://doi.org/10.1080/00220270210151089

Fleras, A., & Elliott, J. L. (2002). *Engaging diversity: Multiculturalism in Canada* (2nd ed). Nelson Thomson Learning.

Frank, M. L. (2013). *Professional identity development: Life positioning analyses of foreign-trained teachers* [Doctoral dissertation, Simon Fraser University].

Giroux, H. A. (2016). Beyond pedagogies of repression. *Monthly Review, 67*(10), 57–71. https://doi.org/10.14452/MR-067-10-2016-03_6

Gomez, M. L., Allen, A.-R., & Clinton, K. (2004). Cultural models of care in teaching: A case study of one pre-service secondary teacher. *Teaching and Teacher Education, 20*(5), 473–488. https://doi.org/10.1016/j.tate.2004.04.005

Grimmett, P. P., & Young, J. C. (2012). *Teacher certification and the professional status of teaching in North America: The new battleground for public education.* Information Age Publishers.

Grubb, W. N., & Lazerson, M. (2007). *The education gospel: The economic power of schooling.* Harvard University Press.

Hargreaves, A., & Fullan, M. (2012). *Professional capital: Transforming teaching in every school.* Teachers College Press.

Harpaz, Y. (2005). Teaching and learning in a community of thinking. *Journal of Curriculum and Supervision, 20*(2), 136–157.

Harvey, D. (2005). *A brief history of neoliberalism.* Oxford University Press. http://dx.doi.org/10.1093/oso/9780199283262.001.0001

Henry, F., & Tator, C. (Eds.). (2009). *Racism in the Canadian university: Demanding social justice, inclusion, and equity.* University of Toronto Press.

Henry, F., Dua, E., James, C. E., Kobayashi, A., Li, P., Ramos, H., & Smith, M. S. (2017). *The equity myth: Racialization and Indigeneity at Canadian universities.* UBC Press. http://books.scholarsportal.info/viewdoc.html?id=/ebooks/ebooks3/upress/2017-07-24/1/9780774834902

Janusch, S. (2015). Voices unheard: Stories of immigrant teachers in Alberta. *Journal of International Migration and Integration, 16*(2), 299–315. https://doi.org/10.1007/s12134-014-0338-4

Johnson, G. F., & Howsam, R. (2020). Whiteness, power and the politics of demographics in the governance of the Canadian academy. *Canadian Journal of Political Science, 53*(3), 676–694. https://doi.org/10.1017/S0008423920000207

Kvale, S. (1996). *Interviews: An introduction to qualitative research interviewing* (1st ed.). Sage.

Ladson-Billings, G. (1998). Just what is critical race theory and what's it doing in a nice field like education? *International Journal of Qualitative Studies in Education, 11*(1), 7–24. https://doi.org/10.1080/095183998236863

Levine-Rasky, C. (2000). The practice of whiteness among teacher candidates. *International Studies in Sociology of Education, 10*(3), 263–284. https://doi.org/10.1080/09620210000200060

Li, G., Anderson, J., Hare, J., & McTavish, M. (Eds.). (2021). *Superdiversity and teacher education: Supporting teachers in working with culturally, linguistically, and racially diverse students, families, and communities* (1st ed.). Routledge. https://doi.org/10.4324/9781003038887

Marom, L. (2017a). Mapping the field: Examining the recertification of internationally educated teachers. *Canadian Journal of Education, 40*(3), 157–190.

Marom, L. (2017b). Eastern/Western conceptions of the "Good Teacher" and the construction of difference in teacher education. *Asia-Pacific Journal of Teacher Education, 46*(2), 167–182. https://doi.org/10.1080/1359866X.2017.1399982

Marom, L. (2019a). From experienced teachers to newcomers to the profession: The capital conversion of internationally educated teachers in Canada. *Teaching and Teacher Education, 78*(2), 85–96. https://doi.org/10.1016/j.tate.2018.11.006

Marom, L. (2019b). Under the cloak of professionalism: Covert racism in teacher education. *Race Ethnicity and Education, 22*(3), 319–337. https://doi.org/10.1080/13613324.2018.1468748

Marom, L. (2021). Outsiders-insiders-in between: Punjabi international students in Canada navigating identity amid intraethnic tensions. *Globalisation, Societies and Education, 20*(2), 221–235. https://doi.org/10.1080/14767724.2021.1882291

Marom, L. (2022a). Market mechanisms' distortions of higher education: Punjabi international students in Canada. *Higher Education., 85*, 123–140. https://doi.org/10.1007/s10734-022-00825-9

Marom, L. (2022b). Putting plagiarism under scrutiny: Punjabi international students and barriers within Canadian higher education. In C. Smith & G. Zhou (Eds.), *Handbook of research on teaching strategies for culturally and linguistically diverse international students* (pp. 168–187). IGI Global.

Maxwell, J. A. (2013). *Qualitative research design: An interactive approach* (3rd ed.). Sage.

Mazzarol, T., & Soutar, G. (2001). *The global market for higher education: Sustainable competitive strategies for the new millennium.* Edward Elgar Publishing.

McCartney, D. M. (2020). Border imperialism and exclusion in Canadian parliamentary talk about international students. *Canadian Journal of Higher Education, 50*(4), 37–51. https://doi.org/10.47678/cjhe.v50i4.188831

Moore, A. (2004). *The good teacher: Dominant discourses in teaching and teacher education.* Routledge. https://doi.org/10.4324/9780203420270

Moore, S. D. M., & Janzen, M. D. (2020, March 03). A largely female teaching force is standing up for public education. *The Conversation.* https://theconversation.com/a-largely-female-teaching-force-is-standing-up-for-public-education-130633

Newkirk, P. (2019). *Diversity, Inc.: The failed promise of a billion-dollar business* (1st ed.). Bold Type Books.

Olssen, M., & Peters, M. A. (2005). Neoliberalism, higher education and the knowledge economy: From the free market to knowledge capitalism. *Journal of Education Policy, 20*(3), 313–345. https://doi.org/10.1080/02680930500108718

Picower, B. (2009). The unexamined Whiteness of teaching: How White teachers maintain and enact dominant racial ideologies. *Race Ethnicity and Education, 12*(2), 197–215. https://doi.org/10.1080/13613320902995475

Pinto, L. E., Portelli, J. P., Rottman, C., Pashby, K., Barrett, S. E., & Mujawamariya, D. (2012). Charismatic, competent, or transformative? Ontario school administrators' perceptions of "good teachers". *Journal of Teaching and Learning, 8*(1), 73–90. https://doi.org/10.22329/JTL.V8I1.3052

Pollock, K. (2010). Marginalization and the occasional teacher workforce in Ontario: The case of internationally educated teachers (IETs). *Canadian Journal of Educational Administration and Policy, 100*, 1–21.

Pratt, D. D. (2002). Good teaching: One size fits all? *New Directions for Adult and Continuing Education, 2002*(93), 5–16. https://doi.org/10.1002/ace.45

Reid, C., Collins, J., & Singh, M. (2014). *Global teachers, Australian perspectives: Goodbye Mr chips, hello Ms Banerjee* (1st ed.). Springer. https://doi.org/10.1007/978-981-4451-36-9

Robertson, S. L. (2012). Placing teachers in global governance agendas. *Comparative Education Review, 56*(4), 584–607. https://doi.org/10.1086/667414

Robertson, S. (2013). *Transnational student-migrants and the state: The education-migration nexus.* Palgrave Macmillan. https://doi.org/10.1057/9781137267085

Rosa, J. (2019). *Looking like a language, sounding like a race: Raciolinguistic ideologies and the learning of Latinidad.* Oxford University Press. https://doi.org/10.1093/oso/9780190634728.001.0001

Schmidt, C. (2010). Systemic discrimination as a barrier for immigrant teachers. *Diaspora, Indigenous, and Minority Education, 4*(4), 235–252. https://doi.org/10.1080/15595692.2010.513246

Schmidt, C. (2016). Herculean efforts are not enough: Diversifying the teaching profession and the need for systemic change. *Intercultural Education, 26*(6), 584–592. https://doi.org/10.1080/14675986.2015.1109776

Scott, C., Safdar, S., Trilokekar, R. D., & El Masri, A. (2015). International students as 'ideal immigrants' in Canada: A disconnect between policy makers' assumptions and the lived experiences of international students. *Comparative and International Education/Éducation Comparée et Internationale, 43*(3). https://doi.org/10.5206/cie-eci.v43i3.9261

Seidman, I. (2006). *Interviewing as qualitative research: A guide for researchers in education and the social sciences* (3rd ed.). Teacher College Press.

Sidhu, R. (2006). *Universities and globalization: To market, to market.* Lawrence Erlbaum Associates Publishers.

Simpson, J. S., James, C. E., & Mack, J. (2011). Multiculturalism, colonialism, and racialization: Conceptual starting points. *Review of Education, Pedagogy, and Cultural Studies, 33*(4), 285–305. https://doi.org/10.1080/10714413.2011.597637

Sleeter, C. E. (2008). Equity, democracy, and neoliberal assaults on teacher education. *Teaching and Teacher Education, 24*(8), 1947–1957. https://doi.org/10.1016/j.tate.2008.04.003

Sleeter, C. E., & Milner, H. R. (2011). Researching successful efforts in teacher education to diversify teachers. In A. F. Ball & C. A. Tyson (Eds.), *Studying diversity in teacher education* (pp. 81–104). Rowman & Littlefield.

Solórzano, D., & Yosso, T. J. (2002). Critical race methodology: Counter-storytelling as an analytical framework for education research. *Qualitative Inquiry, 8*(1), 23–44. https://doi.org/10.1177/107780040200800103

Solórzano, D., Ceja, M., & Yosso, T. J. (2000). Critical race theory, racial microaggressions, and campus racial climate: The experiences of African American college students. *The Journal of Negro Education, 69*(1/2), 60–73.

Sorensen, T. B, & Robertson, S. L. (2018). The OECD program TALIS and framing, measuring and selling quality teacher™. In M. Akiba & G. K. LeTendre (Eds.), *International handbook of teacher quality and policy* (pp. 117–131). Routledge. https://doi.org/10.4324/9781315710068

St. Denis, V. (2011). Silencing Aboriginal curricular content and perspectives through multiculturalism: 'There are other children here'. *Review of Education, Pedagogy & Cultural Studies, 33*(4), 306–317. https://doi.org/10.1080/10714413.2011.597638

Statistics Canada. (2019). *Number and salaries of full-time teaching staff at Canadian Universities (final), 2018/2019.* https://www150.statcan.gc.ca/n1/daily-quotidien/191125/dq191125b-eng.htm

Statistics Canada. (2020). *Survey of postsecondary faculty and researchers, 2019.* https://www150.statcan.gc.ca/n1/daily-quotidien/200922/dq200922a-eng.htm

Statistics Canada. (2021). *Visible minority of person.* https://www23.statcan.gc.ca/imdb/p3Var.pl?Function=DEC&Id=45152

Sue, D. W. (2010). *Microaggressions in everyday life: Race, gender, and sexual orientation.* Wiley.

Tran, L. T., & Vu, T. T. P. (2016). "I'm not like that, why treat me the same way?" The impact of stereotyping international students on their learning, employability, and connectedness with the workplace. *The Australian Educational Researcher, 43*, 203–220. https://doi.org/10.1007/s13384-015-0198-8

Trilokekar, R. D., & El Masri, A. (2019). "International students are...golden": Canada's changing policy contexts, approaches, and national peculiarities in attracting international students as future immigrants. In M.-J Kwak & A. H. Kim (Eds.), *Outward and upward mobilities: International students in Canada, their families, and structuring institutions* (pp. 25–55). University of Toronto Press. https://doi.org/10.3138/9781487530563

Vertovec, S. (2019). Talking around superdiversity. *Ethnic and Racial Studies, 42*(1), 125–139. https://doi.org/10.1080/01419870.2017.1406128

Walsh, S. C., Brigham, S. M., & Wang, Y. (2011). Internationally educated female teachers in the neoliberal context: Their labour market and teacher certification experiences in Canada. *Teaching and Teacher Education, 27*(3), 657–665. https://doi.org/10.1016/j.tate.2010.11.004

Weis, L., & Dolby, N. (Eds.). (2012). *Social class and education: Global perspectives*. Routledge. https://doi.org/10.4324/9780203829202

Lilach Marom is an assistant professor at Simon Fraser University. In her research Lilach draws on critical social theories to focus on questions of diversity, anti-racism, and social justice in teacher education. Her research aims to highlight structural and institutional barriers to the diversification of teacher education and the teaching profession. Lilach has worked as an educator in multiple locations and countries (Israel, the United States, and Canada) with culturally, linguistically, and ethnically diverse populations. Her research has appeared in publications such as *Review of Education, Pedagogy, and Cultural Studies* (2017), *Teaching and Teacher Education* (2019/2020), Race *Ethnicity and Education* (2019), *Critical Studies in Education* (2019), Globalisation, *Societies and Education* (2021), and Higher Education (2022). Email: lmarom@sfu.ca

Sensitising Teachers to Prejudices in Representations of Indigenous Peoples in EFL Textbooks

Helen Margaret Murray

Abstract This chapter considers how teachers can be sensitised to prejudices in representations of minority groups in EFL textbooks, focusing in particular on the teaching of topics relating to Indigenous peoples. The importance of heightening teachers' critical awareness of these portrayals is linked to the development of intercultural and pluricultural competences, and how teaching materials may promote or hinder the development of these competences. Extracts from a chapter in an EFL textbook used in Norway for students aged 13–16 are discussed and both strengths and weaknesses in the representations of Indigenous peoples in texts and the content of the tasks are highlighted. Finally, this chapter considers how textbook analysis can be included in modules in teacher education programmes to encourage teachers to gain critical awareness, to make them sensitive to the challenges and to give them tools for teaching topics relating to minority groups in the classroom.

Keywords Textbook · Intercultural competence · Pluricultural competence · Indigenous peoples · Teacher education

1 Introduction

Teaching in the language classroom should not only focus on the development of learners' linguistic abilities but should also include learning about cultural diversity and understandings that enable learners to communicate successfully with people from backgrounds other than their own. Topics relating to culture should therefore be a central feature of language teaching, and it is important that we, as teacher

H. M. Murray (✉)
Department of Teacher Education, Norwegian University of Science and Technology (NTNU), Trondheim, Norway
e-mail: helen.m.murray@ntnu.no

A. Sahlane, R. Pritchard (eds.), *English as an International Language Education*, English Language Education 33, https://doi.org/10.1007/978-3-031-34702-3_7

educators, encourage teachers in the acquisition of knowledge and abilities necessary to teach cultural aspects in their classrooms.

Cultural elements in language teaching are found in wide ranging documents that influence language teaching internationally; among these is the Council of Europe's Framework of Reference (CEFR) (Council of Europe, 2001). The aim of the CEFR is "to train citizens, who can not only live together harmoniously in their multilingual and multicultural society but also act effectively in their school and workplace" (Acar, 2021, p.1). In the Common European Framework of Reference Companion Volume, learners are represented as *social agents*, and "as a social agent, each individual forms relationships with a widening cluster of overlapping social groups, which together define identity" (Council of Europe, 2001, p.1). Therefore, education should aim to nurture in students the skills needed to enable them to live and participate in multilingual and multicultural societies, and to successfully build relationships within diverse social groups.

An important element in the CEFR's approaches to language learning is seeing knowledge as both plurilingual and pluricultural. One general *knowledge bank* is created, which the individual can access and draw on in different contexts. Language learning is linked to cultural learning as it allows the learners "to use all their linguistic resources when necessary, encouraging them to see similarities and regularities as well as differences between languages and cultures" (Council of Europe, 2020, p.30). This encourages a holistic approach to learning about cultures where culture is seen as behaviours, ways of living and thinking, rather than being object-based (Murray, 2021). This approach may also be present in national curricula, such as in the author's own home country, Norway, where students are required to learn in all subjects about Indigenous peoples, and in particular the Indigenous people of Norway, the Sámi. In the Norwegian curriculum, classroom content should be cross-curricular, and activities should draw on topics covered in other classes, build connections, and consider knowledge as a whole, rather than regarding each subject knowledge as a separate entity.

Textbooks are still a major resource in English as a Foreign Language (EFL) teaching, and it is important that teacher education programmes train pre-service teachers in how to be critical users of educational materials, especially when working with texts and tasks involving minorities and/or groups that have been historically oppressed. Regarding the inclusion of Indigenous materials, teachers should be aware that representations in textbooks can make many books dangerous to Indigenous readers: "(1) they do not reinforce our values, actions, customs, culture and identity; (2) when they tell us about others they are saying that we do not exist; (3) they may be writing about us but are writing things which are untrue; and (4) they are writing about us but saying negative and insensitive things which tell us that we are no good" (Smith, 2012, p.36).

Such representations are not only biased against students from Indigenous or other minority backgrounds, but they are also problematic regardless of the learners' ethnicity, as they reinforce and create negative stereotypes, and perpetuate historical inequalities. It is vital that we have a two-sided approach to working with these challenges in teacher education programmes. Firstly, we should educate teachers by increasing their knowledge about minority cultures, and by sensitising them to the need to challenge stereotypes about cultural others. Secondly, we should empower teachers by training them to tackle social justice topics to promote intercultural sensitivity and empathy in their own multicultural classes.

This chapter will focus on an example from one particular EFL textbook in Norwegian secondary schools that is used by the author when educating teachers about the representations of Indigenous peoples in Norwegian EFL textbooks. The aim of textual analysis of this example is to sensitise teachers to prejudices that may occur towards Indigenous peoples and the social injustices that textbook portrayals may engender, and to promote a critical awareness of teaching materials. From the author's own experiences in teacher education programmes, activities like these can be eye-opening for teachers and can help them develop important analytical skills that they can use in their classrooms.

The texts and tasks from the textbook analysed in this chapter aim to teach students about Indigenous cultures and identities in Australia and New Zealand. While the textbook is published for the Norwegian curriculum, the topics of the chapter are those commonly found in textbooks for intermediate learners of English worldwide. Although the discussion in this chapter focuses on teaching about Indigenous peoples specifically, the points made here are relevant for teaching about all cultures outside of the learners' own and can be directly transferred to the creation and selection of teaching materials about diverse cultural topics, also those found on websites both in written and oral form.

2   Theoretical Background

The following section will discuss several theoretical aspects of learning about cultures that have particular relevance for teaching about minority cultures. Interculturality and intercultural competence are fundamental elements in the Norwegian curriculum, and students are to work with developing competence throughout their education. However, for all language learners, not only those in Norway, developing cultural awareness is an important part of improving language skills, as these skills will not be used in isolation, but in interaction with people from other cultures and with diverse social identities.

2.1   Intercultural Competence, Pluriculturalism and Inclusion of Diversities

A focus on intercultural competence should be included in the language classroom to encourage learners to become *social agents* who can live with and form relations with people from different backgrounds and cultures. According to Byram et al.

(2002), for learners to develop intercultural competence, activities involving development of attitudes, skills, and knowledge must be included in teaching modules. Learners should be encouraged to meet other cultures with curiosity and openness, improve their communication skills and their knowledge of how social groups and identities function and interact with each other. They must foster an understanding of how people from different social groups might interpret the same situation differently, and how their own beliefs and values affect how they view the world and relate to other people. Relating new cultural knowledge to existing knowledge, and to their experience of their own cultures, learners should be encouraged to see both similarities and differences between known and unknown cultures. In addition, they must also learn strategies for acquisition of new knowledge and the flexibility to be able to add to or amend existing knowledge (Byram et al., pp.11–13).

The multifaceted skills and knowledge that the learners gain through acquiring intercultural competence may also be linked to the development of learner's plurilingual and pluricultural competence. By attaining pluricultural competence, learners gain insight into how "the various cultures (national, regional, social) to which [a] person has gained access do not simply co-exist side by side; they are compared, contrasted and actively interact" (Council of Europe, 2001, p.6). Plurilingualism and pluriculturalism are closely tied together and are seen as two parallel sides of learners' developing competence. In teaching about culture, "language is not only a major aspect of culture, but also a means of access to cultural manifestations" (Council of Europe, 2001, p.6). This means that "words and contexts are two mirrors facing each other, infinitely and simultaneously reflecting each other" (Gee, 2014, p.190).

In developing both intercultural and pluricultural competences, we want, as educators, to avoid the replication and reinforcement of pre-existing prejudices in societies, and *essentialist* understandings of culture. *Essentialism* encompasses "the idea that cultural identity is tied to country or a language, and that a person from a given culture is essentially different from someone with another cultural background" (Hoff, 2018, p. 76). An essentialist outlook focuses on group behaviours rather than on the individual's opinions and choices, and may reduce cultures to one single representation, which can in turn lead to reinforcements of stereotypes. When discussing cultural topics, we should rather aim for non-essentialist representations which portray the dynamic and diverse nature of cultures (Murray, 2022).

It is important to emphasise that people's cultural backgrounds are not the same as their national identity. In the modern world, with international activities online and widespread migration, individuals may have membership of several different cultures, which are utilised or discarded depending on the setting (Zhu, 2015, pp. 72–73). For example, people may be united across nations in interests such as supporting football teams, or in online gaming sites, or in political or social interest groups. For some people, these cultures may be stronger than any tie to the nation in which they live. Social identities are also not static, and throughout their lives learners will change and develop their own identity and similarly meet others of different and changing identities. Dervin (2016) discusses how, rather than talking of a single *diversity*, we should talk of *diversities*. This is important for teachers to be aware of when working with topics involving ethnic minority groups, as currently "while the word diversity should refer to multiplicity, it often means difference and 'oneness'" (p.28). This *oneness* is common in the representations of Indigenous peoples in teaching materials, which are often stereotypical and lacking in meaningful engagement (Murray, 2021). For teacher educators, encouraging the inclusion of *diversities* in teaching materials means making teachers firstly aware that the range of authentic perspectives in textbooks may be lacking, and secondly, training them to find and include a wider range of perspectives in the classroom.

2.2 Textbook Representations of Indigenous Peoples

Textbooks are a widely used educational resource in schools across the world. Educating teachers on how to assess textbook suitability should be an important element in teacher education programmes. This includes creating an awareness of textbooks' potential shortcomings, and encouraging teachers' acquisition of tools to use in the analysis of teaching materials. EFL textbooks may contain representations of cultures that present artificial environments, as choices are made by authors and editors about what to include and exclude as examples of the target cultures, and the ways in which people from diverse backgrounds are presented. These prevalent tendencies in textbooks constitute "very particular constructions of reality in which English is given a range of specific associations" (Gray, 2010, p.12) and may potentially encourage the creation and perpetuation of essentialist or stereotypical representations of Indigenous and marginalised cultures.

Research into textbook portrayals of Indigenous peoples has often revealed them to be stereotypical (Brown & Habegger-Conti, 2017; Lund, 2016; Olsen, 2017). These one-sided depictions may reduce cultures to specific, often exotic, characteristics rather than looking at present day ways of living and ways of thinking (Brown & Habegger-Conti, 2017). Indigenous cultures are presented in a selection of static objects rather than as living cultures, including belief systems and ways of life. Indigenous peoples are often shown only in traditional clothing and settings, which can "run the risk of reinforcing the stereotype of Indigenous people as traditional, primitive, and unable to assimilate with the modern world" (Brown & Habegger-Conti, 2017, p.23). Relations to coloniser nations are often skimmed over briefly, or direct reference to invasion and oppression is bypassed by presenting information in the passive voice. In this way, direct reference is avoided as to who did what to whom.

Stereotyping within portrayals of Indigenous peoples may lead to the *othering* of people from Indigenous cultures. *Othering* occurs when a group of people is set apart from the majority society, and is often imbued with negative characteristics. Words such as *we, us* and *our* are widely used about the majority society, while the Indigenous group is referred to as *them* (Smith, 2012, p.37). With *othering* a power imbalance may be recreated and reinforced. It is essential to be aware of this when working with teaching materials about Indigenous peoples, as the inequality in the balance of power is a characteristic of relations between Indigenous and mainstream white settler societies. Teachers should be aware that teaching materials often skim over larger, controversial issues such as racism and colonial oppression (Smith, 2012, p.37). For example, when learners are invited to discuss positive and negative sides of colonisation, the story is often told from Western perspectives; for instance, saying that Columbus *discovered* the Americas. Including an Indigenous point of view would require presenting this historical event differently or offering an alternative interpretation, such as describing the arrival of Europeans as an "invasion" and Columbus as a villainous figure.

Teaching materials should focus on both similarities and differences that exist between cultural groups; they may disregard the differences that can perpetuate historical power imbalances. Teachers need to learn how to create teaching modules and promote practices that focus on developing intercultural understanding and addressing inequalities in the relations between social and cultural groups. Bringing inequalities to light can be an important aspect of working with these topics in the classroom.

2.3   Approaches to Teaching about Indigenous Peoples

One approach to counteract essentialist and stereotypical portrayals of Indigenous peoples in textbooks, and to include diverse voices and perspectives in the classroom, can be through the *indigenisation* of teaching materials. This means using a range of authentic content in which Indigenous voices are included, by referencing Indigenous perspectives on topics, and by the inclusion of texts written by Indigenous authors (Olsen, 2017, p.72). When working with topics that explicitly mention Indigenous peoples, it is natural to include these authentic voices. However, these voices need not be restricted to topics in the curriculum where explicit focus is required, but also where Indigenous perspectives on the issues may be anticipated (e.g. when working on environmental issues, land ownership, etc). Exactly how much of the teaching material for a module should include authentic Indigenous perspectives can depend on the topic being studied and how relevant it is to the lives of Indigenous communities. While all students should learn about Indigenous perspectives, for those of Indigenous background or living in areas with an Indigenous population, it is natural to include a greater amount of Indigenous content. Teachers may also want to focus more on Indigenous perspectives at certain times of year, such as around Australia Day or Columbus Day, and depending on current affairs, both in their locality and worldwide. While *indigenisation* is focused particularly on Indigenous peoples, the concept is equally valid for all minority groups, and the inclusion of minority voices should be a natural part of discussion in the classroom. Including these perspectives can give the learners a greater insight into the complexities and challenges of societies worldwide and improve their cultural knowledge repertoires.

In addition to giving access to a range of authentic teaching materials, meaningful dialogue is an essential element in the development of linguistic and cultural competence. This *meaningfulness* in the dialogue requires learners to engage in activities that demand real communication in authentic situations. Activities can be action-oriented, focused on being realistic, engaging and encouraging students to work with real life situations where intercultural communication takes place. Actions can, for example, take the form of mini projects where they work with a particular issue. These mini projects should aim to equip them with skills "such as personal autonomy, collective responsibility, group work, information management, negotiation, design and implementation of complex actions since these skills are important for language learners to live and work successfully in their democratic society" (Acar, 2019, p.122).

Dialogue is an essential element in intercultural competence as skills are developed through communication with others and it "lays the ground for the formation of values and democratic thinking" (Hoff, 2018, p.80). Activities involving dialogue can also enable students to build their pluricultural repertoires which enables them "to communicate effectively in a multilingual context and/or in a classic mediation situation in which the other people do not share a common language" (Council of Europe, 2020, p.127). It is through meetings with individuals from other cultural backgrounds, with concomitant misunderstandings, communication successes and breakdowns, that learning about other cultures can occur (Dervin, 2016, pp.83–84). Consequently, challenging topics should not be avoided in the classroom, but should rather be seen a starting point for dialogue that can promote personal growth and intercultural awareness.

3   Methodology

In the following section, a chapter from an EFL textbook used in Norway is analysed for strengths and weaknesses in how Indigenous peoples are portrayed and in how students are to engage with the topics covered. Textbook chapters like this one are used by the author in pre-service and in-service teacher education programmes to illustrate how minorities can be portrayed in foreign language textbooks. The textbook chapter discussed here is from *Enter 9* (Diskin & Winsvold, 2020), an EFL book aimed at grade nine students (15 years old) in Norwegian schools. This textbook has been chosen as it is produced by one of the four major Norwegian publishing houses and is currently used in Norwegian schools. The analysed chapter is about the topic "Australia and New Zealand", which is common in EFL textbooks in global teaching contexts. Therefore, while the comments here are specific to the Norwegian textbook, the texts and tasks should be relatable for teachers working in EFL classrooms worldwide.

As this textbook is aimed at upper-intermediate learners, the chapter contains longer written texts, and is less illustration-based than textbooks for lower grades and levels of language competency. I have chosen to focus on these written texts in the following analysis. For a project of larger scope or when working with textbooks for lower grades or for learners with lower levels of competency, it may also be useful to analyse multimodality in the textbooks, for example, the use of pictures and illustrations, as these may play a larger role in the learning materials.

In this chapter, I have primarily considered the content included and the discourses on Indigenous peoples. Discourses can reflect power relations in society, and critical discourse analysis can reveal how patterns of domination and inequalities in power are maintained through normalising ways of speaking about relevant topics in mainstream society. While a detailed analysis is not attempted here, some general tendencies are highlighted. An awareness of these tendencies can be transferred to other situations and used by teachers when creating teaching materials or working with course textbooks.

4 Analysis and Discussion

The chapter "Australia and New Zealand" in the EFL textbook *Enter 9* aims to cover the requirements of the Norwegian EFL curriculum which is mandatory in all schools in Norway. The chapter focuses on the curriculum goal "explore and reflect on the situation of Indigenous peoples in the English-speaking world and in Norway" (The Norwegian Directorate for Education and Training, 2019). Certain elements of the chapter may also relate to another goal, to "explore and describe ways of living, thinking, communication patterns and diversity in the English-speaking world" (The Norwegian Directorate for Education and Training, 2019). Similar goals may be found in other curricula, such as those suggested in the CEFR for developing pluricultural competence, including building relations between learners' own and foreign cultures, building knowledge to enable successful communication and being culturally sensitive in communication.

The chapter is 43 pages long and is split between Australia and New Zealand. The primary focus of the chapter is on the Indigenous peoples of both Australia and New Zealand, as is reflected in the introductory page of the chapter, where the chapter's "Topic Words" are "way of life, identity, respect, Indigenous people, Aboriginal, Māori, sacred and discrimination". Students are also encouraged to activate their previous knowledge by the introductory question "What do you know about Australia and New Zealand? What would you like to know?" (Diskin & Winsvold, 2020, p.155). For students, this activation of previous knowledge and interests may encourage a closer relationship between known and unknown materials and help them to gain awareness of the gaps in their knowledge that they need to fill.

There are ten different texts in the chapter, and they offer the students a range of genres to read, including a longer quotation from a speech by the Prime Minister, an extract from a novel, a traditional story, two poems and other factual articles and interviews with young people. The wide range of genres exposes the learners to diverse voices and perspectives, both those of young people and older people, Indigenous and non-Indigenous. Three of the texts are written by Indigenous authors, one is a traditional Māori myth with author unknown, and Indigenous young people's voices are heard in a fifth text in which several Māori teens are interviewed, along with teens of other ethnic backgrounds. This means that half of all the texts clearly reflect Indigenous voices, an excellent step towards an *indigenisation* of teaching materials and diversity in representations.

Considering the images and other illustrations used in the chapter, over half of all photos or drawn illustrations show people. These people range in age from teenagers to adults, both male and female. There are slightly more young than older people, as may be expected in a textbook aimed at teenagers. There are more depictions of Indigenous peoples than non-Indigenous, which fits with the themes of the chapter, and most of these photos involve people making direct contact with the reader and/or looking happy. The Indigenous peoples are shown in different situations, such as a photo of a young girl surfing on the first page of the chapter, or a group of teenagers in modern clothing lying on grass together. There are also a few photos of Indigenous peoples in traditional dress. Hence, the photos and illustrations in the chapter reflect Indigenous cultures as modern and living, and people as part of contemporary life.

4.1   Analysis and Discussion of Texts

The chapter starts off with a text called "Q&A" in which ten questions about Australia and New Zealand are answered (Diskin & Winsvold, 2020, pp.156–160). The questions cover the history of Australia and New Zealand and briefly discuss several terms commonly used in relation to Indigenous peoples. In the answer to the question "How did things change in Australia after the Europeans arrived?", a number of different active and passive constructions are used:

> The Europeans drove the Aboriginal people off their land, and many died during conflict or of European diseases. The Aboriginal Australians were generally treated badly and discriminated against by the Europeans. In fact, many Aboriginal children were removed from their families (…) It is estimated that over 25,000 children were taken from their families (Diskin & Winsvold, 2020, p.159).

This extract contains a strong opening sentence with an active voice, which clearly states who has done what to whom. The following sentence contains a passive construction, but it is made clear in the prepositional phrase at the end of this sentence who has done this action to the Aboriginal Australians ("by Europeans"). However, further in this same text, the author has chosen to use passive constructions without including a prepositional phrase. Use of the passive form, like is exemplified here, can be a way of avoiding the inclusion of an explicit agent with an active voice. Passive constructions are common in texts discussing Indigenous people's history and relations to the coloniser nations, as they remove focus from the person who is involved in the action (Olsen, 2017, p.77). By using passive constructions, textbook authors can avoid directly addressing inequalities in power relations and problematic historical relations. Using examples, such as the one from this text, can encourage teachers to become aware of this tendency in the teaching materials that they use in their classrooms. However, it is also important to point out that all use of passive constructions is not necessarily a deliberate avoidance of an active agent. Passives can also be used to create variety in language use within a text and they can improve textual fluency. So, while teachers should be made aware of tendencies, over-generalisations should be avoided.

Other questions in this text refer to Indigenous cultures. For example, the question "Were Europeans the first people in Australia and New Zealand?" discusses Indigenous peoples and their cultures:

> They were organized in tribes, each with their own identity traditions and culture. The Māori came from Polynesia in canoes or waka. They called New Zealand Aotearoa, or Land of the Long White Cloud. The Māori settled on the coast and ate food as they hunted, gathered and farmed. They lived in groups, usually peacefully, and developed a strong identity and a tradition of story-telling and art, mainly wood carvings (Diskin & Winsvold, 2020, p.158).

In this extract, the Māori are active agents, and the story is told from their perspectives. Reference is made to diverse ways of living, identity, and cultural expressions. Culture is shown through ways of life rather than through only object-based representations. It is also notable that a word from Te Reo, the Māori language, is referenced. Words in Te Reo are integrated throughout the chapter in the different texts and show the language in use in a natural setting, including a short wordlist with some key Māori words and terms in connection with the poem *I am Māori* by Marilyn Gardiner (Diskin & Winsvold, 2020, p.195).

While the example above shows a good response, the answer to the question "What do Aboriginal people mean when they talk about the Dreaming?" is less informative:

> According to Aboriginal belief, all life as it is today can be traced back to the Great Spirit Ancestors of the Dreaming. This is the beginning of knowledge from which all the great stories and Aboriginal laws have their origin. For survival, these laws and stories must be respected even today (Diskin & Winsvold, 2020, p.159).

While this extract is clearly focused on Aboriginal cultures, it is lacking in informative content, making it hard to engage with. What sort of knowledge? What stories and what laws? What is meant by "for survival"? Who is going to survive and how? The extract needs to be developed and explored further for it to have real meaning for learners. Textual extracts like this one, can be used to improve teachers' awareness of the potential limitations of textbook content and invite discussion of how adjustments or extra teaching material can foster greater student engagement.

Discussion of modern-day cultures is found later in the same chapter, in a text about results from a study published in the *New Zealand Journal of Psychology* where young people discuss their relationship to their own ethnicity. This text explicitly discusses the imbalance of power between Indigenous and non-Indigenous peoples. Regarding the attitudes of the non-Indigenous teens, the text includes the statement that "Pākehā[1] teens felt proud to be Kiwi and acknowledge the privileges of being part of the dominant culture" (Diskin & Winsvold, 2020, p.177). The following paragraph in this text starts by stating Māori teens are "proud of their Indigenous culture, language and kapa haka, showing a sense of pride. "It's just cool being Māori"" (Diskin & Winsvold, 2020, p.177). People from both cultural backgrounds are portrayed as equals, proud of their heritage. The text continues to discuss racism, discrimination, and stereotyping, with multiple direct references to comments made by teens from different ethnic backgrounds. Such reference to situations where racism occurs makes it easier for students to grasp a sense of how and which issues might arise, "When we go to the shops after school, I'm the only one who gets asked to leave my bags at the door" (Diskin & Winsvold, 2020, pp.177–178). This rule is commonly imposed in shops where shoplifting is a problem and will be recognisable to many of the students reading this text. However, here it reflects racism within society as it is only the Indigenous young people who are considered as potential shoplifters. This text concludes with the Pākehā (European) perspective, where the teen interviewed comments "It's just so much easier to fit in, just socially it is easier". Apart from that she is unwilling to comment on other positive aspects of being part of dominant European settler community, commenting "I don't have a culture".

The final section is a list of pros and cons for "Being Pākehā", "Being Māori", "Being Samoan" and "Being Chinese" (Diskin & Winsvold, 2020, p.178). The pros for each group refer to cultural aspects. These are presented in terms that are recognised as positive cultural features, such as "feeling proud about tangata whenua" (Māori), "strong emphasis on family and values" (Samoan) and "delicious food, a rich heritage" (Chinese). It is interesting to note that the pros for being Pākehā are not so openly positive, but rather the interview mentions the focus on being "part of majority group, feel[ing] normal and blend[ing] in". The cons for the being Māori, Samoan and Chinese refer mainly directly to negative stereotypes, such as "violent and criminal" (Māori), "act[ing] like "gangsters" or be[ing] dumb and "fresh off the boat" (Samoan) and "one-dimensional" (Chinese) (Diskin & Winsvold, 2020, p.178). Again, the cons for Pākehā are slightly different in that the focus is on what non-Pākehā perceive Pākehā as thinking about people of another background, rather than focusing on features of their own culture; "being racist, teased for being white, guilty about past" (Diskin & Winsvold, 2020, p.178).

This text is interesting in that it directly addresses issues around identity, stereotyping and racism and shows a diversity of perspectives from multiple ethnic minorities within New Zealand. It can engage learners in the topic and can relate to their own experiences of living in multicultural societies. The positioning and the comments from the Pākehā teen can also be addressed and the reasons why she might claim "I don't have a culture". What ideas lie behind this statement? Do they relate to an awareness of privilege and history and a wish to distance oneself from history, or do they reflect that the European New Zealander culture is the norm for this teen and therefore doesn't feel like a particular culture?

---

[1] New Zealander with European heritage.

Considering the examples from two texts from this textbook chapter, Indigenous peoples are shown as diverse, linked to different cultures and ways of living, and both historical and current day aspects of Indigenous lives are discussed. Indigenous peoples are shown as clear participants in modern day life. Some parts of the text are lacking in further explanation and need development, while some parts could be rewritten to include an active agent. These texts presents both common shortcomings and strengths in textbooks in general and are aspects that teachers can find in the teaching materials used in their own classes.

4.2   Analysis and Discussion of Tasks

As well as exposure to relevant textual content to facilitate the development of intercultural and pluricultural competences, it is necessary to create tasks that encourage learners to increase skills in reflection, expression and interaction with other people. Therefore, as well as looking at strengths and weaknesses of texts presented in teaching materials, it is equally important to consider the content and aims of the tasks.

In the chapter on Indigenous peoples in the textbook, there is one task that comes up seven times throughout. In this task students are asked to "Find words and phrases that describe the Māori and Aboriginal people. Are these words positively or negatively loaded?" (Diskin & Winsvold, 2020, p.161). This task is notable as it encourages the development of learners' critical awareness of texts, and of how cultures are represented and how these representations may be biased. This can lead to discussions of the ways in which power imbalances can be recreated in texts and how they can be addressed. The repetition of this task in connection with several texts throughout the chapter enables students to practise and develop their critical thinking skills in class discussion. In the final set of tasks in the chapter, they are encouraged to test their abilities outside of the textbook, in a task where they are to find a website about Aboriginal Australians or Māori and "find examples of words that are positively or negatively loaded" (Diskin & Winsvold, 2020, p.198). By completing this task, the students have made a connection from the artificial environment of the textbook to the real world. This is then a skill that they can take into reading in other subjects and in other situations, both within and outside of the school setting.

Other tasks in the chapter, this time related to an extract from Kevin Rudd's apology to the Indigenous peoples of Australia in 2008, ask the following three questions as well as the question about positively and negatively loaded words:

1. This speech is one of the most important speeches in the history of Australia. Why do you think this is?
2. Who are "we" in this speech?
3. This is an example of a successful speech. Why do you think this is so? (Diskin & Winsvold, 2020, p.169)

These three questions encourage students to engage with the content of the speech in depth. The speech is described in the first and third questions using positive words such as *important* and *successful*. These reveal the author's attitude to the topic and it is clear that they think an apology to Indigenous peoples was necessary and that this speech was a positive event. Using this text as an example, teachers can then be encouraged to consider use of adjectives in other texts and what they reveal about the writer's perspectives, which can enable them to make informed choices over which teaching materials they want to use in their classrooms.

The first and third questions also involve the students thinking about why the speech was made, which encourages reflection over Aboriginal history in Australia and relations between Indigenous and non-Indigenous communities, and inequalities in the balance of power between these communities. The second question, where learners consider who *we* are, encourages them to think about how pronouns are used in texts to construct in-group and out-group identities. Here in this text, the *we* are the members of parliament of Australia, the chosen representatives of the people and the governing body of the country. While this *we* (ingroup) does exclude Indigenous peoples (outgroup), the speech is directly spoken to them, as is natural in an apology. This question could be used as a springboard into the topic of *othering* in texts. While *othering* is not discussed in this chapter in *Enter 9*, this is a point at which a teacher could add extra teaching materials to show how *we* may be used to exclude certain groups in society.

In several tasks throughout the chapter, the students are encouraged to bring the knowledge they have gained back to their understanding of their own cultures. For example, one task asks them to:

(a) Discuss how you feel when you are negatively stereotyped.
(b) Come up with good ideas for how to avoid stereotypes (Diskin & Winsvold, 2020, p.179).

The first question asks the students to relate what they have read about ethnic minorities being stereotyped to their own experiences; this both encourages in-depth and emotional engagement with the topic and the development of awareness of the learner's own cultures, which is an aspect of intercultural competence. The second question promotes meaningful interaction with the reflections from the first question, by asking them to come up with their own ideas for avoiding stereotypes. This encourages social action and the development of skills that can be used in real life when meeting and communicating with people from other countries.

There are two tasks in the chapter that ask the students to relate what they have just learnt to what they know about the Sámi in Norway. While it is positive that the Sámi are mentioned, these questions could be developed further. Cross-curricular links could be made to what is learnt in other subjects where the Sámi are mentioned in specific curriculum aims. The first task, following from Rudd's speech, prompts learners:

The Australian prime minister apologized to the Indigenous peoples of Australia. Find out whether the Norwegian authorities have done the same to the Indigenous peoples of Norway (Diskin & Winsvold, 2020, p.169).

The second task, coming after the poem *Spiritual Song of the Aborigine* by Hyllus Maris, asks:

> Choose some words that could have been used in a similar poem about the Indigenous peoples of Norway, the Sámi (Diskin & Winsvold, 2020, p.197).

Both these are examples of tasks that can potentially be interesting and engaging for learners, but which need further development. The first is a yes/no question and is lacking the *why* follow-up that encourages them to engage more deeply. The teachers may choose to add this aspect to the task themselves. The second question would require that students have a good previous knowledge of Sámi cultures to avoid the reproduction of stereotypes. This task, while interesting, needs guidance from the teacher in content and potential input on Sámi cultures. Again, there is a *why* aspect lacking. For example, in the second task, students could also reflect on why they have chosen these particular words. If they find them linked to stereotypical ideas about Sámi people, an opportunity could arise in class to discuss and address these concerns.

While teachers outside of Norway are unlikely to focus on the Sámi in their classes, similar questions about Indigenous peoples in other parts of the world could be included in modules about Indigenous peoples. These questions would tie learners' new knowledge of Australia and New Zealand to what they have learnt about other countries, helping them to see their knowledge about Indigenous peoples holistically, rather than as a series of separate entities, encouraging a pluricultural approach to learning about cultures.

5   Implications for Teacher Education Programmes

Working with an analysis of the texts and tasks in a school textbook, as is exemplified in the previous section, may be used in training programmes to sensitise teachers to the portrayals of Indigenous peoples in educational materials. By analysing materials from a textbook that is currently in use in schools, both pre-service and in-service teachers can critically engage with materials in their daily teaching activities. Together with teacher educators, strengths and weaknesses of the textbooks can be explored, and general points for critically assessing teaching materials extrapolated.

Regarding choice of texts, teachers should be made aware of the importance of using textbooks or creating teaching materials that offer a diverse range of voices and perspectives. When working with learning modules about ethnic minority groups, texts should as far as possible be written by authors from the ethnic minority. Authentic materials in a range of genres can encourage real engagement in learning about cultural topics in the classroom. It is important that sufficient information is given about the topics for them to be meaningful for learners and to promote the development of intercultural and pluricultural competences.

Teachers should also be encouraged to consider the language used in texts and tasks. For example, is the passive voice used and if so, why? They can look at who the active agents are, which may in turn encourage an awareness of the perspectives from which the texts and tasks are written. Illustrations can also be considered. Teachers can look at these and discuss who is shown in pictures and photos and what are they doing? Is there diversity in the representations and how do they compare with portrayals of other minoritised and marginalised groups in the textbook? A critical awareness of the perspectives shown in a text can be developed. For example, teachers can look at whether *othering* of minorities occurs, and what words and phrases are used in describing ethnic minority groups. If texts include negative attitudes and prejudices towards them, or if power imbalances are shown, students should be encouraged to become critically aware of such tendencies. Tasks such as the one in the textbook chapter which considered positively and negatively loaded words can aid the development of this awareness.

In working with this topic in teacher education programmes, teachers should look at the tasks found in textbooks. They can also consider if tasks may potentially reproduce essentialist or stereotypical attitudes or if they encourage students to reflect over their own attitudes and consider why people behave in certain ways. The promotion of learners as social actors will require an action-oriented approach and training programmes should include content in how to create tasks that encourage this critical approach. In classroom activities, teachers should aim to involve their students in real actions rather than in simulations. When working with topics involving minority groups such as Indigenous peoples, there is no reason why they should not engage in histories and issues in contemporary societies, as this engages them in real, on-going debates.

Taking the new knowledge learners develop and relating it to their own cultural background is important in the development of intercultural competence. Tasks should also encourage them to relate the knowledge they have gained to what they have learnt about other cultures in previous lessons and in other subjects. This encourages them to develop pluricultural competence, where their cultural knowledge is a resource that they can draw on in different situations rather than relating to specific and separate cultures. In the modern world, cultures transcend boundaries, and it is more natural to see cultural knowledge as a whole rather than as separate units.

6 Conclusion

This chapter has aimed to show how discourse analysis of textbooks in teacher education programmes can increase critical awareness of inequalities in representations of minority groups. By discussing how to address these imbalances in the classroom, teacher educators can contribute to the development of the teacher's role as an agent of reform and encourage the acquisition of critical pedagogical approaches. While the textbook extract discussed above is specific to EFL teaching at Norwegian secondary schools, the points for consideration regarding texts and tasks are relevant for educational institutions worldwide where the curriculum requires students to gain cultural insight and to develop communicative skills.

When working with cultural topics in teacher education programmes, while we can expect some level of intercultural competence in our teachers, it is also important to remember that the development of this competence is a life-long process. Teacher educators should both encourage the advancement of teachers' own knowledge and skills, as well as helping them acquire didactic tools to use in their classrooms. The textbook chapter discussed here is used in the author's own classes in teacher education programmes in a lesson where representations of Indigenous peoples in textbooks are in focus. In the author's class, the results of this lesson are then used by teachers in an assignment where they assess a chapter in a textbook of their choice, based on the rules that they have created together from the example chapter. This assignment enables teachers to choose a subject and a year group that they are aiming to teach themselves, which makes this task meaningful for all teachers, independent of their subject affiliation and the age-group that they plan to teach.

References

Acar, A. (2019). The action-oriented approach: Integrating democratic citizenship education into language teaching, 5. *English Scholarship Beyond Borders*, (1), 122–141.

Acar, A. (2021). An alternative mini-project design proposal for the English textbook mastermind. *Ahi Evran Üniversitesi Sosyal Bilimler Enstitüsü Dergisi, 7*(1), 307–320. https://doi.org/10.31592/aeusbed.833588

Brown, C. W., & Habegger-Conti, J. (2017). Visual representations of indigenous cultures in Norwegian EFL textbooks. *Nordic Journal of Language Teaching and Learning, 5*(1). https://doi.org/10.46364/njmlm.v5i1.369

Byram, M., Gribkova, B., & Starkey, H. (2002). *Developing the intercultural dimension in language teaching*. Council of Europe.

Council of Europe. (2001). *Common European framework of reference for modern languages: Learning, teaching, assessment*. Council of Europe.

Council of Europe. (2020). *Common European framework of reference for modern languages: Learning, teaching, assessment*. Companion Volume. Council of Europe.

Dervin, F. (2016). *Interculturality in education*. Palgrave Macmillan.

Diskin, E., & Winsvold, K. G. (2020). *Enter 9*. Gyldendal.

Gee, J. P. (2014). *An introduction to discourse analysis theory and method*. Routledge.

Gray, J. (2010). *The construction of English: Culture, consumerism and promotion in the ELT global*. Palgrave Macmillan.

Hoff, H. E. (2018). Intercultural Competence. In A.-B. Fenner & A. S. Skulstad (Eds.), *Teaching English in the 21st century*. Fagbokforlaget.

Lund, R. E. (2016). Searching for the indigenous: Urfolk i engelskverket searching. In N. Askeland & B. Aamotsbakken (Eds.). *Folk uten land? Å gi stemme og status til urfolk og nasjonale minoriteter* [People with a country? Giving a voice and status to indigenous peoples and national minorities]. CappelenDamm.

Murray, H. M. (2021). Intercultural competence in the curriculum and in textbooks—Which lessons can be learnt from EFL textbooks in Norwegian schools? In M. Victoria & C. Sangiamchit (Eds.), *Interculturality and the English language classroom*. Springer International Publishing. https://doi.org/10.1007/978-3-030-76757-0

Murray, H. M. (2022). Teaching about indigenous peoples in the EFL classroom: Practical approaches to the development of intercultural competence. *TESOL Journal, 13*(1). https://doi.org/10.1002/tesj.645

Olsen, T. A. (2017). Colonial conflicts: Absence, inclusion and indigenization in textbook representations of indigenous peoples. In J. Lewis, B.-O. Andreassen, & S. Thobro (Eds.), *Textbook violence*. Equinox.

Smith, L. T. (2012). *Decolonizing methodologies* (2nd ed.). Zed Books.

The Norwegian Directorate for Education and Training. (2019). *The English subject curriculum.* The Norwegian Directorate for Education and Training.

Zhu, H. (2015). Negotiation as a way of engagement in Intercutural and lingua Franca communication: Frames of reference and Interculturality. *Journal of English as a Lingua Franca, 4*(1), 63–90. https://doi.org/10.1515/jelf-2015-0008

Helen Margaret Murray is an Assistant Professor at the Department of Teacher Education in the Norwegian University of Science and Technology in Trondheim (NTNU), Norway. She works in the English Section and is also the leader of the interdisciplinary research group "Indigenous Topics in Education". Her research interests include curriculum analysis and representations of Indigenous peoples in textbooks. She is also engaged in creating teaching materials about Indigenous peoples, writing for teaching magazines and holding courses for teachers. Before starting work at NTNU, Helen worked for seventeen years as a teacher at lower and upper secondary schools in Norway. Email: helen.m.murray@ntnu.no

Building on and Sustaining Multilingual Children's Cultural and Linguistic Assets in Superdiverse Early Childhood Education

Criss Jones Díaz

Abstract Australia is characteristically a super-diverse nation. This superdiversity includes varieties of cultural, linguistic, social, and religious practices that operate simultaneously within contexts of economic mobility, ethnicity, income, education, and immigration. Young children and their families living in super-diverse post-multicultural societies, such as Australia, encounter new potentialities and multiple experiences of identity negotiation, affirmation, and connection across diverse cultural, linguistic, and social landscapes. Growing up multilingual with diverse cultural practices means that identity is fluid and multiple, often changing and influenced by contemporary global issues. This chapter argues that educators can acknowledge this fluidity through representing children's cultural, linguistic, and social experiences that are contextual and reflective of their everyday life. In highlighting the significance of superdiversity, frameworks of critical intercultural theory and cultural literacy are used to examine data from two studies, the first of which examines discourses of deficit that are applied to Indigenous families and immigrant multilingual communities' approach to (dis)ability. The second study examines the impact of culturally and linguistically responsive pedagogies that position multilingual children and their families as capable, and agentic communicators. Conclusions highlight the importance of superdiversity, interculturality and cultural literacy that enable pedagogies to build on and sustain the diverse linguistic and cultural assets of young multilingual children and their families.

Keywords Early childhood education · Superdiversity · Critical intercultural theory · Cultural literacy · Pedagogical practices

C. J. Díaz (✉)
Western Sydney University, Penrith, NSW, Australia
e-mail: c.jonesdiaz@westernsydney.edu.au

© The Author(s), under exclusive license to Springer Nature
Switzerland AG 2023
A. Sahlane, R. Pritchard (eds.), *English as an International Language
Education*, English Language Education 33,
https://doi.org/10.1007/978-3-031-34702-3_8

141

1   Introduction

Australia is one of the most diverse multicultural/multilingual nation states in the world with more than 250 ancestries and 350 languages spoken in the community. The numbers of people who use a language other than English at home have increased to more than 5.5 million since the 2016 census, 24% speaking a language other than English at home. Almost half of the population have a parent born overseas (Australian Bureau of Statistics ABS, 2021). Like many other post-colonial nation states, Australia has a vibrant Indigenous history, a colonial past and an increasing diversity of languages, dialects, cultures, gender fluidity, family types (including LGBQIA+), lifestyles, income levels, abilities, urban and regional communities. Vertovec's (2010) notion of super-diversity encapsulates the mixing of cultural, linguistic, and social groups within multiple identity locations, often influenced by contradictory socio-cultural, religious, and political allegiances. Superdiversity goes beyond ethnicity as a singular social category to encompass the layering of other variables such as immigration status, restriction of rights, global labour markets shaped by the interplays of gender, age, religious values, regional, national and local cultural values and practices (Jones Díaz, 2016; Vertovec, 2007; Vertovec et al., 2018). It also adopts an intersectionality approach that does not essentialise 'race', ethnicity, and cultural and linguistic practices, but rather permits a greater incorporation and recognition of cultural, linguistic, and social difference beyond multiculturalism. This is increasingly relevant to post multicultural countries, as well as other immigrant-receiving nation states that in the past were countries from which people emigrated (Jones Díaz, 2016). In this chapter, I draw on Vertovec's (2010) notion of post-multiculturalism that recognises the significance and value of cultural differences (alongside gender, sexuality, age and (dis)ability).

Therefore, in a globalised world, finance, media, communication technologies, free markets, and global capitalism merge in the context of rapid change and ongoing technological advances, consequently extending their reach and impact across multiple fields. Globalisation has also resulted in not only the global rise of English, but transmigration and transnational population flows, fluid labour markets, advanced technologies, and media communications (Jones Díaz, 2016). Moreover, with the intensification of migration, contact between languages, cultures and identities has reached unprecedented levels (Blommaert, 2010; Li, 2018; Romaine, 2011).

1.1   Super-Linguistic Diversity

Vertovec's (2007) notion of super-diversity can be extended to include super-linguistic diversity where there is growing emphasis on the relationships between multilingual practices and globalisation. The reality is that most of the world's population are multilingual, and there are large numbers of languages spoken in many immigrant-receiving superdiverse countries. The life-trajectories of culturally and linguistically diverse (CALD) communities encompass thriving hybrid language practices that operate across multiple social, cultural, and economic domains (Creese & Blackledge, 2018; Jones Díaz, 2016). Within these domains, there are contact zones where encounters of linguistic and cultural diversities become interconnected with power and identity negotiations.

Super-linguistic diversity operates at communicative levels of society where linguistic practices go beyond co-existence to an interconnected and combined use of resources to generate new identities, values and practices (Li, 2018). In this context, Blommaert's (2010) notion of multilingual repertoires is useful in understanding the complex use of linguistic resources in more than one language for meaning making in social settings within contexts of 'extreme mixedness' (p. 102). King and Bigelow (2018) argue that in fluid and multilingual contexts individuals use a wide range of linguistic resources to communicate and connect with others.

Therefore, in many super-diverse nation states, linguistic diversity is the norm, often characterised by cultural and linguistic practices operating simultaneously in contexts of postcolonialism and immigration. For example, much of Australia's diversity is found in the cultural and linguistic repertoires of adults and children living in multilingual families and communities in linguistically diverse highly urbanised and peri urban communities. In this chapter, I use the term multilingualism to also include bilingualism as the issues addressed are relevant to both bilingualism and multilingualism.

1.2 Super-Diversity and Equity

King and Bigelow (2018) suggest that when considering all the dimensions of superdiversity, greater educational equity can be achieved, in which educators and policymakers are able to re-frame outdated notions of difference. They argue that this would entail the recognition of heterogeneity of student populations through which a social justice framework is adopted and the quest for universal approaches to learning in policy is abandoned, where the focus is more on strengthening the capacities of students. This is most pertinent for multilingual children who spend many hours in early childhood education (ECE) settings where the official language is used exclusively, and often minimal opportunities are available for them to use and extend their diverse linguistic repertoires in their home language. This may include children from Indigenous backgrounds and children with disabilities. It is within this context that educators can recognise and acknowledge the diverse experiences of language, identity and communication practices significant to children's and families' lived experiences of ECE (Chan & Ritchie, 2020; Jones Díaz, 2016; Poyatos Matas & Cuatro Nochez, 2011).

The research problem highlighted in this chapter examines the differences between pedagogies of deficit versus pedagogies of possibility in view of how these discourses inform educator's practice when working with diverse children, families and communities. The research question inherent in both studies is: How do educators' views and understandings of superdiversity in relation to multiculturalism, multilingualism, Indigeneity and refugees influence their pedagogical practices? Therefore, this chapter examines data from two studies, the first of which examines the impact of deficit narratives on cultural minorities. The second study underscores the significance of strength-based multilingual pedagogy that builds on the cultural and linguistic capital of multilingual children, families, and educators. However, before embarking on this discussion, it is important to provide an overview of deficit theories and assumptions applied to children from super-diverse backgrounds, particularly those from CALD and Indigenous communities and families with disabilities.

1.3   Deficit Theories and Assumptions About Children from Super-Diverse Backgrounds

In Australian education, notions of deficit have been applied to children from minority backgrounds since colonisation. Throughout the 1950s and 1960s, theories of cultural deprivation or 'deficit theory' were applied to Indigenous, working-class and immigrant communities. During this period, genetic deficiency was the popular explanation for the failure of these communities to succeed in education (Germov, 2004; Knight, 2002). These deficit explanations were informed by assimilationist social policies of monoculturalism through which cultural and linguistic difference was directly equated with cultural deficiency. There was denial that difference mattered and children from Indigenous and immigrant backgrounds were constructed as 'underachievers', 'slow learners', 'lazy' and expected to assimilate. Representations of Australian Aboriginality were constructed by discourses of deficit which framed Aboriginality in a "narrative of negativity, deficiency and disempowerment" (Fforde et al., 2013, p. 162).

As the language and cultural backgrounds of children from Indigenous and immigrant communities were viewed as an impediment to their educational capabilities, the solution to correcting these linguistic deficits was to teach them English to overcome the handicap. They were viewed as victims of their cultural, linguistic, social, and racial backgrounds and their families and communities were to blame for their situation (Robinson & Jones Díaz, 2016).

Assumptions of deficit are also applied to children with disabilities. Macartney and Morton's (2013) study of families' experiences of early education with children identified as '(dis)abled' highlights ways in which children's impairments were the ultimate defining explanation for behaviour, participation, and learning. They argue that this perspective not only decontextualises learning and teaching but also draws attention away from the multiple influences that the environment has on children's learning. They also assert that a singular focus on the 'individual' further attributes the problem to that person with little regard for the importance of pedagogical practices on children's learning. These issues also apply to children and families from immigrant, refugee, and CALD backgrounds in their approach to (dis)ability.

In ECE, a dominant theoretical framework that underpins policy, curriculum and pedagogy is developmental psychology (Pacini-Ketchabaw & Taylor, 2015; Robinson & Jones Díaz, 2016) Within this paradigm, notions of childhood and identity are limited to chronological, fixed, linear and universal stages of growth and development. Little attention is paid to the diverse influence of social and cultural lived experience, rendering children from diverse backgrounds devoid of agency and lacking in cultural and linguistic assets. Such denial of children's multiple and often contradictory experiences of social, cultural and linguistic practices patholo-gises difference as abnormal, deficient, lacking and at risk. This is embedded in discourses of deficit, characterised by assumptions most often applied to socio-cultural minorities which for the most part belong to super-diverse communities.

2   Theoretical Frameworks

In highlighting the significance of superdiversity and its implications for pedagogy, the discussion below examines frameworks of interculturality, cultural literacy and critical intercultural literacies in relation to post-multicultural, superdiverse societies in the context of communication practices, relationships, inequality, power and identity.

2.1   Critical Interculturalism

Questions of interculturality co-exist in super-linguistic diversity, and are major issues for post multicultural nation states, as well as for linguistic majorities and minorities (Blommaert, 2010; May, 2012). According to UNESCO (2006), inter-culturality aims to achieve "a developing and sustainable way of living together in multicultural societies through the creation of understandings of, respect for, and dialogue between different cultural groups" (p. 18). However, Caneva (2012) argues that interculturality is limited in its critique of ethnocentrism, racism and inequality, and falls short of providing a critique for examining ethnocentric attitudes towards cultural differences. Interculturality emphasises interpersonal relations, rather than group exchange, which underestimates the structural problems faced by cultural minorities and immigrants (Barrett, 2013). Importance is on the processes of interactions and relationships between different cultural groups, rather than understanding that these interactions are often constructed within broader societal structures and inequalities. Furthermore, Reid et al. (2016) argue that the presence of children from multiple language and cultural backgrounds alone does not neces-sarily mean an openness to the linguistic and cultural assets that they bring to edu-cational settings, and that diversity itself does not produce equity and inclusion automatically. Therefore, a theoretical approach that requires a more nuanced and critical understanding of the construction of power relations and how diverse children negotiate their multiple identities in contexts of diversity and difference is of crucial importance.

Guilherme and Dietz (2015) argue that the tendency to use interculturality uncritically, manifesting as a softer version of multiculturalism, needs to be challenged. This involves the recognition that interculturality should encourage critical reflection on the 'self' and the 'other' in contexts of inequality and difference. This requires a recognition that the use of language and communication occurs in culturally, linguistically, and socially situated contexts where power relations and diversity co-exit.

2.2 Cultural Literacy

Cultural literacy has its roots in the early work of Street (1984), who argued against traditional notions of literacy as static and autonomous. He proposed an ideological model of literacy "as a social process, in which socially constructed technologies are used within institutional frameworks for specific social purposes" (p. 97). Therefore, literacy constitutes much of our everyday social practice through which meanings are represented in oral, written and visual contexts; this enables us in a variety of ways to 'read' and interpret situations, share, construct or deconstruct meanings about the world. In this process, our values, attitudes, aspirations, opinions, goals, and ideas about the world are communicated.

Contemporary views of literacy as social practice can be extended to textual and communicative practices of interaction. Maine et al. (2019) argue that cultural literacy engenders intercultural dialogue, through the opening of communicative spaces with inherent democratic potential. They suggest that if Street's ideological model of literacy as social practice can be understood as fluid and dialogical, a similar view of cultural literacy can be applied. There is less emphasis on accessing fixed cultural knowledge and more attention to "creating and responding to culture through social practices and engagement" (p. 388). Informed by Street's definition of literacy as social practice, they propose the concept of a dialogic model of cultural literacy which addresses the importance of going beyond individuals and their relationship to culture, towards engagement with others through which social interaction is key to understanding both one's own cultural identity and that of others. This includes the recognition that cultural and linguistic practices create fluid and changing interactions within the dialogic space of communication. Therefore, given our increasingly globalised, super-diverse world, the relationship between communication and culture is ever more present as we progressively encounter people from different social, cultural, and linguistic backgrounds. In this context, interactions and communication styles are mediated by diverse cultural norms, values, beliefs, ways of knowing and describing objects, events, practices, and relationships (Reid et al., 2016; Robinson & Jones Díaz, 2016).

2.3   Critical Intercultural Literacies

Critical intercultural literacies aim to go beyond negotiating meaning systems in different cultural contexts to critical reflection of how one's cultural knowledge and experiences inform and construct communication practices. This requires reflexivity which involves a critical awareness of the 'self' in relation to others (McNay, 2013). Reflexivity refers to the awareness of one's own biases and prejudices which influence the way one operates in the world (Robinson & Jones Díaz, 2016). An important aspect of intercultural communication necessitates a disposition of engaging in and learning from matters of difference, marginalisation, and otherness. To enact critical cultural literacy within contexts of intercultural communication, the willingness to be transformed and changed is crucial. This implies going beyond one's familiar cultural and linguistic mindset to engage with and be transformed by cultural and language differences, diverse identities and power relations that impact on communication.

3   Methodological Approach of Study 1 and Study 2

The data from the two studies discussed in this chapter incorporated case study approaches informed by critical theory and cultural studies (Bhabha, 1994; Bourdieu, 1977, 1990; Foucault, 1974; Hall, 1994, 1996). The aim of the first study was to investigate the impact of contemporary social issues of diversity and difference in the lives of children and families in Australia in view of how they are addressed in ECE settings. The second study aimed to investigate educators' and parents' perspectives on pedagogical approaches that support and extend children's home languages. In both studies, the data were analysed using Nvivo software to organize the data into key themes and sub-themes (Hughes & Jones, 2003). Nvivo was also used to manage the organization of coded data into nodes, which were subsequently sorted into categories, common themes and patterns of meaning, using Critical Discourse Analysis (CDA) (Mullet, 2018). This was then applied to the research questions underpinning these studies. CDA is a qualitative approach that describes, interprets, and explains the operations of discourse in maintaining and legitimising inequalities (Mullet, 2018). In education it is useful in examining the relationship between teaching and learning and the influence of teachers' ideological perspectives on their practice (Llewellyn, 2009; Tamatea et al., 2008). The discussion that follows presents the findings of each study after the methodology pertaining to that study.

4 Study 1: Diversity and Difference in the Lives of Children and Families

This research was conducted across six ECE settings in metropolitan and regional areas of New South Wales (NSW). Data collection practices included interviews; focus groups and participant observation; and field notes to ascertain the contradictions, and fluidity of pedagogical practices and family lived experiences of diversity and difference. Nine interviews were conducted with educators (directors, teachers, and playgroup workers) and three focus groups were held involving seven parents and three educators. In total there were 19 participants. In this chapter, the data from one director, one teacher, one playgroup worker and one parent are reported. Ethics approval was granted for this research by the Human Research Ethics Committee of the researchers' university (Ethics no H12055). Pseudonyms are used for all participants' names in this study.

The questions in both the interviews and focus groups centred on three key areas, including: (a) the impact of contemporary social issues on the lives of children and families in view of how children understood and responded to topics relating to diversity and difference; (b) the study of how discourses of contemporary global problems are constructed in news media and by educators, families and children; and (c) the analysis of how ECE settings addressed these concerns in pedagogy, policy and practices in terms of how educators understood superdiversity in relation to multiculturalism, Indigeneity, refugee and asylum seeking, gender and sexual diversity. This also included their understandings of equity, economic disadvantage, and globalisation. In this chapter, matters pertaining to the third key area are discussed in view of educators' understandings of the impact of superdiversity in relation to multiculturalism, Indigeneity, and refugees. During the interviews, questions related to (dis)ability were raised, and therefore the intersections between cultural and linguistic diversity and (dis)ability are also examined.

4.1 Findings and Discussion

The following discussion reports on the findings of Study 1. Highlighted is how the persistence of deficit approaches applied to Indigenous and immigrant multilingual communities reinforce normative discourses of deficit which position these communities as victims of their own circumstances. This study also draws attention to educators' reluctance to engage in critical reflexivity in their communication practices with Indigenous families and the tendency to apply deficit discourses to culturally and linguistically diverse (CALD) families in their approach to (dis)ability.

4.2   Persistence of Deficit and White Australia Narratives

Australia's colonial past is embedded in Eurocentric constructions of white supremacy and institutional racism. This has led to the persistence of deficit and white Australian narratives about Indigenous people. The comment below from Helen, a parent from one of the focus groups, highlights the persistence of these narratives around Indigenous Australians:

> It is really interesting that the Aboriginal people, being the traditional owners of this land, actually stand out more than people from other countries. They [migrants] seem to blend in quite well unless there's extreme headwear and that sort of stuff. I just find that … Aboriginal people do stand out a little bit more …. I think because they go more by their traditional way, whereas people who come over here are more wanting to do things our way; not speaking in Indian or whatever, that they really want to blend in. Yeah … I guess there's still a little bit of anger there from the Aboriginal community. I don't know if that's got anything to do with the divide, but I guess, yeah, it's interesting that they do; they do stand out more (Helen).

Helen's view of difference is constructed through a deficit lens using normative assimilationist comparisons between Indigenous and migrant Australians. She draws on the discourse of the model minority suggesting that migrants who *'blend in quite well'* and *'do things our way'* show a sign that they want to blend in. Stratton (2009) argues that the key to model minority status is through the acceptance of the dominant white culture's values and goals, which implies a version of assimilation. In this context, blending in and conforming to dominant cultural norms and language is indicative of the good migrant. Fforde et al. (2013) argue that while deficit discourses are expressed through overt racism, there are also covert, "nuanced subtle and insidious manifestations" of racism (p. 166). Helen's reference to *'our way'* suggests that Indigenous people remain outsiders, incapable of blending into the Western system. They are blamed for their marginalisation and their anger is constructed as failure to *'blend in'* at the expense of following *'their traditional way'*.

Helen's views raise critical issues in view of how educators work with families, in the recognition that family perspectives and attitudes towards minority groups, particularly Indigenous Australians, impact on children's understanding of racial minorities and racial inequality. Robinson and Jones Díaz (2016) argue that matters deemed controversial or difficult, that are associated with social justice, are often considered by educators as 'private' family matters, and consequently are avoided and silenced. They propose that educators' responsibility is to engage and communicate with families, offering alternative narratives and discourses around inequality and discrimination. This involves a critical reflexive approach through which intercultural literacy plays an important role. As highlighted earlier, central to reflexivity is developing critical self-consciousness in relation to the Other. In this context, educators are prepared to involve parents, such as Helen, in deconstructing deficit, colonialist and assimilationist discourses about Indigenous and immigrant Australians.

4.3   They Didn't Feel That They Connected

Discourses of managerialism have become normalised within the last 20 years, whereby pedagogy has become the tool in which market-oriented skills are prioritised to compete in the global economy (Giroux, 2011). Giroux argues that there has been a move away from teachers as being transformative intellectuals informed by principles of social justice and equity. This has resulted in the stifling of critical thought in education at all levels to produce student passivity and teacher routinisation. In the interview below with two educators from one of the ECE settings, Sandra, the educator and Jessica, the Director, reflect on an incident involving an Indigenous family who left the centre:

> We … had a family that … they didn't feel that they connected … and felt they didn't build the relationship. That ended up quite a … concern … We … discussed and revisited our approach and our attitude … but that was disappointing … to feel that someone hasn't built that relationship. (Sandra).

It appears that the onus was on 'them' (the family) to connect and build relationships with the educators. While there was an attempt by the ECE setting to revisit their approach, it didn't seem to go far enough and perhaps the focus was limited to the management of the issue. In the extract below, Jessica reflects on the conversational practices between the educators and the families:

> You know if we're thinking about families that [are] hard to connect with, it wouldn't necessarily just be related to [cultural diversity] … It's more families that we connect with personally. … that we would have things in common with. We've had several conversations in staff meetings around that for us just to be … aware. Because we noticed that there are some families who are coming in and staff will just naturally be drawn to them. They're very chatting. They're very friendly. So, we're having more conversations with those families about their children, and their children's interests. I had become aware that there were several families who were more introverted, tended to slip in quietly, get their children, and away, and staff were just allowing them to do that. So, I raised that as a concern because I felt the children of those families then were really being quite disadvantaged because we knew less about them. So, staff really took that on board, and … made efforts towards going to those families, striking up conversations. So, that has been an improvement in our practice, I think. But that wasn't necessarily related to cultural diversity, I don't think. (Jessica).

While Jessica reflects on the importance of making a concerted effort to communicate with families on a day-to-day basis with whom that they have less in common, the focus appears to be making the ECE setting more parent friendly. Jessica's comment that this strategy *'wasn't necessarily related to cultural diversity'* suggests a reluctance to engage in critical reflexivity into how the setting could have prevented this situation from re-occurring, particularly in view of communicating with Indigenous families. It appears that the focus remains at a mainstream level of communicating with all families. The settings' solution to make 'efforts to strike up conversations' may not necessarily prove effective, especially for Indigenous families who may shy away from this, feeling intimidated and overwhelmed. In this context, families are seen as homogeneous entities through which a monocultural approach is adopted. Rather than disrupting or challenging communication practices that are limited to symbolic gestures of inclusion, deficit systems and ideologies remain intact, which only serves to perpetuate inequality and uniformity.

4.4 Deficit Discourses Applied to CALD Families in Their Approach to (Dis)ability

Frameworks of cultural practices and ethnicity are partial explanations of the diversity of experiences in terms of how families access services (Cardona et al., 2005). When ethnicity and culture are understood as 'problems' that need to be 'fixed', this reinforces cultural practice and identity as static and unified (Hall, 1994, 1996). In the extract below, the playgroup worker, Fay, reflects on her interactions with a woman from a CALD and refugee background whose child has a (dis)ability.

> Explaining the ... problems with their children are often difficult because the parents don't want to accept it ... one mother did not want to recognise there was a problem with her boy. I observed him interacting with other children and he was borderline autistic but to make sure, we needed a medical examination of the child. The mother was very upset. (Fay).

From the mother's perspective, her doctor had said that her child, 'was normal'. Perhaps it would have been a surprise for her to learn about an impending medical examination of her child. In this context, Fay appears to be more focussed on the mother's denial of the possibility that her child could be borderline autistic, and less interested in the mother's previous cultural lived experiences and medical knowledge of her child. This in turn produces a narrative of deficit, where the educator has perhaps positioned the mother as difficult, and therefore a problem. Macartney and Morton (2013) argue that it is dangerous to assume that providing 'inclusive' environments is a straightforward and predictable process. They emphasise the importance of educators developing open, responsive and attentive listening practices towards Others, which include immigrant parents' approach to their children's (dis) ability. Furthermore, the prevalence of discourses explaining the reluctance of CALD families to access (dis)ability services because of shame was noted by Cardona et al. (2005). They argued that despite existing differences between CALD and Anglo-Australian families, in terms of cultural perceptions of family responsibility, (dis)ability and illness, viewing culture and ethnicity as homogenised frameworks of reference offers limited explanations about the diversity of experiences of service usage, including ECE. These concepts run the risk of becoming a singular framework of reference to explain disadvantage and exclusion from participation in service usage. Often ethnicity and culture are understood in terms of 'problems' or 'barriers' inherent in CALD communities.

5   Study 2: Supporting and Extending Children's Home Languages

The study was conducted across two ECE settings in urban regions with CALD communities in Sydney, Australia. These settings included a Spanish bilingual long day care (LDC)/preschool setting for children 6 months – 6 years of age, and a preschool for children four-five years of age which employed a Mandarin-speaking educator whose specific role was to support and extend children's Mandarin. Data collection practices included interviews, participant observation and field notes to ascertain the level of multilingual support afforded to the children attending these settings.

Interviews were conducted with four educators (one director and room leader/educator from the Spanish bilingual LDC / preschool setting, and one director and EC teacher from the preschool setting), and four parents from each setting to investigate their perceptions of the settings' programs to examine the ways in which children's home languages were valued and supported at the settings. Eight children (one child of each parent) were observed for the duration of the study. In total there were 20 participants. In the broader study, both qualitative and quantitative approaches were incorporated, using participant observations and field notes to capture children's use of their home languages and English throughout the day in the ECE settings. Since the focus of this chapter is based on educators' perspectives, information from the children and parents is not included (see, Escudero et al., 2020 for quantitative findings from the participant observation data from the bilingual long day care / preschool setting). Ethics approval was granted for this research by the Western Sydney University Human Research Ethics Committee (Ethics no H12904). Pseudonyms are used for all participants' names in in this study.

The research questions in the interviews with educators and parents focussed on four key areas, including: (a) validation and support to children's home languages at the setting; (b) opportunities afforded to children to use their home languages throughout the day at the setting; (c) parents' perspectives and experiences of their children's maintenance and use of the home language in the setting and (d) the pedagogical practices and policies implemented at the settings that support the retention and extension of children's home languages. As this chapter is a critical contrastive analysis of deficit-based discourses versus cultural and linguistically responsive discourses applied to Indigenous and CALD communities, information pertaining to the preschool setting is the primary focus because it highlights educators' critical reflexive positioning in discourses of multilingualism. Therefore, matters pertaining to the first key area are discussed in view of educators' perceptions of the impact of home language validation and support at the setting.

5.1   Findings and Discussion

In contrast to the ways in which families with (dis)ability are constructed as deficient in Study 1, the data reported below highlight the effectiveness of strength-based culturally and linguistically responsive pedagogies. Study 2 draws attention to the impact of culturally and linguistically responsive pedagogies of multilingualism where the educators engage in critical intercultural reflexivity and cultural literacy in relation to their work with Mandarin-speaking families, children, and educators to build on and sustain multilingual children's linguistic capabilities at the setting. In this study, the role of reflexive and supportive communication is key to the maintenance of home languages and cultural practices. It also highlights the importance of critical reflexivity in legitimising the cultural and linguistic capital of multilingual educators.

5.2   Supporting Multilingual Families in Raising Multilingual Children

Questions of identity constructed through cultural and linguistic practices are major issues for both linguistic majorities and minorities (Blommaert, 2010; May, 2012). For multilingual families, these issues are significant due to pressures from community attitudes, educators, and other professionals to abandon their home language in preference for English. As information about the benefits of multilingualism is not often made known to young parents, silences are created around their capacity to raise concerns regarding their children's multilingual trajectory (Jones Díaz, 2018). Consequently, these families often consider the home language as an impediment to their children's academic success, insisting that their children rapidly learn English as they transition into the ECE setting and beyond into primary school. This often results in the abandonment of the home language in preference for Speaking English (Schwartz, 2010). Newly arrived migrant families can be unsupportive of home language use in ECE settings, and this was evident at the preschool setting. In the extract below, the Director, Molly, from the preschool setting comments on concerns of parents from Mandarin-speaking backgrounds regarding English:

> I know a few of the parents, no no no, …, we don't want our children speaking Mandarin all day, we want our children to speak English. And at that point, I really recognize [the] dilemma that they had. (Molly).

Molly's critical reflection highlights the need for educators to fully engage in conversations with families around the importance of maintaining the home language. In understanding the complexities of raising multilingual children, particularly when English unknowingly 'takes over' family interactions, it is crucial that educators develop respectful and sensitive communicative practices around these issues. This is especially relevant for interracial or interethnic families where more than one language and/or dialect is spoken. Ongoing support and encouragement regarding families' concerns is necessary. This involves conversations with families about the importance of the home language as a resource and asset for learning and the negotiation of identity and sense of 'self'.

Furthermore, challenges that are linked to the immigration experience can include anxiety and separation from family and the home country. For young multilingual children, these issues are exacerbated when there is no home language support at the EC setting. In the comment below, the educator Kiera, from the preschool setting reflects on her lack of insight into one of the children's cultural and linguistic isolation as that child transitioned into the preschool setting:

> She misses her friends. She misses school … she misses everything there. And … she … just … didn't want to invest in friendships here, or really have anything to do with the teachers because she missed her teachers [from her home country]. And … it wasn't until the bilingual teacher came and talked to her that we understood this situation, … how she's been feeling for months and months …. And I didn't know because I didn't speak [her] language. (Kiera).

Kiera's reflexivity of her limitations as a monolingual educator enables a recognition of her lack of preparedness to facilitate the child's linguistic and emotional needs. She was not aware of the power of home languages in supporting multilingual children's emotional needs and communicative capacity until the arrival of a bilingual teacher, whose multilingual assets not only helped appease the child, but to extend her learning in Mandarin. This highlights the need for professional development for educators to understand the crucial benefits of early childhood multilingualism in promoting intellectual, linguistic, sociocultural, and familial benefits for children and families. This also points to the important role multilingual educators play in supporting and extending children's multilingual potential (Jones Díaz et al., 2022).

5.3 The Role of Multilingual Educators in Pedagogies of Cultural and Linguistic Responsiveness

In the extract below, Molly reflects on the importance of being strategic in the employment of multilingual educators:

> … we aren't strategic about how we support children's linguistic needs. … And this is where we really need to attract … people to the industry who have diverse backgrounds, because otherwise, … these children are going to lose their language. (Molly).

Molly's admittance to not being strategic in supporting children's linguistic potential is highly reflexive when she recognises that being strategic around employing multilingual educators builds on and recognises the expertise of early childhood multilingual educators. Bourdieu (1990, 1991) argues that cultural capital ascribes forms of advantage that some people acquire through family and life experiences. This includes linguistic capital inherent in the language resources and literacy practices acquired in childhood. Bourdieu (1993) claims that linguistic markets operate within social fields when "someone produces an utterance for receivers capable of assessing it, evaluating it and setting a price on it" (p. 79). His use of a market analogy draws attention to the ways in which languages have certain value in social fields and the value ascribed to a particular language depends on the laws that are determined by the market operating in various social fields (Jones Díaz, 2011). Therefore, in ECE settings, where multilingual educators are strategically employed to extend and sustain children's multilingual repertoires, this in turn legitimises children's and families' cultural and linguistic capital.

In understanding the specific expertise of multilingual educators in building and supporting the cultural and linguistic assets of multilingual children, the extracts below highlight the connections with multilingual families by integrating the home language into the curriculum as a bridge to learning:

> Bilingual education is about trying to connect the home language with what's happening within the … environment. So, … [a bilingual teacher] who can facilitate that, [is] important. … and just having the connection with the families in that way as well. (Kiera)

Below, Molly describes specifically how multilingual educators scaffold and extend children's home languages:

> [The children] seem … a lot more confident [and] … more involved in the program. … we are getting insight into their thinking that we never had before. You know … [the bilingual educator] is sharing with Kiera and … me and we're going wow, imagine that they were thinking that! … So it's been quite … a … revelation … how much more comfortable our families are feeling, how … a lot more [are] smiling and … I can see … [that] they feel really valued. (Molly)

Molly and Kiera's emphasis on the cultural and linguistic expertise that multilingual educators bring to their setting highlights the interconnections between social, linguistic, and cultural capital. Bourdieu and Wacquant (1992) define social capital as accumulated resources that are accessed through networks, relationships, and social groups. It provides a potential tool for conversion to other forms of capital such as linguistic and cultural capital. In settings where there is a healthy appetite for multilingualism to flourish, the role of multilingual educators strengthens relationships with all families through their cultural and linguistic connections. These conversion strategies facilitate intercultural communication through the accumulation of linguistic, cultural, and social capital as children develop friendships and relationships with peers and educators at the ECE setting.

6 Conclusion

In post multicultural societies such as Australia, super-diversity, globalisation, interculturalism and cultural literacy is of increasing importance due to the layering of variables related to immigration, human rights and global labour markets — all of which are shaped by interactions of gender, sexuality, age, (dis)ability, class, religious values, languages and cultural practices. Therefore, an intersectionality approach towards diversity and difference permits a greater incorporation and recognition of cultural, linguistic, and social difference beyond multiculturalism. In this context, notions of super-linguistic diversity enable greater insights into how communication, interactions and relationships between people are central to social, cultural, and linguistic practices.

In understanding the socio-historical context of educational approaches towards difference, deficit discourses have often been applied to children and families from Indigenous and immigrant backgrounds, and families and children living with (dis) abilities. Unfortunately, the implications of these deficit narratives continue to linger where minorities are often constructed as devoid of agency, with limited capacity. This in turn constructs children and families from diverse communities as marginal, unequal and culturally deficient. In response to these issues, critical interculturalism and cultural literacy are useful in enabling a move beyond a simplistic focus on the 'Other' to a more nuanced and reflexive approach that recognises the power relations that exist between social, cultural and language groups. This requires critical reflexivity of the 'self' in relation to the 'Other', particularly in contexts of diversity and difference, inequality, and marginalisation.

In highlighting the utility of critical interculturalism and cultural literacy for ECE, educators' perspectives of diversity and difference are key to building and sustaining children's cultural and linguistic potential. This also includes facilitating equitable relationships and communication practices with Indigenous families, CALD families of children with (dis)abilities and multilingual families. Furthermore, culturally and linguistically responsive pedagogies of multilingualism, informed by critical intercultural reflexivity and cultural literacy, effectively facilitate the cultural and linguistic assets of multilingual children, families and educators.

References

Australian Bureau of Statistics (2021). *Census: Nearly half of Australians have a parent born overseas.* https://www.abs.gov.au/media-centre/media-releases/2021-census-nearly-half-australians-have-parent-born-overseas. Accessed 5 Sept 2022.

Barrett, M. (2013). *Interculturalism and multiculturalism: Similarities and differences.* Council of Europe Publishing.

Bhabha, H. (1994). *The location of culture.* Routledge.

Blommaert, M. (2010). *The sociolinguistics of globalisation.* Cambridge University Press.

Bourdieu, P. (1977). *Outline of a theory of practice.* Cambridge University Press.

Bourdieu, P. (1990). *The Logic of practice* (R. Nice. Trans). Polity Press.

Bourdieu, P. (1991). *Language and symbolic power.* Harvard University Press.

Bourdieu, P. (1993). *Sociology in question.* Sage.

Bourdieu, P., & Wacquant, L. (1992). *An invitation to reflexive sociology.* Blackwell.

Caneva, E. (2012). Interculturalism in the classroom. The strengths and limitations of teachers in managing relations with children and parents of foreign origin. *Italian Journal of sociology of education, 4*(3), 33–58.

Cardona, B., Chalmers, S., & Neilson, B. (2005). *Diverse strategies for diverse carers: The cultural context of family carers in NSW.* Centre for Cultural Research, University of Western Sydney for the Department of Ageing, Disability and Home Care.

Chan, A., & Ritchie, J. (2020). Exploring a Tiriti-based superdiversity paradigm within early childhood care and education in Aotearoa New Zealand. *Contemporary Issues in Early, 24*, 5–19. https://doi.org/10.1177/1463949120971376

Creese, A., & Blackledge, A. (Eds.). (2018). *The Routledge handbook of language and superdiversity*. Routledge. https://doi.org/10.4324/9781315696010

Escudero, P., Jones Díaz, C., Hajek, J., Wigglesworth, G., & Smit, E. A. (2020). Probability of heritage language use at a supportive early childhood setting in Australia. *Frontiers in Education Psychology, 5*(1), 1–11.

Fforde, C., Bamblett, L., Lovett, R., Gorringe, S., & Fogarty, B. (2013). Discourse, deficit, and identity: Aboriginality, the race paradigm and the language of representation in contemporary Australia. *Media International Australia, 149*(1), 162–173. https://doi.org/10.1177/1329878X1314900117

Foucault, M. (1974). *The archaeology of knowledge*. Tavistock.

Germov, J. (2004). Which class do you teach? Education and the reproduction of class. In J. Allen (Ed.), *Sociology of education: Possibilities and practices* (3rd ed., pp. 250–269). Social Science Press.

Giroux, H. (2011). *On critical pedagogy*. The Continuum International Publishing Groups.

Guilherme, M., & Dietz, G. (2015). Difference in diversity: Multiple perspectives on multicultural, intercultural, and transcultural conceptual complexities. *Journal of Multicultural Discourses, 10*(1), 1–21. https://doi.org/10.1080/17447143.2015.1015539

Hall, S. (1994). Cultural identity and diaspora. In P. Williams & L. Chrisman (Eds.), *Colonial discourse and post-colonial theory* (pp. 392–403). Columbia University Press.

Hall, S. (1996). Who needs 'identity'? In S. Hall & P. du Gay (Eds.), *Questions of cultural identity* (pp. 1–17). Sage Publications.

Hughes, J., & Jones, S. (2003). Reflections on the use of grounded theory in interpretive information systems research. In *Proceedings of the European conference on information systems (ECIS)* (Vol. 62). https://aisel.aisnet.org/ecis2003/62/

Jones Díaz, C. (2011). Children's voices: Spanish in urban multilingual and multicultural Australia. In K. Potowski & J. Rothman (Eds.), *Bilingual youth: Spanish in English-speaking societies* (pp. 251–281). John Benjamins.

Jones Díaz, C. (2016). Growing up bilingual and negotiating identity in globalised and multicultural Australia. In D. Cole & C. Woodrow (Eds.), *Super dimensions in globalization and education* (pp. 37–53). Springer.

Jones Díaz, C. (2018). Silences in growing up bilingual in multicultural globalised societies: Educators' and families' and children's views of negotiating languages, identity and difference in childhood. In T. Ferfolja, C. Jones Díaz, & J. Ullman (Eds.), *Understanding sociological theory and pedagogical practices* (2nd ed., pp. 121–139). Cambridge University Press.

Jones Díaz, C., Cardona, B., & Escudero, P. (2022). Exploring the perceptions of early childhood educators on the delivery of multilingual education in Australia: Challenges and opportunities. *Contemporary Issues in Early Childhood, 1-15*, 146394912211379. https://doi.org/10.1177/14639491221137900

King, K. A., & Bigelow, M. (2018). Multilingual education policy, superdiversity and educational equity. In A. Creese & A. Blackledge (Eds.), *The Routledge handbook of language and superdiversity* (pp. 459–472). Routledge.

Knight, T. (2002). Equity in Victorian education and 'deficit' thinking. *Critical Studies in Education, 43*(1), 83–105. https://doi.org/10.1080/17508480209556394

Li, W. (2018). Linguistic (super) diversity, post-multilingualism and translanguaging moments. In *The Routledge handbook of language and superdiversity* (pp. 16–29). Routledge.

Llewellyn, A. (2009). "Gender games": A post-structural exploration of the prospective teacher, mathematics and identity. *Journal of Mathematics Teacher Education, 12*, 411–426. https://doi.org/10.1007/s10857-009-9109-0

Macartney, B., & Morton, M. (2013). Kinds of participation: Teacher and special education perceptions and practices of 'inclusion' in early childhood and primary school settings. *International Journal of Inclusive Education, 17*(8), 776–792. https://doi.org/10.1080/13603116.2011.602529

Maine, F., Cook, V., & Lähdesmäki, T. (2019). Reconceptualizing cultural literacy as a dialogic practice. *London Review of Education, 17*(3), 383–392. https://doi.org/10.18546/LRE.17.3.12

May, S. (2012). *Language and minority rights: Ethnicity, nationalism and the politics of language* (2nd ed.). Routledge.

McNay, L. (2013). *Foucault: A critical introduction*. John Wiley & Sons.

Mullet, D. R. (2018). A general critical discourse analysis framework for educational research. *Journal of Advanced Academics, 29*(2), 116–142.

Pacini-Ketchabaw, V., & Taylor, A. (Eds.). (2015). *Unsettling the colonial places and spaces of early childhood education*. Routledge.

Poyatos Matas, C., & Cuatro Nochez, L. (2011). Reluctant migrants: Socialization patterns among Salvadorian children. In K. Potowski & J. Rothman (Eds.), *Bilingual youth Spanish in English-speaking societies* (pp. 309–330). John Benjamins Publishing Company.

Reid, C., Jones Díaz, C., & Alsairai, H. (2016). Cosmopolitanism, contemporary communication theory and cultural literacy in the EAL/D classroom. *TESOL in Context, 25*(2), 44–63.

Robinson, K. H., & Jones Díaz, C. (2016). *Diversity and difference in childhood: Issues for theory and practice* (2nd ed.). Open University Press.

Romaine, S. (2011). Identity and multilingualism. In K. Potowski & J. Rothman (Eds.), *Bilingual youth: Spanish in English-speaking societies* (pp. 7–30). John Benjamins.

Schwartz, M. (2010). Family language policy: Core issues of an emerging field. *Applied Linguistic Review, 1*(1), 171–192. https://doi.org/10.1515/9783110222654.171

Stratton, J. (2009). Preserving white hegemony: Skilled migration, 'Asians' and middle-class assimilation. *Borderlands, 8*(3). https://espace.curtin.edu.au/handle/20.500.11937/31744. Accessed 23 June 2022.

Street, B. V. (1984). *Literacy in theory and practice* (Vol. 9). Cambridge University Press.

Tamatea, L., Hardy, J., & Ninnes, P. (2008). Paradoxical inscriptions of global subjects: Critical discourse analysis of international schools' websites in the Asia–Pacific Region. *Critical Studies in Education, 49*, 157–170. https://doi.org/10.1080/17508480802040241

UNESCO. (2006). *UNECSO guidelines on intercultural education*. UNESCO. https://unesdoc.unesco.org/ark:/48223/pf0000147878. Accessed 27 Sept 2022

Vertovec, S. (2007). Super-diversity and its implications. *Ethnic and Racial Studies, 30*(6), 1024–1054. https://doi.org/10.1080/01419870701599465

Vertovec, S. (2010). Towards post – Multiculturalism? Changing conditions, communities, and contexts of diversity. *International Social Science Journal, 61*, 83–95. https://doi.org/10.1111/j.1468-2451.2010.01749.x

Vertovec S., Hiebert, D., Gamlen, A. & Spoonley, P. (2018). *Superdiversity*. https://superdiv.mmg.mpg.de/ – sydney national?bubble;filter:Total population?map;variables:0,0;mode:superdiversity?tree;year:2012;category:Humanitarian?sankey;year:2016?dashboard;filters:Persons,Total Persons 18-64,Total persons (ANC1P),Total

Criss Jones Díaz (PhD) is a senior lecturer at Western Sydney University. Her research and publications focus on languages, literacies and identity negotiation in contexts of diversity and difference. Her focus is a critical reframing of languages inequality, within a context of culturally and linguistically relevant pedagogy. The implications of her research inform equitable policy and pedagogy to address these issues which have a critical impact on the lived experiences of multilingual families and children. Her current research aims include a broader national research and publications agenda to address the multilingual policy gap in the provision of bilingual education and home language support for children and their families in early childhood and primary education. Email: c.jonesdiaz@westernsydney.edu.au

Challenging Invisibility in a Privileged Discourse Space: Culturally and Linguistically Inclusive University Teaching

Toni Dobinson

Abstract Australia is a multilingual country with many international students and heritage language students in its universities. However, there is still a tendency to expect students from diverse cultural and linguistic backgrounds to just 'fit in' with the dominant discourse, both culturally and linguistically. In this chapter, I describe an approach to tertiary teaching which is inclusive of language and culture and which (1) utilises the skills of lecturers who are plurilingual and local to the context in which students are being taught, (2) gives careful attention to the inclusion of teaching material which reflects all contexts and languages, (3) incorporates storytelling, reimagines students as partners and promotes message abundancy. This response is shaped by socio-linguistic research in linguistic racism/equality, a Global South stance on interculturality focused on political and transformative change, and my own related research in the area. Using this approach, I hope to diminish educational disparity between students and motivate other university lecturers to develop culturally and linguistically responsive pedagogies, both informally and formally, at course, unit of study and workshop level.

Keywords Culturally and linguistically inclusive approach · Storytelling · Students as partners · Message abundancy

1 Introduction

There were 640,362 international students in universities in Australia in 2018 (Australian Government Department of Education and Training, 2018). However, there is still a tendency in Australia to expect students from diverse cultural and linguistic backgrounds, especially students from the Global South, to just 'fit in'

T. Dobinson (✉)
Curtin University, Perth, WA, Australia
e-mail: T.Dobinson@curtin.edu.au

© The Author(s), under exclusive license to Springer Nature
Switzerland AG 2023
A. Sahlane, R. Pritchard (eds.), *English as an International Language Education*, English Language Education 33,
https://doi.org/10.1007/978-3-031-34702-3_9

with the dominant discourse in educational institutions (Dobinson & Mercieca, 2020; Liddicoat, 2016). Australian universities are opening up globally but do not engage enough with issues surrounding the acceptance of bi/multilingual/translingual perspectives (Liddicoat, 2016) and cultural diversity. This denies certain students an identity and diminishes learning for all. Lecturers become pre-occupied with 'problematic' cultural and linguistic differences in their students or are blind to differences, focusing on students 'blending in' with the dominant cultural and linguistic discourse (Dobinson & Mercieca, 2020). Students are not valued for their translingual repertoires nor seen as cultural resources.

This chapter refers to literature in the area of interculturality, linguistic privileging and internationalization. Research in these areas provided the motivation for the approach to teaching that I came to adopt; an approach focused on ensuring cultural and linguistic inclusivity at course, unit of study and lesson level, in the Australian university in which I work. This is an approach which can be realized inside or outside the classroom by recognizing the importance of emotion and relevance for student engagement and learning (Immordino-Yang & Faeth, 2010) as well as the encouragement of *storytelling*, *students as partners* and *message abundancy*.

Storytelling serves to connect students (and the lecturer). It breaks down cultural, linguistic and social barriers. Both the lecturers and students tell stories, give personal testimonies, and analogies to illustrate complex theories, thus attaching meaning and memorability, stimulating curiosity, and influencing new learning (Koehne, 2005). Stories can be short narratives which are "unrehearsed" and immediate. They might contain false starts, hesitations, unfinished sentences, interruptions, and contradictions (Ochs & Capps, 2002, p. 56). They may not unfold sequentially or even have a plot line. They are not practised or contrived, and may not be completely coherent, but they are more ubiquitous and central to ordinary social encounters. They explore "the human condition" (p. 57).

Students as partners involves lecturers accepting students as equals, diminishing power relations in learning (Matthews, 2017; Smith et al., 2020), creating inclusivity and mediating teachers' tendencies to dominate the discourse of the classroom/ curriculum both culturally and linguistically. It draws on the concept of "belongingness" (Bowles & Brindle, 2017), which describes a situation where students feel part of an institution or a course and identify with the culture, goals and relationships in that setting. According to Matthews (2017, p. 1), "students as partners is a metaphor for university education which challenges traditional assumptions about the identities of, and relationships between, learners and teachers". It involves making places where students can participate and form partnerships across social classes, countries, backgrounds, religions, and disciplines. This approach challenges existing discourses and practices in university contexts and reframes them to include extra-curricular events which connect the campus to the local or the international.

Message or input abundancy is the notion that students should be saturated in similar, repeated messages and concepts, through different mediums and modes, to promote more opportunities for understanding and learning (Gibbons, 2009). In this way, meaning is mediated through multiple exposures to content via a variety of tasks and texts, such as group discussions, listening to aural texts, reading written texts, watching audio-visual texts, such as group discussions, aural text, written texts, audio-visual and visual texts (Dobinson & Nguyen, 2018).

2 Interculturality, Linguistic Privileging and Internationalization

This section draws on sociolinguistic research in the area of interculturality, linguistic privileging and internationalization. These concepts form the backdrop to my approach to coordinating units in our provider institution in Vietnam and teaching international and local students, from culturally and linguistically diverse backgrounds, in my undergraduate and postgraduate education and applied linguistics courses.

2.1 Interculturality

Higher Education in Australia often champions the idea that international students, local students and staff will involve themselves in two-way learning through interaction on Australian university campuses (Leask & Carroll, 2011; Marginson, 2003). The reality is, however, that co-existence does not guarantee intercultural interaction (Colvin et al., 2014; God & Zhang, 2019; Lantz-Deaton, 2017; Leask & Carroll, 2011). The potential for *interculturality* and linguistic exchange often remains unrealized (Marginson & Sawir, 2011) with limited 'shaping' of the intercultural and linguistic environment on campus by the multicultural and multilingual university community (Colvin et al., 2014, p. 442).

Culture is seen as multiple, incomplete, relational, discursive (Risager, 2006) and socially constructed (Kramsch, 2011). While there can be large culture views (e.g., more stable and homogeneous strands of culture such as religion (Byram, 2013; Freitag-Hild, 2018; Holliday, 2016)), there can also be small culture views in which culture can mean feelings, beliefs, values and behaviours that form within any small group (Holliday, 2016). In Global Northern academic stances on interculturality there is a prescriptive tendency towards management of diversity as static competences (Meyer, 1991) packaged up and delivered in handbooks. In Global Southern perspectives the emphasis is on political and transformative change (Dietz, 2018), seeing transcultural experiences as dynamic and co-constructed between participants over time, what has been called "double-voiced discourse" (p. 13). By engaging in this two-way learning (Ryan, 2011; Singh & Nguyen, 2018), international students can grow multiple or hybrid identities which enable them to function and thrive in a third space (Kramsch, 1993) on their own terms. Central to this perspective is dialogue and criticality (Dervin & Simpson, 2021), with interculturality seen as transformational, unfolding and situational. Interculturality refers to emancipation, decolonization and criticism of the assimilationist currents that have imposed an ideology of social injustice (Aman, 2015; Dietz, 2018; Li & Garcia, 2022). From this conceptual framework, interculturality comprises a broad spectrum of ideologies throughout the world. These seek to redefine the traditional relationships between the hegemonic minority of the Global North and the oppressed majority of the Global South (including minority groups and Indigenous communities located in the Global North due to increased mobility and globalisation).

Informal learning can facilitate the development of interculturality and social justice in education, particularly in relation to those who are marginalized (Kraidy, 2017; Rogoff et al., 2016). On university campuses, international students can join clubs and attend social activities to meet other students. This has been shown to encourage interaction amongst students (McDermott-Levy, 2011; McLachlan & Justice, 2009). Shepherd and Rane (2012, p. 6) suggested that such a رحلة (*rihla*) can provide "deeper understanding" of host cultures and contexts. Having its origins in the Arabic language, *rihla* means journey or travel. Students endeavour to seek knowledge of the new cultures and languages while travelling to "find the familiar in the strange" (Abdul-Jabbar, 2019, p. 258). A study carried out in 2020 (Dobinson et al., 2020) drew on this idea and brought students and academics together on one Australian university campus as travellers through a dynamic landscape of interculturality and language (Behar, 1996). This was mediated through the screening of Arabic language films on campus curated by the Arab Film Festival Australia (AFFA) and Information and Cultural Exchange (ICE), Sydney, Australia, a community arts organization association that works with emerging communities, artists and creative producers. The films were written and directed by Arab-background artists and promoted respectful, critical thinking and conversations about issues that were common to all human social experience. They shone a light on the notion of diversity within cultures and languages, calling into question culturalist, monolithic images and mediating transcultural understanding amongst the participants. Any perceived misrepresentation or culturalism initiated dialogue crucial to interculturality amongst participants (Dervin & Simpson, 2021) with transformative stances facilitated (Dietz, 2018) (See Dobinson et al., 2020 for details).

2.2   Linguistic Privileging

Linked with interculturality can be *linguistic privileging*. This concept refers to the situation where "speakers of certain languages and varieties of languages enjoy a status which may be sealed off to those who do not speak those languages" (Dobinson & Mercieca, 2020, p. 792). In the university context I describe in this chapter, this refers to students feeling deviant or uncomfortable when they use any language which is not English even when interacting with speakers of their own heritage languages. It also refers to students being mandated to use one particular variety of English even though many varieties are present. Many contexts in

Australia can be described as linguistically unequal (Piller, 2016), with linguistic racism (Dovchin, 2019), and linguistic invisibility, being the norm (Dobinson & Mercieca, 2020). Occupying this space requires the promotion of linguistic strategies such as translanguaging (Li & Garcia, 2022), with students using their full *spatial translingual repertoire* (Canagarajah, 2018). This repertoire involves students moving between organised and defined languages as well as utilizing all resources at their disposal to shape meaning. Languages, paralinguistic behaviours, use of objects in space and time i.e., whiteboards, note pads, artefacts (material ecology), use of multimodal tools accessible on digital platforms (Canagarajah, 2018) come together to help students express themselves.

However, despite advocacy for the merits of translanguaging (Yanaprasart & Lüdi, 2018), national language planning/policies in Australia are overwhelmingly hegemonic and monolingual, with the almost exclusive use of Standard English mandated in most areas at multilingual Australian universities (Dovchin et al., 2018; Liddicoat, 2016). This creates linguistic inequality and disadvantage (Piller, 2016). Students are dissuaded from using their own heritage languages in university classroom contexts, leading some observers to comment that Australia is a multicultural community but not a multilingual one (Earshot, ABC Radio National, 2019), with some languages remaining invisible, peripheral and unacknowledged while others take up central roles. Linguistic privileging also occurs, with speakers of certain languages and varieties of languages attaining a social and educational status which is not attainable by those who do not speak the preferred languages. Of course, it opens up status to those who do learn to speak the language of the dominant discourse.

Signage saying "Speak English only (and you will get better faster)" at the entry to an English language teaching centre triggered my project on English privileging and linguistic racism on one Australian university campus (see Dobinson & Mercieca, 2020 for details). While it is common for English language centres to display signs like this, to make sure that students use every opportunity, while in an English setting, to improve their English, this sort of signage reinforces English medium campus norms and inculcates feelings of language prohibition in students with culturally and linguistically different backgrounds (Shohamy, 2013). Policy documents on this campus, despite claiming to promote equity in terms of cultural considerations, do not address or include explicit statements about equity in language use. Interviews with international students revealed they felt pressured to use English the entire time on campus. They could not comfortably speak their own languages on campus due to the subliminal "English only" mandate (Dobinson et al., 2020). This mandate was not explicit outside of the English language centre but was a legacy of their time there. They had become used to rules imposed and also wanted to please other stakeholders such as their parents who believed that an "English only" environment would promote greater English language acquisition. This acted as a barrier with local students because they would rather say nothing than attempt a conversation which included translanguaging (Dobinson et al., 2023). They got excited when they were able to speak their own languages and expressed interest in seeing and hearing languages other than English written and spoken on campus. The idea that they could bring related texts written in their own languages to tutorials and workshops to discuss and translate was appealing to many students. Local students, who spoke heritage languages, described talking with those who spoke their own language as connecting with their history. Academics also felt it was important for students to have linguistic visibility on campus to increase a sense of belonging. They admitted they were embarrassed to say they could not identify different languages when they heard them.

2.3   Internationalisation

Internationalisation and widened participation in higher education in Australia has meant that there are more students who come to universities with different cultural schemas and their own legitimate varieties of English. This increasing diversity, however, has not been met with practices which sanction linguistic diversity, and, in some cases, there has been a move towards even greater standardisation, especially in written assessment practices (Dobinson et al., 2019). This can leave students from diverse linguistic backgrounds disadvantaged. Against the backdrop of increasing validation of World or Global Englishes (Jenkins, 2006, 2014; Kirkpatrick, 2007, 2011), and intentional and unintentional translanguaging practices (Canagarajah, 2018; Garcia & Li, 2014; Li & Garcia, 2022; Li & Ho, 2018), the importance of language identity retention seems to have been largely ignored with language varieties seen in a deficit light and students' full spatial and linguistic repertoires underutilized.

In a project undertaken in 2019 (see Dobinson et al., 2019 for more details), on an Australian university campus, the written work of students who speak English as an Additional Language or Dialect (EAL/D) was analysed to find out, (1) if students were incorporating Global English forms into their written assessments and, (2) how lecturers reacted when they did this. Findings revealed few examples of Global Englishes in students' scripts with students mostly writing in academic English, the favoured discourse for the setting in which they found themselves. There was, therefore, little opportunity for lecturers to be able to comment on the use of Global English forms in students' written work. While this could be regarded positively, it also shows that students had adopted the dominant academic discourse, resisting any urge to translanguage or use their own variety of English and retain their linguistic identity. This is testimony to the fact that increasing linguistic diversity, as mentioned earlier, has not been accommodated or sanctioned on Australian campuses. There may be a cause to celebrate students achieving standards mandated in most educational settings in Australia (and elsewhere), but there is a mismatch between the literature which sees translanguaging as valuing plurilingual students, their communities, language practices and language rights (Garcia, 2009; Young, 2010) and the situation on the ground in tertiary, and most educational, settings in Australia

Studies that were carried out painted a picture of a university which needed to pay more attention to interculturality, linguistic privilege and the underlying principles of internationalisation if students from diverse cultural and linguistic backgrounds were to feel valued and less marginalised (Piller, 2016). The following section outlines my pedagogical response to this research.

3 Pedagogical Response: Valuing and Recognising Cultures and Languages on Campus

I needed to think carefully about my approach to teaching and unit/course coordination on my campus in Australia as well as transnationally in our provider institution in Ho Chi Min City, Vietnam, if I was to practise what I preached. I had to encourage interculturality, more significant diverse linguistic representation and better understanding/awareness of, and support for, the use of Global Englishes and language varieties at course, unit of study and workshop level. Attention to this would diminish educational disparity between students and inculcate a sense of responsibility in academics to develop culturally and linguistically responsive pedagogies at all levels, as well as a sense of mission about inclusivity of staff with diverse linguistic and cultural backgrounds. I was guided in the formulation of my teaching approach by the philosophy that, (1) learning is made more memorable and engaging once emotion and relevance are attached (Immordino-Yang & Faeth, 2010), (2) learner-centredness involves diminished power relations and students as equal partners in learning (Matthews, 2017; Smith et al., 2020) and, (3) cognitive and social constructivist pedagogies facilitate learning. Central to my approach was acknowledgement of the need to be flexible in content and assessments in the transnational space and to be inclusive of local academics working in this space. I also felt strongly about including language and content from outside the dominant discourse. Storytelling, students as partners and message abundancy could be powerful learner-centred pedagogical tools when it came to ensuring cultural and linguistic inclusivity. I tried to apply all of what I had learned from the research to the courses and units I coordinated in the MA Applied Linguistics, MTESOL, Graduate Certificate in TESOL and Bachelor of Education.

4 Ensuring a Culturally and Linguistically Inclusive Approach at Course Level

As already mentioned, the principles enshrined in striving for inclusivity of culture and language apply not only to units of study and workshops, but to entire courses. The MA Applied Linguistics course has been taught in Australia since 1999 and transnationally in Vietnam since 2006. I have had to make decisions about course design and curriculum in these two settings. The question of inclusivity was raised when it came to the transnational Vietnamese lecturers and the units of study taught by Australian lecturers in Ho Chi Min City. Early in the partnership, Vietnamese lecturers reported "a desire to place the input in a more localised context… deliver information in a way that might be more accessible for Vietnamese English language teachers living and teaching in Vietnam" (Dobinson, 2013, p. 256) as well as a desire for Vietnamese students to keep their identity (p. 259). Together we co-designed changes to the curriculum, and re-imagined several units to reflect the contexts of the Vietnamese students taking the course. We included Vietnamese English in the MA unit *Special Topics in Applied Linguistics* which focuses on Global Englishes, and we fostered inclusivity by having assessments designed to allow Vietnamese students a choice of topics relevant to their contexts. We also discussed the marking of assessments, how we would deal with Vietnamese varieties of English if they arose (Dobinson et al., 2019) and the legitimacy, and desirability, of translanguaging between Vietnamese and English in the workshops taught by the Vietnamese lecturers (Li & Garcia, 2022). After peer observations and workshops, the Vietnamese lecturers were encouraged to take over four of the eight units taught by pre-dominantly monolingual Australian lecturers.

5 Adopting Approaches that Are Inclusive of Culture and Language at Unit of Study Level

Work Integrated Learning experiences in my Bachelor of Education *Language and Diversity* unit were reimagined based on my research. This unit is taken in the third year of the Bachelor of Education course by local Australian and international students all destined to be teachers in schools. Ways of assessing Culturally and Linguistically Diverse (CALD) students' writing were explored in the unit with a view to, (1) widening their perspectives on students' plurilingualism and spatial translingual repertoires (Canagarajah, 2018), (2) encouraging greater acceptance of varieties of English used by students in their classes. Initial teacher educators were able to integrate this knowledge and insight into their second assessment in the unit in which they have to adapt their teaching to a class largely comprised of CALD students. By making pre-service teachers aware of the plurilingual prowess of their students, and the legitimacy of their students' varieties of English, I attempted to move them away from a pre-occupation with a deficit view of EAL/D students' speaking and writing and towards the idea that Australian Standard English (something few of them speak themselves) is only one of many varieties spoken around the world (Jenkins, 2014).

Content in the post graduate unit *Transcultural Communication* was previously selected from a Western or Global North 'us and them' perspective (Dietz, 2018) and divided into nationality groups (i.e., Japanese speech styles, Aboriginal speech styles, etc.). After a light bulb moment at a conference, I realised that I was in fact guilty of culturalism myself by continuing to adopt this approach. The premises underlying the unit design resembled a large culture view of culture as static, stable and homogeneous (Byram, 2013; Freitag-Hild, 2018; Holliday, 2016) rather than a small culture view in which culture can mean feelings, beliefs, values, and behaviours that form within any small group. My experience with the Arab Film festival project showed me the value of incorporating a small culture view into my teaching. I re-designed the unit to focus on awkward moments across all cultures (e.g., inviting, apologizing, complimenting, directness/indirectness; shifting the emphasis from 'othering' to inclusivity (Dobinson et al., 2020)). If students were critical of what they were being taught, and saw outdated or misrepresented large culture stereotypes, they were encouraged to speak up. Dialogue, central to interculturality, was then initiated (Dervin & Simpson, 2021) and transformative stances made possible (Dietz, 2018). The original materials were also text-based, 'theory heavy' and from the perspective of a white, middle class, middle aged academic, lacking any recognition of intersectionality (e.g., social class, age, gender). There was little inclusion of multimodality such as SMS text messaging, Facebook posts, popular music videos and graffiti. Moreover, students had no ownership over the materials in the unit. Motivated by a first-year local student in my research project, who said he would like to know about the cultural backgrounds and languages of his classmates, but was too shy to ask, I made materials more interactive and accessible.

Inspired by the learning opportunities that students (and lecturers) said they had gained from films in an informal setting, and the *rihlas* these had provided, I set about incorporating different kinds of films into the unit. All the films had different messages relevant to the content of the unit. Some were short YouTube videos; some were advertisements and others were more substantial films. Many were in languages other than English or different varieties of English such as Aboriginal English. All depicted scenarios in which students were able to conduct a *rihla* together and "find the familiar in the strange" (Abdul-Jabbar, 2019, p. 258) as well as the strange in the familiar. One video depicted a Saudi Arabian artist and activist called Hisham Fageeh singing a song with locally relevant lyrics in English to the tune of Bob Marley's *No woman no crime* (Fageeh, 2013). The second example depicted Australian Aboriginal children singing a hip hop song but using Aboriginal English and local language to do so in their own bush setting (Monkey Marc, 2011).

5.1   Workshop Level

As mentioned earlier, a culturally and linguistically inclusive university classroom can be achieved by the use of approaches which allow students to bring their personal lives into the classroom, feel respected and valued and have many opportunities to make meaning out of what is being taught. I have found the encouragement of storytelling by both the lecturer and the students, the reimagining of students as partners with lecturers in learning and the exposure of students to messages in many different mediums and modes to facilitate inclusivity. Each one of these components is outlined in more detail in the sections that follow.

5.2   Inclusivity as Storytelling

Personalized storytelling can break down cultural, linguistic, and social barriers (Koehne, 2005) and make international students comfortable in their new setting while enabling all students (and the teacher) to learn about other cultures and languages. It is a powerful tool for making CALD students, in particular, feel noticed, valued and more permanent. As previously mentioned, stories can be "small", disjointed, full of hesitations, unfinished ideas and interruptions (Ochs & Capps, 2002). An example of this, in my undergraduate *Language and Diversity* unit, is when I introduce the concept of Schema Theory on a PowerPoint slide. Noting the students' blank stares, I put them at ease by telling a humorous story of a friend's disorientation when his schema is upset by staying in a hotel room rather than his own bedroom. I then get students to relate their own similar stories of schema disequilibrium to each other in groups. The group decides whether the students' individual stories are examples of schema theory or not. We then discuss this in a mini plenary session. Afterwards, the more advanced topic of cultural schema can be introduced, and students can compare their own cultural experiences and note the similarities and differences in the way they responded in certain situations and settings and the language they might have used. These language related stories were especially significant during COVID-19 disruptions when the students in my unit suddenly found themselves fully online. Nearly every day I would tell my small story to students while they responded with stories of their own COVID experiences set, either locally or in their own states or countries, against diverse cultural and linguistic backdrops. Storytelling created intimacy, and was an effective and inclusive teaching tool, in my virtual classroom (Baskerville, 2011; Csikar & Stefaniak, 2018) and higher education setting (Abrahamson, 1998) (Fig. 1).

If I do seem a little bit out of kilter today ....I encountered ...the most alarming kind of COVID rage ...I've had so far .... at the erm checkout ...you know how you have to do your own bags now ... I was going as fast as I could and this chap ...I don't know ...he must have been in his late 60s ... starting commenting ...saying you know ...something like erm 'Well if you could just get a move on I would be able to get through here'...I went 'Oh sorry I can't go any faster... I'm just packing as fast as I can' and then he said 'Well if you just stop faffing around and get them in' and I was like (puffs air out) ...'Excuse me' ...so I said 'Would you mind not being so rude' and then he said 'Well would you mind just getting a fxxxing move on'...so I was like 'Oh ok' ...so I just silently went as slow as I could.

Fig. 1 My Covid story as a lead into students telling their stories

5.3   Inclusivity: Re-imagining Students as 'Partners'

Learner-centredness can sometimes be more 'talk than walk' with lecturers who are used to being in control in their classrooms dominating the discourse, without even realising it. I try to combat this by giving short mini-lectures then long learner-centred tasks which require a group leader to keep the discussion going and then feedback to the larger group. I try to give the role to a student who may not otherwise say very much, especially someone whose first language is not English. In other words, I turn them into partners. I encourage students who have access to a language other than English to use some of their own language whether there is someone in the group who speaks the same language or not. In this way the student can become a teacher of their language at a very basic level. Alongside the use of their L1 they can make use of their full spatial repertoires. This includes gesture, paralinguistic behaviour, visuals, realia, devices which allow for the negotiation of meaning and the making of successful self-expression (Kim & Park, 2019) such as when using Google translate. All of this encourages translanguaging practices. Such practices have been discussed in the context of expressiveness and linguistic creativity (Dovchin et al., 2018), with users combining multiple first language (L1), additional language (LX) explicit verbal and written linguistic resources, modes and repertoires (Van Viegen, 2020) to help them process information and communicate effectively. Explicit translanguaging can also be achieved by the incorporation of varied linguistic resources to talk about interlocutors' lives and events occurring around them (Li & Zhu, 2013, 2019). This can improve expressive interactions between both students & teachers and students & students. It can make learning more memorable and increase the involvement of learners who speak English as one language in their broader repertoire, in the discourse of the workshops. It can mitigate any pressure students might feel to constantly speak or write in English and enable them to grapple more effectively with newly learned concepts (Young, 2010). It is also a way of bringing students' home languages into the context of the dominant monolingual setting. As one West Papuan university student said about his university bible group, where members read a section of the Bible in their language each meeting, "You could say it is a bit confusing…you can't understand what they are saying…but what is really good you know like how they [languages] sound like". The auditory sensation of hearing languages different to his own was appreciated by the student (Dobinson & Mercieca, 2020, p. 795).

Another way to appreciate students as partners is through increased personalization and the use of students' linguistic and cultural backgrounds as essential authentic resources. This builds a greater pool of knowledge for the entire group. Being informed about other cultures and languages is key to student-lecturer partnerships. One way of informing myself, and the rest of the class, is to get students to bring their own materials to workshops in their own languages so that we can make meaningful connections between unit content and their everyday realities. An example of this can be seen in my *Transcultural Communication* unit where a Chinese student brought the Chinese national anthem in Mandarin (which she sang to the class) and an English translation to compare with the New Zealand and Australian national anthems for language style and content. All students were then very motivated to discuss their own national anthems. To highlight different writing styles across cultures, I bring emails sent to me by students (after seeking approval from the authors of course) or emails sent to other students. Emails from Vietnamese and Omani students written in English often demonstrate an unusual shift in writing style, mixing the formal with the very personal. Students can then explain the differences in styles and tell us the translations in their own languages. When looking at linguistic theory, such as Accommodation Theory, I bring a series of emails between an Australian student and a Japanese exchange student written in English. These can capture cultural schemas and also the language of youth, showing how the two interlocutors accommodate and converge towards each other, with the L1 English speaker converging towards the Japanese English speaker in both style and level of complexity in writing. Students analyse the emails collaboratively in groups and bring in their own emails in their own languages or in English to translate and/or analyse. The following email chain, which the participants gave permission to use, is an example of this.

Figure 2 (names have been changed to pseudonyms) shows how the inclusion of authentic texts from both the lecturer's and the students' lives, can foster students' active engagement, collaboration, and opportunities for choice. International students can feel empowered and included in an approach which breaks down power relationships and moves away from didacticism. They take on a consultant role common to any partnership arrangement. Formative feedback (with students handing in first drafts for guidance) is also part of students being seen as partners. A dialogic approach is taken towards assessed work, which resembles the way that academics, who are collaborating on articles together, give each other feedback. This ensures that students are perceiving the requirements of the task in the same way as the lecturer. Students are encouraged to post first drafts and road map plans to a blog for comment by peers and the lecturer before embarking on the final draft of an assessment for submission.

> Hello
> Luciano and Luciano's family.
> I am Yoshi.
> Now able to use this computer.
> My mother couldn't send mail for Luciano yesterday.
> Please tell me Luciano's address.
> Thank you
> Hello Yoshi.
> I am Luciano.
> I think maybe you have the wrong address.
> Here is my address luciano_mercieca@hotmail.com
> if it does not work you can use my mums.
> When you come to my house you will be sleeping in my brother's room.
> We are looking forward to meeting you.
> Thank You

Fig. 2 Emails between a Japanese student and an Australian student

5.4   Inclusivity as Message Abundancy

Ensuring an abundance of input on one particular topic, theme, or message allows students who are operating in an LX to get multiple opportunities to decode important content. They require scaffolding in their learning using a combination of traditional paper and digital resources to create message abundancy. Curricula need to be carefully crafted to include multimedia. Teaching approaches should take advantage of the multimodality that is possible on digital platforms (i.e., video, audio and side text chat). These features allow the lecturer to relate to students' backgrounds, cultures, languages and interests with diverse delivery of content and multifaceted tasks in different media. This might mean utilizing written text, YouTube videos, social media, SMS text messaging, personal emails, music, poetry anthologies and any authentic texts with which students have daily contact. For example, when discussing language contact and translanguaging, students engage interactively with prescribed readings on this topic in groups before I summarise the main points. Students then listen to a recording of a song in which translanguaging takes place and try to work out what is being said. After that, they watch a video of a musician singing the same song. Next, they fill in the gaps on the lyric sheet and watch again to check what they have filled in. Once they have the transcript complete, they revisit what the singer is describing and the meaning behind his lyrics. They then analyse the lyric sheet for instances of creole using a list of characteristics I provide. Finally, students are shown poems written by the same artist in Standard British English to highlight the artist's plurilinguality and capacity to translanguage. This teaching cycle encourages collaboration and confidence building in students, recognising those who have done the prescribed reading as mentors of those who have not done the reading. Of course, if the relationship becomes one-sided, with the same students doing all the reading, then the teacher intervenes and allocates reading tasks equitably. The video gives a multimodal perspective, and the content validates CALD students' translingual repertoires. Students ultimately achieve success in a difficult task, and they use this learning process as a blueprint for their own teaching when they return to teach in schools in their own countries. Having all the different kinds of materials for the same topic pre-loaded onto the Blackboard site also facilitates student independence through a 'flipped' approach. Assuring the same message is conveyed in many different ways is especially inclusive for CALD students who may need examples reiterated several times to be able to fully comprehend the message. Digital tools, such as recorded lectures and live online sessions, support students to revisit their learning in their own time.

Figure 3 illustrates how common practice it is for plurilingual, bidialectal or even monolingual individuals to move easily between two or more languages or styles, thus endorsing students' capacity to do the same and encouraging them to feel comfortable doing so. It also shows them that judging people on their variety of English is not legitimate as many plurilingual people maintain successful hybrid identities and do so on a regular basis.

Sonny's Lettah	Jamaica Lullaby
from brixton prison, jebb avenue london s.w. 2 inglan	*(to the memory of Olive Morris)*
	So soon
dear mama	the moon
good day	rises tonight
i hope that when these few lines reach you they may find you	making fire
in the best of health	making sparks
i doun know how to tell ya dis for i did mek a solemn promise	piercing spots of dark
to tek care a lickle jim an try mi bes fi look out fi him	
mama, i really did try mi bes but none a di less	stars gather gold
sorry fi tell ya seh, poor lickle jim get arres	making holes
it was de miggle a di rush hour	in the vast body of night
hevrybody jus a hustle and a bustle	dogs begin
to go home fi dem evenin showermi an jim stan up waitin pon	their ritual barks
a bus	and howls as fowls
not causin no fuss	steal sleep to meet
	tomorrow face to face

Fig. 3 Example of translanguaging shown to students

6 Concluding Remarks

Being culturally and linguistically inclusive requires a bottom-up approach to teaching students. Communities and contexts need to be closely researched to explore where the gaps are in terms of equitable and transformative approaches in both formal and informal learning environments. Keeping in touch with communities ensures a dynamic rather than static view of culture and language, a small culture rather than large culture view, which avoids essentialist tendencies (Holliday, 2016). The studies I have alluded to in this chapter gave rise to a teaching approach focused on cultural and linguistic inclusion. Without such an approach, certain students would be denied the opportunity to establish and display their cultural and plurilingual identities. This perspective does not cancel out the importance of developing and operating in the new LX, but it recognises the benefits of using the first language as an additional resource. Studies have found that when home cultures and languages are seen as valuable learning resources in classrooms, and incorporated into workshops, students whose first language is not English tend to engage more in learning and show better academic gains (Langdon & Cheng, 1992). The bolstering of learners' linguistic and cultural identities through their L1 has a positive effect on their LX probably because learners can maintain their L1 self while developing their ideal LX self rather than replacing their L1 self. Moreover, all students in the class, even monolingual students, are encouraged to develop a hybrid identity. Immersion in language in mainstream subjects has proved to be successful in Australia in recent years with First Nations/ Aboriginal and Torres Strait Islander languages. The use of Noongar language in signage, labelling of emails and events, acknowledgements of country and greetings in university classrooms, has produced students who are now familiar with, and able to use, some basic Noongar language. The point is not necessarily for them to learn the language, but to respect both the language and the people who speak it.

Rather than focusing on cultural and linguistic differences as 'problematic', resorting to deficit views of difference, and becoming pre-occupied with students 'blending in' with the dominant cultural and linguistic discourse (Dobinson & Mercieca, 2020), students can have their first languages and cultures privileged alongside those of the dominant discourse. They can be seen as linguistic and cultural resources, valued for their translingual repertoires and visible in their identities. Relationships between lecturers and students can be dynamic, with the materials and tasks underpinning the workshops co-constructed and co-designed between participants (Ryan, 2011; Singh & Nguyen, 2018). Being inclusive at course level can mean utilising the skills of lecturers who are plurilingual and local to the context in which students are being taught. At unit level, it may mean careful attention to the inclusion of material which reflects all contexts and languages. At workshop level, it may involve storytelling which brings in students' personal lives and cultural/linguistic backgrounds. It may also mean engaging students as partners to co-design workshop content and provide snapshots of other cultures and languages for their peers. Finally, it also means incorporating different media into workshops to allow the same messages to be available to learners in very many modes, providing learners with abundant opportunities to consolidate meaning. These are just a few insights I have had about making my tertiary teaching more culturally and linguistically inclusive. Fundamental to this is a dialogic and critical approach which reshapes traditional relationships not only between lecturers and students, but between the hegemonic minority and the oppressed majority (Dervin & Simpson, 2021).

References

Abdul-Jabbar, W. K. (2019). The intercultural deterritorialization of knowledge: Al-Ghazali and the enunciation of the educator's rihla. *Teaching in Higher Education, 24*(3), 318–331. https://doi.org/10.1080/13562517.2018.1542378

Abrahamson, C. E. (1998). Storytelling as a pedagogical tool in higher education. *Education, 11*(3), 440. https://global.factiva.com/ha/default.aspx#./!?&_suid=16573572236750705382861610672

Aman, R. (2015). Why Interculturalidad is not Interculturality. *Cultural Studies, 29*(2), 205–228. https://doi.org/10.1080/09502386.2014.899379

Australian Government Department of Education and Training (DET). (2018). *International student data monthly summary*. Retrieved from: https://internationaleducation.gov.au/research/International-Student-data/Documents/MONTHLY20SUMMARIES/2018/Aug202018%20MonthlyInfographic.pdf

Baskerville, D. (2011). Developing cohesion and building positive relationships through storytelling in a culturally diverse New Zealand classroom. *Teaching and Teacher Education, 27*, 107–115. https://doi.org/10.1016/j.tate.2010.07.007

Behar, R. (1996). *The vulnerable observer: Anthropology that breaks your heart*. Beacon Press.

Bowles, T. V., & Brindle, K. A. (2017). Identifying facilitating factors and barriers to improving student retention rates in tertiary teaching courses: a systematic review. *Higher Education Research & Development, 36*(5), 903–919. https://doi.org/10.1080/07294360.2016.1264927

Byram, M. (2013). Foreign language teaching and intercultural citizenship. *Iranian Journal of Language Teaching Research, 1*(3), 53–62.

Canagarajah, S. (2018). Translingual practice as spatial repertoires: Expanding the paradigm beyond structuralist orientations. *Applied Linguistics, 39*(1), 31–54. https://doi.org/10.1093/applin/amx041gs

Colvin, C., Volet, S., & Fozdar, F. (2014). Local university students and intercultural interactions: Conceptualising culture. *Higher Education Research & Development, 33*(3), 440–455. https://doi.org/10.1080/07294360.2013.841642

Csikar, E., & Stefaniak, J. E. (2018). The utility of storytelling strategies in the biology classroom. *Contemporary Educational Technology, 9*(1), 42–60. https://doi.org/10.30935/cedtech/6210

Dervin, F., & Simpson, A. (2021). *Interculturality and the Political Within Education*. Routledge. https://doi.org/10.4324/9780429471155

Dietz, G. (2018). Interculturality. In H. Callan (Ed.), *The international encyclopedia of anthropology* (pp. 1–19). Wiley & Sons.

Dobinson, T. (2013). *Encountering the "Asian learner": Teaching and learning experiences of post graduate Asian learners and their lecturers in Australia and Vietnam*. (Doctoral Dissertation). Retrieved from: https://api.research-repository.uwa.edu.au/ws/portalfiles/portal/3360204/Dobinson_Toni_2013.pdf

Dobinson, T., & Mercieca, P. (2020). Seeing things as they are, not just as we are: Investigating the visibility of languages on an Australian university campus. *International Journal of Bilingual Education and Bilingualism, 23*(7), 789–803. https://doi.org/10.1080/13670050.2020.1724074

Dobinson, T., & Nguyen, B. (2018). Teaching young EAL/D learners in mainstream contexts. In R. Oliver & B. Nguyen (Eds.), *Teaching young second language learners: Practices in different classroom contexts*. Routledge.

Dobinson, T., Mercieca, P., & Kent, S. (2019). World Englishes in academic writing: Exploring markers' responses. In T. Dobinson & K. Dunworth (Eds.), *Literacy unbound: Multiliterate, multilingual, multimodal* (pp. 11–29). Springer Nature.

Dobinson, T., McAlinden, M., Mercieca, P., & Bogachenko, T. (2020). Finding the familiar in the strange: Transcultural learning as rihla رحلة at an Australian university. *Higher Education Research Development., 40*, 476–490. https://doi.org/10.1080/07294360.2020.1765317

Dobinson, T., Dryden, S., Dovchin, S., Gong, Q., & Mercieca, P. (2023). Translanguaging and "English only" at universities. *TESOL Quarterly*. https://onlinelibrary.wiley.com/doi/10.1002/tesq.3232

Dovchin, S. (2019). Language crossing and linguistic racism: Mongolian immigrant women in Australia. *Journal of Multicultural Discourses, 14*(4), 1–18. https://doi.org/10.1080/17447143.2019.1566345

Dovchin, S., Pennycook, A., & Sultana, S. (2018). *Popular culture, voice and linguistic diversity: young adults on-and offline*. Palgrave-MacMillan.

Earshot, ABC Radio National. (2019). Is Australia ready for the multilingual mindset? Tongue tied and fluent part 1. Retrieved from https://www.abc.net.au/radionational/programs/earshot/is-australia-ready-for-the-multilingualmindset/11658608

Fageeh, H. (2013). *No woman no drive.* Retrieved from https://www.youtube.com/watch?v=aZMbTFNp4wI

Freitag-Hild, B. (2018). Teaching culture – intercultural competence, transcultural learning, global education. In C. Surkamp & B. Viebrock (Eds.), *Teaching English as a foreign language* (pp. 159–175). JB Metzler.

Garcia, O. (2009). Education, multilingualism and translanguaging in the 21st century. In T. Skutnabb-Kangas, R. Phillipson, A. K. Mohanty, & M. Panada (Eds.), *Social justice through multilingual education* (pp. 140–159). Multilingual Matters.

García, O., & Li, W. (2014). *Translanguaging: Language, Bilingualism and education.* Palgrave Macmillan Pivot.

Gibbons, P. (2009). *English learners' academic literacy and thinking.* Heinemann.

God, Y. T., & Zhang, H. (2019). Intercultural challenges, intracultural practices: How Chinese and Australian students understand and experience intercultural communication at an Australian university. *Higher Education, 78,* 305–322. https://doi.org/10.1007/s10734-018-0344-0

Holliday, A. (2016). Revisiting intercultural competence: Small culture formation on the go through threads of experience. *International Journal of Bias, Identity and Diversities in Education, 1*(2), 1–13. https://doi.org/10.4018/IJBIDE.2016070101

Immordino-Yang, M. H., & Faeth, M. (2010). The role of emotion and skilled intuition in learning. In D. A. Sousa (Ed.), *Mind, brain and education: Neuroscience implications for the classroom* (pp. 1–23). Solution Tree Press.

Jenkins, J. (2006). Current perspectives on teaching WEs and English as a Lingua Franca. *TESOL Quarterly, 40*(1), 157–181. https://doi.org/10.2307/40264515

Jenkins, J. (2014). *English as a Lingua Franca in the international university: The politics of academic English language policy.* Routledge.

Kim, K. M., & Park, G. (2019). "It is more expressive for me": A translingual approach to meaningful literacy instruction through Sijo poetry. *TESOL Quarterly, 54*(2), 281–309. https://doi.org/10.1002/tesq.545

Kirkpatrick, A. (2007). *World Englishes: Implications for international communication and English language teaching.* Cambridge University Press.

Kirkpatrick, A. (2011). English as an Asian lingua franca and the multilingual model of ELT. *Language Teaching, 44*(2), 212–224. https://doi.org/10.1017/S0261444810000145

Koehne, N. (2005). (Re) Construction: Ways international students talk about their identity. *Australian Journal of Education, 49*(1), 104–119. https://doi.org/10.1177/000494410504900107

Kraidy, M. (2017). *Hybridity, or the cultural logic of globalization.* Temple University Press.

Kramsch, C. (1993). *Context and culture in language teaching.* Oxford University Press.

Kramsch, C. (2011). The symbolic dimensions of the intercultural. *Language Teaching, 44*(3), 354–367. https://doi.org/10.1017/S0261444810000431

Langdon, H. W., & Cheng, L. R. L. (1992). *Hispanic children and adults with communication disorders: Assessment and intervention.* Aspen.

Lantz-Deaton, C. (2017). Internationalisation and the development of students' intercultural competence. *Teaching in Higher Education, 22*(5), 532–550. https://doi.org/10.1080/13562517.2016.1273209

Leask, B., & Carroll, J. (2011). Moving beyond 'wishing and hoping': Internationalisation and student experiences of inclusion and engagement. *Higher Education Research & Development, 30*(5), 647–659. https://doi.org/10.1080/07294360.2011.598454

Li, W., & Garcia, O. (2022). Not a first language but one repertoire: Translanguaging as a decolonizing project. *RELC Journal, 53,* 1–12. https://doi.org/10.1177/00336882221092841

Li, W., & Ho, W. Y. (2018). Language learning sans frontiers: Translanguaging view. *Annual Review of Applied Linguistics, 38,* 33–59. https://doi.org/10.1017/S0267190518000053

Li, W., & Zhu, H. (2013). Translanguaging identities and ideologies: Creating transnational space through flexible multilingual practices amongst Chinese university students in the UK. *Applied Linguistics, 34*(5), 516–535. https://doi.org/10.1093/applin/amt022

Li, W., & Zhu, H. (2019). Tranßcripting: playful subversion with Chinese characters. *International Journal of Multilingualism, 16*(2), 145–161. https://doi.org/10.1080/14790718.2019.1575834

Liddicoat, A. (2016). Language planning in universities: Teaching, research and administration. *Current Issues in Language Planning, 17*(3–4), 231–241. https://doi.org/10.1080/1466420 8.2016.1216351

Marginson, S. (2003). Higher education reform in Australia – an evaluation. In H. Eggins (Ed.), *Globalisation and reform in higher education* (pp. 133–163). Open University Press.

Marginson, S., & Sawir, E. (2011). *Ideas for intercultural education*. Palgrave-Macmillan.

Matthews, K. (2017). Five propositions for genuine students as partners practice. *International Journal for Students as Partners, 1*(2), 1–9. https://doi.org/10.15173/ijsap.v1i2.3315

McDermott-Levy, R. (2011). Going alone: The lived experience of female Arab-Muslim nursing students living and studying in the United States. *Nursing Outlook, 59*, 266–277. https://doi.org/10.1016/j.outlook.2011.02.006

McLachlan, D., & Justice, J. (2009). A grounded theory of international student well-being. *Journal of Theory Construction and Testing, 13*, 27–32.

Meyer, M. (1991). Developing transcultural competence: Case studies of advanced foreign language learners. In D. Buttjes & M. Byram (Eds.), *Mediating languages and cultures* (pp. 136–158). Multilingual Matters.

Monkey Marc. (2011). *Bikey Boys from Nyirripi, NT*. [video] YouTube. Retrieved from https://www.youtube.com/watch?app=desktop&v=1_oKO76OApk

Ochs, E., & Capps, L. (2002). *Living narrative*. Harvard University Press.

Piller, I. (2016). *Linguistic diversity and social justice: An introduction to applied sociolinguistics*. Oxford University Press.

Risager, K. (2006). *Language and culture: Global flows and local complexity*. Multilingual Matters.

Rogoff, B., Callanan, M., Gutiérrez, K. D., & Erickson, F. (2016). The organization of informal learning. *Review of Research in Education, 40*(1), 356–401. https://doi.org/10.310 2/0091732X16680994

Ryan, J. (2011). Teaching and learning for international students: Towards a transcultural approach AU. *Teachers and Teaching, 17*(6), 631–648. https://doi.org/10.1080/13540602.2011.625138

Shepherd, G., & Rane, H. (2012). *Experiencing Australia: Arab students' perspectives and perceptions informing enhancement strategies*. Paper presented at the 23rd ISANA conference, Auckland.

Shohamy, E. (2013). A critical perspective on the use of English as a medium of instruction at Universities. In A. Doiz, D. Lasagabaster, & J. M. Sierra (Eds.), *English-medium instruction at universities: Global challenges* (pp. 196–212). Multilingual Matters.

Singh, M., & Nguyen, T. H. N. (2018). *Teaching students through localizing Chinese*. Springer.

Smith, C., Beltman, S., Dinham, J., Dobinson, T., & Jay, J. (2020). Supporting undergraduate university students through instrumental mentoring. *Australian Journal of Teacher Education, 45*(1). https://doi.org/10.14221/ajte.2020v45n1.6

Van Viegen, S. (2020). Remaking the ground on which they stand: Plurilingual approaches across the curriculum. In S. M. C. Lau & S. Van Viegen (Eds.), *Plurilingual Pedagogies: Critical and creative endeavours for equitable language in education* (pp. 161–183). Springer.

Yanaprasart, P., & Lüdi, G. (2018). Diversity and multilingual challenges in academic settings. *International Journal of Bilingual Education and Bilingualism, 21*(7), 825–840. https://doi.org/10.1080/13670050.2017.1308311

Young, V. A. (2010). Nah, we straight: An argument against code-switching. *Journal of Advanced Composition JAC, 29*(1–2), 49–76.

Toni Dobinson is Associate Professor, coordinator and teacher of the Post Graduate Programmes in Applied Linguistics at Curtin University, Australia. She researches and publishes in the areas of language teacher education, language and identity, language and social justice, translingual practices and is the co-editor of the book, *Literacy Unbound: Multiliterate, Multilingual, Multimodal*. Email: T.Dobinson@curtin.edu.au

Teacher – Culture – Pluri: An International Initiative to Develop Open Educational Resources for Pluralistic Teaching in FL Teacher Education

María-Elena Gómez-Parra and Joanna Pfingsthorn

Abstract Preparing teachers for responsible plurilingual/pluricultural foreign language education is a challenging task. Despite the availability of extensive literature on intercultural teaching, there are very few comprehensive open educational, digital resources devoted specifically to plurilingualism/pluriculturalism that could be applicable in various educational systems as well as on various levels of teacher education. In this contribution we describe a successful attempt to alleviate this problem by an international team (Erasmus+ Project "TEACUP: Teacher – Culture – Pluri") composed of researchers, policy makers and teacher educators from four European countries (Spain, Poland, Hungary and Germany) and the USA, who have jointly developed a large set of comprehensive open educational resources that are intended to provide a theoretical foundation and practical materials for plurilingual and pluricultural foreign language teaching and assessment. We focus on the application of the developed open educational resources dealing with key concepts around pluriculturalism and plurilingualism in an international workshop for both pre- and in-service teachers of English as a foreign language. Upon discussing the underlying structure of the materials, we report on their perceived quality and the shortcomings of their application in this concrete educational setting. We round off the discussion with comments and implications for foreign language teacher education programs.

Keywords Plurilingualism · Pluriculturalism · International project · Teacher educators · In-service teachers · Pre-service teachers

M.-E. Gómez-Parra (✉)
University of Córdoba, Córdoba, Spain
e-mail: elena.gomez@uco.es

J. Pfingsthorn
University of Bremen, Bremen, Germany
e-mail: pfingsthorn@uni-bremen.de

© The Author(s), under exclusive license to Springer Nature Switzerland AG 2023
A. Sahlane, R. Pritchard (eds.), *English as an International Language Education*, English Language Education 33,
https://doi.org/10.1007/978-3-031-34702-3_10

177

1 Introduction

Plurilingualism views individual language components as "uneven, differentiated according to the learner's experience and in an unstable relation as that experience changes" (Council of Europe, 2001, p. 34). Plurilinguals are assumed to have the ability to call flexibly upon their "single, inter-related" repertoire, which manifests, for instance, in the capacity to "switch from one language, dialect or variety to another", to "bring the whole of one's linguistic equipment into play, experimenting with alternative forms of expression" or to "call upon the knowledge of several languages (or dialects, or varieties) to make sense of a text or experiment with alternative forms of expression" (Council of Europe, 2018, p. 28). The fluidity with which these various language components interact is believed to promote the development of linguistic and cultural awareness, and to contribute to global understanding and acceptance of diversity. It is also interwoven with the concept of pluriculturalism – an approach that perceives individuals as complex beings shaped by multiple cultural experiences and identifications (Runnels, 2021).

If we assume – following Pennycook (2010) that "languages are a product of the deeply social and cultural activities in which people engage", and are "central organizing activities of social lives" (pp. 1–2), then it becomes clear that viewing and teaching languages as compartmentalized structures or pre-given entities instead of dynamic, local practices is not accurate. In fact, such a view can even limit our understanding of how languages and speakers truly operate. As Makoni and Pennycook (2006, p. 2) suggest, "languages do not exist as real entities in the world and neither do they emerge from or represent real environments; they are, by contrast, the inventions of social, cultural and political movements."

Yet, languages (and their cultural contexts) are still typically taught in isolation. In the EU, for instance, although each member state is free to shape its own educational system individually, a monolingual and compartmentalized approach to foreign languages (FL) seems to be a common ground, with English being the most common compulsory foreign language at upper secondary general education level. In 2019, 96% of European students were, in fact, learning English, followed by other languages typically listed as separate entities: Spanish (26%), French (22%), German (20%) and Italian (3%) (Eurostat, 2019). In addition, in most EU member states, more than three fifths of students, in general upper secondary education, were reported to be learning two or more foreign languages in 2019. However, this number reached only 12.1% in Ireland, 6.3% in Portugal and 0.7% in Greece (Eurostat, 2021[1]). Given that politically, the EU strives to reach the Barcelona Summit (2002) "mother tongue + 2" objective, these numbers are rather disappointing, especially in the face of the European labour market's growing demand for effective multi- and plurilingual communication skills and (pluri)cultural awareness (OMC group, 2020). Thus, apart from potentially failing to do justice to the

---

[1] https://ec.europa.eu/eurostat/statistics-explained/index.php?title=Foreign_language_learning_statistics

complex reality of learners' linguistic/cultural repertoires (Blommaert & Backus, 2013), monolingual teaching also creates "limitations in terms both of learning capacity and space in the curriculum" (Candelier et al., 2012, p. 8) that constrict the exposure to a diverse spectrum of languages and cultures.

At the same time, there is ample evidence to support the notion that adopting plurilingualism can be a challenge for teachers. As Hélot and Laoire (2011, p. xi) put it,

> teachers in the multilingual classroom may continue to underestimate the competence of plurilingual students and to silence their voices, rather than using cross-linguistic learning strategies and learners' metalinguistic awareness as learning resources across languages and even across school disciplines.

In fact, stigmatization or marginalization in foreign language education is not an issue that the field of second language acquisition or foreign language education has managed to eradicate or avoid completely. A good example is the complex status or significance of bi/multilingualism. As Ortega (2017, p. 288) points out, many ideologically monolingual societies have the tendency to impose the monolingual ethos onto multilingual speakers, and while multilingualism should "neither be demonized nor romanticized", "it is the socially constructed hierarchical valuing of different languages and different degrees and shapes of multilingualism that creates a boon for some and a liability for others". Given such challenges, it is plausible that preparing foreign language teachers for responsible plurilingual/pluricultural foreign language education can present itself as a difficult task, especially in the face of relatively scarce resources that could aid the process. Foreign language education can rely on extensive literature on intercultural teaching, and learn from the attempts to make such academic content more accessible to teachers (e.g., "[d]eveloping teacher competences for pluralistic approaches" (ECML, 2021)). However, to date there exist no comprehensive open educational, digital resources for foreign language teacher education which could offer a broad look into plurilingual/pluricultural language education and be applicable in various educational systems as well as on various levels of teacher education.

In this contribution we demonstrate an attempt to alleviate this problem, namely through the foundation of an international project team composed of researchers, policy makers and teacher educators from four European countries (Spain, Poland, Hungary and Germany) and the United States under the umbrella of an Erasmus+ Project "TEACUP: Teacher – Culture – Pluri" funded by the European Union (ref. no. 2019-1-ES01-KA203-064412). The project team have been tasked to jointly develop, test, and evaluate a large set of comprehensive open educational resources that are intended to provide a theoretical foundation and practical materials for plurilingual and pluricultural foreign language teaching and assessment. These modules offer teachers an insight into the principles of pluricultural/plurilingual education in FL learning settings with a focus on three issues: Key Concepts, Classroom Applications and Assessment.

More specifically, in this chapter we focus on learning materials belonging to the area of Key Concepts and demonstrate an attempt to evaluate their application in the context of an intensive course for pre- and in-service teachers. We use this example to display the underlying structure of the materials as well as their potential pedagogical versatility and shortcomings. We round off the discussion with comments and implications for foreign language teacher education programs.

2   Plurilingualism and Pluriculturalism as Educational Goals: Pluralistic Approaches

From the plurilingual/pluricultural point of view, borders between languages become irrelevant. García (2009, p. 45) suggests a shift away from the monolingual and compartmentalized perspective and the adoption of the concept of "translanguaging" – an attempt at "describing the language practices of bilinguals from the perspective of the users themselves, and not [...] from the perspective of the language itself". Focusing on translanguaging practices of multilingual learners "disrupts the hierarchy that sees 'native' English speakers as possessing English and thus superior to those who acquire English as a 'second' language" (García et al., 2017, p. 4). In this sense, plurilingual language learning approaches distance themselves from three ideologies: (1) the native speaker serving as the ideal model of language proficiency; (2) the assumption that the ideal bilingual speaker is fluent in one or more languages; and (3) the conviction that partial competences in different languages, varieties or dialects are a deficiency (Runnels, 2021, p. 9). Seen from the plurilingual/pluricultural perspective, language learning is, thus, a way to enhance learners' repertoires without compartmentalizing languages; it does not necessarily target a native speaker-like mastery of one or more languages. The Companion Volume to the Common European Framework of Reference (Council of Europe, 2018) attempts to further specify plurilingual competence (i.e., "the ability to call flexibly upon an inter-related, uneven, plurilinguistic repertoire" (p. 28)) as the ability to:

- switch from one language or dialect (or variety) to another;
- express oneself in one language (or dialect, or variety) and understand a person speaking another;
- call upon the knowledge of a number of languages (or dialects, or varieties) to make sense of a text;
- recognise words from a common international store in a new guise;
- mediate between individuals with no common language (or dialect, or variety), even with only a slight knowledge oneself;
- bring the whole of one's linguistic equipment into play, experimenting with alternative forms of expression;
- exploit paralinguistics (mime, gesture, facial expression, etc.).

(Council of Europe, 2018, p. 28)

Plurilingual/pluricultural approaches steer away from pre-defined notions or preconceptions of what languages, dialects, or varieties these should be. These languages, varieties or dialects do not necessarily need to be taught within the educational system and can exist in any societal domain. This is also true for cultures, which can be "individual, societal and geographic" (Runnels, 2021). Pluricultural individuals do not necessarily adopt or identify with traits or practices of other cultures through "eclectic fusion of resources and elements drawn from multiple cultures to create a novel cultural synthesis" (p. 3); they do not necessarily have to be members of a cultural minority or majority or individuals living in ethnically homogeneous communities, who come to the realization that their own society is diverse, as Byram (2009, p. 326) suggests. Rather, their pluricultural repertoire is shaped by their individual life experience. Hence, people who are "born in the same place, live in the same neighbourhood, speak the same languages, have the same interests and experience the same type of (formal or informal) education" end up developing their individualized pluricultural profiles (Runnels, 2021, p. 11). Runnels (2011, p. 11) suggests the following influences that shape how individual pluricultural repertoires develop: "life trajectory, job or occupational paths, geographic space, family mobility, travel expatriation, emigration, family experience and history, changing personal interests, reading and through the media". In this sense, pluricultural approaches reject the notion that culture can be equated with nationality or ethnic heritage and that certain values, beliefs or practices are reserved for given cultural groups. Pluricultural approaches also embrace the dynamic nature of cultural repertoires, which change over time.

Pluricultural and plurilingual – or pluralistic – approaches strive to increase learners' awareness of linguistic and cultural diversity and its role in communicative situations. There are a few pluralistic approaches to language learning that have been commonly recognized, such as awakening to languages or inter-comprehension (Candelier et al., 2012). Awakening to languages is based on the notion that linguistic diversity can be introduced to learners at an early age, both within and beyond their communities. Learners should be exposed to languages and learn about them, which ideally leads to the development of curiosity and interest in said languages and cultures. In an inter-comprehension approach, learners focus on two or more languages from the same linguistic family and use the knowledge of a related language to learn a new one. In both approaches, relationships among the studied languages and cultures are identified, recognized, and then optimized for the learning process.

3 Plurilingualism and Pluriculturalism in Foreign Language Teacher Education: Demands and Challenges

For the last 20 years, the European Commission has explicitly promoted plurilingualism, notably through the Common European Framework of Reference for Languages (CEFR) (Council of Europe, 2001), a pan-European guideline used to describe the achievements of foreign language learners in the subject matter, and, more recently through the Framework for Pluralistic Approaches (FREPA; Candelier et al., 2012). The FREPA builds on the CEFR's groundwork and endorses an integrated approach to language education, fostering language awareness, intercomprehension and transculturality. These publications can be viewed as cornerstone elements of the academic and political discourse in the field of European foreign language education that took place over the last few decades and focused on the ever-increasing role of cultural and linguistic diversity (e.g., De Florio Hansen, 2011), the essence of which can be summarized as follows (Council of Europe, 2001, p. 2):

> The rich heritage of diverse languages and cultures in Europe is a valuable common resource to be protected and developed, and (…) a major educational effort is needed to convert that diversity from a barrier to communication into a source of mutual enrichment and understanding.

These assumptions are noticeable in the EU teacher education policy, which recognizes the need to "empower and equip teachers to take an active stand against all forms of discrimination, to meet the needs of pupils from diverse backgrounds, to impart common fundamental values and to prevent racism and intolerance" (Public Policy and Management Institute, 2017, p. 13). In Germany, for example, standards for teacher education, defined by the Standing Conference of the Ministers of Education and Cultural Affairs (KMK) and recognized as guidelines by all the federal states (KMK, 2014, p. 3), emphasize the importance of linguistic and cultural diversity. As such, prospective teachers should acknowledge diversity as an integral part of successful learning (KMK, 2014, p. 10), be informed about theoretical concepts and aspects of diversity/heterogeneity (KMK, 2014, p. 11), and be able to reflect upon the challenges that diversity and heterogeneity pose for the teaching profession (KMK, 2014, p. 13). In a more recent guideline published by the Standing Conference of the Ministers of Education and Cultural Affairs of the States in Germany (Kultusministerkonferenz (KMK) and Hochschulrektorenkonferenz (HRK)), 2015, p. 2), educational policy makers view teachers as the central agents that have the capacity to endorse a positive, appreciative, and inclusive attitude to all forms of learners' diversity:

> Teachers need professional competences to allow them to recognize pupils' special gifts and any disadvantages, impediments and other obstacles that they might exhibit or experience and to put in place appropriate pedagogical measures for prevention or support.

In fact, it is assumed that creating environments in which diversity is acknowledged and appreciated as norm and strength is fundamental for the promotion of an inclusive educational system, which "aims to make the education of every pupil as successful as possible, to promote social cohesion, social participation and to avoid any kind of discrimination" (KMK & HRK, 2015, p. 2). In Spain, several authors belonging to the Thematic Network on Language Education and Language Training (*Temática sobre la Educación Lingüística y la Formación de Enseñantes en Contextos Multiculturales y Multilingües*, for its Spanish title) published a manifesto in 2004 entitled *Multiculturalismo y plurilingüismo escolar. La formación inicial del profesorado de enseñanza obligatoria* [*Multiculturalism and plurilingualism in schools. The initial training of school teachers in compulsory education,* 2004]. A number of institutions and universities adhered to this, though teachers in other school types do not need to comply with this publication. This text was intended to provide a synthetic reflection on the phenomena of multiculturalism and plurilingualism in schools and on the role of universities in the teaching and learning process. In a nutshell, the aim was to provide a common frame of reference for Spanish universities in charge of the first phases of teacher training. This manifesto contained three sections: a) "Society, Languages and Cultures"; b) "School, languages and cultures"; and c) "Teacher training, multiculturalism and multilingualism".

Yet, decisions made on the educational policy level, or on the level of the "intended curriculum" as Cuban (2012) calls it, do not warrant an immediate or complete adoption in teaching practice, or, in Cuban's terms on the level of the "taught curriculum". In fact, studies show that despite the efforts made on the educational policy level, linguistic diversity can, in some contexts, still be perceived as a hindrance rather than an asset in the classroom. Marshall (2020, p. 12), for example, reports that instructors at a Canadian university weighed acknowledging or encouraging students' plurilingual language practice, and thereby their linguistic variety, against the necessity to deliver the final product for assessment and communication of knowledge in formal, academic English and concludes that:

> Attitudes about plurilingual students were framed within a backdrop of pervasive institutional discourses about plurilingual/EAL students around which their presence in classes is often seen in terms of deficit, problems, and a lowering of standards.

Similar forms of resistance to the presence of linguistic variety in teaching practice can be observed in the context of heritage languages, which can be perceived as an obstacle to learning rather than an enrichment. As Helot and Ó Laoire (2011, p. xi) noted:

> Teachers in the multilingual classroom may continue to underestimate the competence of plurilingual students and to silence their voices, rather than using cross-linguistic learning strategies and learners' metalinguistic awareness as learning resources across languages and even across school disciplines.

This hierarchical approach to various languages observed in educational landscapes stands in direct opposition to the actual goals set for the provision of teacher education on the policy making level. These include the development of tolerance, respect, and positive attitudes towards diversity. In addition, plurilingual/pluricultural education may need a reconceptualization of the role of the teacher and a shift away from the assumption that language teachers act solely as transmitters of linguistic and/or communicative skills. Teachers' tasks also include understanding of and mediation between various cultures, languages, perspectives, discourses, and identities. As Kramsch (2004, p. 37) puts it:

> In a world of increased multilingualism and multiculturalism, foreign language teachers seem to be challenged to be less authoritative transmitters of linguistic or pragmatic knowledge, than mediators between various identities, discourses and worldviews.

Kramsch (2004, p. 44) goes on to suggest that language teachers need to be perceived "as the quintessential go-between among people with various languages, and of different cultures, generations, and genders". The implementation of this notion in practice means, however, that teacher education needs to incorporate sufficient pluralistic content, which is not always straightforward. Runnels (2021, p. xiii) points out that several issues or aspects of the plurilingual/pluricultural approach, such as "the relationships between pluricultural, plurilingual, general and communicative language competences and the role of mediation" remain unclear. Although the FREPA lists various competences and the ability to put them into action via strategies to communicate effectively (Candelier et al., 2012), concrete strategies associated with the support of plurilingual and pluricultural competence that could be integrated in teacher education programs are not explicitly discussed. In addition, the document employs many terms relevant to the development of plurilingual/pluricultural competences that are not explicitly defined, for instance, "cultural identity", "cultural sensitivity" or "sociocultural awareness", which leaves space for individual interpretation.

Several projects (partially) dealing with various aspects of plurilingualism and pluriculturalism have been able to deliver materials that could be adapted to the use in teacher education programs, for instance: (a) the "Language Educator Awareness" (LEA) (2007) training-kit, which comprises a relatively short set of practical instruments designed to help teacher educators introduce the essential aspects of plurilingualism and pluriculturalism to language teachers and learners; (b) the "Majority language in multilingual settings" (MARILLE) project (2008), which provides five practice examples and reflective materials for majority language teachers to promote the idea of plurilingualism; (c) The Plurilingualism Project: Tertiary Language Learning – German after English (2004), which presents examples of how to apply the plurilingual method in teaching in the "German after English" sequence; (d) the ELICIT-PLUS (2014–2017) project, which designed resources to prepare teachers for intercultural education and European citizenship; (e) The PluriMobil (2015) and IEREST (2015) projects, which include resources that help teachers and teacher trainers prepare their students for participation in international-project activities and guide them through it.

However, what these highly resourceful projects do not offer yet are comprehensive solutions for foreign language teacher education programs that could be integrated as separate sessions, thematic foci modules or complete courses in various educational systems and offer an in-depth look into the topics of plurilingualism and pluriculturalism. The aim of the Teacher – Culture – Pluri (TEACUP) project is to offer such sustainable and comprehensive solution to foreign language teacher educators interested in the topics of pluriculturalism and plurilingualism. Moreover, the focus of TEACUP is on both pre- and in-service teachers, which is also new in comparison to the above-mentioned projects.

4 Teacher – Culture – Pluri (TEACUP): An Attempt to Integrate Plurilingualism into Teacher Education

In an attempt to alleviate the problem of scarce resources for teacher education programs focused on the development of pluralistic competences, an international project team composed of researchers, policy makers and teacher educators from four European countries (Spain, Poland, Hungary, and Germany) and the United States joined forces under the umbrella of an Erasmus+ Project "TEACUP: Teacher – Culture – Pluri" funded by the European Union. The project team have been given the task to jointly develop, test, and evaluate a large set of comprehensive, versatile, open educational resources that are intended to provide a theoretical foundation and practical materials for plurilingual and pluricultural foreign language teaching and assessment. The developed resources encompass six learning modules, which focus on the area of plurilingualism (ML1, ML2, ML3) and on the area of pluriculturalism (MC1, MC2, MC3) see Fig. 1; for more information visit https://teacup-project.eu/site/#materials).

Thematically the six modules are devoted to three focal points: Key Concepts, Classroom Applications and Assessment. Overall, the modules present (pre-service) language teachers with theoretical and research-oriented insights into the principles of pluricultural/plurilingual education in foreign language learning settings. They

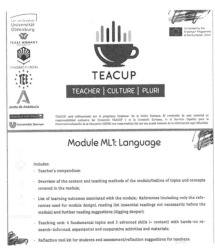

Fig. 1 TEACUP ML1 and MC1

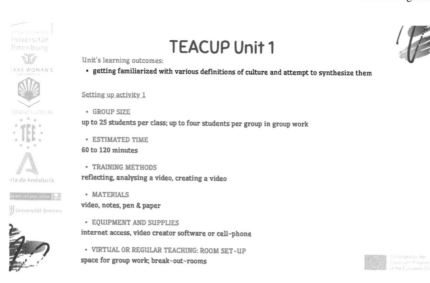

Fig. 2 TEACUP unit 1

also provide the potential users with examples of classroom activities that can foster pluricultural and plurilingual skills (see Fig. 2 as an example of the assigned activities).

In addition, the modules contain various tools that can be useful in the process of assessment and evaluation of plurilingual and pluricultural competences. Structurally, all of the modules contain: (a) a compendium providing an overview of the thematic content specifically tailored to the needs of teacher educators, including the relevant theories, models/ frameworks and state of the art research findings; (b) multiple teaching units for teacher education programs, including hands-on, research-informed, interactive and collaborative activities and materials; (c) an instructor's companion with a transparent description of desired learner outcomes (can-do descriptors), didactic commentary for the teaching unit and examples of possible teaching scenarios; and (d) a reflection tool-kit for monitoring the learning process of the module users.

The project team aim at developing modules that are versatile in terms of their structural flexibility: the learning materials should be available for use both as complete regular university courses or intensive workshops, and/or as individual smaller-scale units/topics, on various levels of teacher education, thereby enhancing systematic and sustainable integration into teacher education structures. During the project, the modules have been embedded into the teaching programs of the involved institutions. The project team have also used the modules in tele-collaboration activities involving pre-service teachers from different project countries. The structural goodness of fit of the modules as well as their quality have been empirically (re) tested, (re)evaluated in different transnational settings, (re)modified and improved accordingly through 3 rounds of reviews by TEACUP partners, as planned in the application of the project to the Spanish National Agency (SEPIE). The TEACUP project encompassed two international workshops for both pre- and in-service foreign language teachers, which provided testing environments for the newly-designed modules.

In the remainder of this chapter, we focus on the implementation of modules MC1 and ML1, dealing with key concepts around pluriculturalism and plurilingualism respectively, in the first international workshop associated with the TEACUP project. We briefly discuss the underlying structure of the applied materials, and subsequently analyse the reception of the modules and feedback on the experience of having worked with the materials as reported by the workshop participants.

Module MC1 "Key concepts: Culture" aims at encouraging students to critically (re)define the term "culture" by taking into consideration its polysemantic nature and a multitude of definitions that have been proposed in the literature. The units within the module encourage learners to reflect on their own understanding of their culture and juxtapose it with other people's culture in order to challenge the notion of (singular) identities. Learners working with the module are also encouraged to focus on the concept of "cultural identity" in connection to the notion of culture. They also reflect on the processes of describing cultures, stereotyping, and "intersectionality". Furthermore, the module also delves into discovering and reflecting upon two different models of "intercultural competence" and realizing their potential in teacher education. Learners are expected to describe and critically reflect on two well-established and frequently applied models of Intercultural Communicative Competence (*ICC*): Byram's ICC model and Bennett's Developmental Model of Intercultural Sensitivity (DMIS). The module further encourages reflecting upon the fluidity of the concept of culture and introducing the *emic* and *etic* view on culture. Learners are then encouraged to discuss the relationship between variability and regularity within cultures and associate it with the perspective of the social constructivist approach to understanding cultures; they deconstruct the notion of transculturality and hybridity and redefine the notion of culture; and they differentiate between *emic* and *etic* views of culture. In addition, the module aims at introducing and reflecting upon different *etic* frameworks. Learners are presented with an *etic* framework and differentiate between *emic* and *etic* views of culture and evaluate their advantages and shortcomings.

Module ML1 "Key concepts: Plurilingualism" encourages learners to reflect on the concepts of plurilingualism, plurilingual competence and their own individual plurilingual profile. In addition, learners get to know tools and instruments that help them (and their future students) to visualize, recognize and describe their individual plurilingual profiles. The module also links the notion of plurilingualism with relevant terms connected to bilingualism and Content and Language Integrated Learning (CLIL). Learners are encouraged to revise key concepts of bilingualism and multilingualism by working with a video and taking a quiz. They are expected to reflect on the potential benefits CLIL offers for plurilingual approaches by studying texts, collecting criteria, and analysing lesson plans. Learners working with the module are also encouraged to critically reflect on pedagogical gains and possibilities of implementing these tools and instruments in EFL classrooms. Furthermore, users of the module are encouraged to study how pluricultural and plurilingual approaches are intertwined in the CEFR (2001) and its Companion Volume (2018) and to present their understanding of pluricultural and plurilingual approaches in different formats, namely as infographics and as a recorded talk (or a script for a recorded talk). Learners working with the module are further familiarized with the concept of translanguaging and discuss its meaning in the context of plurilingualism theory. This is associated with a deeper reflection on the implications of "plurilingual stance" to establish change in TESOL classrooms. In addition, learners working with the module get familiarised with the FREPA framework and practise working with the scales provided within it. Ideally, this raises the awareness of the FREPA's relevance and viability within plurilingual (and pluricultural) education.

5 Testing TEACUP: Reception of the Materials

In September 2021, the TEACUP project team organized an international, five-day long, hybrid workshop for pre- and in-service foreign language teachers, which implemented the above-mentioned modules. A total of fourteen pre- and in-service language teachers, and ten staff, from Spain, Poland, Hungary, Germany and the United States, actively partook in the event. The pre- and in-service teachers were associated with the institutions involved in the project and were invited to participate in the workshop. They did so on a voluntary basis. The staff responsible for the provision of the modules to the workshop participants were members of the TEACUP project consortium.

The workshop consisted of face-to-face and online sessions. Social forms of activity during the workshop included group discussions, work in small groups as well as individual work. Upon the completion of the workshop, participants were requested to provide trainers with feedback on the workshop and its contents. Then, participants filled out a questionnaire, which was an adapted version of the reflection tool included in the modules, based on Gibbs' reflective cycle (1988) and Bain et al.'s (2002) 5R framework for reflection (see Fig. 3). Firstly, participants were asked to briefly describe or report on the experience of the workshop (questionnaire section on "Description/reporting"). In order to gain insights into the participants' emotional or personal response to the workshop, the project managers enquired about the feelings and thoughts that the teachers associated with the workshop (questionnaire section on "Feelings/responding"). Subsequently, the participants were asked to describe their familiarity with the concepts and relate them to their work as foreign language teachers (questionnaire section on "Relating"). In addition, the participants were required to evaluate the experience during the workshop, including the extent to which they found it interesting and difficult as well as aspects that they considered positive and negative (questionnaire section on "Analysis/ evaluation"). Data were tapped into through content analysis (Krippendorf & Bock, 2008), which involved the systematic reading and observation of the texts obtained

TEACUP

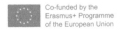

Co-funded by the
Erasmus+ Programme
of the European Union

Reflection tool for students:

The reflection tool is loosely based on Gibb's (1988) reflective model and Bain et al. 5R Framework for reflection (e.g. 2002).

Description/Reporting: Summarize the content of the unit in five sentences. What are the key elements of the unit?
Feelings/Responding: What are your feelings and thoughts about the content of the unit?

not at all--------- ---------very much

How interesting was this set of activities for you?	👍	👍	👍	👍	👍
How informative/helpful was this set of activities?	👍	👍	👍	👍	👍

Relating: Were you familiar with some of the concepts introduced in the unit before? What does the unit mean for your work as a foreign language teacher?

Analysis/Evaluation: How difficult was this set of activities? Why? What would have made it easier?	☹	☹	☹	☹	☹

What did you like about the unit?

DSW University of Lower Silesia WROCŁAW   Universität Bremen   TEXAS WOMAN'S UNIVERSITY   TEE   universität OLDENBURG

Fig. 3 Reflection tool developed as part of the TEACUP modules

from participant teachers. Their responses were labelled to pinpoint categories to identify similarities (comparison) and differences (contrast).

In the following section, we present the results of the evaluation of the workshop and the implemented modules.

5.1 Description/Reporting

All participants identified "bilingualism", "multilingualism", "plurilingualism", "pluriculturalism", "identity" and "culture" as the main notions that the workshop was centred on. They also listed "translanguaging" among the focal points of the course. As participant 1 summarizes:

> The content of the course was integrating the notions of plurilingualism and pluricultural-ism into foreign language teaching. The key elements were: Translanguaging, Language, Culture, Plurilingualism, CLIL, Identity.

Some participants offered insights into how they perceived the processing of the content that we tried to implement in the workshop. Participant 3 highlights some dependencies and relationships between the key focal points that were covered along the sessions:

> We talked about different cultural aspects. How our culture and our identity as individuals and as social beings affect how we behave and interact with our environment. Moreover, we reflected on how we perceive our own culture vs. others and other cultures vs. ours. We also talked about how, even if one belongs to a certain social group, they can stop following the social norms or conventions, and change their routines.

Based on these summaries, it can be concluded that the presentation of the key concepts implemented in the two modules yielded the expected results in the context of the workshop: The participants reflected on their own understanding of their culture and juxtaposed it with other people's culture. They also focused on the concept of "cultural identity" in connection to the notion of culture and reflected on the processes of describing cultures, stereotyping, and intersectionality. How they conceive of "intersectionality", however, remained unexplored.

5.2 Relating

Most pre- and in-service teachers that were involved in the workshop expressed their general familiarity with the notions of "multiculturalism" and "bilingualism", which was to be expected given that these notions typically occur in teacher education contexts and in teaching practice. Some participants concluded that, with the exception of one or two notions, the course contained topics that they were already familiar with, as pointed out by participant 9, "I guess the only concepts I didn't know before this course were ETICS and EMICS." However, most participants recognized the potential of the course to expand and systematize their knowledge of the topics, as pointed out by participant 1:

> Many of the contexts of the topics covered were generally familiar to me. I practice many of them in my daily work. It was not revealing, but it allowed me to expand my knowledge and make it more systematic. And I love it.

Participant 4 shared a similar insight and commented on how the course helped them build on their existing knowledge and reflect on its meaning in teaching practice. It also seems that this participant used the course as a chance to reframe the concepts in a new context:

> I have heard about interculturality before or multicultural or pluricultural, however I have heard about them as an abstract concept; however, in this course I have reflected deeply about these concepts and how we can incorporate them in our daily lessons and how important is to do it in order to promote not only learning but also social and cultural inclusion.

Participant 2 describes themselves as open to new ideas and concepts. They mention that the workshop had a motivating effect on them leaving them "hungry" for more. In addition, the participant underscores the willingness to implement the ideas shared during the workshop related to learner autonomy and emphasizes how important it is for them as a teacher to support learners in their learning process:

> I am always open to new ideas and new concepts. I am learning something new every day and I think that this course made me feel like I need to learn even more now. I am 'hungry' for more. I want to implement the ideas shared during the course in my everyday work with young learners to help them develop their autonomy; to help them discover THEIR best way of learning.

5.3 Feelings/Responding

The participants reported having generally positive feelings in response to the workshop experience. Some participants mentioned feeling amazed or surprised by the impact that the reflection on the significance of the discussed topics exerted on them. Participant 4 highlights the role of the teacher in the context of the plurilingual/pluricultural approach, who acts more as a guide facilitating the students' learning rather than the ultimate source of knowledge. This participant also reflected on the change in the traditional perception of role of the mother tongue that is associated with the plurilingual/pluricultural approach:

> I am amazed how important and at the same time insignificant role is played by the teacher in the process of teaching a language, whose aim is to navigate the student in the process of shaping the skills of learning how to learn. What surprised me was that this modern view of teaching English as a foreign language shows how not to downgrade the importance of the mother tongue in acquiring a foreign language. This breaks the traditional approach to language teaching.

A similar insight was reported by participant 5, who also focused on the role of the mother tongue and expressed their determination to assign a different status to the "national" languages in their teaching:

> Now I am determined not to decrease the importance of the national language in teaching. What's more, I want to give my students independence, help them develop autonomy and a sense of ownership during language acquisition.

Other participants signalled that the course resonated with them to a degree that they described it as leading to significant changes in their approach as language teachers. Participant 6 even used the adjective "mind-blowing" and expressed the readiness to change the way in which they plan their lessons:

> This course was an absolutely mind-blowing experience for me. The content of the course is a very important topic especially during the time when our kindergartens, schools, universities are open places to all nations. We are listening to more languages; we are interrelating with other cultures. I am changing my priorities when planning my lessons with young pupils now.

The sentiment was shared by participants 7 and 9, who also mentioned that the content moved them personally and changed their views as language teachers:

> I feel these ideas in me. I want to follow them in my work at school as a teacher because they are easier for me and more joyful for children.
> Everything I have learnt in this course opens a new paradigm in teaching learning process of languages. I'm changing the view and the way in which I'm going to focus my lessons on my school. Something has changed inside of me as a language teacher forever.

Participant 6 also expressed the willingness to share the materials and the main idea behind the course with their colleagues:

> I am sure that I will make even more use of my students' linguistic potential. I will also use the materials provided during the training - I will share them with other language teachers in our school, while conveying the idea of the course, and the work with children.

Participants 10 and 9 additionally expressed having enjoyed working on the content of the modules in the international context. The TEACUP consortium had the advantage of having access to teaching staff from five countries, who were willing to moderate the sessions and took over the responsibility for the provision of their content.

> I really liked having the opportunity to talk about such an interesting topic with people from other countries. That helped me getting to know other cultures through members of such cultures.
> TEACUP online training was an excellent experience for me. The fact that I attended talks of great lecturers from Germany, Spain, the USA, and Hungary at one course was a fascinating experience for me. I like this kind of international cooperation, which is a usually valuable opportunity for the audience to meet and discuss thoughts worldwide.

5.4 Analysis/Evaluation

The course participants were asked to reflect on the positive and negative aspects of the workshop and the materials that it incorporated. In their feedback, the participants also considered the social interaction forms and general organization of the workshop, such as timing, and provided instruction and/or explanations. Their overall evaluation of the event was quite positive. The participants mentioned that they enjoyed the atmosphere of the workshop. In this example, participant 1 lists the things that they enjoyed about the workshop:

– A company of smiling, kind, wise and open-minded people ready to share their experiences.
– An international environment and the opportunity to share opinions and ask questions.

Participant 8 also emphasized the interactive nature of the workshop, which they perceived as significant in making such events enjoyable. It has to be noted that the modules could also be used in more individual settings, which may be more appropriate for learners who feel less comfortable participating in group discussions.

> I liked having interactions with the speaker and the audience. I liked being separated in small groups so that we could be able to speak to each other and learn from each other. Interaction in such meetings (even more when they're online) can be the key to make them more enjoyable and profitable.

Another participant (no. 5) underscored the importance of concrete examples in the provision of the content that, from their perspective, contributed to a better understanding of the content:

> Bringing real life experiences and examples were to me important for understanding definitions of the course. Knowing that language and culture influence everything that surrounds this course opened my eyes even more.

Several participants suggested that the topics needed deeper reflection, which is associated with sufficient time to process them. They generally did not seem to think that the materials lacked clarity or that they were too easy or too demanding. However, they often expressed the opinion that, due to the fact that the plurilingual/pluricultural approach breaks with what the participants considered to be the traditional view on foreign language education, the re-conceptualisation of this notion requires an open-minded stance. One participant (7) suggested accompanying course materials, which would include excerpts from relevant publications with even further additional reading assignments.

> Sometimes the topic required deeper reflection. It was not the exercise itself that was difficult but trying to understand and explore it, breaking with the traditional approach. It required a lot of open-mindedness and knowledge of linguistic issues. (Participant 3)

> Sometimes the activity is clear and can be done easily, but some other times, it needs more time to think about it. (Participant 6)

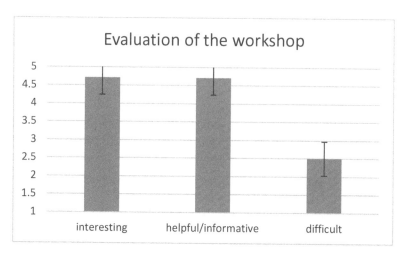

Fig. 4 Evaluation of the workshop. (N = 10. Answers provided on the Likert scale: 1 = not at all; 5 = very much)

> Overall, I liked the assignments that connected the subject matter to relevant, contemporary issues. I appreciated that everything was straightforward. There was no confusion on assignments, which is always a plus with online courses. I'm not sure what I would change about the course. Maybe some supplemental reading. (Participant 7)

In addition to open-ended questions, participants were offered an option to evaluate the extent to which they perceived the workshop as interesting, helpful, and informative. In addition, they were also asked to estimate its level of difficulty. The participants used a Likert scale ranging from 1 = not at all to 5 = very much (see Fig. 4).

The data revealed that the participants considered the workshop to be very interesting (Mean = 4,71, SD = 0,47), very helpful and informative (Mean = 4,71, SD =0,47) and neither very difficult nor very easy (Mean = 2,5, SD. = 1,01). These findings reinforced the insights found in the open answers discussed above.

6 Conclusion and Discussion

Despite great efforts made on the educational policy level, in some contexts teachers seem to struggle with embracing linguistic and cultural diversity in the foreign language classroom and still perceive it as a hindrance rather than an asset to the learning process. This implies that the plurilingual/pluricultural perspective may not necessarily be seen by teachers as a desirable approach to foreign languages. At the same time, it is teachers that are the agents of reform, who have the choice or carry the responsibility to implement ideas formulated on the level of policy making into actual teaching practice. This assumption reflects Borg's (2003, p. 81) insights from a review of studies in teacher cognition, which presents teachers as "active, thinking decision-makers who make instructional choices by drawing on complex, practically-oriented, personalized, and context-sensitive networks of knowledge, thoughts, and beliefs". If foreign language education is to respond to the ever-growing fluidity of contemporary EU societies and help create settings that are truly inclusive, language teachers first need to understand, recognise, and acknowledge the complex reality of learners' linguistic/cultural repertoires (Blommaert & Backus, 2011).

This contribution aimed at illustrating the efforts of an international team of teacher educators, researchers, policy makers and teachers to alleviate that issue through the development and evaluation of comprehensive learning and teaching materials focusing on the implementation of the plurilingual/pluricultural approach in foreign language education. Insights were gained from this attempt, especially from having tested the developed educational resources among a relatively small international group of pre- and in-service foreign language teachers; they point to the conclusion that plurilingualism/pluriculturalism is, indeed, a topic that requires more structured attention in international foreign language teacher education programs. These results mirror the findings of Yilmaz (2016), who states that teacher candidates report the need to focus on multicultural education as the basis of social tolerance and the training for recognizing other cultures. They are also in line with the argumentation proposed by Paul-Binyamin and Reingold (2014), who emphasize the importance of incorporating multicultural policies into virtually any institution in a democratic society, but especially in educational institutions, as they are responsible for the primary socialization of society's members.

Although the TEACUP participants involved in the evaluation of the resources reported being generally familiar with notions such as multilingualism, translanguaging, plurilingualism or cultural identity, they welcomed the opportunity to study their interrelations and dependencies in a more thorough way. They described this experience as one offering them a chance to expand and reflect on their existing knowledge and reported being willing, or even determined to change their teaching practice and align it more with the assumptions of pluralistic teaching approaches. Some participants even underscored their surprise that certain presuppositions traditionally associated with communicative foreign language teaching, such as a limited importance of the mother tongue, can and should be questioned from the plurilingual and pluricultural perspective. These results are in line with a corpus of studies (Czura, 2016; Larzén-Östermark, 2009; Sercu, 2005) that have also reported on foreign language pre- and in-service teachers' selective and often inconsistent understanding of concepts such as "intercultural communicative competence". Such insights into pre- and in-service teacher's cognition suggest that providing them with points to ponder and reflect can exert an influence on their professional identity, which Sachs (2005, p. 15) defines as a framework that lets them form ideas on "how to be", "how to act" and "how to understand" their work and place in a society. It has been suggested that teachers' professional identities influence their classroom choices (Coldron & Smith, 1999).

However, the inferences that we draw from the TEACUP project so far, and especially from the workshop, need to be interpreted with a degree of scepticism. Although the modules have been developed, continuously evaluated, and adapted by a relatively large consortium consisting of over 30 language education professionals from five different countries, who aimed to create content that could be applied in various cultural educational settings, the materials may not necessarily serve that purpose in all teaching contexts and with all learner groups. In addition, the individuals involved in the workshop engaged with the materials intensively and over the course of a week. Yet, their experience may not necessarily be generalizable. They were a relatively small sample, who had voluntarily agreed to participate in the workshop as a part of their pre- or in-service training. In this sense, there are grounds to believe that their feedback is not representative (of all FL teachers) and displays how a group of highly motivated, experienced, and knowledgeable professionals react to the products of the project. At the same time, given that pre- and in-service teachers (both novice and experienced) are more likely to use particular teaching tools or techniques in their teaching practice if they have a chance to experience them themselves during their teacher education program (Guichon & Hauck, 2011, p. 195), it is possible that these highly motivated teachers act as multipliers in their teaching practice by implementing their newly acquired insights and sharing them with their colleagues.

What also seems to have maximised the learning benefits associated with the use of the modules was the international and telecollaborative aspect of the experience, i.e., the fact that international teachers, both pre- and in-service worked with international teaching staff. Engagement in collaborative discussions and exchanges of thoughts on selected facets of the plurilingual and pluricultural approach with student teachers and/or practitioners from other countries may encourage (future) teachers to reflect in a greater depth on their own experiences (Sadler & Dooly, 2016).

References

Bain, J. D., Ballantyne, R., Mills, C., & Lester, N. C. (2002). *Reflecting on practice: Student teachers' perspectives*. Post Pressed.

Blommaert, J., & Backus, A. (2011). Repertoires revisited: 'Knowing language' in superdiversity. *Working papers in urban language and literacies*, paper 67.

Blommaert, J., & Backus, A. (2013). Superdiverse repertoires and the individual. In I. de Saint-Georges & J.-J. Weber (Eds.), *Multilingualism and multimodality: Current challenges for educational studies* (pp. 14–33). Sense Publishers. https://doi.org/10.1007/978-94-6209-266-2

Borg, S. (2003). Teacher cognition in language teaching: A review of research on what language teachers think, know, believe, and do. *Language Teaching, 36*(2), 81–109. https://doi.org/10.1017/S0261444803001903

Byram, M. (2009). The intercultural speaker and the pedagogy of foreign language education. In D. K. Deardoff (Ed.), *The SAGE handbook of intercultural competence* (pp. 321–332). SAGE Publications.

Candelier, M., Daryai-Hansen, P., & Schröder-Sura, A. (2012). The framework of reference for pluralistic approaches to languages and cultures - a complement to the CEFR to develop plurilingual and intercultural competences. *Innovation in Language Learning and Teaching, 6*(3), 243–257. https://doi.org/10.1080/17501229.2012.725252

Coldron, J., & Smith, R. (1999). Active location in teachers' construction of their professional identities. *Journal of Curriculum Studies, 31*(6), 711–726.

Council of Europe. (2001). *Common European framework of reference for languages: Learning, teaching, assessment.* Cambridge University Press.

Council of Europe. (2018). CEFR Companion Volume. *Council of Europe.* https://rm.coe.int/cefr-companion-volume-with-new-descriptors-2018/1680787989

Cuban, L. (2012). *The multi-layered curriculum: Why change is often confused with reform.* https://larrycuban.wordpress.com/2012/01/14/the-multi-layered-curriculum-why-change-is-often-confused-with-reform/

Czura, A. (2016). Major field of study and student teachers' views on intercultural communicative competence. *Language and Intercultural Communication, 16*(1), 83–98. https://doi.org/10.1080/14708477.2015.1113753

De Florio Hansen, I. (2011). *Towards Multilingualism and the Inclusion of Cultural Diversity.* Kassel University Press.

ECML. (2021). Developing teacher competences for pluralistic approaches. *Training and reflection tools for teachers and teacher educators.* https://www.ecml.at/ECML-Programme/Programme2020-2023/Developingteachercompetencesforpluralisticapproaches/tabid/4300/language/en-GB/Default.aspx

ELICIT-PLUS. (2014). *European literacy and citizenship education-plus.* http://www.aede-france.org/SUMMARY-EN.html

Eurostat. (2019). *Pupils by education level and modern foreign language studied – absolute numbers and % of pupils by language studied.* https://ec.europa.eu/eurostat/databrowser/view/EDUC_UOE_LANG01__custom_1310816/bookmark/table?lang=en&bookmarkId=3569e58e-bba8-43a9-8fc4-6048e86daa4a

García, O. (2009). *Bilingual education in the 21st century: A global perspective.* Basil/ Blackwell.

García, O., Johnson Ibarra, S., & Seltzer, K. (2017). *The translanguaging classroom: Leveraging student Bilingualism for learning.* Caslon Pub.

Gibbs, G. (1988). *Learning by doing: A guide to teaching and learning methods.* Further Educational Unit, Oxford Polytechnic.

Guichon, N., & Hauck, M. (2011). Editorial: Teacher education research in CALL and CMC: More in demand than ever. *ReCALL, 23*(3), 187–199. https://doi.org/10.1017/S0958344011000139

Hélot, C., & Laoire, M. Ó. (Eds.). (2011). *Language policy for the multilingual classroom: Pedagogy of the possible* (Vol. 82). Multilingual Matters.

IEREST. (2015). *Intercultural education resources for Erasmus students and their teachers.* http://www.ierest-project.eu

Kramsch, C. (2004). The language teacher as go-between. *Utbildning & Demokrati – Tidskrift För Didaktik Och Utbildningspolitik, 13*(3), 37–60. https://doi.org/10.48059/uod.v13i3.781

Krippendorff, K., & Bock, M. A. (Eds.). (2008). *The content analysis reader.* SAGE.

Kultusministerkonferenz [KMK]. (2014). *Standards für die Lehrerbildung: Bildungswissenschaften.* https://www.kmk.org/fileadmin/Dateien/veroeffentlichungen_beschluesse/2004/2004_12_16-Standards-Lehrerbildung-Bildungswissenschaften.pdf

Kultusministerkonferenz and Hochschulrektorenkonferenz [KMK HRK]. (2015). Lehrerbildung für eine Schule der Vielfalt. *Gemeinsame Empfehlung von Hochschulrektorenkonferenz und Kultusministerkonferenz.* https://www.kmk.org/fileadmin/veroeffentlichungen_beschluesse/2015/2015_03_12-Schule-der-Vielfalt.pdf

Larzén-Östermark, E. (2009). Language teacher education in Finland and the cultural dimension of foreign language teaching - a student teacher perspective. *European Journal of Teacher Education, 32*(4), 401–421. https://doi.org/10.1080/02619760903012688

LEA. (2007). *Plurilingual and pluricultural awareness in language teacher education: A training kit (LEA).* https://www.ecml.at/Resources/ECMLresources/tabid/277/ID/56/language/en-GB/Default.aspx

Makoni, S., & Pennycook, A. (2006). Disinventing and Reconstituting Languages. *Multilingual Matters.* https://doi.org/10.21832/9781853599255

MARILLE. (2008). *Majority language in multilingual settings.* https://www.ecml.at/ECML-Programme/Programme2008-2011/Majoritylanguageinmultilingualsettings/tabid/5451/Default.aspx

Marshall, S. (2020). Understanding plurilingualism and developing pedagogy: teaching in linguistically diverse classes across the disciplines at a Canadian university. *Language, Culture and Curriculum, 33*(2), 142–156. https://doi.org/10.1080/07908318.2019.1676768

Multiculturalisme i plurilingüisme escolar. (2004). La formació inicial del professorat de l'ensenyament obligatori. *Articles de Didáctica de la Llengua i de la Literatura, 34*, 87–97.

OMC group "Languages for jobs". (2020). Languages for jobs. *Providing multilingual communication skills for the labour market.* https://ec.europa.eu/assets/eac/languages/policy/strategic-framework/documents/languages-for-jobs-report_en.pdf

Ortega, L. (2017). New CALL-SLA research interfaces for the 21st century: Towards equitable multilingualism. *CALICO Journal, 34*, 285–316. https://doi.org/10.1558/cj.33855

Paul-Binyamin, I., & Reingold, R. (2014). Multiculturalism in teacher education institutes – The relationship between formulated official policies and grassroots initiatives. *Teaching and Teacher Education, 42*, 47–57. https://doi.org/10.1016/j.tate.2014.04.008

Pennycook, A. (2010). *Language as a local practice.* Routledge. https://doi.org/10.4324/9780203846223

Plurilingualism Project: Tertiary Language Learning – German after English. (2004). http://archive.ecml.at/documents/pub112E2004HufeisenNeuner.pdf

PluriMobil. (2015). Plurilingual and intercultural learning through mobility. *Practical resources for teachers and teacher trainers.* https://plurimobil.ecml.at

Public Policy and Management Institute [PPMI]. (2017). *Preparing teachers for diversity: The role of initial teacher education.* Publications Office of the European Union.

Runnels, J. (2021). *Pluricultural Language Education and the CEFR.* Cambridge University Press.

Sachs, J. (2005). Teacher education and the development of professional identity: Learning to be a teacher. In P. Denicolo & M. Kompf (Eds.), *Connecting policy and practice: Challenges for teaching and learning in schools and universities* (pp. 5–21). Routledge.

Sadler, R., & Dooly, M. (2016). Twelve years of telecollaboration: What we have learnt. *ELT Journal, 70*(4), 401–413. https://doi.org/10.1093/elt/ccw041

Sercu, L. (2005). *Foreign language teachers and intercultural competence: An investigation in 7 countries of foreign language teachers' views and teaching practices.* Multilingual Matters. https://doi.org/10.21832/9781853598456

Yılmaz, F. (2016). Multiculturalism and multicultural education: A case study of teacher candidates' perceptions. *Cogent Education, 3*(1), 1172394. https://doi.org/10.1080/2331186X.2016.1172394

María-Elena Gómez-Parra, PhD, graduated from the University of Granada as an English Philologist and then from the University of Córdoba as a PhD. She holds a Master's in Distance Education (UNED). Currently, she is a Full Professor in the Faculty of Education at the University of Córdoba and an interdisciplinary researcher working mainly within the field of Intercultural Education, Bilingual Education, and English as a Foreign Language. Her key research areas include: interculture, bilingual education, early second language acquisition. Email: elena.gomez@uco.es

Joanna Pfingsthorn is a senior researcher at the department of Foreign Language Education at the University of Bremen. Her main research interest is inclusive education in foreign language teaching. From 2007–2019 she worked as a lecturer and research associate at the Institute of English and American Studies at the University of Oldenburg, where she trained prospective EFL teachers. She holds a PhD in Foreign Language Education from the University of Oldenburg, an M.Sc. in Cognitive Science from the University of Amsterdam and a B.A. in Psychology from Jacobs University Bremen. Email: pfingsthorn@uni-bremen.de

Teachers' Perceptions of Cultural Otherness in Sri Lanka: Bridging the Gap in ELT Interculturality

Shashini Rochana Tennekoon

Abstract Sri Lanka is a multi-ethnic country where schools are segregated based on medium of instruction. However, the teachers of English are increasingly being required to work in schools where the medium of instruction is not their mother tongue and students come from culturally and linguistically diverse backgrounds. Therefore, communication across cultural boundaries has become a prerequisite for their professional competence. This research is an attempt to identify whether the teachers of English trained by pre-service teacher education institutes in Sri Lanka possess this mandatory competency. The chapter reports findings from a mixed method study carried out in a College of Education in Kalutara district. Data include an attitudinal survey based on a purposive sample of 63 first- and second-year teacher trainees to ascertain their intercultural sensitivity. Findings revealed that the majority of the student teachers have negative perceptions of cultural diversity which would ultimately have a negative impact on their teaching. The present chapter suggests practical ways to overcome this challenge with a specially designed curriculum and introduces a context-based definition of intercultural competence.

Keywords Cultural perceptions · Intercultural competence · Pre-service teacher training · Cultural and linguistic diversity · Sri Lanka

1 Introduction

Out of the many benefits of education it is perceived that developing intercultural citizenship can be rated amongst the highest as it helps one to survive in a diverse world. Education can pave the way to developing solidarity in an ethnically divided

S. R. Tennekoon (✉)
Maharagama National College of Education for Preservice Teachers, Maharagama, Sri Lanka

© The Author(s), under exclusive license to Springer Nature
Switzerland AG 2023
A. Sahlane, R. Pritchard (eds.), *English as an International Language
Education*, English Language Education 33,
https://doi.org/10.1007/978-3-031-34702-3_11

society like Sri Lanka inculcating knowledge, skills and especially attitudes necessary to survive in a plural society where the majority group, Sinhalese, make up 74.9% of the population; the Tamils, who are an ethnic group, form 9.3% of the population according to the latest official statistics (Census of Housing and Population Sri Lanka, 2012). The history of the country demonstrates the continued antagonism between different ethnic groups as evidenced in the 30-year long ethnic war between Tamil militant groups and the Sri Lankan armed forces with the Sinhalese majority. Recent ethno-religious conflicts, such as the anti-Muslim riots undertaken by extreme Sinhala-Buddhist *Bodhu Bala Sena* groups (the Buddhist Power Force) in 2014, which were the result of a wave of Islamophobic rhetoric and violence against the Sri Lankan Muslim community, and the terrorist Easter Sunday attacks in 2019 by radicalised Muslim extremist groups (*National Tawheed Jamaat*), show the growing polarisation of the Sri Lankan political scene, based on racial, religious and ethno-nationalist identity politics. Thus, it has become an important need of the Sri Lankan educational system to make their citizens interculturally competent in order to establish complete peace among them.

One way of promoting peace is to educate citizens to combat prejudice and develop intercultural competence (Lynch & Lodge, 2002). English language teachers should be trained to develop in their students a sense of compassion and empathy towards cultural others (Lynch, 1992). In other words, as Lynch stated, education should

> foster social literacy including the intercultural competence to relate creatively to the diversity of human cultures, to give awareness of the way in which human conflicts arise at the personal, inter-group and international level and to develop the ability to resolve conflicts creatively and justly, combat prejudice, discrimination and social injustice wherever they arise (p. 32).

Thus, this chapter discusses what intercultural competence is and how it is developed in prospective teachers of English studying in a preservice teacher education course. It describes an intervention in the form of an intercultural syllabus and proposes some pedagogical recommendations for future changes.

According to Hammer et al. (1978), intercultural competence is "the ability to think and act in interculturally appropriate ways" (p. 422). Lustig and Koester (2003) stress three key elements of intercultural competence: interpersonal and situational context; the degree of appropriateness and effectiveness of the interaction; and sufficient knowledge, motivation and action. Specifically, they emphasise that competence is dependent on "the relationships and situations within which the communication occurs" (p. 65). Thus, in its broadest sense, intercultural competence can be defined as "a complex of abilities needed to perform effectively and appropriately when interacting with others who are linguistically and culturally different from oneself" (Fantini, 2009, p. 12). Fantini further notes that the "effective" aspect relates to the individual's competencies and the "appropriate" aspect to the receiver's perception of the speaker's competencies and states that there are four dimensions to intercultural competence: knowledge, skill, attitude, and awareness.

Hence, it is in this context that Deardorff (2004) attempts to document consensus among top intercultural scholars and academic administrators on what constitutes intercultural competence and the best ways to measure this complex construct, thus representing the first crucial step toward definition and measurement. According to her findings, intercultural competence is defined as "the ability to communicate effectively and appropriately in intercultural situations based on one's intercultural knowledge, skills, and attitudes" (p. 247). This is the working definition used throughout this research.

The present chapter seeks to give a clear picture of key components of intercultural competence (IC) as delineated in the relevant literature by showing their relevance in the Sri Lankan context, e.g., by promoting IC as a desirable outcome of English language teaching and learning. Specifically, it tries to understand what it means to be interculturally competent, how to develop IC in student teachers and how to identify the best ways to measure it. Therefore, the following research questions were addressed.

1. What are student teachers' current perceptions of cultural diversity?
2. How would they respond to an intervention which would provide extensive opportunities that promote a greater understanding of intercultural issues?
3. Which strategies used by the researcher in curriculum implementation are most effective in enhancing prospective teachers' intercultural competence?

Consequently, the study's objectives are as follows, the aim being to achieve them through the proposed intervention.

- Evaluate the student teachers' current perceptions of cultural diversity and determine whether they are more inclined towards "ethnocentrism" or "ethnorelativism" (Bennett, 1993).
- Assess how effective is the specially designed intercultural curriculum in developing the intercultural competence of pre-service teachers of English.
- Identify the most and least effective activities in the intercultural curriculum designed to enhance the student teachers' intercultural competence; and propose a course of action accordingly.

2 Research Context

This research was carried out in a National College of Education (NCOE), one of the nineteen pre-service teacher education institutes that train teachers to be deployed in the Sri Lankan school system. The training period is of 3 years and in the third-year trainees are placed in schools for their practicums during which they work as 'tenured' teachers. However, the NCOE in which the research is conducted is different from other National Colleges where the medium of instruction is the mother tongue, because pre-service teachers from all three major ethnic groups study together here as the medium of instruction is English. Therefore, this has provided a unique opportunity to promote intercultural competence in Sri Lankan teacher education programs. In here, there are about four hundred residential students at any time of the year, representing all three major ethnic groups (but with a majority of Sinhala students), which necessitates the use of English as a lingua franca in such an intercultural situation. Nevertheless, it is observed that rather than developing intercultural relationships, student teachers tend to opt for more ethnolinguistic comradeship.

2.1 The Sample

The sample is composed of 63 student teachers from both first and second year of their residential course in the NCOE. The second-year group had spent more time in the institution and there was a chance of them being more interculturally competent due to their exposure to more cultural diversity. To determine the impact of cultural diversity, a first-year sample too was selected from the freshers. Two classes were selected from the 2 years purposely as they manifest the highest ethnic diversity in the college. Since the research methodology was more qualitative in nature, using purposive sampling techniques assured ample representation of different cultural groups to match the purpose of the research. The representation of ethnic groups in the sample is illustrated in Tables 1 and 2.

When looking at Table 1, it is clear that in the second year Sinhala students formed the largest proportion with 74.19%, which is almost ¾ of the whole sample. Next came the Muslim students with 19.35% and the smallest number was the

Table 1 Distribution of sample according to ethnic/religious affiliations

Ethno-religious identity	Tamil		Muslim		Sinhala	
	No	%	No	%	No	%
No. of Students in Second Year	2	6.45	6	19.35	23	74.19
No of Students in First Year	3	9.38	6	18.75	23	71.88
Total	5	7.91	12	19.05	46	73.03

Table 2 Distribution of sample according to religion

Religion	Hindu		Buddhist		Islam		Roman Catholic		Total
	No	%	No	%	No	%	No	%	
No. of Students in Second Year	2	6.45	20	64.52	6	19.35	3	9.68	31
No of Students in First Year	2	6.25	21	65.63	6	18.75	3	9.38	32
Total	4	6.35	41	65.08	12	19.05	6	9.53	63

Tamils with 6.45%. The first-year student sample also consisted of more Sinhala students with 71.88% and the smallest number coming from Tamils with 9.38% while the Muslim participants represented 18.75%.

When the religious representation was considered, it was noticed that the sample consisted of major religious groups in the country (i.e., Buddhists, Hindus, Muslims, and Roman Catholics). However, there were lesser numbers of student teachers from other religions when compared with majority group, the Buddhists (see Table 2).

The majority of both 1st and 2nd year student teachers were Buddhists (i.e., 64.52% and 65.63%, respectively). They were followed by the Muslims, with 19.35% in the second year and 18.75% in the first year. Roman Catholics represented 9.68% in the second year and 9.38% in the first year. The least represented were the Hindus, who were 6.45% in the second year and 6.25 in the first year. The first cycle of the research was implemented with the second-year teacher trainees and the second cycle was implemented with the first-year teacher trainees. The intervention was carried out over a period of 3 months for the first cycle and 6 months for the second cycle respectively, with 8 hours of contact lessons per week for each class.

2.2   Research Design

This study is aiming at changing a situation as well as studying a phenomenon. Therefore, it is a sort of action research. Action inquiry was chosen for several reasons. First, action research seeks not only to understand and interpret the world but to change it (Cohen et al., 2007; McNiff & Whitehead, 2006) and as such it clearly suited this study's purpose of using education for social change. Second, it is expected that all involved educational stakeholders would benefit from such an endeavour in their actual context of practice by developing the required knowledge, skills, attitudes and behaviours during the process. Furthermore, a main difference between action inquiry and other research paradigms is that "knowing becomes a holistic practice and that theory is lived in practice and practice becomes a living theory" (McNiff & Whitehead, 2000, p. 35). Traditionally, the difference between theory and practice is exaggerated in that research is supposed to give priority to knowing through thinking whereas application is knowing through doing. However, such demarcation is viewed as obsolescent because both fields complement each other (Darder et al., 2003). Both theoretical and action research paradigms require rigour and objectivity. Social reality is characteristically 'subjective' and discursively constructed, especially in the field of education because education is always a value laden activity.

2.3   Mixed Method Approach

A classroom-based research study was conducted with 63 student teacher participants, using both quantitative and qualitative methods in the data collection and data
analysis. According to intercultural scholars, the best way to assess intercultural
competence is through a mix of qualitative and quantitative measures (Deardorff,
2006, p. 250). In action research everything that happens in the setting could be
described and used as data, and could be interpreted to understand behaviour.
Therefore, the following data collection methods were used in this research: attitudinal scale, observation, reflective journals, student diaries and field notes.

2.4   Attitudinal

The attitudinal scale was used as it provided the opportunity to collect information
on attitudes and perceptions of a large number of student trainees in the shortest
possible time. It consisted of sixty statements spread on the intercultural competence continuum specified by Bennett (1993) which has six stages basically divided
into 'ethnocentric' and 'ethnorelative' orientations. There are three ethnocentric
stages (i.e., "denial," "defence" and "minimization") and three ethnorelative stages,
namely "acceptance", "adaptation" and "integration" (Bennett, 1993, p. 46). The
sixty statements were designed in such a manner that they fell into one of the six
stages, and they were equally distributed into a set of thirty statements for each of
the two phases. The Likert attitudinal scale was adapted, based on five ratings from
strongly agree to strongly disagree on sixty items. Half of the attitudinal statements
were ethnocentric statements, and the other half were ethnorelative. The marks were
given in such a way that the respondent needed to acquire more than 35 marks to be
rated, for example, on the ethnorelative continuum.

2.5   Observation

Observation was used as a tool to understand the nature of changes that occur in the
participants. It was utilised as a method of enriching or supplementing the data
gathered by other methods. Therefore, a colleague teaching the same subject was
used as a non-participant observer and her field notes were analysed and compared
with those of the researcher in order to find answers to the research questions. There
was a checklist too used for logging the observations. The observation checklist was
designed based on the pyramid model (Deardorff, 2006) and five factor model
(Byram, 1997). The checklist was divided into three different components (i.e.,
knowledge, skills and attitudes) and a rubric system was devised to quantify the
observed behaviours and thereby to allocate a total mark for each student for each
lesson.

2.6   Student Diaries, Observer Field Notes and Researcher's Reflective Journal

Narrative accounts play an important role in classroom-based qualitative approaches, and therefore one of the main data sources was the reflective journal maintained by the researcher. All observations related to "what happened in the classroom" were documented in this journal together with the thoughts and personal reflections of the researcher. Journal entries were basically divided into three categories and logged under three columns: (a) what actually happened in the class, (b) what the researcher thought about what happened and (c) what she learnt from what happened. Student teachers were also instructed to keep a diary during and after the class to document their reflections about the class activities. The non-participant observer too maintained a field notebook and both of these were divided into columns, same as the reflective journal of the researcher for the purposes of comparing and contrasting the observations entered.

2.7   Intervention

The intervention was done in the form of a curriculum specially designed with intercultural material. The first cycle of action was conducted with the sample from the second years. Based on the feedback from it, a second cycle was conducted with the first-year students. The intercultural materials aimed at teaching students English language skills from an intercultural perspective. English language skills are taught for 8 hours a week for both first and second years in the 2-year training period. However, this special intercultural syllabus was followed for 3 months with the second-year trainees and 6 months with the first-year trainees. The period consists of sixty-hour contact sessions with the second-year students and 100 hours with the first years. The rationale of the course was to improve the four skills of English (i.e., listening, speaking, reading, and writing).

Although there is a set syllabus for English with specified competencies and lists of topics, no detailed content is prescribed such as a particular textbook or a course of lessons. Thus, this 'gap' provided an opportunity to design the researcher's own materials referred to as the "Intercultural Syllabus". These intercultural materials were carefully selected to develop student trainees' attitudes, knowledge, skills, and critical cultural awareness necessary to improve intercultural interactions, taking the findings from the literature review into consideration. Since the target of the activities was to increase the critical cultural awareness and sensitivity to otherness of the student teachers while improving their English language skills, the content of the activities was on social and cultural information that promotes reflections on intercultural issues. The ultimate goal was to help student teachers to establish successful interactions with people from other cultures using English. There was a

Table 3 Sample activities

Competency Level
Identify writer's purpose and infer implied meaning [Reading]
Use English creatively and innovatively in written communication [Writing]
Report ideas and views clearly and concisely [Listening]
Apply critical thinking skills to determine bias/accuracy of information presented orally and make decisions. [Speaking]
Description of the activity and the procedure implemented
Display the title of the poem "culture clash" by Sally Odger and get the students to predict the content. Put the rest of the poem on the board and get them to complete the task sheet individually. Discuss whether they agree with the poet's ideas. Ask them to write a similar poem based on their personal experiences. [Reading]
Ask the students to work in groups and comment on pictures by describing, interpreting and evaluating their responses. The rationale is to decipher cultural predispositions that govern the perception of social reality. [Writing]
Students listen to "The Story of Abigail" and then arrange the characters in their order of preference by taking into consideration how they behaved in the story. First, they do it individually and then in groups and present the agreed list to the class and justify their choices. [Listening]
Students are presented with some pictures of Indian culture and are required to predict what they are about. Students then discuss their personal opinions about Indian Culture, both negative and positive. Next, they watch the film "Outsourced" and find out situations in which Mr. Todd, an American who got himself appointed to a company as a manager in India, is in trouble with Indian culture and how he manages to come out of it finally. After that, students select one of the incidents and explain to the class how they would have reacted in such a situation. Students also discuss and emphasise the qualities and characteristics that helped Mr. Todd to adjust to India. [Speaking]

pre- and post-discussion session for each activity to develop participants' critical thinking. The details of some activities are given in Table 3 to illustrate the nature of the intervention activities.

3   Data Analysis

The data of this study are presented based on two categories. One is quantitative data and the other is qualitative data. The quantitative data were collected from the questionnaire and the checklist. The qualitative data were collected from the reflective journal of the researcher, field notes of the non-participant observer and diaries of the students. These data were analysed in such a manner that they answer the primary concerns of this research i.e., to understand the cultural perceptions of the student teacher participants at the beginning and the end of the intervention and how they have responded to the intercultural syllabus. It also allowed the researcher to understand better strategies and material that were more effective in developing intercultural competence of the student teachers. How the data are analysed is described under each data collection tool as follows.

Table 4 Scores of the attitudinal scale

No	Ethnicity/religion	Second year		First years	
		Student's name	Score	Student's name	Score
1	Tamil Hindu	Maha	37	Abinaya	33
2	Tamil Hindu	Nihamath Hayam	30	Radha	32
3	Muslim	Farvin	16	Zinda	29
4	Muslim	Nuzrath	18	Ruzaira	
5	Muslim	Fazeeha	11	Zaina	08
6	Muslim	Raza	35	Fathima Manal	35
7	Muslim	Hazeena	30	Zeenath	29
8	Muslim	Maf	16	Hazeema	44
9	Sinhala Catholic	Jacky	11	Ann	
10	Sinhala Catholic	Gabrielle	09	Mar	19
11	Sinhala Catholic	Maf	06	Sharmane	
12	Sinhala Buddhist	Ashaya	29	Shadsavi	25
13	Sinhala Buddhist	Sachi	28	Sara	29
14	Sinhala Buddhist	Radeeka	11	Shenali	21
15	Sinhala Buddhist	Induwari	13	Sherin	12
16	Sinhala Buddhist	Samanthi	34	Manel	18
17	Sinhala Buddhist	Upamali	06	Vimeka	22
18	Sinhala Buddhist	Randhi	26	Pahansilu	18
19	Sinhala Buddhist	Samadhi	17	Udaka	21
20	Sinhala Buddhist	Nishu	31	Saumya	22
21	Sinhala Buddhist	Sadeesha	29	Dineni	09
22	Sinhala Buddhist	Saranya	16	Samanali	30
23	Sinhala Buddhist	Tharika	16	Chichee	36
24	Sinhala Buddhist	Samudini	25	Thilini	29
25	Sinhala Buddhist	Parami	39	Seya	36
26	Sinhala Buddhist	Sithari	53	Sajeewani	31
27	Sinhala Buddhist	Melanthi	30	Ayesha	21
28	Sinhala Buddhist	Sanjana	26	Arundathi	31
29	Sinhala Buddhist	Priyandhi	48	Daham	24
30	Sinhala Buddhist	Bopath	19	Piumi	15
31	Sinhala Buddhist	Sepali	24	Anu	08
32	Tamil Christian	–		Sharon	26

3.1 The Analysis of Data from the Attitudinal Scale

The attitudinal scale of cultural perceptions based on Bennett's (1993) Intercultural Sensitivity Development Model that was used to understand whether student teachers' cultural perceptions were more inclined towards ethnocentric or ethnorelative attitudes was analysed by giving an appropriate mark based on its stage and these scores are analysed in Table 4.The real identity of the student participants is concealed by pseudonym i.e., using typical names representing their ethnicities in this Table and on all such occasions.

3.2   Findings of the Attitudinal Scale

When discussing the scores obtained by the second-year participants, it was observed that the highest and the lowest scores i.e., 53 and 6 were obtained by Sinhala Buddhist student teachers. Conversely, the highest score obtained by a Tamil student is 37 while the highest score obtained by a Muslim student was 35 and the lowest was 6. The three Sinhala Roman Catholics had scores of 11, 9 and 6, respectively. The mean score of the total sample was 16.93, which is only the half of the required score. The mean score of the Tamils was 33.5 and the Muslims was 21.4. The Sinhala Roman Catholics had a mean score of 10 whereas Sinhala Buddhists had a mean score of 15.52. Accordingly, the Tamils had the highest mean score, and the Roman Catholic Sinhalese had the lowest mean score. The highest number of student scores lay in the range of 31–40 which is 35.5% of the total population. The mode of the score was 33.

In relation to First Year sample's score the highest mark obtained was 38 and the lowest was 5. Both were obtained by Sinhala Buddhist students. The highest score of Muslims was 44 and the lowest was 08. The highest score of Tamils was 33. The highest score of Roman Catholics was 29 and the lowest was 19. The mean score of the Sinhala Buddhists was 19.18. The mean score of Tamils was 33 and of the Muslims 29.5. The mean score of Sinhala Roman Catholics was 25. The highest number of scores lay in the range of 21–30 which consisted of 31.25% of the population. The mode of the score was 29. The range of scores of the total sample, and the mean score of each ethnic group are presented in Tables 5 and 6.

Table 5 Mean score of the sample

Range	Second years		First years	
	Number of students	Percentage %	Number of students	Percentage %
0–10	02	6.45	06	18.75
11–20	12	38.7	04	12.5
21–30	06	19.35	13	40.63
31–40	05	16.13	07	21.88
41–50	00	00	02	6.25
51–60	00	00	00	00
Over 61	00	00	00	00

Table 6 Mean score based on ethno-religious identity

Ethnicity/Religion	Tamil	Muslim	Sinhala Buddhist	Sinhala Roman Catholic
Mean Score of the Second Years	33	21.4	15.52	10
Mean Score of the First Years	22	29.5.	19.18	25

Table 7 Deviation of scores from the mean

Ethno-religious identity	Deviation
Tamils	1.9
Muslims	3.0
Sinhala Buddhists	−1.0
Sinhala Roman Catholics	−3.3

The highest percentage of student scores (19.35%) of the second years lay in the range of 11–20 and 40.63% of the first-year student scores lay in the range of 21–30, just at the margin of gaining intercultural competence. The lowest percentage, 6.45% of the second years, lay between 0–10 and 6.25% scores of first years were between 41–50. None of the students from any batch scored marks above 60. When the mean scores were analysed based on the ethnicity the result was as shown in Table 6.

From the second-year batch the highest mean score 33 was achieved by Tamils and from the first years the highest mean score 29 was achieved by Muslims. Thus, the tables exemplified the fact that the majority Sinhala Buddhists are more inclined towards ethnocentrism. Table 7 displays how far the mean score of each ethnic group deviated from the expected score.

When focused on how far the mean score of each ethnic/religious group deviated from the original it is clear that Muslims have the highest positive deviation whereas the Roman Catholic Sinhalese have the highest negative deviation. Thus, the findings from the attitudinal scale show that the cultural perceptions of both first- and second-year students are more inclined towards ethnocentrism which means they believe their culture is superior to others at the beginning of the intervention. However, when the same attitudinal scale was implemented at the end of the intervention, the picture changed. This is clearly evident in Table 8 where both the marks students scored at the beginning of the intervention and at the end of the intervention are compared side by side.

When the scores of the first-year students taken before the intervention are compared with the ones taken after the intervention, it can be seen that out of the 32 participants only two have not increased their scores and one student has stayed at the same score. If this is taken as a percentage, 90.63% of the student teachers can be said to have improved their scores after being subjected to intercultural sensitivity training. Those who have scored more than 35 can be considered as in the ethnorelative phase of intercultural competence. Thus, 17 people have scored more than 35 after the intervention which is an average of 53.13%. None of the participants of the second year sample have gone down in their scores after the intervention and they all have improved their scores generally at a 100% success rate. 19 participants have scored more than 35, an average of 59.38. Hence, when considering the numbers of the sample, the intercultural learning seemed to be successful. However, many other strategies described below were used to corroborate the findings.

Table 8 Marks of the attitudinal scale before and after intervention

No	Ethnicity/religion	Second year			First years		
		Student's name	SBI	SAI	Student's name	SBI	SAI
1	Tamil Hindu	Maha	37	38	Abinaya	33	36
2	Muslim	Nihamath Hayam	35	63	Maiza	32	47
3	Muslim	Fazeeha	11	35	Zaina	08	28
4	Muslim	Raza	35	44	Fathima Manal	35	44
5	Muslim	Hazeena	35	41	Zeenath	33	45
6	Muslim	Maf Ali	06	28	Hazeena	34	52
7	Sinhala Catholic	Jacky	25	33	Zinda	24	36
8	Sinhala Catholic	Gabrielle	16	24	Mar x	23	31
9	Sinhala Buddhist	Ashaya	08	40	Shadsavi x	25	40
10	Sinhala Buddhist	Sachi	28	38	Sarah	29	40
11	Sinhala Buddhist	Radeeka	11	37	Shenali	21	52
12	Sinhala Buddhist	Induwari	13	46	Sherin	15	20
13	Sinhala Buddhist	Samanthi	34	44	Manel	18	40
14	Sinhala Buddhist	Upamali	06	25	Vimeka	22	36
15	Sinhala Buddhist	Randhi	26	34	Pahansilu	18	30
16	Sinhala Buddhist	Samadhi	17	34	Udaka	21	29
17	Sinhala Buddhist	Nishu	31	47	Saumya	22	29
18	Sinhala Buddhist	Sadeesha	29	36	Dineni	09	32
19	Sinhala Buddhist	Saranya	16	27	Samanali	15	30
20	Sinhala Buddhist	Tharika	16	19	Chichee	20	36
21	Sinhala Buddhist	Samudini	25	29	Thilini	29	29
22	Sinhala Buddhist	Parami	39	41	Seya	36	51
23	Sinhala Buddhist	Sithari	53	55	Sajeewani	31	45
24	Sinhala Buddhist	Melanthi	30	43	Ayesha	21	22
25	Sinhala Buddhist	Sanjana	26	28	Arundathi	31	39
26	Sinhala Buddhist	Priyandhi	48	59	Daham	24	52
27	Sinhala Buddhist	Bopath	19	35	Nihara	13	15
28	Sinhala Buddhist	Amanda	32	49	Piumi	5	24
29	Sinhala Buddhist	Devi	16	31	Nayana	12	14
30	Sinhala Buddhist	Samuduni	29	48	Sheshadri	38	28
31	Sinhala Buddhist	Sepali	24	25	Anu	08	38
32	Tamil Christian				Sharon	26	28

Note: SBI: Score Before Intervention; SAI: Score After Intervention

4 Analysis of Student Diaries, Observer Field Notes and Researcher's Reflective Journal

As mentioned earlier the data from classroom proceedings were logged on using three strategies, namely student diaries, field notes of the non-participant observer and the researcher's reflective journal. Although student diaries did not feature entries related to observation, they were used to access direct responses of students to the intercultural syllabus as well as their cultural perceptions. The entries in the student diaries also enabled the researcher to access personal thoughts, feelings and opinions of the participants which she could not have done otherwise. Besides, the key objective of maintaining the reflective journal was to reflect on the researcher's practice and class activities. The data collected from these three sources were interpreted using the content analysis method. While analysing student diaries, emergent categories were identified. For example, student notes revealed different variables, such as the content relevant to student knowledge about other cultures, their skills to interact with people from other cultures, their attitudes towards the culturally different others and their critical awareness about intercultural issues. Thus, the researcher followed an 'emerged coding' method after initial analysis of data. Nevertheless, her coding and categorisation were greatly influenced by the theories of intercultural competence discussed in the literature review. Thus, the student diaries were read several times in order to identify perceptions and group them into categories to work out patterns and decode meaning. It was considered necessary that groups of words which give the sense of similar meaning or undertone were in the same categories and if similar words were used, they too were interpreted as connected to the same ideas and concepts. Tables based on these categories were drawn up, findings were analysed, and conclusions were drawn based on the major themes.

From these data the researcher wanted to find answers for the research questions; particularly the focus was on finding out whether the student teachers responded positively to the activities in the specially designed curriculum and changed their ethnocentric cultural perceptions over the time of the intervention. The researcher was also interested in understanding what types of activities were more/less effective in developing intercultural competence of the student teachers. Therefore, when finding categories of similar ideas, the focus was also on gathering up statements related to the obtained categories. For the purposes of triangulation, the researcher's reflective journal entries and non-participant observer's field notes based on the same activity were analysed simultaneously to work out patterns and connections between and among them.

The reflective journal helped the researcher to reflect on what happened in the class and also acted as an aid to memory. To analyse the entries of the reflective journal the content analysis method was used. After reading the entries several times, themes were developed on which the analysis was based. The focus of these themes was on finding out the cultural perceptions of the prospective teacher participants, and thus the same categorisations related to student diaries were used in analysing both the reflective journal entries and entries in the field notes of the observer. As mentioned earlier, the field notes and reflective journal entries were divided into three segments as follows: (a) what I did, (b) what happened, and (c) what I think about what happened.

In the data analysis, extensive attention was paid to the last two segments since they gave better insight into answering the research questions. When maintaining the student diaries, the students were instructed to invent a name representing their cultural identity and stick to it to preserve their anonymity; these were the names used throughout.

What was found in the student diaries related to the activities logged in Table 9. When similar ideas/phrases/words were found, the names of all of those students were mentioned against the comment. Since they take lots of space, only an excerpt of the first activity is included here as a sample to give a brief idea.

5 Findings of Student Diaries, Observer Field Notes and Researcher's Reflective Journal

The comments in all three rows of the Student Diaries section of Table 9 show that the students were very reluctant to use a greeting from another culture, which clearly illustrated their ethnocentric attitudes. However, they also gave evidence as to the keenness of students to learn about other cultures which happened as a result of the promotion of intercultural competence in the intercultural curriculum. When comparing the entries in the student diaries, field notes and reflective journal it can be concluded that student teachers had very 'culture centred' opinions and most of them believed their culture was superior to other cultures at the beginning of the intervention. Also, students who belonged to minority groups were much more culture conscious than students coming from the majority group. However, they responded positively to the activities in the intercultural curriculum, and it was obvious they improved their knowledge about each other's cultures, developed skills required to handle intercultural encounters effectively and changed their negative attitudes towards culturally different others during the course of the intervention to a significant extent.

The Observation Field Notes were maintained by the non-participant observer during the activities. Through the checklist the observer tried to quantify intercultural competence by allocating a designation for different IC components. Thus, a rating system was given to each component as follows: Inadequate – 1; minimal – 2; moderate – 3; extensive – 4. For each of the activities discussed above, the checklist was used for observation, and students' knowledge, attitudes, and skills were given a score. In some instances, some of the students were not actively participating in the lesson. In such circumstances it was difficult for the observer to quantify their intercultural competence. Thus, no marks were given. After each lesson the marks of the individuals were totalled up and their progress recorded. The mean scores obtained by these students are included in Fig. 1. A slight increase in marks in the activities towards the end was obvious in most cases. Only a few students did not show an evident change. However, when considering the mean score, it is obvious that progress has taken place. This shows that students' intercultural awareness has improved in all three aspects of knowledge.

Table 9 Analysis of attitudes towards greetings and intercultural information exchange

Student diaries	
Ethnocentric	"It was first time I did a different greeting. It was somewhat uncomfortable for me" Fathima Manal "I am very comfortable when I used my own greeting *Ayubowan* to greet others" Sachi/Piumi "Using previous one's gestures was a trouble to me" Hazeema "It is a bit odd to say *ayubowan*" Fathima/Zeenath
Ethnorelative	"It was the very first time I greeted in a different way I was happy to learn it"-Sajeewani "Got familiarised with others' cultural patterns" Seya "We have to respect other cultures. By knowing about other cultures, we can respect them strongly" Maiza
Effectiveness of the activity	"Happy to know the way they greet" Fathima Manal "I learnt how they celebrate, how they feel about their festivals" Udaka "Able to collect much information about other cultures; I enjoyed very much" Abinaya "I understood about other cultures" Zinda "It is useful to know about other cultures" Nihamath/ Hazeena/ Maiza/ Mar/ Priyandhi
Field Notes of the Observer	
Ethnocentric	"Although this was the very first activity done with the class, it was not difficult to identify how reluctant the majority of the students were, to use a greeting from another culture. I noticed that many students quickly finished up the greeting part when they were using a greeting from another culture. Some were very shy to use them. Also, some students were making sour faces when using them. It was evident that they are not used to this type of activity from their behaviour."
Ethnorelative	The general idea accepted by everybody was that it was an interesting experience to share knowledge with friends from other cultures. I noticed students enthusiastically taking part in friendly discussions.
Effectiveness of the activity	Majority of the students enjoyed the activity. They seemed to have learnt a lot of facts about other cultures from the interactions, which was revealed in the post discussion stage.
Reflective Journal of the Researcher	
Ethnocentric	"Students were very reluctant to use the greeting they learnt from the friend, if the friend belonged to another culture. At first, I thought the reluctance was due to shyness at using an unfamiliar gesture. But later my close observations revealed the dislike merely because the greeting belonged to another culture. I noticed they were making faces as if they are touching something 'yuki' when using these gestures. This uneasiness was specifically evident between Sinhalese and Muslims."
Ethnorelative	"I was glad to notice that participants were very keen to ask questions that enhanced their knowledge about each other's cultures and attentively listened to the answers given by their friends."
Effectiveness of the activity	"Most of the participants were very keen to interact with each other and they said activity was interesting. They said they learnt a lot of new things about other cultures."

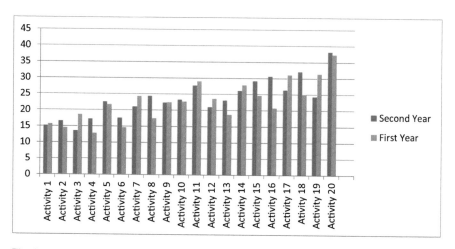

Fig. 1 Mean of the marks of the sample for each activity

In relation to the Researcher's Reflective Journal, serious issues emerged that may reflect the political discord in Sri Lanka. Students were ethnocentric enough to view with distaste greetings from another culture and were reluctant to take the role of the Other by using such greetings themselves. This is not altogether surprising, especially as people from different cultures might have been opponents in the civil war between the Tamils and the Sinhalese (1983–2009). Language was an issue that contributed to that war. In 1956, a "Sinhala Only Act" was passed which replaced English as the official language. The Tamil-minority population found this unfair because it impeded their recruitment to public service, and was discriminatory in linguistic, cultural and economic terms. The ethno-relative stage of the current research showed some willingness of participants to reach out and learn about each other's cultures. As such, it can be regarded as a success for the intervention.

6   Conclusion:(Re)defining 'Intercultural Competence'

The findings helped in concluding that at the beginning of the intervention the participants were more inclined towards ethnocentrism. All data collection tools indicated that the major reason for this is the negative picture they had of their cultural counterparts because of lack of knowledge about other cultures. With every activity in the intervention the participants were given the opportunity to reflect on their preconceived ideas and critically analyse them during the pre-discussion stage. Then, they were in a position to unlearn their biased preconceptions about other cultures. With the passing of time, they learnt to listen and respect cultural difference, critically analyse intercultural issues, and show empathy towards cultural others. This ethnorelative stage of intercultural sensitivity development can be

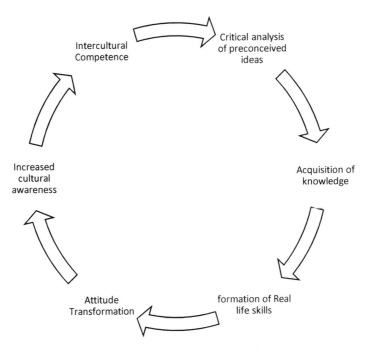

Fig. 2 Intercultural competence as a cyclic process

illustrated by using the following cycle (see Fig. 2). Thus, the development of intercultural competence is a lifelong process in which you acquire knowledge, form skills, transform attitudes and increase cultural awareness.

The present study explored how Sri Lankan student teachers perceive "intercultural competence" (IC) by inviting them to give their own definitions before and after the training intervention. The student teachers' understanding of IC improved along the road. The analysis showed that there are three common phrases found in the majority of the students' definitions of the concept of IC, in relation to (a) knowledge about other cultures, (b) the ability to communicate across cultural differences, and (c) tolerance of cultural difference. Based on the findings of the current study, a context-based definition of intercultural competence would read as follows: "Intercultural competence means the acquisition of knowledge, formation of real-life skills and the transformation of attitudes necessary to communicate across cultural boundaries with minimum conflict" (Tennekoon, 2021, p. 148).

Thus, this study has contributed in identifying a context-based definition for intercultural competence from a non-Eurocentric perspective. It also sheds a significant light on the English Language Teaching in Sri Lanka by illuminating the importance of Intercultural Competence in making English a true lingua franca among different cultures in Sri Lankan multiethnic society.

It is obvious that English Language Learning in Sri Lanka has neglected the intercultural dimensions of English language learning, making learners inadequately prepared for challenges in their real-life language use which is more of a communication tool than a linguistic tool. Thus, it is high time we include intercultural aspects within language learning programs in Sri Lanka. In addition, English language teacher training programs in the country have not paid much attention to the challenges encountered by English language teachers as they are constantly required to cope with culturally and linguistically diverse students in their language classrooms. Therefore, English language teacher educators should be prepared to address intercultural competence both theoretically and practically in their teacher training courses through curriculum, syllabi and pedagogic revisions. Moreover, the notion of reaching native speaker competence must be replaced with the model of intercultural speaker, which fosters the ability to relate to other cultures in a way that helps in realising the goals of English as a link language. Intercultural learning should be made an integral part of foreign language education, and not some peripheral component. This is necessary to reach intercultural communicative competence in addition to linguistic or lexical competence.

References

Bennett, M. J. (1993). Towards ethnorelativism: A developmental model of intercultural sensitivity. In R. M. Paige (Ed.), *Education for the intercultural experience* (2nd ed., pp. 21–71). Intercultural Press.

Byram, M. (1997). *Teaching and assessing intercultural communicative competence*. Multilingual Matters.

Cohen, L., Manion, L., & Morrison, K. (2007). *Research methods in education* (6th ed.). Routledge/Taylor & Francis Group.

Darder, A., Baltodano, M., & Torres, R. (2003). *Critical pedagogy: an introduction in the critical pedagogy reader* (pp. 1–21). Routledge.

Deardorff, D. K. (2004). *The identification and assessment of intercultural competence as a student outcome of international education at institutions of higher education in the United States*. Unpublished EdD dissertation, North Carolina State University. http://www.lib.ncsu.edu/resolver/1840.16/5733

Deardorff, D. K. (2006). Identification and assessment of intercultural competence as a student outcome of internationalization. *Journal of Studies in International Education, 10*, 241–266.

Department of Census and Statistics, Sri Lanka. (2012). *Census of Population and Housing in Sri Lanka*. Ministry of Finance.

Fantini, A. E. (2009). Assessing intercultural competence. Issues and tools. In D. Deardorff (Ed.), *The sage handbook of intercultural competence* (pp. 456–476). Thousand Oaks.

Hammer, R. M., Gudykunst, W. R., & Wiseman, R. L. (1978). Dimensions of intercultural effectiveness: An exploratory study. *International Journal of Intercultural Relations, 2*, 382–393. https://doi.org/10.1016/0147-1767(78)90036-6

Lustig, M. W., & Koester, J. (2003). *Intercultural competence: Interpersonal communication across cultures* (4th ed.). Allyn & Bacon.

Lynch, J. (1992). *Education for citizenship in a multicultural society*. Cassell.

Lynch, K., & Lodge, A. (2002). *Equality and power in schools: Redistribution, recognition and representation*. Routledge Falmer.

McNiff, J., & Whitehead, J. (2000). *Action research in organisations*. Routledge.

McNiff, J., & Whitehead, J. (2006). *All you need to know about action research*. Sage.

Tennekoon, S.R. (2021). Crossing the cultural boundaries: Developing intercultural competence of teachers of English. Stamford Lake.

Shashini Rochana Tennekoon is a senior lecturer in English at Sri Lanka Teacher Educators' Service-Class 1 attached to Maharagama National College of Teacher Education. Presently she is the Vice President of Academic and Quality Assurance of the institute in charge of planning, organizing, and implementing all academic activities. She has eleven years of experience as a Teacher of English in Public Schools from Primary to High School in Sri Lanka and 21 years as a Teacher Educator in English in National Colleges of Education. She holds an MA in TESOL from University of Ulster, UK and received her doctoral degree from University of Colombo, Sri Lanka. Email: shashinirt@gmail.com

Pre-service Teachers' Difficulty Understanding English as a Lingua Franca for Intercultural Awareness Development

Ayako Suzuki

Abstract Communication in English as a Lingua Franca (ELF) is one of the features of our contemporary society. Because of this role of the language, English Language Teaching (ELT) now needs teachers who possess good intercultural awareness of communication and can effectively engage with a variety of multilingual users of English, while also incorporating linguistic diversity into their teaching. This chapter reports on a short-term educational intervention implemented for Japanese pre-service English teachers to develop their intercultural awareness. The intervention consisted of four lectures on the present-day realities of English communication, and the participants' responses to the lectures were collected for analysis. The findings from a pre-intervention questionnaire and reflection writing tasks after the lectures suggest that the intervention relatively easily developed the pre-service teachers' open attitudes to the diversity of English but did not help them fully understand the complex realities of ELF communication. By investigating why it was difficult to understand these realities, the chapter draws insights into English teacher education in the era of ELF communication.

Keywords English as a Lingua Franca · Educational intervention · Intercultural awareness · Pre-service English teachers · Multilinguality

1 Introduction: Communication in English as a Lingua Franca

Communication in English as a common international lingua franca, or ELF, can be one of the essential features of our contemporary society. English is often used as an additional language by different language speakers in many intercultural

A. Suzuki (✉)
College of Humanities, Tamagawa University, Tokyo, Japan
e-mail: ay-suzuki@lit.tamagawa.ac.jp

© The Author(s), under exclusive license to Springer Nature Switzerland AG 2023
A. Sahlane, R. Pritchard (eds.), *English as an International Language Education*, English Language Education 33,
https://doi.org/10.1007/978-3-031-34702-3_12

219

contexts, including politics, education, business, and entertainment. As such, the ability in the language is seen as part of global literacy for people living in the present and coming ages. The worldwide use of English necessarily entails great variety and diversity in its linguistic form, function, and identity because multilingual users employ the language for their own purposes to interact with linguistically and culturally diverse others. The great diversity in its use is a key characteristic of ELF (for an overview see Jenkins et al., 2018), and the degree of diversity can be further intensified by the increasing mixing of heterogeneous people. It is certain that the language people encounter in situations of ELF communication is usually not standard English, which is often presented as a model in the language classroom.

While the diversity of English in ELF communication should never be ignored, it also has to be noted that English is not the only language used for ELF communication. Other languages available to interlocutors are often utilised to facilitate interactions, and thus it is more appropriate to understand ELF within multilingualism as a multilingual franca (Makoni & Pennycook, 2012) or "English as a multilingua franca" (EMF), as reframed by Jenkins (2015a), emphasising multilingualism. Given that each multilingual speaker uses his/her own idiolect (Li, 2018), or "MY English" (Kohn, 2018), constructed through an individual process of social and educational experiences, a wide range of multilingual, pragmatic, semiotic, and multimodal resources are also used in ELF communication to succeed in their linguistic and cultural negotiations (see Zhu, 2018). Therefore, today it is difficult to predict what types of multilingual English users you will encounter, and how and what English and resources they will deploy for interaction with you.

These complex realities of ELF communication call the current practices of English language teaching (ELT) into question as it generally assumes a particular type of English speakers—native English speakers (NESs)—as target interlocutors. To better respond to the realities, English teacher education is required to equip (pre-service) teachers with knowledge and skills to prepare students for such complex and unpredictable encounters. The present chapter is a report on an initial short-term educational intervention aimed at helping university students who aspired to be English teachers depart from the NES- and monolingual-oriented views of English through the instruction on intercultural communication in English exploring key ideas relating to linguistic diversity, including native-speakerism, World Englishes (WE), ELF, and intercultural communication (ICC). The intervention was carried out by the author as a lecturer in Japan where English is chiefly learnt as a foreign language (EFL) in the classroom, and the report describes students' difficulties in understanding ELF communication within this EFL setting.

2   Background of the Intervention: Linguistic Diversity as Language Teacher Knowledge

ELT and its teacher education are expected to change in response to the complexities of ICC in English. Investigating the variety and diversity in English, researchers of Global Englishes (GE) call for a departure from NES-focused practices of ELT. GE indicates the use and users of English for ICC mainly outside the Anglophone world, and it is used as an umbrella term covering the research fields of WE, ELF, and English as an International Language (EIL) (Baker & Ishikawa, 2021, p. 318). Although these three fields look into English from different perspectives, they share a common awareness of problems with the current ELT: That is, ELT inadequately addresses the sociolinguistic realities of English in the actual world. GE researchers have pointed out that the present configuration of ELT depends heavily on the linguistic competence of NESs and cultural knowledge of the Anglophone world as a norm (e.g., Baratta, 2019; Bayyurt & Akcan, 2015; Rose & Galloway, 2019; Matsuda, 2012), and such a monolithic approach to English results in learners' limited intercultural awareness.

To change the present situation, many ELT practitioners and teacher trainers are striving to incorporate the multifaceted nature of English and the complex realities of ELF communication into classroom practices. In recent years, the accumulating research about the nature of ELF communication is very significant (e.g., Kiczkowiak & Lowe, 2019; *ELT Journal* 2020 Special issue on English as a lingua franca and language teaching), but at present what attracts more attention is the incorporation of theoretical knowledge into teacher training practice. The main reason is that "… the transformation of the conventional modes of thinking, principles, and practices into socioculturally informed pedagogy can only happen with the education of teachers both at pre- and in-service levels" (Selvi & Yazan, 2021, p. 3). If teachers continue to adhere to the monolithic approach, their students will fail to acquire ICC, necessary for effective communication with English users from diverse cultural backgrounds. This may be particularly true in places where English conversations are not regularly heard in the street, such as the East Asian region, including Japan, because the classroom may be the only space where students are exposed to the language (Suzuki et al., 2018). Therefore, to change ELT, the first step should be to support teachers in developing an awareness of the complexities of ELF communication and taking a flexible approach to the language.

Then, what attempts have been made to support teachers' development? Sifakis and Bayyurt (2018) promote ELF-aware teacher education. It is designed to encourage teachers to reflect on how and why their teaching is constructed in light of changing sociolinguistic realities of English and potential challenges to ELT. The goal is to enable teachers to create more learner- and context-sensitive classroom activities. This "transformative" teacher education (Sifakis & Bayyurt, 2018, p. 460) consists of three phases: *exposure* to the variety and diversity of

English, *critical awareness* of own teaching practice based on the exposure, and *action plan* for ELF-aware classroom activities appropriate for learners and contexts. Organized in alignment with this framework, Selvi and Yazan's book on teacher education (2021) presents many innovative activities, including, for example, listening to different varieties of English using video materials, discussing common views about English through direct interaction with different types of English users, exploring the evolving nature of language by referring to a dictionary, and understanding diverse linguistic resources for writing through the use of corpora. The teacher-training practitioners who contributed to the book reported positive changes in their trainees' attitudes, although they were also aware of limitations with their attempts.

Focusing on research methodology, Rose et al. (2021) conducted a review of GE-related classroom-based language teacher education research between 2010 and 2020. They also found that instruction on GE was likely to elicit teacher trainees' sympathetic reactions to the diversity of English. However, they noted that available studies tended to remain in the attitudinal investigation, making it difficult to know whether changed attitudes actually translate into changes in their classroom practices. Referring to Suzuki's (2011) research, they also pointed out that raising teacher trainees' awareness of the diversity of English would not ensure changes in the classroom (see also Blair, 2015). However, acknowledging the diversity of English is still a crucial part of teacher education, particularly for those who operate in the EFL contexts.

Research in the field of multilingualism confirms the importance of awareness-raising by showing the significance of language teachers' self-recognition as multilingual. Focusing particularly on European contexts, Vetter (2011), who promotes "multilingualism pedagogy", argues that learning one specific language is necessarily intertwined with a learner's existing linguistic resources. Therefore, language teacher education needs to address multilingualism to encourage teachers to adopt pluralistic approaches to language and cultures. However, according to Vetter, teacher education commonly does not support teachers to value their own multilinguality as an advantage for teaching (see also Iversen, 2020).

Calafato (2019) reviewed research on the identity of "non-native speaker teachers" (NNSTs) who engaged in language teaching. Like Vetter (2011), Calafato was concerned that teachers who do not embrace a multilingual identity would not be able to effectively raise their students' language awareness. Of the 84 studies published between 2009 and 2018 that he reviewed, Calafato found that, although multilinguality was generally perceived positively by NNSTs in any region, unlike in Europe, the studies conducted in Asia showed that NNSTs were more likely to struggle with linguistic and cultural legitimacy of being teachers of the target language, very often English. In the Asian contexts where native-speakerism tends to prevail and monolingual ideology is pervasive, Calafato argues that teacher education needs to promote "multilingual practices like translanguaging, code-switching, and cross-linguistic comparisons, as well as encourage self-reflection in teachers about their language awareness and associated abilities" (p. 20). Therefore, one task for English language teacher education in the age of GE is to enhance teachers' understanding of their own and their students' multilinguality and multilingual practices to overcome the monolingual ideology within teaching.

3   ELT and Teacher Education in Japan

Japan is one of the East Asian countries which subscribes to native-speakerism and a monolingual ideology (Houghton & Rivers, 2013; Konakahara & Tsuchiya, 2020), and the intervention on which the present chapter reports was conducted there. To contextualise the intervention, this section provides an overview of ELT and English teacher education in this country.

In response to globalisation, Japan as a nation has been striving to improve ELT by implementing a series of educational reforms over the last two decades to equip young Japanese nationals with ICC skills in English as global literacy (Yoshida, 2021). The main rationale behind these reforms is the recognition of the English language as a necessary international lingua franca (Seargeant, 2020), and this point is explicitly stated in the policy documents such as *Five Proposals and Specific Measures for Developing Proficiency in English for International Communication* (Commission on the Development of Foreign Language Proficiency, 2011). Despite such a rationale, what has been implemented in the classroom seems contradictory. Let us first look into the national curriculum for students in junior high schools (7th–9th graders), known as the *Course of Study* (the Ministry of Education, Culture, Sports, Science, and Technology [MEXT] 2017a,[1]b).

3.1   School English Education Reform

First of all, the *Course of Study* shows great reliance on NESs for teaching, although it makes brief mentions of the diversity of English and indicates the need to consider it (Naka, 2018; Yoshida, 2021). It states that learning with NESs can enhance Japanese students' speaking and listening skills because NESs speak "natural English" (MEXT, 2017b, p. 55) with "standard" and "correct" accents, and thus students can be exposed to "real foreign language" (pp. 89–90). Also, it advises Japanese English teachers to seek assistance from their NES colleagues with lesson planning and delivery because of their "effective" ways of speaking (p. 64) (for details see Suzuki, 2020). Another important point in the *Course of Study* is the principle that "[English] Lessons, in principle, should be conducted in English."

---

[1] The English version of the *Course of Study* is available at https://www.mext.go.jp/content/20220603-mxt_kyoiku02-000005242_003.pdf

This monolingual principle first appeared in the curriculum for junior high schools in 2017, while it had been introduced for senior high school students (10th–12th graders) in 2008. The use of Japanese is not banned but discouraged, because the principle is "to enhance opportunities for the students to use English and turn classes into communication situations" (MEXT, 2017a, p. 151). From these descriptions of NESs and the monolingual policy, it can be understood that the *Course of Study* regards monolingual NESs who use standard English as a model to emulate and values their nativeness to English as teacher quality, dismissing Japanese English teachers' multilinguality.

In terms of the monolingual principle, Noda and O'Regan (2020) investigated how it was received and practised at senior high schools by interviewing three types of stakeholders: national and local government officials, and senior high school teachers. They discovered that government officials strongly preferred the monolingual teaching strategy, whereas the teachers were aware of the advantages of using the students' L1 in the classroom. They concluded that the policy made it difficult for teachers to use L1 and thus distorted local teaching practices. Glasgow (2018) also looked into high school teachers' understanding of the policy by surveying 40 practitioners' opinions. The teachers surveyed reported using L1 in the classroom, but they themselves perceived it as an illegitimate teaching practice. These two studies suggest that the monolingual principle has made monolingual practice the norm, causing teachers to view their own multilinguality as an encumbrance. One underlying reason for the neglect of the multilinguality of both teachers and students has been the belief among Japanese policymakers that advanced ability for ICC in English is equivalent to high linguistic proficiency in standard English, and thus the government tends to emphasise the development of linguistic skills (Kubota & Takeda, 2021). In sum, it is clear that Japanese ELT on the levels of policy as well as practice subscribes to native-speakerism and prioritizes monolingual approaches to the target language, and this causes multilingual teachers to struggle.

3.2   Teacher Education Reform

In 2017, English teacher education also underwent a major reform at the national level to improve teacher quality after a gap of twenty years. MEXT commissioned Tokyo Gakugei University (TGU) to identify the essential abilities and knowledge areas required by school English teachers to be able to perform successfully. TGU developed the *Core Curriculum* for English language teacher education (TGU, 2017[2]), which is a standardised common curriculum. All universities that offer English teacher training programmes had to revise their teaching modules and contents to align with the new curriculum and be authorised by MEXT by the time of official implementation in April 2019.

---

[2]The English version can be assessed at https://www2.u-gakugei.ac.jp/~coretgu/pdf/koakari_digest_en.pdf

The *Core Curriculum* has two major subject areas, "English class teaching methods" and "technical matters relating to English class[3]" (TUG, 2017). The latter consists of four categories: communication in English, English linguistics, English literature, and cross-cultural understanding. Under the category of English linguistics, "historical development of English language, English as a global common language" is newly specified as required learning content for pre-service teachers. They are now expected "to acquire a basic knowledge of the historical evolution of the English language in terms of speech, writing, vocabulary, and grammar, and to understand the reality of English as a global common language in the English-speaking world and throughout the world" (TGU, 2017 p. 114, the author's translation). Although what contents are covered and how many hours are spent on "English as a global common language" is up to each university's decision, this is the very first time that teachers have been required to take this course. This change should be welcomed, even though the requirement and the *Course of Study*'s reliance on NESs and the monolingual principle are not necessarily compatible. Moreover, we do not know much about whether the change in the teacher education curriculum has contributed to pre-service teachers' awareness development of linguistic diversity because the curriculum is still new. Therefore, the present study (detailed in the next section) was conducted to seek answers to the following research questions:

(a) Can a short-term educational intervention that addresses the linguistic diversity of English invite changes in Japanese pre-service English teachers' intercultural awareness?
(b) If any, what changes can be observed?

The current chapter may be one of the first studies on the influences of curriculum reform on teachers' views of English.

4   The Present Study

Within the contexts outlined above, a short-term educational intervention was conducted in 2021 to develop pre-service English teachers' awareness of ICC in English at a university in Tokyo. The intervention was part of a semester-long compulsory module of language studies for second-year English majors, consisting of fifteen 100-minute classes. This introductory module fell under the category of English linguistics in the *Core Curriculum* and aimed at equipping the students with basic knowledge of concepts and technical terms necessary for language studies. Five faculty members of the university delivered lectures in turn according to each specialization, including English linguistics, psycholinguistics, and sociolinguistics. The author was responsible for four lectures on the "historical development of English language' and "English as a global common language" (TGU, 2017).

---

[3] TUG's original English version calls this "technical matters on English class" (p. 8).

Table 1 Details of intervention lectures

Week (mode)	Lecture theme	Topics
1 (Face to Face)	Concepts of native English speakers (NESs)	Concepts of standard language Concepts of NESs Native-speakerism Language learning and NESs
2 (Online)	World Englishes (WE)	The global spread of English Types of English use and speakers Kachru's three circles model of WE Diversification of English
3 (Online)	English as a Lingua Franca (ELF)	Criticism of WE History of research on international English Features of ELF communication EFL and ELF
4 (Online)	Intercultural Communication (ICC)	Definitions of culture and nature of communication ICC ICC in ELF Communication strategies

4.1 The Intervention

The four lectures the author provided were specifically designed to raise the pre-service teachers' awareness of linguistic diversity by exposing them to key academic arguments about the global use of English, including native-speakerism, WE, ELF and ICC. Table 1 shows details of the intervention lectures, including teaching modes, themes, and topics covered in each lecture. Because the module had a large number of registered students (see the following section) and was conducted during the COVID-19 pandemic situation, the lectures took a teacher-centred style. Due to the university's decision, only the first lecture was conducted face-to-face, while the other three were synchronically delivered via an Internet video conference system. In the classroom, because oral interactions were restricted by the university, the video conference's chat function was utilized to elicit the students' responses. The lectures and interactions with the students were all in the students' L1, Japanese.

4.2 Research Participants and Data Collection

The number of students who registered for the module was 93. In the first lecture, the author explained the purpose of the current research, and all students except four absentees were provided with an online research consent form that asked whether they agreed to provide the following as data for the current research:

answers to a pre-intervention questionnaire (hereafter, questionnaire), pre-lecture preparation questions (preparation tasks), and post-lecture reflection questions (reflection tasks). The students were also informed that they could withdraw at any time if they changed their minds. Of the 89 students, 72 consented to the use of all their data for the research. Among these students, about 85 per cent completed all the tasks, while some students missed one or two tasks and/or were absent from one of the four lectures.

Of the 72 participants, the majority were pre-service teachers who were seeking an English teacher certificate for secondary education, although not all intended to pursue a teaching career. The ratio of males to females was about two to one, and the majority of them were 18 or 19 years old. It is worth noting that these students were going to join a study abroad programme in one of three English-speaking countries, the USA, the UK, or Ireland, which was a requirement for their graduation. The intervention was carried out during their pre-departure period, and thus they were also taking other modules that covered preparatory information about the destination countries' cultures, as well as English language learning. Therefore, their comments introduced in this chapter may have been reflected by what they learned in those modules.

The questionnaire consisted of two parts with the first one containing 17 questions asking about the students' ideas of the global use of English and linguistic norms of English for global communication. The second part had 11 questions about their general awareness of global participation, but these are not discussed in this chapter. The main purpose of the first part was to capture the students' initial views of English before the intervention. As the 17 questions used a six-point Likert scale, from Strongly Agree (6), Agree (5), Slightly Agree (4), Slightly Disagree (3), Disagree (2) to Strongly Disagree (1), the simple mean scores and standard deviations of the collected answers were calculated using statistical software, Bell Curve for Excel.[4] Out of the 17 questions, this chapter only shows the results of ten questions (Table 3) because these are directly related to the chapter's theme. The remaining seven are excluded from the analysis.

Table 2 shows the details of preparation and reflection tasks which required the participants to answer the given questions in writing. All the answers were stored and analysed using NVivo. First, each task was analysed separately to identify prominent topics, and then all the written data were thematically analysed cross-sectionally. The questionnaire and reflection tasks are the main focus of this chapter. The questionnaire could give an overview of the pre-service teachers' existing perceptions of English, and the reflection tasks could reveal what they learnt from the lectures and what they did not. Note that all data were in the students' L1, Japanese, and pieces of the data shown below have been translated by the author.

---

[4]The package is the product by Social Survey Research Information Co., Ltd.

Table 2 Details of preparation and reflection tasks

Lecture theme	Preparation task: Three short questions	Reflection task: An extended question
NESs	NA	If becoming like NESs is not the goal of language learning, what can be the goal?
WE	What type(s) of English have you learnt? What English do you want to acquire? What does "real English" mean to you?	Do you support the idea of World Englishes? Why or why not?
ELF	What English is "international common English" in your understanding? Do you think the existence of WE hinders global communication? Can you think of any other possible hindrances to global communication?	Some people argue that even NESs need to learn English for intercultural communication. What do you think of this opinion?
ICC	When you hear "different culture(s)," what comes to your mind? What does "communication" mean to you? Do you think understanding cultures in English-speaking countries is important for global communication in English?	When someone has said "s/he is good at intercultural communication in English," what kind of person is s/he?

Table 3 Pre-intervention questionnaire results

Questions	Mean	Standard deviation
1. I want to be able to use standard English.	5.71	0.70
2. For global communication, it is important to know the cultures in English-speaking countries.	5.04	0.97
3. In order to improve English proficiency, it is important to communicate with native English speakers.	4.98	0.93
4. I want to pronounce English like native English speakers.	4.96	1.17
5. I'm interested in English used by non-native English speakers.	4.92	1.10
6. Odd expressions are acceptable as long as they are intelligible.	4.88	0.99
7. It is important to be able to use correct English grammar.	4.65	0.98
8. It is beneficial to learn English with non-native English-speaking teachers (other than Japanese).	4.63	1.09
9. English language classes should be conducted in English.	4.18	1.13
10. I want to learn English with native English-speaking teachers rather than with Japanese English teachers.	3.99	1.09

5 Findings

This section offers the findings of the current investigation, starting from the pre-intervention questionnaire through the first two lectures on NESs and WE and to the last two on ELF and ICC in sequence. By looking into these in turn, it is possible to track the progression of the students' awareness of linguistic diversity. As the main aim of this chapter is to trace how they broadened their views of ICC in English through the intervention, the findings illustrated below are general tendencies of the students' responses to the intervention, rather than intricate individual progressions.

5.1 The Pre-intervention Questionnaire: Standard English Is the Target Language

The results of the ten question items in the questionnaire are shown in Table 3 in the rank order of mean scores from high to low. In the results, what is outstanding is the students' very strong adherence to standard English (Question 1), as evidenced by the mean score of 5.71. Of the 72 students, 57 chose Strongly Agree and 12 chose Agree. Then, what kind of English was standard English in their minds? From the items related to linguistic forms of English, it is noticed that their desires for native-like pronunciation (Question 4) and correct grammar (Question 7) were not necessarily very intense, and they were relatively tolerant of unconventional expressions (Question 6). Thus, it can be understood that, in the students' minds, standard English did not refer to particular linguistic forms of English. Indeed, there were no significant correlations between Question 1 and the other three question items. This suggests that although the students did not have substantial knowledge of standard English, at the same time acquiring it appeared to be a pre-established goal of learning English due to their learning practices at the school, as discussed in Sect. 3.1.

Another notable point is that while there is a relatively close link between students' association of standard English, the cultures in English-speaking countries and NESs as desirable English proficiency models (Questions 2 and 3), they did not necessarily dismiss the importance of multilingual English users and their English varieties (Questions 5 and 8). However, they exhibited ambivalent attitudes towards Japanese English teachers (Question 10) because two-thirds of the students chose either Slightly Agree (32 students) or Slightly Disagree (16 students). Their ambivalence might have come from their experiences that sharing L1 with an English teacher in the classroom had benefits for their L2 learning (Question 9). Therefore, it can be said that despite their strong desire for standard English, their views of the use and users of English were relatively open. Then, from such existing perceptions, how did the students develop and what changes did they show?

5.2 Lectures 1 and 2: NESs and WE

The first two lectures were devoted to expanding the students' views of English use and users by exploring the concepts of NESs (Lecture 1) and introducing the idea of WE (Lecture 2). The first lecture started with the topic of standard and regional variations of Japanese to help them recognise linguistic diversity in their familiar contexts. Referring to this, the lecture moved to the issues of standard English and its relationship with NESs, taking into account multilingual users of English. Then, the students were encouraged to think about the benefits of learning English with NESs. Towards the end of Lecture 1, they were introduced to movements against native-speakerism (Holliday, 2006) in language teaching, including the TESOL International Association's "Position Statement Against Discrimination of Nonnative Speakers of English in the Field of TESOL" (2006).[5]

Lecture 2 explored the idea of WE, considering the history of the global spread of English. Showing Kachru's three-circle model of WE (Kachru, 1992, p. 356) and examples of varieties of English, different types of English use and users, such as ENL (English as a Native Language), ESL (English as a Second Language), and EFL (English as a Foreign Language) were introduced. Then, the lecture moved on to the inseparable relationship between the globalisation and diversification of English because of the intensive contact between English and local language(s) and culture(s). The lecture ended by encouraging the students to consider their own English from the perspective of WE, which sees all varieties of English as equal.

5.2.1 Findings in Lectures 1 and 2: Diversity Should Be Celebrated

Lectures 1 and 2 revealed the students' open and inclusive attitudes towards different speakers and varieties of English. They readily acknowledged the diversity of English and exhibited respect for linguistic differences and individual choices. For the reflection task of Lecture 1, students were invited to answer the question "if to be like NESs is not the goal of language learning, what can be the goal?" to make them explore why people, including themselves, learn English. Out of the 72 students, 67 completed the task, and there were two frequent themes: 1) The goal is to become able to communicate with any type of people who use English, and 2) There should not be a one-size-fits-all goal as each person sets different goals according to their objectives in learning English. The following answer covered both types of themes:

> Although the goals of language learning vary according to the ability that individuals require, I believe that the ultimate goal for everyone, including those who do not like English or have no goals in English, should be to be able to communicate without difficulty with English speakers around the world. The goal for them should be to be able to confidently use their own English to communicate, not the standard variety of English that serves as a norm. This is because there are many non-native English speakers in the world. (Student 52)

Out of 67 posts, 57 (85%) could fall into these two themes, and what we can observe in them is the students' respect for each person's unique version of English, or, as Kohn (2018) puts it, "MY English." Although the questionnaire results showed a

---

[5] https://www.tesol.org/docs/pdf/5889.pdf (last accessed 29th March 2023).

strong preference for standard English, few students mentioned this as part of a learning goal. This is probably because the students' knowledge of standard English was rather insubstantial: Their ideas could be easily overwritten by the new knowledge of the variability of English.

As for the reflection task of Lecture 2, the students were asked whether they supported the idea of WE. All but two of the 72 participants provided answers, and the great majority of the responses (66) basically favoured the idea. Several students expressed concerns, while only a few (4) explicitly made a denial. The most typical reasons for support were that 1) different Englishes should be respected because there should be no hierarchy among them and 2) it is natural that various varieties of English exist due to cultural and societal differences. One typical comment is below.

> I agree with the idea of World Englishes. I think it is unique and interesting that English varies from region to region. To deny this is not only discriminatory but also seems to be deciding a superiority or inferiority of the language. It is fine to have a wide variety of English that has developed into a form that is unique to each region due to exposure to different cultures and societies. English does not have to be one variety, all should be respected equally with ENL. (Student 10)

The students adopted liberal approaches to the diversity of English, in many cases, from moral points of view. However, the posted answers generally did not show a deep interest in *why* differences were produced between the varieties of English, though they enjoyed superficial differences, such as vocabulary. Also, there seemed to be a lack of perspective on communication as an interactive process because about two-thirds of the posts did not consider the possible difficulties caused by the differences in English, although this may be reasonable since the lectures had not necessarily focused on interactional aspects of English use.

5.3   Lectures 3 and 4: ELF and ICC

Lectures 3 and 4, building upon the first two lectures, aimed at developing the students' awareness of the communicative and flexible use of English. Lecture 3 started with criticism of WE to assist the students in anticipating possible communication difficulties that linguistic differences might cause. Then, the lecture moved to the current empirical research of ELF whose focus is on the users of English as an additional language. Features of ELF communication, including non-normative use of English in phonology and lexicogrammar (see Jenkins, 2015b), were described to make the students realise that particular linguistic forms of English, or standard English, were not always necessary for communicative success. The final part of the lecture invited the students to think about the differences between learning EFL and ELF.

Lecture 4 focused on ICC, particularly pragmatic strategies used for ELF communication. The lecture first addressed definitions of culture and communication, emphasising communication as a bi-directional process between interlocutors.

Then, referring back to the features of ELF communication discussed in Lecture 3, examples of pragmatic strategies, such as negotiation of meaning and paraphrasing, were looked into. Stressing the importance of skills to accommodate communicational norms according to interlocutors and situations, Lecture 4 ended with the exploration of the role of English in ICC among multilingual users of English.

5.3.1 Findings in Lectures 3 and 4: Positive Attitudes Can Solve Problems in ICC

The students' raised awareness of the diversity of English through Lectures 1 and 2 seemed to have facilitated their understanding of communication as an interactional process in Lecture 3. However, what Lecture 4 exposed was the limitation in their development of awareness. As the students had not had rich intercultural experiences, their discussions on successful ICC tended to remain at a superficial level.

As the reflection question of Lecture 3, the students considered whether NESs needed to learn English for ICC. Out of 65 answers, 52 (80%) showed supportive opinions. They appeared to have shifted away from the common idea among L2 learners that responsibilities for communicative success depended on themselves as non-L1 speakers of English (Shibata, 2021; see also Suzuki, 2021). This shift was likely due to their realisation that mutual cooperation was indispensable to overcome linguistic differences in intercultural encounters, like the comment below.

> … [I agree with the idea because] as for English as ELF, it is English for successful communication, and native English speakers should learn English that is clear and understandable to others as any other English speaker. … If we think about ELF, whose goal is communication in English, there are many barriers to communicating with other English speakers in terms of grammar, idioms, vocabulary, pronunciation, and many other aspects of native English. Therefore, to communicate more smoothly, it is necessary to learn English that is easy to understand. (Student 29)

Although the answers commonly exhibited positive attitudes towards ELF communication, when it came to considering the qualities of a good intercultural communicator in English in Lecture 4, their responses concentrated on liberal democratic ideals rather than the practicalities of communication. One typical comment is the following:

> I believe that a person who is curious is a good intercultural communicator. … Especially in different cultures, most of what we see and hear is new to us. By being interested in and acknowledging these differences, other people will appreciate us, which leads to mutual appreciation with them. … From this, it can be said that a person who is a good intercultural communicator is one who actually makes use of his or her curiosity, not the ability to use language. (Student 60)

In the lecture, the emphasis was placed on the use of pragmatic strategies for successful communication, but these were not taken up by most of the students in the answers. About 70 per cent (51 posts) of the 69 answers focused on people's respect for and/or friendliness towards others, and about 45 per cent of them (21 posts) did not even make any mention of language or English.

Then, why did the students overlook the role of language in communication and the use of pragmatic strategies? The main reason might be the students' lack of direct experience with ICC. This point is clearly described in Student 34's comment:

> [For answering the question] I have never met anyone I thought was a good intercultural communicator, so I read some articles on the Internet and referred to the ones I agreed with the most. (Student 34).

Comments like this were scarce, but it may be true that several students had limited experiences with direct communication with multilingual users of English. Even if they had, they might not have counted these encounters as authentic English communication due to the monolithic image of the language (Suzuki, 2021). In the context of Japan, students' opportunity to have English communication tends to be only with their English teachers and peer students in the classroom, and therefore they could not envision how English is used for ICC and how pragmatic strategies could be helpful for them. In this way, their exclusive focus on attitudinal issues could be understandable.

6   Discussion and Conclusion

The present educational intervention was carried out to develop the intercultural awareness of pre-service English teachers by contesting the prevailing native-speakerism and monolingualism in the Japanese ELT context. The contributions of the intervention could be summarised as twofold. First, it helped the pre-service teachers foster open and inclusive attitudes towards the diverse uses and users of English because their existing knowledge of standard English was found to be superficial. The superficiality could be improved to some extent by providing robust knowledge of social and historical developments of the dominant use of English as a global language (see Chap. 7 in Baker & Ishikawa, 2021). Second, because of the lectures focusing on ELF in ICC, the pre-service teachers could realise that communication in English is an equally collaborative process, even when communicating with NESs, and that it was not always necessary for them to take all communicative responsibility just because of their non-nativeness to English (see Shibata, 2021; Subtirelu et al., 2022). However, it is difficult to know whether these trainees retain their developed intercultural awareness after the intervention. As it was a short-term, one-off process, its effects may not be long-lasting (Suzuki, 2011).

At the same time, the limitations of the intervention also became apparent. One of these is that despite the emphasis given to the multilinguality of users of English as an additional language during the intervention, it did not capture the pre-service teachers' attention. While they well understood the diversity of English and showed respect for it, their understanding seemed to remain on the surface level. This may be because they continued to see English and L1 as completely separate languages (Li, 2018) owing to the monolingual practices in Japanese ELT they had undergone, as addressed in Sect. 3.1. Another limitation was that ELF communication was difficult to envisage without direct experiences of communication with other multilingual users (Mayumi & Hüttner, 2020). Although the importance of pragmatic strategies for communication in multilingual encounters was discussed in the lectures, it was not well recognised by the lecture participants. Compared to the intervention conducted by Ishikawa (2020) in a similar context, which successfully raised Japanese university students' awareness of multilingual communication practices, the present intervention lacked the offering of first-hand experiences of ELF communication.

Then, what insights could be drawn from the current intervention for teacher education? One can be that, as discussed in Sect. 2 above, teacher education should explicitly acknowledge the multilinguality of both teachers and learners to nurture the trainees' views of their L1 as a valuable resource for language learning as well as teaching. This then would lead them to build up self-confidence as legitimate multilingual language teachers (Vetter, 2011; Calafato, 2019; Glasgow, 2018; Krulatz et al., 2022). Also, it is desirable that teacher education programmes provide the trainees with opportunities for first-hand experiences of ELF communication because without them it is difficult for the trainees to understand what role English would play and how pragmatic strategies can be helpful to negotiate meaning in ELF settings (cf. Ishikawa, 2020). It could be difficult to incorporate such opportunities into a short-term intervention like the present one, but it may be still feasible to seek possibilities for out-of-class and virtual communication activities to develop the trainees' consciousness of ELF communication (Sung, 2018), even in EFL contexts like Japan.

Acknowledgements *This work is supported by the Japan Society for the Promotion of Science (JSPS) KAKENHI Grant Number 21K00659.*

References

Baker, W., & Ishikawa, T. (2021). *Transcultural communication through global Englishes: An advanced textbook for students*. Routledge. https://doi.org/10.4324/9780367809973

Baratta, A. (2019). *World Englishes in English language teaching*. Palgrave Macmillan. https://doi.org/10.1007/978-3-030-13286-6

Bayyurt, Y., & Akcan, S. (Eds.). (2015). *Current perspectives on pedagogy for English as a Lingua Franca*. De Gruyter. https://doi.org/10.1515/9783110335965

Blair, A. (2015). Evolving a post-native, multilingual model for ELF-aware teacher education. In Y. Bayyurt & S. Akcan (Eds.), *Current perspectives on pedagogy for English as a Lingua Franca*. De Gruyter. https://doi.org/10.1515/9783110335965.89

Calafato, R. (2019). The non-native speaker teacher as proficient multilingual: A critical review of research from 2009–2018. *Lingua, 227*, 1–25. https://doi.org/10.1016/j.lingua.2019.06.001

Commission on the Development of Foreign Language Proficiency (2011, June). *Five proposals and specific measures for developing proficiency in English for international communication*. https://www.mext.go.jp/component/english/__icsFiles/afieldfile/2012/07/09/1319707_1.pdf

Glasgow, P. G. (2018). Curriculum reform and professional development: The problems faced by Japanese senior high school teachers. In K. Hashimoto & V. Nguyen (Eds.), *Professional development of English language teachers in Asia: Lessons from Japan and Vietnam* (pp. 45–60). Routledge. https://doi.org/10.4324/9781315413259

Holliday, A. (2006). Native-speakerism. *ELT Journal, 60*(4), 385–387. https://doi.org/10.1093/elt/ccl030

Houghton, S. A., & Rivers, D. J. (Eds.). (2013). *Native-speakerism in Japan: Intergroup dynamics in foreign language education.* Multilingual Matters.

Ishikawa, T. (2020). EMF awareness in the Japanese EFL/EMI context. *ELT Journal, 74*(4), 408–417. https://doi.org/10.1093/elt/ccaa037

Iversen, J. Y. (2020). Pre-service teachers' narratives about their lived experience of language. *Journal of Multilingual and Multicultural Development, 43*(2), 140–153. https://doi.org/10.1080/01434632.2020.1735400

Jenkins, J. (2015a). Repositioning English and multilingualism in English as a lingua Franca. *Englishes in Practice, 2*(3), 49–85. https://doi.org/10.1515/eip-2015-0003

Jenkins, J. (2015b). *Global Englishes: A resource book for students* (3rd ed.). https://doi.org/10.4324/9781315761596

Jenkins, J., Baker, W., & Dewey, M. (Eds.). (2018). *The Routledge handbook of English as a Lingua Franca.* Routledge. https://doi.org/10.4324/9781315717173

Kachru, B. B. (1992). Teaching world Englishes. In B. B. Kachru (Ed.), *The other tongue: English across cultures* (pp. 355–366). University of Illinois Press.

Kiczkowiak, M., & Lowe, R. J. (2019). *Teaching English as a lingua Franca: The journey from EFL to ELF.* Delta Publishing.

Kohn, K. (2018). MY English: A social constructivist perspective on ELF. *Journal of English as a Lingua Franca, 7*(1), 1–24. https://doi.org/10.1515/jelf-2018-0001

Konakahara, M., & Tsuchiya, K. (2020). *English as a Lingua Franca in Japan: Towards multilingual practices.* Palgrave Mcmillan. https://doi.org/10.1007/978-3-030-33288-4

Krulatz, A., Neokleous, G., & Dahl, A. (2022). Multilingual approaches to additional language teaching: Bridging theory and practice. In A. Krulatz, G. Neokleous, & A. Dahl (Eds.), *Theoretical and applied perspectives on teaching foreign languages in multilingual settings: Pedagogical implications* (pp. 15–29). Multilingual Matters. https://doi.org/10.21832/9781788926423-006

Kubota, R., & Takeda, Y. (2021). Language-in-education policies in Japan versus transnational workers' voices: Two faces of neoliberal communication competence. *TESOL Quarterly, 55*(2), 458–485. https://doi.org/10.1002/tesq.613

Li, W. (2018). Translanguaging as a practical theory of language. *Applied Linguistics, 39*(1), 9–30. https://doi.org/10.1093/applin/amx039

Makoni, S., & Pennycook, A. (2012). Disinventing multilingualism: From monological multilingualism to multilingua francas. In M. Martin-Jones, A. Blackledge, & A. Creese (Eds.), *The Routledge handbook of multilingualism* (pp. 439–453). Routledge. https://doi.org/10.4324/9780203154427

Matsuda, A. (Ed.). (2012). *Principles and practices of teaching English as an international language.* Multilingual Matters. https://doi.org/10.4324/9780203819159

Mayumi, K., & Hüttner, J. (2020). Changing beliefs on English: Study abroad for teacher development. *ELT Journal, 74*(3), 268–276. https://doi.org/10.1093/elt/ccaa020

MEXT. (2017a). *Chugakko gakushu shido yoryo* [The course of study for junior high schools]. https://www.mext.go.jp/content/1413522_002.pdf

MEXT. (2017b). *Chugakko gakushu shido yoryo kaisetsu: Gaikokugo* [The commentary on the course of study for junior high schools: Foreign language]. https://www.mext.go.jp/content/20210531-mxt_kyoiku01-100002608_010.pdf

Naka, K. (2018). Professional development for pre-service English language teachers in the age of globalisation. In K. Hashimoto & V. Nguyen (Eds.), *Professional development of English language teachers in Asia: Lessons from Japan and Vietnam* (pp. 76–91). Routledge. https://doi.org/10.4324/9781315413259

Noda, N., & O'Regan, J. P. (2020). L1 marginalisation in Japan: Monolingual instrumentalism and the discursive shift against *yakudoku* in the Japanese government's course of study. *Current Issues in Language Planning, 21*(2), 135–152. https://doi.org/10.1080/14664208.2019.1647998

Rose, H., & Galloway, N. (2019). *Global Englishes for language teaching*. Cambridge University Press. https://doi.org/10.1017/9781316678343

Rose, H., McKinley, J., & Galloway, N. (2021). Global Englishes and language teaching: A review of pedagogical research. *Language Teaching, 54*(2), 157–189. https://doi.org/10.1017/S0261444820000518

Seargeant, P. (2020). English in Japan. In K. Bolton, W. Botha, & A. Kirkpatrick (Eds.), *The Handbook of Asian Englishes* (pp. 569–584). https://doi.org/10.1002/9781118791882.ch24

Selvi, A. F., & Yazan, B. (2021). Introduction: Integrating global Englishes in language teacher education practices. In A. F. Selvi & B. Yazan (Eds.), *Language teacher education for global Englishes: A practical resource book* (pp. 1–8). Routledge. https://doi.org/10.4324/9781003082712

Shibata, M. (2021). Japanese L2 English learners' positions in miscommunication: Who is responsible for failures? *Journal of Language, Identity & Education*. https://doi.org/10.1080/15348458.2021.1938572

Sifakis, N. C., & Bayyurt, Y. (2018). ELF-aware teacher learning and development. In J. Jenkins, W. Baker, & M. Dewey (Eds.), *The Routledge handbook of English as a Lingua Franca* (pp. 456–467). Routledge. https://doi.org/10.4324/9781315717173

Subtirelu, N. C., Lindemann, S., Acheson, K., & Campbell, M. (2022). Sharing communicative responsibility: Training US students in cooperative strategies for communicating across linguistic difference. *Multilingua, 41*(6), 689–716. https://doi.org/10.1515/multi-2021-0013

Sung, C. C. M. (2018). Out-of-class communication and awareness of English as a Lingua Franca. *ELT Journal, 72*(1), 15–25. https://doi.org/10.1093/elt/ccx024

Suzuki, A. (2011). Introducing diversity of English into ELT: Student teachers' responses. *ELT Journal, 65*(2), 145–153. https://doi.org/10.1093/elt/ccq024

Suzuki, A. (2020). ELF for global mindsets? Theory and practice of ELT in formal education in Japan. In M. Konakahara & K. Tsuchiya (Eds.), *English as a lingua franca in Japan: Towards multilingual practices* (pp. 71–89). Palgrave Macmillan. https://doi.org/10.1007/978-3-030-33288-4_4

Suzuki, A. (2021). Changing views of English through study abroad as teacher training. *ELT Journal, 75*(4), 397–406. https://doi.org/10.1093/elt/ccab038

Suzuki, A., Liu, H., & Yu, M. (2018). ELT and ELF in the East Asian contexts. In J. Jenkins, W. Baker, & M. Dewey (Eds.), *The Routledge handbook of English as a Lingua Franca* (pp. 494–505). Routledge. https://doi.org/10.4324/9781315717173

Tokyo Gakugei University. (2017, March). *Eigo kyoin no eigoryoku, shidoryoku kyouka no tame no chosa kenkyu* [Research on the development of English language teachers' proficiency and teaching competencies]. https://www2.u-gakugei.ac.jp/~estudy/28file/report28_all.pdf

Vetter, E. (2011). Multilingualism pedagogy: Building bridges between languages. In J. Hüttner, B. Mehlmauer-Larcher, & S. Reichl (Eds.), *Theory and practice in EFL teacher education* (pp. 228–245). Multilingual Matters. https://doi.org/10.21832/9781847695260-015

Yoshida, T. (2021). English education reform, teacher education, and the Tokyo Olympics: Perfect timing? In A. B. M. Tsui (Ed.), *English language teaching and teacher education in East Asia: Global challenges and local responses* (pp. 135–157). Cambridge University Press. https://doi.org/10.1017/9781108856218.008

Zhu, H. (2018). *Exploring intercultural communication: Language in action* (2nd ed.). https://doi.org/10.4324/9781315159010

Ayako Suzuki (PhD) is a Professor in sociolinguistics and language teaching at the Department of English Language Education, the College of Humanities, Tamagawa University, where she also serves as an Associate Director of the Centre for English as a Lingua Franca. She has researched and published in the areas of ELT, ELF, and intercultural citizenship. Her most recent work appears in *ELT Journal* and *Journal of English as a Lingua Franca*. Email: ay-suzuki@lit.tamagawa.ac.jp

Re-envisioning EIL-Informed TESOL Teacher-Education Curriculum

Roby Marlina

Abstract As a result of the intercultural nature of communication in the twenty-first century and the kaleidoscopic plurality of the English language, its users, and cultures, the discipline of TESOL has shifted its paradigm from Teaching English as a Second/Foreign Language (ESL/EFL) to English as an International Language (EIL). One implication of EIL on TESOL teacher-education is the need for a teacher-education curriculum that engages teacher-candidates in developing a repertoire of pedagogical strategies to foster intercultural understanding and respect for lingua-cultural diversity in ELT classrooms. Although such implication has been repeatedly proffered by EIL scholars and researchers, its operationalisation in teacher education courses is still not visible. Since there is a paucity of teacher-education curricula for preparing teachers to promote intercultural understanding and respect for lingua-cultural diversity in ELT classrooms, this chapter will discuss what can or should be incorporated in the curriculum of an EIL-informed teacher education programme. In particular, what can be the overall goals of an EIL-informed TESOL teacher-education programme? What should form the key content of the programme? What teaching and assessment practices can teacher-educators use to help meet the goals of the programme? It is hoped that upon completion of reading this chapter, readers will be able to see that the curriculum of an EIL-informed teacher education programme should go beyond simply raising teacher-candidates' awareness of lingua-cultural diversity or 'talking about' lingua-cultural differences.

Keywords Curriculum · TESOL · Teacher education · English as an international language · Intercultural communication · World Englishes

R. Marlina (✉)
Training, Research, Assessment, and Consultancy Department, SEAMEO-RELC,
Singapore, Singapore
e-mail: Roby.Marlina@relc.org.sg

© The Author(s), under exclusive license to Springer Nature
Switzerland AG 2023
A. Sahlane, R. Pritchard (eds.), *English as an International Language
Education*, English Language Education 33,
https://doi.org/10.1007/978-3-031-34702-3_13

237

1 Introduction

As a result of the intercultural nature of communication in the twenty-first century, and the kaleidoscopic plurality of the English language, its users, and cultures, the discipline of TESOL has shifted its paradigm from Teaching English as a Second/Foreign Language (ESL/EFL) to English as an International Language (EIL), placing a strong emphasis on teaching intercultural communication skills and fostering awareness of World Englishes.

One implication of EIL on TESOL teacher-education is the need for a teacher-education curriculum that engages teacher-candidates in developing a repertoire of pedagogical strategies to foster intercultural understanding and respect for lingua-cultural diversity in ELT classrooms. Although such implication has been repeatedly proffered by EIL scholars and researchers, its operationalisation in teacher education courses is still not visible (Selvi & Yazan, 2021). This is because, as Bayyurt and Sifakis (2017) explained, "while ESL/EFL is readily specified as teaching and learning construct, EIL/ELF (English as a Lingua Franca) is still not (p. 6).

Since there is a paucity of teacher-education curricula for preparing teachers to promote intercultural understanding and respect for lingua-cultural diversity in ELT classrooms (Bayyurt & Sifakis, 2017; Marlina, 2021; Selvi & Yazan, 2021), this chapter will discuss what can or should be incorporated in the curriculum of an EIL-informed teacher education programme.

As goals, content, and assessment practices form the fundamentals of curriculum development, this practice-oriented chapter uses the EIL paradigm as well as Sifakis and Bayyurt's (2017) model of EIL-aware teacher education to address the following questions: what can be the overall goals of an EIL-informed TESOL teacher-education programme? What should form the key content of the programme? In other words, what should teacher-candidates be engaged in learning? What teaching and assessment practices can teacher-educators use to help meet the goals of the programme?

Prior to addressing the aforementioned questions, the following section explains the paradigm of EIL and its implications for TESOL teacher-education.

2 The EIL Paradigm

As previously mentioned, the changing sociolinguistic reality of English, evidenced in the pluralisation of the use, users, and cultures of English in the world, has led to a paradigm shift in the field of TESOL (Selvi & Yazan, 2021). The traditional ESL/EFL paradigm of language teaching and research, advocating the teaching of the so-called 'native' English speakers' linguistic and cultural practices, has been deemed anachronistic, irrelevant, and pragmatically counter-productive (Marlina, forthcoming; Matsuda, 2020). Variationist scholars have also been casting doubts upon the relevance of classroom practices informed by the aforementioned paradigm to the real communicative needs of today's English language users whose communicative encounters in English often do not involve 'native'-English speakers (Marlina, 2018; Matsuda, 2020). Prompted further by the unprecedented growth in the number of multilingual users of English and their dominance in today's exchanges in English, the plurilithic nature of English, and the forces of globalisation that have made the nature of today's communication dizzyingly diverse and complex, the paradigm of language teaching and research has shifted towards what seems to be a more liberal and democratic one, i.e., the EIL (English as an International Language) paradigm (Sharifian, 2009; McKay, 2018; Matsuda, 2020). This paradigm provides researchers, scholars, and educators with a lens to critically:

- revisit and reconsider their ways of conceptualising English,
- re-assess their analytical tools and the approaches they adopt in the sociolinguistics of English and TESOL disciplines, and
- revise their pedagogical strategies for English language education in the light of the tremendous changes that English has undergone as a result of its global expansion in recent decades (Marlina, 2014, p. 4).

Scholars and researchers working within the scholarship of EIL have been urging ELT researchers and practitioners to critically re-examine their teaching methodologies, instructional variety and model, curriculum and syllabus materials, language assessment and testing, and TESOL teacher-education program. Specifically, what implications does this paradigm shift have for TESOL teacher-education program? This question is addressed in the next section.

3 Implications of EIL for TESOL Teacher Education

Given the complex nature of English and communicative encounters in the twenty-first century, TESOL teacher-educators have been advised to provide their teacher-candidates with "a comprehensive education that fosters an understanding of language variation and change, the new forms and functions of English, the relationship between language and identity, the negotiated nature of intercultural communication and a more nuanced understanding of bilingual language proficiency" (Dogancay-Aktuna & Hardman, 2017, p. 19). Extending this suggestion, Sifakis and Bayyurt (2017, p. 7) have further proposed a specific model (see Fig. 1 below) that EIL-inspired teacher-educators can refer to when designing or delivering an EIL-informed teacher-education programme:

In phase A or the Exposure stage, Sifakis and Bayyurt (2017) advise that teacher-educators expose teacher-candidates to various literature and research on the global expansion of the English language, its positive and negative outcomes, and the characteristics of successful intercultural interactions between users of English from different lingua-cultural backgrounds. In phase B, teacher-educators invite their teacher-candidates to critically reflect on their own assumptions or deepest convictions about language use, language learning, and language teaching in light of what

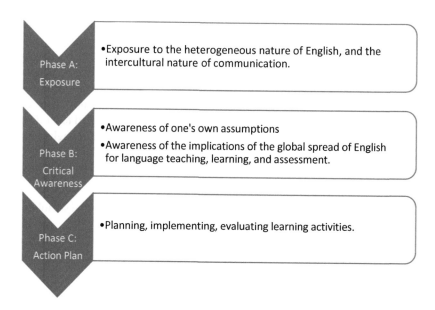

Fig. 1 Foundations of an EIL-aware teacher education

they have learned in the previous phase. Finally, in phase C, teacher-candidates are tasked to plan or develop EIL-oriented learning activities based on what they have learned in the previous two phases, and on the needs analysis results of their own learners. They then trial these activities with their students in a real classroom setting, and critically evaluate the effectiveness of the activities.

Though there has been a collection of literature showcasing how EIL can be incorporated into a TESOL teacher-education programme (see Galloway, 2017; Matsuda, 2017), empirical research has revealed that many teacher-education programmes are still dominated by the native-speakerism ideology (Snodin & Resnik, 2019). As Wheeler (2016) once asserts, "so much research, and yet so little change" (p. 367). Even after a series of exposures to literature on World Englishes, English as a Lingua Franca or Global Englishes, many teacher-candidates still show strong preferences towards learning and teaching native-speakers' linguistic and cultural practices, and hold a deficit perspective of those classified as 'non-native' speakers (Marlina, 2019; Prabjandee, 2020; Chen et al., forthcoming). For example, after completing a 3-week professional development course on World Englishes and Intercultural Communication, linguistic and cultural differences were 'patronisingly sympathised' – rather than recognised as legitimate and sociolinguistically normal – by a group of in-service ELT teachers from the ASEAN region (Marlina, 2019). In a study by Prabjandee (2020) who used transformative-learning-theory-informed activities in a 16-hour workshop on Global Englishes Language Teaching, preferences towards teaching and learning native-speakers' lingua-cultural practices were still observed in the attitudes of Thai ELT teachers upon completion of the workshop. This has suggested three things.

Firstly, any future writings about teaching EIL should attempt to avoid what Canagarajah (1999) once referred to as "bury[ing] our eyes ostrich-like to the political evils and ideological temptations outside" (p. 201). Secondly, in order to inspire teachers to develop respect for lingua-cultural diversity and to see this diversity as sociolinguistically normal, an EIL-informed TESOL teacher-education programme should "go beyond simply 'talking about' the current reality of English or how to teach EIL" (Marlina, 2017, p. 107). Lastly, EIL-inspired teacher-educators may wish to consider critically revisiting their EIL-oriented teacher-education curricular materials, courses, or programmes in order to bring about long-lasting effects on their teacher-candidates' ideological beliefs and pedagogical practices (Rose et al., 2021; Galloway & Rose, 2021; Selvi & Yazan, 2021). Based on a review of various empirical studies and one's extensive experiences in teaching EIL to both language practitioners and teacher-educators, the following section presents suggestions on possible goals, curricular materials, and assessment practices that EIL-inspired teacher educators may wish to consider or re-consider when designing an EIL-oriented TESOL teacher-education programme.

4   Goals of an EIL-Informed TESOL Teacher-Education Curriculum

In various writings on EIL-informed TESOL teacher-education (Bayyurt & Sifakis, 2017; Dogancay-Aktuna & Hardman, 2012, 2017), EIL-inspired teacher-educators have been advised to gear their teacher-education programmes towards "teacher-development, not the indoctrination of EIL" (Bayyurt & Sifakis, 2017, p. 15). With 'teacher-development' as an overarching orientation, the goals of an EIL-informed TESOL teacher education curriculum are to:

- "critically engage teachers into forming a comprehensive understanding of EIL (ELF/WE) construct;
- prompt teachers to become conscious of their deeper convictions about teaching, learning, assessing etc., vis-à-vis English, and to help them begin to change these perspectives to the extent they want/are able to;
- prompt teachers to understand the implications of the EIL construct for their own teaching context; and
- assist teachers in applying the EIL construct in their own teaching context, to the extent they want/are able to" (p. 15).

Though the above goals seem achievable, and should continue to serve as the guidelines for developing an EIL-informed TESOL teacher education curriculum, it is equally important to be aware of the possibility of experiencing 'cognitive disequilibrium' when engaging teacher-candidates in learning to achieve those goals, or more specifically to think and act differently from usual. One often encounters tensions, dilemmas, and conflicts when one's deeply-ingrained convictions are challenged or when one is prompted to learn to think and act differently (Marlina, 2018). In the journey of forming a comprehensive understanding of EIL constructs and, therefore, learning to develop appreciative attitudes towards lingua-cultural diversity, one is likely to encounter moments whereby one questions whether diversity is welcomed or positively constructed in the socio-political context in which one lives (Nieto, 2018). As Tupas (2018, 2021) has observed, varieties of English may be sociolinguistically acceptable and yet still socio-politically unacceptable. Hence, in addition to the listed goals above, an EIL-informed teacher education curriculum should prompt teachers to avoid falling into the trap of romanticising the equality of all languages, cultures, and lingua-cultural practices. In other words, teachers can be prompted to avoid assuming that all Englishes and languages spoken within a community exist in harmony or all lingua-cultural practices are legitimately recognised and valued. As language and culture are also sites of struggle whereby the existing relations of domination and marginalisation are constantly (re) negotiated and (re)defined, EIL-informed teacher-educators can engage teachers in unpacking the politics of lingua-cultural differences in their respective contexts, learning how to grapple with various elitist and ethnocentric discourses, and assisting them in finding ways to address these politics in a language-learning classroom. The following section will discuss a possible way of fostering critical dialogues on linguistic diversity as well as the politics of differences in an EIL-informed teacher education curricular content.

5   Re-envisioned Curriculum Content

In order to achieve the goals outlined in the previous section, Sifakis and Bayyurt's (2017) framework has suggested that teacher-candidates should be firstly exposed to scholarly works on the global expansion of the English language, its positive and negative outcomes, and the characteristics of successful intercultural interactions between users of English from different lingua-cultural backgrounds. They then reflect critically on their own assumptions or convictions about the global spread of English and its implications for teaching, learning, and assessment. Though Sifakis and Bayyurt's (2017) framework is useful and implementable, one would like to propose a different way of approaching this framework especially in light of the persistent favourable attitudes towards the lingua-cultural practices of the so-called 'native' English speakers even after being exposed to scholarly works on World Englishes (Marlina, 2019; Prabjandee, 2020).

5.1 Exploration of the Nature of Language Variation

ELT teacher-candidates may come to the classroom with a particular view of or ideological belief about the English language. Prompting them to engage with research studies on the global expansion of English at the early stage of learning with a hope of fostering respect and appreciation for lingua-cultural diversity might run the risk of being interpreted as an act of indoctrination. It may even, as Marlina's study (2018) has revealed, lead to a strong resistance towards the perspectives advocated by EIL scholars.

In the spirit of teacher development and of inspiring ELT teachers to develop respect for lingua-cultural diversity (including their own lingua-cultural practices), one would like to propose the possibility of raising at the outset teacher-candidates' awareness of the *nature* of language variation. This awareness goes beyond knowing about the structural aspects of language. Awareness of the nature of language as a dynamic entity entails knowing (1) how language is a complex system of choices, (2) how these choices are not stochastic, and (3) how language users are linguistically creative in nature. As Seidlhofer (1996) suggested, teacher education courses should get the candidates "to stand back and think hard about not only the [linguistic] choices that have to be made, but also about the choices that can be made" (p. 6), especially when they deviate from the established norms or so-called the 'standard variety'.

Undergirded by the philosophy of language as a dynamic entity and a complex adaptive system, teacher-candidates can be engaged in a series of dialogues on how language, as a self-regulating system, varies at national, regional, social, contextual, and individual level. For example, if teacher-candidates speak languages other than English, they can be engaged in exploring or reflecting on how their L1 or dominant language varies. If English is the dominant language or the only language spoken by the teacher candidates, then teacher educators should involve them in learning activities that raise their awareness of the complexity of dialect variation in their own communities. Most importantly, an in-depth reflection about why language naturally varies should be promoted to stimulate a further general discussion on the intricate relationship between language, cultures, and identities, and the interplay between social/contextual variables and language variation or change. One practical way to explore language variation is, as Li (2017) suggested, "an autobiographic sketch or linguistic self-study in which teachers are asked to write (through traditional essays or using new technologies) their reflection on their own language and cultural experiences in their homes, schools and communities such as family cultural histories, language and literacy practices in their lives" (p. 260). Not only should the above learning activities help to prompt teacher-candidates to develop linguistic self-respect (Li, 2017) and to debunk various myths arising from a view of language as a static and monolithic entity, but it should also prompt a critical reflection on their views of normativity, appropriateness, accuracy, intelligibility, comprehensibility, and linguistic ownership.

In brief, the overall key teaching points that need to be established at the early stage of a re-envisioned EIL-oriented teacher education programme are that:

1. language is protean in nature,
2. language variation is socio-linguistically normal and necessary,
3. no one can avoid bathing in the sea of linguistic variety (Crystal, 1999),
4. language users are linguistically creative in nature,
5. those who use language differently have their reasons for doing so, and
6. language variation is a reflection of diverse and complex interplay of values, beliefs, and identities.

5.2   The Global Expansion of the English Language

To expose teacher-candidates to the multiplicity and complexity of the English language, teacher-candidates can be prompted to use the above established six key teaching points as a conceptual lens or frame in guiding their exploration of the recent development of the English language. To what extent is the English language dynamic in nature? How does it vary? Why does it vary? How does English acquire the status of an international lingua franca? Their exploration should aim to professionally foster the development of a well-informed understanding of the outcomes of the global spread of the language that lead English to acquire the status of an international heterogeneous language. Hence, in order to scaffold their understanding of the pluralisation of the uses, users, and forms of English (as a result of its expansion) and provide a more solid intellectual ammunition to help contest the monolithic view of English, teacher-candidates, as suggested by Sifakis and Bayyurt (2017), should be engaged with some of the following key research areas in the field of World Englishes or English as a Lingua Franca.

Firstly, the diaspora of the English language: in addition to reading about the global expansion of English, there should also be discussions on how language contact situations ecologically contribute to the plurality of the linguistic and cultural practices even within a single community. For example, as opposed to learning about a monolithic variety of Australian English and reified forms of Australian cultures, teacher-candidates can explore the rich and complex sociolinguistic reality of English in Australia and the Englishes spoken in Australia, such as Aboriginal Englishes and other varieties of Englishes as a result of the increased human mobility across the globe e.g., migration, travel, or study-abroad.

Secondly, the emergence of different varieties of English in the world: discussion on this will include the newly emerged or emergent varieties of English in countries where English does not hold an official or administrative status and is used in conjunction with other languages. Scholarly works from the journal of *World Englishes*, *Asian Englishes*, or *English Today* can be prescribed either as mandatory or supplementary readings. In their engagement with the literature, teacher-candidates can be prompted to explore the ecological influence of other languages on the role of

English, its uses, and its usage. Most importantly, they need to see how English and other languages co-exist and are used meaningfully and effectively by the multilingual locals. At the same time, teacher-educators can engage the candidates in critical dialogues, wherein concepts such as 'native/non-native', 'Standard English', 'norm-providing countries', and 'norm-dependent countries' are problematized.

Thirdly, moving from exploring the sociolinguistic reality of English in the above-mentioned multilingual countries, teacher-candidates should be also exposed to various samples of successful interactions between multilingual users of English. This can be done in two ways. First, as suggested by Sifakis and Bayyurt (2017), teacher-candidates should be given the opportunity to engage in authentic communicative exchanges with 'non-native' users. Second, there should also be an opportunity to study and analyse excerpts from available ELF corpora such as the VOICE corpus, the ELFA corpus, and the ASEAN corpus (see Sifakis & Bayyurt, 2017 for more details). Most importantly, the analysis of the interactions between multilingual users of English should be informed by key learning points from the earlier stage, paying specific attention to (1) how these users creatively draw on their communicative strategies and plurilingual repertoires to negotiate meanings and to ensure mutual intelligibility, comprehensibility, and interpretability; and (2) how they use accommodation skills and compensatory strategies to reduce the likelihood of intercultural miscommunication.

Lastly, the hegemonic spread of English: teacher-candidates should also be exposed to discourses about both positive and negative outcomes of the English language (Sifakis & Bayyurt, 2017). Although English is often chosen to be the medium of communication in various international economic and cultural arenas, ELT teachers may need to be aware and critical of the imperialistic nature and possible undesirable consequences of the language being a popular medium for global communication. In the re-envisioned EIL-oriented teacher education curriculum, there need to be critical dialogues on linguistic imperialism (Phillipson, 2018), linguicism (Skutnabb-Kangas, 2015), and language commodification (Cameron, 2012). In addition to discussing these issues or getting teacher-candidates to critically explore the implicit unequal importance placed on English vis-à-vis other languages (national, regional, minority, migrant, or foreign) in their context, they can be engaged in a critical reflective inquiry into their own awareness of how their values, biases, or ideological beliefs about the English language may cloud their interpretations of prospective learners' needs of learning the language.

As a part of the process of inspiring ELT teachers to develop respect for linguacultural diversity, the overall key teaching points that need to be established at this stage of a re-envisioned EIL-oriented teacher education programme are that:

1. English, as a result of its global spread, is no longer a unitary concept, but a heterogeneous language, reflecting complex or diverse identities, worldviews, and practices.
2. As a result of the emergence of World Englishes, concepts such as 'standard', 'native/non-native', and 'norm-providing / norm-dependent' countries are problematic and are likely to become anachronistic. This is evidenced in the

successful interactions between multilingual users of English who creatively use various communicative strategies and rich linguistic repertoires to achieve their immediate communicative aims (see Matsumoto, 2011 for more details).

3. Though the choice of English as a tool for international communication may bring communicative conveniences, it may also bring undesirable consequences or disruptions to the local linguistic ecosystems.

5.3   The Politics of Differences

To inspire teachers to learn to develop respect for lingua-cultural diversity, teacher-education curriculum should go beyond simply getting them to read scholarly works on world Englishes, intercultural communication, and their pedagogical implications with a hope that their view and attitudes towards diversity will change. This liberal approach to the teaching of linguistic and cultural diversity (Banks & Banks, 2006) has been proven by EIL-oriented pedagogical research studies to be relatively ineffective in changing pre-/in-service teachers' negative attitudes towards the so-called 'non-native' English speakers' lingua-cultural practices (Marlina, 2019; Prabjandee, 2020). What needs to be further emphasised is that this approach may fail to "deal adequately with the politics of difference and all too often declines into a romantic and anti-intellectual celebration of individual difference" (Pennycook, 1990, p. 308). Kubota (2021) also cautioned that "the celebration of superficial diversity obscures deep-rooted inequalities of race, gender, class, sexuality and so on, as well as unequal power relations of power in society and institutions" (p. 139). Therefore, educational programmes that specialise in teaching linguistic and cultural pluralism should attempt to avoid distancing themselves from socio-political questions especially when many Englishes are still not yet socio-politically legitimate (Tupas, 2021). These kinds of arguments suggest that in terms of EIL-oriented teacher-education curriculum, political issues need to be taken into consideration or openly discussed. How are these everyday political issues different from the one about linguicism or linguistic imperialism?

In order to organise the huge complexity of issues associated with politics, Janks (2010) divides the notion of politics into two areas of exploration: Politics (with a "big P") and politics (with a "little p"). By big-P Politics, she refers to "the big stuff, worldly concerns…[such as] government and world trade agreements and the United Nations peace-keeping forces, ethnic or religious genocide, money laundering, and linguistic imperialism" (p. 40). Little-p politics refers to the "micro-politics of everyday life…[such as] the minute-by-minute choices and decisions that make us who we are; it is about politics of identity and place such as how we treat people day-by-day" (p. 40). In relation to EIL, Matsuda (2003) and Kubota (2012) emphasise the importance of incorporating these issues in an EIL-oriented curriculum. However, these issues are mainly big-P ones. For example, Matsuda (2003) asserts that an EIL curriculum "must address the politics of the language [such as] the colonial and possibly the postcolonial presence of the language and the power inequality associated with its history" (p. 722). Echoing a similar viewpoint, Kubota (2012) also argues about the importance of raising awareness of the global expansion of English as a potential threat to the multilingualism of a nation. Though these big-P issues should remain in the curriculum, they may not necessarily be the politics that teacher-candidates may encounter in their everyday lives. As transformative intellectuals, teacher-educators should enable their teacher-candidates to "critically engage with the conditions of their lives and thereby achieve a better sense of their possibilities as human beings and members of a larger community" (Doecke & Kostogriz, 2008, p. 82). Therefore, the re-envisioned EIL-oriented teacher-education curriculum can engage teacher-candidates in unpacking the everyday politics of lingua-cultural differences in their respective contexts and in learning how to grapple with various elitist and ethnocentric discourses.

To be more specific, teacher-candidates can observe their surroundings and share critical incidents whereby people are unjustly treated on the basis of their racial backgrounds, socio-economic status, and sexuality; racial violence, assimilationist policy, accent-reduction therapy, and linguistic/racial discrimination may impact language teaching employment. Not only are these politics of differences encounterable, but also "working with the politics of the local enables us to effect small changes that make a difference in our everyday lives and those of the people around us" (Janks, 2010, p. 41). One acknowledges that simply having a dialogue about these issues is not likely to be sufficient as they may end up becoming a rather tired set of social issues. Another mechanism of challenging oppression is by making visible and audible the underlying assumptions that (re-)produce structures of domination or possibly institute any ideologies that may favour certain groups and marginalise others. Specifically, teacher-candidates can be prompted to question how those elitist/ethnocentric discourses have come to be as they are, and how discourses have structured peoples' lives. In light of their responses to these questions, they envisage or propose versions of a more just world, or alternative possibilities for organising social life (Marlina, 2018). It is through this questioning that teacher-candidates can learn to be critical of their sociopolitical surroundings as well as their own ideological beliefs, especially the implications of those beliefs on themselves and others.

In short, the key learning points that need to be clearly established after engaging teacher-candidates in learning about the plurality of the English language are:

1. Language and culture are also sites of struggle whereby certain practices are intentionally or unintentionally constructed as more favourable than others. In relation to Englishes, although all varieties of English are sociolinguistically legitimate, the political legitimacies of those Englishes may not necessarily be evenly weighted. Hence, discussions on world Englishes need to be situated within one's socio-political context.
2. Given the prevalence of unjust ideologies and treatments arising from those ideologies, teacher-candidates need to be aware of their roles in helping to deal with the everyday politics of differences in their own socio-political surroundings. Through a series of professional dialogues on dominant ideologies, they should learn to equip themselves with sufficient intellectual strategies to critically contest elitist discourses or ideological beliefs (including their own, if any).

6 Re-envisioned Curriculum: The Action Phase – *"So What?" and "So How?"*

Similar to the Sifakis and Bayyurt's (2017) framework of EIL-oriented teacher education, the last phase of this re-envisioned teacher education curriculum is the 'Action Phase' (cf. Sifakis & Bayyurt, 2017) where teacher-candidates are prompted to suggest pedagogical implications of what they have learned about the pluralisation of English, to try translating these implications into classroom practice, and to critically reflect on the efficacy of their classroom practices. This phase is crucial for teacher-candidates' ideological development as they are provided with opportunities for hands-on experiences in developing pedagogical strategies to foster understanding and respect for lingua-cultural diversity in ELT classrooms, and in developing themselves as twenty-first century language educators. As Doecke and Kostogriz (2008) remind us, "challenging ideology can never be a matter of simply persuading people to think otherwise" (p. 82). They have to experience various learning encounters and learn from those experiences. In the next section, I will discuss some assessment tasks that EIL-inspired teacher-educators may wish to use to assess their candidates' learning in this proposed teacher-education curriculum. In particular, as the 'Action Phase' involves planning, implementing, and evaluating, I will describe what teacher-candidates can be engaged in doing in each stage.

6.1 The Planning Stage

In the planning stage, teacher-educators should engage teacher-candidates in developing an EIL-oriented lesson plan which they can implement in the next stage (Sifakis & Bayyurt, 2017). To plan a lesson, the teachers need to know their classroom contexts as well as that of the learners. Therefore, prior to lesson plan development, teacher-candidates should firstly be assessed on how much they know about their learners' sociolinguistic, sociocultural, and sociopolitical contexts, and how this knowledge can be used to inform their pedagogical strategies and instructional materials. Here are some examples of assessment tasks:

1. *Ethnographic work*: teacher-candidates can be tasked to carry out ethnographic research exploring the linguistic variations found in their own respective contexts. They can observe and document the linguistic choices made by speakers in the community, how these speakers switch judiciously between codes, dialects, or languages, and most importantly in what communicative situations the switching takes place. The results of this ethnographic work are likely to provide ample information about the linguistic or communicative needs of their prospective learners, which can then be used later to design their lessons and instructional materials/activities.

2. *A sociolinguistic sketch of (a country)*: after a series of discussions on the global expansion of English, teacher-candidates can choose a country in which they are likely to teach upon completion of the teacher-education programme. In a form of an oral presentation or a written report, they explain the historical spread of English in the country, the role and function of English in the country, the specific contexts in which English is used, the demographics of English language users, any instance of indigenisation of English, and any competing language ideologies as a result of the status of English in the country. This will add to the sociocultural profile of the learners that the teacher-candidates are likely to teach and to design the instructional materials for.

3. *Reflective journal entries*: Teacher-candidates can be required to submit two entries. For the first entry, teacher-candidates suggest the implications of the above ethnographic work and sociolinguistic sketch on language teaching, learning, and assessment in their own contexts. In light of the scholarly works on the pedagogy of EIL (Marlina, 2014; McKay & Brown, 2016; Matsuda, 2020) where those scholars put forward general implications of the pluralised uses, users, and forms of English on language learning, teaching, and assessment, they can be tasked in the second entry to respond to and/or critique the implications. Specifically, they will explain and justify which of the implications are (or are not) relevant as well as feasible within their context. While discussing those that are not relevant, teacher-candidates can be prompted to situate the discussions within their own socio-political contexts, addressing how the politicisation of differences hinders the implementation of the implications, and proposing (if possible, together with the teacher-educators) alternative ways of operationalising them.

4. *Textbook evaluation*: There are two versions of this task that have been suggested by EIL scholars (see details in Selvi & Yazan, 2021). For the first version, teacher-candidates choose any prescribed ELT textbooks in their contexts, and evaluate them in light of what they have learned from the above ethnographic work and the sociolinguistic sketch of the country of their choice. For the second version, teacher-candidates evaluate the prescribed textbooks in light of the diversification of the uses, users, and forms of English. Framed within the EIL paradigm, teacher-candidates critically consider the extent to which linguistic and cultural aspects of the textbooks have sufficiently equipped language learners with knowledge, skills, and attitudes for operating effectively in today's communicative exchanges that are international and intercultural in nature. In terms of the linguistic aspect, they can analyse whether the textbook exposes learners to diverse varieties of English or prioritises certain varieties. Based on the characters in the textbook, who are portrayed as the linguistic role models? In terms of the cultural aspect, the analysis can focus on whose cultures are represented, and whether they all equally portrayed. Are learners' cultures respectfully referred to? Are there tasks where students are engaged in learning how to use English to communicate across cultures? Are there questions that prompt learners to explore lingua-cultural norms and practices beyond the ones found in the textbooks? If not, what should teachers do especially when they have no control

over what goes into the curriculum? What are the instructional questions that teachers can supplement so that they still teach the prescribed materials and, at the same time, engage students in learning to communicate across cultures and Englishes? (see Marlina, 2021). Not only will this task allow teachers to develop their own original EIL-informed instructional materials for their learners, but it will also alleviate the dearth of instructional materials that are based on a paradigm that advocates the development of respectful attitudes towards lingua-cultural diversity in ELT classrooms (Vettorel, 2021).

5. *Field Observation 1* (ES/FL-based classroom): teacher-candidates can be tasked with observing language lessons that may be largely informed by the traditional ESL/EFL paradigm. While observing these lessons, they critically analyse whether the materials, pedagogical strategies, corrective feedback strategies, and assessment practices (a) respond to the learners' needs (gathered from the ethnographic work and sociolinguistic sketch) and (b) prepare learners to use English effectively across cultures and Englishes. If the classroom observation analyses have revealed shortcomings, they can suggest ways to improve them. For example, if the teacher-candidates notice that the learners' lingua-cultural knowledge is not appreciated and not treated as an invaluable source of knowledge, they should propose some pedagogically efficacious ways of leveraging learners' linguistic and cultural capital in an ELT classroom. This proposal can be used as a stepping stone to develop an EIL-oriented lesson plan. At the time of coming up with a proposal, teacher-candidates need to think about potential resistance from various stakeholders that may prevent them from operationalising those changes. Such scenarios may need to be acknowledged, foregrounded, and critically addressed.

6. *Field Observation 2* (TEIL-based classroom): Before developing and implementing their own EIL-informed lesson plan, teacher-candidates need to be given a model of what is considered to be an EIL-oriented ELT lesson, one that inspires learners to develop respect for lingua-cultural diversity (Marlina, 2017). If possible and available, they can observe these lessons, compare what they have observed in Field Observation 1, and analyse aspects of the lessons that are reflective of the EIL paradigm. In their observational report, they can be prompted to discuss, as I outlined elsewhere (Marlina, 2017, p. 104–105):

- What have you learned from the lessons you have observed?
- How does the teacher implement the principles of teaching EIL?
- Do you believe that his or her teaching materials and pedagogical approaches have raised his/her students' awareness of linguistic and cultural diversity, and have inspired them to appreciate this diversity? Explain.
- Is there anything you would have done differently? If yes, what is it and why?

7. *TEIL-lesson plan development or adaptation:* In light of what they have learned from their sociolinguistic enquiry, reflective entries, textbook evaluation exercises, and field observations, teacher-candidates are required to develop an original EIL-informed ELT lesson that suits their targeted learners' communicative

needs (see an example in Marlina, 2017). Alternatively, they can critically analyse any pre-existing lesson plans, and then revise those lesson plans based on the principles of teaching EIL. Prior to implementation, there needs to be a pre-conferencing session wherein the teacher-educator and teacher-candidate discuss the overall effectiveness of the lesson plan, and the unexpected awkward/ unpleasant encounters (e.g., ethnocentric speech or culturally insensitive remarks observed during an intercultural learning activity) as well as any intervention strategies in response to the encounters.

6.2 The Implementing Stage

This is the stage whereby the teacher-candidates put into practice the lesson plan that they have developed. Two assessment tasks that can be carried at this stage are:

1. *Teaching Demonstration or Peer Teaching*: before getting the teacher-candidates to implement the lesson plan in a classroom setting with language learners, teacher-educators may wish to consider getting them to try out the lesson plan or to do a 'teaching demonstration' on their fellow teacher-candidates first. They then make adjustment to their lesson plan upon receiving feedback from their peers after the demonstration.
2. *Teaching practicum*: this is where the teacher-candidates implement the above adjusted or revised lesson plan in a classroom setting with language learners under the teacher-educators' supervision. During the lesson, the candidates can be prompted to constantly monitor and observe their students' responses to the EIL-informed teaching materials, their students' discourses of linguistic and cultural diversity, and their students' attitudes towards their classmates from different linguistic and cultural backgrounds (if the lesson is conducted in a multicultural classroom setting).

6.3 The Evaluating and Future Goal-Setting Stage

This is the post-conferencing stage in which teacher-candidates are engaged in self-reflection (Sifakis & Bayyurt, 2017; Chen et al., forthcoming) as well as critical dialogue with the teacher-educators on the efficacy of their lessons in terms of their strengths and areas of improvement. Since lingua-cultural differences may still be socio-politically illegitimate in some contexts, teacher-educators should also engage the candidates in thinking about the potential struggles that they are likely to encounter when teaching students to appreciate lingua-cultural diversity. Therefore, the reflective dialogue can be guided by the following questions:

- Do you believe that your lessons have successfully raised students' awareness of linguistic and cultural diversity, and have inspired them to appreciate this diversity? If so, what did you do?
- Did you experience any challenges in teaching intercultural communication skills, or inspiring your learners to appreciate lingua-cultural diversity? If so, what are the challenges, and why?
- Did you encounter any unexpected awkward/unpleasant scenarios? What did the learners say/do? What do you think are the reasons underlying what they said/ did? How did you respond to it? Do you think you were successful?
- If you are to implement it again, do you think you will face similar problems, scenarios, or constraints? What strategies do you think you can employ when encountering similar problems or scenarios?

It is hoped that these critical reflective practice and critical thinking tasks can help "teachers become not only aware of current concerns in English language teaching, learning and communication, but also more autonomous practitioners and, by extension, develop themselves and their practice" (Sifakis & Bayyurt, 2017, p. 462).

7   Conclusion

In this chapter, I have attempted to propose a re-envisioned EIL-oriented teacher education curriculum in response to a paucity of teacher-education curriculum that engages prospective ELT teachers in learning how to promote intercultural understanding and respect for lingua-cultural diversity in ELT classrooms (Selvi & Yazan, 2021; Chen et.al, forthcoming). Like many other EIL/WE/ELF scholars, I have argued throughout the chapter that prospective ELT teachers need to be aware of the nature of language variation and the messy sociolinguistic reality of English as a result of its global expansion. This can be done through engagement with EIL/WE/ELF research that contests perspectives and practices informed by a monolithic view of English and a monolingual/cultural-chauvinistic approach to language teaching. However, as proven by some research studies, such engagement does not seem to be sufficient especially when there is a scholarly call for developing teacher-candidates to be autonomous ELT teachers who can continue fostering intercultural understanding and respect for lingua-cultural diversity in ELT classrooms. Therefore, in addition to familiarising themselves with current EIL theoretical assumptions, teacher-candidates need to be engaged in various experiential learning assessment tasks whereby they explore the nature of language variation and the current sociolinguistic reality of English in their choice of context. The results from this sociolinguistic exploration should be constantly used as frames of reference to inform their choice of ELT instructional materials, pedagogical strategies, lesson plan development, and lesson delivery.

Although no one can "avoid bathing in the sea of linguistic variety" (Crystal, 1999, p. 19), I and other critical applied linguists (Kubota, 2021; Tupas, 2021) have also argued that no one can avoid encountering scenarios wherein differences are politicised on the basis of race and other social variables. As revealed in Marlina (2018), these everyday micropolitics of differences and their disturbing ideologies are often the ones that cause teachers the struggle to continue advocating the EIL perspective in their own practices. Hence, these little-p issues need to be acknowledged and addressed in an EIL-oriented teacher education curriculum. While addressing these issues, teacher-candidates need to be given the opportunity to anticipate potential struggles or scenarios they may face when teaching an EIL-informed ELT lesson, and be ready to propose communicative and pedagogical strategies that can help to minimise the possibilities of those ideologies being normalised, perpetuated, or instituted. As there has been a dearth of scholarly writing on this, I would like to encourage future pedagogical research to enquire into ways to incorporate little-p issues or Unequal Englishes (Tupas, 2021) in an ELT-teacher education programme. This is so that the TESOL community can have a more solid teacher-education curriculum that not only produces twenty-first century language educators, but also ones who can help to continue advocating linguistic equality and social justice in ELT and through EIL.

References

Banks, J. A., & Banks, C. A. M. (2006). *Multicultural education: Issues and perspectives* (6th ed.). Jossey-Bass. https://doi.org/10.1080/14675986.2020.1766194

Bayyurt, Y., & Sifakis, N. C. (2017). Foundations of an EIL-aware teacher education. In A. Matsuda (Ed.), *Preparing teachers to teach english as an international language* (pp. 3–18). Multilingual Matters. https://doi.org/10.21832/9781783097036

Cameron, D. (2012). The commodification of language: English as a global commodity. In T. Nevalainen & E. C. Traugott (Eds.), *The Oxford handbook of the history of English* (pp. 352–361). Oxford University Press. https://doi.org/10.1093/oxfordhb/9780199922765.001.0001

Canagarajah, A. S. (1999). *Resisting linguistic imperialism in English teaching*. Oxford University Press.

Chen, Z., Chen, X., & Fang, F. (forthcoming). Global Englishes and teacher education: Present cases and future directions. *RELC Journal*. https://doi.org/10.1177/00336882211044872

Crystal, D. (1999). From out in the left field? That's not cricket: Finding a focus for the language curriculum. In R. S. Wheeler (Ed.), *The workings of language: From prescriptions to perspectives* (pp. 91–105). Praeger.

Doecke, B., & Kostogriz, A. (2008). Becoming a professional (and other dissident acts): Language and literacy teaching in an age of neoliberal reform. *L1-Educational Studies in Language and Literature, 8*(4), 63–84. https://doi.org/10.17239/L1ESLL-2008.08.04.04

Dogancay-Aktuna, S., & Hardman, J. (2012). Teacher education for EIL: Working toward a situated meta-praxis. In A. Matsuda (Ed.), *Principles and practices of teaching English as an international language* (pp. 103–118). Multilingual Matters. https://doi.org/10.21832/9781847697042-009

Dogancay-Aktuna, S., & Hardman, J. (2017). A framework for incorporating an English as an international perspective into TESOL teacher education. In A. Matsuda (Ed.), *Preparing teachers to teach English as an international language* (pp. 19–31). Multilingual Matters. https://doi.org/10.21832/9781783097036-004

Galloway, N. (2017). *Global Englishes and change in language teaching: Attitudes and impact.* Routledge. https://doi.org/10.4324/9781315158983

Galloway, N., & Rose, H. R. (2021). The global spread of English and global Englishes language teaching. In A. F. Selvi & B. Yazan (Eds.), *Global Englishes language teaching: A practical guide for teachers and teacher-educators* (pp. 11–19). Routledge. https://doi.org/10.4324/9781003082712

Janks, H. (2010). Language, power, and pedagogies. In N. Hornberger & S. L. McKay (Eds.), *Sociolinguistics and language education* (pp. 40–61). Multilingual Matters. https://doi.org/10.21832/9781847692849

Kubota, R. (2012). The politics of EIL: Toward border-crossing communication in and beyond English. In A. Matsuda (Ed.), *Principles and practices of teaching English as an international language* (pp. 55–69). Multilingual Matters. https://doi.org/10.21832/9781847697042-006

Kubota, R. (2021). Global Englishes and teaching culture. In A. F. Selvi & B. Yazan (Eds.), *Global Englishes language teaching: A practical guide for teachers and teacher-educators* (pp. 135–143). Routledge. https://doi.org/10.4324/9781003082712

Li, G. (2017). Preparing culturally and linguistically competent teachers for English as an international language. *TESOL Journal, 8*(2), 250–276. https://doi.org/10.1002/tesj.322

Marlina, R. (2014). The pedagogy of English as an international language: More reflections and dialogues. In R. Marlina & R. Giri (Eds.), *The pedagogy of English as an international language: Perspectives from scholars, teachers, and students* (pp. 1–19). Springer International Publishing. https://doi.org/10.1007/978-3-319-06127-6_1

Marlina, R. (2017). Practices of teaching Englishes for international communication. In A. Matsuda (Ed.), *Preparing teachers to teach English as an international language* (pp. 100–113). Multilingual Matters. https://doi.org/10.21832/9781783097036-009

Marlina, R. (2018). *Teaching English as an international language: Implementing, reviewing, and re-envisioning world Englishes in language education.* Routledge. https://doi.org/10.4324/9781315315768

Marlina, R. (2019). *Englishes in TESOL Teacher-Education Programme: From the Unequal Englishes perspective.* Conference Paper presented at the 58th JACET International Convention, "Beyond 'Borderless': English Education in a Changing Society", 28th–30th August, 2019, Nagoya Institute of Teaching.

Marlina, R. (2021). Curriculum development in global Englishes. In A. F. Selvi & B. Yazan (Eds.), *Global Englishes language teaching: A practical guide for teachers and teacher-educators* (pp. 239–247). Routledge. https://doi.org/10.4324/9781003082712

Marlina, R. (forthcoming). World Englishes and the teaching of oral communication. In K. Bolton (Ed.), *The Encyclopaedia of world Englishes.* Wiley-Blackwell.

Matsuda, A. (2003). Incorporating world Englishes in teaching English as an international language. *TESOL Quarterly, 37,* 719–729. https://doi.org/10.2307/3588220

Matsuda, A. (2017). *Preparing teachers to teach English as an international language. Multilingual Matters.* https://doi.org/10.21832/9781783097036

Matsuda, A. (2020). World Englishes and pedagogy. In C. L. Nelson, Z. G. Proshina, & D. R. Davies (Eds.), *The handbook of world Englishes* (pp. 686–702). Wiley Blackwell. https://doi.org/10.1002/9781119147282

Matsumoto, Y. (2011). Successful ELF communications and implications for ELT: Sequential analysis of ELF pronunciation negotiation strategies. *The Modern Language Journal, 95,* 97–114. https://doi.org/10.1111/j.1540-4781.2011.01172.x

McKay, S. (2018). English as an international language: What it is and what it means for pedagogy. *RELC Journal, 49*(1), 9–23. https://doi.org/10.1177/0033688217738817

McKay, S. L., & Brown, J. D. (2016). *Teaching and assessing EIL in local contexts around the world.* Routledge. https://doi.org/10.4324/9781315769097

Nieto, S. (2018). *Language, culture, and teaching: Critical perspectives for a new century* (3rd ed.). https://doi.org/10.4324/9781315465692

Pennycook, A. (1990). Critical pedagogy and second language acquisition. *System, 18*(3), 303–314. https://doi.org/10.1016/0346-251X(90)90003-N

Phillipson, R. (2018). Linguistic imperialism and NNESTs. In J. I. Liontas (Ed.), *TESOL Encyclopaedia of English language teaching: Non-native English speaking teachers* (pp. 1–7). Wiley-Blackwell. https://doi.org/10.1002/9781118784235.eelt0023

Prabjandee, D. (2020). Teacher professional development to implement global Englishes language teaching. *Asian Englishes, 22*(1), 52–67. https://doi.org/10.1080/13488678.2019.1624931

Rose, H., McKinley, J., & Galloway, N. (2021). Global Englishes and language teaching: A review of pedagogical research. *Language Teaching, 54*(2), 157–189. https://doi.org/10.1017/S0261444820000518

Seidlhofer, B. (1996). 'It is an undulating feeling …': The importance of being a non-native teacher of English. *VIEWS (Vienna English Working papers), 5*, 63–79.

Selvi, A. F., & Yazan, B. (2021). *Language teacher education for global Englishes: A practical resource book.* Routledge. https://doi.org/10.4324/9781003082712

Sharifian, F. (2009). *English as an international language: Perspectives and pedagogical issues.* Multilingual Matters. https://doi.org/10.21832/9781847691231

Sifakis, N. C., & Bayyurt, Y. (2017). ELF-aware teacher learning and development. In J. Jenkins, W. Baker, & M. Dewey (Eds.), *Handbook of English as a lingua Franca* (pp. 456–467). Routledge. https://doi.org/10.4324/9781315717173

Skutnabb-Kangas, T. (2015). Linguicism. In C. Chapelle (Ed.), *The encyclopedia of applied linguistics* (pp. 1–6). https://doi.org/10.1002/9781405198431.wbeal1460

Snodin, N., & Resnik, P. (2019). WE, ELF, EIL and their implications for English language teacher education. In S. Walsh & S. Mann (Eds.), *The Routledge handbook of English language teacher education.* Routledge. https://doi.org/10.4324/9781315659824

Tupas, R. (2018). Singlish in the classroom: Is Singapore ready for additive bidialectalism? *International Journal of Bilingual Education and Bilingualism, 21*(8), 982–993. https://doi.org/10.1080/13670050.2016.1226757

Tupas, R. (2021). Fostering translingual dispositions against unequal Englishes. *English in Education, 55*(3), 222–238. https://doi.org/10.1080/04250494.2020.1786367

Vettorel, P. (2021). Fostering teachers' awareness of global Englishes in primary teacher education in Italy. In A. F. Selvi & B. Yazan (Eds.), *Global Englishes language teaching: A practical guide for teachers and teacher-educators* (pp. 239–247). Routledge. https://doi.org/10.4324/9781003082712

Wheeler, R. (2016). "So much research, so little change": Teaching standard English in African American classrooms. *Annual Review of Linguistics, 2*, 367–390. https://doi.org/10.1146/annurev-linguistics-011415-040434

Roby Marlina (Ph D) is a Senior Language Specialist at SEAMEO-RELC (Regional Language Centre, Singapore) and the Editor of the Scopus-indexed (Q1) *RELC Journal.* His works appear in various international journals including *International Journal of Educational Research, World Englishes, Asian Englishes, RELC Journal,* and *Multilingual Education.* He is one of the main editors of the book, *The Pedagogy of English as an International Language: Perspectives from Scholars, Teachers, and Students* (Springer International Publishing). He is also the author of a monograph, Teaching English as an International Language: Implementing, Reviewing, and Re-Envisioning World Englishes in Language Education (Routledge). Email: Roby.Marlina@relc.org.sg

Part III
Intercultural Communication, EIL Education and Diversity Management

In Part III, Ashraf's study delineates how social media networking is deployed to enhance people's trust in medical expertise through the conjunction of transliteration, translanguaging (English & Urdu) and health communication; it analyses how plurilingual and semiotic practices intersect and transform each other against the backdrop of the surging COVID-19 crisis. It demonstrates the important role of micro-influencers in facilitating health knowledge translation. Hence, crisis networking and digital platforming can play a vital role in the trust-based construction of global public health discourses. Due to the language barrier, ordinary foreign language illiterate Pakistanis were getting most of their information during the pandemic from social media.[1]

Ashraf's chapter describes a networked translation model of health communication initiated by a Facebook group in Pakistan that incorporates circular and dialogic communication modes to alleviate people's sufferings during the COVID-19 pandemic by providing greater social support for its members and by engaging in building Covid literacy through multilingual and translingual semiotic practices that form the symbolic capital of the created online community. By exchanging lived experiences during the pandemic and disseminating expert opinion to educate people about the pandemic, the evolved interpersonal bonds cultivated a sense of belonging, trust, solidarity, and cooperation. Translation has transformed health communication into a non-hierarchical, horizontal, dialogic, and adaptive process, changing the dynamics of health information exchange conceptually from 'transmission' to 'translation'. Thus, non-expert actors have gained voice by sharing COVID-related health issues, which may, sometimes, contest 'scientific' discourses. Therefore, the importance of trust in the source (not just in the content) is very crucial.

---

[1] This study corroborates the influence of online social media platforms, which have always provided access to trusted translated communications (networked model) for Syrian refugee communities and have helped them to keep connected with displaced family members while navigating the perilous European borders seeking help.

Ashraf's study shows that while in a volatile media landscape social media can be weaponised as conduits for disseminating fake news and misinformation, and thus undermining institutional and professional trust, they can also be deployed as valuable tools to educate people and promote public engagement. They can be used as parallel communicative spaces in disasters and humanitarian response or health crisis settings to disseminate information (whether accurately or not); foster community bonding (earthly and spiritual); and engage people who have a shared faith (as a source of social capital) and a common destiny (as a human condition).

In our increasingly interconnected world, globally minded and culturally literate leaders are in high demand. Therefore, one of the essential tasks of educators and business administrators is to promote critical intercultural and transnational literacies and enhance cultural intelligence (appreciation of cultural diversity) and global intercultural awareness (the ability to function effectively across different cultures) to prepare tomorrow's leaders for employment in the twenty-first century global workplaces. To this effect, ElKaleh and Stryker propose a model of effective practice for global administration and leadership consisting of foundational requirements that include global mindset dispositions (i.e., flexibility, respect for cultural difference, ability to adapt, and empathy) and competencies (e.g., cross-cultural collaboration skills, cultural sensitivity & readiness to learn) that are relevant to the changing dynamics of our globalised job markets. Effective global leadership across cultures presupposes that intercultural leaders must fully assume their central role of cultivating empathy, critical intercultural understanding, and promoting more just, tolerant, and inclusive communities of practice by nurturing an openness to alternative cross-cultural perspectives and worldviews.

Likewise, Fazel delineates the difficulty facing novice multilingual researchers while trying to publish in English, pointing to the need to consider the intercultural challenges that early-career scholars encounter when navigating the communicative problems inherent in Eurocentric academic spaces, especially in relation to interaction with editors and peer reviewers. The author critically reflects upon his first-hand experience (as a foreign-born Canadian) in writing for scholarly publication. The study also presents a longitudinal (16-month) project investigating the writing-for-publication experiences of a group of bilingual and monolingual (post)graduate students in English language education at a Canadian university. The chapter concludes by offering pedagogical recommendations to surmount intercultural hurdles that may obtain while communicating across cultures in academic spaces. The study highlights how multilingual/multicultural approaches should feature in the development of the authorial agency of a novice multilingual researcher. Fazel analyses how this could broaden the inclusivity of academic spaces that remain characteristically monolithic and Eurocentric by requiring multilingual scholars to comply with rigid linguistic and cultural norms entrenched in neocolonial ideologies that exclude culturally sustaining pluriversal modes of knowing as valuable resources for co-production of knowledge.

Health Communication in Pakistan: Establishing Trust in Networked Multilingualism

Hina Ashraf

Abstract This case study of covid literacy addresses a vital question about how language practices can reflect and transform social realities to create trust and social capital. Language is central to this exchange, and with the technologically supported affordances of digital social media, users actively co-construct, translate and disseminate information to both known and unknown audiences. However, during the last two and half years of the pandemic crisis so far, information flows from the Global North to the South primarily in English, and is often complemented with conflicting discourses and ambiguous scientific information. Often this information is convoluted in issues related to translations, limited functional literacy, and access to trustworthy resources of knowledge in developing countries of the South. Yet some studies claimed clarity in health literacy in Pakistan's relatively successful communication campaign during the covid pandemic despite the country's highly populous status, its multilingual repertoires, and 50% literacy rates. Using Gee's relationship building tool as a cue, in this chapter I delineate the knowledge, assumptions and inferences embedded in translingual language practices that contribute to trustworthy information. I specifically present findings from an investigation of the literacy practices from a popular Facebook group in Pakistan during the first two episodes of the covid pandemic. The findings demonstrate that trust is embedded in communication comprising an intriguing interplay of languages and digital tools representing the evolving features of contemporary communicative practices among plurilingual English speakers.

Keywords Plurilingual · Covid literacy · Trust · Social capital · Networked multilingualism · Pakistan

H. Ashraf (✉)
Initiative for Multilingual Studies, Department of Linguistics, Georgetown University, Washington, DC, USA
e-mail: Hina.Ashraf@georgetown.edu

© The Author(s), under exclusive license to Springer Nature Switzerland AG 2023
A. Sahlane, R. Pritchard (eds.), *English as an International Language Education*, English Language Education 33, https://doi.org/10.1007/978-3-031-34702-3_14

1   Introduction

The global pandemic brings to limelight aspects of communication that are not just those of language, but also of trust and relationship building, complicated in countries in the Global South, where, in general, public access to information is limited by internet, media and literacy rates. In linguistic research, during the last two and half years of the covid[1] global pandemic crisis thus far, many issues have been covered with regard to language and culture related inequities. In the Asian context, for example, Piller et al. (2020) detailed the multilingual settings that have been impacted by digital emergency communication being mostly in English or by translations of pandemic information not sitting well with oral traditions or minoritized languages and cultural practices. Efforts launched in response to those challenges include using local languages in public service announcements, interviewing local leaders to ensure culturally appropriate information reaches the public, or drawing from the genre of story-telling and oral traditions to disseminate scientific pandemic content (see for example Binder & Gago, 2020, for South America; see Vita, 2020, for Central Africa). These studies raise questions of how the efficacy of health communication is impacted by availability of translations, accessibility to disadvantaged populations, acceptability of accuracy and appropriateness of covid literacy, and adaptability of provisions for the shifting requirements of diverse populations (Piller et al., 2020; Jang & Choi, 2020). By comparison, elements of trust and relationship building within covid-19 discourse are yet to be explored in multilingual research. This chapter is a step in that direction.

I draw attention to the roles that languages and shared repertoires of multilingual speakers play in establishing trust and exchange of information in online communities during the covid pandemic. Diverse groups network and access shared language resources, information channels, and opportunities to increase their social mobility and social capital (Ashraf, 2008; Bourdieu, 1986; Nahapiet & Ghoshal, 1998; Putnam, 1994; Thoresen et al., 2021). Capabilities of social media platforms to build trust derive from a range of associated factors, and taking an analytical view of a social media platform's linguistic features can illuminate textual and discourse elements that inspire bonding and networking among people with diverse backgrounds. I argue that because language practices create the bridges to facilitate discussion, and are the vehicle to promote health literacy and collaboration, there is a need to recognize and theorize how through multilingual literacies as deployed by many plurilingual online communities, collaborations, dissemination of information, and advancement of scientific knowledge are nurtured. I use Androutsopoulos's (2015) "networked multilingualism", Bourdieu's (1985) theory of social capital, and Gee's (2010) discourse as relationship building tool to analyse the literacy practices of a Pakistani online community during the Covid-19 pandemic.

---

[1] I refer to the Covid-19 Sars-II virus as Covid capitalized when it is used as a proper noun. All other uses are covid.

Pakistan, similar to some other densely populated and linguistically diverse countries in the Global South, was also impacted by the lack of accuracy in translations (Abbasi, 2020), low literacy rates and poor access to information. Yet owing to various communication campaigns, in Pakistan the covid crisis was regarded relatively mild despite its highly populous status, and 50% literacy rates (Akhtar et al., 2021; Anwar et al., 2020; Noreen et al., 2021; Siddiqui et al., 2021, WHO, 2020). It would be helpful, therefore, to shed light on the language in the communication practices that have bridged intercultural diversity and built trust and networking during the pandemic. For this case study, these communicative practices are located in informally structured and locally grounded horizontal information channels in a Pakistani Facebook group. My own background as a multilingual Pakistani gives me the advantage of insight into the intercultural practices and linguistic ecology in which the online community operates. In an effort to systematically document these communicative practices, and articulate how trust and social capital is cultivated, I postulate that Pakistan's online community offers a window into the interpersonal strategies that create health literacy within the uncertainty of a pandemic.

2   Theoretical Framework

Below I detail the social capital theory, networked multilingualism, and the relationship building tool to explain how I conceptualize users' ways of interacting, valuing and connecting contribute to the D/discourses underlying multilingual health communication.

2.1   Social Capital in Online Health Communities

In the works of Pierre Bourdieu (1986), James Coleman (1988), and Robert Putnam (2001), social capital is conceptualized as intangible elements and dispositions (e.g., education or individual and collective habitus) that contribute to social and economic mobility, and opportunities. Nahapiet and Ghoshal (1998) include the sum of the actual and potential resources embedded within, available through, and derived from the network of relationships that provide access to information channels or intellectual capital. With some differences, three primary dimensions of social capital stand out in these formulations. Accordingly, the *cognitive dimension* enables members to access information through networks of shared knowledge (i.e., what one knows about individual and social mobility); the *structural dimension* is concerned with the configuration of network ties, their density, hierarchy, and connectivity; the *relational dimension* of social capital is embedded within one's personal relationships formed through shared identity or common destiny that influences behaviours and self-identification (Ashraf, 2008; Nahapiet & Ghoshal, 1998).

Similarly, a correlation between health outcomes of an individual and their network contacts demonstrates the potential influences of the diffusion of information and belief on health behaviours, social learning, norm adoption, and peer imitation, and in creating a sense of community, trust, and solidarity among their members (Kawachi et al., 2008; Kye & Hwang, 2020; Zhang & Centola, 2019). In Norway, Thoresen et al. (2021) compared levels of personalized and generalized trust via Facebook to study their influence on behavioural tendencies. In South Korea, Jang & Choi, (2020) highlight the role of the online community of *Fenhan* in providing international students with information and emotional support through language brokering that involved translating, mediating, highlighting and disseminating key information, thereby promoting trust, a sense of belonging and connectedness. Advances in free online translation services and translanguaging offer opportunities to network on the web, overcome intercultural barriers, and increase user participation (Lee & Barton, 2013; Sato, 2022).

2.2 Plurilingual or Translingual Norms in Online Communities

Given the literacy practices and unique orthographies of each language, the normative discourses, indexicalities and subjectivities of members are juxtaposed in novel traditions in online communities (Androutsopoulos, 2020; Spilioti, 2019). Urdu on the web is written through the Perso-Arabic script *nasta'liq* from right to left unlike English, or is transliterated to Romanized Urdu. In a combination of these different techniques the multilingual users' choice of script, directionality, and competence reflect different identities and motivations. Additionally, trans-scripting involves creative semiotic resources that are not legitimized in offline literacy practices but accepted in ingenious meshing of codes to serve different purposes. Since the affordances of social media and keyboards offer more options to plurilingual web users and audiences in Pakistan, in this investigation, I mostly refer to these unique multilingual literacy encounters as *translingual*.

Technology also enables contextualized actions through the modalities of status updates, posts, images, content sharing, and user comments referred to as *affordances* (Earl & Kimport, 2011; Faraj & Azad, 2012). A combination of translingual communication with the social media affordances, inspires online community members to engage in the use of multiple languages within a single literacy event through multiple and online keyboards, or transliteration and translations that Androutsopoulos (2015) conceptualizes as "networked multilingualism". Networked multilingualism encompasses how individuals deploy the entire range of linguistic resources within three sets of constraints: mediation of written language by keyboard-and-screen technologies, access to network resources, and orientation to networked audiences. Users create their own rules for establishing in-group solidarity, familiarity and proactive content in languages of their own choices (Pérez-Sabater, 2022; Androutsopoulos, 2015) simultaneously opening windows into several communicative encounters (Androutsopoulos, 2015), presenting increasing fluidity, diversity and mobility as people move resources across online and offline spaces (Spilioti, 2019).

Societal multilingualism is typical of Global South contexts, and it is widely accepted that plurilinguals in these contexts fluidly switch between languages without any specific or consistent pattern of code switches (Canagarajah, 2009) that are complementary, unique in each context, and inherent to the linguistically diverse repertoire of South Asia (Ashraf, 2022; Canagarajah & Ashraf, 2013).

2.3 Discourse/discourse, Context, Language-in-Use

Code-meshing to co-construct trust and promote health literacy during the covid pandemic in Pakistan is more of a process rather than a product. While trust is an intangible concept, which may be traced in discourse in co-constructed acts of mutual aid, the expectation of receiving and providing help, and a sense of common faith and destiny (Liu et al., 2019). According to Gee (1999), while "discourses" are forms of "language in use" when melded in non-language phenomena (e.g., actions, interactions, history, values and beliefs) through which individuals and groups enact certain activities and identities, the big D Discourses are involved (p. 2). In this sense, members of the online group engage in the Discourse of Health Literacy and Covid Literacy, and the Discourse of Public Health, and the Discourse of Facebook Groups, who enact certain identities and roles to be able to "walk the walk, and integrate the walk with the talk" (Gee, 1999, p. 2), adjusting, hybridizing, and evolving in different *contexts* to enable trust, networking or social capital.

Gee (2010) regards *context* as a space of reflexive perspective in which relationship building occurs in a synergy of language-in-use, non-verbal cues, and shared cultural knowledge. For the purpose of the present study, this *context* is a Pakistani Facebook group that covers covid literacy and support. *Language-in-use* in this sense is not just language for saying or doing things, but also building and sustaining relationships that are enacted in a series of actions in related contexts, over a long stretch of time. Building on these elements of discourse, to explicate the construction of social capital in online communities, Gee's (1999) Discourse "relationship building toolkit" offers a set of questions through which an analyst can unpack the Discourses in discourses. The guiding principle is how words and various grammatical devices are used to build and sustain or change relationships of various sorts among the speaker, other people, social groups, cultures, and/or institutions (Gee, 2010, p. 116).

3   Methodological Framework

My interest in this chapter is to build on the above-detailed conceptualization of networked multilingualism and the theory of social capital as integrated in the D/discourses of plurilingual online communities, in order to understand better how they communicate about the pandemic and what roles trust and information exchange play in that communication.

3.1   The Present Framework

In this chapter, I reason people's habitus is disposed to the affordances of social media, and they accommodate to the interface and online communities to increase their reach and access the resources, which is how social capital is created in these online networks. The following research questions are asked to explore how the cognitive, relational and structural social capital are cultivated with language practices in the networked multilingual space of a Pakistani Facebook group:

(a) What knowledge, assumptions, and inferences do users bring to bear to create clear and understandable health communication as they alternate their language-in-use preferences?
(b) What knowledge, cultural resources and grammatical devices are privileged and de-privileged (e.g., translation vs transliteration, words vs images) to achieve clarity and increase social capital?
(c) How are various discourse strategies used to build and sustain, or change relationships of various sorts among users, social groups, cultures, and institutions?

Table 1 presents the theoretical model that guides my analysis of social capital and the construct of its key dimensions in Pakistani online communities through language practices. The investigation foregrounds the premise that during the covid pandemic successful networks generated trust, and thereby promoted health literacy through networked multilingualism, both of which are the product and the cause of shared cultural communication and discourses.

Table 1 Theoretical and analytical framework

Dimensions of social capital in discourse	Social mobility	Language preferences
Cognitive—building information through networks of shared knowledge in assumptions and inferences	*What you know*	{English, Urdu, Translingual}
Structural—developing societal, kinship bonds, or knowing people with cultural knowledge and linguistic elements	*Who you know*	
Relational—identifying with network members who have similar identities or common destiny	*Who you want to be*	

3.2   Data

Data for this study come from a health-related Facebook group, *Corona Warriors Recovered!* (*CWR!* onwards). The virtual hub serves a "home base" (Stellefson et al., 2019) for different contextualized actions e.g., covid health literacy, alternative medication, nutrition, disease-management and its prevention. The success of the group's solidarity campaign was recognized in national and international forums to offer crisis support, network building and information channels (e.g., *Reuters*; see Farooq, 2020). When I began collecting the data for this study, *CWR!* had more than 338,000 members that open a window into symbiotically created diverse literacy practices and covid discourses in Pakistan. To narrow down the scope of the communication on the Facebook group, I first created boundaries through an event-based approach (see also Lee, 2022). Using the search option in Facebook terms related to health, its Urdu variant *sehat,* vaccination, and the oldest and latest posts, data were copied and then manually coded for analysis. Details of the data, and the number of posts from each time period are provided in Table 2. This resulted in a total of 308 posts, in addition to user comments.

4   Analysis

4.1   Assumptions and Inferences in Alternate Language-in-Use Preferences

Building on the framework presented in Table 1, the initial coding of data identifies seven different functions performed by members through different languages. Each function corresponds to social capital dimensions as created through member's interactional intentions, and the context of the language-in-use itself that fulfils their motivations and needs. This is summed up in Table 3.

Table 2   Description of data from facebook

Data	Time period		Total no. of posts
	From	To	
Posts tagged COVID (the oldest posts)	July 8, 2020	December 19, 2020	39
Posts tagged "vaccination"	December 30, 2021	March 24, 2022	65
Posts tagged "sehat"	January 20, 2022	January 26 2022	55
Posts tagged COVID (the latest posts)	January 21, 2022	March 8 2022	45
Unfiltered latest posts	February 25, 2022	March 8, 2022	104
			308

Table 3 Initial coding of data: function, feature, language and social capital dimension

Function	Facebook tools	Language and grammatical features	Language-in-use	Social capital dimension
Covid information: direct, literal communication	Status updates Images: screenshots User comments	Epistemic: facts, figures, statistical data, news headlines Personal information: telephone number, address Legitimacy	English	Cognitive aspect building information channels
Affirmation of faith; Prayer: pragmatic	User posts User comments Images	Request: asking for help, inviting Lexical pragmatic markers to bring about an action Persuasive; Lending authenticity; Emphatic Arabic script, centrality of religion	Translingual English	Relational dimension; identification with members through common destiny and belief
Seeking help	User posts User comments	Request; Emotion; Persuasive	English Urdu Translingual	Cognitive: seeking information
Clarification about medical report	User posts User comments Images	Personal narrative: patterns of personal reference; Emotion; Synopsis of events Personal information Enquiry; Anticipation; Modals	English; Translingual	Cognitive: seeking information Structural: establishing connections; knowing people
Health literacy: medical information	Status updates User comments Images	Epistemic; Assessment: emphatic; Predicting often with conditionals; Evaluative: positive	English Urdu Translingual	Cognitive: seeking information Structural: providing connections; knowing people
General updates; news, group rules	Admin User posts Images	Deictic: anaphoric; contextualized; Progressive aspect (continuous tense)	English Translingual	Cognitive: sharing information Structural: contacts; knowing people
Personal experiences	User posts User comments	Personal narratives: synopsis of events; emotion; distrust/ gratitude; request for prayer or prayer; Agentive; perfect aspect; Evaluative	English Translingual	Relational dimension: identification; ways of doing things; commonalities Structural: knowing people Cognitive: information about

A few deductions can be made here. *One*, members produce, attend to, and respond to the emerging conversation in the posts revealing rich and complex translingual practices in a collaboratively sustained online space. And *two*, scrutiny of the knowledge, assumptions, and inferences that users bring to the group in their distinct roles and functions, contribute to the three dimensions of social capital. In line with the theories of social capital the dimensions are inter-related. Below I elucidate how the languages, cultural practices, and lexical devices that users bring to the group to network facilitate trust and action.

4.2 The Cognitive Dimension in Information Exchange

People employ languages to build or sustain relationships, distribute or hold back social goods and share information using different vocabulary and grammatical devices (Gee, 1999, p. 138). As information exchange is central to social capital formation, an analysis of the cognitive dimension shows how it is created and accessed by *CWR!* members in the knowledge and inferences they bring to the posts or to their requests of information in the group.

4.2.1 Informational Posts

By leveraging their agency, social media administrators negotiate the terms for members, and moderate topics and languages that were critical during the pandemic. Through different modalities, *CWR!* administrators (henceforth "admin") disseminate general covid literacy, vaccine information, medical and plasma treatment, invitations to provide details through google forms, captions for expert interviews, and group and membership rules. The informational updates from official bureaucratic organizations privileging English over Urdu, are supported epistemically with data, and characterized by shorter, straightforward statements. A significant number of these posts include screenshots of official tweets with number of vaccines administered, the count of cases, and updates from the government agencies e.g., *National Command and Operation Center* (NCOC, a central organization to synergize and articulate the national covid policy), and *National Institute of Health, Islamabad* (NIH) as shown in Fig. 1. In this sense, *CWR!* includes as Paton and Irons (2016) indicate, not just timely information, but also the ability of its recipients to interpret it, use it and respond to it.

These covid updates in English imply its official language status for transmitting covid related news, in spite of the fact that by and large these practices conflict with the status and ideologies of languages in a postcolonial country like Pakistan (Abbasi, 2020; Ashraf, 2022). In conflating these two contrasts, whenever state information is presented in English, it glosses over the absence of languages besides English in professional, STEM, and higher education, and over the vast majority of the 50% literate population of Pakistan who do not necessarily learn their school science or STEM courses in English. Nonetheless, as English is part of the plurilingual repertoire, these posts reveal that both admin and members do seek out and attempt to interpret health literacy transmitted in English by the group, make sense of it, and make decisions about how to act when dealing with the pandemic.

Fig. 1 NCOC post shared
by administration

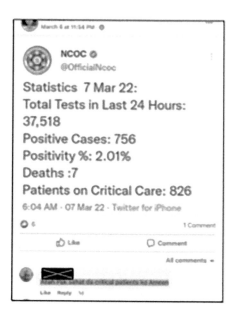

From time to time, members function through translingual codes presenting information with Urdu, English, Romanized Urdu or trans-scripting literacy practices within the same post or comment. Language and local knowledge are, in fact, key to this sense-making and relation-building where local literacies, religion, homeopathic and home remedies offer cure as is illustrated in Example A in Fig. 2 below.

For the admin, local knowledges and language brokering to address myths, and bridge gaps between the physicians and laypersons is mostly translingual. Interviews incorporate a blend of English and Urdu codes, translations and repetitions that facilitate connections and health communication. In the interviews, the founder of the group, Zoraiz, opens up the session, introduces and thanks the invited medical expert, and moderates the conversation between the experts, live audiences, and their posted comments. In Example B (Box 1), I provide the admin's introduction of a pulmonologist's interview that was run live and involved audience questions, with Urdu words in bold. Transmitting information from both ends, and mediating the information to and from, he takes on the role of a health literacy language broker. He selects and highlights topics to support informed decision and understanding of the pandemic, and remediates key information by rephrasing, translating or expanding it. While doing this, he fluidly shifts between Urdu and English, translates some of his own words and of the invited expert, thereby exhibiting a dynamic plurilingual competence in which Urdu or English can interchangeably be the matrix language of an exchange.

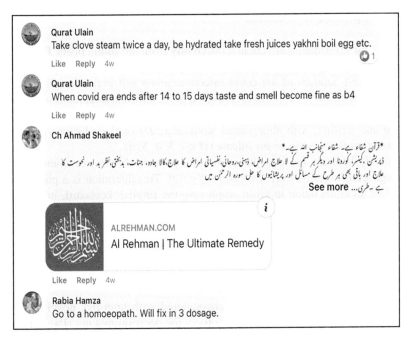

Qurat Ulain
Take clove steam twice a day, be hydrated take fresh juices yakhni boil egg etc.

Like   Reply   4w

Qurat Ulain
When covid era ends after 14 to 15 days taste and smell become fine as b4

Like   Reply   4w

Ch Ahmad Shakeel

قرآن شفاء ہے۔ شفاء منجانب اللہ ہے۔
ڈپریشن، کینسر، کورونا اور دیگر ہر قسم کے لا علاج امراض، ذہنی، روحانی، نفسیاتی امراض کا علاج، کالا جادو، جنات، بدبختی، نظر بد اور نحوست کا علاج اور باقی بھی ہر طرح کے مسائل اور پریشانیوں کا حل سورہ الرحمٰن میں ہے ۔۔طرح
See more ...

ALREHMAN.COM
Al Rehman | The Ultimate Remedy

Like   Reply   4w

Rabia Hamza
Go to a homoeopath. Will fix in 3 dosage.

Fig. 2 Example A of user comments in a translingual script and local health literacies

---

Box 1 Example B: A Post by the Founder of the Group Depicting Plurilingual Competence

Eik mahina complete **honay per**… is important **moqa per, jinhun nay** concept **diya hae, jinhun nay** plasma therapy **ka** concept **diya hae**, hopeless **logon ko umeed di hae, mushkil se nikala hae; humaray saath** live **haen,** public **ke saath** direct inquiries **ko** handle **bhi kerein gay; ye hoti kya hae;** doctor **sahab** will update us what is this. Thank you so much for coming to this session. It is an honor for us; **aap ka bari shiddat se intezar tha is pooray** group **ko, aur un ki** basic queries **ko** solve **bhi kerein. Logon ko is se kya kya cheezein jaan ni haen.** Salam Everyone. **Jitni bhi der aap chahein gay hum is per beth ker baat kerein gay**, status **kya hae is ka poori dunya mein;** pandemic is half way through; **buhut** time **aesa guzray ga is ko buhgata rahay houn gay; is ki tabahkariyon ko dekhein gay.**"

In the above example, Zoraiz says that after a month of plasma treatment advances, it was important to have the person on the show who had introduced it, as he has *given hope to hopeless people and taken them out of hardship* (literal translation). Unlike the continuous shifts in the first part, the last 5 lines use detailed Urdu clauses with English noun insertions only.

4.2.2 Requesting Information

Requests for information are curated differently from the admin posts. First, beginning mostly in English, members present a synopsis of events that opens with the prognosis and duration of the covid infection, and a self-evaluation of symptoms interwoven with emotion. As in Examples C to G, informational requests are structured tentatively, and informally in similar trends to online posts as hybrids of speech and writing, with abbreviated words e.g., *Dr* or *doc* (doctor), and lexical pragmatic markers as *Plz* or *pls* (please) (Figs. 3, 4, 5, 6).

Second, there are few exceptions of Urdu posts in the dataset where members privilege transliteration over the nasta'liq script. Transliteration is a phonetic rendering of an enunciation in Urdu employing the English keyboard, indexicalized more with the discourse function than the spelling. In Examples F and G, the members open the post with the Muslim greetings of salam presented in a variety of forms: transliterated as *Assalam o alaikum* and *Assalam u Alaikum*, abbreviated as *Aoa, AOA, AoA* or typed out as *Salam*. Symbolizing a common faith, it serves to engage the larger audience with the post and introduces the poster through shared cultural etiquette.

Third, in providing details when encountered with high-risk novel situations, people actively seek out the views of others for decision-making (Paton & Irons, 2016), which is different from their general disposition as passive risk-perceivers (Lion et al., 2002). Answers to difficult but direct questions like, *Should we be wearing masks around each other?* and *How can two people living together have different results?* as in Examples C and D, remain vague in members' responses. In Example E, a member provides a disclosure of their covid experience, followed by an expression of gratitude i.e., *Allhumdollilah* (all praise to Allah; also spelt *Alhamdolillah* elsewhere in the dataset), repeated after describing convalescence, and ending with the request for information from any doctor.

Fourth, explicit knowledge to disambiguate myths is constructed in the interaction itself. The symptoms of fever, chest x-ray, weakness, chest heaviness, and relapse after some days are helpful to document the varied complications of the coronavirus. Members seek clarifying questions about the test results, x-rays, blood

January 26 ·

Me and my family are covid positive. We are making food ourself, for each other too. Should we be constantly wearing masks around each other?

In terms of laundry, should everything in the cupboard (unworn items) be washed again? If I wash clothes for myself, will they be considered clean when I test negative? I just need a bit of guidance in terms of eliminating cross contamination so life can come back to a semblance of normal.

I would be very grateful if a medical professional can answer these questions please.

12   0 Comments

Fig. 3 Example C of request

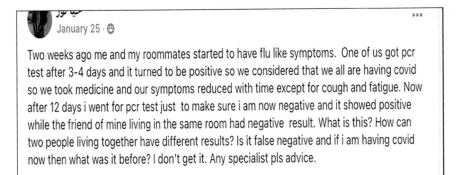

Fig. 4 Example D of seeking information

My covid test came out to be positive on 24th of January, 2022. I kept myself isolated for 10 days. I was having fever, cough and stomach cramps. Symtoms vanished after 8-9 days. Three days ago, I started to have the symptoms once again, feeling feverish and having severe cough.
What could be the reason? Am I still positive even after 2 weeks?

Fig. 5 Example E of seeking medication information

January 19 ·

Assalam u Alaikum,
Needs guidance to get the first dose of Pfizer.
Background: My brother, 26yo, unvaccinated, will relocate for studies as soon as the concerned country issues study permits to international students. He visited CVC & has been told that currently, Pfizer is only for children aged 12-18 and adults who need a booster having valid travel documents. Now, he can get a jab of any vaccine, but if his visa came within 6 months period, he can stuck coz of an unapproved vaccine as the booster shot is administered after 6 months of dual dosage; that's why he wants to get a Pfizer shot in the first place. Can anyone pls guide how he can get it in Rwp/Isb? JazakAllah.

Fig. 6 Example F about Pfizer vaccine

tests, prescriptions, and resources to access that information. Often the medical information request is authenticated with a snapshot of the test results or doctor's prescription. In Example G (Fig. 7), information about CRP blood test, as a marker of infection, engages members with similar experience, but also provides knowledge about the symptoms for members unfamiliar with it. Response comments continue to enrich covid literacy as Example H illustrates (Box 2).

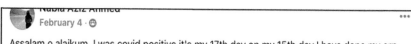

Nabia Aziz Ahmed
February 4 · 🌐   •••

Assalam o alaikum, I was covid positive it's my 17th day on my 15th day I have done my crp
test which was 28 nd mild infection in xray mujhe ab rooz raat ko 98 or 99 fever ho jata hai us
k bad weakness bht ho jati hai cbc test was all ok Allhumdollilah baki no cough Allhumdollilah
just chest me Zara heavy feel hota Hai... Plz any Dr here guide krden 😔

👍😊🥰 6   36 Comments

Fig. 7 Example G about CRP blood test

Box 2 Example H: User Comments Creating Covid Literacy while Deploying both English and Urdu

A: Allah **pak sehatyaab**

B: Aameen

C: Bump

D: Rest **na lenay say b hota hai**. (Also happens if rest is not taken) Dr suggested only panadol for fever. Take proper rest if all other reports r ok

X: only crp is high cbc is all okay

D: i cant say anything about high crp as i m not dr. But fever **mujhe b hota tha** after **recovering jab mai nay kam start kia aik dam**. **Tu** tiredness caused fever in my case **jo aik do** panadol n surbex z dr **nay** recommend **kia tha bas**.

X: **Mera b jb kaam Thora krlon tu** start **ho jata raat mein Apko kitny** days **raha Tha**

D: 2 days **shayad bus ziada** fatigue **say bachein**

mujhe buhat days **hogye hn** 99 **py fever rehta hai** fatigue **Har waqt** weakness **se hath b** shiver **krty** sometimes (it's been several days for me 99 fever stays fatigue all the time weakness also causes hands to shiver) Box [Example 8] ends

---

Finally, how the translingual code glosses over the fluid shifts between both languages is striking. As represented in the post and comments, both Examples G & H are in a mix of Urdu and English codes transliterated into the Roman script, and non-standard punctuation. Composed translingually, this parlance with English and transliterated Urdu comments does not follow the normative literacy practices of medical scripts, or the syntax expected in writing. Amidst these unconventional practices, covid literacy evolves in the flow of user comments including lay knowledge about the levels of the CRP blood tests and over the counter medicine that may help people lacking access to medical experts.

Posts and comments convey anticipation and expectation as both the poster and commenter tentatively share information about their covid experience, and make recommendations. Cultural and religious etiquette is visible in the responses to the post serving different purposes. A, B and C in Example H offer good wishes through supplications that God may grant health followed by an amen and "Bump" that increases audience to the post. Members perceive the group's potential in understanding their account, and audiences assisting them with symptom management, emotional support and optimism constituting a literacy event of information exchange. This is similar to a medical history often taken down in a doctor's office, sans the questions being asked of the patient. With limited physical interaction impacting patients' ability to access medical care in person, the indirect, greater social support from the members of the group, and friends of those members illuminates the passive but robust engagement of the online community in building covid literacy. I suggest that this evolving health discourse supplemented with nonmedical information in a translingual code augments the exchange of covid information in Pakistan.

In this section, I delineated how pragmatic and discourse markers, and the choice of languages, contribute to the cognitive dimension of social capital. Next, explicating the structural dimension, I show members' acceptability of information is tied to the strength of their relationship with the people disseminating the information.

4.3   Tracing the Structural Dimension in Shared Norms

The structural dimension of social capital is related to the strength of members' bonds in their network and reflected in the trust created through shared norms and values (e.g., beliefs) that promote a stable pattern of interaction, cooperation and social relationships (see Borgonovi & Andrieu, 2020; Liu et al., 2019). In this section, I draw on the networking norms of Facebook, and the distinctive use of hashtags that contribute to the cultivation of trust.

4.3.1   Establishing Trust Through Norms of Hierarchy, Appropriacy, and Shared Values

With the Facebook technology that enables meshed languages, images, gifs, and emojis, user options surpass the offline literacy norms in establishing linkages and trust. In Example I while strictly detailing the rules of the group, emotions and emojis lend more clarity to the norm expectations of membership. Choosing to begin with a personal sentiment, the founder, Zoraiz Riaz, shares the experience of losing a loved one to covid, commits to not leaving the general (unknown) audience or the Pakistani people without information and resources, and inserts URLs of websites and emojis (e.g., lightning bolt, the big red cross). These alternative semiotic practices are multi-layered. For example, the flag of Pakistan symbolizes a nation itself, but also invites nationalism or patriotism, prioritizing commitment to bring together both online and offline Pakistanis. Such affordances lead to a sense of community and belonging among members and support the information channels (Jang & Choi, 2020; Paton & Irons, 2016). Zoraiz's reference to a digital community of 250,000 members is indicative of the strength of the connections and significance of relationships. The note of optimism to rise to the challenge lends more credence to his role, while simultaneously establishing his hierarchy as a group administrator. Similarly, the use of block letters, and punctuation to convey the good news are resounding and dialogical. Towards the close, a marked shift to Urdu in the insertion of the single word, *Baqi* (*The rest*), and the return to personal tone strengthens trust in his message, and in the appropriacy of these translingual practices. The use of the term *Baqi* also implies a sense of resignation with an underlying religious faith that there is also much that is beyond human control. This tone is sustained in "I pray," and "Love!" at the end of the post, weaving together common faith, destiny and the perils of the pandemic. We see here the group does not just provide information on specific issues, but also creates "an embryonic space" of emotional support (Paton & Irons, 2016), and value co-creation (Liu et al., 2019) (Fig. 8).

Trust is often created in tacit ways. Blurring the boundaries between the public and the private, the members' norm of keeping their data private is frequently

Zoraiz Riaz
June 11, 2020 ·

Yesterday was rough as I had lost my friend's father because of Covid-19, I had a lot of queries but let me tell you, I'm not leaving you all alone in this.

Enough negativity! ✕
Let's fast forward and look up to the new stats, voice notes, pictures of the donors and screenshots 📱
1- Group Strength of 250,000 in 13 days.
2- Plasma requests across Pakistan on www.plasmaportal.org were 530.
3- 350 Donors have been connected. (Difference because of donor unavailability)
4- 75+ cases connected themselves through the group themselves as the donors are they are secretly looking for potential recipients.
5- Up to 75% recovery reports have been recorded in the mild/moderate cases because of plasma therapy and YES IT IS SOME GOOOOOD NEWSSS!!!

6- Patients on ventilators develop multiple complications and hence plasma therapy is not very effective in them but let me tell you one thing, when they were injected plasma, they were recovered and stable but after a few days their condition was back and not much could be done. 😔

7- Convalescent plasma therapy is not always effective and not always recommended but the patients who are moderate and have the tendency to worsen can definitely improve through this.

Baqi progress is visible in the following stuff.

I pray that this small idea of connecting people which has become so big saves a lot of lives!
Love!
Zoraiz Riaz

#WeWillWinThisWar #GoodTimesAhead #CoronaWar — with **Sarim Saeed Bhatti.**

Fig. 8 Example I: Presenting admin post with hashtags and emoticons

abandoned in favour of sharing their personal information signalling trust and benevolence in the organization of information by this group. Incorporating personal introductions and contact information lends legitimacy and continuity to the online interaction (Burke et al., 2007), and facilitates the overall pattern of relationships, helping *CWR!* members decide who to reach and how.

4.3.2 Hashtags and Pinned Topics

Predictably, *CWR!* makes use of several hashtags that draw attention to people and topics, and increase accessibility of information. In Example I above, before signing off, Zoraiz adds the tags, "We Win!", "Good Times Ahead", and "Corona War", all of which are metaphors of hope, commitment, and optimism amidst the despair of the pandemic. As with other studies, Zoraiz's hashtags serve the discourse functions of fact, opinion, and emotion (Papacharissi, 2015) convey self-presentation and linguistic acts of evaluation (Lee, 2022), and inclusivity as captured in the collective pronoun *we*. The widespread use of the war metaphor for the Covid-19 pandemic implies resonance, improved communication, an ability to simplify complex issues, and an all-in-this-together mentality (e.g., Isaacs & Priesz, 2021); but also, an inappropriate personification of the virus as a vilifying opponent, producing anxiety and unrest (Semino, 2021). Zoraiz's post suggests both of these impressions in the details of his personal experience, converting it into the bigger purpose of the group that reiterates who members should reach out to when in need of any kind of help (Fig. 9).

While hashtags in pinned topics are created in translingual codes, the practices suggest a pattern. Informative topics related to critical issues e.g., آپ خود چیسٹ ایکسرے دیکھنا سیکھیں (learn yourself how to view a chest x-ray) or آکسیجن کے استعمال کے متعلق ضروری باتیں (important topics about the use of oxygen), or دمہ اور کرونا مریض کو کیسے پہچانیں (how to distinguish between an asthma and corona patient) are in Urdu for outreach. Topics hashtagged in both Urdu and English combine scripts and reading directionality e.g., ونٹیلیٹ ventilator-مشین کے بارے میں. (about the machine ventilator) and خوراک اور کرونا مریض medical perspective (medical perspective diet and corona patient). Though Urdu is the matrix language in these translingual hashtags, English nouns either trans-scripted in Urdu, or repeated in English, suggesting their higher degree of familiarity with the terms

English	Urdu	translingual
drtahirshamsilive	آکسیجن کے استعمال کے متعلق ضروری باتیں	ونٹیلیٹ ventilator مشین کے بارے میں
helmetmaskventilationabridgetherapy	دمہ اور کرونا مریض کو کیسے پہچانیں	medicalperspective خوراک اور کرونا مریض
coronadiseasespectrumexplained	آکسیجن کے استعمال کے متعلق ضروری باتیں	asthma دمہ کیا ہے کیسے علاج کیا جائے
coronadiseasespectrumexplained	آپ خود چیسٹ ایکسرے دیکھنا سیکھیں	inhaler مشین کے مریض اور انہیلر
howyoucanreadecg	کرونا ڈی سیز متعلصر الہ و جہبی سمجہیں	
coronarecoveryexpectationvsreality	سٹیلو ڈی سیز کے بارے میں ہر ہیں	
drsomiaiqtadartalksaboutcovid 19	کرونا ڈی سیز کیس کا ری نو ٹری	
coronapatientdietbypulmonologist		
recoveryfromcorona		

Fig. 9 Pinned topics Hashtagged in English, Urdu and Translingual codes by the group admin

in English. These translingual practices may carry no socio-pragmatic inference (Androutsopoulos, 2020); instead, as Spilioti (2019), suggests, the interplay of languages creates shared semiotics, identities and reciprocity in creative ways that facilitate mobility of resources across online and offline spaces.

4.4   The Relational Dimension in a Common Destiny

The relational dimension of social capital, though tied inextricably to the structural, has its roots in people's dispositions to identify with members and networks having similar interests and stories. In *CWR!*, admin support in dissemination of information is complemented with user stories and reflections attesting to a common interest that emerges in expressions of shared faith and destiny. Below I discuss their role in cultivating and sustaining relationships.

4.4.1   Personal Reflections and Shared Sentiments

By enabling a platform to share personal experiences, *CWR!* also provides a reflexive perspective where users build relationships in a synergy of language-in-use, non-verbal cues, and shared cultural knowledge (Gee, 2010). Example J below, addresses the general unknown audience and engages in three discourse functions: imparting news, bonding, and identifying with readers through a shared faith and common destiny. These discourses are packed in a translingual message scripted in English, Romanized Urdu and plurilingual codes as if one language would not be enough to describe the emotional granularity of the experience (Fig. 10).

Opening in Urdu, the first statement fully (*Helping all of you it has been 2 years*), the third partially (*Not to worry*) and last before closing (*Still a lot to do*) are scripted in Roman. The sentiments expressed here, on the one hand, record an instant and personal connection with the readers for having a shared language and identity, and on the other, benefit from the technology of social media and the ease of the English

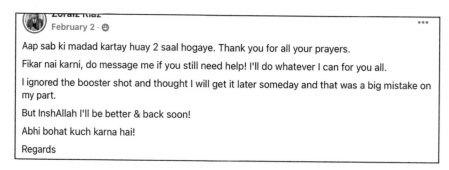

Fig. 10 Example J of personal reflections

keyboard. Carrying personal undertones, each of these Urdu statements has been interspersed with information regarding the covid infection that Zoraiz got for missing a booster shot, admitting the oversight, and affirming the commitment to help even if he is unwell. The sense of shared religion and tenets of religion expressed here in the Arabic expression *Insha'Allah* (God-Willing) in line 5 denote a) commitment, b) faith that God will help him accomplish his goals, and c) a sense of optimism in *'Still a lot to do'*, that is bred into cultural and religious commitment not to give up. In such translingual encounters, English and Urdu languages become the vehicle of both connection and information. As identified by studies (e.g., Paton & Irons, 2016; Thoresen et al. 2021), personal stories in *CWR!* also increased generalized trust among participants, and provided a context to members so that those with similar needs and experiences responded more meaningfully to each other, while also making sense of the pandemic travails by identifying with members who shared the same fate and destiny. Thus they lend more weight to the theory that a shared language and faith builds a sense of trust, identity and opportunity that bridge the gaps in the online spaces (Paton & Irons, 2016).

4.4.2 Praying Together During the Pandemic

Coping with a crisis through individual and communal prayers is common among world religions, and studies have shown that shared religion is a source of social capital (Coleman, 1988; Furseth, 2017). Referring to the Quran, and sending goodwill prayers to the wider known and unknown audiences is salient in *CWR!* In fact, almost each post by users or admin is reciprocated in a prayer, an expression of faith or a common destiny in the comments. The most frequent responses to updates about covid, for example, are in the original or transliterated Arabic phrase *Alhamdolillah*, and a translingually composed prayer, *Allah critical patients ko sehat de Ameen* (May Allah bless critically ill patients with health. Amen). The phrase *Alhamdolillah* is a form of gratitude to God literally meaning that all praise is to God, and a popular response in stating one's well-being. This phrase functions along with *Jazak'Allah* (may God reward you) abbreviated as *jzk* to thank, *Masha'Allah* (if God wills) to express faith in God, and *Insha'Allah* (God-willing) to commit. Their deployment illustrates people's dispositions to draw upon local literacies and practices in online groups to create a shared sense of religiosity and contentment among members. Because disaster management in Islam is treated as an opportunity for people to purify their faith (Nuryana & Fauzi, 2020), *CWR!* petitionary requests are often relational. Instead of religious norm enforcement, seeking prayers is invitational, persuasive and interpersonal in *CWR!*, knitting together a diverse virtual community similar to offline religious communities that create civic engagement and social capital (Sarkissian, 2012). Though to actuate how such expressions of faith play a role in the shared happiness or emotional capital of the society would need to be empirically researched, here it suffices that these forms of prayer and the Arabic script itself encapsulate both physical and metaphysical connections that are simultaneously worldly and spiritual. Reference to the suffering

Figs. 11 and 12 Requests for prayer accompanied by the prayer and its translation

and request for collective prayers are frequently supplemented with images of the original text from Scripture, an authentic reference to religious books, and translation (as in Figs. 11 and 12). Besides English, Arabic and Urdu, a combination of images and other visual resources juxtaposed in the online post with the written word, do not replace the language, but just represent new modes working together in powerful ways (see also Lee & Barton, 2013).

The supplication in Example 12 that God is my Lord, and I do not associate a partner with Him" affirms the Muslim belief that though medical information and aide is helpful, only God has the ultimate power of alleviating the epidemic. The prayer thus strengthens the relational ties among people in Pakistan—a country that has more than 96% Muslim population.

5   Conclusion: Social Capital in Networked Translingual Spaces

In some earlier research, I traced the cultivation of social capital in the language of schooling in Pakistan (Ashraf, 2008) that showed people's affinity with languages is often through varied patterns of their individual and cultural habitus. In this chapter, I have returned to that conceptualization to draw upon the cognitive, structural and relational dimensions of social capital showing how language-in-use fosters health literacy discourse and intercultural communication. I have presented a comprehensive set of data from different time segments and modalities that give an overview of a popular Facebook group's affordances in building bridges and bonding among a highly diverse population during the pandemic in Pakistan. Doing so, I demonstrate that in influencing health outcomes and healthy behaviours, language as a code and as a discourse of multilingual literacies is reciprocated in the group through norm adoption, cultural terminologies and the affordances of social media thereby granting it legitimacy. The multilingual analysis is illustrative of social capital in intercultural online communication. Given the dearth of literature on the intercultural communicative practices of Pakistani users' linguistic practices in web-bound spaces, this study is representative of the content and engagement to which a typical Pakistani is generally exposed on Facebook, especially with regard to COVID (health) literacy practices.

Examining the interplay of languages, shifts to and from the two dominant languages, English to Urdu, emoticons and other digital tools, in fact, confer more autonomy upon members of online communities, though such practices are discouraged in educational settings and education policy (Ashraf, 2022; Ashraf et al., 2014). Given that Pakistan's national language is Urdu, the government. or the Facebook group would normally disseminate the information in Urdu or translate English to Urdu. However, the posts by the administrators or the government do not follow a uniform consistent language policy throughout my dataset. Nor do the members. Rather they emerge as participants in the co-construction of a health narrative in the translingual code. The study probed whether there were any rules that directed these norms. By examining the languages and practices that users privilege, it is obvious that the central languages in their literacy practices are English and Urdu, and are often plurilingual, aligning with the offline Pakistani experience (see also Khan et al., 2022). Though in discussing the varied patterns of member posts and comments, Urdu cannot be decoupled from English, translingual norms show that phoneme representation outperforms the orthographic representation of Urdu language. Transliteration is privileged over translation, and lay terms over technical. Members exert a distinct control over their language choices and their manner of engaging with the audience. For English language educators, it increases the significance of translanguaging pedagogies, as networked multilingual spaces create their own norms in using English. The wealth of data on language and intercultural communication on the web, in fact, affirms the call to revisit health literacy and general standards as languages which were earlier only recognized as oral repertoires now are increasingly being written down. To conclude, increased trust is conducive to the production of social capital because as theorists acknowledge "who you know" affects "what you know" (Nahapiet & Ghoshal, 1998; Coleman, 1988) and *how you redefine yourself and your options.* This discourse analysis of Pakistani health literacy clearly demonstrates the point.

References

Abbasi, K. (2020, December 11). Mismatched public health communication costs lives in Pakistan. *Language on the Move.* https://www.languageonthemove.com/mismatched-public-health-communication-costs-lives-in-pakistan/

Akhtar, H., Afridi, M., Akhtar, S., Ahmad, H., Ali, S., Khalid, S., Awan, S. M., Jahangiri, S., & Khader, Y. S. (2021). Pakistan's Response to COVID-19: Overcoming National and International Hypes to Fight the Pandemic. *JMIR Public Health and Surveillance, 7*(5), e28517. https://doi.org/10.2196/28517

Androutsopoulos, J. (2015). Networked multilingualism: Some language practices on Facebook and their implications. *International Journal of Bilingualism, 19*(2), 185–205. https://doi.org/10.1177/1367006913489198

Androutsopoulos, J. (2020). Trans-scripting as a multilingual practice: the case of Hellenised English. *International Journal of Multilingualism, 17*(3), 286–308. https://doi.org/10.1080/14790718.2020.1766053

Anwar, A., Malik, M., Raees, V., & Anwar, A. (2020). Role of Mass Media and Public Health Communications in the COVID-19 Pandemic. *Cureus, 12*(9), e10453. https://doi.org/10.7759/cureus.10453

Ashraf, H. (2008). The language of schooling and social capital in Pakistan. *National University of Modern Languages Research Magazine, 1*, 73–89.

Ashraf, H. (2022). The ambivalent role of Urdu and English in multilingual Pakistan: a Bourdieusian study. *Language Policy.* https://doi.org/10.1007/s10993-022-09623-6

Ashraf, H., Hakim, L., & Zulfiqar, I. (2014). English for Academic Purposes in Plurilingual Pakistan. In I. Liyanage & T. Walker (Eds.), *English for academic purposes (EAP) in Asia. Critical new literacies* (pp. 33–49). Sense Publishers.

Binder & Gago (2020). *Radios in the post-pandemic world—Tools and strategies to confront the new normal: Powerful voices.* Community Media in Latin America. https://www.comminit.com/content/radios-post-pandemic-world-tools-and-strategies-confront-new-normal. Accessed 3 Dec 2022.

Borgonovi, F., & Andrieu, E. (2020). Bowling together by bowling alone: Social capital and Covid-19. *Social Science & Medicine, 265*, 113501. https://doi.org/10.1016/j.socscimed.2020.113501

Bourdieu, P. (1985) The forms of capital. In J. Richardson (Ed.), *Handbook of theory and research for the sociology of education* (pp. 241–258). Greenwood.

Bourdieu, P. (1986). The forms of capital. In J. G. Richardson (Ed.), *Handbook of theory and research for the sociology of education* (pp. 241–258). Greenwood.

Burke, M., Joyce, E., Kim, T., Anand, V., & Kraut, R. (2007). Introductions and requests: Rhetorical strategies that elicit response in online communities. In *Communities and technologies* (pp. 21–39). Springer.

Canagarajah, S. (2009). The plurilingual tradition and the English language in South Asia. *AILA Review, 22*(1), 5–22. https://doi.org/10.1075/aila.22.02can

Canagarajah, S., & Ashraf, H. (2013). Multilingualism and education in South Asia: Resolving policy/practice dilemmas. *Annual Review of Applied Linguistics, 33*, 258–285. https://doi.org/10.1017/S0267190513000068

Coleman, J. S. (1988). Social capital in the creation of human capital. *American Journal of Sociology, 94*, S95–S120.

Earl, J., & Kimport, K. (2011). *Digitally enabled social change: Activism in the internet age.* MIT Press. https://www.jstor.org/stable/j.ctt5hhcb9

Faraj, S., & Azad, B. (2012). The materiality of technology: An affordance perspective. In *Materiality and organizing: Social interaction in a technological world, 237*, 258.

Farooq, U. (2020, June 30). *Drugs, doctors and donors: Pakistan turns to Corona Warriors Facebook Group.* Reuters. https://www.reuters.com/article/uk-health-coronavirus-pakistan-facebook/drugs-doctors-and-donors-pakistanis-turn-to-corona-warriors-facebook-group-idUKKBN2412DO. Accessed 3 Dec 2022.

Furseth, I. (2017). Social capital and immigrant religion. *Nordic Journal of Religion and Society, 21*(2), 147–164. https://doi.org/10.18261/ISSN1890-7008-2008-02-02

Gee, J. P. (1999). *An introduction to discourse analysis: Theory and Method.* Routledge.

Gee, J. P. (2010). *How to do discourse analysis: A toolkit.* Routledge.

Isaacs, D., & Priesz, A. (2021). COVID-19 and the metaphor of war. *Journal of Paediatrics and Child Health, 57*(1), 6–8. https://doi.org/10.1111/jpc.15164

Jang, I., & Choi, L. (2020). Staying connected during COVID-19: The social and communicative role of an ethnic online community of Chinese international students in South Korea. *Multilingua, 39*(5), 541–552. https://doi.org/10.1515/multi-2020-0097

Kawachi, I., Subramanian, S., & Kim, D. (2008). Social capital and health. In I. Kawachi, S. Subramanian, & D. Kim (Eds.), *Social capital and health* (pp. 1–26). Springer.

Khan, U., Khan, A., Khan, W., Su'ud, M., Alam, M., Subhan, F., & Asghar, Z. (2022). A review of Urdu sentiment analysis with multilingual perspective: A case of Urdu and roman Urdu language. *Computers, 11*(3), 1–29. https://doi.org/10.3390/computers11010003

Kye, B., & Hwang, S.-J. (2020). Social trust in the midst of pandemic crisis: implications from COVID-19 of South Korea. *Research in Social Stratification and Mobility, 68*, 100523. https://doi.org/10.1016/j.rssm.2020.100523

Lee, C. (2022). Researching multilingual digital discourse. In C. Vasquez (Ed.), *Research methods for digital discourse analysis* (pp. 139–158). Bloomsbury.

Lee, C., & Barton, D. (2013). *Language online: Investigating digital texts and practices.* Routledge.

Lion, R., Meertens, R. M., & Bot, I. (2002). Priorities in information desire about unknown risks. *Risk Analysis: An International Journal, 22*(4), 765–776. https://doi.org/10.1111/0272-4332.00067

Liu, W., Fan, X., Ji, R., & Jiang, Y. (2019). Perceived Community Support, Users' Interactions, and Value Co-Creation in Online Health Community: The Moderating Effect of Social Exclusion. *International Journal of Environmental Research and Public Health, 17*(1), 204. https://doi.org/10.3390/ijerph17010204

Nahapiet, J., & Ghoshal, S. (1998). Social capital, intellectual capital, and the organizational advantage. *Academy of Management Review, 23*(2), 242–266. https://doi.org/10.2307/259373

Noreen, N., Atta-Ur-Rehman, S., Naveed, I., Khan Niazi, S., & Furqan, I. (2021). Pakistan's COVID-19 Outbreak Preparedness and Response: A Situational Analysis. *Health Security, 19*(6), 605–615. https://doi.org/10.1089/hs.2021.0006

Nuryana, Z., & Fauzi, N. A. F. (2020). The Fiqh of disaster: The mitigation of covid-19 in the perspective of Islamic education-neuroscience. *International Journal of Disaster Risk Reduction, 51*, 101848.

Papacharissi, Z. (2015). *Affective publics: Sentiment, technology, and politics.* Oxford University Press.

Paton, D., & Irons, M. (2016). Communication, sense of community, and disaster recovery: A Facebook case study. *Frontiers in Communication, 1*(4), 1–12. https://doi.org/10.3389/fcomm.2016.00004

Piller, I., Zhang, J., & Li, J. (2020). Linguistic diversity in a time of crisis: Language challenges of the COVID-19 pandemic. *Multilingua, 39*(5), 503–515. https://doi.org/10.1515/multi-2020-0136

Putnam, R. D. (1994). Social capital and public affairs. *Bulletin of the American Academy of Arts and Sciences*, pp. 5–19.

Putnam, R. D. (2001). *Bowling alone: The decline of social capital in America.* Simon & Schuster.

Sarkissian, A. (2012). Religion and civic engagement in Muslim countries. *Journal for the Scientific Study of Religion, 51*(4), 607–622. https://doi.org/10.1111/j.1468-5906.2012.01677.x

Sato, E. (2022). *Translanguaging in Translation: Invisible Contributions that Shape Our Language and Society.* Multilingual Matters.

Semino, E. (2021). "Not Soldiers but Fire-fighters" – Metaphors and Covid-19. *Health Communication, 36*(1), 50–58. https://doi.org/10.1080/10410236.2020.1844989

Siddiqui, A., Ahmed, A., Tanveer, M., Saqlain, M., Kow, C. S., & Hasan, S. S. (2021). An overview of procurement, pricing, and uptake of COVID-19 vaccines in Pakistan. *Vaccine, 39*(37), 5251–5253. https://doi.org/10.1016/j.vaccine.2021.07.072

Spilioti, T. (2019). From transliteration to trans-scripting: Creativity and multilingual writing on the internet. *Discourse, Context & Media, 29*, 100294. https://doi.org/10.1016/j.dcm.2019.03.001

Stellefson, M., Paige, S., Apperson, A., & Spratt, S. (2019). Social Media Content Analysis of Public Diabetes Facebook Groups. *Journal of Diabetes Science and Technology, 13*(3), 428–438. https://doi.org/10.1177/1932296819839099

Thoresen, S., Blix, I., Wentzel-Larsen, T., & Birkeland, M. S. (2021). Trusting others during a pandemic: Investigating potential changes in generalized trust and its relationship with pandemic-related experiences and worry. *Frontiers in Psychology, 12*, 698519. https://doi.org/10.3389/fpsyg.2021.698519

Vita, V. (2020, August 12). Bridging new and traditional media in the fight against Covid-19. *Language on the Move.* https://www.languageonthemove.com/bridging-new-and-traditional-media-in-the-fight-against-covid-19/. Accessed 3 Dec 2022.

WHO (2020). Covid-19 in Pakistan: WHO fighting tirelessly against the odds (Nov. 9, 2020). *World Health Organization.* Accessed from https://www.who.int/news-room/feature-stories/detail/covid-19-in-pakistan-who-fighting-tirelessly-against-the-odds.

Zhang, J., & Centola, D. (2019). Social networks and health: New developments in diffusion, online and offline. *Annual Review of Sociology, 45*, 91–109. https://doi.org/10.1146/annurev-soc-073117-041421

Pérez-Sabater, C. (2022). Mixing Catalan, English and Spanish on WhatsApp: A case study on language choice and code-switching. *Spanish in Context, 19*(2), 289–313.

Hina Ashraf is Associate Research Professor in the Department of Linguistics at Georgetown University, USA. Her research has focused on the negotiation strategies employed by multilingual speakers in various global settings through a sociologically oriented discourse analysis. She has engaged in language policy making by taking up the call to develop and implement innovative and equitable pedagogies that acknowledge and build upon students' diverse language and educational backgrounds across a range of proficiency levels. As a native speaker of Urdu and Punjabi, with beginner Arabic proficiency, she also has a deep understanding of the linguistic and cultural complexities that arise in multilingual settings. Email: Hina.Ashraf@georgetown.edu

Cultural Competency as a Critical Component of Quality Public Administration Services: A Model for Leading Multicultural Teams

Eman S. ElKaleh and Courtney Stryker

Abstract The chapter discusses cultural competency and global mindset development as a critical approach for providing high quality public administration services. It investigates the main factors that lead to effective leadership practices within a multicultural working environment and proposes a model that aims to assist public and higher education administrators to achieve high levels of performance and leadership by providing them with a self-reflective tool that guides and informs their work practices, career plans, and professional growth. The Global Cultural Leadership Competency (GCLC) model, proposed here, was developed based on a comprehensive and critical review of relevant literature supplemented by open-ended interviews with higher education professionals who have cross-cultural working experience in different cultural contexts. The model outlines the core competencies, skills, attitudes and behaviours that leaders need to develop in order to operate with greater impact and effectiveness. Finally, the chapter argues that developing cultural competency will lead to positive organisational outcomes such as improved organisational learning, creating a culture of collaboration, innovation and creativity, enhanced performance, coherent teams, and high-quality public administration services.

Keywords Cultural competency model · Cross-cultural leadership · Leading multicultural · Teams · Global leadership · Higher education · Public administration

E. S. ElKaleh (✉)
Emirates College for Advanced Education, Abu Dhabi, UAE

C. Stryker
Qatar University, Doha, Qatar

© The Author(s), under exclusive license to Springer Nature Switzerland AG 2023
A. Sahlane, R. Pritchard (eds.), *English as an International Language Education*, English Language Education 33,
https://doi.org/10.1007/978-3-031-34702-3_15

1 Introduction

In response to the increasingly expansive impacts of globalisation on higher educa-tion, universities around the world are implementing a broad spectrum of interna-tionalisation strategies, such as the recruitment of international students, faculty and administrators, offering study abroad programs, providing offshore branch cam-puses and/or programs, and establishing transnational alliances and research part-nerships (ElKaleh, 2021). These initiatives, coupled with the myriad impacts of the global COVID-19 pandemic, have led to an increase in the range, diversity and social complexity of the higher education landscape, putting more responsibility and pressure on its administrators to develop the skills needed to address the com-plex and challenging needs of such a varied population in a culturally competent manner (Lopez-Littleton & Blessett, 2015). The ability to lead teams effectively in a culturally diverse context—whether in-person, online, or via hybrid delivery methods—necessitates a clear understanding of the intricacies involved in intercul-tural communication, cognition, and competence (Berardo & Deardorff, 2012; Shuffler et al., 2016). When leading through cultural complexities that extend beyond language comprehension, it is vital that public and higher education admin-istrators at the managerial and executive levels have a roadmap to help them navi-gate the delicate balance between recognition and empathy, valuing and stereotyping, and exchanging information and effectively communicating to be impactful (Nielsen, 2018).

The purpose of this chapter is to discuss cultural competency and global mindset as a critical approach for providing quality and relevant public administration ser-vices and programs (Rice, 2007) and offer a cultural competency model or concep-tual framework for leading multicultural teams in higher education. The chapter highlights how leaders can utilise a framework model to develop a set of cultural competencies that may help to drive organisational transformation through com-munity building and intercultural work environments; it examines how global mind-set leadership can help operationalise and improve competency development and application. This novel approach to intercultural professional development, through a competencies-based framework and a cognitively based mindset approach, helps focus staff behaviour in a way that best reflects the values and mission of an organ-isation, as well as contributing to its success (Intersectoral Platform for a Culture of Peace and Non-Violence, Bureau for Strategic Planning, 2013). The chapter begins with an overview of the global higher education sector and the various challenges and opportunities that leaders encounter when working with culturally diverse pop-ulations. This is followed by a discussion of the different factors contributing to the development of cultural competency and global mindset such as emotional intelli-gence (EI), cultural intelligence (CQ), and personality traits. Research methodology and results of a qualitative study conducted with higher education professionals to identify the four dimensions of cultural competency (knowledge, attitude, skills, behaviours), and the dynamic and developmental process associated with gaining these skills (Getha-Taylor et al., 2020) are discussed next. The final section proposes a cultural competency and global mindset model for leading multicultural teams in a public administration/higher education ecosystem, and considers how it may be applied in a professional development context.

2 Overview of Higher Education: Challenges and Opportunities

In their chapter *Trends in global higher education and the future of internationalization*, Rumbley et al. (2022) aptly describe the global higher education landscape and the culturally diverse populations therein as "a complex panorama of challenges, opportunities, and shifting realities" (p. 3). They further note that internationalisation is one of the most important aspects of higher education—especially when considered in a global context—and is a phenomenon that "can be considered both an object and agent of change across the sector" (p. 3). While there are innumerable variables that impact higher education in a global context, and it is clear that the consequences of the COVID-19 pandemic for higher education and higher education leaders will take several years to understand fully, it is vital that all higher education professionals get a "handle on how higher education will be impacted" (p. 3). The global pandemic and its collateral impacts on all sectors of society and the economy remain one of the largest challenges on higher education leaders' horizons.

Pulling back from the major challenges resulting from the pandemic, Rumbley et al. (2022, p. 4) highlight seven major trends that have emerged over the last decade and have had a direct impact on higher education leadership in a multicultural context:

- the "massification of higher education" and the striking increase in international student mobility;
- globalisation and "the evolving global knowledge economy";
- "concerns around access, equity, and persistence" in global higher education (HE);
- increase of "commercialization and privatization" throughout HE;
- a concerted effort to focus on "all aspects of the student experience" as well as "the nature of teaching, learning, and assessment";
- the impact and "evolving role" of technology on all aspects of instruction, research and global diversity; and
- new HE paradigms that range from "competency-based degrees to microcredentials and many additional nascent structures for delivery and evaluation" (p. 4).

Additional challenges faced by higher education leaders working in a multinational context include the socio-political and environmental forces that have a major impact on the content, quality and openness to cross-cultural interactions (Deardorff et al., 2022).

In contrast to the above challenges, diversity can also offer many opportunities. It helps us gain new knowledge, ideas, experiences, skills, and innovations, leading to what Wildman et al. (2016, p. vi) call "collective wisdom". Diversity widens our perspectives and helps us challenge assumptions, and even our worldviews, that we may take for granted. It encourages us to try new things, go beyond the norm and develop new patterns of thinking, eventually leading to what cross-cultural scholars call global mindset (Den Dekker, 2016; Nielsen, 2018).

Similar to existing literature on cross-cultural competence (Abramson & Moran, 2018; Berardo & Deardorff, 2012; Carrizales, 2010; Carrizales et al., 2016; Derr et al., 2002) and the notion of developing a 'global mindset' (Den Dekker, 2016), Nielsen (2018) presents a compelling argument for considering a global mindset as a 'meta-competence' for organisational leaders. This competence can be viewed "as a way to address the increased strategic and cultural complexity that occurs when international or global corporations have to create, coordinate, and control across both borders and boundaries" (p.147). A wide range of studies (Jeannet, 2000; Lane et al., 2009; Levy et al., 2008) highlight the important connection between global mindset leadership and improved performance in an international context. Context, in this sense, is key to developing this cognitive capacity which can be explained as the ability "to develop and interpret criteria for personal and business performance that are independent of the assumptions of a single context; and to implement those criteria appropriately in different contexts" (Lane et al., 2009, p.14).

Despite the fact that cultural competency is the key to working in a multicultural setting, some argue that it is language that presents the most challenging barrier to success. Some scholars maintain that monolingualism as a so-called 'best practice', is due for a critical review and reconsideration in light of global decolonisation efforts. Using English as the 'lingua franca' of higher education is limiting in terms of cognition, comprehension, expression, cultural identity and values, and meaningful social interaction (Herlihy-Mera, 2022, para 4–5), and is not enough to bridge the gap when working with culturally diverse populations. Other researchers highlight several challenges that hinder working across cultures, borders and languages in a broader context, and note these challenges may negate the benefits of cross-cultural work (Reynolds, 2019). For example, not all team members may feel empowered to contribute opinions or ideas based on their culture of origin; fully integrating team members or individuals in an organisation may be a challenge "particularly if there are underlying prejudices between cultures, making them less inclined to work together". Therefore, both language and cultural barriers may impact effective communication creating a "lost in translation' [scenario] among multicultural colleagues"; "individuals from different cultures can also bring with them different workplace attitudes, values, behaviours, and etiquette", resulting in misunderstandings and negative feelings; working styles and attitudes are a direct reflection of an individual's culture and language—"formality (or relative informality), organizational hierarchy, and even working hours can conflict across cultures" along with matters of punctuality, confrontation and interpersonal conflict; and highly variable attitudes towards working styles and approaches to teamwork also pose challenges as some cultures value collective consensus over independence, spontaneity over order/rigour, flexibility over organisation (Reynolds, 2019, para. 11–13). Language, as discussed by Bok (2009) is not the only factor contributing to cultural competency. The implication is that knowing another language may help one to understand some aspects of another culture, but it is not enough to make one culturally competent.

Building on the challenges and opportunities that higher education leaders face working with multicultural teams in a diverse and globalised environment, it is essential that they should be able to develop a roadmap or framework that affords them the opportunity to navigate intercultural encounters with confidence and a measure of flexibility. The following section presents a practical and normative approach to leading multicultural teams in a higher education environment via the different dimensions of cultural competency.

3 Developing Cultural Competency and Global Mindset

The idea of cultural competency is part of a family of concepts that are directly related to the notion of globalisation (Deardorff, 2009). Concepts like global competence, global employability, global citizenship, and global stewardship underscore the need for individuals leading teams and providing professional development in higher education to have a clear understanding of the attributes that define this idea. The thread that links each of these concepts is the recognition of globalisation as a worldwide changing force. Building on this presumption, cultural competency became an essential skill in an increasingly globalised world. Globalisation mandates higher education leaders be able to interact with people from different cultures and countries who have been shaped by different values, beliefs, and experiences. Using this imperative as a context, it is vital to develop a working definition of cultural competency that frames this chapter. Leung et al. (2014) present a straightforward account of this competence by indicating that (inter)cultural competence is the ability to function effectively across cultures, to think and act appropriately, and to communicate and work with people from different cultural backgrounds both locally and internationally. However, cultural competency may go beyond that to include a deep understanding of "historic oppression and discrimination" issues and the development of a moral obligation to resist all forms of racism, prejudice, and unjust social practices (Barakat et al., 2019, p. 7).

Leadership style preferences and behaviour vary widely across cultures (House et al., 2004). In response to this broad variation, leaders need to develop a set of core competencies that allow them to adapt their leadership styles and behaviours based on the characteristics of their teams and the multicultural situations in which they may be required to operate. As Berardo and Deardorff (2012) highlight, core competencies centred around skills, knowledge, attitudes and behaviours provide the foundational, heuristic approach that can guide higher education and other public administration leaders in a manner that transcends leadership style preferences.

This method of incorporating cross-cultural leadership competencies along with multiple intelligences and cognitive practice is considered in greater detail below.

Fischer and Wildman (2016, p. 16) argue that emotional intelligence, cultural intelligence, and personality play a crucial role in developing effective global leadership. Goleman (1998, p. 2), who was the first scholar to discuss the concept of emotional intelligence, argues that what makes "superb leaders" is not general intelligence (IQ) or technical skills but rather a high level of emotional intelligence (EI). He defines emotional intelligence as the ability to understand and manage one's emotions and those of others. According to him, EI consists of five skills that allow leaders to maximise their own and others' capabilities: (1) self-awareness, a deep understanding of one's emotions, drives, strengths, weaknesses, and values and how they impact others; (2) self-regulation, the ability to manage and redirect negative and disruptive emotions; (3) motivation, a strong drive or passion to achieve work for its own sake—beyond extrinsic motivators such as money and/or status; (4) empathy, the ability to understand and consider people's emotions and thoughtfully respond to them especially during decision making; and (5) social skills, the ability to build effective relationships and rapport with others and help them move toward a desired direction. Goleman (1998) indicates that, while we are born with a certain level of EI, this level can be further developed through practice, persistence, and constructive feedback from coaches and colleagues. Research studies on EI have provided substantial evidence that EI plays a crucial role in developing effective global leaders as it allows leaders to build trusting, respectful, and caring relationships with followers, leading to effective communication and enhanced work performance (Fischer & Wildman, 2016; Gabel-Shemueli & Dolan, 2011; George & Zhou, 2001; Lillis & Tian, 2009).

Cultural intelligence (CQ) is another multifactor concept that significantly contributes to the development of cultural competency and effective global leadership. CQ is defined as an individual's ability to perform effectively in cross-cultural contexts, and explains why some individuals are more capable of performing better than others when interacting with people from different cultural backgrounds (Earley & Ang, 2003; Dean, 2008). As suggested by Ang et al. (2007) and Earley and Ang (2003), cultural intelligence consists of four components: (a) metacognitive, which refers to the cognitive processes used to acquire and comprehend cultural knowledge; (b) cognitive, which reflects one's general knowledge of the culture such as its norms, values, artifacts, and practices; (c) motivational, which represents the volume and direction of one's energy toward learning and succeeding in cross cultural contexts; and (d) behavioural, which refers to one's ability to demonstrate appropriate actions when dealing or working with people from different cultural backgrounds.

Personality is the third pillar that contributes to the development of effective global leadership as proposed by Fischer and Wildman (2016). According to cross-cultural research, the Big Five personality traits—which are the most accepted classification of personality—can strongly predict work performance, completion of overseas assignments, and ability to adapt to and cope with uncertain and new situations (Ang et al., 2006; Barrick & Mount, 1991; Caligiuri, 2000; Witt et al., 2002).

The Big Five personality traits include: (1) extraversion, which refers to being sociable, adventurous, optimistic, energetic, and self-confident; (2) agreeableness, which include being friendly, cooperative, courteous, flexible, forgiving, and nurturing; (3) conscientiousness, which represents individuals who are high achievers, persistent, good planners, dependable, organised, and thorough; (4) emotional stability, which refers to calm, less anxious, and more secure personalities; (5) openness to experience, which includes being intellectual, creative, broad-minded, and curious to acquire new knowledge and skills (Barrick & Mount, 1991; Caligiuri, 2000; Mount et al., 1998). Ang et al. (2006) argue that personality traits are significantly related to the four components of cultural intelligence (cognitive, metacognitive, motivational, and behavioural) and can strongly predict effective leadership-performance in cross-cultural contexts. Their results confirm that openness to experience is highly related to the four aspects of cultural intelligence mainly because, when people are open to learning and willing to try new things, they have higher cognitive, metacognitive, motivational, and behavioural characteristics. They also tend to be non-judgemental, forgiving, and willing to change and adapt to new environments (Fischer & Wildman, 2016, pp. 22–23). This is followed by extraversion, which proved to be highly correlated with cognitive, motivational, behavioural aspects, and conscientiousness which was positively related to metacognitive and behavioural facets.

Fischer and Wildman (2016, p. 17) also suggest that general IQ, which is an important predictor of one's capabilities and performance, combined with overseas experience, which helps in developing a deep understanding of the different patterns of thinking and living, are also important variables that contribute to the development of effective global leadership. They found that a combination of high IQ and experience working abroad with multicultural teams leads to the development of global leadership competencies. Other factors that also contribute to the development of intercultural competence, according to Barakat et al. (2019) and Smith et al. (1997) include: (a) lived experience in cross-culture contexts, (b) exposure to or interacting with people from different cultures, (c) experiencing discrimination against oneself (e.g., treated unfairly due to race, ethnicity, language, citizenship status, etc.), and (d) education or taking a cultural diversity course. However, according to Barakat et al. (2019), it is important to note these factors may not always overcome any pre-existing negative beliefs, values and/or attitudes that leaders may have as some individuals do not possess the emotional and/or intellectual agility or flexibility to do so.

4   Practitioners' Lived Experiences

While there are several seminal works addressing the theoretical underpinnings of intercultural competence and heuristics supporting their attainment (Deardorff, 2009; Barakat et al., 2019; Getha-Taylor et al., 2020; Henson, 2016; Newman et al., 1978), it is vital to explore further the lived experiences of higher education practitioners in order to gain a clearer, more enhanced understanding of what it takes to work effectively in a multicultural higher education and/or public administration context. Illuminating the experiences and perspectives of these individuals brings a level of authenticity to the findings that guide the development of a practical model designed for effective implementation and further evaluation. In a deliberate effort to highlight practitioner input, supplement our literature review findings, and develop a better understanding of the factors that contribute to the development of cultural competency and effective global leadership, we conducted a qualitative study with experienced higher education professionals who have cross-cultural experience.

Data were collected to explore higher education professionals' practical attitudes and experiences in leading teams through the cultural complexities extant in an international higher education context. Respondents included faculty, higher education administrators, mid-level managers and entry-level staff (a total of 28 participants). A series of open-ended questions were posted to higher education 'communities of practice' via two social media platforms (LinkedIn and Facebook) and data were gathered using the following techniques:

- *Posts and discussions* on both social media platforms.
- *Direct messaging* from participants wishing to address the questions in a more private manner.
- *Follow-up interviews* with 10 of the 28 respondents. All follow-up interviews were conducted in English and nine were conducted asynchronously via Facebook Messenger.

Critical discourse analysis (CDA) was used to analyse the data collected from participants through social media posts and interview transcripts. CDA is a type of analysis that investigates the problem from social, political, and cultural perspectives, allowing the researcher to uncover and understand the hidden ideological assumptions in the text and spoken words (Fairclough, 1993; McGregor, 2004). CDA can be conducted, according to Huckin (1997), in two stages: (a) approaching the text as an ordinary reader attempting to understand its content; and (b) critically revisiting the textual content at different levels to uncover implicit assumptions that may be embedded in it. CDA helped us uncover participants' attitudes, values, beliefs, and hidden assumptions about the multicultural contexts they work in. Follow up interviews revealed participants' different opinions about effective leadership. For example, Participant 1 argues for the importance of creating just and equally engaging learning opportunities where all voices are heard and respected. It also foregrounds a teaching persona where tolerance, forgiveness, support and other teaching characteristics are important:

> Depending on the culture one is working with, a larger-than-life teaching persona (if teaching) is helpful. It's not just about communicating to students; one must actively work to engage them in learning and appearing interesting/engaging is a major asset. [Participant 1]

In contrast, Participant 3 reflects a prejudice and holds a superior attitude toward non-native English speakers viewing them as lazy learners instead of perceiving their request for professional feedback as an opportunity to build mutual collaborative relationship where knowledge and experience are exchanged and further developed:

> One of the struggles I faced working abroad with folks that were not fluent in English and/or comfortable with English professionally meant that they often relied on native English speakers to constantly edit their work... instead of working to improve their language skills. Personally, I had to completely stop helping others in this way. [Participant 3]

Unlike the above negative attitude, Participant 4 shows the value of learning from others and a belief that one's own culture and perspective is neither universal nor applicable to other contexts:

> I wish it was more obvious, but in my experience, those with a US background come in not understanding that their perspective is not shared universally, and without that understanding at the forefront, it makes productive engagement, communication, and mutual understanding so much harder. Especially across those who may not use English as a first language. [Participant 4]

Developing such learning attitude or mindset where one is open to new experiences and knowledge can be achieved through on-going critical reflection, as indicated by participant 1:

> It's easy to assume that, as an outside expert, you will know just what is wanted and how to do it. Until you experience and understand a critical mass of the many subtle cross-cultural dynamics at play, your first responses and reactions will likely be wrong. In a worst-case scenario, these ever-present, but initially hard-to-detect misalignments between cultures, expectations, and procedures could quickly wind up negatively impacting how valuable your skills and abilities are perceived. You need to be constantly thinking about what you're doing and why. [Participant 1]

Finally, participant 6 discusses the importance of learning the local language and how a moderate level of the language can facilitate one's learning and working experience:

> Knowledge of foreign languages always helps. If you don't understand the language, you won't understand the culture, let alone people you work with. [Participant 6]

Applying the CDA on all the 28 responses, we categorised all findings across the four cultural competency dimensions discussed by Getha-Taylor et al. (2020) and Geleta and Amsale (2016) as follows: skill, knowledge, attitude, and behaviour. A summary of these results is presented in Table 1. Our results were consistent with the main factors discussed by management and cross-cultural literature. Participants' explicit and implicit responses fell into the different categories of emotional intelligence, cultural intelligence, and the Big Five personality traits. For example, characteristics such as persistence, negotiation, and patience fall into the social skills aspect of EI. Also, tolerance, forgiveness, humility, and flexibility are part of the agreeable personality trait. Similarly, critical reflection is included within the EI self-awareness component.

Table 1 Critical discourse analysis of emergent themes

Skill	Knowledge	Attitude	Behaviour
Observation	Local language	Patience, Hope	Openness to learning/new experiences
Critical analysis	Cultural norms, values, artifacts, and practices	Flexibility	Listening/considering other perspectives
Problem solving	Work practices	Forgiveness	Engaging others
Negotiation, resilience, adaptability	Cultural knowledge	Tolerance	Slow speech, simple language, visual aids
Emotional intelligence	Cultural knowledge	Perseverance	Critical reflection

Fig. 1 Global cultural leadership competency model

CDA themes that had no equivalent in these three pillars such as observation, listening, critical analysis, and problem solving were grouped together under a 'personal skills' section. Responses that included factors such as overseas living/working experience, finding a cultural mentor, or taking a culture training course were grouped together as external factors. Finally, having hope and resilience, self-efficacy, and learning the local language were categorized together as facilitating factors.

The final step of our research included combining the main findings of the literature review with the themes that emerged from the CDA to build the Global Cultural Leadership Competency (GCLC) Model in Fig. 1.

5 The Global Cultural Leadership Competency (GCLC) Model

The following section presents a practical and flexible framework for the codification, delivery, development, and assessment of its components, and highlights how this framework may be applied in a professional development context. As noted above, several CDA themes emerged from participants' responses that underscore the very practical nature of leadership development within the higher education and public administration contexts. One of the other issues to acknowledge is the fact that most institutions included internationalisation and/or global engagement as part of their mission statements or strategic outcomes. This further supports the development of a framework that lends itself to the practical application of professional development programs across these wide and varied institutions.

A cultural competency model refers to the personality traits, skills, knowledge, attitudes, and behaviours that enable successful adaptation, effective communication and work performance in a multicultural context (Campion et al., 2011; Sieck et al., 2016). This section proposes a Global Cultural Leadership Competency (GCLC) model that has a theoretical and empirical foundation. It is argued here that this model can promote high levels of cultural competency, global mindset, effective global leadership practices, and enhanced organisational performance in higher education and other public administration sectors. The model is developed based on a comprehensive review of management, leadership, and cross-cultural literature in addition to critical discourse analysis of the empirical data collected from interviewing HE professionals, who reflected on their professional and personal experiences with multicultural teams in different cultural contexts. The model aims to provide public administrators with a framework and assessment tool that guides and informs their professional development, career plans, and work practices with multicultural teams. The GCLC model also can serve as a human resources management tool assisting public administration organisations in planning and implementing recruitment and career advancement processes, such as job selection, assignment, training, promotion, and retention by hiring, training, and retaining talented employees who have high potential to perform well in a multicultural context.

The GCLC model presented in Fig. 1 suggests that developing key personality traits such as openness to experience, extraversion, conscientiousness, and agreeableness, coupled with developing one's emotional intelligence, helps individuals achieve higher levels of cultural learning and cultural intelligence. When cultural learning is further supported by (a) a number of facilitating factors, such as having self-efficacy (Bandura, 1977), hope, resilience and moderately competent language; (b) some external factors, such as having overseas experiences, cultural mentorship, and cultural training; and (c) a number of personal skills, such as observation, listening, critical analysis, and creative problem solving, eventually leading to the development of cultural competency and global mindset. This combination of characteristics can be considered a meta-competence that facilitates the development of highly effective global leaders. Finally, we posit that effective global leadership will lead to many positive organisational changes and outcomes, such as improved organisational learning; creating a culture of collaboration, innovation and creativity; enhanced organisational performance; and coherent teams and high-quality public administration services. However, it is important to notice that people may respond differently to such developmental frameworks based on their ability to change and the pre-existing beliefs and attitudes they may have, as noted by Barakat et al. (2019).

The practical implications of the proposed GCLC model can be addressed by higher education and public administrators using the basic steps outlined below. These steps are designed to facilitate the incorporation of the GCLC model into regular institutional practices and highlight the emphasis on learning as a key component of global leadership competency development. In general, institutions need to

Step 1: Develop a clear operational definition for GCLC within the context of their own work ethos and in accordance with their institutional missions and goals;
Step 2: Develop a set of desired learning outcomes based on Step 1;
Step 3: Create strategies to support and enable the mission, goals and learning outcomes;
Step 4: Implement strategies based on the GCLC and the institutional context;
Step 5: Assess the learning outcomes; and
Step 6: Evaluate the impact of the program based on mission, goals, strategies and participant learning outcomes.

Some selected strategies for developing global leadership competencies might include:

- Auditing and revising professional development and other training materials to include multiple cultural perspectives and approaches;
- Including international readings, interactions (via technology), and meaningful international engagement opportunities;
- Allowing time for self-reflection and introspection via institutional surveys and evaluations, as well as personal, self-evaluations and inventories with appropriate follow-up and processing;
- Providing well-structured opportunities for cross-cultural interactions across the organization; and
- Creating physical and virtual spaces where staff can interact informally.

This list is not exhaustive but may be used as a jumping off point for promoting GCLCs within and among HE and public administration organizations.

6   Research Implications

This chapter presents a critical consideration of the competencies needed to develop effective global leaders and presents two key meta-competencies—cultural competence and global mindset—that support a model of effective practice for intercultural leadership learners. The authors suggest careful and purposeful planning and effective global mindset interventions—that include both training and practice—to facilitate transformative professional development opportunities across institutions and organisations. Adding to the suggestions in the section above, the structure and content of global leadership professional preparation programs should focus on developing culturally competent leaders who advocate and strive for social justice, equity, and inclusion within the HE and public administration communities. As the GCLC model suggests, programs need to engage leaders in "ontological and epistemological" debates on the competing worldviews, values, beliefs, and experiences that go beyond "a mere consciousness of diversity and equity issues" allowing leaders to understand the social challenges that minority groups go through to find their way within the society and become proactive change agents who can anticipate and resolve unjust social practices, conflicts, and diversity related issues (Barakat et al., 2019, pp. 4–5).

7   Recommendations and Next Steps

The GCLC model is a first step in promoting and developing the learning and experiential capacities to acquire the meta competencies needed to become impactful global leaders. Developing cultural competence and global mindset requires time, practice, and hands-on experience. Therefore, leadership preparation programs should be supplemented with work experience opportunities in a multicultural context (Barakat et al., 2019) as well as with opportunities for ethnographic study, self-introspection and critical analysis.

The following list highlights next steps to take in order to study further, develop and implement the GCLC model within a HE and public administration context.

(a) Develop and test a cultural competence and global mindset (CCGM) inventory.
(b) Develop and test a heuristic approach to CCGM development that can be applied in context-specific environments.
(c) Continue to develop an evolving set of terms to support, scaffold and sustain CCGM development in a critical intercultural competence context.
(d) Expand further the GCLC model to include beginning, intermediate and advanced-level competencies to promote scaffolded global leadership development
(e) Create learning and/or performance outcomes to guide, assess and evaluate leadership development.
(f) Create a set of rubrics to measure, assess and evaluate learning/performance outcomes at the beginning, intermediate and advanced levels.
(g) Establish outcomes-based professional development programs to support the successful acquisition of GCLCs.

8 Conclusion

This chapter departs from the existing literature on interculturally competent leadership and global mindset research in that it combines a visual model for learning and development with a cognitive mindset practice. The Global Cultural Leadership Competency model outlines the fundamental personal attributes, skills, knowledge and attitudes needed to achieve cultural competency and global mindset, and suggests ideal and practical skills, factors and practices for becoming an effective global leader. This nascent model is a first step in developing impactful and engaging training for globalised leadership and mindset.

Developing cultural competency and global mindset is a life-long learning process. Leaders who are about to start a cross-cultural work assignment can use the GCLC model as a roadmap and developmental tool to assist them in finding their way in the new cultural context. Additionally, leaders who are working with multicultural teams can use the model as an assessment and self-reflective tool that guides and informs their practice and professional development. It is argued here that possessing cultural competence and global mindset will require: (a) a high level of emotional intelligence, especially the empathy and social skills aspects; (b) personality traits of openness to experience, conscientiousness, agreeableness, and extraversion; (c) high self-efficacy, knowledge of local language, hope, and resilience; (d) personal skills of observation, listening, critical analysis, and problem solving; and (e) having a hands on experience by interacting with people from different cultural backgrounds, taking a cultural training course and/or finding a cultural mentor. Future research may expand this process by testing the GCLC model and proposing additional developmental approaches.

It is essential in today's multicultural, international higher education and public administration environments that individuals in leadership positions know how to navigate the perils and pitfalls, serendipity and success of a globalised organisation. Left to chance, the provincial may prevail over the progressive and hinder the overall effectiveness of teams and individuals. The GCLC model proposed here aims to start an ongoing debate on what constitutes cultural competency, global mindset development, and effective global leadership. This chapter further outlines a deliberate and comprehensive approach to developing essential professional meta-competencies that may positively impact an institution's ability to operate effectively in a multicultural context. Without a model, an organisation cannot develop a strategy; and, without a strategy, an institution has no roadmap to follow when running day-to-day operations or pursuing new opportunities. Recognising globalisation as a force for change in nearly all aspects of higher education and public administration, the GCLC model seeks to empower leaders and their teams to engage and thrive.

References

Abramson, N. R., & Moran, R. (2018). *Managing cultural differences* (10th ed.). Routledge. https://doi.org/10.4324/9781315403984

Ang, S., Van Dyne, L., & Koh, C. (2006). Personality correlates of the four-factor model of cultural intelligence. *Group and Organization Management, 31*(1), 100–123. https://doi.org/10.1177/1059601105275267

Ang, S., Van Dyne, L., Koh, C., Ng, K. Y., Templer, K. J., Tay, C., & Chandrasekar, N. A. (2007). Cultural intelligence: Its measurement and effects on cultural judgment and decision making, cultural adaptation and task performance. *Management and Organization Review, 3*(3), 335–371. https://doi.org/10.1111/j.1740-8784.2007.00082.x

Bandura, A. (1977). Self-efficacy: Toward a unifying theory of behavioral change. *Psychological Review, 84*, 191–215. https://doi.org/10.1037/0033-295X.84.2.191

Barakat, M., Reames, E., & Kensler, L. A. (2019). Leadership preparation programs: Preparing culturally competent educational leaders. *Journal of Research on Leadership Education, 14*(3), 212–235. https://doi.org/10.1177/1942775118759070

Barrick, M. R., & Mount, M. K. (1991). The big five personality dimensions and job performance. *Personnel Psychology, 41*, 1–26. https://hdl.handle.net/10520/EJC88938

Berardo, K., & Deardorff, D. (Eds.). (2012). *Building cultural competence: Innovative activities and models*. Stylus.

Bok, D. (2009). *Our underachieving colleges: A candid look at how much students learn and why they should be learning more* (New Edition). Princeton University Press. https://doi.org/10.1515/9781400831333.

Caligiuri, P. M. (2000). The big five personality characteristics as predictors of expatriate's desire to terminate the assignment and supervisor-rated performance. *Personnel Psychology, 53*, 67–88. https://doi.org/10.1111/j.1744-6570.2000.tb00194.x

Campion, M., Fink, A., Ruggeberg, B., Carr, L., Phillips, G., & Odman, R. (2011). Doing competencies well: Best practices in competency modeling. *Personnel Psychology, 64*, 225–262. https://doi.org/10.1111/j.1744-6570.2010.01207.x

Carrizales, T. (2010). Exploring cultural competency within the public affairs curriculum. *Journal of Public Affairs Education, 16*(4), 593–606. https://doi.org/10.1080/15236803.2010.12001616

Carrizales, T., Zahradnik, A., & Silverio, M. (2016). Organizational advocacy of cultural competency initiatives: Lessons for public administration. *Public Administration Quarterly, 40*(1), 126–155. https://www.jstor.org/stable/24772945

Dean, B. P. (2008). *Cultural intelligence in global leadership: A model for developing culturally and nationally diverse teams*. Doctoral dissertation. Regent University. https://www.proquest.com/docview/304713848?pq-origsite=gscholar&fromopenview=true

Deardorff, D. (Ed.). (2009). *The SAGE handbook of intercultural competence*. SAGE.

Deardorff, D., Wit, H., Leask, B., & Charles, H. (Eds.). (2022). *The handbook of international higher education* (2nd ed.). Stylus.

Den Dekker, W. (2016). *Global mindset and cross-cultural behavior: Improving leadership effectiveness*. Palgrave Macmillan.

Derr, C. B., Roussillon, S., & Bournois, F. (Eds.). (2002). *Cross-cultural approaches to leadership development*. Quorum.

Earley, P. C., & Ang, S. (2003). *Cultural intelligence: Individual interactions across cultures*. Stanford University Press.

ElKaleh, E. (2021). Internationalisation models and strategies in higher education: A conceptual model for internationalizing the curriculum. In E. Samier, E. ElKaleh, & W. Hammad (Eds.), *Internationalisation of educational administration and leadership curriculum: Voices and experiences from the peripheries* (pp. 69–88). Emerald.

Fairclough, N. (1993). Critical discourse analysis and the marketization of public discourse: The universities. *Discourse and Society, 4*(2), 133–168. https://doi.org/10.1177/0957926593004002002

Fischer, J., & Wildman, J. (2016). Globally intelligent leadership: Toward an integration of competencies. In J. Wildman, R. Grifith, & B. Armon (Eds.), *Critical issues in cross cultural management* (pp. 15–32). Springer. https://doi.org/10.1007/978-3-319-42166-7

Gabel-Shemueli, R., & Dolan, S. (2011). Do emotions matter? The role of emotional intelligence
   competences in cross-cultural adjustment for international assignment. *Management Research,
   9*(3), 207–229. https://doi.org/10.1108/1536-541111181912

Geleta, A., & Amsale, F. (2016). An assessment of educational Leaders' multicultural competences in Ethiopian public universities. *Online Submission, 12*(10), 387–402. https://eric.
   ed.gov/?id=ED574384

George, J. M., & Zhou, J. (2001). When openness to experience and conscientiousness are related
   to creative behavior: An interactional approach. *Journal of Applied Psychology, 86*, 513–524.
   https://doi.org/10.1037/0021-9010.86.3.513

Getha-Taylor, H., Holmes, M. H., & Moen, J. R. (2020). Evidence-based interventions for cultural
   competency development within public institutions. *Administration & Society, 52*(1), 57–80.
   https://doi.org/10.1177/0095399718764332

Goleman, D. (1998). What makes a leader? *Harvard Business Review, 76*(6), 93–102.

Henson, R. (2016). *Successful global leadership: Frameworks for cross-cultural managers and
   organization.* Palgrave Macmillan.

Herlihy-Mera, J. (2022). A case for multilingual universities. *Inside Higher Education.* Accessed 19
   May 2022. https://www.insidehighered.com/views/2022/05/19/multilingual-university-model-
   brings-benefits-opinion?utm_source=Inside+Higher+Ed&utm_campaign=387e49f96c-
   DNU_2021_COPY_02&utm_medium=email&utm_term=0_1fcbc04421-387e49f96c-
   197367693&mc_cid=387e49f96c&mc_eid=3d711ed74d

House, R., Hanges, P., Javidan, M., Dorfman, P., & Gupta, V. (Eds.). (2004). *Culture, leadership,
   and organizations: The GLOBE study of 62 societies.* Sage.

Huckin, T. (1997). Critical discourse analysis. In T. Miller (Ed.), *Functional approaches to written
   text: Classroom applications* (pp. 78–92). United States Information Agency.

Intersectoral Platform for a Culture of Peace and Non-Violence, Bureau for Strategic Planning.
   (Ed.). (2013). *Intercultural competences: Conceptual and operational framework.* UNESCO.

Jeannet, J. P. (2000). *Managing with a global mindset.* Financial Times Prentice Hall.

Lane, H. W., Maznevski, M. L., DiStefano, J. J., & Dietz, J. (2009). *International management
   behavior: Leading with a global mindset.* Wiley.

Leung, K., Ang, S., & Tan, M. (2014). Intercultural competence. *Annual Review of Organizational
   Psychology and Organizational Behavior, 1*(1), 489–519. https://doi.org/10.1146/
   annurev-orgpsych-031413-091229

Levy, O., Beechler, S., Taylor, S., & Boyacigiller, N. A. (2008). What we talk about when we
   talk about 'global mindset.' managerial cognition in multinational corporations. *Journal of
   International Business Studies, 38*(2), 231–258. https://doi.org/10.1057/palgrave.jibs.8400265

Lillis,M.P.,&Tian,R.G.(2009).Cross-culturalcommunicationandemotionalintelligence.*Marketing
   Intelligence & Planning, 27*(3), 428–438. https://doi.org/10.1108/02634500910955272

Lopez-Littleton, V., & Blessett, B. (2015). A framework for integrating cultural competency into
   the curriculum of public administration programs. *Journal of Public Affairs Education, 21*(4),
   557–574. https://doi.org/10.1080/15236803.2015.12002220

McGregor, S. (2004*). Critical discourse analysis: A primer* [online]. Accessed 30 June 2022.
   http://www.kon.org/archives/forum/15-1/mcgregorcda.html

Mount, M. K., Barrick, M. R., & Stewart, G. L. (1998). Five-factor model of personality and
   performance in jobs involving interpersonal interactions. *Human Performance, 11*, 145–165.
   https://doi.org/10.1080/08959285.1998.9668029

Newman, J., Bhatt, B., & Gutteridge, T. (1978). Determinants of expatriate effectiveness: A
   theoretical and empirical vacuum. *Academy of Management Review, 4*, 655–661. https://doi.
   org/10.5465/ambpp.1976.4975877

Nielsen, R. K. (2018). Managerial practices of strategic global mindset: Forging the connection between individual competence and organizational capability. *Advances in Global Leadership*, 145–172. https://doi.org/10.1108/S1535-120320180000011005

Reynolds, K. (2019). 13 benefits and challenges of cultural diversity in the workplace. *HULT Blogs*. https://www.hult.edu/blog/benefits-challenges-cultural-diversity-workplace/

Rice, M. F. (2007). A post-modern cultural competency framework for public administration and public service delivery. *International Journal of Public Sector Management, 20*(7), 622–637.

Rumbley, L., Altbach, P., Reisberg, L., & Leask, B. (2022). Trends in global higher education and the future of internationalization. In D. Deardorff, H. Wit, B. Leask, & H. Charles (Eds.), *The handbook of international higher education* (2nd ed., pp. 25–44). Stylus.

Shuffler, M., Kramer, W., & Burke, S. (2016). Team leadership: Leadership for today's multicultural virtual, distributed teams. In J. Wildman, R. Grifith, & B. Armon (Eds.), *Critical issues in cross cultural management* (pp. 1–14). Springer. https://doi.org/10.1007/978-3-319-42166-7

Sieck, W., Rasmussen, L., & Duran, J. (2016). Considerations and best practices for developing cultural competency models in applied work domains. In J. Wildman, R. Grifith, & B. Armon (Eds.), *Critical issues in cross cultural management* (pp. 33–52). Springer. https://doi.org/10.1007/978-3-319-42166-7

Smith, R., Moallem, M., & Sherrill, D. (1997). How preservice teachers think about cultural diversity: A closer look at factors which influence their beliefs towards equality. *Educational Foundations, 11*(2), 41–61. https://eric.ed.gov/?id=EJ551351

Wildman, J., Griffith, R., & Armon, B. (Eds.). (2016). *Critical issues in cross cultural management*. Springer. https://doi.org/10.1007/978-3-319-42166-7

Witt, L. A., Burke, L. A., Barrick, M. R., & Mount, M. K. (2002). The interactive effects of conscientiousness and agreeableness on job performance. *Journal of Applied Psychology, 87*, 164–169. https://doi.org/10.1037/0021-9010.87.1.164

Eman S. ElKaleh is the Director of the Academic Support Division at Emirates College for Advanced Education. Before that, she served as a Lecturer and Senior Administrator at Zayed University. Eman worked also as a Lecturer in Management and Leadership at University of Wollongong Dubai. She has a Master's of Business Administration from University of Wollongong and a PhD in Management, Leadership and Policy from the British University in Dubai in association with Birmingham University, UK. Her research interests and publications revolve around leadership from Islamic and cross-cultural perspectives, curriculum development, Indigenous research and teaching leadership from critical and cross-cultural approaches. She serves as a reviewer for a number of international peer-reviewed journals and has been a keynote speaker and guest lecturer at the MENASA NASPA Conferences, Oxford Brookes University, Humboldt University of Berlin and a number of universities in the Middle East. Email: eman.salah2@gmail.com

Courtney Stryker most recently lived in Doha, Qatar and served as a consultant-advisor to the Vice President for Student Affairs at Qatar University. Before moving internationally, she served as both Assistant Dean and then Dean of Students at Montana State University during her twelve years there. Seeking new challenges after a twenty-year career in student affairs in the United States, she accepted a position at the United Arab Emirates University in Al Ain, UAE as Assistant Provost and Dean of Students. She served in similar capacities at Zayed University in Abu Dhabi and Dubai. Courtney has consulted in several countries/regions including Fiji, Oman, Europe, Kazakhstan and Mexico. She is the founding director of the Middle East, North Africa, South Asia (MENASA) Area and National Association of Student Personnel Administrators (NASPA) Board. Email: courtney.stryker@gmail.com

Novice Multilingual Writers Learning to Write and Publish: An Intercultural Perspective

Ismaeil Fazel

Abstract This chapter brings to the fore the common intercultural complexities and challenges facing novice multilingual scholars in the high-stakes genre of writing for scholarly publication in English. Framed within the concept of intercultural competence (Deardorff, 2006). *Journal of Studies in International Education*, the chapter draws on relevant autoethnographic and empirical data to foreground the intercultural issues and complexities in navigating interactions inherent to the process of writing for scholarly publication. The thrust of the chapter is to demonstrate the importance of intercultural competence and literacy in writing for scholarly publication. Findings overall highlight the need for support and training of novice scholars in terms of intercultural knowledge, skills and attitudes needed to deal with the complexities of the power-infused intercultural interactions with gatekeepers of publication (i.e., editors and anonymous peer reviewers). Key areas of difficulty which emerged from the study include the challenge of handling the socio-pragmatic and interpretive aspects of peer review. The chapter concludes by offering pedagogical suggestions as to how intercultural competence and awareness can be cultivated amongst novice multilingual scholars in graduate education and writing-for-publication training.

Keywords Multilingualism · Novice scholars · Writing for publication · Intercultural competence · Academic communication

I. Fazel (✉)
University of British Columbia, Vantage College, Vancouver, BC, Canada
e-mail: ismaeil.fazel@ubc.ca

© The Author(s), under exclusive license to Springer Nature
Switzerland AG 2023
A. Sahlane, R. Pritchard (eds.), *English as an International Language
Education*, English Language Education 33,
https://doi.org/10.1007/978-3-031-34702-3_16

1   Introduction

The pervasiveness of the pressure to publish in the current neoliberal academia has extended beyond faculty to include graduate, especially doctoral, students. As apprentices in academia (Belcher, 1994; Hyland, 2009), graduate students are increasingly expected or compelled to engage with writing for scholarly publication early on to enhance their chances of employment in today's increasingly competitive job market (Aitchison et al., 2010; Casanave, 2014; Kwan, 2010; see Habibie & Hyland, 2019 for a detailed discussion).

However, getting published is arguably no easy task even for experienced academics, let alone for those new to the fraught and complex terrain of academic publication. While writing for scholarly publication can be challenging for all novice academic writers, including those speaking English as their first language (L1), it can conceivably be even more challenging for those using English as a second language (L2) (e.g., Curry & Lillis, 2017, 2019; Flowerdew, 2015, among others). Attempting to achieve academic publication can be particularly challenging and burdensome during graduate studies, while dealing with graduate coursework and thesis writing.

Learning how to publish academically in English involves not only knowing how to rhetorically compose a scholarly text, but also – equally if not more importantly – learning how to manage the intricate intercultural interactions with gatekeepers of scholarly publication (i.e., editors and peer reviewers), which can be particularly daunting and challenging for novice L2 scholars.

This chapter aims to bring to the fore the intercultural issues and challenges facing multilingual graduate students, as novice scholars, in the process of scholarly publication in English. The chapter begins by providing an overview of the relevant literature and the conceptual framework used to analyse and interpret the findings. It will then describe the study and present the findings and discussion. The chapter will conclude by offering pedagogical suggestions as to the possible ways in which intercultural competence can be cultivated amongst novice multilingual scholars in graduate education and writing-for-publication training.

2   Background to the Study

In response to the widespread pressure on scholars the world over to publish in English-medium scholarly venues, a considerable body of research in English for Academic Purposes (EAP) has investigated issues and challenges facing multilingual scholars in writing for publication. Burgeoning research and scholarship in this area – now categorised under English for Research Publication Purposes (ERPP) as an emerging sub-field of EAP (Cargill & Burgess, 2008) – has highlighted several major discursive challenges, an important one being deviation from the standard (i.e., Anglophone) rhetorical and stylistic conventions of English, as the *de facto* language of academic publication (e.g., Connor, 2011; Englander, 2006; Mur-Dueñas, 2011). Research in this area has been mainly influenced by Intercultural Rhetoric – formerly called Contrastive Analysis – which is conceptualized as "the study of written discourse between and among individuals with different cultural backgrounds" (Connor, 2011, p.1).

Research in this vein tends to use the methodology of Corpus Linguistics to compare academic texts written by non-Anglophone writers with similar texts written by Anglophone writers, with a view to illuminating discursive and rhetorical challenges in academic writing for non-Anglophone scholars from a variety of linguistic and cultural backgrounds, or linguacultures (Risager, 2006).

This strand of corpus-based contrastive research has made cross-comparisons between Anglophone and non-Anglophone writing conventions and rhetorical features of academic genres (especially research articles and research article abstracts). These studies have, for example, analysed the rhetorical and discursive features of published research articles in Chinese versus English (e.g., Loi, 2010; Loi & Evans, 2010); Spanish versus English (e.g., Burgess, 2002; Moreno, 2004; Mur-Dueñas, 2007, 2011), among many other comparative studies (see Mur-Dueñas & Šinkūnienė, 2018, for a full review).

These studies have shown that texts written by non-Anglophone writers may, for example, lack the necessary rhetorical moves (e.g., Dontcheva-Navratilova, 2016; Hu & Wang, 2014) or critical stance (e.g., Martín-Martín & Burgess, 2004; Salager-Meyer et al., 2003), which are typical features of research articles written by Anglophone authors. These cross-cultural, text-based studies have served to shed valuable light on the issues and challenges facing non-Anglophone scholars when writing for publication in English. Importantly, they have provided useful insights into "potential transfer of differing rhetorical and discursive conventions" from first language (L1) to English texts written by non-Anglophone scholars for international publication (Mur-Dueñas, 2018, p. 278). The findings of such contrastive studies have in turn informed pedagogical interventions in ERPP. Nonetheless, the main caveat with this contrastive approach (intercultural rhetorical), according to Hyland (2018), is that it "runs the risk of static and reductive over-generalisations about cultures, disciplines or genres" (p. ix).

Another limitation with these contrastive, text-based studies is their predominant focus on the analysis of published texts. Often neglected in this line of research is the process leading up to the production and eventual publication of texts. In the often-lengthy process of academic publication, texts are more often than not subject to revision and modification to one degree or another by different mediators – called "literacy brokers" (Lillis & Curry, 2006) or "shapers" (Burrough-Boenisch, 2003) – involved in the process of the production of the final text. Very often it is the case that "literacy brokers" (Lillis & Curry, 2006) suggest changes so that texts approximate the expected prevailing Anglophone rhetorical norms or standards.

Overall, there appear to be multiple gaps in intercultural research on writing for scholarly publication. In terms of theoretical lens, the extant research in this area has been heavily influenced by (contrastive) intercultural rhetoric, which – while not without value – has been amply and extensively researched. In the past few decades, several informative and noteworthy theoretical models and perspectives have emerged, especially in the field of intercultural communication, which can be taken up and explored by research in this area. Furthermore, only few studies (e.g., Mur-Dueñas, 2012, 2013) have attended to the process of getting academically published from an intercultural perspective. There is also a clear paucity of process-oriented research that seeks to understand the intercultural challenges facing multilingual, especially novice, scholars (including early-career academics and doctoral students) in steering the process of writing to publish academically. Particularly useful would be research on the complex communicative interactions and negotiations with editors and reviewers, from an intercultural perspective.

Given these gaps in interculturally-oriented research on academic publication, the study reported in this chapter aims to explore and discuss the intercultural issues and challenges facing novice multilingual scholars in the process of scholarly publication in English.

3 Conceptual Framework

In this chapter Deardorff's (2006) model of intercultural competence will be utilised, as a conceptual lens, to better understand and interpret the intercultural experiences and challenges of the multilingual graduate students, as novice scholars, in the study. Before proceeding to discuss the conceptual model, a brief explanation of the concept of culture is warranted. The notion of culture was traditionally conceived as being fixed, discrete and often equated with national or ethnic entities, largely influenced by anthropological perspectives. However, over time, and in light of postmodern and post structural influences, culture as a concept has evolved from an essentialist view (culture as nationality) to a more dynamic and complex view, which includes shared values, practices and interests of social groupings "within and across national boundaries" (Kramsch, 2002, p. 276).

Of relevance here is Holliday's (1999) oft-cited distinction between 'large culture' and 'small culture', which has been influential in intercultural research. Holliday proposed the term 'small culture' in contrast to the more traditional 'large culture' – national, ethnic, geographical and other entities. Small culture, as conceived by Holliday (1999), characterizes "small social groupings or activities wherever there is cohesive behaviour" (p. 237). Small cultures are grounded in routinized activities, discourses and practices associated with social groups. Such small cultures could be a wide variety of social groupings ranging from academic (e.g., classroom culture) to professional (e.g., workplace), to other social and community-based groups (e.g., youth culture). Viewed within this lens, "the discourse community is a small culture" (p. 252). Holliday (1999) argues that a large-culture approach cannot account for complexities of intercultural interactions in an increasingly global context. From his perspective, the small culture approach "is most appropriate for a world which is increasingly multi-cultural at every level." (p. 260) The shifting conceptualisations of the notion of culture have clearly had important implications for intercultural research and scholarship.

In what follows, the notion of intercultural competence and Deardorff's (2006) model of intercultural competence development will be laid out.

3.1   Intercultural Competence

Since its inception a few decades ago, the term 'intercultural competence' has been subject to different interpretations and evolving definitions, reflecting the paradigm shift from essentialist to constructivist and critical perspectives, due in large part to the shifting views of the concept of culture (See Rings & Rasinger, 2020 for a detailed discussion).

Various definitions have been proposed in the literature to delineate the concept of intercultural competence (e.g., Deardorff, 2006, 2009; Fantini, 2009; Spitzberg & Changnon, 2009, among others). Intercultural competence has been broadly defined as "complex abilities that are required to perform effectively and appropriately when interacting with others who are linguistically and culturally different from oneself" (Fantini, 2009, p. 458). Intercultural competence has also been defined as "the appropriate and effective management of interaction between people who … represent different or divergent affective, cognitive, and behavioural orientations to the world" (Spitzberg & Changnon, 2009, p. 7).

Two key aspects highlighted in the oft-cited definitions of intercultural competence are effectiveness – being able to achieve one's communicative purpose in a given interactional exchange – and appropriateness – interacting successfully in a manner that is mutually acceptable to the involved parties (Arasaratnam-Smith, 2017).

Intercultural competence as conceptualised by Deardorff (2006) refers to "the ability to communicate effectively and appropriately in intercultural situations based on one's intercultural knowledge, skills, and attitudes" (p. 247). Importantly, Deardorff (2006) notes that, "just as culture is ever changing, scholars' opinions on intercultural competence change with time" (p. 258), which premises a fluid and dynamic view of culture.

3.2   The Process Model of Intercultural Competence

Deardorff's (2006) model has been arguably one of the most influential models in research on intercultural competence development in recent years. Based on the consensus of leading intercultural experts, Deardorff (2006) proposed a dynamic model of intercultural competence development that identifies the fundamental attributes (attitudes, knowledge, and skills) which can be conducive to desired internal and external outcomes in intercultural situations. The components and sub-components comprising the composite construct of intercultural competence in this model (Deardorff, 2006, pp. 247–248) are as follows:

- *Attitudes*
- Fundamental to the model are the intercultural attitudes, which include respect (toward other cultures), openness (to intercultural learning and cultural differences), as well as curiosity (tolerance of uncertainty and ambiguity).
- *Knowledge*
- Intercultural knowledge refers to cultural self-awareness, culture-specific knowledge, and sociolinguistic awareness needed for communication across cultural boundaries.
- *Skills*
- Intercultural skills include listening, observation and interpretation of cultural differences, and analysis, evaluation and relation to culturally different others. The two components of knowledge and skills in Deardorff's (2006) model interact and are interrelated in the sense that they influence, reinforce, and supplement each other.
- *Internal outcome*
- Desired internal outcome refers to shift in one's frame of reference, which includes empathy, adaptability (to different behaviours and communication styles), flexibility (flexible selection and use of appropriate communication styles and behaviours; cognitive flexibility). In essence, the internal outcome is the ability to adapt to various cultural contexts and to flexibly use appropriate communication styles to treat culturally different others' worldviews and values with equal empathy to their own.
- *External outcome*
- The desired external outcome would be behaving and communicating effectively and appropriately in intercultural situations. The model posits that the extent to which individuals can communicate appropriately and effectively in intercultural environments is predicated on how far they have acquired the underlying elements (attitudes, knowledge, skills). In Deardorff's (2006) model, intercultural competence progressively advances from an individual plane (i.e., attitudes, knowledge, and skills) to an interactive plane of external outcome.

For Deardorff (2006, 2009), intercultural competence development is a lifelong and ongoing process; it is not a one-off act of acquisition or achievement but rather a continuous journey and trajectory of 'becoming' and 'being' across time and cultural space. Moreover, and crucially, Deardorff (2009) notes that intercultural experience per se does not necessarily lead to the development of intercultural competence. Rather, intercultural competence needs to be cultivated deliberately "through adequate preparation, substantive intercultural interactions, and relationship building" (p. xiii).

In this chapter, I extend Deardorff's (2006) model of intercultural competence to the realm of scholarly publication to explore intercultural issues and challenges experienced by a group of multilingual graduate students, as novice academics, in the process of writing for scholarly publication. I should note that I also reflectively analyse my own relevant experiences with academic publishing when doing my doctorate. It is important to note that, given the limitations of the available data, I only focus on the three foundational components (knowledge, skills and attitudes) of intercultural competence as laid out in Deardorff's (2006) intercultural competence framework.

4 The Study

The research question guiding this chapter is: What intercultural issues and challenges do multilingual graduate students, as novice scholars, encounter in the process of getting published in English-medium scholarly venues? This research question has been adapted and modified from a larger qualitative, 16-month, multiple case study which explored the writing for publication practices and experiences of graduate students – both multilingual and Anglophone – in language and literacy education at a Canadian research-intensive university.

The inclusion criteria, in the larger study, required the participants to (a) be enrolled as full-time graduate students in a Canadian university, (b) have had prior (successful or otherwise) experience with writing for scholarly publication in English (journal articles, book chapters, books, book reviews), and (c) intend to write for publication within the time span of the study—16 months from the commencement of the study. The larger project recruited four Anglophone, two bilingual, and nine EAL doctoral students as well as three EAL Master's students, all of whom met the inclusion criteria. Participation in the study was on a voluntary basis, and informed consent, in accordance with the institutional ethics policy, was sought prior to data collection. For the purposes of this chapter, however, I draw on data and relevant examples from four multilingual – two doctoral and two Master's – graduate students in the study to address the aforementioned research question.

To preserve confidentiality, the participants' countries of origin have not been specified; instead, the broader geographical regions where their countries are located have been indicated. In addition, other potential identifiers including the participants' year of study in the program and age – have also been excluded to help protect the participants' identities. All the names used in this study are pseudonyms.

It is worth noting that, as graduate students in language and literacy education, all participants had a decent command of English language skills and proficiency, and had served as language teachers in their home countries. Thus, the participants in this study comprised a somewhat unique sample. Also, all participants had some experience with academic publication in English, prior to their participation in the study. Before proceeding further, and in order to better interpret the findings and salient themes, a brief description of the selected participants is warranted.

4.1 Participants

The selected doctoral students were Sam (Male from Latin America) and Yelena (Female from East Europe), and the Master's students in the study were Mohammad (Male from the Middle East) and Cho (Female from East Asia). I should note that henceforth the letters "M" (male) and "F" (female) will be used after the participants' names to specify gender. As earlier noted, all participants had published academically in English prior to the study. Sam (M) had previously co-authored three journal articles, a book chapter, and two conference proceedings. Yelena (F) had published a conference proceeding paper prior to study. Mohammad (M) had co-authored an educational book on English for academic purposes in his home country, prior to starting his Master's program, and Cho (F) had published a co-authored journal article in her first language, prior to the commencement of her Master's studies.

As noted earlier, where relevant, I will also refer to my own first-hand experiences and observations in scholarly publishing, particularly during my doctoral studies. I should note that I am a naturalized citizen of Canada, originally from Iran (born and raised), and I speak Persian (Farsi) as my first language and English as an additional language.

4.2 Data Collection and Analysis

In this 16-month, qualitative, multiple case study, data were collected through questionnaires, multiple semi-structured interviews, submission trajectories, emails and communications with journal editors and reviewers. The data used here, though, are mainly from the interviews conducted with the selected participants in the study. Over the course of the study (16 months), multiple one-on-one, semi-structured interviews were conducted with each participant – Yelena and Cho (three interviews each) and Sam and Mohammad (four and five interviews respectively). Duration of the interviews ranged from 20 to 60 minutes; the first and final interviews with each participant were longer. The collected data were then subject to iterative thematic analysis (Clarke & Braun, 2014) to identify salient themes and patterns relevant to the research question.

5 Findings and Discussion

In what follows, drawing on the process model of intercultural competence (Deardorff, 2006), the participants' intercultural experiences and challenges in writing for publication are presented and discussed under respective sub-headings corresponding to the intercultural attitudes, knowledge, and skills, as the foundational elements of intercultural competence (Deardorff, 2006).

5.1 Intercultural Attitudes

Based upon Deardorff's (2006) theoretical framework, attitudes constitute a fundamental part of intercultural competence; this in practice means being respectful, open-minded, and unbiased toward other cultural and linguistic groups. The findings indicated that while all participants expressed positive attitudes towards other cultures, they showed a biased preference for native-speakerism and its associated cultural capital, as illustrated in the quote by Mohammad (M), who said, "they [native speakers] have not just the language but … they also have the upper hand culturally, I mean." The presumed superiority of the cultural and linguistic capital of the native speakers can also be seen in the quote below by Cho (F), who had experienced co-authoring a journal article with her Anglophone peer; she remarked:

> native speakers have a huge advantage … throughout the publication journey, pre-submission and post-submission. Pre-submission in the sense that first language writers know better about the conventions, about the academic writing in their own language and in the post-submission area in the negotiation stage, L1 writers they have more cultural capital to negotiate with people from their own culture.

Encapsulated in the quote above is the presumed superiority of "the cultural capital" of the native speaker. Moreover, and surprisingly, the findings suggested that this presupposition was not just confined to the novice multilingual scholars in the study. "Non-English evident" was the verbatim phrase in a peer review report that Sam (M), a doctoral student in the study, received after having submitted his first sole-authored manuscript to a reputable journal in the field. The above-mentioned comment quite clearly indicates the peer reviewer's subscription to "the ideology of native-speakerism" (Holliday, 2015, p. 12).

My contention is that the uncritical presumption of the superiority of "the embodied linguistic/cultural capital of the native speaker" (Pennycook, 2001, p. 154) is counterproductive and antithetical to the ethos and spirit of interculturalism (Short, 2009), which advocates for inclusivity and diversity. Rather than uncritically valorise the cultural and linguistic capital of the native speaker, it would be productive to adopt the more apt notion of competent "intercultural speaker" (Byram, 1997, 2008, 2021), which was proposed as a viable alternative to the almost unattainable native speaker ideal (Boye & Byram, 2017; Wilkinson, 2012). A competent intercultural speaker transcends the specific cultural and linguistic boundaries and is able to "navigate and negotiate the space between languages and cultures that opens whenever communication takes place between speakers of different linguistic and/or cultural backgrounds" (Wilkinson, 2020, p. 286). Such a perspective, I would argue, is more compatible with and conducive to interculturalism and the development of intercultural competence.

Reflecting on my own experiences of publishing during the doctorate, much like the participants in the study, I too initially considered myself to be at a linguistic disadvantage vis-à-vis my so called 'native speaker' peers, but over time, as I progressed further in my doctoral studies, I revisited and revised my initial uncritical acceptance of the linguistic "disadvantage orthodoxy" (Hyland, 2019, p. 27), which I have discussed elsewhere in more detail (Fazel, 2021).

5.2   Intercultural Knowledge

The knowledge component of the intercultural competence model by Deardorff (2006) includes a deep understanding of one's own culture and beliefs and those of others as well as sociolinguistic awareness of communication etiquettes (including unwritten norms and conventions) in different cultures including theirs, which is particularly pertinent to communications and intercultural interactions between novice writers and journal editors and peer reviewers in the process of writing for publication.

The findings indicated an understanding among the participants that language and culture are inextricably linked, and that translation is not always the way to convey the meaning of a word or phrase, as illustrated in the quote below by one of the participants (Sam):

> I cannot translate like I mean it would be really easy if I could just translate … my native language to English but that's not the way it works. I mean there are many nuances and things that have to do with culture, things like that … for example literacy. We don't have a word for literacy, we just don't … in … [his first language] … the idea of literacy as a social practice is really hard to grasp because we don't have a word for that term.

The quote above represents an awareness that some concepts may exist in one language but not in another, and that language is bound up with and embedded in culture in a complex way. As noted earlier, intercultural knowledge also implies an awareness of the sociolinguistic aspects of communication in different cultures. In this regard, the participants were overall aware of the importance and influence of sociocultural factors in communication in general and in scholarly communication in particular; nevertheless, they were not confident in their grasp of the socio-pragmatic aspects of communications and negotiations in the process of academic publishing. On a relevant note, Sam (M), despite being proficient in English, enlisted the help of Anglophone "literacy brokers" (Lillis & Curry, 2006), professional paid editors, both in the pre- and the post-submission phases of writing for publication. When asked why he would seek help from Anglophone copy editors even in response to peer review reports, he remarked:

> It's not just the language, grammar or vocabulary, … what I may see as polite disagreement may be seen as disrespect by them [reviewers], so I am not sure. I do not wanna step on their toes unintentionally, you know what I mean?

In the quote above, Sam (M) is concerned about miscommunication in responding to the peer reviewers. He is in particular unsure as to the socio-pragmatic nuances of expressing disagreement with peer reviewers in English, which is understandable given that "pragmatic norms vary across languages and cultures or even within a single language, language variety, or culture" (Ishihara & Cohen, 2022, p. 2).

Thinking back to my own experiences with publication endeavours during doctoral years, I can attest to the challenge of responding to reviewers, especially where it involved objection or rebuttal of an argument. Quite clearly, arguing against or disagreeing with peer review comments, which decide the fate of the publication, is no easy task, especially for a novice multilingual writer. Part of the challenge, as noted above, lies in the pragmatic complexities of communication, which can be "even more challenging in intercultural communication, where all interactants may not rely on the same cultural literacy" (Ishihara & Cohen, 2022, p. 1).

Effective intercultural communication, in part, necessitates a pragmatic awareness of the socially and culturally preferred language (Bardovi-Harlig, 2019, 2020). Attaining the pragmatic knowledge in an additional language is of paramount importance in that it is key to intercultural interactions, particularly when it comes to writing for publication, which inherently and consequentially involves engagement with gatekeepers of scholarly publication.

5.3   Intercultural Skills

The intercultural skills noted by Deardorff (2006) include the prowess and ability to listen, observe, interpret, analyse, evaluate, and relate to intercultural communicative events and experiences. An interculturally competent individual needs to possess and apply these interpretive, analytical and evaluative skills so as to successfully grapple with intercultural interactions and encounters. These skills are directly essential to writing for publication, particularly when it comes to the interpretation of comments and feedback in peer review reports, an "occluded genre" (Swales, 1990, 1996), which is generally hidden from public view, yet crucially important in academic publication.

A salient theme indicated by the findings was the differential perceptions of peer review feedback on the part of the participants. Interestingly, there appeared to be differences among the participants in terms of their perception of the harshness and directness in the peer review feedback. For example, Cho (F), a participant coming from an East Asian country, was demonstrably shocked and offended to have received harsh and critical feedback on her submitted article, which had received a revise-and-resubmit verdict. Sharing her perception of the feedback she had received, and while trying to control her emotions, she remarked, "it is so impersonal, just like 'hello, correct this and that', … so abrupt, direct and inconsiderate, you know…, even rude where I come from." Interestingly, a somewhat similar scenario happened to Yelena (F), another participant in the study from an East European country; that is, she too received impersonal and critical feedback on a submitted (conference proceedings) paper, which similarly received a revise-and-resubmit decision. Strikingly, however, Yelena (F) had a notably different perception and reaction to the critical and impersonal feedback. Commenting on the feedback received, she said:

> the response was so impersonal and abrupt, yes. I guess for me it's cultural in a way, ... I was not really offended by the impersonal, how impersonal and direct it was you know ... I think like in my country people don't sugar up things. They say 'wonderful, your grammar is wrong and nothing that you just said made sense please try again' ... More frank and quite often I do the same just because I am socialized into this way of thinking and talking, ... like we never start our feedback with I like the way you did this and I like the way you did that because if you like somebody or something you don't comment on it. If it's not good, why should you say that it's good? So, we only focus on the bad, something that can be improved.

The quotes above show the different perceptions between the participants regarding harshness and directness of feedback. It is worth acknowledging that Yelena's reaction to the peer review feedback seems to be culturally determined, likely influenced by the prevailing zeitgeist of socialism in her country. Cho's response, on the other hand, might be somewhat personal in nature rather than being necessarily determined by her sociocultural background.

On a relevant note, another source of confusion for the participants in the study was interpretation of feedback comments by peer reviewers, as shown in the following anecdote that happened to Mohammad (M). He had written a review of an influential book as an assignment in one of his graduate courses, and he had received an A for the assignment. Encouraged by his supervisor's positive feedback, he had decided to send his review to a reputable journal in the field for publication. This was in fact his first attempt at publishing in a scholarly journal. Based on his supervisor's glowing feedback, he expected an easy road to publication. Contrary to his expectations, though, the feedback he received from the editor and peer reviewers was unexpectedly harsh, critical, and confusing to him. He had been particularly critiqued for his use of "flowery language" and lack of critical engagement with the book he had reviewed, which he found both demoralising and rather confusing. When I asked him in the interview about his perception of the feedback he had received, he commented:

> I do not understand what they mean. This is how I write. I wanted to write beautifully and elegantly. There is nothing grammatically wrong or in terms of words. I like to write beautifully. What is wrong with that? I have written this way before, and my profs did not say anything against it... I am a huge fan of literature, both in .... [his first language] ... and in English. I studied literature before [in his bachelor's program]. Also, where I come from writing in a literary style is considered elegant. What's wrong with that? I do not understand.

Regarding his lack of critical stance in the book review, he remarked: "the authors of the book are authorities, big wigs in the field ... I know how to criticise, but I am generally not used to challenging or criticising authority...that's part of my upbringing you know". As illustrated in the above quotes, Mohammad (M) found it hard to challenge and critique the authority figures in the field due to his "upbringing" and his socio-cultural background.

It is also interesting to note that he attributes his style of writing to his interest in literature both in his first language and in English. The journal editor and peer reviewers though seemed to prefer a more conventional style of writing for publication. It is worth pointing out that Mohammad's initial decision was not to pursue the publication any longer; however, after having consulted his more experienced peers in the department who had already published book reviews, he changed his mind. Eventually, after revising and resubmitting the book review based on the feedback from peer reviewers, and after another round of minor revisions, he got published. Salient here is the supportive role of Mohammad's peers in the department. Turning again to my own experiences of publishing during the doctoral years, I can attest to the key role of peer learning and support, which helped me deal with the critical engagements in peer review (Fazel, 2021).

It is worth noting that, notwithstanding the challenges in the process, all participants managed to publish academically during the study period. Within the study period, Sam (M) managed to publish two sole-authored journal articles and a co-authored conference proceedings volume with his supervisor. Yelena (F) published a book review and co-authored two journal articles with an Anglophone peer of hers in the department. Mohammad (M) successfully published two sole-authored book reviews in scholarly journals, and Cho (F) managed to co-author a conference proceedings paper and a journal article in collaboration with her Anglophone peer who was also doing her Master's degree in the department.

6   Conclusion

The overarching aim of this study was to explore the intercultural challenges facing multilingual graduate students, as novice academics, in the process of writing for scholarly publication. Deardorff's (2006) model of intercultural competence was used as a conceptual lens to interpret the participants' intercultural attitudes, knowledge, and skills – affective and cognitive domains – in the process of writing for academic publication. Developing these foundational affective and cognitive attributes, according to Deardorff (2006), is a key precursor to the attainment of the desired (internal and external) behavioural outcomes in intercultural communication with other culturally different interactants – which, as mentioned earlier, lies beyond the scope of the present study.

By and large, the findings indicated challenges mainly stemming from the domains of intercultural knowledge and skills. More specifically, the findings showed that the participants struggled to one degree or another with the intercultural interactions in the high-stakes peer review process. Two specific challenges underlying this struggle were identified to be difficulty in interpreting and unpacking the peer review feedback as well as the sociopragmatic aspect of engaging with and responding to peer reviewers.

Quite clearly, successful navigation of the process of academic publishing demands, among other things, the sensibility of knowing how to skilfully communicate and negotiate with the publication gatekeepers – i.e., journal editors and reviewers – and, where possible and apropos, disagree with or argue against their comments and positions in peer review reports – which requires one to know how to interpret peer review reports as well as manifest an adept awareness of socio-pragmatic nuances and complexities inherent in any power-infused negotiation.

Particularly of note is that the participants all received some sort of support in the process of scholarly publication, particularly when faced with intercultural challenges. Cho (F) and Yelena (F) managed to publish in collaboration with their Anglophone peers. It is worth remembering that Mohammad (M) also received support and guidance from his departmental peers in his publication endeavour, and Sam (M) enlisted the help of professional editors – literacy brokers (Lillis & Curry, 2006) – in his publication attempts. The findings highlight the importance of the mediating role of literacy brokers (Lillis & Curry, 2006) and academic mentors in supporting the participants in their publication endeavours – which has implications for ERPP pedagogy and graduate student education.

The burgeoning global spread of English and emergence of varieties of English in diverse settings has led to increasing calls in the scholarly community (e.g., Hynninen & Kuteeva, 2017; Kuteeva & Mauranen, 2014) for more tolerance and variation in English scholarly communication and publication. The fact remains though that the so-called "standard" English continues to be the default frame of reference in scholarly journals (Flowerdew & Habibie, 2022). In fact, research on the role played by academic mediators and literacy brokers in scholarly publication has revealed "a strong incentive" on the part of brokers and even authors to "follow Standard English correctness norms" (Hynninen, 2020, p. 20).

The findings also point to the need for further support and scaffolding in intercultural competence training of novice scholars, including graduate (especially doctoral) students and early-career scholars. I would argue that such training needs to be discipline-specific and tailored to meet the varying needs of novice authors within discourse communities. Experts in ERPP and intercultural rhetoric can help identify the common conventions of disciplinary discourse communities and also their members' tolerance for variation from the 'standard' English. Understandably, it is not easy for novices to know how much leeway from the norms (including standard English) is allowed in a given disciplinary discourse community. It is immensely and consequentially important for novice scholars to learn how to skilfully yet appropriately communicate – and, where necessary, negotiate or disagree – in their intercultural communications with the publication gatekeepers (i.e., journal editors and reviewers).

It is crucial to note though that intercultural experience per se, as rightly noted by Deardorff (2009), does not necessarily or automatically lead to the development of intercultural competence. Rather, intercultural competence needs to be cultivated deliberately "through adequate preparation, substantive intercultural interactions, and relationship building" (p. xiii).

Given the key role of intercultural competence (knowledge, skills, and attitudes) in handling intercultural communication in the process of writing for publication, ERPP initiatives and pedagogical programs need to embed intercultural competence training as an integral part of their curriculum. Equipped with these sensibilities, novices would be better poised and prepared to handle the intercultural exchanges and encounters inherent in the process of scholarly publication and communication. I would argue that intercultural competence training should also be embedded into the graduate, especially doctoral, education curriculum, given the burgeoning importance of intercultural competence not only in scholarly publication but also in navigating communications in today's increasingly connected world, where there are endless opportunities for scholars to interact in a variety of modes and milieus.

On a different level, I would argue that journals too need to consider offering intercultural training aimed at peer reviewers with a focus on intercultural dimensions of peer review reports, such that they would be more mindful of intercultural considerations in their feedback provision. These intercultural exchanges, if used appropriately and mindfully, can serve as opportunities for intercultural training of novices, both multilingual and Anglophone writers wishing to enter their academic discourse communities.

The limited scope of the data available for the purposes of this chapter did not allow for an analysis of the internal and external outcomes of intercultural communication, as conceptualised in Deardorff's (2006) framework. A proper assessment of these interactional and relational aspects (internal and external intercultural outcomes) would require extensive and in-depth relevant data on the intricate intercultural interactions and exchanges taking place between the key interactants (i.e., journal editors, peer reviewers, academic mentors, etc.) involved in the process of scholarly publication, which future research in this vein should investigate.

References

Aitchison, C., Kamler, B., & Lee, A. (Eds.). (2010). *Publishing pedagogies for the doctorate and beyond*. Routledge. https://doi.org/10.4324/9780203860960

Arasaratnam-Smith, L. A. (2017). Intercultural competence: An overview. In D. K. Deardorff & L. A. Arasaratnam-Smith (Eds.), *Intercultural competence in higher education* (pp. 7–18). Routledge. https://doi.org/10.4324/9781315529257

Bardovi-Harlig, K. (2019). Routines in L2 pragmatics research. In N. Taguchi (Ed.), *The Routledge handbook of second language acquisition and pragmatics* (pp. 47–62). Routledge. https://doi.org/10.4324/9781351164085

Bardovi-Harlig, K. (2020). Pedagogical linguistics: A view from L2 pragmatics. *Pedagogical Linguistics, 1*(1), 44–65. https://doi.org/10.1075/pl.19013.bar

Belcher, D. (1994). The apprenticeship approach to advanced academic literacy: Graduate students and their mentors. *English for Specific Purposes, 13*(1), 23–34. https://doi.org/10.1016/0889-4906(94)90022-1

Boye, S., & Byram, M. (2017). Language awareness and the acquisition of intercultural communicative competence. In P. Garrett & J. M. Cots (Eds.), *The Routledge handbook of language awareness* (pp. 435–449). Routledge. https://doi.org/10.4324/9781315676494-27

Burgess, S. (2002). Packed houses and intimate gatherings: Audience and rhetorical strategies. In J. Flowerdew (Ed.), *Academic discourse* (pp. 196–225). Longman. https://doi.org/10.4324/9781315838069

Burrough-Boenisch, J. (2003). Shapers of published NNS research articles. *Journal of Second Language Writing, 12*(3), 223–243. https://doi.org/10.1016/s1060-3743(03)00037-7

Byram, M. (1997). *Teaching and assessing intercultural communication competence.* Multilingual Matters.

Byram, M. (2008). *From foreign language education to education for intercultural citizenship.* Multilingual Matters. https://doi.org/10.21832/9781847690807

Byram, M. (2021). *Teaching and assessing intercultural communicative competence: Revisited* (2nd ed.). Multilingual Matters. https://doi.org/10.21832/9781800410251

Cargill, M., & Burgess, S. (2008). Introduction to the special issue: English for research publication purposes. *Journal of English for Academic Purposes, 7*(2), 75–76. https://doi.org/10.1016/j.jeap.2008.02.006

Casanave, C. P. (2014). *Before the dissertation: A textual mentor for doctoral students at early stages of a research project.* University of Michigan Press. https://doi.org/10.3998/mpub.7111486

Clarke, V., & Braun, V. (2014). Thematic analysis. In T. Teo (Ed.), *Encyclopedia of critical psychology* (pp. 1947–1952). Springer. https://doi.org/10.1007/978-1-4614-5583-7

Connor, U. (2011). *Intercultural rhetoric in the writing classroom.* University of Michigan Press. https://doi.org/10.3998/mpub.3488851

Curry, M. J., & Lillis, T. (Eds.). (2017). *Global academic publishing: Policies, perspectives and pedagogies.* Multilingual Matters. https://doi.org/10.21832/9781783099245

Curry, M. J., & Lillis, T. (2019). Unpacking the lore on multilingual scholars publishing in English: A discussion paper. *Publications, 7*(2), 1–14. https://doi.org/10.3390/publications7020027

Deardorff, D. K. (2006). Identification and assessment of intercultural competence as a student outcome of internationalization. *Journal of Studies in International Education, 10*(3), 241–266. https://doi.org/10.1177/1028315306287002

Deardorff, D. K. (2009). *The sage handbook of intercultural competence.* Sage. https://doi.org/10.4135/9781071872987.n28

Dontcheva-Navratilova, O. (2016). Rhetorical functions of citations in linguistics research articles: A contrastive (Czech-English) study. *Discourse and Interaction, 9*(2), 51–74. https://doi.org/10.5817/di2016-2-51

Englander, K. (2006). Revision of scientific manuscripts by nonnative-English-speaking scientists in response to scientific journal editors' language critiques. *Journal of Applied Linguistics, 3*(2), 129–161. https://doi.org/10.1558/japl.v3i2.129

Fantini, A. E. (2009). Assessing intercultural competence. In D. K. Deardorff (Ed.), *The sage handbook of intercultural competence* (pp. 456–476). Sage. https://doi.org/10.4135/9781071872987.n27

Fazel, I. (2021). Socialization into scholarly publication as a multilingual, early-career scholar. In P. Habibie & S. Burgess (Eds.), *Scholarly publication trajectories of early-career scholars* (pp. 189–205). Palgrave Macmillan. https://doi.org/10.1007/978-3-030-85784-4_11

Flowerdew, J. (2015). Some thoughts on English for research publication purposes (ERPP) and related issues. *Language Teaching, 48*(2), 250–262. https://doi.org/10.1017/s0261444812000523

Flowerdew, J., & Habibie, P. (2022). *Introducing English for research publication purposes.* Routledge. https://doi.org/10.4324/9780429317798

Habibie, P., & Hyland, K. (Eds.). (2019). *Novice writers and scholarly publication: Authors, mentors, gatekeepers.* Palgrave Macmillan. https://doi.org/10.1007/978-3-319-95333-5

Holliday, A. (1999). Small cultures. *Applied Linguistics, 20*(2), 237–264. https://doi.org/10.1093/applin/20.2.237

Holliday, A. (2015). Native-speakerism: Taking the concept forward and achieving cultural belief. In A. Swan, P. Aboshiha, & A. Holliday (Eds.), *(En) countering native-speakerism* (pp. 11–25). Palgrave Macmillan. https://doi.org/10.1057/9781137463500_2

Hu, G., & Wang, G. (2014). Disciplinary and ethnolinguistic influences on citation in research articles. *Journal of English for Academic Purposes, 14*, 14–28. https://doi.org/10.1016/j.jeap.2013.11.001

Hyland, K. (2009). English for professional academic purposes: Writing for scholarly publication. In D. Belcher (Ed.), *English for specific purposes in theory and practice* (pp. 83–105). University of Michigan Press. https://doi.org/10.3998/mpub.770237

Hyland, K. (2018). Preface: Academic writing and non-Anglophone scholars. In P. Mur-Dueñas & J. Šinkūienė (Eds.), *Intercultural perspectives on research writing* (pp. vii–x). John Benjamins. https://doi.org/10.1075/aals.18

Hyland, K. (2019). Participation in publishing: The demoralizing discourse of disadvantage. In P. Habibie & K. Hyland (Eds.), *Novice writers and scholarly publication: Authors, mentors, gatekeepers* (pp. 13–33). Palgrave Macmillan. https://doi.org/10.1007/978-3-319-95333-5

Hynninen, N. (2020). Moments and mechanisms of intervention along textual trajectories: Norm negotiations in English-medium research writing. *Text & Talk, 42*(2), 209–232. https://doi.org/10.1515/text-2019-0303

Hynninen, N., & Kuteeva, M. (2017). "Good" and "acceptable" English in L2 research writing: Ideals and realities in history and computer science. *Journal of English for Academic Purposes, 30*, 53–65. https://doi.org/10.1016/j.jeap.2017.10.009

Ishihara, N., & Cohen, A. D. (2022). *Teaching and learning pragmatics: Where language and culture meet* (2nd ed.). Routledge. https://doi.org/10.4324/9781003168188

Kramsch, C. (2002). *Language acquisition and language socialization: Ecological perspectives.* Continuum.

Kuteeva, M., & Mauranen, A. (2014). Writing for publication in multilingual contexts: An introduction to the special issue. *Journal of English for Academic Purposes, 13*, 1–4. https://doi.org/10.1016/j.jeap.2013.11.002

Kwan, B. S. C. (2010). An investigation of instruction in research publishing offered in doctoral programs: The Hong Kong case. *Higher Education, 59*(1), 55–68. https://doi.org/10.1007/s10734-009-9233-x

Lillis, T., & Curry, M. J. (2006). Professional academic writing by multilingual scholars: Interactions with literacy brokers in the production of English-medium texts. *Written Communication, 23*(1), 3–35. https://doi.org/10.1177/0741088305283754

Loi, C. K. (2010). Research article introductions in Chinese and English: A comparative genre-based study. *Journal of English for Academic Purposes, 9*(4), 267–279. https://doi.org/10.1016/j.jeap.2010.09.004

Loi, C. K., & Evans, M. S. (2010). Cultural differences in the organization of research article introductions from the field of educational psychology: English and Chinese. *Journal of Pragmatics, 42*(10), 2814–2825. https://doi.org/10.1016/j.pragma.2010.03.010

Martín-Martín, P., & Burgess, S. (2004). The rhetorical management of academic criticism in research article abstracts. *Text & Talk, 24*(2), 171–195. https://doi.org/10.1515/text.2004.007

Moreno, A. (2004). Retrospective labelling in premise-conclusion metatext: An English-Spanish contrastive study of research articles on business and economics. *Journal of English for Academic Purposes, 3*(4), 321–339. https://doi.org/10.1016/j.jeap.2004.07.005

Mur-Dueñas, P. (2007). 'I/We Focus on…': A cross-cultural analysis of self-mentions in business management research articles. *Journal of English for Academic Purposes, 6*(2), 143–162. https://doi.org/10.1016/j.jeap.2007.05.002

Mur-Dueñas, P. (2011). An intercultural analysis of metadiscourse features in research articles written in English and in Spanish. *Journal of Pragmatics, 43*(12), 3068–3079. https://doi.org/10.1016/j.pragma.2011.05.002

Mur-Dueñas, P. (2012). Getting research published internationally in English: An ethnographic account of a team of finance Spanish scholars' struggles. *Ibérica, 24*, 9–28.

Mur-Dueñas, P. (2013). Spanish scholars' research article publishing process in English medium journals: English used as a lingua franca? *Journal of English as a Lingua Franca, 2*(2), 315–340. https://doi.org/10.1515/jelf-2013-0017

Mur-Dueñas, P. (2018). Exploring ELF manuscripts: An analysis of the anticipatory it pattern with an interpersonal function. In P. Mur-Dueñas & J. Šinkūienė (Eds.), *Intercultural perspectives on research writing* (pp. 277–297). John Benjamins. https://doi.org/10.1075/aals.18.13mur

Mur-Dueñas, P., & Šinkūíenė, J. (Eds.). (2018). Intercultural perspectives on research writing. *John Benjamins.* https://doi.org/10.1075/aals.18

Pennycook, A. (2001). *Critical applied linguistics: A critical introduction.* Routledge. https://doi.org/10.4324/9781410600790

Rings, G., & Rasinger, S. (Eds.). (2020). *The Cambridge handbook of intercultural communication.* Cambridge University Press. https://doi.org/10.1017/9781108555067

Risager, K. (2006). *Language and culture: Global flows and local complexity.* Multilingual Matters. https://doi.org/10.21832/9781853598609

Salager-Meyer, F., Ariza, M. Á. A., & Zambrano, N. (2003). The scimitar, the dagger and the glove: Intercultural differences in the rhetoric of criticism in Spanish, French and English medical discourse (1930–1995). *English for Specific Purposes, 22*(3), 223–247. https://doi.org/10.1016/s0889-4906(02)00019-4

Short, K. G. (2009). Critically reading the word and the world: Building intercultural understanding through literature. *Bookbird: A Journal of International Children's Literature, 47*(2), 1–10. https://doi.org/10.1353/bkb.0.0160

Spitzberg, B. H., & Changnon, G. (2009). Conceptualizing intercultural competence. In D. K. Deardorff (Ed.), *The sage handbook of intercultural competence* (pp. 2–52). Sage. https://doi.org/10.4135/9781071872987.n1

Swales, J. M. (1990). *Genre analysis: English in academic and research settings.* Cambridge University Press.

Swales, J. (1996). Occluded genres in the academy: The case of the submission letter. In E. Ventola & A. Mauranen (Eds.), *Academic writing: Intercultural and textual issues* (pp. 45–58). John Benjamins. https://doi.org/10.1075/pbns.41.06swa

Wilkinson, J. (2012). The intercultural speaker and the acquisition of intercultural/global competence. In J. Jackson (Ed.), *The Routledge handbook of language and intercultural communication* (pp. 296–309). Routledge. https://doi.org/10.4324/9780203805640.ch18

Wilkinson, J. (2020). From native speaker to intercultural speaker and beyond: Intercultural (communicative) competence in foreign language education. In J. Jackson (Ed.), *The Routledge handbook of language and intercultural communication* (pp. 283–298). Routledge. https://doi.org/10.4324/9781003036210-22

Ismaeil Fazel has a PhD in Language and Literacy Education and a sub-specialization in Measurement, Evaluation, and Research Methodology from the University of British Columbia. He is currently teaching EAP courses in the Vantage One Academic English Program at the University of British Columbia in Vancouver, Canada. Ismaeil has been actively engaged in the field of English for Academic and Professional Purposes for over 15 years now, serving in a variety of leading roles such as practitioner, teacher trainer, curriculum developer, and researcher. His publications have appeared in reputable journals including the *Journal of English for Academic Purposes, English for Specific Purposes,* and *Journal of English for Research Publication Purposes.* He has also published numerous refereed book chapters and a co-authored encyclopedia entry on English for Specific Purposes (Abrar-ul-Hassan & Fazel) in the TESOL Encyclopedia of English Language Teaching (2018). Email: ismaeil.fazel@ubc.ca

Part IV
Intercultural Literacy Assessment in EIL Education

Part IV is about critical discussion of the place of culture in English language teaching (ELT) textbooks. This section interrogates the discursive dimensions of representation related to discriminatory practices, based on sociocultural and gender differences. For example, in recent years there has been a conspicuous shift in Saudi English ELT education in favour of an emergent global cosmopolitan and consumerist culture. The commodification of the English language has shifted the role of English from the language of national/cultural identification to that of global communication. With the ever-increasing interconnectedness of the world, the argument for the need to train learners to become 'global citizens' and 'cultural cosmopolitans' has gained a lot of pedagogical credence. The current 'glocalisation' of the ELT profession in the Global South involves Westernisation of teaching materials, research methods and language teaching approaches, irrespective of the local cultural particularities.

However, such a glocalising tendency has not always been the case in the first Saudi ELT curricula. Sahlane and Pritchard's study demonstrates how alternative local sources of language teaching materials designed by local educators for the Saudi context have helped to safeguard Islamic tenets and values in the teaching of English as a foreign language (EFL). The study examines cultural dimensions of Saudi EFL textbooks for Elementary, Intermediate and Secondary Education (Saudi Ministry of Education, 2006). Drawing on critical discourse analysis methodology, the authors analyse the cultural content in the 'Say It In English' Series (SIIE) and in 'English for Saudi Arabia' Series (EFS). The study also investigates how visual and verbal discourses operate together to produce cultural representations. The chapter critically interrogates the discursive construction of cultural otherness and the implications that categorisation and hierarchisation (mediated in/by the text) may have for the positionings of sociocultural actors in textbook discourse. Emphasis is put on the (de)construction of subjectivities through the unravelling of labelling/naming strategies deployed to categorise 'us' vs 'them' in Saudi K-12 textbooks. Thematic and content analysis is used, inspired by methodological insights from critical discourse analysis, with the aim of deciphering meanings associated with the discursive construction of cultural identity and intercultural sensitivity in Saudi EFL textbooks. The chapter also shows how ethnocentrism needs to be problematised to counteract tendencies to regard one's own culture as the centre of human experience and meaning making.

Likewise, Moutia's chapter aims at exploring how the gender perspective is incorporated in nine locally designed (glocalised) Moroccan EFL textbooks. The study has adopted a qualitative-quantitative content analysis approach in examining how gender stereotyping characterises the textbook visual discourse in terms of gender visibility (visual illustrations), "frequency of appearance", "space" (male images outweigh those of their female counterparts) and "firstness" (foregrounding). The chapter reveals that patriarchal ideology is ingrained in the way EFL textbooks' visual discourse depict gendered social roles in modern Moroccan society. This might have detrimental effects in the way students (as target consumers of the visual contents of EFL textbooks) would conceive of gender relations in their lives outside the classroom.

Drawing on the data generated by a questionnaire, Tian and Yao's chapter investigates the impact of English proficiency on sociocultural and academic adaptation of 530 Chinese students (from different disciplines) in short-term study-abroad exchange programmes in Anglophone countries. The results show that students with high English proficiency successfully manage to navigate the varied demands of the host cultures by adopting higher-order cognitive strategies to 'decentre' (i.e., behave appropriately in host cultures, cultivate empathy towards cultural others, and appreciate cultural diversity). The study also reveals that higher metacognitive, motivational, and behavioural cultural intelligence is a significant predictor of academic (but not sociocultural) adaptation. It delineates the importance of English proficiency and its relation to social connectedness in intercultural encounters. The analysis concludes that short-term study-abroad exchange programs enhance the four factors of cultural intelligence (CQ): metacognition, cognition, motivation, and behaviour. However, the reason why sociocultural adjustments are not achieved might be because adapting to a new culture implies a dynamic shift in personal and cultural identification; low language proficiency may also be another reason. Moreover, monocultural networking may significantly delay such sociocultural adaptation. Adapting to a new culture is one of the biggest adjustments that must be made when transitioning to college in a new country. For monocultural individuals, cultural intelligence tends to be higher after studying abroad than before studying abroad. Because the study is short-term, such variables might not be easy to investigate.

Assessing Perspectives on Culture in Saudi EFL Textbook Discourse

Ahmed Sahlane (ID) **and Rosalind Pritchard**

Abstract Because of the increased mobility and high interconnectivity characterising the modern world, the incorporation of intercultural communicative competence in foreign language education has gained more pedagogical credence. However, the challenge is how to create a reflexive and critical space for intercultural diversities within English as a Foreign Language (EFL) classrooms in a way that empowers learners to successfully navigate intercultural encounters. The purpose of the present chapter is to examine how 'interculturality' is integrated into the Saudi EFL textbooks for K-12 public education. Drawing on critical discourse analysis methodology, we examine how visual and verbal discourses operate together to inspire students to navigate intercultural encounters. The findings suggest that the cultural content in 'Say It In English' Series (SIIE) and 'English for Saudi Arabia' Series (EFS) is mainly motivated by the need to acquire skills for 'global communication' and 'intercultural awareness' in the context of the conservation and appreciation of Arab/Islamic culture.

Keywords English as a foreign language · Critical discourse analysis · Culture · Interculturality · Intercultural competence · Islam · Saudi Arabia · Textbook

A. Sahlane (✉)
English Language Institute, University of Jeddah, Jeddah, Saudi Arabia
e-mail: asahlan1@uj.edu.sa

R. Pritchard
Faculty of Arts, Humanities & Social Sciences, Ulster University, Coleraine, UK
e-mail: R.Pritchard@ulster.ac.uk

1   Introduction

The present study investigates how cultural diversity is integrated in Saudi K-12 foreign language education textbooks. The analysis is done in light of Bennett's (1986) developmental model of intercultural sensitivity (DMIS), Byram's (1997) intercultural communicative competence (ICC) model, and Liddicoat's (2005) approach to intercultural language teaching (ILT). This chapter is organised in five parts. First, we discuss the theoretical framework that will serve as a basis for investigating intercultural language teaching in the Saudi EFL context (Bennett, 1986; Byram, 1997; Liddicoat, 2005). Then, methods used in this study are delineated. Next, we examine how foreign culture is represented in the Saudi EFL textbooks. After that, we undertake a critical discourse analysis (CDA) to illustrate how text can do ideological work. Finally, some concluding comments are made.

1.1   Intercultural Approaches to Foreign Language Education

Bennett's (1986, 1993) model of intercultural sensitivity posits that cultural learning is a developmental process extending along a continuum of six stages of personal growth. Three of these are 'ethnocentric' (denial, defence, and minimisation), and three are 'ethnorelative' (acceptance, adaptation, integration). As individuals become more interculturally sensitive, they move through the ethnocentric stages and progress toward more ethnorelative stages. For example, 'denial' of difference may occur within ethnically segregated communities (e.g., ideologically oriented groups or gated selective 'clubs.'). As cultural difference might seem threatening to such ethnocentric groups, 'defensive' strategies might range from 'denigration' (e.g., negative stereotyping: Donald Trump's xenophobic rhetoric toward Muslims and Latinos), 'superiority' (e.g., Eurocentric depiction of Global Southern cultures as 'backward' and 'inferior') and 'reversal' (e.g., Peace Corps volunteers' rethinking of Western misrepresentations of local 'Third World' cultures after first-hand experience). 'Defensive' 'ethnocentrism' may also reflect the struggle of minoritised and Indigenous communities to preserve their ways of life. Conversely, the 'minimisation' stage involves progressing towards being less judgmental or derogatory of cultural diversity (Bennett, 1986, p. 1993).

On the other hand, the 'acceptance' of cultural difference is a major shift towards 'ethnorelativism', which entails acknowledgement of and respect for alternative worldviews (Bennett, 1986, p. 184). This stance may lead to 'adaptation', which involves a non-assimilative upgrade of one's intercultural communicative skills repertoire by means of continuous socialisation (enculturation) into particular networks of communities of practice. Hence, "[o]ne does not have culture; one engages in it" (Bennett, 1993, p. 52). One of the most central aspects of 'adaptation' is the nurture of 'empathy.' Empathy engages "the ability to experience some aspect of reality differently from what is 'given' by one's own culture" (Bennett, 1993, p. 53). The "ability to formulate appropriate questions" is a very important manifestation of empathy (Bennett, 1986, p. 185). For example, settler lawyers in the Euro-Canadian tradition may fail to respectfully engage with indigenous Elders (as witnesses and revered knowledge-keepers) in their cross-examinations by inappropriately disregarding Aboriginal protocols within Canadian court proceedings (Healey, 2018). A more advanced form of 'adaptation' is the ability to immerse oneself in different world cultures, which ideally leads to the development of a pluralist and multiculturalist mindset ("integration"): a "holistic, coherent sense of self that somehow integrates … multiple frames of reference" (Bennett, 1993, p. 59). Therefore, being a competent language user implies the ability to appropriately call upon one's linguistic and intercultural repertoires based on contextual demands.

Another influential model of teaching language and culture is Byram's (1997) intercultural communicative competence (ICC). It comprises the following five 'savoirs' (knowledge types). These various competences involve the ability to negotiate cultural meanings and perform appropriately in multicultural contexts. These *savoir* types mark several thresholds representing different stages of ICC, as follows.

1. *Savoir (knowledge)*: It involves knowledge about how social groups interact and perceive each other across cultures. From a pedagogical perspective, uncovering stereotypical cultural misrepresentations in textbooks or other mediated discourses (e.g., Hollywood depiction of cultural others) is a first step in acquiring knowledge of the target language sociocultural processes and intercultural interaction.

2. *Savoir comprendre (skills of interpreting and relating)*: It engages the skills of relating new information to existing knowledge, comparing cultural values, resolving communication misunderstandings, and analysis and interpretation of texts and events. In brief, this *savoir* type involves the skill of interpreting texts or social events from other cultures by relating them to those from one's own culture.

3. *Savoir être (attitudes)*: It reflects the foreign language learners' need to cultivate an attitude of open curiosity (withholding judgement), tolerance for ambiguity, and cultural empathy. The ability to look upon oneself from the outside and to visualise the world from others' point of view (perspective shifting) is very critical. Classroom activities might include raising awareness about cultural similarities and differences in order to promote learners' understanding that cultures carry diverse worldviews. Developing cultural openness and readiness to unlearn unthinking belief about one's own culture and suspend disbelief in the views of cultural others (by relativising self and valuing the other) is a crucial step towards the promotion of ICC.

4. *Savoir apprendre/faire (skills of discovery and interaction)*: It requires the ability to acquire new knowledge of cultural practices and apply it under the constraints of real-time communication. Involving students in role-play activities and interviews or encouraging them to analyse critical incidents and cultural misunderstandings is useful for the development of discovery skills. Discovery skills have a pivotal role in Byram's ICC model because they involve asking

questions to elicit further knowledge from an interlocutor. Interaction skills (*savoir faire*) are very crucial in that they operationalise and integrate all the other ICC components.

5. *Savoir s'engager* (*critical cultural awareness*): It is the ability to critically evaluate the cultural behaviours and social perspectives in one's own and other cultures. Foreign language educators should encourage students to reflect on the ways language and culture are intertwined, thus enabling them to successfully manage cultural misunderstandings (e.g., how particular sociocultural problems are dealt with in different cultures). (Byram, 1997, p. 31–54)

In Byram's ICC model, linguistic proficiency in the foreign language plays a salient part in enhancing the learner's intercultural competence, which is an ongoing lifelong learning journey.

As the goal of EFL education is to train learners to be able to "understand, reflect on and mediate cultures" (Liddicoat, 2005, p. 201–202), they should be encouraged to actively engage with the cultural contexts of communication in ways that appropriately frame interpretation (p. 203). Speakers are "constantly invoking, interpreting and confirming social relationships through talk" (Liddicoat, 2005, p. 202). Hence, the concept of 'culture' can be conceived as a complex "dynamic set of practices rather than as a body of shared information" and 'culture learning' can be said to involve "an engagement with cultural practices rather than exposure to information about a [monolithic] culture" (p. 204). According to Liddicoat (2005), culture teaching involves four stages:

1. *Awareness-raising*: Exposing students to more authentic learning tasks (e.g., video and newspaper materials) can help students to 'notice' differences between the new foreign culture input and their own culture.
2. *Skills development*: The goal is to empower students to perform successfully in intercultural interaction situations by "trying out native speakers' ways of acting and speaking" (Liddicoat, 2005, p. 207). Practice enhances communicative language and intercultural skills (p. 208).
3. The *Production* stage: This output stage involves the learners' integration of the acquired foreign cultural knowledge in their repertoire of actual (foreign) language use (e.g., through 'role play' activities). The goal is to raise learners' awareness of any knowledge gap in their learning process along their journeys to become 'intercultural speakers.'
4. The F*eedback* stage: It encourages learners to reflect upon their learning experiences and discover their 'third culture,' a 'sphere of interculturality' that "enables language students to take an insider's view as well as an outsider's view on both their first and second cultures" (Kramsch, 2011, p. 354–5).

The acquisition of ICC begins with knowledge of home culture (L1 cultural practices) and gradually progresses through the acquired 'intercultural' practices towards the acquisition of an approximative system of L2 cultural practices (Liddicoat, 2005, p. 209). Liddicoat prescribes four teaching steps in the learning process (i.e., Input – Notice – Practice – Output). Though Liddicoat's model is inspired by traditional 'deficit' theories (i.e., 'interlanguage' and 'transfer'), it does not necessarily entail assimilation to the target culture norms. The 'intercultural learner' is seen as a 'mediator' between their own culture and the foreign cultural frameworks. The process of acquiring intercultural competence is cyclical. Acquiring L2 culture begins with a cultural difference 'input.' Then, the learner's 'noticing' of the 'input' (with the support of the teacher) is required. Next, the learner decides how to accommodate the 'input' within his intercultural repertoire (through reflection and experimentation). This leads to an 'output,' using a modified set of cultural norms. The output itself provides opportunities for *new noticing* (which becomes the target of further reflection) (p. 211).

2   Materials and Methods

The present study uses critical discourse analysis (CDA) to explore how 'intercultural sensitivity' materialises in the Saudi EFL textbooks. The instantiation of aspects of (foreign) 'culture' in textbook discourse takes the form of texts, exercises, tasks, and visuals that refer implicitly or explicitly to products, places, perspectives, historical facts, and (imagined) identities (Canale, 2016, p. 227). The Saudi EFL curriculum (Ministry of Education, 2006; cited in Al-Hajailan, 2006) is based on seven locally produced textbooks, 'English for Saudi Arabia' (*EFSA*) series and 'Say It in English' (*SIIE*) series (see Table 1). They cover from grade 6 to grade 12. EFSA textbooks are taught in Grade 6 (Book 1), Grades 10, 11 and 12 (Books 5, 6 and 7, respectively). Each book consists of 6 units based around a particular language function and communicative activities, and each unit consists of eight lessons. SIIE textbooks, on the other hand, are taught in grade 7, 8 and 9 (Books 2, 3, and 4, respectively). This series consist of 16 units; each of which is divided into four lessons. Greater focus is on the development of listening and speaking skills.

Intercultural communicative competence (ICC) involves the learner's need to nurture greater self-confidence, cultivate empathy towards cultural others, and appreciate cultural diversity. The importance of ICC in Saudi foreign language education is clearly reflected in the Saudi EFL textbooks' main objectives which include the need to (1) "acquire the linguistic basis that would enable [learners] to participate in transferring the scientific and technological advances …. in accordance with Islamic teachings," (2) the need to "enhance the concepts of international cooperation that develop understanding and respect of cultural differences among nations" and the aim to (3) "participate in the spreading of Islam and serving humanity" (Ministry of Education, 2006; cited in Al-Hajailan, 2006, p. 23–25). This chapter investigates to what extent the curriculum goals cited above are aligned to the cultural content in the Saudi EFL textbooks. Conducting a critical discursive analysis is guided by the following questions:

Table 1 List of the Saudi public EFL textbooks used in this study

Book #	Title	Level	Authors/Reviewers
Book 1	*English for Saudi Arabia* Pupil's Book (2006 ed.)	6th year elementary (grade 6)	Ahmad Al-Mofareh Rashid Al-Abdulkareem Mohammad Al-Muhanna Abdulaziz Al-Subai
Book 2	*Say it in English* Pupil's Book (2006 ed.)	1st year intermediate (grade 7)	Hanan Al-Saroji Hanan Al-Rayis Saher Al-Admah Hana Mojdali
Book 3	*Say it in English* Pupil's Book (2006 ed.)	2nd year intermediate (grade 8)	Hanan Al-Saroji Hanan Al-Rayis Saher Al-Admah Hana Mojdali
Book 4	*Say it in English* Pupil's Book (2006 ed.)	3rd year intermediate (grade 9)	Hanan Al-Saroji Hanan Al-Rayis Saher Al-Admah & others
Book 5	*English for Saudi Arabia* Student's Book (2006 ed.)	1st year secondary (grade 10)	Mohammed Al-Aohaydib Abdulkareem Al-Hameed Abdullah Al-Badri & others
Book 6	*English for Saudi Arabia* Student's Book (2006 ed.)	2nd year secondary (grade 11)	Mohammed Al-Aohaydib Abdulkareem Al-Hameed Abdulaziz Al-Amer & others
Book 7	*English For Saudi Arabia* Student's Book (2006 ed.)	3rd year secondary (grade 12)	Mohammed Al-Aohaydib Abdulkareem Al-Hameed Abdulaziz Al-Amer & others

(a) What opportunities for intercultural exploration of meaning-making do the text-books afford students? (e.g., do reading texts incorporate multiperspective approaches to meaning negotiation?).

(b) Is any cultural othering depicted through textual and visual portrayals (e.g., ethnic and gender hierachisation)?

(c) Do Saudi EFL textbooks cater for the development of identity as an enculturating process, which departs from 'ethnocentrism' and promotes intercultural sensitivity?

3   A Content Analysis of 'Interculturality' in the Saudi EFL Textbooks: Review of Literature

As there are very few studies that addressed the issue of interculturality in the 2006 version of Saudi EFL curriculum, we will restrict our review by outlining the findings of Bayhan's (2011) study. In this study of *English for Saudi Arabia* series (*EFSA*) & *Say It in English* series (*SIIE*) (see Table 1 above), Bayhan (2011) found that an extensive integration of language and culture is clearly evident in Book Four and Book Seven. It is assumed that for foreign language learners to develop ICC, they need to understand their own culture first. EFL learners are primarily encouraged to draw on their native linguistic and communicative resources rather than to learn about the foreign language culture. Consequently, 'culture' tends to be a mere accompanying pedagogical tool to language learning. Likewise, the study concluded that 'simplified' cultural content predominates in the EFL textbooks. Moreover, communication settings predominantly feature local cultural values, identities and cultural activities, both at elementary and secondary levels, wherein home culture is prioritised over foreign culture. For example, the exclusion of foreign language culture (visual and textual) in grade 6 elementary textbook is very conspicuous (see Table 2 (adapted); Bayhan, 2011, p. 70).

The frequency of cultural features (both textual and imagery) is delineated in Fig. 1 (Bayhan, 2011, p. 75).

The data in Fig. 1 show that when religion is mentioned in the EFL textbooks, there is an overwhelming focus on Islam (24.9% of all content). In fact, the only occurrence of religious content other than Islam is two items in Book 4. The commitment to the Islamic faith is obvious in that despite exposing students to foreign cultures, Islamic religion remains the sole spiritual reference endorsed in the English language teaching (ELT) materials. The highest religious content features in Book 2 (29 occurrences) followed by book 4 (22 occurrences) and Book 5 (21 occurrences).

Bayhan's study also revealed that in terms of cultural lifestyle, there is relatively a balanced portrayal of Saudi/Arab and foreign cultures. However, if the frequencies of Arab and Saudi contents are combined, then Arab/Muslim culture is more abundant than other foreign cultures (118 as opposed to 92 occurrences). Book 2 (18 occurrences), 3 (25 occurrences) and 4 (28 occurrences) contain the highest content of non-Arab cultures. The frequencies for the naming of characters show that the majority are Arab names (140 out of 187). This applies to both males and females, although male Saudi names dominate the books (52%). Saudi women feature less frequently in the ELT textbooks than do Saudi men. Non-Saudi females are the least present in both series (14%). Hence, women are less visible, relatively lower in social status (they are more likely to be stereotypically portrayed in traditional jobs) and less active as conversational actors. Such underrepresentation might assume an indication of women's unworthiness. For all three types of content, Book 4 stood out in having content in all the forms including non-Islamic religious content, non-Saudi females, and especially content about other (non-Saudi and non-Arab) lifestyles.

Table 2 Cultural representation in the Saudi EFT textbooks

Book/Title	Characters	Representation of other cultures
Book 1 [a]*EFSA*, sixth elementary	All Arab	Underrepresented
Book 2 *SIIE*, first year intermediate	Arab, except for Alan	Few and indirect forms of representation (e.g., queuing, clothing items, and English idioms)
Book 3 [b]*SIIE*, second year intermediate	Arab and non-Arab	Moderate representation (e.g., famous people, greeting customs, foreigners in Saudi Arabia, travelling abroad, and shopping).
Book 4 *SIIE*, third year intermediate	Arab and non-Arab	Intercultural awareness-raising (e.g., inclusion of manifold cultural elements, such as world historical monuments, famous world destinations, comparisons of nations, and different cultural customs).
Book 5 *EFSA*, first year secondary	Mostly Arab	Moderate inclusion of intercultural elements, with respect to school life, housing, landmarks, and dining customs.
Book 6 *EFSA*, second year secondary	Arab	Representation of Muslim and Western cultures (e.g., shopping habits, health care system, etc.)
Book 7 *EFSA*, third year secondary	Arab and several non-Arab	Plentiful inclusion of intercultural components (e.g., a historical visit to China, welfare of animals in Africa, English literature, and international calligraphy).

[a]*English for Saudi Arabia (EFSA)*
[b]*Say It in English (SIIE)*

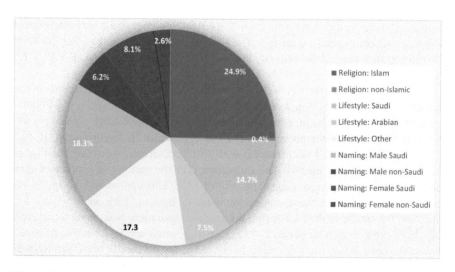

Fig. 1 Chart of content data

As regards the visual content of the textbooks, image analysis shows that the most popular character is the Saudi male (115 occurrences, books 1–7, Table 2). In contrast, there are fewer Saudi female occurrences (70) and very few non-Saudi females (13). Some books fail to feature a single non-Saudi female. Book 4 has the greatest number of non-Saudi characters of both genders (23), and this is reflective of its pedagogical orientation towards the inclusion of more intercultural content. As to clothing habits, this roughly mirrors the proportions assigned for the gender of characters. However, Book 5 is the richest in terms of male clothing (43 out of 166) and Book 2 features the most female clothing (23 out of 73). Textbook imagery tends to focus mainly on Saudi culture (86 out of 244 or 35%) although non-Saudi images are also significant (28%), especially in Book 4 (42 out of 69). Mixed cultural images feature in all books, apart from Book 1. In terms of the variation in all types of imagery, again Book 4 stands out, but Book 5 is not far behind, and Book 2 has exhibited the greatest multicultural imagery (Bayhan, 2011). Consider the illustration in Fig. 2 (Bayhan, 2011, p. 76).

The ordering of the textbooks in terms of their integration of foreign cultural content yields the following information (from the least to the most) (see Table 3, Bayhan, 2011, p. 71).

As is clear from Table 3, Book 1 has the least foreign cultural content representation and Book 4 contains the most foreign cultural content. Hence, it seems that the EFL learner goes through a journey from a monocultural stage (elementary) to reach a stage of more openness to foreign culture (intermediate) before regressing into cultural protectionism again (secondary). Further remarks are noteworthy:

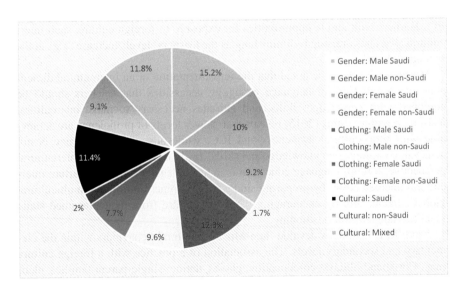

Fig. 2 Chart of image data

Table 3 Ascending ordering of foreign cultural content in the textbooks

Book 1 *EFSA (Grade 6)	Book 6 EFSA (Grade 11)	Book 7 EFSA (Grade 12)	Book 5 EFSA (Grade 10)	Book 2 **SIIE (Grade 7)	Book 3 SIIE (Grade 8)	Book 4 SIIE (Grade 9)
6th year elementary	2nd year secondary	3rd year secondary	1st year secondary	1st year intermediate	2nd year intermediate	3rd year intermediate

*English for Saudi Arabia (EFSA)
**Say It in English (SIIE)

1. The SIIE series has greater foreign cultural content than the *EFSA series*. SIIE book for grade 7 (Book 2) has more foreign cultural content than any secondary year textbook in the *EFSA* series.
2. There is a gradual progression in foreign cultural content at the Intermediate level (Grades 7, 8, 9).
3. Foreign culture is underrepresented in elementary level (Grade 6) and the incorporation of foreign culture in the teaching materials decreases as the learner's level increases. For example, while Intermediate textbooks integrate more foreign cultural content, foreign cultural representation decreases at the secondary level (Grade 10, 11, 12). Besides, it also decreases within levels. For example, Book 5 (Grade 10) contains more foreign cultural content than the subsequent books 6 and 7 (Grade 11 and 12, respectively) (Bayhan, 2011).

Therefore, it is clear that while the *SIIE* series provides more settings for foreign cultural exposure, the *EFSA* series tends to favour Arab/Muslim culture. Students are emotionally involved in the local culture at the elementary levels and such ethnocentric approaches decrease as the textbooks reach higher levels; there is a tendency to align the development of intercultural understanding with the development of language proficiency. However, while intermediate level textbooks present Saudi EFL learners with ample opportunities for exposure to foreign culture, such intercultural awareness-raising is diminishing as the learners' levels increase (e.g., at the secondary level).

Moreover, it should be noted that the implementation of an intercultural dimension into Saudi English language pedagogy necessities that teachers should be equipped with knowledge, skills, and attitudes necessary to make intercultural learning possible. Ennis (2015) reveals that "lower levels of proficiency are achievable with little cultural awareness and ICC, while advanced proficiency is not achievable without such knowledge and skills" (p. 17). Hence, from an intercultural perspective, foreign language education is in a privileged position to nurture intercultural understanding by preparing students to become multilingual/multicultural global citizens, and by encouraging them to decentre from their presumed static identities and cultural positioning.

Saudi EFL textbooks devalue 'non-Muslim' cultural behaviours within the elementary and secondary levels. The association of a practice with a foreign culture (e.g., Christian holidays, co-education, ghosts, dating, single-parent families, alcohol, pork, etc.) is clearly done through the exclusion of such culturally 'inappropriate' manifestations from both text and visuals. Hence, this attempt to counter a "perceived threat" to Muslim culture (assumed to be superior) can be viewed as an instance of "defence strategy" implicitly enacted through implied "negative stereotyping" of difference (Bennett, 1986, p. 183).

Bayhan (2011) mainly restricted his analysis to coding and counting uses of cultural items in the Saudi textbooks, as opposed to interrogating the very nature of 'interculturality' in actual (con)textual use. Hence, the present study addresses the reasoning contained within the process of communication itself. In this chapter, therefore, we intend to extend Bayhan's (2011) study by offering a more critical focus on the details of textual ideation, using critical discourse analysis.

4 Interrogating Cultural Representations: A Critical Discourse Perspective

Critical discourse analysis (CDA), which studies how language as a cultural tool mediates power relations in social encounters, is a powerful methodological approach that helps to examine how text and imagery can be used as a rhetorical resource to legitimate, perpetuate, or contest a hegemonic status quo. For example, discourses that privilege whiteness, native-speakerism, and cultural 'deficit' theories try to stabilise their Eurocentric epistemological worldviews as 'universal' and 'natural' by destabilising any pluriversal knowledge forms that involve a struggle over the symbolic and material capital (see Sahlane, this volume, Chapter "(En) Countering the 'White' Gaze: Native-speakerist Rhetorics and the Raciolinguistics of Hegemony"). Likewise, media visual and textual (mis)representation of political conflicts may be done through the deployment of an arsenal of topoi, stories, and textual/visual frames to manufacture a hegemonic perspective that does not simply reflect reality but actively seeks to shape it (Sahlane, 2022). Similarly, textbook discourse can create a discursive space for ideological struggle in that (foreign) language curriculum policymakers draw on discursive resources that frame a social reality in a way consonant with their ideological aims. Hence, "the study of representations requires us to consider not only what textbook discourse represents and how it chooses to represent it, but also what it chooses to leave out" (Canale, 2016, p. 232). In what follows, we will illustrate "how language conventions and language practices are invested with power relations and ideological processes which people are often unaware of" (Fairclough, 1992, p. 7).

Book 1 (Grade 6) introduces Saudi EFL learners to the basics of learning English. The characters, clothing styles, and religious or civic symbols tend to be mainly Muslim/Arab. Images that strengthen the Saudi cultural practice of enforcing a strict dress code on women (Saudi men also wear traditional *thobe*) are abundant. They may serve to help activate students' schematic knowledge as an aid to comprehending reading texts (see Fig. 3).

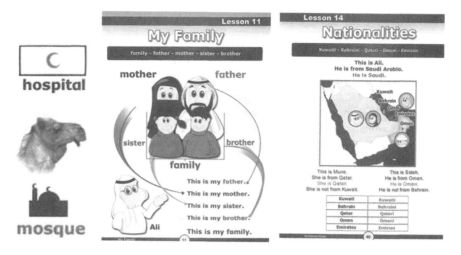

Fig. 3 Imagery and symbolic representations of Arab/Muslim culture

Fig. 4 Presentation of alphabet and vocabulary as cultural representation

In Book Two (Grade 7), the audiolingual teaching methodology prescribed focuses mainly on language usage and drilling. However, practised teachers can exploit these materials to help students fulfil a variety of communicative needs (e.g., greetings, farewells). The topics covered are all related to life in Saudi Arabia, specifically the home and school environments. The words used to introduce the English alphabet, practise spelling, or teach new vocabulary also represent the Muslim/Saudi culture (see Figs. 4 and 5).

Although most of the characters used in Book 2 have Arabic names and wear Arab clothing, there are also a few English characters with English names. However,

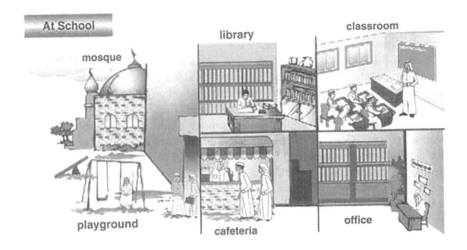

Fig. 5 Verbal and visual cultural representation and language tasks

Fig. 6 Appropriating Western clothing style

the few English personalities (see Fig. 6) that are included are simply meant to familiarise the student with them as they appear in the subsequent books. The professions and interests of Nabeel (male) and Salwa (female), for example, could be said to transcend traditional gender boundaries (e.g., sports, hobbies, and cooking). Likewise, relative engagement with other cultures involves clothing habits (unit 9). For instance, the way a Saudi guy travelling to London is dressed looks Western (see Fig. 6). Unit 11 also compares the traditional Arab *souq* (marketplace) with American shopping malls. The unit with a significant multicultural orientation is about 'countries' (unit 15). The power of language to name and portray cultural 'others' is illustrated in a reading passage about Africa (its weather, people and clothing habits). Students are also encouraged to discuss "Why is learning other languages important?" The introduction of idiomatic expression and proverbs presupposes some foreign culture awareness.

In Book 3 (Grade 8), Arabic names (e.g., Ahmad, Amina), Arab/Muslim clothing, eating habits, traditions, and lifestyles continue to predominate, with rare exceptions of people's names from Asian cultural backgrounds. Most of the photographs depicting people represent Saudis or Middle Eastern people. A reading text invites students to guess which three "famous cities" are described (Jeddah, Damascus and Geneva). These sociopolitical spaces serve to reinforce 'our' nationalistic constructions of 'cultural' identity. For example, to teach superlatives, the textbook gives such examples: "*Mamlaka Tower* is the highest in Saudi Arabia" and "The highest fountain in the world is in Jeddah." A reading text about "a special moment in your childhood" narrates a story by a Saudi schoolboy about his "happiest memories" at elementary school in the US, where he lived with his family. He states that "I liked life in the United States and got used to it easily. However, I was always proud of being a Saudi national" (p. 14). On a school field trip to the *John F. Kennedy Centre* in Washington DC., he passed by the *Hall of Flags* and asserted that,

> Hurriedly my eyes searched for the Saudi flag. I simply stood under it and saluted it. My teacher and classmates were touched by my patriotism. They spent the rest of the day telling everyone how wonderful it was for a child to love his country so much (p. 14).

The Saudi boy's behaviour is moving and praiseworthy, but the textbook misses a good opportunity to introduce students to other cultures. This story also intertextually features an image of a Saudi schoolboy saluting the national flag in the courtyard of a local Saudi school. The use of this perspective-based story and the tendency towards narrativisation (use of first person narrative) has a rhetorical function: it engenders positive self-presentation ('I miss my home country' is a performative message) and it engages the target audience through pathos ('while abroad, you will feel homesick') and commands action ('be proud of your country while abroad'). The 'flag' event implicitly argues that Saudi Arabia is a great place to live, with its fantastic coasts, foods, traditions, and people (invoking an implicit comparison with the host country). Hence, "cultural diversity" is presented as "something that is to be evaluated from one's own cultural perspective" as it "is constructed in terms of one culture being in some sense better than another" (Liddicoat & Scarino, 2013, p. 91).

Such study-abroad experience gives the EFL learner the opportunity to get involved in "direct experience of lived reality as a text for interpretation" (Liddicoat & Scarino, 2013, p. 97). However, the positioning of the Saudi student as immune from outside 'acculturation' influences (perceived as a threat to their Muslim identity) fails to empower them to 'entertain' alternative voices within the 'school field trip' multicultural context, and thus closes the Bakhtinian sense of heteroglossic space for intercultural dialogue. 'Task authenticity' was also discounted because a multi-perspective approach to the text would engender different interpretations of the 'flag' situation, and thus accommodate multi-voiced understandings that co-exist in a coherent way with the effect of promoting real life intercultural communication. In other words, there is a conflict with the learner's identity as a potentially intercultural 'mediator' of home and target culture in the 'real world' and this conventionally assigned collective national identity ('culture' as a nation-bound static entity). Individuals should be "seen as dynamic co-creators of their realities" (Bennett, 1986, p. 185). "The concomitant construal of cultural reality as consensual and mutable is essential to ethnorelativism and necessary for further development of intercultural sensitivity" (p. 185). Encouraging students to view their own culture as fundamental to world reality construction (e.g., sidelining their lived experiences as Saudi sojourners in a foreign country by prioritising feelings of nostalgia and the reverence of the Saudi flag) may reduce their ability to become intercultural mediators and global citizens.

'Home culture' predominates in Book 3. For example, to introduce comparatives, students read a text about how "travelling your homeland" is "less expensive"; "the people are friendlier, and the local food is tastier." A follow-up topic for class discussion is "Which Islamic countries would you like to visit?" (p. 54). Then, pictorial exploitation of Saeed's family in Malaysia is used to write a paragraph, using present continuous (e.g., "They are performing *Dhuhr* prayer) (see Fig. 7) In addition, great Muslim scholars (e.g., Ibn Khaldun, Al-Ghazali, Ahmad Zuwail) are proposed as subjects for writing a biographical paragraph. Another reading passage is about the Prophet Mohamed, which is used to reinforce the use of past tense. Finally, King Faisal's life is assigned as a timeline writing activity. The focus of activities in most images covers work, family, school and shopping in Muslim settings. However, intersectional bias is clear in the way social actors are assigned roles in the textbook. While men are represented in wider contexts (work, science, adventure, sport, etc.) women are stereotypically assigned subordinate social roles (e.g., accompanying

Fig. 7 Cultural visual content and gender roles

their husbands to do shopping, taking care of children or being involved in traditional nurturing roles). Hence, the inclusion of a pan-Arab/Muslim cultural diversity forms a backdrop in Saudi EFL textbooks (e.g., Syria, Morocco, Egypt, Malaysia, Pakistan) and silences many facets of local cultural divergences.

However, to promote 'cultural diversity,' Book 3 contains a reading text about West Edmonton Mall, the world's "largest shopping and entertainment centre" (p. 53). Moreover, "Time around the world" introduces different world time zones, followed by a reading passage entitled "Around the world in eighty days". This is followed by another reading passage about Ali Habeeb, an Egyptian tourist guide. Finally, students are invited to compare the famous traveller Marco Polo with the Muslim explorer, Ibn Battuta (speaking activity). Each student has a reading passage containing biographical information about their traveller (either Ibn Battuta or Marco Polo). Then students need to ask their partners questions about their travellers to elicit biographical information and fill a table with the right information. A follow-up activity invites students to reflect about the benefits of travelling abroad. Likewise, a "greeting customs" reading passage introduces students to cultural disparities. Finally, "talking about jobs" is a speaking task that features many nationalities. Hence, students are encouraged to rationalise their strong appeals to pride in their own culture by inviting them to talk about "good" things within other cultures (Bennett, 1986, p. 189) or reflect on the commonalities among own and foreign culture before exploring the differences. However, it is clear that cultural 'pluralism' is celebrated only when "perspectives, cosmogonies and ideologies are not at stake, so that they cannot be contested" (Canale, 2016, p. 236). As "culture is assumed to be the accumulation of historical facts or the crystallised and homogeneous behaviours of a group, often times associated with national boundaries" (p. 239), this process of cultural representation fails to provide an open space for reflection and the promotion of the learner's critical intercultural awareness.

In Book 4 (Grade 9), Unit 4 features more multicultural textual and visual content representation. For example, there is a reading about "Eiffel Tower". However, such selective touristic icons reduce foreign culture to mere essentialised accounts of the foreign culture. Moreover, to teach reported speech, quotations from famous international figures have been used (Einstein, Helen Keller, Neil Armstrong). Students are also invited to name famous international touristic city attractions; they also compare countries, populations, languages, religions and currencies. Then, students take the role of foreign visitors to Saudi Arabia and write postcards to their friends worldwide about their hometowns. A listening activity features Asim, who talks about his trip to Singapore. Another reading passage is about Western "women inventors." Muslim women are conspicuously excluded, thereby omitting their important active role in Islamic history and their contribution to nation-building. This gendered perspective in Saudi EFL textbooks homogenises the experiences of women in a way that codifies culturally naturalised norms of 'femininity'. Saudi women's struggle to promote gender equality is viewed as uncultural, and thus at odds with the discursively manufactured consensus about national identity. Women's identity is typically constructed within the confines of the domestic sphere ('harems'). Any transgression of the institutionalised and socially constructed gender boundaries might pose a threat to the established patriarchal social order.

The book also focuses more on debating pressing global issues (e.g., environment protection, healthy eating, cultural tolerance). However, it tends to "guide semiosis so that a particular and unproblematic understanding of culture becomes naturalised" (Canale, 2016, p. 240). In this sense, intercultural sensitiity is reduced to essentialised traditions across cultures (e.g., greetings by rubbing noses in the Middle East; eating with chopsticks in Asia; traditional clothes, festivals, etc.). However, these are mere observable surface cultural norms that are stereotypically static and fail to account for the fact that culture is dynamic and heterogenous because it transforms over time, across generations and cuts across national boundaries. Learners should be sensitised to the conflictual sociocultural realities of our modern world through the adoption of a critical pedagogy that promotes rational dialogue and contestation rather than congratulatory rhetorical accounts of surface culture (e.g., tourist attractions, holidays, celebrations). In other words, teaching students survival strategies or useful tips to manage and appreciate cultural differences while they visit foreign countries fails to promote students' critical thinking.

A shortened version of Charles Dickens' novel *David Copperfield* represents an opportunity to introduce students to the English work of literature. Intercultural engagement with literature is a vital source of cultural learning, as the act of reading may be transformed into meaning negotiation across cultures by exploring the context of discourse (at the situational, interactional, cultural and intertextual levels), and thus may promote a deeper reflection and understanding of cultural sensitivity by encouraging students to engage in a "dialogic relationship with the text in which they recognize the gaps and dissonances as they read" (Liddicoat and Scarino, 2013, p. 96). Hence, such engagement with literary texts promotes the language learner's awareness that language is not only a means of communication and a 'neutral' reflection of social reality, but it is rather a "socially and historically situated mode of action" in that "it is socially shaped, but it is also socially shaping, or constitutive" (Fairclough, 1995, p. 131). However, the problem is that Saudi EFL students are positioned as 'strangers' to the target language culture. This "naturalises the idea that only certain facts and practices are legitimate within the culture, and that these need to be known and mastered in order to have full access to the target language and community" (Canale, 2016, p. 240).

A reading passage entitled "Your ID, please" reads as follows:

> Trends started in the West are immediately accepted in the East. Young people from different countries are becoming more alike. They wear the same clothes, have the same haircuts, listen to the same type of music and eat the same type of food. ... Leaving your traditions behind makes you a slave to others. This will make you lose your individuality and thus your freedom. So, be proud of your culture and traditions (Book 4, Unit 12, p. 37).

Though Book 4 adopts a cross-cultural approach (mainly by conceiving of culture as behavioural performance), the warning that 'acculturation' can lead to cultural alienation reframes the globalising youth lifestyles in an ethnocentric way to the effect that ideological standpoints are constructed as taken-for-granted 'truth' claims. However, practices in actual classrooms might promote more inclusion of different perspectives and discursive spaces, wherein teachers and students "may become agents in the process of reinforcing, appropriating, or contesting the representations textbooks (re)produce" (Canale, 2016, p. 226).

Book 5 (Grade 10) deals at length with foreign culture. For example, Ahmad Al-Ali interviews Mr. Jones (a Saudi private English language school director) to highlight the cultural differences between learning English at home and studying abroad. Then, there is an interview with James Brown (a schoolboy). Such ethnographic interviews serve as a valuable source for intercultural learning. Likewise, a reading passage about "going to school in the USA" (unit 3) and authentic reading texts (e.g., a brochure of a language school in England; a school registration form; job application letter) provide learners with a good opportunity to engage in (intercultural) authentic tasks.

However, a reading passage, which is about vocational training, argues that "[m]any jobs which are now filled by foreign workers can … be done by Saudis". The writer fails to interrogate the existing structures of inequality and discrimination in Saudi workplaces. The arguer also contends that "[m]ale students may apply to go to any of these [technical colleges]." Hence, women are excluded from certain jobs, despite the fact that Saudi women today represent over 60% of enrolments in Saudi universities and 25% of enrolments in Master's and doctoral degrees at Saudi universities (Sulaimani and Elyas, 2018, p. 56). Therefore, textbook discourse fails to address pressing contentious issues of modern-day slavery in the Middle Eastern context (e.g., domestic worker abuse, gender inequality, social injustice, 'sponsorship' system). However, it is fair to point out that such problems have recently gained the attention of the current Saudi government. Drastic steps have been taken to alleviate such abuses. For example, Saudi Arabian females were finally allowed to get behind the wheel in July 2018. The strict male guardianship laws have been eased; women can conduct bank transactions and travel without a male guardian's permission.

Using local cultural context can motivate students and enhance their reading comprehension. For example, a Sudanese pilgrim, called Hamza, is interviewed about his first Hajj journey experience (see Fig. 8). In a role-play activity, students

Fig. 8 Interviewing Hamzah about his first pilgrimage to Makkah

are invited exploit pictures and notes and write their stories about their first Hajj (pilgrimage) journey. They are also invited to write a guided paragraph about the rituals of Hajj. A map visualising the Hajj rituals step by step is provided. Hence, the sacred temporality and spatiality of students' life-worlds are shaped by a combination of Islamic cultural elements (e.g., qibla, Al-Ka'abah, Makkah, Hajj). These institutionalised cultural spaces reinforce Islamic identity by excluding all cultural content that is inconsistent with Islamic practices; the aim is to avoid potential disaffection and conflict.

Book 6 (Grade 11) deals with the early spread of Islam (see Fig. 9) in unit 3. The students are grounded in early history in which parts of Europe were under the Islamic civilisation rule while the West was in the grip of the dark ages, and the Arabic language held a far more prestigious status than it does today. In Unit 4 students write a description of a mosque in China (based on pictorial prompts and guiding questions). Another reading passage ("Ibn Battuta travels") describes the Muslim exlorer's adventures and displomatic responsibilities while on his long journey. The role of Islam in international trading during this historical era is also highlighted. Many other themes are tackled (e.g., the history of the Saudi Post, starting from the use of watchtowers and pigeons in the fourteenth century Muslim empire). The glorious Muslim scientific past is echoed by the present Saudi economic progress in oil industry, championed by ARAMCO (the Saudi public oil company). However, the historical and political factors that led to the expulsion of Muslims from the Iberian peninsula are silenced. Students have been passively crammed with selective historical 'facts' and no opportunities have been offered for students to explore different perspectives for themselves. For examples, field trips to historical sites in Saudi Arabia might involve students in gathering information themselves. Similarly, a virtual exploration of the importance of Al-Qarawiyyin University in Fez, Morocco, (founded in 859 AD) or the city of Córdoba in Spain could encourage students to reflect upon the legacy of Islamic civilisation.

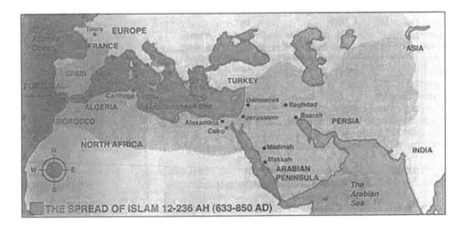

Fig. 9 The early spread of Islam and Islamic civilization

An extensive reading passage encourages students to reflect about different eating habits and daily lifestyles in global societies and their relationship with the individual's wellbeing. Another reading passage talks about the poor health care system before Islam and how the "progress of Arab medicine" has led to the tremendous "improvements in health care" in Saudi Arabia today. However, visual representations (see Fig. 10) reveal that the writer resorts to discursive strategies of 'collectivisation' and 'homogenisation' to conflate all involved medical actors within the Arab labelling category superimposed on Saudi. For example, Al-Razi and Ibn Sina (Muslim Persian scholars) are represented as "Arab doctors" (Unit 6, lesson 2). However, pharmacy clerks are depicted as expatriate workers.

Many other themes are tackled (e.g., multicultural beverages). For example, the book delineates the history of tea and discusses its worldwide popularity and different drinking customs (e.g., 'the British are the biggest tea drinkers in the world'; 'it is normal for guests in Morocco to accept three glasses of tea'; 'Indian tea has a lot of milk in it, whereas the Russians prefer it sweet and black'; 'Tibetan tea is usually in the shape of a brick'; 'the use of tea bags originated in the United States'). However, it is clear that there is an avoidance of discussing alcoholic drinks since they are prohibited in Islam. Intercultural awareness also involves comparing shopping customs in different nations. For example, a "European greengrocer might become quite angry if you touch his fruits or vegetables. In Middle Eastern bazaars, on the other hand, shoppers are usually free to handle the goods" (p. 95). A similar point is made about bargaining – prices are fixed in Western stores, and Westerners shopping in the Middle East find bargaining a difficult skill.

It is important to problematise the essentialising representations delineated above because they deny culture its complex hybridity and ignore its heterogeneity. Assigning deterministic traits to people based on their place of origin or ethnoreligious background is constrictive and potentially harmful. Pushing assumptions on interactants based on stereotypes may prove misguided. Besides, by referring to the 'greengrocer' as culturally a male job ('his'), the writer depicts the business from an ethnocentric perspective (i.e., based on gender roles in the traditional Saudi

Fig. 10 The visual depiction of Muslim pioneers of medicine

society). However, the changing roles of Saudi women today have moved from being primarily housewives to being partners at work in domains conventionally reserved for male expatriates.

Book 7 (Grade 12) equally adopts a multicultural perspective on a variety of global topics and/or issues (e.g. calligraphy, space exploration, poaching, deforestation, environment conservation, etc.). There are also some examples of well-known English literature (e.g., a simplified version of Charles Dickens' *Great Expectations* and Mark Twain's *The Adventures of Tom Sawyer*). However, Ibn Battuta's travel to China is revisited to reinforce some Muslim cultural/religious values ('Ibn Battuta did not bow to the Chinese emperor'). In the same vein, a reading text about the two Saudi explorers who participated in a multinational scientific mission to the Antarctic in 1989 concludes that

> The Saudis in the team were the *first Arabs and Muslims to perform their prayers* at the South Pole. The *Saudi flag* was raised there together with those of other countries. This action was a symbol of Saudi Arabia's cooperation with other countries for scientific discovery. (Emphasis added, p. 49)

Another interesting reading text entitled "Arab aid" (see Fig. 11) depicts the Third World countries as beneficiaries from the generosity of the "very rich" Gulf States (ignoring unequal distribution of wealth in these countries; see Thompson, 2017). It is also argued that "Gulf states see their aid as a way of making friends in the Third World. But Arab Aid is also the result of the religious duty called Zakat (alms-giving): giving to those who have less than we do" (Book 7, p. 73). This is preceded by a listening text (involving a reporter interviewing an expert); it concerns a Malaysian agricultural project, which was financed by Saudi Arabia (p. 65).

Hence, again patriotism ('flag') 'benevolence' ('aid') and religious identity ('prayers') are foregrounded in Saudi EFL textbooks. Textbook discourse reproduces and reinforces the socially sanctioned codes of behaviour and values deemed important in socialising the Saudi youth. Individuals are represented as static role-bearers and carriers of pre-specified social roles. Such 'nationalist' discourse creates and supports hierarchical relations of power ('aid-providers' vs.

Arab Aid goes to countries all over the world.

Building a dam with Arab Aid in Morocco

A canal for a Sudanese irrigation project

Fig. 11 Framing 'Arab Aid' as Zakat

'alms-receivers'). Third world countries are constructed as non-agentive recipients of Saudi/Arab 'aid.' Besides, 'aid' and 'loan' are fallaciously conflated. In contrast, foreign workers' contribution to the development of Saudi/Gulf states' economies is muted. Success and virtue are more associated with material wealth than with human capital. The promotion of the cooperative ethic in Islam (alms-giving) is nullified by this 'neoliberal' mentality. Such ideological discourse tacitly constructs 'poverty' or 'Third Worldness' as self-inflicted social problems perpetuated by the have-nots themselves (the adverse role of neocolonial powers today in Africa is muted).

Book 7 also describes the development of the Saudi higher education system, the history of domestic travel (e.g., air travel) and the expansion of the Holy Mosque at Makkah. A listening activity about King Abdulaziz, the founder of Saudi Arabia, is followed by a class discussion about "What do you know about King Abdelaziz's life and achievements?" (p. 28). Then, students read a text about King Abdulaziz and how he was "a great and fair leader with a strong faith in Islam" and answer comprehension questions (p. 36). Another reading text (Unit 4) is about the "Holy month of Ramadan," its religious duties, social customs and celebrations (*Eid-Al-Fitr*). Hence, though the textbook fosters cultural literacy through encouraging learners to read English literature and relate to the target culture, more attention is attached to the promotion of patriotic feelings and the maintenance of an endangered Islamic cultural identity.

5   Concluding Comments

Saudi EFL textbooks have encouraged learners to embrace intercultural sensitivity within an essentially monocultural educational frame in that teaching materials were designed to project particular images of Saudi/Muslim culture rather than engaging with the various cultural worldviews of the foreign language. In other words, the conception of English as a mere 'communication tool' (instead of a 'cultural carrier' and a "bearer of a particular vision of the world" (Phillipson, 2017, p. 314)) has transformed English into a useful vehicle for expressing Islamic beliefs and Saudi local cultural norms and traditions. Hence, the representation of 'cultural diversity' boils down to comparing products, practices and persons (e.g., historical facts, famous people, touristic cities, rituals, etc.) in a stereotypically essentialising way in that culture is conceived as a stable finished 'commodity' that we are predetermined to share with our presumed 'homogeneous' national or ethnic groups.

In this sense, the textbooks failed to adopt a processual view of culture as a dynamic (continually evolving), heterogeneous and de-territorialised process in that values and practices are being continuously (re)shaped across time and place. Lack of 'cultural diversity' may be manifested in the clear domination of Arab/Muslim worldviews, perspectives and ideologies in the textbooks. The static view of comparing practices, products or behaviours across cultures involves the reification of culture and its reduction to mere essentialising practices. Moreover, the ultimate aim of most intercultural awareness-raising activities is to teach lexico-grammatical items and not to promote the learner's critical engagement with the textbook topics.

Language is principally a social phenomenon which is intimately intertwined with culture. However, culture is regarded as the 'hidden curriculum' in that it is a site of struggle for voice, agency, and the legitimation of knowledge production. Hence textbook discourses are grounded in ideologies that often legitimise, naturalise, and stabilise dominant forms of knowledge construction. Far from being repositories of objective historical facts, textbooks are value-laden as they are the results of sociopolitical, economic, and cultural struggles and compromises (Canale, 2016). Education policymakers can subtly mould the beliefs and behaviours of key educational stakeholders towards the advancing of their own ideological interests. Saudi EFL textbooks dedicated whole units to Islam and Saudi Arabia; they contained abundant references to Islamic teachings, history, and cultural practices. In addition, despite the diversity of intercultural topics and themes that serve to potentially boost learners' cultural awareness, lexicogrammatical patterns remained the core focus of foreign language education, with a clear foregrounding of ethnocentric representations of self (and sometimes the stereotypical portrayals of cultural others).

Likewise, authentic materials are very crucial for intercultural language learning, especially when culture is viewed as an integral part in the process of 'authentic' language learning. However, authenticity should not be reduced to 'native-speakership' because the monolingual native-speaker model may actually hinder any ample opportunity for effective intercultural learning. Today's lingua franca situations entail that 'authenticity' can be enhanced when multilingual/multicultural learners of English engage in intercultural encounters demanding meaning negotiation and critical perspective-taking across cultural boundaries. Hence, as Saudi EFL textbooks require teachers to limit cultural learning to transmitting factual knowledge about culture, culture is reduced to a mere set of learnable cultural tips, a situation that fails to position the EFL students as important intercultural actors who are actively involved in a dynamic and embodied process of meaning and relationship negotiation. The role of teachers is not to bring the foreign language society into the classroom for learners to experience interculturality; rather, their main responsibility as 'intercultural mediators' is to prioritise students' development of critical intercultural awareness so that they can relativise their own cultural values, beliefs and behaviours and investigate for themselves those of the cultural others. However, teachers' concern about engaging with controversy may discourage them from training their students in critical cultural engagement.

The focus on mere knowledge transmission means that teachers are mainly concerned with teaching the language; the focus on other sociological facets (family/home life, customs, institutions, interpersonal relations, etc.) and aesthetic aspects of culture (e.g., literature, music, theatre) plays a mere ancillary role to language study. However, it is clear that the Saudi EFL curriculum needs to attach a significant importance to the development of learners' critical intercultural awareness that is necessary to appropriately interpret cultural difference and critically evaluate perspectives and discursive practices in their own and foreign cultures. Though Saudi

EFL textbooks contain plenty of authentic materials, such resources alone do not guarantee relevant intercultural learning because the whole teaching environment (teacher preparedness, continuous professional development, etc.) is what really makes a big difference. As the EFL curriculum does not prescribe specific intercultural teaching strategies, teachers need to make independent efforts to provide learners with opportunities to translate the stated cultural objectives into practice. Hence, while at the heart of debates about teaching EIL is the selection of teaching methodology, the most salient mediators of learning remain the language teaching materials because textbooks often serve to legitimise what cultural content to pass on to learners.

In recent years there has been a conspicuous shift in Saudi EFL education in favour of an emergent global cosmopolitan and consumerist culture. The commodification of the English language has shifted the role of English from the language of national/cultural identification to that of global communication. With the ever-increasing interconnectedness of the world, training learners to become 'global citizens' and 'cultural cosmopolitans' has gained a lot of pedagogical credence. The current 'glocalisation' of the English language teaching profession in Saudi Arabia takes the form of the Westernisation of teaching materials, research methods and language teaching approaches, irrespective of the local cultural particularities. However, the appropriateness of the cultural materials in the textbooks is of paramount importance. There has been a growing awareness among international publishers that not all cultural content can be suitable for different teaching contexts. For example, in Saudi Arabian EFL context, various aspects of national cultures (geography, social norms, history, iconography, etc.) are presented, together with sanitised references to some aspects of global cultures.

Hence, the indigenisation movement that catered for the 'Islamisation' of the foreign language education by 'purifying' ELT textbooks from Western 'values', belief systems and foreign identities is losing ground to a more globally oriented view of coursebook design. For example, Foundation Year curriculum at most Saudi universities is no longer designed by local educational stakeholders (e.g., teachers, teacher educators) who are better equipped (than international commercial textbook designers) with relevant knowledge of the local communities they are supposed to serve. In addition, with the poor achievement of EFL learners and the increasing global tendency to learn English, and in line with the trending approach to teaching language and culture (e.g., CEFR), the Saudi Ministry of Education (MoE) has sought to 'modernise' its EFL curriculum by opting for the inclusion of more foreign cultural content in its English language curriculum. Hence, extensive investment in educational 'reform' came with King Abdullah's Foreign Scholarship Program (KAFSP) launched in 2005. It was the largest in the kingdom's history. Over 207,000 students and dependants benefited from KAFSP in 2014, at a cost of $6 billion (Reuters, Feb. 1, 2016).

Starting from 2021, English is taught from First Elementary (MoE, 2021). However, tensions between conservative and 'liberal' social actors in the Saudi society (religious leaders, media, etc.) have continued to fuel public discourses about the merit of teaching English at early stages of K-12 education and the need to maintain the dominant status of Arabic whilst safeguarding national Muslim identity. Hence, the challenge remains: how can we design glocal English textbooks linking the foreign language into local worldviews in a way that can mediate between indigenous realities and the Saudi youth's hybrid pluralistic identities & globalising cultural lifestyles? Losing ownership over the content and process of curriculum design is not the right solution; it can be equated with loss of epistemic agency and the recolonising of the Muslim mind. For textbooks to be socially empowering, they should nurture intercultural sensitivity in a way that prepares learners to become responsible global citizens and intercultural speakers. EFL teaching materials and teacher education programs should focus more on developing learners' intercultural and critical thinking skills. Intercultural competence requires not only awareness of one's own culture but also a good understanding of how different cultures interact. Hence, teaching of intercultural communication skills is vital for creating educational safe environments in our diverse modern societies, and thus for promoting a sustainable world peace.

Acknowledgement This work was funded by the University of Jeddah, Jeddah, Saudi Arabia, under grant No. (UJ-22-SHR-2). The authors, therefore, acknowledge with thanks the University of Jeddah for its technical and financial support.

References

Al-Hajailan, T. (2006). *Teaching English in Saudi Arabia*. Dar Al-Sawlatia.

Bayhan, A. (2011). *How are English cultural elements presented in the Saudi English learning textbooks series?* Unpublished Master of TESOL thesis, Faculty of Education, La Trobe University, Australia.

Bennett, M. J. (1986). A developmental approach to training for intercultural sensitivity. *International Journal of Intercultural Relations, 10*(2), 179–196. https://doi.org/10.1016/0147-1767(86)90005-2

Bennett, M. J. (1993). Towards ethnorelativism: A developmental model of intercultural sensitivity." In R. M. Paige (Ed.), Education for the intercultural experience (2nd ed.). Intercultural Press.

Byram, M. (1997). *Teaching and assessing intercultural communicative competence*. Multilingual Matters.

Canale, G. (2016). (Re)searching culture in foreign language textbooks, or the politics of hide and seek. *Language, Culture and Curriculum, 29*(2), 225–243. https://doi.org/10.1080/0790831 8.2016.1144764

Ennis, M. J. (2015). Toward an integrated approach to language, culture, and communication in the foreign language classroom. In E. Nash, N. C. Brown, & L. Bracci (Eds.), *Intercultural horizons volume III: Intercultural competence: Key to the new multicultural societies of the globalized world* (pp. 3–33). Cambridge Scholars.

Fairclough, N. (1992). *Critical language awareness*. Longman.

Fairclough, N. (1995). *Media discourse*. Edward Arnold.

Healey, N. (2018). Ethics, legal professionalism and reconciliation: Enacting reconciliation through civility. *Dalhousie Journal of Legal Studies, 26*, 113–135.

Kramsch, C. (2011). The symbolic dimensions of the intercultural. *Language Teaching, 44*(3), 354–367. https://doi.org/10.1017/S0261444810000431

Liddicoat, A. J. (2005). Teaching languages for intercultural communication. In D. Cunningham & A. Hatoss (Eds.), *An international perspective of language policies, practices and proficiencies* (Fédération Internationale des Professeurs de Langues Vivantes (FIPLV)) (pp. 201–214). https://doi.org/10.1007/s10993-007-9059-2

Liddicoat, A. J., & Scarino, A. (2013). *Intercultural language teaching and learning.* Wiley-Blackwell.

Ministry of Education-Saudi Arabia. (2021, 28 September). *Teaching English from the first primary school to enhance students' language abilities from an early age.* https://www.moe.gov.sa/en/mediacenter/MOEnews/Pages/english-tech-2021-76.aspx. Accessed 24 Apr 2022.

Phillipson, R. (2017). Myths and realities of 'global' English. *Language Policy, 16,* 313–331.

Sahlane, A. (2022). Covering Iraq: The pragmatics of framing and visual rhetoric. In I. Chiluwa (Ed.), *Discourse, media & conflict* (pp. 93–116). Cambridge University Press. https://doi.org/10.1017/9781009064057.006

Sulaimani, A., & Elyas, T. (2018). Contextualizing gender representation in EFL textbooks in Saudi Arabia: A critical discourse analysis perspective. In A. F. Selvi & N. Rudolph (Eds.), *Conceptual shifts and contextualized practices in education for glocal interaction: Issues and implications* (pp. 55–76). Springer Nature.

Thompson, M. C. (2017). 'Saudi vision 2030': A viable response to youth aspirations and concerns? *Asian Affairs, 48*(2), 205–221. https://doi.org/10.1080/03068374.2017.1313598

Ahmed Sahlane (PhD, University of Ulster, Belfast) is Senior Lecturer in English at University of Jeddah (English Language Institute). He coordinated several EAP/ESP programs at Saudi universities, where he served in a variety of leadership roles such as business English program academic advisor and curriculum designer. He has taught English at all levels (K-12 and tertiary) in Morocco, Oman, Saudi Arabia, and Canada. He was the winner of Top Gun Master Teacher's Award, CDIS, Burnaby, Canada, 2001. His publications focus on the critical analysis of mediated political discourse from the perspective of argumentation theory and critical linguistics. He has published several articles and book chapters about the coverage of the 2003 Iraq War in Western opinion-editorial press. Sahlane's current research interests revolve around the rhetorics of populist discourse and media (mis)representation of cultural otherness. His research interests also include intersectionality and decoloniality studies, social semiotics, and critical pedagogy. Email: asahlan1@uj.edu.sa

Rosalind Pritchard is Emeritus Professor of Education and Senior Distinguished Research Fellow at Ulster University, where she was Head of the School of Education and Coordinator of Research. Her research interests include higher education and TESOL (especially cross-cultural adaptation and teaching strategies). She is a member of the British Academy of Social Sciences, an Honorary Member of the British Association for International and Comparative Education, Secretary of the European Association for Institutional Research and a Member of the Royal Irish Academy, of which membership is considered the highest academic honour in Ireland. She has held grants from the Leverhulme Trust, the Economic and Social Research Council, the UK Council for International Education, the German Academic Exchange Service and the Higher Education Innovation Fund. Email: R.Pritchard@ulster.ac.uk

Gender and Visual Representation in Moroccan ELT Textbook Discourse

Fatimazahrae Moutia

Abstract The present chapter aims at analysing the construction of identities and the representations of gender in the English language teaching (ELT) curriculum discourses in the Moroccan context. It examines the ELT discursive portrayal of women and evaluates to what extent these textbook narratives have been successful in (de) legitimising the traditional stereotypes that have been associated with gender in Muslim communities. The study aims to (a) give a new understanding of the localising of the global ELT profession in relation to gender identity, and (b) to address the methodological tools used to analyse the representation of women in the Moroccan ELT Textbooks. The analysis of ELT materials intends to deconstruct gender ideologies entrenched in K-12 textbook content. Power dynamics defining Moroccan culture include religion and identity politics (gender, social class, ethnicity, language, etc.). The findings revealed that textbooks indicate instances of gender-biased representation concerning visibility, occupations, and appearance. The chapter makes recommendations for circumventing gender inequalities in forthcoming Moroccan ELT textbooks.

Keywords Bias · Culture · Discourse · ELT · Gender · Morocco · Representation stereotypes · Textbook

1 Introduction

Gender equality is a relatively controversial policy concern in Morocco. One of its responsibilities is to implement the Gender Discrimination Ordinance to promote "equality" and "equal opportunities for all" (Sadiqi & Ennaji, 2006). With the increasing progress in modern technology, visual images have become a principal

F. Moutia (✉)
Sidi Mohamed Ben Abdellah University, Fes, Morocco

University of Pavia, Pavia, Italy

© The Author(s), under exclusive license to Springer Nature
Switzerland AG 2023
A. Sahlane, R. Pritchard (eds.), *English as an International Language Education*, English Language Education 33,
https://doi.org/10.1007/978-3-031-34702-3_18

characteristic permeating the contents of most foreign language textbooks. They are meant to consolidate the understanding of the reading passages they accompany as well as serve their pedagogical goal of raising students' interest in reading (Yassin et al., 2019).

The present study investigated the extent to which selected Moroccan English language teaching (ELT) textbooks succeed in depicting gender without stereotyping and inequality tendencies. It addressed the frequency of occurrence of feminine and masculine nouns and pronouns, the space allocated to feminine and masculine characters in texts and dialogues, the visibility of these characters in pictures and images, and their primacy in dialogues, texts, and examples. The study was conducted within the framework of the standards-based approach (SBA) (American Council on the Teaching of Foreign Languages). This choice was dictated not only by the Guidelines for Teaching English in Secondary Education (Ministry of National Education (MNE), 2007), which designates the SBA as the official framework for ELT in Morocco, but also by the opportunity to study, contrast, and understand the components of foreign and Indigenous cultures that this approach offers. The SBA aims to promote foreign language teaching through the development of a framework aimed at achieving eleven content standards contained in five main goal areas: Communication, Cultures, Comparisons, Connections, and Communities. While the Communication goal area promotes interpersonal, interpretive, and presentational forms of communication, the Cultures and Comparisons goal areas enable students to discover, contrast, and compare local and foreign languages and cultures. The Connections component encourages learners to use English to learn new information about other school subjects accessible only in English, while the Communities goal aims to equip learners with lifelong learning skills that enable them to confront the ever-changing realities of modern communities and prepare them for global citizenship (ACTFL, 1996; Ministry of National Education, 2007).

This study will examine some of the recurring patterns that characterise the visual representations of women and men in a variety of social contexts. The visual discourse of six Moroccan English as a Foreign Language (EFL) textbooks will be analysed in conjunction with two analytical techniques, namely content analysis and critical image analysis (Newfield, 2011). Particular attention will be paid to the categorisation of the two gender groups in terms of agency roles in images (e.g., active vs passive). The paper also examines how women and men are portrayed in visual images, what kinds of activities they engage in, in what settings, what occupational roles they play, and what kinds of power and dominance relationships can be inferred from their interactions.

2   Literature Review

Gender equality has been an issue for gender and language research from as early as the 1970s to the contemporary era, and gender stereotyping in textbooks is an issue in many different countries (Blumberg, 2007). For example, Western texts have generally promoted fixed Orientalist images of Muslim women and have presented them as poor, veiled, illiterate, victimised, sexually constrained, docile housewives (Said, 1978). In lacking a polyvalent dynamic approach to the real workings and functioning of concepts like monolingualism, multilingualism, code-switching, Islam, and illiteracy in real social everyday life, the Western image often remains essentialist and stereotypical, as it hides the wide disparities that exist between Moroccan women and that deeply affect the way they perform gender.

Gender performance and women's agency in the Moroccan socio-cultural context need to be examined in relation to four sets of factors: (a) the larger power structures that constitute Moroccan culture: history, geography, Islam, multilingualism, orality, social organisation, economic status, and political system, (b) social variables (geographical origin, class, level of education, job opportunity, language skills, and marital status), (c) contextual variables (physical setting, interlocutor, topic, and purpose of conversation), and (d) identity variables including motives, saliency, and immediate interest (Benattabou, 2014). These factors interact in a dialectic way and deeply influence the system of viewing the world conceptually, the ideology, beliefs, values, and meaning for Moroccan men and women. It is in this interaction that individual and collective identities, as well as gender roles, are continuously constructed, negotiated, and subverted. The interaction of the three factors which influence gender perception, gender subversion, and language use shows that the social and individual differences of Moroccan women can be understood only within the Moroccan sociocultural context.

The term 'gender' was first used in linguistics and other areas of social sciences. In linguistics, the term referred to the grammatical categories that indexed sex in the structure of human languages. Feminist theorists of the 1960s and 1970s used the term 'gender' to refer to the construction of the categories 'masculine' and 'feminine' in society. This construction was related to biological sex in contested ways. There have been two influential views in theorising about language and gender: the essentialist view and the constructionist view. The terms 'essentialist' and 'constructionist' have been used as 'qualifying' terms to refer to ways in which particular works in language and gender may be 'evaluated'. Hellinger (1980) and Sunderland (2000) also identified three types of gender bias based on the results of content analyses of EFL textbooks published in the 1970s and 1980s: 'exclusion', 'subordination and distortion', and 'degradation'. Exclusion refers to the phenomenon of females being relatively 'excluded' while males are over-represented (Sunderland, 2000). Subordination and distortion are concepts that allude to a situation in which gender relationship is represented in terms of power imbalance. In most cases, women are classified in lower positions and under the domination of men. Thus, there is a constant distortion bias that tempts us to believe that men are the cultural standard. Within this context, degradation indicates how females are degraded and denied the rights and dignity that are given to men.

The notion of identity is attracting growing attention in ELT research generally (Tsui, 2007). However, a corresponding interest within empirical ELT textbook research is hardly evident. Aside from gender-oriented studies, empirical studies in ELT textbook deal with the textual and linguistic construction of language identity. Three key studies in this thin literature are Hicks (2000), Kullman (2003) and Gray (2007). Kullman (2003) is an investigation into the construction of the learner's identity in ELT textbooks. The study develops a protocol of analysis based on an array of methodologies from cultural studies, social constructionism and deconstructionism, semiotics, social semiotics, and critical discourse analysis to uncover the meanings of the learner's identity construction in ELT textbooks (p. 160). Meanwhile, Hicks (2000) helps to develop an understanding of the role of others in shaping and constructing identity. How identity shapes literacy practices in an individualistic manner and how schooling and textbooks have a strong influence on learners. She based her studies on Bakhtin's issue of predicting the identity-forming paradigm of self and others in dialogue, time, and space. The process of identity's shaping and re-shaping continually occurs through interactions with newly gained knowledge and skills, which change perspectives and understandings (p. 19). This goes hand in glove with Gray's argument that views learning as an essential part of identity. Put differently, teaching offers learners with necessary academic, cultural, and social experiences to build up their personalities and interact in society (p. 122).

The fact that language teaching materials tend to project the ideological attitudes and cultural beliefs and values of the community in which they operate can hardly be denied. Sexism is reported to occur among a host of many other dimensions of these ideological attitudes. Sex stereotyping has often been the concern of a substantial body of research studies. Much of the existing literature on gender bias in ELT studies was basically concerned with the study of textbook discourses.

Researchers have investigated the representations of gender bias in various ELT textbooks. Their findings revealed different instances of gender bias, stressing the dominance of male characters over females (Ait Bouzid, 2016). For instance, various studies explored gender stereotypes in texts, dialogues, and tasks that feature in ELT textbooks and identified instances where female characters were mainly associated with indoor domestic activities that portray them as housewives, care-takers, nurses, babysitters, and teachers Otlowski, M. (2003). In addition, Ghorbani (2009) observed that female characters were often described using adjectives that portray their emotional and physical appearance, while men were represented using adjectives depicting their performance and personality.

Moreover, Amini & Birjandi (2012) found that ELT textbooks tend to present male characters in the first position in texts, dialogues, and language tasks. Such personae were given more space in texts and dialogues and uttered more words than female characters. Cunningsworth (1995) asserts that though textbooks present characters belonging to different social classes and racial groups, there is still an unequal division of space allotted to these categories. Litz (2005) adds that ELT textbooks maintained dominance of the Caucasian (white) race as characters belonging to this group are more frequently mentioned, more visible in pictures, and were given more space in dialogues and texts. Similarly, Yamada (2011) agrees that in spite of the diversity of races identified throughout ELT textbooks, Caucasians appeared more than Asians in Korean and Japanese ELT textbooks and that the Black population, within the general history textbooks, is highly underrepresented. Interestingly enough, Yaqoob & Zubair (2012) claim that ELT textbooks may work to disempower certain social classes and that they perpetuate the uneven division of power between different social classes by keeping the lower class powerless and the upper class more powerful. To avoid such discrepancies, Richards (2001) suggests a thorough investigation of the representation of social and racial representations in ELT textbooks; this might help to ensure an equal representation that does not privilege one class or one race over the other.

Other studies investigated the visibility of male and female characters in illustrations. Their findings indicated that male characters are more frequently identified in pictures and images throughout several ELT textbooks (Amini & Birjandi, 2012). These studies demonstrated that men appeared more in outdoor activities associated with sports, hobbies, and work, while women were often pictured in domestic activities such as household chores and care-taking activities. By contrast, a study conducted by Kazemi et al. (2013) revealed that men are invisible in some ELT textbooks and that women are represented as first-class citizens. Cunningsworth (1995) suggested that the textbooks that were investigated presented a balanced gender representation both quantitatively and qualitatively. In their evaluation of the pictorial representation of women and men, Hogben & Waterman (1997) focused more on the qualitative features of images. High-status occupational roles are attributed to men far more often than to women. When a man is visually represented juxtaposed with a woman in a hospital, for instance, the usual biased pattern is that the male character is a doctor while the female acts merely as his assistant nurse. Men are commonly depicted taking more active leadership roles. Utilising the tools of critical image analysis, Ziad & Ouahmiche (2019) found more instances of visual sexism in textbooks. Apart from very few bias-free gender images, the overwhelming majority of the photographic data examined in this study indicates more biased images discriminating against female characters. Male characters are visually more strongly represented, perform more social roles, and enjoy a more privileged status than their female partners.

The studies stated above evaluated locally designed textbooks in various countries: Morocco, Iran, Pakistan, the USA, Brazil, and England. The findings are generally in harmony despite some differences that are caused by the contextual variations of socio-cultural realities. Unfortunately, the results are quite disturbing: it appears that the way these ELT textbooks represent females does not foster gender equality. On the contrary, the way these textbooks represent men as more active, competent, and socially important eventually results in promoting stereotypes against women. This study is an endeavour to examine select Moroccan ELT textbooks in the light of these studies and to investigate whether Moroccan textbook writers have succeed in avoiding gender-biased representations that hinder the achievement of gender equality.

3   Research Methodology

The general objective of this chapter is to explore how women and men are represented in the visual discourse of Moroccan English as foreign language textbooks. In the present study, a mixed-methods design was used in which quantitative and qualitative data analysis techniques were combined in equal measure. The goal of such a design was to determine whether the two techniques converged toward an understanding of the problem under study. In addition, a mixed-methods design allowed complementary use of the strengths of quantitative and qualitative data analysis techniques. It was a single-phase design that allowed the two data sets to be analysed separately and then merged in the interpretation phase. Thus, the two data sets were integrated into an overall interpretation that related the quantitative findings to the qualitative findings of the content analysis (Krippendorff, 2013). This chapter examines a corpus of visual data in which female characters, male characters, or both appear in the visual discourse of EFL textbooks in Morocco. Nine textbooks were selected based on purposive sampling criteria. First, they are still currently used in all public educational institutions. Second, they have been written by Moroccan textbook authors, approved and officially recommended by the Ministry of Education, and widely used by teachers throughout Morocco. Third, like any other textbook, they have been examined, reviewed, and recommended by the Bureau of the Textbook Committee of the Ministry of Education. The last criterion for the selection of these textbooks is based on the year of their publication, which is between 2008 and 2010. This means that they are expected to have a balanced distribution and fair representation of the two gender groups, as recommended by the guidelines for avoiding gender bias documented in Sabir (2005). They represent nearly 100 percent of all textbooks currently used in the classroom.

The present study formulates two research questions to be addressed:

(a) To what extent do Moroccan ELT textbooks provide an authentic representation of gender in terms of frequency of appearance, visibility, space, and firstness?
(b) To what extent is the gendered textbook visual discourse well balanced?

The sampled textbooks covered the following four levels, which are currently used in teaching 9th grade, common core, first and second baccalaureate:

1. *Focus* (2008). Nadia Edition, Rabat, 4th grade.
2. *Window on the World* (2008). Rabat, Nadia Edition, common core, 5th grade.
3. *Outlook* (2010). Inter Graph, Rabat,5th grade.
4. *Visa to the World* (2010). Dar Nachr Almaarifa, Rabat,4th grade.
5. *Gateway to English*. Book 1 (2010). Nadia Edition, Rabat,6th grade.
6. *Ticket to English*. Book 1(2009). Casablanca, DIO. El Hadita, 6th grade.

Additionally, the qualitative analysis aimed at describing the nature of the gender references depicted throughout the six textbooks, explaining how gender roles were portrayed, and exploring the implications of biased gender categorisation. The description was supported by visual evidence from the six textbooks. The combination of quantitative and qualitative data allowed for the triangulation of the findings and helped in verifying the validity and the quality of interpretations. The quantitative analysis consisted of making frequency counts and illustrating them in tables followed by a descriptive qualitative analysis, which describes ways in which both sexes were represented through texts, dialogues, tasks, and images identified in the six textbooks. The interpretation of both quantitative and qualitative data is fused with the qualitative description that follows each table since it is impossible to separate qualitative analysis from interpretation.

4   Findings and Discussions

This section presents and discusses the results obtained from the analysis of the visual data using a bimodal approach. They are organised according to certain themes that are dominant in the visual discourse of the textbooks studied.

The pictorial representations of the contents of the Moroccan EFL textbooks were analyzed to determine the distribution of women and men by their visibility and frequency of appearance. As shown in Fig. 1, there are significant differences in the frequency distribution of the visibility of females and males in the images studied. The visual representation of the two gender groups indicates significant instances of hidden gender stereotypes and prejudice against women. In examining the visual content of the selected textbooks, a total of 2712 visual representations of women and men were collected. Male figures are identified more frequently than the corresponding female images. In total, there are 1602 images depicting male figures, which corresponds to 59.07%, while those reserved for women include 1110, which corresponds to an average of only 40.93% (see Table 1).

Figure 2 in *Visa* (p. 27), as a case in point, shows a tendency among male characters to outstrip females in the visual discourse of the sampled textbooks. The picture puts more emphasis on the explanation of the ten activities. As expected, nine out of ten (90%) of these visual images displaying a wide range of activities are all male-centred. The only exception is one picture displaying a woman drawing artistic pictures representing merely 10% of the whole group of images. Given the

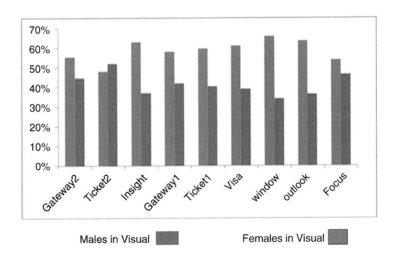

Fig. 1 Gender visual representations in Moroccan EFL textbooks

Table 1 The visual representation of gender in Moroccan EFL textbooks

The visual distribution of women and men	Males	Females	Total
Pictures	1602	1110	2712
Frequency	59.07%	40 .93%	100%

Fig. 2 Gendered occupations in ELT textbooks

social activities attributed to men, there is a tendency to see male figures in a variety of activities playing multiple roles. They are depicted in occupations such as pilot, dentist, engineer, doctor, bus driver, and others. They are also seen in roles related to public services, public speaking, and politics (see Fig. 3; *Insights*, p. 105).

Conversely, the activities assigned to women are invariably rooted in housework (see Fig. 4): cooking, washing dishes, preparing meals in the kitchen, and wearing an apron as a common sign of domestic life (*Ticket* 2, p. 79, and *Visa*, p. 42). They are also portrayed as mothers and housewives whose main job is to take care of their babies and children (*Ticket* 2, p. 79), or as nurses who take care of other people's health (Visa, p. 76). They also work in the world of shopping (*Window*, p. 72) or as saleswomen in a traditional food market (*Focus*, p. 118).

Even more stereotypical representations can be observed when women and men are juxtaposed. There is a general tendency to portray women as at the mercy of men. Male figures are depicted as protagonists grasping women's hands, clasping their bodies, or holding out their hands to help them. In Fig. 5 (*Focus*, p. 65), for example, a woman can be seen prostrating and kneeling before a man, as if asking him for mercy or protection, and extending her hand to him. Similarly, in *Ticket* 1

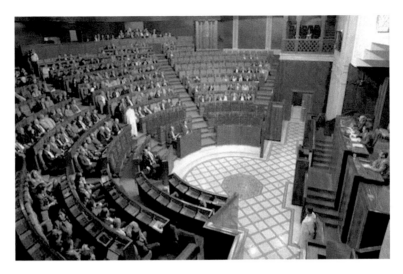

Fig. 3 Exclusion of women as political actors

Fig. 4 Perpetuating traditional gender roles

(p. 138), a male figure is shown rescuing a woman from danger. The man is placed in the position of a rescuer, standing in the centre and looking down at the girl, extending his arm to grasp her hand firmly as a gesture to save her life. Masculinity is seen in terms of control and power over the powerless (in this case, the girl and, by extension, women). Masculinity could also be conveyed through the brave decision of the man who takes all the risks to save the girl. The man is placed in the

Fig. 5 Chivalrous portrayal of men as saviours of women

Fig. 6 Woman as a chemist

foreground while the girl is shown from behind, symbolically deprived of her own personality and identity.

Although the visual discourse of EFL textbooks seems to be more male-oriented, especially in terms of activities associated with women and men, there are some images of women working on computers, giving presentations, and playing the role of chemists (see Fig. 6; Insights, p. 45).

Likewise, an image in *Gateway* 1 (p. 29) shows a group of elderly women in very traditional dress attending a class in a classroom (see Fig. 7). The text that accompanies this picture conveys the message that these women are illiterate and therefore still in desperate need of help, guidance, and supervision. The way they sit quietly suggests that they are passive recipients, forced to attend schools to combat illiteracy even in adulthood. However, it is important to mention that, nowadays, women's access to education, work, and politics in postcolonial Morocco has resulted in the inclusion of women in many different fields and the feminization of the public space (see Sadiqi, 2008).

Fig. 7 Oldish illiterate women

Whenever the subject of illiteracy is raised, women in traditional dress are shown. Almost the same image is found in other textbooks that address the same one-sided topic (see *Ticket* 2, p. 38 and p. 43). As anticipated, the male characters are exempted from all these prejudices as if the problem of illiteracy concerned only women but not men. Examining literacy levels in Morocco, the urban/rural division remains alarming. It has recently been found, in the Moroccan context, that illiteracy levels represent 25.6 percent among urban males, 48.5 percent among urban females, 62 percent among rural males, and 64.1 percent among rural females (UNESCO, 2019). Such an attitude seems to divert our attention from considering women as active agents who contribute to the progress of their social environment. As a matter of fact, women have launched into new fields of work including education, health and law, and they are engaged in political and social work. However, the exaggerated stereotypical images in textbooks under investigation do not reflect the current educational status of Moroccan women due to the huge progress that has been made in recent decades, especially with the new family code that enhances women's rights in different spheres.

This is consistent with evidence from studies in clinical psychology. This research trend has provided more evidence that psychology textbooks seem to be more biased. It is usually female characters that are blatantly used to illustrate prototypical examples of mental disorders in that anxiety or distress seem to be typically female attributes (Vikram, 2005).

In addition, male characters seem to appear in a number of sports competitions. The predominant tendency in these activities is that they guarantee strength, hard muscles, endurance, and stamina. In addition to football and basketball, men are also much more frequently depicted in images showing male-oriented sports such as wrestling, cycling, playing baseball, and swimming or running in tough competitions (*Focus*, p. 72). Similar visual images are used to depict men demonstrating their strength, masculinity and high endurance in very tough athletic competitions (*Ticket* 1, p. 37 and p. 43) or standing upright to show their willingness to fight in karate (Outlook, p. 89). However, the exclusion of women in sports in these

Fig. 8 The sports world as a male-dominated space

textbooks does not reflect the reality of their participation in many sports, including handball, football, golf, tennis, basketball, and athletics (see Fig. 8).

There is also a tendency for men to be overrepresented in an abundance of activities such as climbing, fishing, and hunting. In addition, they are depicted as having supernatural powers, being daring, and possessing extraordinary abilities such as a Spiderman (*Focus*, p. 63) and a gladiator (*Gateway* 2, p. 126). These athletic activities are traditionally associated with men because they require strong endurance, courage, and robust physical fitness. Female figures, on the other hand, are stereotypically underrepresented, as they are found in only a few sports. On the contrary, both sexes should be equally visible throughout the textbooks and more active roles should be given to women. Their visual representation, in fact, in such activities is very limited and restricted, both quantitatively and qualitatively. They are present in only 15 images (26.78%) in all the current textbooks, while men are represented in 41 images with an average distribution frequency of 73.22%.

Another prevalent theme, more common in Moroccan EFL textbooks aimed specifically at high school graduates is entitled "Women and Power". This separate unit was introduced in three textbooks, namely *Insights, Gateway* 2, and *Ticket* 2, to give due consideration to women's issues and women in positions of influence. *Insights* (p,63), for example, has integrated this unit to introduce some famous women. Figure 9 below shows five different images of women, including Nawal El Moutawakel as a "goodwill ambassador" for UNICEF, Fatima Mernissi as a "sociologist", Farida Benlyazid as a "filmmaker", Malika El Fassi as a "nationalist" and Meryem Chahid as an "astronomer".

In the list of famous men visually presented in the same textbook (*Insights,* p. 60), six other prominent figures are depicted, but with completely different captions. Females are portrayed as historically, socially, and politically unimportant figures, contributing little to society. These leaders are not given any details about their achievements, and they are not discussed in sections examining major political and economic events. It is argued that no space was devoted to Moroccan women's experiences and perspectives or to their contribution to knowledge production. The wording in these captions is more biased toward men, as too many adjectives are

Fig. 9 Moroccan female leaders

Fig. 10 Recognition of male scholars throughout history

used to emphasise male supremacy: Albert Einstein is introduced to the reader as a "Nobel Laureate"; Louis Pasteur as "known for his remarkable breakthrough in microbiology"; Ibn Khaldun as a "brilliant and prolific scientist"; Thomas Edison as "one of the most prolific inventors in history"; Alexander Graham Bell as the "inventor of the telephone at age 29"; and Bill Gates as the software developer and co/founder of Microsoft (see Fig. 10). Indeed, there is strong evidence that EFL textbooks are highly stereotypical in their visual representations and strongly discriminate against women.

Similarly, *Ticket* 2 (see Fig. 11) contains only four visual representations of famous women, namely Margaret Thatcher, chancellor Angela Merkel, Nawal El-Moutawakel and Shirin Ebadi (pp. 66–67, n. 25). There is little information about Fatema Mernissi (p. 74) and Leila Abouzeid (p. 76). They are Moroccan scholars and intellectuals who should occupy a big part of these textbooks, but they have been neglected. Women are almost exclusively portrayed in the roles of mothers, housewives, caretakers, and servants. But none of the men are represented in conducting traditionally feminine activities. This fosters sexism, unequal and unfair treatment based on gender.

Fig. 11 Female activists and leaders

Fig. 12 The Green March of 1975 for the liberation of the Moroccan Sahara

Another example of male domination in the EFL textbook is illustrated in the context of the historical Green March (see Fig. 12), which shows the victory of Morocco in the liberation of the Moroccan Sahara (*Gateway* 1, p. 68). The image shows a group of males proudly crossing the borders to the exclusion of women, standing at the front and raising their hands in the air to express their triumph. They are also depicted holding the Moroccan flags, the images of King Hassan II, and the holy Quran in victory. Although women were pivotal activists in this historical event, they are completely marginalised and excluded in the visual scenes celebrating the liberation of the Moroccan Sahara from Spanish colonialism. Women actively participated in political resistance and led the movement side by side with

Fig. 13 Gender in Moroccan currency

men. Men, on the other hand, are foregrounded and assume a dominant role throughout the frame of this image. This observation is consistent with Sadiqi's (2008) argument that "the role of women is either ignored or subordinated to that of men, thus constructing the subordination of Moroccan women and supporting patriarchy for centuries" (p. 166).

Likewise, official documents, embodied in stamps and banknotes, were also portrayed as male dominated. Ibn Battuta is visually represented within the frame of the Moroccan postage stamp (see Fig. 13; *Gateway* 1, p. 146). Similarly, Fig. 13 (*Visa*, p. 118) shows five banknotes, four of which (80%) feature only men, while only one banknote is reserved for a female figure, which is a very small minority with an average share of only 20%.

Therefore, there is a danger that Moroccan students reading the EFL textbooks will be ideologically indoctrinated to understand that the huge strides that have been made on a global scale have been achieved thanks to the influential contributions of men to the exclusion of women. Students are more likely to feel that women have no part in all of these so-called man-made achievements. Despite all these challenges, women lead various social and political movements; they have contributed to the democratisation and modernisation of the country by lobbying the government to sign a number of international conventions which would give rights to women by making huge changes in the family code. Men, on the other hand, are far more likely to be portrayed in professional attire. But in many Muslim societies, the traditional dress code for women is rule-governed, though in some, like Uzbekistan, the rules are more liberal, and women have more choices. Men are usually shown wearing a suit and tie, which gives them the image of gentlemen or businessmen. In these textbooks, there are more pictures of men in professional and business attire than of women. Such a visual tendency seems to associate men with wealth, professional prosperity, and social dominance. (see Fig. 14; *Ticket 2*, p. 40; *Insights*, p. 119; & *Ticket 1*, p. 133).

There was a major imbalance between pictures that featured only female characters and those that featured only males not only in terms of quantity but also in terms of quality. Male-centred pictures portrayed a variety of conventionally accepted images of politicians, soldiers, doctors, and judges.

Fig. 14 Male-dominated occupations

Furthermore, the objective of this study was also to identify which gender frequently came first in the sequence, the order of mention of female/male names, nouns, pronouns, and voices in texts, dialogues, and sentences of exercises where both female and male characters were sequenced. Indeed, out of 304 sequences, male characters appeared first in 182 (59.86%) instances, which significantly exceeds the 122 (40%) instances in which females came first. The six textbooks maintained the dominance of the male-first order since males were mentioned, for instance, in 56.6%, 58.4% and 59.7% instances in *Gateway to English* 2, *Insights into English* 2 and *Ticket 2 English*, respectively. Females occurred in the pole position only in 43.4% of sequences in *Gateway to English* 2, 41.6% in *Insights into English* 2 and 40.3% in *Ticket 2 English*.

The male dominance in the six textbooks was extended to include firstness. Male characters usually appeared first in exercises and texts, while female characters often spoke first in conversations. For instance, vocabulary and grammar exercises usually started with examples that referred to male characters either by names or pronouns. In conversations and dialogues, female characters usually initiated the conversation by asking questions to or greeting the male character. In some journalistic texts found in the textbooks, female characters appeared as interviewers and thus spoke first to ask the male interviewee a question. In most cases where various characters gave their opinion about a specific subject, male opinions were usually shown first, while female opinions were listed second or third. In fact, it seemed that the criteria of firstness, visibility, and frequency were in harmony as the findings attributed to each one of them indicate the dominance of males over females over the six examined textbooks. In terms of space and voice, female speeches were often reported indirectly while males spoke in direct speech, which made female voices less audible, and thus the space they were allotted was shortened. Additionally, most texts that featured male characters were autobiographical, whereas the female-centred texts were usually biographical. The textbooks that were analysed showed how males reign over space available to both genders.

5 Discussion of the Results

The results of this study show that Moroccan EFL textbooks are replete with countless instances of gender stereotyping. This bimodal analysis of the visual discourse in the textbooks studied has attempted to highlight some instances of gender imbalance that subtly shape the visual representation of the two gender groups. This lends more credence to and underpins, to a greater extent, our textual analysis of the same topic in the same textbooks studied in another paper (Benattabou, 2014).

The overall results of this study indicate that the visual representation of female characters is disproportionately high in the domestic environment while their representation is rendered almost invisible in relation to the world of work, especially when it comes to leadership roles. In contrast, the proportion of males in domestic settings is relatively low. However, they seem to be more represented, and they tend to take up the lion's share of almost all leadership roles. In addition, men's physical appearance appears to be predominant, as their images outweigh those of their female partners, which tends to reinforce women's invisibility. Hence, it is very unfortunate that despite the considerable contributions of a large percentage of women in the labour force (Sadiqi & Ennaji, 2006), such a colossal effort on the part of women has not been projected in these textbooks.

The present study fits into the burgeoning field of ELT textbook research. It contributes to this field of research by examining the largely contested phenomenon of gender representation in textbook discourse. The analysis of the above figures confirms both the dominance of men and the under-representation of women. As for the visual representation of gender, although there are more men than women in the illustrations of the textbook series, the phenomenon of gender stereotyping in terms of occupations and activities in the illustrations of the selected books is very conspicuous.

This study shows that women in English textbooks are not only represented in different occupational roles than men, but also in a narrower range of roles. It illustrates that women are mainly constructed as housewives or childcare workers, while men are in a wide range of occupations, such as engineer and scientist, and women are in less prestigious occupations, such as waitress, office lady, maid, and housewife. It is very surprising that even in Window textbook, which is written by an equal number of textbook authors, namely two males and two females, gender differences in the portrayal of women and men persist. This could explain, at least in part, that the gender of the author may not be a significant factor in the use of gender stereotypes in textbooks. However, even though this textbook was designed by both sexes, gender stereotypes endure and seem to offer strong resistance to changing the ways women are portrayed in the EFL textbooks. This proves the subtlety of the problem as it lurks beneath the surface, and without conscious awareness, any attempts to combat it will undoubtedly be futile and unsuccessful.

As regards discourse representation and gender in textbook dialogues, previous studies have often shown that male speakers are more visible than female speakers, with both more male and female speakers appearing in dialogues (Hellinger, 1980;

Mukundan & Nimehchisalem, 2008), and males producing more and longer utterances than females. Consequently, even in these textbooks, it could be argued that male speakers dominated the single-sex or mixed-sex dialogues by producing more words and longer utterances than females. In the light of textbooks under study, there is a greater number of "nominations" for males than for females when counted as "tokens". Both men and women were represented by proper names in formal, semi-formal, or informal ways, although both were most often referred to by their first names only. Thus, the phenomenon of women often being anonymous in the English textbooks studied by Hellinger (1980) is not found. However, men were represented in outdoor activities, as opposed to women, who were represented in a number of domestic spheres. Despite the fact that the status of Moroccan women's rights has witnessed a huge advance and the Moroccan Constitution empowers women, these changes have not been extended to EFL textbook representations, wherein women are confined to the traditional domestic and nurturing roles.

Another more biased description prevalent in the visual discourse of these textbooks, and which proves that the sampled textbooks have been designed through male lenses, is the exclusion of women from history. The progress humanity has gone through, and the remarkable accomplishments so far throughout the history of all nations at a worldwide level are invariably referred to as man-made. In Visa, for example, seven prominent scholars who have marked history at different levels are portrayed visually; all of them are men (*Visa*, p. 15). Also, on the same page, six famous stars are identified in pictures; only one of them is a woman, yielding on the whole a male-to-female ratio of 12:1 (*Visa*, p. 15). This implies that for every twelve male portrayals there is only one for females. This exclusion of women from history resonates well with the findings of Sadker and Sadker (1986). The present investigation seems to suggest that patriarchal attitudes and social expectations are invariably projected through the visual discourse of these textbooks, with male characters figuring significantly far more often in most of the occupational roles in the public and private sectors. This may also imply that past traditions which perpetuate a binary and dualistic vision of female and male gender roles remain relatively stable.

The findings of this study corroborate prior research arguments that mainstream media discourse has accentuated women's invisibility. In line with this, Moroccan EFL textbooks seem to have marginalized the contribution of women and are therefore far away from any adequate reflection of women's real occupations and accomplishments. This may surely inhibit both girls' and boys' worldviews regarding who they are and what are their true aspirations for the future. The type of gendered messages transmitted to students through these pictorial images tends to perpetuate certain attributes as being highly associated with either males or females. This pattern of representation might have been deployed, intentionally or not, as an effort to draw our attention away from the actual contribution of women as professional and managerial leaders, and seems to evoke and over-emphasize merely their indoor duties. Subsequent research indicates that continuous exposure of students to such biased representations may surely induce them to formulate inappropriate conclusions regarding their future participation in high managerial positions.

6 Conclusion

This chapter presented a study of the representation of gender in six Moroccan ELT textbooks currently used to teach first and second-year Baccalaureate levels in public high schools. The aim was to investigate the extent to which these textbooks include textual and visual gender content that provided an unbiased representation of females. This analysis of the pictorial representation of women and men in Moroccan EFL textbooks reasonably leads one to conclude that the textbook content is far removed from any fuller consideration of gender bias checklists documented at worldwide level against which the production of instructional materials could be evaluated (CEDAW, 1979).[1]

The textbooks appeared to be fraught with a wide range of gender misrepresentations favouring male characters. Qualitatively, 'exclusive' positive adjectives were used to describe both males and females in the reading passages of the six-textbook series; both males and females were portrayed engaging in household chores. The findings were in line with the literature and revealed that there was a noticeable shortage in the recognition of women's contributions in these textbooks which undoubtedly failed to contribute to promoting equality, justice, and peaceful coexistence for both sexes among learners. As a matter of fact, the contributions and accomplishments of famous female scholars have not been recognised in textbook discourse, as if their achievements and success are not worth knowing and unessential to be acknowledged. This, in fact, led to the exclusion and dismissal of their historical, political, and political presence.

These heavily biased portrayals may certainly have adverse psychological and educational effects on foreign language learners as target consumers of the visual contents of these textbooks. Subsequent research indicates that repeated exposure of students to biased visual portrayals of women and men similar to the ones investigated herein may do more harm than good to Moroccan EFL female learners; they may create learning inequalities in the classroom and set limits on women's future endeavours. This chapter can be located in the area of the intersection of language, gender, and women in Morocco. The male dominance in language was ascribable to the political and cultural dominance of men over women in society, and how the politics of representation work to perpetuate and strengthen gender stereotypes. In the overall Moroccan culture, women's voices lack discursive authority because of underrepresentation and politics of exclusion.

To improve the representation of women in EFL textbooks Moroccan ELT textbooks designers should (1) include authentic female names belonging to different fields and nations, (2) foster values of tolerance, understanding, coexistence, and equality between the sexes, (3) adopt inclusive pedagogies that recognize the contributions of women beyond the domestic sphere, and (4) present reading or

---

[1] CEDAW is an abbreviation that refers to the Convention on the Elimination of All Forms of Discrimination Against Women. It is an international treaty adopted in 1979 by the United Nations to proclaim all human rights, and those of women in particular.

listening activities that inform learners about success stories of some historical female figures from different disciplines, (5) textbooks should avoid textual and visual content that features women in stereotypical roles related to domestic, indoor and household activities, and should ensure that female and male characters are given equal space in images, dialogues, and texts.

References

ACTFL (1996). *Standards for foreign language learning: preparing for the 21st century.* https://www.actfl.org/educator-resources/world-readiness-standards-for-learning-languages. Accessed 1 Apr 2023.

Ait Bouzid, H. (2016). Race and social class in Moroccan ELT textbooks. *EFL Journal, 1*(2), 113–127. https://doi.org/10.21462/eflj.v1i2.11

Amini, M., & Birjandi, P. (2012). Gender bias in the Iranian high school EFL textbooks. *English Language Teaching, 5*(2), 134–147.

Benattabou, D. (2014). The representation of women in language teaching materials: A discourse analysis of gender bias in Moroccan EFL textbooks. In *Proceedings of the international conference on discourse in/and cultures in contact*, held in 22–23 December/2010 at the Faculty of Arts and Humanities Fes-Saiss. Conferences and Colloquia Series.

Blumberg, R. L. (2007). *Gender bias in textbooks: A hidden obstacle on the road to gender equality in education.* UNESCO. http://unesdoc.unesco.org/images/0015/001555/155509e.pdf

Cunningsworth, A. (1995). *Choosing your Coursebook.* Heinemann.

Ghorbani, M. R. (2009). ELT in Iranian high schools in Iran, Malaysia and Japan: Reflections on how tests influence use of prescribed textbooks. *Reflections on English Language Teaching, 8*(2), 131–139.

Gray, J. (2007). *A Study of cultural content in the British ELT global coursebook: A cultural studies approach.* Unpublished PhD Thesis. Institute of Education, University of London.

Hellinger, M. (1980). "For men must work, and women must weep": Sexism in English language textbooks used in German schools. *Women's Studies International Quarterly, 3*(2/3), 275–267. https://doi.org/10.1016/S0148-0685(80)92323-4

Hicks, D. (2000). Self and Other in Bakhtin's early philosophical essays: Prelude to a theory of Prose consciousness. *Mind, Culture, and Activity, 7*, 227–242. https://doi.org/10.1207/S15327884MCA0703_10

Hogben, M., & Waterman, C. (1997). Are all of your students represented in their textbooks? A content analysis of coverage of diversity issues in introductory psychology textbooks. *Teaching of Psychology, 24*, 102. https://doi.org/10.1207/s15328023top2402_3

Kazemi, S., Aidinlou, N., Savaedi, S., & Alaviniya, M. (2013). Subliminal culture, sexism and hidden curriculum in the internationally distributed interchange textbooks. *Australian Journal of Applied Sciences, 7*(9), 182–191.

Krippendorff, K. (2013). *Content analysis. An introduction to its methodology* (3rd ed.). Sage.

Kullman, J. P. (2003). *The Social construction of learner identity in the UK-published ELT coursebook.* Unpublished Ph.D. thesis, University of Kent.

Litz, D. R. A. (2005). Textbook evaluation and ELT management: A South Korean Case Study. *Asian EFL Journal, 48*(1), 1-53.

Ministry of National Education (2007). *English language guidelines for secondary schools: Common core, first-year, and second-year baccalaureate.*

Mukundan, J., & Nimehchisalem, V. (2008). Gender representation in Malaysian secondary school English language textbooks. *Indonesian Journal of English Language Teaching, 4*(2), 155–173.

Newfield, D. (2011). From visual literacy to critical visual literacy: An analysis of educational materials. *English Teaching: Practice and Critique: University of the Witwatersrand, 10*(1), 81–94. http://education.waikato.ac.nz/research/files/etpc/files/2011v10n1art5.pdf

Otlowski, M. (2003). Ethnic diversity and gender bias in EFL textbooks. *Asian EFL Journal. The EFL Professional's Written Forum*. Microsoft Word - june_03_mo.doc (asian-efl-journal.com).

Richards, J. (2001). *Curriculum development in language teaching*. Cambridge University Press.

Sabir, M. (2005). *Gender and public spending on education in Pakistan: A case study of disaggregated benefit incidence. Public Economics 0503005*. University Library of Munich.

Sadiqi, F. (2008). Language and gender in Moroccan urban areas. *International Journal of the Sociology of Language*, (190), 145–165.

Sadiqi, F., & Ennaji, M. (2006). The feminization of public space: Women's activism, the family law, and social change in Morocco. *Journal of Middle East Women's Studies, 2*(2), 86–114.

Sadker, M., & Sadker, D. (1986). Genderism in the classroom: From grade school to graduate school. *Phi Delta Kappan, 67*, 512–515.

Said, E. W. (1978). *Orientalism*. Pantheon Books.

Sunderland, J. (2000). Issues of gender representations in textbooks: A state of the art studies. *Language Teaching, 33*(4), 203–223.

The Ministry of National Education. (2007). *The National Curriculum for Basic Education*. http://www.nied.edu.na/assets/documents/05Policies/NationalCurriculumGuide/Po_NationalCurriculumBasicEducation_

Tsui, A. (2007). Complexities of identity formation: A narrative inquiry of an EFL teacher. *TESOL Quarterly, 41*, 657–680. https://doi.org/10.1002/j.1545-7249.2007.tb00098.x

UNESCO (2019). *Participation in Education.* https://uis.unesco.org/en/country/ma?theme=education-and-literacy

Vikram, P. (2005). Gender and mental health: A review of two textbooks of psychiatry. *Economic & Political Weekly, 40*(18), 1850–1858.

Yamada, M. (2011). Awareness of racial and ethnic diversity in Japanese junior high schools' English language textbooks. *Critical Inquiry in Language Studies, 8*(3), 289–312. https://doi.org/10.1080/15427587.2011.592131

Yaqoob, T., & Zubair, S. (2012). Culture, class, and power: A critique of Pakistan English language textbooks. *Pakistan Journal of Social Sciences, 32*(2), 529–540.

Yassin, A. A., Razak, N. A., & Maasum, N. R. M. (2019). Investigating the need for computer assisted cooperative learning to improve reading skills among Yemeni university EFL students: A needs analysis study. *International Journal of Virtual and Personal Learning Environments, 9*(2), 15–31.

Ziad, K., & Ouahmiche, G. (2019). Gender positioning in the visual discourse of Algerian secondary education EFL textbooks: Critical image analysis vs. teachers' perceptions. *Journal of Language and Linguistic Studies, 15*(3), 773–793.

Fatimazahrae Moutia is a final-year PhD candidate at the University of Sidi Mohamed Ben Abdellah, Fes, Morocco. She is working on Anthropology of the Female Body, affiliated with Psychology, Sociology, and Cultural Studies laboratory. She is currently a visiting scholar at University of Pavia, Italy. Her primary academic research interests are focused on the novel, cultural studies, gender issues analysis, and postcolonial theory. She is the author of two articles entitled "Can the Subaltern Body Perform? Moroccan *Shikhat* as Living Heritage in the Virtual" (2020) and "Politics of the Female Body" (2021). Email: fatimazahraemoutia96@outlook.com

The Impact of English Proficiency on the Sociocultural and Academic Adaptation of Chinese Students in Short-term Exchange Programs: The Mediating Effects of Cultural Intelligence

Dandan Yao and Mei Tian

Abstract This chapter examines the impact of English proficiency on sociocultural and academic adaptation through the mediating effects of cultural intelligence. Data were generated by a web-based survey involving 530 Chinese students having participated in short-term exchange programmes in English-speaking countries. A partial least square structural equation modelling analysis was performed. The results revealed that English proficiency and the four dimensions of cultural intelligence explained 81.6% of the variance in academic adaptation and 15.9% in sociocultural adaptation, indicating that English proficiency and cultural intelligence significantly predicted the participants' sociocultural and academic adaptation. The bootstrapping results indicated that the four dimensions of cultural intelligence partially mediated the relationship between English proficiency and academic adaptation, while only cognitive cultural intelligence serves as a mediator between English proficiency and sociocultural adaptation. The results confirmed the significant mediating role of multi-faceted cultural intelligence in the relationship between English competence and adaptation among Chinese students in short-term study-abroad programmes.

Keywords Chinese students · Study abroad · Exchange programme · Cultural intelligence · Sociocultural adaptation · Academic adaptation · Intercultural competence

D. Yao
School of Foreign Studies, Xi'an Jiaotong University (City College), Xi'an, China

M. Tian (✉)
School of Foreign Studies, Xi'an Jiaotong University, Xi'an, China
e-mail: Temmytian@mail.xjtu.edu.cn

A. Sahlane, R. Pritchard (eds.), *English as an International Language Education*, English Language Education 33,
https://doi.org/10.1007/978-3-031-34702-3_19

1 Introduction

Organization for Economic Cooperation and Development (OECD) statistics (2020) show that around 5.6 million students pursued higher education outside their home countries in 2018, more than twice the number in 2015. China has long been the world's largest international student source country. With Chinese universities' growing emphasis on international cooperation in the endeavour of building world-class academic excellence, an increasing proportion of the total Chinese students abroad, roughly 662,100 in 2018 (China Ministry of Education, 2019), is enrolled in the universities' short-term study-abroad (STSA) programmes. Previous research has explored STSA students' experiences, of which the findings highlighted language barriers as a major problem affecting these students' intercultural learning (Cao & Meng, 2019; Peng & Patterson, 2022; Shafaei & Razak, 2016; Martirosyan et al., 2015; Neumann et al., 2019; Quiñones et al., 2021; Smith & Khawaja, 2011; Wilson et al., 2013; Wright & Schartner, 2013; Young et al., 2013; Yu et al., 2019). For Chinese STSA students studying in English-speaking countries, insufficient English proficiency negatively influenced their academic performance (Doiz et al., 2011; Hellekjaer, 2010; Kim & Shin, 2014), while limiting their interaction in daily life (Wang & Hannes, 2014).

Cultural intelligence (CQ), proposed by Ang and her colleagues, refers to culture-specific knowledge, attitudes, and behaviours that enable individuals to "function …effectively in culturally diverse settings" (Ang et al., 2007, p. 336; Earley & Ang, 2003). Studies have reported the positive relationship between international students' English proficiency and CQ (e.g., Jurasek & Potocky, 2020; Poort et al., 2021; Uen et al., 2018), and the positive link between their CQ and intercultural adaptation (Ang et al., 2007). These studies, however, focused on international students from English-speaking countries, particularly the US. Given the increasing number of STSA students from China, an investigation into their CQ, and how CQ relates to English proficiency and intercultural adaptation is imperative.

The current study examined the effect of English proficiency on the sociocultural and academic adaptation of Chinese STSA students, mediated by CQ. Data were generated by a web-based survey involving 530 Chinese students across disciplines at a national key university in China. When the survey was conducted, the respondents had just completed short-term programmes in English-speaking countries. Using the adapted Cultural Intelligence scale (Ang et al., 2007), the survey explored the characteristics of the respondents' CQ, the predictive power of their English proficiency and CQ for sociocultural and academic adaptation, and the mediating effects of CQ between their English proficiency and adaptation. Although focusing on Chinese students, the research holds implications for home and host universities to support international students' positive experiences in short-term exchange programmes.

2 Literature Review

In this section, we first introduce the concept of cultural intelligence. We then review empirical research on the relationships between English proficiency and cultural intelligence, between English proficiency and sociocultural and academic adaptation, and between cultural intelligence and sociocultural and academic adaptation. Based on previous research findings, a research model is proposed for the current research, aiming to explore the predictor power of English proficiency and cultural intelligence on sociocultural and academic adaptation.

2.1 Cultural Intelligence

Cultural intelligence is defined as "a set of malleable capabilities developed and improved through exposure to other cultures" (Earley & Ang, 2003, p. 108). It is a "culture-free", multi-faceted construct (Ng & Earley, 2006, p. 7), consisting of meta-cognitive CQ (MCCQ), cognitive CQ (CCQ), motivational CQ (MCQ), and behavioural CQ (BCQ) dimensions. MCCQ involves high-order mental abilities to anticipate the cultural preferences of others and to adjust cultural knowledge during and after intercultural interactions. Students with high MCCQ have the abilities to process cultural information and incorporate it into their cultural understandings (Earley & Ang, 2003). CCQ refers to the abilities to acquire cultural knowledge, such as norms and conventions, and culture-specific differences in academic and social communications (Ang et al., 2004). MCQ focuses on individuals' attitudes towards learning cultural knowledge and functioning in target cultures. Those with high MCQ demonstrate their interest and confidence in studying in a multicultural environment, despite the challenges they may encounter. BCQ refers to the abilities to demonstrate appropriate verbal and nonverbal behaviours during interaction with people from different cultures (Ang et al., 2004).

2.2 English Proficiency and CQ

Previous studies have explored the relationship between English proficiency and cultural intelligence (e.g., Eisenberg et al., 2013; Huff, 2013; Jurasek & Potocky, 2020; Poort et al., 2021; Uen et al., 2018). Jurasek and Potocky (2020) empirically confirmed that international students' English competence significantly affected their overall CQ rating. Other studies reported a significant correlation between English proficiency and CCQ (see also Eisenberg et al., 2013; Huff, 2013; Remhof et al., 2012). The higher the international students' language proficiency, the more capable they were of performing well in intercultural contexts. Earley (2002) and Earley and Ang (2003) reported that English proficiency positively affected BCQ and MCQ. Good command of the English language could support appropriate behaviours and desirable engagement in culturally "new" environments. Based on the research reviewed above, the following hypothesis was proposed:

H1 English proficiency has a positive influence on MCCQ (H1a), CCQ (H1b), MCQ (H1c) and BCQ (H1d).

2.3 English Proficiency and Sociocultural and Academic Adaptation

Ward (1996) defined sociocultural adaptation as "behavioural competence or skills" within "a cultural learning paradigm". Many studies have established a positive relationship between English proficiency and international students' sociocultural adaptation (Cao & Meng, 2019; Wilson et al., 2013; Yu et al., 2019). Accordingly, English proficiency is a prerequisite for cultural learning. An adequate level of English enables the initiating and managing of daily interactions with locals in diverse intercultural settings.

Academic adaptation refers to the degree to which international students meet and deal with various educational demands of their host universities (Beyers & Goossens, 2002; Meng et al., 2018). Previous research has pinpointed the significant influences of English proficiency on international students' academic adaptation. For example, Hung and Hyun (2010) reported language challenges that non-native English speakers face when learning English, ranging from reading academic articles to comprehending lectures and interacting with peers and local faculty. Cao and Meng (2019) focused on Chinese students in Belgium and found that Chinese international students with higher levels of English reported better academic adaptation in English-mediated courses. Based on these studies, we put forward the following hypotheses:

H2 English proficiency has a positive effect on sociocultural adaptation.
H3 English proficiency has a positive effect on academic adaptation.

2.4 CQ and Sociocultural and Academic Adaptation

Earley and Ang (2003) proposed the direct effect of CQ on international students' sociocultural adaptation, suggesting that individual students with higher CQ would adapt more effectively to host cultural environments. Other studies have tested the hypothesis, the findings of which, however, are inconclusive. For example, Ang et al. (2004) and Templer et al. (2006) confirmed that MCQ significantly positively influenced international students' sociocultural and academic adaptation. Similarly, Earley and Peterson (2004) stated that the higher MCQ international students had, the higher degree of adaptation they would achieve in a new cultural setting. Moreover, Ang et al. (2007) confirmed that MCQ and BCQ predicted sociocultural adaptation. Ward et al. (2011) reported that higher levels of MCCQ and MCQ facilitated sociocultural adaptation. In contrast, Mokhothu and Callaghan (2018) found that MCQ was significantly related to international students' sociocultural adaptation and academic performance. Based on the previous research's findings, the following hypotheses are posed.

H4: MCCQ (H4a), CCQ (H4b), MCQ (H4c) and BCQ (H4d) have a positive effect on sociocultural adaptation.

H5: MCCQ (H5a), CCQ (H5b), MCQ (H5c) and BCQ (H5d) have a positive effect on academic adaptation.

2.5 Cultural Intelligence as a Mediator

Previous scholarship has investigated the mediating effects of CQ. For example, Eisenberg et al. (2013) reported that CCQ mediated the relationship between students' proficiency in the target language and their intention to work in the host culture. In addition, Mokhothu and Callaghan (2018) found that MCQ mediated the relationship between international students' sociocultural adaptation and academic performance. Although empirical studies indicated that CQ was both an outcome influenced by foreign language proficiency and a determinant influencing international students' adaptation to the host culture, the mediation effect of CQ between Chinese students' English proficiency and their intercultural adaptation has been inadequately examined. Hence, we propose the following hypotheses:

H6: MCCQ (H6a), CCQ (H6b), MCQ (H6c) and BCQ (H6d) mediate the relationship between English proficiency and sociocultural adaptation.

H7: MCCQ (H7a), CCQ (H7b), MCQ (H7c) and BCQ (H7d) mediate the relationship between English proficiency and academic adaptation.

3 The Proposed Research Model

A hypothesized research model was established (see Fig. 1). The research model illustrates the direct effects of English proficiency on sociocultural and academic adaptation, the direct effects of CQ on sociocultural and academic adaptation, and the indirect effects of English proficiency on sociocultural and academic adaptation mediated by CQ.

The research model proposed above consists of one independent variable (i.e., English proficiency), two dependent variables (i.e., sociocultural and academic adaptation), and four mediators (i.e., MCCQ, CCQ, MCQ, and BCQ). As shown in Fig. 1, English proficiency may directly affect the four facets of CQ (i.e., MCCQ,

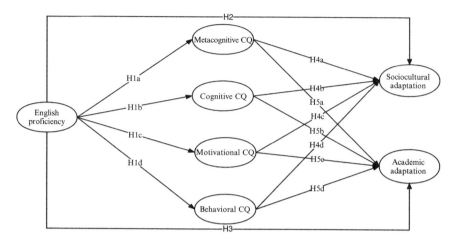

Fig. 1 The proposed research model

CCQ, MCQ, and BCQ), sociocultural adaptation, and academic adaptation. The four facets of CQ (MCCQ, CCQ, MCQ, and BCQ) may directly affect sociocultural and academic adaptation. The four facets of CQ (i.e., MCCQ, CCQ, MCQ, and BCQ) may mediate the relationship between English proficiency and sociocultural adaptation, and the relationship between English proficiency and academic adaptation.

In the following sections, we will briefly present our methodology, including information on participants, instruments and data analysis methods. We then report research results before discussing the identified relationships between predictors and outcome variables. Finally, research implications, limitations and recommendations for future research are presented.

4   Research Methodology

4.1   Participants

In the 2018/19 academic year, with the consent of the office of academic affairs at a national key university in China, an online anonymous questionnaire survey was conducted, involving 530 Chinese students taking part in short-term study abroad programmes in English-speaking countries. The informed consent was obtained before the participants filled in the questionnaire. Among all participants, 247 (46.6%) were female and 283 (53.4%) were male; 346 were undergraduates (65.29%), 115 (21.7%) were Master's students and 69 were PhD students (13.02%); 105 (19.81%) majored in natural sciences, 159 (30%) in engineering technology, 182 (34.34%) in humanities and social sciences, 49 (9.25%) in medical sciences, and 35 (6.6%) in agricultural sciences. Table 1 presents the demographic information of the survey respondents. According to Hair et al. (2016), the sample size

Table 1 Participants' demographics[a]

	Category	No.	Percent
Age	≤20	120	22.6%
	21–25	297	56%
	26–30	91	17.2%
	≥31	22	4.2%
Gender	Female	247	46.60%
	Male	283	53.40%
Areas	Asia	111	20.94%
	North America	240	45.29%
	Oceania	37	6.98%
	Europe	142	26.79%
Academic level	Undergraduate	346	65.29%
	Master's	115	21.7%
	PhD student	69	13.02%
University disciplines	Natural Sciences	105	19.81%
	Engineering and Technology	159	30%
	Humanities and Social Sciences	182	34.34%
	Medical Science	49	9.25%
	Agricultural Science	35	6.6%

[a](N = 530)

using partial least square structural equation modelling (PLS-SEM) should be greater than ten times the maximum number of links associated with a latent variable in the structural model. In this survey, the sample size (N = 530) was greater than the required sample size estimation, satisfying the model testing conditions.

4.2 Instrument and Measures

All respondents were invited to complete an online questionnaire (see Table 2). In this questionnaire, English language proficiency was measured by students' self-reported English skills and abilities (3 items) on a 6-point Likert scale from *very poor* (1) to *excellent* (6), where higher scores demonstrated higher levels of English proficiency. The 19-item Cultural Intelligence scale (CQS) (Ang et al., 2007) was adapted and used to measure MCCQ (4 items), CCQ (6 items), MCQ (5 items), and BCQ (4 items). The items were tested by a 7-point Likert scale, ranging from 1 *strongly disagree* (1) to *strongly agree* (7), with higher scores exhibiting higher CQ. Ten items from the academic adaptation subscale of the Student Adaptation to College Questionnaire (Baker & Siryk, 1999) were adopted to measure students' academic adaptation. This questionnaire has been validated by various studies (e.g., Meng et al., 2018). A 5-point Likert scale, ranging from *strongly disagree* (1) to *strongly agree* (5), was used, with higher scores indicating better academic adaptation.

Table 2 Constructs, number of items, and representative examples

Construct	Number of items	Representative examples
*EP	3	Please indicate your overall English proficiency.
MCCQ	4	I am conscious of my cultural knowledge when interacting with people with different cultural backgrounds.
CCQ	6	I know other languages' rules (e.g., vocabulary, grammar).
MCQ	5	I enjoy interacting with people from different cultures.
BCQ	4	I change my verbal behaviour (e.g., accent, tone) when an intercultural interaction requires it.
**SCA	13	I understand local jokes and humour
***AA	10	My academic goals and purposes are well defined.

*EP = English proficiency, **SCA = sociocultural adaptation, ***AA = academic adaptation

Sociocultural adaptation was measured by the adapted Sociocultural Adaptation Scale (SCAS, Ward & Kennedy, 1999), a 13-item scale assessing the difficulties international students perceive when living in cross-cultural environments and socialising with people from diverse cultures. A 5-point Likert scale, ranging from *extreme difficulty* (1) to *no difficulty* (5), was used to rate the perceived levels of difficulty in "making friends", "using the transport system", "going shopping", "understanding jokes and humour", "dealing with the climate", "getting used to the local food/finding food you enjoy", and "adapting to local accommodation". Higher scores demonstrate less difficulty in conducting these social activities and better sociocultural adaptation in a foreign country.

5 Data Analysis

This study performed PLS-SEM to test the hypothesized relationships between the latent variables. PLS-SEM was designed to test a prediction model and identify key predictors for dependent variables, and has been verified as a highly effective tool to examine theoretically supported casual models (Hair Jr et al., 2016). This research then used StataSE-64 to analyse the impact of control variables on key constructs.

5.1 Results

5.1.1 Descriptive Statistics and Correlations

Table 3 presents descriptive statistics. As displayed, the mean of the respondents' self-rated English proficiency was 3.36, indicating that their English proficiency was almost "good" (4 = good). The means of the four dimensions of CQ were between 4.12 and 4.58, higher than the median value (4), indicating that the

Table 3 Descriptive statistics and correlations of the variables

Variables	M	SD	Min	Max	1	2	3	4	5	6	7
1. EP	3.36	1.37	1.00	6.00	0.891						
2. MCCQ	4.55	1.83	1.00	7.00	0.763**	0.949					
3. CCQ	4.12	1.69	1.00	7.00	0.769**	0.908**	0.931				
4. MCQ	4.30	1.77	1.00	7.00	0.756**	0.921**	0.910**	0.939			
5. BCQ	4.58	1.39	1.00	7.00	0.752**	0.899**	0.896**	0.899**	0.963		
6. SCA	3.80	1.05	1.00	5.00	0.376**	0.234**	0.286**	0.234**	0.252**	0.937	
7. AA	3.25	1.11	1.00	5.00	0.763**	0.883**	0.823**	0.869**	0.851**	0.185**	–

Note 1. *M* mean, *SD* standard deviation. The diagonal elements are the square roots of AVEs
Note 2: (N = 530)
**p < 0.01

respondents tended to slightly agree that they were capable of functioning in their host cultures. Moreover, the mean of the self-reported SCA was 3.80, revealing that, on average, the participants tended to have "slight difficulty" (4 = slight difficulty) in sociocultural adaptation. The mean of the self-reported AA was 3.25, indicating that Chinese students tended to have "moderate difficulty" (4 = moderate difficulty) in academic adaptation. Moreover, Table 3 presents correlations of the variables, revealing that all variables were positively and significantly correlated.

5.2 Construct Validity and Reliability

The convergent validity of each variable was measured by the analysis of factor loading, composite reliability (CR), Cronbach's alpha, and average variance extracted (AVE). Table 4 displays the results of the convergent validity analysis. All indicators' outer loadings were above 0.7, ranging from 0.713 to 0.980, higher than the benchmark value of 0.7 (Fornell & Larcker, 1981). The values of Cronbach's alpha ranged from 0.932 to 0.974, showing the high reliability of the constructs. The CR values of the constructs ranged from 0.950 to 0.981, higher than 0.6, exhibiting its high internal consistency. The AVE values of all the constructs ranged from 0.593 to 0.927, higher than 0.5, confirming the convergent validity of the constructs. The discriminant validity was also confirmed, as the square roots of AVEs of each construct were greater than other correlation values (see Table 3).

Table 4 Measurement items and loadings

Constructs	Indicators	Cronbach' α	Weight/loadings	*T* value	CR	AVE
EP	EP1	0.932	0.942	131.973	0.957	0.881
	EP2		0.947	172.308		
	EP3		0.926	127.095		
MCCQ	MCCQ1	0.974	0.961	165.200	0.981	0.927
	MCCQ2		0.980	463.688		
	MCCQ3		0.955	302.604		
	MCCQ4		0.954	144.425		
CCQ	CCQ1	0.969	0.914	95.083	0.975	0.866
	CCQ2		0.926	131.735		
	CCQ3		0.935	106.296		
	CCQ4		0.949	176.391		
	CCQ5		0.928	88.327		
	CCQ6		0.932	115.824		
MCQ	MCQ1	0.965	0.951	172.544	0.973	0.877
	MCQ2		0.957	183.554		
	MCQ3		0.948	105.160		
	MCQ4		0.885	77.122		
	MCQ5		0.940	123.887		
BCQ	BCQ1	0.963	0.933	106.515	0.973	0.901
	BCQ2		0.949	141.827		
	BCQ3		0.954	130.662		
	BCQ4		0.961	220.690		
AA	AA1	0.971	0.886	66.119	0.975	0.794
	AA2		0.844	51.121		
	AA3		0.902	102.023		
	AA4		0.878	73.865		
	AA5		0.886	68.642		
	AA6		0.908	99.537		
	AA7		0.871	62.810		
	AA8		0.920	105.051		
	AA9		0.911	99.615		
	AA10		0.900	91.646		
SCA	SCA1	0.943	0.713	26.664	0.950	0.593
	SCA2		0.820	47.020		
	SCA3		0.815	45.693		
	SCA4		0.719	27.442		
	SCA5		0.760	28.597		
	SCA6		0.810	39.670		
	SCA7		0.797	41.478		
	SCA8		0.783	33.141		
	SCA9		0.734	29.475		
	SCA10		0.748	28.749		
	SCA11		0.788	36.610		
	SCA12		0.747	29.092		
	SCA13		0.766	33.243		

CR composite reliability, **AVE* average variance extracted

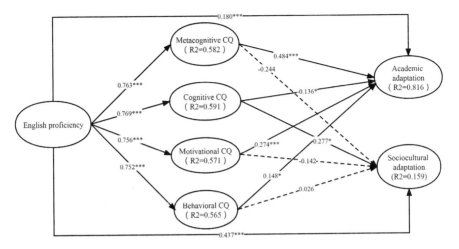

Fig. 2 Results of the PLS-SEM Analysis. (*Note.* *p<0.05 ***p<0.001)

6 Hypotheses Testing

6.1 Coefficient of Determination, f² Effect Size, and Predictive Relevance

PLS-SEM was performed to test the hypothesized model. The coefficient of determination (R^2) represents the model's prediction accuracy on the endogenous variables. As shown in Fig. 2, the R^2 values of MCCQ (0.582), BCQ (0.565), CCQ (0.591), MCQ (0.571) were all high, indicating the model's high prediction accuracy on the endogenous variables. The R^2 value of academic adjustment (0.816) was substantially high, showing that 81.6% of the variance in AA was explained by English proficiency, MCCQ, CCQ, MCQ, and BCQ.

The change of the R^2 value assessed the influence on the endogenous constructs when one of the endogenous constructs was deleted from the model. It was measured by the f² effect size, with the values of 0.02, 0.15, and 0.35, respectively, representing small, medium, and large effect sizes. The results showed that English proficiency had large effect sizes on MCCQ (1.395), CCQ (1.444), MCQ (1.333), BCQ (1.301), and small effect sizes on AA (0.067) and SCA (0.086). MCCQ had a medium effect size on AA (0.150), while MCQ had a small effect size on AA (0.037).

The blindfolding procedure was applied to measure the predictive relevance (Q^2) of the path model. Values greater than 0 indicate that the model has predictive relevance for a certain endogenous construct (Hair Jr et al., 2016). The higher the Q^2 value, the stronger the predictive relevance. If the value is equal to or greater than 0.50, it demonstrates large predictive power. The Q^2 values of MCCQ, CCQ, BCQ, and AA range from 0.507 to 0.643, indicating the large predictive power of these constructs.

6.2 Direct Effects of English Proficiency on CQ, Sociocultural Adaptation, and Academic Adaptation

The effects of English proficiency on CQ, SCA, and AA were tested. As indicated in Fig. 2, English proficiency had significantly positive effects on the four dimensions of CQ; thus, H1a, H1b, H1c, and H1d were supported. Moreover, the positive associations of English proficiency with MCCQ ($\beta = 0.763$, $p < 0.001$), CCQ ($\beta = 0.769$, $p < 0.001$), MCQ ($\beta = 0.756$, $p < 0.001$), and BCQ ($\beta = 0.752$, $p < 0.001$) were substantial, indicating a strong effect of English proficiency on the four-faceted CQ. In addition, the results exhibited strong positive links between English proficiency and AA ($\beta = 0.180$, $p < 0.001$) and SCA ($\beta = 0.437$, $p < 0.001$), thereby supporting H2 and H3. Among the direct paths between the four CQ dimensions and SCA, only one link between CCQ and SCA was positively significant ($\beta = 0.277$, $p < 0.05$), while MCCQ, MCQ, and BCQ failed to predict SCA, and thus only H4b was supported. Moreover, MCCQ ($\beta = 0.484$, $p < 0.001$), CCQ ($\beta = -0.136$, $p < 0.05$), MCQ ($\beta = 0.274$, $p < 0.001$), and BCQ ($\beta = 0.148$, $p < 0.05$) were significantly associated with AA, while CCQ was negatively associated with AA. Therefore, H5a, H5c, and H5d were supported, while H5b was rejected.

6.3 Mediating Effects of CQ

Mediation involves strong correlations between an independent variable and a mediating variable, and between the mediating variable and a dependent variable. Baron and Kenny (1986) suggested that to test the mediating effect of a variable, four conditions should be satisfied. First, an independent variable should have a significant effect on a dependent variable. Second, the independent variable should significantly predict the mediator. Third, the mediator should significantly affect the dependent variable. Fourth, the strong impact of the independent variable on the dependent variable would be diminished or eliminated if the mediating variable is removed from the model.

To test the mediating effects of CQ in the relationship between English proficiency and SCA/AA, a bootstrapping estimation with a sample of 5000 was used. Five mediating effects proved evident as the 95% confidence intervals (CI) did not contain zero (see Table 5). Results also indicated that MCCQ ($\beta = 0.369$, $p < 0.001$), CCQ ($\beta = -0.105$, $p < 0.05$), MCQ ($\beta = 0.207$, $p < 0.001$), and BCQ ($\beta = 0.111$, $p < 0.05$) partially mediated the relationship between English proficiency and AA. Thus H7a, H7b, H7c, and H7d were supported. Moreover, CCQ ($\beta = 0.231$, $p < 0.05$) mediated the relationship between English proficiency and SCA; thus, H6b was supported. MCCQ, MCQ, and BCQ failed to mediate the relationship between English proficiency and SCA, thereby rejecting H6a, H6c, and H6d.

Table 5 Mediating effects of the four dimensions of CQ

Independent variable	Mediators	Dependent variable	β	SD	T value	95% CI
English proficiency	MCCQ	AA	0.369***	0.050	7.426	[0.272, 0.467]
English proficiency	CCQ	AA	−0.105*	0.048	2.194	[−0.201, −0.014]
English proficiency	MCQ	AA	0.207***	0.058	3.573	[0.089, 0.320]
English proficiency	BCQ	AA	0.111*	0.051	2.197	[0.014, 0.208]
English proficiency	CCQ	SCA	0.213*	0.098	2.184	[0.030, 0.417]

Note. *p<0.05 ***p<0.001

6.4 Results of Hypotheses Testing

The results of the hypotheses testing are presented in Table 6. The table shows that 15 hypotheses were supported, while seven were rejected.

7 Discussion

The present study focused on Chinese students in short-term programmes in English-speaking countries. Drawing on the data generated by a questionnaire study, the research examined the impact of the respondents' English proficiency on their SCA and AA in host countries. It also explored whether and how the students' CQ mediated between their English proficiency and sociocultural/academic adaptation.

7.1 Characteristics of Chinese Students' English Proficiency, CQ, SCA, and AA

Descriptive statistics showed that, on average, the respondents reported lower than the "good" level of English proficiency. In addition, they tended only slightly to agree that they had sufficient cognitive, meta-cognitive, motivational and behavioural abilities to manage academic studies and daily life. It is worth noting that among the four dimensions of CQ, BCQ was the highest rated while CCQ was the lowest rated, showing that the respondents reported comparatively higher abilities to adjust behaviours to fit host cultures, and lower abilities to understand and acquire host cultural knowledge. Moreover, the students reported slightly higher levels of SCA than AA, reflecting more difficulties they encountered in adapting to academic cultures in their host universities.

Table 6 Results of hypotheses testing

	Hypothesis	Supported?
H1	H1a English proficiency has a positive influence on MCCQ.	yes
	H1b English proficiency has a positive influence on CCQ.	yes
	H1c English proficiency has a positive influence on MCQ.	yes
	H1d English proficiency has a positive influence on BCQ.	yes
H2	English proficiency has a positive effect on sociocultural adaptation.	yes
H3	English proficiency has a positive effect on academic adaptation.	yes
H4	H4a MCCQ has a positive effect on sociocultural adaptation.	no
	H4b CCQ has a positive effect on sociocultural adaptation.	yes
	H4c MCQ has a positive effect on sociocultural adaptation.	No
	H4d BCQ has a positive effect on sociocultural adaptation.	No
H5	H5a MCCQ has a positive effect on academic adaptation.	Yes
	H5b CCQ has a positive effect on academic adaptation.	No
	H5c MCQ has a positive effect on academic adaptation.	Yes
	H5d BCQ has a positive effect on academic adaptation.	Yes
H6 H7	H6a MCCQ mediates the relationship between English proficiency and sociocultural adaptation.	No
	H6b CCQ mediates the relationship between English proficiency and sociocultural adaptation.	Yes
	H6c MCQ mediates the relationship between English proficiency and sociocultural adaptation.	No
	H6d BCQ mediates the relationship between English proficiency and sociocultural adaptation.	No
	H7a MCCQ mediates the relationship between English proficiency and academic adaptation.	Yes
	H7b CCQ mediates the relationship between English proficiency and academic adaptation	Yes
	H7c MCQ mediates the relationship between English proficiency and academic adaptation.	Yes
	H7d BCQ mediates the relationship between English proficiency and academic adaptation.	Yes

7.2 Impact of English Proficiency on CQ, SCA, and AA

Performing PLS-SEM, the research revealed that the participants' levels of English proficiency significantly predicated the four dimensions of CQ. The results showed that the Chinese participants with higher English proficiency levels were more capable of adopting higher-order cognitive strategies to deepen cultural understandings, learn local cultural norms and conventions, regulate their emotions, and behave appropriately in host cultures. Our results are consistent with those of the previous studies on the positive impact of English proficiency on CCQ (Shannon & Begley, 2008; Eisenberg et al., 2013; Huff, 2013; Remhof et al., 2012), MCQ (Earley &

Ang, 2003), and BCQ (Earley, 2002). The findings of this research expand the research literature to Chinese STSA learners in English-speaking countries, verifying significant positive influences of these students' English proficiency on their MCCQ.

In addition, in the present study, the participants' levels of English proficiency were significantly related to their SCA and AA. Previous research has repeatedly reported linguistic challenges faced by non-native speakers in Anglophone countries (e.g., Cao & Meng, 2019; Wilson et al., 2013; Yu et al., 2019). Consistently with the findings of previous studies, the results of this research confirmed the positive impact of Chinese students' English proficiency on their sociocultural and academic adaptation in host universities.

7.3   Impact of CQ on SCA and AA

The PLS-SEM analysis revealed the positive impact of the participants' MCCQ, MCQ, and BCQ on their self-reported AA in host countries. In line with Lee and Sukoco (2010), the participants with higher MCCQ, MCQ, and BCQ presented higher abilities to monitor mental processes for academic cultural understandings, more effectively control anxieties and stresses in intercultural learning, and behave appropriately in academic contexts, all of which may have helped to reduce intercultural learning uncertainty and therefore, support their AA. However, inconsistent with the findings of some previous research (Ang et al., 2004; Templer et al., 2006; Ward et al., 2011; Mokhothu & Callaghan, 2018), MCCQ, MCQ, and BCQ were not significant predictors of SCA. One explanation is that the participants' reported MCCQ, MCQ, and BCQ were low, and hence, could not have a significant impact on their social adaptation.

In addition, the PLS-SEM analysis revealed that CCQ was significantly positively associated with SCA, but significantly negatively related to AA. Since the participants voluntarily selected STSA destinations, they would be willing to know about their host cultures. Those reporting higher CCQ may learn more about local food, custom, and traditions, which could have boosted their confidence, encouraged their interaction with locals, and facilitated their social adaptation. In contrast, academic adaptation involves more complex cognitive processes, requiring an in-depth understanding of new academic systems, educational beliefs, expectations, and conventions, and teaching and learning approaches and strategies. It is worth noting that the short length of study-abroad exchange programmes allowed limited meaningful interactions with host academic contexts, resulting in the danger that the knowledge these students acquired regarding academic differences can be superficial, "static", or stereotypical. In these cases, CCQ can negatively affect international students' AA.

7.4 Mediating Effects of CQ

This research confirmed that all four dimensions of CQ, namely, MCCQ, CCQ, MCQ, and BCQ, partially mediated the relationship between English proficiency and academic adaptation. The results indicated that for Chinese students in short-term exchange programmes, the effect of English proficiency on their academic adaptation was actualised through their CQs. These findings were consistent with those of the previous research (e.g., Ang et al., 2004; Templer et al., 2006), which identified the positive effects of the CQ dimensions on international students' AA. The mediating role of CCQ in the relationship between English proficiency and SCA was also confirmed in the present study, which was in line with Mokhothu and Callaghan (2018).

8 Implications

The research results hold the following implications. Firstly, previous studies on STSA programmes mainly focused on international students from the US and Europe. The current study extended the focus of the research to Chinese STSA students, highlighting "the value of STSA programmes for participants in other countries" (Iskhakova et al., 2021, p. 409). Secondly, the current study contributes to the research literature on the relationships between English proficiency, CQ, and sociocultural and academic adaptation. Particularly, the research results confirmed the significant positive impact of English proficiency on sociocultural and academic adaptation, and the significant positive impact of the four CQ dimensions on sociocultural and academic adaptation. This research also revealed the mediating effects of the four dimensions of CQ in the relationship between English proficiency and academic adaptation, and the mediating effect of CCQ in the relationship between English proficiency and sociocultural adaptation. Based on the findings, it is suggested that universities organizing short-term exchange programmes well design cultural orientation and language courses to support the development of Chinese STSA students' proficiency in English. It is also imperative for programme managers and university administrators to provide cultural and intercultural intervention programmes, which incorporate "the cultural knowledge of the host country into academic requirements of the host university" (Meng et al., 2018, p. 13). The courses are suggested to provide rich opportunities for Chinese STSA students to interact with local students and residents, engage in host academic cultures, and challenge cultural assumptions and stereotypes to support their sociocultural and academic adaptation.

9   Limitations and Future Research

The current research has the following limitations to be addressed in future studies. First, the participants were from a single university, and the findings may not be generalised to students at other Chinese universities involved in short-term study-abroad programmes. Secondly, CQ is pliable, highlighting individual differences. Future research can explore whether and how individual demographics of Chinese STSA students, such as gender, age, levels of education, and prior study abroad experiences, affect their CQ. In addition, this research revealed English proficiency as a significant determinant of the participants' sociocultural adaptation. Further research is needed to explore how other factors, including mono-cultural networking and mental and psychological problems, affect such sociocultural adaptation.

Fourthly, this research found no significant mediating effect of MCCQ, MCQ, and BCQ in the relationship between English proficiency and sociocultural adaptation. Future studies can further explore the predictive power of English proficiency toward sociocultural adaptation through MCCQ, MCQ, and BCQ. Moreover, adapting to a new culture is a complex process, which often involves a dynamic shift in personal and cultural identification. A longitudinal research design using qualitative methods is suggested to explore (re-)formation of individual identities to deepen our understanding of the acculturation processes among Chinese college students in short-term study-abroad programmes.

Acknowledgement *The authors would like to thank Dr. Chen Duan and the office of academic affairs of the sampling institute for the kindly support in data collection.*

References

Ang, S., Van Dyne, L., Koh, C., & Ng, K. Y. (2004). *The measurement of cultural intelligence.* Paper presented at the Academy of Management Meeting's Symposium on Cultural Intelligence in the 21st Century. New Orleans.

Ang, S., Van Dyne, L., Koh, C., Ng, K. Y., Templer, K. J., Tay, C., et al. (2007). Cultural intelligence. Its measurement and effects on cultural judgment and decision-making, cultural adaptation, and task performance. *Management and Organization Review, 3*(3), 335–371. https://doi.org/10.1111/j.1740-8784.2007.00082.x

Baker, R. W., & Siryk, B. (1999). *SACQ: Student adaptation to college questionnaire: Manual.* Western Psychological Services.

Baron, R. M., & Kenny, D. A. (1986). The moderator–mediator variable distinction in social psychological research: Conceptual, strategic, and statistical considerations. *Journal of Personality and Social Psychology, 51*(6), 1173–1182. https://doi.org/10.1037/0022-3514.51.6.1173

Beyers, W., & Goossens, L. (2002). Concurrent and predictive validity of the student adaptation to college questionnaire in a sample of European freshman students. *Educational and Psychological Measurement, 62*(3), 527–538. https://doi.org/10.1177/00164402062003009

Cao, C., & Meng, Q. (2019). Mapping the paths from language proficiency to adaptation for Chinese students in a non-English speaking country: An integrative model of mediation. *Current Psychology, 38*(6), 1564–1575. https://doi.org/10.1007/s12144-017-9708-3

China Ministry of Education. (2019). *News of Ministry of Education*, http://www.moe.gov.cn/jyb_xwfb/gzdt_gzdt/s5987/201903/t20190327_375704.html.

Doiz, A., Lasagabaster, D., & Sierra, J. M. (2011). Internationalization, multilingualism and English-medium instruction. *World Englishes, 30*(3), 345–359. https://doi.org/10.1111/j.1467-971X.2011.01718.x

Earley, P. C. (2002). Redefining interactions across cultures and organizations: Moving forward with cultural intelligence. *Research in Organizational Behavior, 24*, 271–299. https://doi.org/10.1016/S0191-3085(02)24008-3

Earley, P. C., & Ang, S. (2003). *Cultural intelligence: Individual interactions across cultures.* Stanford University Press.

Earley, P. C., & Peterson, R. S. (2004). The Elusive Cultural Chameleon: Cultural Intelligence as a New Approach to Intercultural Training for the Global Manager. *Academy of Management Learning &Education, 3*(1), 100–115. https://doi.org/10.5465/AMLE.2004.12436826

Eisenberg, J., Lee, H. J., Brueck, F., Brenner, B., Claes, M. T., Mironski, J., & Bell, R. (2013). Can business schools make students culturally competent? Effects of cross-cultural management courses on cultural intelligence. *Academy of Management Learning & Education, 12*(4), 603–621. https://doi.org/10.5465/amle.2012.0022

Fornell, C., & Larcker, D. F. (1981). Evaluating structural equation models with unobservable variables and measurement error. *Journal of Marketing Research, 18*(1), 39–50. https://doi.org/10.2307/3151312

Hair, J. F., Jr., Hult, G. T. M., Ringle, C., & Sarstedt, M. (2016). *A primer on partial least squares structural equation modeling (PLS-SEM)*. Sage publication.

Hellekjaer, G. O. (2010). Language matters: Assessing lecture comprehension in Norwegian English-medium higher education. In C. Dalton-Puffer, T. Nikula, & U. Smit (Eds.), *Language use in content-and-language-integrated learning (CLIL)* (pp. 233–258). John Benjamins.

Huff, K. C. (2013). Language, cultural intelligence and expatriate success. *Management Research Review, 36*(6), 596–612. https://doi.org/10.1108/01409171311325750

Hung, H. L., & Hyun, E. (2010). East Asian international graduate students' epistemological experiences in an American University. *International Journal of Intercultural Relations, 34*(4), 340–353. https://doi.org/10.1016/j.ijintrel.2009.12.001

Iskhakova, M., Bradly, A., Whiting, B., & Lu, V. N. (2021). Cultural intelligence development during short-term study abroad programmes: the role of cultural distance and prior international experience. *Studies in Higher Education.* https://doi.org/10.1080/03075079.2021.1957811

Jurasek, M., & Potocky, T. (2020). Management of innovations in cross-cultural communication within an organization. *Marketing and Management of Innovations, 2*, 108–121. https://doi.org/10.21272/mmi.2020.2-08

Kim, E. G., & Shin, A. (2014). Seeking an effective program to improve communication skills of non-English-speaking graduate Engineering students: The case of a Korean Engineering school. *IEEE Transactions on Professional Communication, 57*(1), 41–55. https://doi.org/10.1109/TPC.2014.2310784

Lee, L. Y., & Sukoco, B. M. (2010). The effects of cultural intelligence on expatriate performance: the moderating effects of international experience. *The International Journal of Human Resource Management, 21*(7), 963–981. https://doi.org/10.1080/09585191003783397

Martirosyan, N. M., Hwang, E., & Wanjohi, R. (2015). Impact of English proficiency on academic performance of international students. *Journal of International Students, 5*(1), 60–71. https://doi.org/10.32674/jis.v5i1.443

Meng, Q., Zhu, C., & Cao, C. (2018). Chinese international students' social connectedness, social and academic adaptation: the mediating role of global competence. *Higher Education, 75*(1), 131–147. https://doi.org/10.1007/s10734-017-0129-x

Mokhothu, T. M., & Callaghan, C. W. (2018). The management of the international student experience in the South Africa context: The role of sociocultural adaptation and cultural intelligence. *Acta Commercii, 18*(1), 1–11. https://doi.org/10.4102/ac.v18i1.49

Neumann, H., Padden, N., & McDonough, K. (2019). Beyond English language proficiency scores: Understanding the academic performance of international undergraduate students during the first year of study. *Higher Education Research & Development, 38*(2), 324–338. https://doi.org/10.1080/07294360.2018.1522621

Ng, K. Y., & Earley, P. C. (2006). Culture plus intelligence-Old constructs, new frontiers. *Group & Organization Management, 31*(1), 4–19. https://doi.org/10.1177/1059601105275251

OECD. (2020). Indicator B2. See Education at a Glance Database http://stats.oecd.org/ for more information and Annex 3 for notes. https://doi.org/10.1787/69096873-en

Peng, A. Q., & Patterson, M. M. (2022). Relations among cultural identity, motivation for language learning, and perceived English language proficiency for international students in the United States. *Language, Culture and Curriculum, 35*(1), 67–82. https://doi.org/10.1080/0790831 8.2021.1938106

Poort, I., Jansen, E., & Hofman, A. (2021). Cultural Intelligence and Openness to Experiences Pave the Way for Cognitive Engagement in Intercultural Group Work. *Journal of Studies in International Education, 27*, 1–21. https://doi.org/10.1177/10283153211042091

Quiñones, A. S., Bustos, C. E., Pérez, M. V., Peralta, D. L., Zañartu, N., & Vergara del Solar, J. I. (2021). Metasynthesis regarding the sociocultural adaptation of International University. *The Qualitative Report, 26*(5), 1567–1600. https://doi.org/10.46743/2160-3715/2021.4623

Remhof, S., Gunkel, M., & Schlagel, C. (2012). Working in the "global village": The influence of cultural intelligence on the intention to work abroad. *German Journal of Research in Human Resources Management, 27*(3), 224–250. https://doi.org/10.1688/1862-0000_ZfP_2013_03_Remhof

Shafaei, A., & Razak, N. A. (2016). International postgraduate students' cross-cultural adaptation in Malaysia: antecedents and outcomes. *Research in Higher Education, 57*, 739–767. https://doi.org/10.1007/s11162-015-9404-9

Shannon, L. M., & Begley, T. M. (2008). Antecedents of the four-factor model of cultural intelligence. In S. Ang & L. Van Dyne (Eds.), *Handbook of cultural intelligence: Theory, measurement, and applications* (pp. 41–55). Armonk, NY, & London, UK, M. E. Sharpe.

Smith, R. A., & Khawaja, N. G. (2011). A review of the acculturation experiences of international students. *International Journal of Intercultural Relations, 35*(6), 699–713. https://doi.org/10.1016/j.ijintrel.2011.08.004

Templer, K. J., Tay, C., & Chandrasekar, N. A. (2006). Motivational cultural intelligence, realistic job preview, realistic living conditions preview and cross-cultural adjustment. *Group & Organization Management, 31*(1), 154–173. https://doi.org/10.1177/1059601105275293

Uen, J.F., Teng, S.K., Wu, L.C., Tsao, S.A. (2018). The antecedents and consequences of cultural intelligence: an exploratory study of taiwanese expatriates. In *5th International Conference on Business and Industrial Research (ICBIR)*, Bangkok.

Wang, Q., & Hannes, K. (2014). Academic and sociocultural adjustment among Asian international students in the Flemish community of Belgium: A photovoice project. *International Journal of Intercultural Relations, 39*, 66–81. https://doi.org/10.1016/j.ijintrel.2013.09.013

Ward, C. (1996). Acculturation. In D. Landis, & R. Bhagat (Eds.), *Handbook of intercultural training* (pp. 124–147). Sage.

Ward, C., & Kennedy, A. (1999). The measurement of sociocultural adaptation. *International Journal of Intercultural Relations, 23*(4), 659–677. https://doi.org/10.1016/S0147-1767(99)00014-0

Ward, C., Wilson, J., & Fischer, R. (2011). Assessing the predictive validity of cultural intelligence over time. *Personality and Individual Differences, 51*(2), 138–142. https://doi.org/10.1016/j.paid.2011.03.032

Wilson, J. K., Ward, C., & Fischer, R. (2013). Beyond culture learning theory: What can personality tell us about cultural competence? *Journal of Cross-Cultural Psychology, 44*(6), 900–927. https://doi.org/10.1177/0022022113492889

Wright, C., & Schartner, A. (2013). 'I can't … I won't?': International students at the threshold of social interaction. *Journal of Research in International Education, 12*(2), 113–128. https://doi.org/10.1177/1475240913491055

Young, T. J., Sercombe, P. G., Sachdev, I., Naeb, R., & Schartner, A. (2013). Success factors for international postgraduate students' adjustment: Exploring the roles of intercultural competence, language proficiency, social contact and social support. *European Journal of Higher Education, 3*(2), 151–171. https://doi.org/10.1080/21568235.2012.743746

Yu, B., Bodycott, P., & Mak, A. S. (2019). Language and Interpersonal Resources Predictors of Psychological and Sociocultural Adaptation: International Students in Hong Kong. *Journal of Studies in International Education, 23*(5), 572–588. https://doi.org/10.1177/1028315318825336

Dandan Yao is a PhD Candidate at Xi'an Jiaotong University, and Associate Professor of City College of Xi'an Jiaotong University. Her research interests include internationalisation of higher education and intercultural competence of Chinese college students. Email: yaodantina@126.com

Mei Tian holds a PhD from the University of Bath, UK. She is a Professor in the School of Foreign Studies at Xi'an Jiaotong University, China. Her current research focuses on international student experiences in China. Her recent publications include *Academic Experiences of International Students in Chinese Higher Education* (London: Routledge). Email: Temmytian@mail.xjtu.edu.cn

Part V
Decolonising Minds, Discourses and Practices

Part V is about how Eurocentric research methodologies, epistemologies, pedagogies, and language policies have continued to be powerful purveyors of enduring coloniality in post-colonial Global South nations. Tupas describes how monolingualist language ideologies and native-speakerist deficit theories continue to permeate postcolonial educational systems globally. The author argues for the need to decolonise the uses of English in the primary curriculum in Southern post-colonial settings, where English is used either as the subject or the medium of instruction. He also advocates the promotion of critical multilingual awareness in Northern countries, where coloniality is still persistent in the way it impacts Aboriginal and minoritised students, who are unfairly subjected to assimilationist monolingualist (English-only) policies that devalue the cultural and linguistic capital they bring to the classroom, by framing it in 'deficit' terms. The author argues for the need to reorient and reposition English language teaching in elementary education in ways that acknowledge the realistic linguistic and cultural needs of the students by challenging the mono-epistemological assumptions and pedagogies of the ex-colonisers, and by granting voice and epistemic agency to local educational stakeholders. For decolonial educational projects in the Global South to succeed, it is vital to 'recentre' local knowledge, take ownership over curriculum development, promote a multilingual and intercultural approach, and make use of the translingual pedagogy in the English language primary classrooms. Besides, the introduction of 'glocalised' and Indigenous teaching methodologies presupposes the fostering of dialogic engagement with relevant community actors.

In a similar vein, Al Tamimi's chapter argues for the need to acknowledge the legitimacy of alternative discursive Indigenous modes of reasoning such as narrative, emotional reasoning, as well as other non-verbal modes that are different from the Northern logico-deductive model. The author questions the hegemonic thinking that delegitimises the argumentation modes of peoples from the Global South. For example, the Indigenous peoples' stories of survivance represent collective resistance to white settler cultural, linguistic, and onto-epistemological domination. Bearing witness is empowering for Indigenous people because it challenges colonial 'benevolent' narratives and helps to decolonise history, legal traditions (i.e., use of 'restorative justice'), and argumentation practices (counter-storytelling). Survivor testimonies are necessarily "dialogical" and "relational", and thus provide a shift in the epistemic frameworks toward Indigenous storytelling as a form of narrative argumentation (Nagy, 2020, pp. 227–234). The author challenges the hierarchisation of modes of reasoning by stressing the value of Indigenous knowledge(s) and different ways of argumentative engagement. The mainstream Western mode of arguing is problematic because it (i) marginalises alternative modes of reasoning and experiencing the world, (ii) feeds into colonialist thinking, and (iii) reduces the possibility of genuine intercultural dialogue.

The purpose of Samier's study is to develop a culturally relevant conceptual framework of professional meritocracy pertaining to educational and organisational leadership from an Islamic perspective. The study draws attention to the way in which leadership which is informed and shaped by Islamic 'spiritual intelligence' and work ethic can positively impact organisational commitment. The argument is that the hegemonic Anglo-American neoliberalist notions of leadership are at odds with the pedagogy and ethos of Islamic leadership ideals. Islamic leadership promotes work for the common good and the collective betterment of the community. Faith-based leadership perspectives are driven by values such as *Sayyid al qawn khadimuhum* [A leader of the nation is their servant]) and they are influenced by personal characteristics that often have a faith-dimension. For example, while the *Qur'an* is the ultimate source of values, the Prophet Muhammad as a *qudwah* (role model), "upon which to base good leadership values and practices," sets the *Sunnah* (the statements, actions, and approbation of the Prophet Muhammad). The chapter argues for the urgent need for educational leadership research that prioritises the influence of cultural context in the (re)conceptualisation of leadership from more diverse perspectives. It seems evident, therefore, that the importance of upholding Islamic values in the Middle East context is considered essential for effective shaping of the ways in which educational leadership and organisational management should be understood and practised. It could also with advantage be applied more widely to humanise management cultures, even in non-Islamic different environments, just as Islamic banking and money conventions have wisdom to impart to Western commerce and economics.

The study by Le et al. is about a transgender teacher of English and a group of English LGBTIQ+ youth learners in Vietnam. The study's use of photovoice method is inspired by Paulo Freire's pedagogy of the oppressed, and thus it is meant to be empowering. By offering LGBTIQ+ communities the chance to publicise their lived experiences, it gives them a voice to present their grievances and create a sense of solidarity amongst their 'community of identity/practice'. The study is based on an emancipatory research method that seeks to generate critical consciousness among marginalised LGBTIQ+ communities in Vietnam in a way that enables them to push back against discrimination and exclusion (based on sexual orientation) with resilience and 'cultural' pride. The authors argue that photovoice method is based on critical intersectionality theory in that it promotes action for social justice through the transformation of power relations.

Photovoice methods expose the subtle societal processes used to marginalise vulnerable social groups by re-envisaging new ways of being and viewing the world, based on lived experience (revealed through photographs accompanied by personal narratives). Such a paradigm shift provides an alternative onto-epistemological orientation to reality in that it is community-based: participants, research partners, and the researcher (who acts as the facilitator) work collaboratively to identify and dismantle the oppressive power dynamics, such as racism, homophobia, or tokenism. More interestingly, emancipatory photovoice research can enhance collective learning, healing, and growth for the involved community members.

Subhan's study discusses relevant theoretical issues pertaining to the status of English as a lingua franca today (e.g., linguistic hegemony/linguicism as a legacy of colonialism, equity and inclusion in education, intersectionality, decoloniality, interculturality, cultural otherness). The author delineates the subtle and pervasive forms of power dynamics in contemporary contexts that shape the (re)production of Northern colonial patterns of domination by normalising the persistent hierarchisation of racial, ethnic, linguistic, and cultural relations and the subalternisation and marginalisation of Southern peoples' epistemological knowledges, experiences, and ways of being. For example, she describes how, as a racialised educator, she experiences "race discordance"[1] when she travels. Her self-identification as British by birth and cultural upbringing is questioned in certain contexts (e.g., in social/academic spaces assumed to be exclusively 'white') despite her 'native speaker' English accent. Hence, this can be distressing because white skin is used as "a badge of identification" (Kowal & Paradies, 2017, p. 109). Such instances of race misrecognition also involve light-skinned Indigenous people who could easily pass for whites, but who, instead, choose to identify as Indigenous and reclaim their Indigeneity by wearing 'Indigenous' jewellery or using specific discursive signals.[2] Such a perspective is motivated by the need to resist assimilation by maintaining their Indigenous identity as "a form of defiance and survival" (Kowal & Paradies, 2017, p. 109). Hence, "when a person who is presumed to be white (by other whites) reveals their indigeneity, the encounter radically shifts from a space of exclusively white sociality to a much more precarious intercultural space between whites and Indigenous people" (p. 109). Moreover, to dismantle such homogenising and assimilationist ideologies, light-skinned Aboriginal people "refuse to disown, attenuate or forgo ties to a history, culture and experience they value" (p. 109). Besides, such Indigenous identity maintenance is a clear contestation of everyday racism and racialisation of cultural others.

---

[1] "a mismatch between personal identification and socially attributed or ascribed race" (Kowal & Paradies, 2017, 106).

[2] This reminds Ahmed Sahlane of his first day in "Pédagogie Générale" class in Faculty of Education (Mohamed V university, Rabat, 1989) when the professor called him *Ahmed* (Arabic pronunciation) and he said, "My name is *Hmad* (Amazigh pronunciation) to reclaim his ethnocultural and linguistic Amazigh identity. In high school, he used to feel very embarrassed whenever his peers would realise he was Amazigh.

References

Kowal, E, & Paradies, Y. (2017). Indigeneity and the refusal of Whiteness. *Postcolonial Studies, 20* (1), 101–117. https://doi.org/10.1080/13688790.2017.1334287

Nagy, R. (2020). Settler witnessing at the Truth and Reconciliation Commission of Canada. *Human Rights Review 21*, 219–241. https://doi.org/10.1007/s12142-020-00595-w

The Struggle to Decolonize English in School Curricula

Ruanni Tupas

Abstract In this chapter, I attempt to introduce broad approaches to decolonizing English in school curricula. It makes the case for a much longer historical trajectory of such efforts, arguing that decolonizing efforts are not simply products of recent awakenings in academia about the need to decolonize power, knowledge and being. Scholars from all over the globe, since the formal ceding of power back to subjugated nations in the 1950s and 1960s, have called for decolonizing the curriculum, including the English language curriculum, in all levels of education, as part of nationalization or cultural indigenization projects aimed at taking ownership of the design of the ex-colonised people's future. This chapter will feature four innovative intercultural and multilingual approaches to decolonizing English-centred curricula: *taking ownership of knowledge, reclaiming local knowledge, embedding English in bi/multilingualism*, and *deploying translingual pedagogy*.

Keywords Multilingualism · Translingual · Decolonization · Mother tongue · K-12 education · Primary education · Curriculum development

1 Introduction

Much has been written about decolonizing curricula around the world (Charles, 2019; Subedi, 2013). There has also been ample work on decolonizing the lenses and research we mobilize in applied linguistics, sociolinguistics, language policy and language education (Cushman, 2016; Hsu, 2015; Kumaravadivelu, 2003; Phyak, 2021; Rubdy, 2015). However, curiously much less has so far been done to explore approaches in transforming the uses of English in K-12 curricula in early schooling through the lens of decolonization. The lower the grade levels are

R. Tupas (✉)
Institute of Education, University College London, London, UK
e-mail: r.tupas@ucl.ac.uk

(kindergarten to primary school), the rarer to find published work which tackles the question of English as a colonial language in curricula and explores how it might be transformed through a decolonizing lens. It is for these reasons that this chapter attempts to assemble broad approaches to decolonizing English in early school curricula. The texts to be used come from different postcolonial contexts, but they share similar broad approaches to transforming the uses of English in school curricula. These approaches are: (a) taking ownership of knowledge, (b) reclaiming local knowledge, (c) embedding English in bi/multilingualism, and (d) deploying translingual pedagogy.

However, in discussing these approaches, I first construct my author positionality concerning decolonization and education in order to explain why I frame my discussion the way I do. I then discuss briefly why English as a colonial language remains central to decolonizing efforts in education today but frame the discussion in the context of global coloniality to assert the fact that countries which have not been formally colonized are now also embedded in colonial logics of policy-making and knowledge production. Scholars such as Escobar (2004), Grosfoguel (2006) and Tlostanova and Mignolo (2009) alert us to extended logics of colonialism today which are embedded in international political relations and economies, such that countries like Thailand and Ethiopia which have not been subjected to direct colonial rule could be seen to be operating within the same logics of global coloniality. In this sense, while we bear in mind that each project of decolonizing English in school curricula "should be historically grounded" (López-Gopar, 2016, p. 195; see also Tuck and Yang, 2012; Loomba, 1998), we nevertheless see similar broad approaches found in different curricular contexts because they all aim to take control of knowledge production and local practices in the teaching and learning of English which historically have been devalued or erased.

2 My Positionality

I come from the Philippines, a country governed by Spain for 333 years, by the United States for around five decades, and by the Japanese during World War II. For much of the twentieth century, however, Philippine education was essentially an American construction (Rafael, 2015). Spain governed through religion, but the US made education its centrepiece tool for the accomplishment of its benevolent assimilation policy. During the Philippine-American War (1899–1902) when thousands of Filipinos were killed or injured, American soldiers simultaneously built schools in towns where they were deployed, and English was the first subject to be taught (Constantino, 1970). After the war formally ended in 1902, colonial pacification took the form of ideological warfare, for example through the provision of universal basic education. English became the centrepiece language of instruction. It remained so until 1970s during which the 'language wars' erupted again which resulted in the implementation of bilingual education in English (in Mathematics and Science) and Pilipino (later renamed 'Filipino') (in all other subjects) (Tupas & Martin, 2017), although still essentially excluding all other Philippine languages from the education system.

Nevertheless, because of decades of colonial education, the status of English as the most symbolically powerful language of education remained unscathed, thus language ideologies embedded in educational practices and policies remained heavily favourable towards English and unwelcoming of Philippine multilingualism. Despite policies affirming the multilingual repertoires of Filipino pupils in recent years, English is still the most desired language in the country purportedly for social mobility and career opportunities (Salonga, 2015).

After the Philippines' nominal independence in 1946, decolonizing efforts since the 1960s ensued, including the so-called nationalization of education, indigenization of knowledge, and the rewriting of history from the perspective of 'the Filipino people' (Agoncillo & Alfonso, 1960; Guillermo, 2003). All these efforts, however, were being mobilized within neocolonial conditions because economic and political ties with the United States were never severed after 'independence' (Constantino, 1970). In academe, the infrastructure of knowledge production (textbook production, theory-building, circulation of 'best practices', etc.), remained controlled by institutions and people sited in global knowledge centres, including the United States (Gray, 2002; Kumaravadivelu, 2003; Pennycook, 2018). Therefore, as an English language major and, later, as an educator, it has constantly been a struggle to be immersed in theories and practices produced by colonialism because they could not account for my multilingual realities.

To give one very specific example, the first undergraduate major course I taught was English phonology. The English sound became a key battleground of identity-making and ideological construction. What counted as the 'correct' transcription of an English sound was based on American rather than on Filipino pronunciation. As the teacher, I struggled to pronounce the sounds in the American way (because this was how 'native speakers' sounded) but they would end up sounding 'Filipino'. Should my students transcribe the sounds as they heard them, or as they thought the sounds should be pronounced? We learned about the phoneme as a psychological reality but the ones that are produced out of it are the allophones or the actual sounds produced by the individual speakers themselves. This was three decades ago and in the context of my own institution at least, native speakerism was deemed unproblematic.

But such classroom experiences began to unsettle me. I felt that my being multilingual (I speak English and three Philippine languages) devalued or erased the manner by which I used and taught English. If I accepted transcriptions of localized English sounds, thus reflecting the influence of phonological systems of the different languages I speak, it would appear that I was legitimizing so-called non-native sounds of English. I had to cling on to the psychological reality of 'native' English sounds and disregard my own multilingual production of these sounds, as well as that of my students'.

This discomfort slowly gained ideological clarity as similar struggles emerged in the teaching of syntax, history of English, and language teaching methodologies. The erasure or devaluation of the multilingual matrix within which my education and the education of my students occurred became a question of coloniality as the theories and sanctioned classroom practices we were expected to learn and perform respectively were all imported and, in fact, could be traced back to colonial education and the colonial history of the introduction of the discipline of linguistics and English language teaching in the Philippines. For more than two decades, therefore, my academic work has been centrally galvanized by my own colonized body and scholarly practice such that my scholarly undertakings, whether they be in applied linguistics, sociolinguistics, language policy, geopolitics of knowledge production, literacy and development, or Teaching of English to Speakers of Other Languages (TESOL), the concern would always revolve around addressing 'inequalities of multilingualism' (Tupas, 2015) and how to decolonize and transform them. This chapter is fully aligned with my longstanding decolonizing agenda, training my lenses on English in school curricula.

3   Global Coloniality and English in School Curricula

Nevertheless, if projects of decolonization began several decades ago, why is it that there remains today an urgent need for "transforming the world by transforming the way people see it, feel it and act in it" (Tlostanova & Mignolo, 2009, p. 131)? The broad intercultural answer to this by scholars of different orientations and approaches is unanimous: colonial structures and practices of everyday life *endure* (López-Gopar, 2016). This essentially means that the colonial situation remains until today – thus the term 'coloniality' because it is colonialism without direct rule – leading some scholars to contend that decolonization has in fact been "a myth" (Fasakin, 2021, p. 902). "We are a far cry from experiencing a post-colonial turn," contends Sugiharto (2013, p. 165) in the context of Indonesia. In academia, there have been serious efforts at epistemic or knowledge decolonization. However, these have devalued structures and practices of coloniality as objects of inquiry in favour of frameworks which focused on the agentive and resistive responses of the colonized to colonial rule (Gonzalez, 1976; Vaish, 2005).

In schools, the common argument thus has been: yes, English was a colonial language but it can now be used to speak against the empire. While this may be true, it does not give the complete picture because it has shifted attention away from enduring structures of colonialism within which resistance through English is mobilized. Postcolonial struggles as practices of resistance by the colonized have been misinterpreted as a thing of the past (for example, see Vaish, 2005, in the case of India; Paterno, 2018, in the case of the Philippines). The presence of one does not necessarily negate the presence of the other; in other words, postcolonial struggles are mobilized within conditions of coloniality.

Thus, the most recent wave of decolonization is born out of the realization yet again of the durable presence of coloniality in our lives, except that this time the "notion of coloniality relates to the global multifaceted system of control and domination designed to succeed direct European colonialism in non-Western contexts"

(Fasakin, 2021, p. 903). This means that countries which were not directly ruled by another country in the past now also contend with global coloniality because the same logics of colonialism operate in the mobilization of knowledge production, the global economy and international relations (Escobar, 2004; Fasakin, 2021). In the context of language education, these proxies take the form of global industry players in knowledge production and dissemination, thus the continuing privileging of native speaker norms and rhetorics, as well as Western-drawn language teaching methodologies and cultural content (Hsu, 2015; Kumaravadivelu, 2003).

For example, Gray (2002) describes "the phenomenon of the global coursebook – that genre of English language textbook which is produced in English-speaking countries and is designed for use as the core text in language classrooms around the world [which are]…highly wrought cultural constructs and carriers of cultural messages" (pp. 151–152). Global coursebook exemplars are the ELT books of Abbs and Freebairn (e.g., 1977, 1979) which "emphasize aspects of UK culture, at the expense, perhaps, of other countries' cultures" (Rixon & Smith, 2012). In a more recent study, Soto-Molina and Méndez (2020) also alert us to recent textbooks around the world which "emphasize the image of the native speaker (man, white, heterosexual) in a superior relation or position to other interactants in dialogues" which "consolidate[s] certain deficient practices, prejudices and stereotypes while at the same time strengthening or weakening local or national awareness" (p. 13; see also Tupas, 2021, for curriculum development and teacher education in general).

4   English-Centred School Curricula in Decolonizing Projects

When direct colonial rule officially ended in one country after the other halfway through the twentieth century, anti-colonial protests grew on the streets demanding the dismantling of economic, cultural and political structures of oppression linked with colonialism. The struggle, in different forms and approaches, took on one central issue: colonialism may have ended officially, but coloniality endured. Colonialism, in this sense, refers to particular historical periods characterized by "the control by individuals or groups over the territory/behavior of other individuals and groups" (Horvath, 1972, p. 46), while coloniality refers to present-day conditions and practices which can be traced back to colonialism. According to Maldonado-Torres (2007), "coloniality survives colonialism" (p. 243). One can argue that colonialism is a thing of the past, but it "is maintained alive in books, in the criteria for academic performance, in cultural patterns, in common sense, in the self-image of peoples, in aspirations of self, and so many other aspects of our modern experience" (p. 243). The economies needed to be nationalized in order to serve the needs of the masses rather than the needs of elites who benefited from collusion with colonial powers. Political structures of governance were still very much colonial in nature to the extent that transfer of power occurred mainly between colonial rulers and the very small local elite, thus protests were likewise focused on opening up the political arena to marginalized voices and sectors in society.

In contexts of continuing direct rule, attempts to challenge systems of power in institutions such as the schools take on unique configurations because people and institutions responsible for the silencing and the dispossession of Indigenous communities continue to rule over their lands and everyday lives. Thus, decolonization cannot be viewed simply as a metaphor (Tuck & Yang, 2012) because the struggle is real and material in nature. Tuck and Yang assert that much of decolonization discourse has moved away from talking about real everyday struggles of people to reclaim their land and other possessions taken away from them (then and now) by their colonizers such that any movement for change becomes a decolonial act or agenda.

Therefore, while this chapter argues for the need to decolonize knowledge and knowledge production because histories were written through the lens of the colonizers, decolonizing education should be seen broadly as the attempt to challenge epistemologies of oppression *as part of* the broad agenda of dismantling all structures of coloniality in society. Epistemic or knowledge decolonization introduces new ways of thinking about the past and creating knowledge for the erstwhile subjugated people, but efforts along this line should not be disconnected from other efforts to help transform society.

It is in this context that the colonial language has been and remains central to the decolonization project both in the symbolic and material sense. This is especially so with English, not only because it has taken on international intercultural functions (Baker, 2009) but also because the world has become obsessed with it through the institutionalization of English-only and English as Medium of Instruction policies in educational systems (Dearden, 2015). Thus, English is central to the decolonization project in the symbolic sense because language is a battleground for identity-making, especially of the 'nationalist' kind. It also has real effects on people, functioning as a socially divisive language. It privileges those sectors proficient in the colonial language with multiple resources needed to uplift their economic and cultural well-being, while marginalizing all others (Salonga, 2015, p. 139).

5 Approaches to Decolonizing English in School Curricula

Thus, decolonizing English in school curricula should be seen, first, as part of a longer historical trajectory of the decolonizing project and, second, as a response to enduring conditions of coloniality. What then have been some broad approaches to decolonizing in English in school curricula? The following discussion will present four predominant ones: taking ownership of knowledge, reclaiming local knowledge, embedding English in bi/multilingualism, and deploying translingual pedagogy.

6   Taking Ownership Over Curriculum Development

First is the demand for ownership of the curriculum design itself. That is, curriculum should not be an overly centralized endeavour but, rather, should be designed with the participation of local stakeholders, such as teachers who are members of the local communities within which the teaching of English occurs. Recognizing local expertise based on knowledge of local customs and traditions, as well as Indigenous ways of teaching and learning, should lead to working *with* teachers and other local stakeholders in matters concerning curriculum development. Decades of top-down decision-making on what is best for non-Western local communities of teachers and learners have created an unequal production of knowledge where local classrooms are treated as sites of theoretical and methodological application, and never as sites of knowledge-making in the first place. Thus, taking back ownership over the content and process of curriculum development would presumably alter the production and use of problematic materials and methodologies respectively.

In the context of China where, according to Guo and Beckett (2007), the presence and the symbolic power of English from kindergarten through all levels of education are products of neocolonial engagements with the United States and United Kingdom, a paradigm shift must be initiated through the lens of glocalization in the curriculum "where local actors can claim their ownership of English and act as active agents to engage in different creative practices" (p. 127). Legitimizing local expertise in this sense means moving away from the harmful practices and ideologies of native-speakerism, monolingualist classroom teaching, and cultural imperialism. Thus, it is "important to validate China English, used for international communication, as one form of World English because Chinese learners are far more likely to use their English with non-native than with native speakers" (Guo & Beckett, 2007, p. 127).

Similarly, as part of its drive to take control of curricula which would not rely on external (read: British) expertise, a body of local educators from different Caribbean countries was convened to set syllabi and evaluate examinations in these countries (Bakker-Mitchell, 2002). This was because examinations were set and evaluated externally based on British standards, leading to an individual's intellectual ability being "measured by that person's performance at these external examinations" (p. 194). Putting together a local body of experts was not undertaken simply because of the assumption that local educators are experts in their own professional and cultural contexts but, more importantly, because taking ownership over the content and practice of teaching and learning is a postcolonial assertion of independent decision-making.

Teachers, however, should not be the only stakeholders who should take control of teaching and learning. In the context of a decolonizing project in Oaxaca, Mexico, López-Gopar (2016) shows the collaborative and dialogic work of student teachers and children as authors and language subjects in the classroom. They co-author 'identity texts' (or materials and final projects which help them affirm their own identities) while "developing authentic syllabi rooted in the children's lives and by bringing different languages, along with their emergent alphabetic literacies, into the classroom" (p. 171).

7 Reclaiming Local Knowledge

Consequently, reclaiming local knowledge (Matemba & Lilemba, 2015; Shizha, 2013; Sugiharto, 2013) is another key approach to decolonizing English in school curriculum. In recent years this has been encapsulated in the term *funds of knowledge* (Gonzales & Moll, 2002) which essentially refers to ignored or devalued knowledge which children bring along with them to the classroom (Thomson & Hall, 2008). Such knowledge is reclaimed in the classroom as a rich resource for teaching and learning. In the case of Singapore, Goh (2015) describes the countering of English-speaking elitism, for example, through the launch of a Confucianization movement with "the introduction of moral and religious knowledge education to combat individualism and westernization in the use of English language and mass consumption of western popular culture" (Goh, 2015, p. 147). TESOL Islamia (2022) is another example in this direction as it commits itself to affirming Islamic values and practices in the teaching of English (see also the Islamisation of EFL textbooks in Saudi Arabia by Sahlane and Pritchard, this volume, chap. 17). In the case of the Philippines, reclaiming local knowledge early on took the form of a 'non-conformist' approach to the postcolonial TESOL movement, where English language textbooks starting at primary education used "English to express Philippine realities and to use English in Philippine situations" (Gonzalez, 1976, p. 445). This was because immediately after independence from the United States in 1946, English language teaching (or TESOL) materials meant for elementary school children not only featured overwhelmingly American content, but were in fact originally written for international students entering the United States to study (Gonzalez, 1976, p. 444).

Concrete efforts are described by Ramanathan (2015) when she tracks the retrieval of community-based cultural content in the form of locally-recognizable everyday practices and landmarks through the medium of Gujarati in primary English classrooms in Ahmedabad, Gujarat, India. Valdez (2020), on the other hand, details an anti-colonial classroom pedagogy which aims to trouble colonial discourses in the academic language development classes of primary students in the United States. Such a design consists of three key stages: (1) identify and examine colonial discourse, (2) engage in anti-colonial vocabulary activities, and (3) contest colonial discourse and writing. For example, to build an alternative vocabulary to the European conquest of American Indians in North America described as a 'competition of things', the word 'exploitation' and other significant words are introduced in PowerPoint slides with visuals, and then students engage in vocabulary games like word wizard, bingo, and acting out.

8   Embedding English in Bi/Multilingualism

A third approach is to acknowledge and affirm the multilingual nature and context of the teaching and learning of English. Multilingual classrooms within which English has operated as the main language have traditionally been treated as *monolingual* classrooms which have – theoretically or ideologically, of course – no place for multilingualism, multiculturalism and intercultural interactions. However, ample research has shown how the teaching, learning and use of English can, in fact, be facilitated more effectively if multilingual and multicultural resources which both learners and students bring into the classroom are utilized as pedagogical resources (Ferguson, 2003). Guo and Beckett (2007) assert this position very clearly in the context of China:

> There is no empirical evidence to support the assertion that English is best taught monolingually. Educators must abolish the harmful idea that students' first languages must be stamped out to ensure educational success. Educators need to recognise that students' first languages are an important component of their identity and a useful tool for thinking and learning (p. 125).

In vernacular-medium primary schools in India, the postcolonial response has been to develop bilingual strategies to teach English (Ramanathan, 2015). Textbooks, for example, shift between the use of a local language, for example Gujarati, and English, to scaffold students' learning of English. Gujarati is used for instructions to students on how to navigate intercultural activities in their English lessons; local names, landmarks and cultural practices are also incorporated into reading and other activities to provide local colour to the English lessons. All this is based on the assumption that Gujarati helps capture cultural nuances and local sensibilities which, in turn, increase students' motivation to learn English. This bilingual approach is clearly a decolonial approach to addressing the divisive nature of English language learning in India. It must be pointed out that in general the "postcolonial Indian ground" (p. 207) which is split between English-medium and vernacular-medium systems follows "a class-based divide" (p. 207). Vernacular-medium schools cater to students who are less privileged socioeconomically and culturally, thus the learning of English requires strategic use of the bilingual approach with the end-view of addressing class-based learning gaps between English-medium- and vernacular-medium-educated students. The use of local languages in primary English language classrooms should prod us "into questioning what passes for 'effective' and 'appropriate' learning and teaching in west-based TESOL" (p. 208).

In the context of the Philippines, a similar approach has also been found to be effective in the teaching and learning of primary English in peripheral communities in the country. The longitudinal Lubuagan experiment aimed to use the local language, Lilubuagen, in delivering formal literacies in formal basic education classrooms, including the English language classroom. It has provided empirical evidence for the effective strategic use of the local language in teaching and learning (Dumatog & Dekker, 2003; Walter & Dekker, 2011). In fact, the use of the local language in the teaching and learning of English was found to have helped pupils perform better in national examinations than pupils who were taught English solely through the use of English as medium of instruction. The institutionalization of Mother Tongue-Based Multilingual Education (MTB-MLE) in 2012, which was later incorporated into the revised basic education law requiring the use of the mother tongues in the early years of elementary education, used the Libuagan experiment as one of the major sources of evidence for the need to move away from the colonial framework of English-medium education (Tupas & Martin, 2017).

9 Deploying Translingual Pedagogy

A fourth approach is the deployment of translingual pedagogy. This is essentially a multilingual-affirming approach to the teaching and learning of English, except that its conceptual framing is different from that of a bi/multilingual approach which essentially assumes the occurrence of separate languages and language varieties in the classroom. According to the translingual framework, teachers and students bring along with them not necessarily separate languages and language varieties, but a wide range of linguistic and communicative practices which cannot be reduced to accounting for the presence of individual languages and language varieties (Dowling & Krause, 2019; Sterzuk & Nelson, 2016). They are "part of one's unique linguistic repertoire" (Portolés & Martí, 2017, p. 65). Students' communicative repertoires are traditionally devalued in the classroom because they presumably indicate lack of competence in any of the languages used when, in fact, these repertoires help teachers and pupils accomplish tasks, thus showcasing their competence in facilitating effective communication. In many classrooms which teach or use English as a 'foreign' language, translanguaging is discouraged for fear of "cross-linguistic contamination, despite the fact that no research has proven the validity of that assumption" (Portolés & Martí, 2017, p. 70). While imperial linguistic and cultural borders have been constructed by colonialism in English classrooms, translingual practices help teachers and students create and navigate alternative spaces of learning and teaching where these constructed borders do not exist (Cushman, 2016). It is in this decolonial frame that translanguaging may be viewed as 'resistance' (de Los Ríos & Seltzer, 2017, p. 60).

In some elementary English language classrooms in the Philippines, Canilao (2020) provides examples of translingual instructional practices of teachers for better comprehension of lesson content. The teachers draw on the multilingual repertoires of the communities where the local language, Bisaya, and the national language, Filipino, find their way into the formal classroom and integrate into the target language, English, in such a way that the instructional practices mobilize a unified intermeshed communicative repertoire. No language in the communicative repertoire is identifiable according to a particular communicative function; rather, while languages are identifiable in form, they collectively perform a function or task. Canilao's (2019) own foray into translingual practices in the classroom has led her to a personal re-evaluation of her own approach to the teaching of English:

> I used to focus on all errors and pour my efforts into correcting mistakes. I used to think that allowing them to use other varieties of English and languages would impede the learning process. Now, I wear a new set of lenses with an appreciation of students' resourceful attempts to enhance communication skills and an understanding of the collective process that "owning English" for a purpose entails (p. 8).

Translingual practices in K-12 classrooms in the United States can similarly be framed as decolonizing strategies. In countries like the Philippines, the US is historically a colonizing country. Colonialism, however, also defines the subjugation of Indigenous peoples of the US by white occupiers except that the colonialists settled in the country rather than left it. "Until the 1970s," according to de Los Ríos et al. (2019), "American Indian children were subjected to forced assimilation in English-only Americanization boarding schools wherein punitive, physically violent, and dehumanizing school practices were utilized in the name of teaching English" (p. 361).

This monolingualist English-only approach to teaching and learning has persisted in US classrooms today, thus marginalizing minoritized students' rich multilinguistic competencies and framing them as linguistically and culturally deviant. Through a decolonizing lens, de Los Ríos et al. (2019) propose that translanguaging be used in minoritized classrooms not only to scaffold the teaching, learning and/or use of English, but to promote critical multilingual awareness which enables the pupils to reflect on their own linguistic practices and how these can be harnessed to their own advantage in the classroom. They urge teachers to ask what counts as language in the classroom beyond an understanding of language as a bounded and discrete entity, and extend the use of translanguaging to all minoritized students whose communicative repertoires continue to be devalued and, worse, mocked (p. 364).

López-Gopar (2016) describes in more detail how translingual pedagogy works, this time in the context of primary English classrooms in Oaxaca, Mexico. Student teachers and Indigenous children produce identity texts which are essentially original materials about families, animals and other entities within their own communities. Children are taught English words which are most likely to be seen and heard in everyday life and urged to use them in creating their multimodal stories which affirm, rather than mock, their cultural identities. These stories are written in ways that children find most comfortable, thus bilingual and/or trilingual use is allowed.

10   Conclusion

Monolingualist and deficit language ideologies continue to pervade postcolonial educational systems around the world today (Ashraf, 2018), and this includes primary and secondary classrooms which use English as either the subject or the medium of instruction (Sterzuk & Nelson, 2016). Structures and practices of coloniality pervade both the everyday life of speakers, as well as broader economic, political and cultural relations between people, institutions and countries. Decolonizing English in school curricula is and will always be a struggle, but it has operationalized various responses to these structures and practices through four key overlapping efforts and approaches: *taking ownership of knowledge, reclaiming local knowledge, embedding English in bi/ multilingualism,* and *deploying translingual pedagogy.*

Early in the paper, however, we have highlighted the need to locate such efforts within larger projects of decolonization. Being able to engage in these very critical and much needed efforts should not blind us to the enduring conditions of global coloniality even if such efforts are directed at addressing these conditions in the first place. At the centre of these decolonizing efforts remains the teaching, learning and use of English; that is, while we interrogate English and everything that it stands for in our lives by reorganizing our classroom practices, reconstituting our identities, and revaluing and incorporating local knowledge, a key aim is still supposedly to help the children learn English. In other words, decolonizing the uses of English in educational systems is unavoidably ironic, but commitment to social justice and equity issues will help us link our efforts in the classroom with our lives and that of our students which are deeply enmeshed in the messy and everyday struggles against ideologies and conditions of coloniality.

References

Abbs, B., & Freebairn, I. (1977). *Starting strategies: An integrated language course for beginners of English.* Longman.

Abbs, B., & Freebairn, I. (1979). *Building strategies: An integrated language course for learners of English* [Students' book]. Longman.

Agoncillo, T. A., & Alfonso, O. M. (1960). *A short history of the Filipino people.* University of the Philippines.

Ashraf, H. (2018). Translingual practices and monoglot policy aspirations: A case study of Pakistan's plurilingual classrooms. *Current Issues in Language Planning, 19*(1), 1–21. https://doi.org/10.1080/14664208.2017.1281035

Baker, W. (2009). The cultures of English as a lingua franca. *TESOL Quarterly, 43*(4), 567–592. https://doi.org/10.1002/j.1545-7249.2009.tb00187.x

Bakker-Mitchell, I. A. (2002). Foreign language education in post-colonial English speaking Caribbean. *Journal of Instructional Psychology, 29*(3), 192–202.

Canilao, M. L. E. N. (2020). Foregrounding Philippine Englishes in fostering linguistic equality. *Asian Englishes, 22*(2), 195–215. https://doi.org/10.1017/S0047404500018583

Canilao, M. L. E. N. (2019). English–mine, yours, and ours: Enabling all learners to own it for a purpose. *The English Connection, 23*(4), 7–8.

Charles, E. (2019). Decolonizing the curriculum. *Insights, 32*(1), 24. https://doi.org/10.1629/uksg.475

Constantino, R. (1970). The mis-education of the Filipino. *Journal of Contemporary Asia, 1*(1), 20–36. https://doi.org/10.1080/00472337085390031

Cushman, E. (2016). Translingual and decolonial approaches to meaning making. *College English, 78*(3), 234–242.

Dearden, J. (2015). English as a medium of instruction-a growing global phenomenon. *British Council*. Retrieved June 10, 2022, from https://www.britishcouncil.org/sites/default/files/e484_emi_cover_option_3_final_web.pdf

de Los Ríos, C. V., Martinez, D. C., Musser, A. D., Canady, A., Camangian, P., & Quijada, P. D. (2019). Upending colonial practices: Toward repairing harm in English education. *Theory Into Practice, 58*(4), 359–367. https://doi.org/10.1080/00405841.2019.1626615

de Los Ríos, C. V., & Seltzer, K. (2017). Translanguaging, coloniality, and English classrooms: An exploration of two bicoastal urban classrooms. *Research in the Teaching of English, 52*(1), 55–76.

Dowling, T., & Krause, L. (2019). 'Ndifuna i meaning yakhe': Translingual morphology in English teaching in a south African township classroom. *International Journal of Multilingualism, 16*(3), 205–225. https://doi.org/10.1080/14790718.2017.1419475

Dumatog, R., & Dekker, D. (2003). *First language education in Lubuagan, Northern Philippines*. Retrieved January 12, 2021, from SIL Philippines: http://www-01.sil.org/asia/ldc/parallel_papers/dumatog_and_dekker.pdf

Escobar, A. (2004). Beyond the third world: Imperial globality, global coloniality and anti-globalisation social movements. *Third World Quarterly, 25*(1), 207–230. https://doi.org/10.1080/0143659042000185417

Fasakin, A. (2021). The coloniality of power in postcolonial Africa: Experiences from Nigeria. *Third World Quarterly, 42*(5), 902–921. https://doi.org/10.1080/01436597.2021.1880318

Ferguson, G. (2003). Classroom code-switching in post-colonial contexts: Functions, attitudes and policies. In S. Makoni & U. Meinhof (Eds.), *African and applied linguistics (AILA volume review)* (Vol. 16). John Benjamins. https://doi.org/10.1075/aila.16.05fer

Goh, D. P. S. (2015). Elite schools, postcolonial Chineseness and hegemonic masculinities in Singapore. *British Journal of Sociology of Education, 36*(1), 137–155. https://doi.org/10.1080/01425692.2014.971944

Gonzales, N., & Moll, L. (2002) Cruzanda el puente: Building bridges to funds of knowledge. *Educational Policy, 16(4)*, 623–641.

Gonzalez, A. (1976). Content in English language materials in The Philippines: A case study of cultural and linguistic emancipation. *Philippine Studies, 24*(4), 443–454.

Gray, J. (2002). The global coursebook in English language teaching. In D. Block & D. Cameron (Eds.), *Globalization and language teaching* (pp. 161–177). Routledge.

Grosfoguel, R. (2006). World-systems analysis in the context of transmodernity, border thinking, and global coloniality. *Postcolonial Studies to Decolonial Studies: Decolonizing Postcolonial Studies, 29*(2), 167–187.

Guillermo, R. (2003). Exposition, critique and new directions for Pantayong Pananaw. *Kyoto Review of Southeast Asia, 3*, 1–20.

Guo, Y., & Beckett, G. H. (2007). The hegemony of English as a global language: Reclaiming local knowledge and culture in China. *Convergence, 40*(1–2), 117–131.

Hsu, F. (2015). The coloniality of neoliberal English: The enduring structures of American colonial English instruction: The Philippines and Puerto Rico. *L2 Journal, 7*(3), 123–145. https://doi.org/10.5070/L27323549

Horvath, R. J. (1972). A definition of colonialism. *Current Anthropology, 13*(1), 45–57.

Kumaravadivelu, B. (2003). A postmethod perspective on English language teaching. *World Englishes, 22*(4), 539–550. https://doi-org.libproxy.ucl.ac.uk/10.1111/j.1467-971X.2003.00317.x

Loomba, A. (1998). *Colonialism/postcolonialism*. Routledge.

López-Gopar, M. E. (2016). *Decolonizing primary English language teaching*. Multilingual Matters.

Maldonado-Torres, N. (2007). On the coloniality of being. *Cultural Studies, 21*(2–3), 240–270. https://doi.org/10.1080/09502380601162548

Matemba, Y. H., & Lilemba, J. M. (2015). Challenging the status quo: Reclaiming indigenous knowledge through Namibia's postcolonial education system. *Diaspora, Indigenous, and Minority Education, 9*(3), 159–174. https://doi.org/10.1080/15595692.2014.997382

Paterno, M. G. (2018). Anguish as mother tongue: English in a multilingual context. In I. Martin (Ed.), *Reconceptualizing English education in a multilingual society* (pp. 67–83). Springer. https://doi.org/10.1007/978-981-10-7528-5_5

Pennycook, A. (2018). Applied linguistics as epistemic assemblage. *AILA Review, 31*(1), 113–134. https://doi.org/10.1075/aila.00015.pen

Portolés, L., & Martí, O. (2017). Translanguaging as a teaching resource in early language learning of English as an additional language (EAL). *Bellaterra Journal of Teaching & Learning Language & Literature, 10*(1), 61–77.

Phyak, P. (2021). Epistemicide, deficit language ideology, and (de) coloniality in language education policy. *International Journal of the Sociology of Language, 2021*(267–268), 219–233. https://doi.org/10.1515/ijsl-2020-0104

Rafael, V. L. (2015). The war of translation: Colonial education, American English, and Tagalog slang in The Philippines. *The Journal of Asian Studies, 74*(2), 283–302. https://doi.org/10.1017/S0021911814002241

Ramanathan, V. (2015). Contesting the Raj's 'divide and rule' policies: Linguistic apartheid, unequal Englishes, and the postcolonial framework. In R. Tupas (Ed.), *Unequal Englishes: The politics of Englishes today* (pp. 203–222). Palgrave Macmillan.

Rixon, S., & Smith, R. (2012). The work of Brian Abbs and Ingrid Freebairn. *ELT Journal, 66*(3), 383–393. https://doi.org/10.1093/elt/ccs022

Rubdy, R. (2015). Unequal Englishes, the native speaker, and decolonization in TESOL. In *Unequal Englishes: Politics of Englishes today* (pp. 42–58). Palgrave Macmillan.

Salonga, A. O. (2015). Performing gayness and English in an offshore call center industry. In *Unequal Englishes: The politics of Englishes today* (pp. 130–142). Palgrave Macmillan.

Shizha, E. (2013). Reclaiming our indigenous voices: The problem with postcolonial sub-Saharan African school curriculum. *Journal of Indigenous Social Development, 2*(1), 1–18.

Soto-Molina, J. E., & Méndez, P. (2020). Linguistic colonialism in the English language textbooks of multinational publishing houses. *HOW Journal, 27*(1), 11–28.

Sterzuk, A., & Nelson, C. A. (2016). "Nobody told me they didn't speak English!": Teacher language views and student linguistic repertoires in Hutterite colony schools in Canada. *Journal of Language, Identity & Education, 15*(6), 376–388. https://doi.org/10.1080/15348458.2016.1233066

Subedi, B. (2013). Decolonizing the curriculum for global perspectives. *Educational Theory, 63*(6), 621–638. https://doi.org/10.1111/edth.12045

Sugiharto, S. (2013). Rethinking globalization, reclaiming the local: A post-colonial perspective of English language education in Indonesia. *The Indonesian Quarterly, 41*(3), 148–166.

TESOL Islamia. (2022). Accessed from https://www.tesolislamia.org/, on July 21, 2022.

Thomson, P., & Hall, C. (2008). Opportunities missed and/or thwarted? 'Funds of knowledge' meet the English national curriculum. *The Curriculum Journal, 19*(2), 87–103. https://doi.org/10.1080/09585170802079488

Tlostanova, M., & Mignolo, W. (2009). Global coloniality and the decolonial option. *Kult, 6* (Special issue: The Latin American decolonial option and its ramifications), Fall, 130–147.

Tuck, E., & Yang, K. W. (2012). Decolonization is not a metaphor. *Decolonization: Indigeneity, Education and Society, 1*(1), 1–40.

Tupas, R. (2021). Afterword: Who controls the production of knowledge? Teacher empowerment in TESOL teacher education. In A. Ahmed & O. Barnawi (Eds.), *Mobility of knowledge, practice and pedagogy in TESOL teacher education*. Palgrave Macmillan. https://doi.org/10.1007/978-3-030-64140-5_16

Tupas, R. (2015). Inequalities of multilingualism: Challenges to mother tongue-based multilingual education. *Language and Education, 29*(2), 112–124. https://doi.org/10.1080/09500782.2014.977295

Tupas, R., & Martin, I. P. (2017). Bilingual and mother tongue-based multilingual education in The Philippines. In O. García, A. Lin, & S. May (Eds.), *Bilingual and multilingual education, encyclopedia of language and education* (pp. 247–258). Springer. https://doi.org/10.1007/978-3-319-02324-3_18-1

Valdez, C. (2020). Disrupting colonial discourses: Anticolonial academic language development for the elementary classroom. *Multicultural Perspectives, 22*(1), 3–11. https://doi.org/10.1080/15210960.2020.1728276

Vaish, V. (2005). A peripherist view of English as a language of decolonization in post-colonial India. *Language Policy, 4*(2), 187–206. https://doi.org/10.1007/s10993-005-3523-7

Walter, S. L., & Dekker, D. E. (2011). Mother tongue instruction in Lubuagan: A case study from The Philippines. *International Review of Education, 57*(5), 667–683. https://doi.org/10.1007/s11159-011-9246-4

Ruanni Tupas (Ph D) teaches sociolinguistics of education at the Institute of Education, University College London. He is an Associate Editor of *The International Journal of the Sociology of Language*. Email: r.tupas@ucl.ac.uk

Coloniality, Interculturality, and Modes of Arguing

Khameiel Al Tamimi

Abstract This chapter argues that including alternative modes of reasoning such as narrative arguments is one way of resisting the Eurocentrism found in dominant accounts of argumentation. Storytelling plays a crucial role in Indigenous and African philosophy. However, African and Indigenous philosophy are denied the credibility that they deserve and are not seen as legitimate philosophy. This problem is due to the way argument is defined and how the philosophical method is conceptualized. The dominant mode of arguing is problematic for three main reasons: first, it marginalises alternative modes of reasoning and experiencing the world; second, it fuels colonialist thinking, which is salient in philosophy; and third, it hinders genuine intercultural dialogue. Broadening our concept of arguments to include narrative and non-standard modes enriches the philosophical method and helps include marginalized voices in the sphere of argumentation.

Keywords Narrative argument · Indigenous philosophy · Domination · African philosophy · Eurocentrism · Decoloniality · Philosophical method · Hegemony

1   Introduction

This chapter argues that expanding the concept of argument to include narrative is one way of resisting the Eurocentrism embedded in the dominant model of arguing that gives rise to colonial and hegemonic thinking in the study and practice of argumentation. The dominant mode of arguing is problematic because it (a) marginalises alternative modes of reasoning and experiencing the world, (b) feeds into colonialist thinking, and (c) reduces the possibility of genuine intercultural dialogue. This model of arguing comes from a Western conception that is Eurocentric and excludes the narrative mode. However, narrative is recognized within many

K. Al Tamimi (✉)
Independent Scholar, Windsor, ON, Canada

social contexts and cultural traditions as a valid mode of argumentation. In fact, women, Indigenous, and African people tend to favour narrative argument. Therefore, recognizing narrative arguments helps incorporate those voices into the debate, helping to decolonise philosophy.

The objective of this chapter is to challenge colonialist notions embedded in the classical concept of arguing by offering alternative models of reasoning. The first part will offer a critique of the traditional model of arguing by showing how it is exclusive of the pluriversal worldviews of Indigenous scholarly communities of practice. My goal is to show how excluding the Indigenous mode of knowledge production further recolonises the minds of Indigenous scholars. In the second part of the chapter, I will delineate how alternative modes of arguing, particularly narrative, are legitimate and can enhance the goal of interculturality and pluralistic argumentation practices. Hence, if we wish to embrace interculturality, we ought to pay attention to all the modes of argument that are used across cultures and argumentation communities.

2 History of Argumentation Theory and Definitions of Argument

Argumentation theory is an interdisciplinary field which draws from a wide range of disciplines and scholars such as philosophers, logicians, computer scientists, linguists, legal scholars and speech communication theorists. Argumentation theorists are interested in the production, structure and evaluation of arguments (Van Eemeren et al., 2009, p.12). The study of argument has historically focused on formal logic, which was an attempt to understand arguments, thinking, and reasoning using formal deductive methods and artificial abstract language.

While the study of argumentation has been part of the field of philosophy ever since Aristotle, who analysed argumentation in terms of formal and deductive logic, argumentation theory is nevertheless a new field that developed in the 1950s (Gilbert, 1997, p. 3). Two of the main scholars who pioneered the study of argumentation are Chaim Perelman and Stephen Toulmin. Both Toulmin and Perelman attack formal logic for being artificial and irrelevant to the natural and everyday language of argumentation. Perelman and Olbrechts-Tyteca's *The New Rhetoric* (1969: originally published in French in 1958) and Toulmin's *The Uses of Argument* (1958) are an attempt to offer an alternative to formal logic that is more suitable and useful for analysing and dealing with everyday interactive argumentation in ordinary language. And both theorists argue that there is a difference between the artificial language of logic and the natural language of argument, and that logic by itself is not sufficient for analysing natural arguments. This rejection of logic for analysing and understanding everyday language became the mainstream perspective during the 1970s (Benoit et al., 1992, p.7). Until the late seventies, argumentation theory was still dominated by the work of Toulmin (1958) and Perelman and Olbrechts-Tyteca (1969).

Since the early 1990s, new approaches to argumentation have emerged that tried to build on Perelman's and Toulmin's models of argumentation. These new approaches include Rhetoric, Formal Dialectics, Pragma Dialectics, Informal Logic and Formal Analysis of Fallacies. Although this list is not exhaustive, these approaches roughly represent the current state of argumentation theory.

The definitions of argument and the methodology and procedure of argumentation vary from one approach to another. However, the dominant understanding defines argumentation as "a verbal and social activity of reason aimed at increasing (or decreasing) the acceptability of a controversial standpoint for the listener or reader, by putting forward a constellation of propositions intended to justify (or refute) the standpoint before a rational judge" (Van Eemeren et al., 2009, p.5). As such, the common understanding of argument among scholars is that an argument has to be explicit, linear, with premises and a conclusion. Recently, the boundaries of what constitutes an argument have been expanded, and more attention has been paid to the role of interpersonal argumentation and context. While the new school of argumentation scholars has broadened this conception of argument, there is still very little work done on narrative argument. Narrative argument continues to be a contested topic along with other multimodal arguments such as emotional and visual arguments (Gilbert, 1997). This is because the traditional, standard model of argumentation only accepts claims, premises and conclusions set out in an explicit and linear fashion as an argument. Narrative does not follow this format, and therefore is not seen as an argument. Other modes of arguing such as emotional and visual arguments are also dismissed. While Indigenous and African cultures rely on multiple modes, I will focus on narrative arguments.

3 What Is a Narrative Argument?

Narrative argumentation is a largely unexplored area that in recent years has received more attention from argumentation theorists. The narrative account I rely on here is a continuation of my PhD dissertation project which, I will show, is compatible with Indigenous and African modes of knowledge. In my dissertation, *A Narrative Account of Argumentation* (2017), I developed a narrative account of argument by showing how storytelling can function as an argument. I define narrative argument as storytelling with the purpose of persuading in the context of disagreement. My account of narrative argument combines features of argument with narrative features (event, plot, audience, time and space). Narrative arguments contain reasons which are unstated and conveyed through the story. Since argumentation is a reason-giving activity, the arguer putting forth a story must do so within the realm of reasons. That is, the story must contain reasons that are embedded in the story, otherwise it is not an argument. With narrative arguments, like traditional arguments, an assertion is made that something has to be done, changed, or believed. My account of narrative is distinct from the dominant model of arguing since narrative arguers utilise all the available modes of communication, such as body language, emotions, and contextual features of the situation.

Moreover, narrative argumentation is a continuation of the debate on multimodal argumentation. The concept of multi-modal argumentation was first introduced by Michael Gilbert (1994), and later developed into coalescent argumentation (1997). Multimodal argumentation emphasises that there are different modes of arguing which include the four pointed out by Gilbert (1997): the logical, emotional, visceral (which relates to the physical mode of arguing that can include a touch or any nonverbal communication such as body language (Gilbert, p. 84)), kisceral (which is the "mode of communication that relies on the intuitive, the imaginative, the religious, the spiritual, and the mystical" (Gilbert, 1997, p. 86), but it can also include visual argumentation (Groarke, 2009), and the musical mode (Groarke & Dewey, 2002). Taste, smell, and actio (as in action), which is a mode found in facial expression, gestures, posture and tone of voice and other non-verbal modes of argumentation, have all been identified as arguments by some argumentation scholars, such as Gilbert (1994), Groarke (1996), Gelang and Kjeldsen (2011) and Groarke (2015, p. 134).

The idea of multimodal argumentation is that the concept of traditional argumentation does not fit the demands of arguers in everyday life, arguers who use whatever means available to make a point. Multi-modal (with hyphen) as used by Gilbert designates four separate and distinct modes that do not necessarily work together. Gilbert argues that in most situations one is able to identify some aspect of a distinct mode. However, multimodal (without hyphen) refers to an argument that uses channels of more than one mode of argumentation. In general, the idea of multimodal (with or without the hyphen) refers to the recognition of different modes of arguing that may or may not work together in an argument. In addition, as noted by Gilbert, arguers rarely utilise one mode alone, for often argumentation is a combination of many modes (1994, p. 166).

Narrative arguments are not based on the traditional model and are not linear, direct or explicit, and as such they exhibit a unique argumentative form (which is that of story). It is no coincidence that narrative, which is associated with marginalised groups such as Indigenous and African people, is not recognised in mainstream traditional argumentation theories. The rejection of narrative and other modes of arguing stems from the ideal of philosophical purity, which will be discussed later in this chapter.

4 Critiques of Traditional Argumentation

There are many ways that feminists have reacted against the existing styles or practices of argumentation. Feminist critiques of argumentation range from critiques about the method of arguing (i.e., the adversarial model), the conceptualisation of reason (as masculine), and the exclusionary definitions of arguments, to questions about gender differences in preferred modes of arguing. However, I will only focus on the critiques relevant to the exclusion of marginalised voices of Indigenous and African people.

Many feminist theorists of argumentation criticise the adversariality that is embedded in classical approaches to argumentation. The practice of argument is often infused with aggression and hostility that puts women at a disadvantage, since women, due to socialisation, tend to use politer forms of argumentation. Feminists, such as Janice Moulton (1983), argue that traditional argumentative styles are rooted in the "adversary method" which accepts aggressive behaviour as a model of philo-sophical reasoning. As Moulton points out, aggression takes on positive connota-tions when it is connected to males or professional workers. Aggression is then connected to more positive concepts, such as power, authority, competence, etc. The conflation of aggression with positive concepts has made it hard to see that polite and non-abrupt speech can be just as effective and persuasive (p. 150).

A major drawback of the adversary method is that it only accepts the kind of reasoning whose goal is to convince an opponent and ignores reasoning that might be used in other circumstances: To figure something out for oneself, to discuss something with like-minded thinkers, to convince the indifferent or the uncommit-ted, are examples (Moulton, 1983, p. 159). That is, the adversary method ignores the multiplicity of goals that argument and arguing has for people. In addition, the adversary method limits and misrepresents what philosophical reasoning is (p. 153). Non-adversarial modes of reasoning, then, are dismissed as non-legitimate modes of arguing. This has implications for argumentation theory. Indigenous and African cultures rely more than the colonial West on narrative and holistic methods to attain knowledge. Narrative is an important mode because it is cooperative and non-aggressive.

Narrative arguing, which is a politer form of dialogue, is not validated in classi-cal argumentation theory because it is not seen as credible. Narrative, much like emotional reasoning, is regarded as non-argumentative or non-persuasive. This nar-row conception of philosophy coincides with a narrow conception of argumenta-tion, reasoning, and rationality. Given that narrative is a polite form of reasoning, it is important to consider what modes of reasoning are legitimised and fostered by philosophy as a discipline and how these impact and shape the dominant discourses of exclusion and dismissal. This is precisely the point that feminist critiques of argumentation engage with and make, i.e., that there is indeed something problem-atic with the way argumentation and philosophy at large conceptualise reasoning--what it means to argue and be a rational person. This adversarial method has led philosophers to ignore ways in which one may argue without being hostile. Arguments that are passive and indirect are not considered arguments due to the dominance of the adversarial method. The problem with this approach to argumen-tation is that those who are not comfortable with it (that is, those who prefer a coop-erative and polite style of reasoning) are disbarred from argumentation. And so, the problem is with how argumentation is defined and conceptualised as adversarial, assertive, explicit and linear (i.e., as masculine). The adversariality of argumenta-tion limits what is and is not credible and stipulates that only the stereotypical masculine mode can be sound and legitimate. This may alienate women who, according to Moulton, favour less adversarial modes of argumentation (like narrative). But it is not just women who are excluded; anyone who uses alternative modes of arguing is discredited.

Other feminist critiques focus on how reasoning has been constructed as a masculine activity since the time of Aristotle. Feminists such as Genevieve Lloyd (1984) and Phyllis Rooney (1991) argue that there is a problem with the way reason has been constructed as exclusive and devaluing of women. That is, there is a metaphorical and literal exclusion of women from the perspective of reason. In *The Man of Reason* (1984), Lloyd offers an historical account of the way reason has been conceived. In doing this, she surveys major philosophers who have theorised reason, and argues that reason has been developed with male ideals of reason, which exclude women and devalue femaleness and ways of knowing associated with women. What Lloyd refers to as the maleness of reason is rooted in a deep philosophical tradition which relegates women to the body, to the part of the person deemed as irrational, which in turn puts women in opposition to reason (1984, p. xviii).

From the beginnings of philosophical thought, femaleness was associated with what reason leaves behind, i.e., the dark forces of earth (Lloyd, 1984, p. 2). Since the Greeks, femaleness was associated with a vague and indeterminate mode of thought, whereas maleness represented a clear and determinate mode of thinking. Similarly, Phyllis Rooney (1991) demonstrates that the pervasive thematic dichotomy in Greek thought aligns reason and form with maleness and matter and formlessness with the female (p. 79). Lloyd's point is that our ideals of reason have excluded the feminine, and that femininity has been historically understood on the basis of this exclusion (1984, p. xix). Lloyd argues that this male bias in reasoning is more than just misogynist attitudes in philosophical thought (p. 37); it is, in fact, the way reason has been understood and developed, in opposition to and exclusive of the female.

In this chapter, I argue that reason has not only been reconstructed to exclude femaleness, but also to exclude racialised voices. Reason has been constructed in opposition to Indigenous and African modes of knowledge. This legacy of exclusion in philosophy relates not just to women, but also to Indigenous, African, and marginalised groups. We see the same happening to minoritised people whose arguments are dismissed due to the way reason and philosophy are theorised. Western conceptualisation of reasons is hegemonic in the sense that it leaves no room for alternative epistemic practices, including narrative.

The traditional model of arguing is a Eurocentric model as it focuses on only one mode of arguing, i.e., the exchange of reasons through premises and conclusions, and excludes narrative and other modes of arguing. As a result, many argumentation theorists (e.g., Gilbert, 1994; Nye, 1990 & Ayim, 1988) have rejected the traditional (critical-logical) model of argumentation, as it ignores the social, contextual, and personal aspects of argumentation. As such, peoples of the global South whose linguistic habits differ from the Northern logico-deductive model are disempowered as arguers. For example, Indigenous knowledge practices, epistemologies and pedagogies are denied legitimacy due to their group-specific linguistic practices, thus reducing the likelihood of genuinely effective cross-cultural dialogue. This exclusion operates partly through the erasure of narrative argument, which does not conform to the Eurocentric model of argumentation.

5   The Eurocentrism of Dominant Argumentation Theory

Traditional modes of argumentation are Eurocentric in that they reject other modes of reasoning associated with other cultures including African and Indigenous people. Alternative modes of arguing such as narrative are associated with the marginalised, and not regarded as valid or equal. Denying legitimacy to other modes of arguing is one way of silencing the cultural others. As discussed earlier, many scholars have criticised the negative effects of mainstream argumentation theories on women. However, little work has been done on how the traditional model is hegemonic and Eurocentric. As such, the damaging effects of the dominant model on Indigenous and marginalised groups from the global south have been ignored.

The idea of rationality was at the heart of colonial exploitation and subjugation where Africans were not seen as rational beings. And insofar as they were seen as irrational, they were then perceived as incapable of producing reason. Hence, "The struggle for reason – who is and who is not a rational animal – is the foundation of racism" (Ramose, 2002, p.3). This racism led to the rejection of African philosophy among Western philosophers. That is because the history of Western philosophy was based on the idea that Africans are not wholly or truly human (p. 5). In other words, Eurocentrism rests on the idea that it is Western knowledge that sets the criteria of what is considered reasonable and what is not reasonable (Doxtater, 2004, p. 629). Western reason excludes everything outside of its dictates. That is, anything outside the realm of reason, such as traditional rites, mystical beliefs and spiritual customs and rituals, is deemed irrational and is discredited. As a result, African societies are viewed as living under the spell of magic and the burden of charm and are consequently resistant to change (Mbembe, 2001, p. 4). African philosophy is contested because African ways of being are not seen as rational.

Walsh (2007) argues that Indigenous and black people are still considered by dominant society as incapable of serious intellectual work due to the Eurocentricity and racialised character of critical thought (p. 229). While logic and critical thought have always existed among Indigenous and Afro-descendent people, it has seldom been recognised because African societies are seen as prelogical and preliterate, as argued by the anthropologist Lévy-Bruhl (1975). However, Fayemi (2020) rejects the racist and obscene claim that there is no logic in African culture, since logic and language are two fundamental features of all human society (Fayemi, 2020, p. 126). Fayemi argues further that every culture, insofar as it contains language, must have logic, and as such language and logic are intertwined. Without language, logic is impossible and without logic, language is unintelligible, i.e., both need each other to work (p. 126).

Further, logic is culturally bound. And much like western concepts of logic, African logic also relies on deduction and experience. That is, a conclusion is reached after many occurrences, enabling a logical connection to be established (Kanu, 2017, p. 13). Kanu (2017) argues that if by logic we mean the ability to be reasonable, critically judge or evaluate evidence and avoid contradiction and inconsistency, then logic can be found in all cultures. Kanu asserts, "There is no culture that does not accommodate a good argument, especially as it concerns their conclusions. Whether in Africa or in Europe or in America or in Asia, if the assumption of an argument is true, the conclusion of the argument would always be true" (2017, pp. 13–14). Therefore, Kanu argues that while the principles of logic are universal, the application of logic is local and specific to a culture. Kanu explains that by African logic we mean the application of reason to the culture and experience of African people (p.13). While African cultural traditions are logical, they also rely heavily on narrative arguments, which are also logical. Understanding the reason-giving force of narrative arguments helps to deflate the Eurocentric conception of African culture as illogical and irrational.

Despite the existence of African logic and hence philosophy, non-western philosophers still rely on the Western philosophical paradigm and categories of thinking. The result is that non-western philosophers are unable to think or express their thoughts in an authentic form without translating them into Western modes. As Chimakonam (2017) points out, western philosophy is Eurocentric in its epistemic vision as it imposes western categories of thought on the philosophies of the Global South, particularly African philosophy. Since survivors of colonisation were robbed of their genuine modes of expression, they were left with no other modes of intellectual expression except the cultural patterns of the rulers (Quijano, 2007, p. 170). Colonisers suppressed Indigenous ways of knowing and the language of knowing. The result of colonisation is that Africa was reduced to silence in the minds of Europeans. Consequently, non-western ways of doing philosophy, such as the use of narrative as a source and method of producing knowledge, are denied credibility. The problem of what counts as philosophy is the same problem as what counts as argument, simply because argument is the method of doing philosophy. Just as alternative modes of arguing are not seen as argumentative or reason producing, alternative methods of doing philosophy, that is African and Indigenous philosophies, are also not seen as real philosophy, but instead as pseudo philosophy because they do not abide by the classical ways of doing philosophy.

Moreover, philosophers from the Global South are denied an equal platform to participate and engage with western philosophers, as evident in the way research and publication is disseminated (Chimakonam, 2017, p. 125). There is a connection between this silencing that takes place in the publication of research and the exclusion of narrative and alternative voices. Part of the reason that some work is being denied legitimacy is precisely because it is narrative-based and defies the canonical method. As such, argumentation becomes a colonising practice when it rejects forms of reasoning and arguing that are associated with minoritised groups, such as

Indigenous communities and African and other non-western people. As a result, both the dominant model of reasoning and the philosophical method are hegemonic and embedded in colonialist contexts and practices. The philosophical method is Eurocentric in the way it is conducted, i.e., what is taught and learned as philosophy in the West remains focused on the methodology and philosophers of the West, including Western approaches to argumentation. The discipline of philosophy remains focused on philosophers of European origins from Plato to Sartre or Wittgenstein. Also, very few philosophy departments in the USA or Europe offer courses on African or Indigenous philosophy. The rejection of the Indigenous and African methods for doing philosophy stems from a deep-rooted bias in philosophical methods and the idea of philosophical purity, i.e., the notion that there is only one way of doing philosophy. As Barry Hallen (2002), asserts,

> There is yet another dimension to the history of philosophy in Africa—the virtual mountain of historical texts, still incompletely catalogued, that have been indiscriminately labelled African 'oral literature.' For it certainly is the case that academic philosophers were for long predisposed to turn up their noses at the suggestion that an anonymous corpus of writings that included myths, legends, poetry, song, and proverbs was truly worthy of the title 'philosophy'. One thing upon which Africana scholars and intellectuals largely agree is that the criteria used to define what is and what is not philosophy in the world today are unfairly biased by and for 'philosophy' as presently construed by western culture. (p. 11)

Therefore, African and Indigenous philosophies still have to conform to Imperial western modes of thought in order to be considered legitimate philosophy, otherwise such philosophies are seen as inferior. As argued by Kanu (2014a), "More so, the denial of philosophy to Africans by some Africans and some Western thinkers is also based on the issue of methodology, precisely on the belief that philosophy everywhere should have a universal methodology" (p. 1). However, the fact is that philosophising is a universal and cultural phenomenon that is not restricted to one method (Rico, 2016, p. 77). In some cultures, such as in Europe and North America, we find more focus on the written and discursive mode of philosophizing (argumentation). In other cultures, and parts of the world, such as Africa and indigenous communities, the act of philosophizing, while still utilizing the principles of reason and logic, is done through different mediums, such as storytelling. As noted by Kanu (2014b), traditional African philosophy is not a written philosophy and is "embodied in proverbs, aphorisms and pithy sayings" (p. 86). Kanu (2014b) argues that the absence of writing does not mean an absence of philosophy. For example, the Upanishads and Vedas were not written down for centuries yet are considered classic Indian philosophy (p. 86).

Moreover, Oruka (1991) argues that philosophy does not have to be discursive or written down to be considered philosophy, but it must have critical and coherent thoughts. Oruka states that to exist as a philosopher, one's philosophy doesn't have to be written and available to future generations. It is enough that a philosopher is deemed as such by his contemporaries and his fellow community members (Oruka, 1991, p. 58). And so, there are many ways of producing philosophical works just as there are many ways of producing arguments and reasoning. This is not to say that Africa lacks a literate or written philosophy but that the non-written modes of philosophical work matter and should be recognized. Since much of African philosophy can be found in stories, proverbs and myths, the rejection of the narrative form is also a rejection and erasure of traditional African philosophical works that are embedded in those stories. To clarify, I am not here making the argument that African or Indigenous people are incapable of producing or using canonical and classical philosophical methods. That is, narrative is not the only method of doing philosophy in Africa, it is one of many. What I'm suggesting is that philosophical ideas in African traditions can be extensively found in storytelling, myths, and legends, and these ideas are dismissed in the West.

Likewise, Rico (2016) offers an example of an African autobiography that can be read as a philosophical work. She looks at one particular African autobiographical work, namely Malidoma Patrice Somé's *Of Water and the Spirit: Ritual, Magic and Initiation in the Life of an African Shaman*. As noted by Rico, Somé in his autobiography challenges western hegemonic thought and western metaphysical conceptions of the ethical self, temporality, and history. African autobiography favours a communal conception of self that differs from the western conceptions of the self as autonomous (p. 78). Somé tells his story of being kidnapped from his village by the French Jesuits as a young boy and forced to leave his Dagara community. After fifteen years of being forced to learn and adapt to the western education, he returns home and begins a journey of self-discovery and the initiation process into adulthood where he learns to see the self differently (p. 84).

Rico explains that it is through spirituality and Somé's connection to his culture and traditions that he comes to see the self as connected to the community and not separate from it. As pointed out by Rico, "the mystical aspects of his initiation lead Somé to believe in an intimate relationship between mind, body, and soul that, for him, involves a close relationship to community and one's ancestors" (p. 84). In his autobiography, Somé's celebration of spirituality and his initiation journey challenges western perceptions of the self and spirituality as in opposition to rational thought. As such, using the mode of autobiography, philosophical ideas can be entertained and contested. Similarly, narrative arguments, such as those present in African autobiographical work, are imbued with philosophical purpose and meaning.

Mungwini et al. (2019) argue that African philosophers must express their philosophical thinking, using their own categories of reflection and conceptual frameworks that are derived from their own African culture (p. 73). The authors critique this reliance on the western conceptual apparatus and argue that the problem is that "Our thinking has remained predominantly Eurocentric even though we are not ourselves Europeans" (p. 73). In the same vein, Dennis Masaka (2018) points out that the liberation of African philosophy requires a change of paradigm in the way African philosophy is understood and studied since western frameworks dismiss and discredit African traditions, stories, and culture as non-philosophical.

6 The Benefits of Recognising Narrative Argumentation

Understanding narrative as a legitimate argument type has important implications for the decolonisation of Indigenous and African epistemologies. Storytelling plays a crucial role in Indigenous and African cultures in that it is the primary method for acquiring knowledge due to the prevalence of an oral tradition. That is, orality is central to Indigenous culture and knowledge production (Dei, 2000). Indigenous epistemic practices are rooted in storytelling, connection to nature, and spirituality. As such Indigenous knowledge is personal, oral, holistic and relies on storytelling. Alternative modes of reasoning such as narrative, emotional reasoning, as well as other modes that are neither verbal nor discursive, are more prevalent in non-western cultures, particularly in Indigenous communities (Iseke, 2013). While narrative is used in all cultures and is a universal human practice, some cultures esteem and value narrative more than others, including Indigenous and African cultures. In some cultures, narrative is more than entertainment or a recalling of events. Narrative is important for transmission of knowledge and for the building and maintenance of ancestral and community bonds. For example, narrative is crucial to how elders in aboriginal communities communicate and share knowledge. Senanayake (2006) explains that Indigenous knowledge "is the unique knowledge confined to a particular culture or society" (p. 87). It is the profound knowledge that Indigenous people have of their local environment that is generated and transmitted by communities over time and passed down from one generation to another. Indigenous knowledge derives from the long residence in a place and the direct experience of nature and the environment and its connection and relationship with the social world (Dei, 2000, p.114). Besides, Indigenous knowledge is difficult to express in Eurocentric thought because it deals not only with the realm of the physical, but also with the metaphysical and the spiritual. It consists of many ways of knowing that are beyond the cognitive, such as dreams, visions, feelings and intuitions. As Shahjahan (2005) points out,

> Neither indigenous knowledges, nor the anti-colonial movements, have ever exclusively been a rationalistic exercise; rather, they involved the emotions, spirits, dreams, intuition, poetry, music, bodies of the colonized in order to resist the colonial encounter. Anti-colonial discourse has to embody these ways of knowing in our own writings and stories. (p. 232)

Shahjahan argues that since Indigenous thought is colonised by the rules of Eurocentric thought, namely the rules of linear, rational and impersonal writing, we need to decolonise our writing styles (p. 231). This means expanding the concepts of arguing to include alternative modes of arguing.

The problem is that the non-standard modes of arguing such as the narrative, the visceral (or physical,) the kisceral (or intuitive), and the emotional (Gilbert, 1997) that are associated with marginalised groups, are perceived as inferior to the Western rational model of arguing, and not regarded as valid forms of persuasion. Hence, the dominant model of arguing feeds into and supports colonialist ideology. For example, narrative, which is central to Indigenous epistemologies and pedagogies, is delegitimised as a form of rational argument. Prioritising the dominant model is colonialist in its essence because it forces Indigenous and other marginalised cultures to assimilate to the dominant model of arguing as premises and conclusion to be considered legitimate forms of critical discussion and participate in western discourse. This is problematic for two main reasons. Using the standard model, Indigenous epistemological and cultural facts are lost because this model requires the deconstruction and abstraction of their arguments from their context and social setting. Second, forcing minoritised groups to submit to the standard model of reasoning disrespects and denigrates their culture.

Since much of African and Indigenous philosophy relies on storytelling and other non-standard modes of arguing, excluding narrative is part of the problem of the colonisation of knowledge. This exclusion can be seen in the way argument is defined, how rationality is understood, and how credibility is distributed among the sexes and those of alternative ethnic backgrounds. The exclusion of non-standard forms of arguments leads to philosophical homogeneity and epistemic injustice, as different forms of knowledge are tied with the multiple modes of communication and arguing.

Hence, widening the concept of argument is a decolonising act, as the narrative mode is associated with Indigenous knowledge. Other modes of arguing are also associated with Indigenous modes of knowledge because Indigenous epistemologies are holistic. Argumentation is tied to epistemic practices since one of the important roles of argumentation is to produce knowledge. Argumentation is the practice of reason giving and as such reasoning is crucial for acquiring and producing knowledge. In addition, through arguments, one can convince another of an alternative point of view. By assessing and criticising, we can accept or reject a claim and a conclusion. And it is through argumentation that we come to accept conclusions and gain knowledge. The inclusion of narrative in the space of argumentation serves the epistemic functions of decolonising Indigenous thought and enhancing uptake for delegitimised and suppressed Indigenous claims. More importantly, diversifying philosophy requires diversifying our concepts of arguments, particularly arguments that have been associated with and used by marginalised groups. Recognising other forms of critical thinking is important for a decolonial project because, as Catherine Walsh (2007) asserts, "To speak of an 'other' critical thought then is to give credence to ongoing struggles — struggles that are epistemic as well as political in character'" (p. 232).

Recovering Indigenous knowledge requires challenging powerful institutions of colonisation that have subverted and dismissed alternative modes of knowledge. As Waziyatawin Angela Wilson (2004) argues, the loss of Indigenous knowledge and culture is the result of "centuries of colonialism's efforts to methodically eradicate our ways of seeing, being, and interacting with the world" (p. 359). These modes of being, as indicated above, are predominately narrative. Wilson argues that colonisers "hammered into our heads that our Indigenous cultural traditions were inferior to those of Euro-Americans and Euro-Canadians, that there was nothing of value in our old ways, and that those ways were incompatible with modernity and civilization" (p. 360). In order to perpetuate their colonial agendas and empire building, colonialists taught Indigenous people that their traditions and epistemologies are worthless and inferio.

Therefore, it is no surprise that we see narrative that is associated with African and Indigenous thought being denied legitimacy and credibility as viable forms of reasoning. If the objective is to validate Indigenous epistemologies, then some modes of arguments need to derive from Indigenous cultures. The inclusion of narrative is one way of overcoming epistemic injustice against non-western testimony. Recovering Indigenous knowledge requires the revalorisation and celebration of these cultural traditions, including narrative. The decolonisation of Indigenous thought is a form of *epistemic* decolonisation that contributes to epistemic justice, i.e., a fairer allocation of credibility to Indigenous testimony. And hence, recovering Indigenous knowledge via the celebration of storytelling is an anticolonial project.

As argued by Aman Sium and Eric Ritskes (2013), Indigenous storytelling is a form of resistance to colonial power that disrupts Eurocentric and colonial norms of objectivity and knowledge. The act of storytelling is an act of the resurgence of Indigenous epistemology and sovereignty that were destroyed by colonialism (p. 3). Storytelling as an epistemic practice disrupts academic notions of intellectual rigour and what counts as legitimate scholarship (p. 4). Iskeke (2013) argues that it is through the telling of stories and the witnessing function of storytelling that indigenous communities can resist colonisation (p. 573). Since argumentation is the practice of debating, reasoning, and negotiation, it is an integral part of social change. Without argumentation and debate, it is difficult to imagine a democratic and pluralistic society. Disagreement characterises public life in democratic societies. Therefore, debates sustain democratic participation and subvert the power of dictatorship (Asen, 2005, p. 121). The primary function of argument as justification identified by Toulmin (1958) serves an important role in democratic societies by legitimating laws and public policies (Asen, p. 123). It is through this justificatory function of arguments that laws get contested and passed. The justificatory function of argument is important for problem-solving, decision-making, and conflict resolution (p. 123).

As such, including silenced voices in argumentation means that these voices will be granted epistemic agency in the reason giving process, and that these arguers will be seen as reasoners who are capable of justifying and refuting claims, which challenges the idea that these marginalised groups are incapable of producing real philosophy. Likewise, the silencing that takes place in argumentation due to the exclusion of alternative modes of reasoning means that marginalised groups cannot reap the benefit of argumentation as a vehicle for behavioural change. Recognising narrative as argument is important because it grants marginalised voices legitimacy as rational arguers in the domain of critical discussion, a domain where actual change can take place.

As important as justification is to democracy, Asen (2005) thinks it is not its only crucial function. He points out that justification doesn't always lead to agreement. However, argumentation serves other purposes. Asen identifies three other functions of argument: agenda expansion, responsibility attribution, and identity formation (p. 128). Argumentation may be used to expand public agendas. As Asen explains, "Drawing attention rather than justifying one's position characterizes the aim of agenda expansion" (p. 129). Hence, by using argumentation, marginalised groups can expand their agenda by having the public understand the significance of their positions and the reasons why they hold those positions. They can also use argumentation for attribution of responsibility. As Asen points out, "Forcing people to accept responsibility may be an important function of argument in cases where people of different social standing interact, especially in cases where these differences are great" (p. 130). Through argumentation ordinary people and politicians can be put on record. Making public arguments means one is responsible for their actions by acknowledging their viewpoints. Responsibility means that there is scrutiny and one's decisions will not go unnoticed. Hence, taking responsibility for one's arguments means that there will be social change. As noted by Asen, "The very records created by advocates in these situations may contribute to wider social change" (p. 131). By putting people in social relations, participating in argumentation encourages a sense of self and others (p. 132).

Invalidating Indigenous and African voices and narrative arguments leads to the erasure of their right to disagree and dissent, and thus to participate in argumentation. This exclusion from the realm of discussing a difference of opinion in the area of argumentation erases the dissenting voices of diverse groups and presents a false reality where there is no dissent. Recognising narrative argument and alternative modes of arguing such as emotions promotes inclusivity and accommodates marginalised cultures, such as African and Indigenous communities. Diversifying argumentation is important for the decoloniality of reasoning. Dismantling the hegemonic power rooted in argumentation and colonisation requires the recognition and celebration of marginalised voices. Furthermore, the inclusion of narrative and alternative voices is important for genuine cross-cultural communication. No authentic debate or negotiation can take place when a segment of humanity is silenced. Communication requires hearing and listening to one another, which requires the recognition of alternative modes of argumentation those voices may use.

7   Conclusion

Decolonizing argumentation holds significant implications for interculturality. Decoloniality requires the recognition of different ways of thinking about argumentation, ones that are non-linear and inclusive of the alternative modes of being, seeing the world and reasoning. As Walter D. Mignolo (2010) argues, "Today, the focus of decolonial thinking is no longer sending the colonizers home but to de-link, in thought and action, in thinking and doing, from the colonial matrix of power" (p. 18). This matrix of power resides in the way dominant accounts of argumentation dismiss alternative ways of arguing. Therefore, the decolonisation of the racialised and marginalised voices in argumentation requires the inclusion of the perspectives of thinkers from the Global South. To include those voices, we need to recognise the different modes of arguments that those oppressed voices may use.

Diversity and decoloniality require taking seriously perspectives and voices of the cultural others, African and Indigenous communities. This decolonisation project, in turn, requires the acceptance of alternative modes of arguing, particularly narrative.

References

AlTamimi, K. (2017). *A narrative account of argumentation.* Unpublished Doctoral Dissertation, York University, Canada.

Asen, R. (2005). Pluralism, disagreement, and the status of argument in the public sphere. *Informal Logic, 25*(2), 117–137. https://doi.org/10.22329/il.v25i2.1115

Ayim, M. (1988). Violence and domination as metaphors in academic discourse. In T. Govier (Ed.), *Selected issues in logic and communication* (pp. 184–195). Wadsworth.

Benoit, W. L., Hample, D., & Benoit, P. J. (1992). *Readings in argumentation.* Foris Publications. https://doi.org/10.1515/9783110885651

Chimakonam, J. O. (2017). African philosophy and global epistemic injustice. *Journal of Global Ethics, 13*(2), 120–137. https://doi.org/10.1080/17449626.2017.1364660

Dei, G. J. S. (2000). Rethinking the role of indigenous knowledges in the academy. *International Journal of Inclusive Education, 4*(2), 111–132. https://doi.org/10.1080/136031100284849

Doxtater, M. G. (2004). Indigenous knowledge in the decolonial era. *American Indian Quarterly, 28*(3&4), 618–633. https://www.jstor.org/stable/4138935

Fayemi, A. K. (2020). Logic in Yoruba proverbs. In J. O. Chimakonam (Ed.), *Logic and African philosophy: Seminal essays on African systems of thought* (pp. 123–139). Vernon Press.

Gelang, M., & Kjeldsen, J. E. (2011). Nonverbal communication as argumentation. In F. H. van Eemeren, B. Garssen, D. Godden, & G. Mitchell (Eds.), *Proceedings of the 7th conference of the International Society for the Study of argumentation* (pp. 567–576). SicSat.

Gilbert, M. A. (1994). Feminism, argumentation and coalescence. *Informal Logic, 16*(2), 95–113. https://doi.org/10.22329/il.v16i2.2444

Gilbert, M. A. (1997). *Coalescent argumentation.* Lawrence Erlbaum. https://doi.org/10.4324/9780203810903

Groarke, L. (1996). Logic, art and argument. *Informal Logic, 18*(2), 105–129. https://doi.org/10.22329/il.v18i2.2376

Groarke, L. (2009). Five theses on Toulmin and visual argument. In *Pondering on problems of argumentation* (pp. 229–239). Springer. https://doi.org/10.1007/978-1-4020-9165-0

Groarke, L. (2015). Going multimodal: What is a mode of arguing and why does it matter? *Argumentation, 29*(2), 133–155. https://doi.org/10.1007/s10503-014-9336-0

Groarke, L., & Dewey, S. (2002). Are musical arguments possible? In F. H. van Eemeren (Ed.), *Proceedings of the fifth conference of the International Society for the Study of argumentation (ISSA)* (pp. 419–423). SicSat.

Hallen, B. (2002). *A short history of African philosophy.* Indiana University Press. https://doi.org/10.3366/afr.2005.75.4.608

Iseke, J. (2013). Indigenous storytelling as research. *International Review of Qualitative Research, 6*(4), 559–577. https://doi.org/10.1525/irqr.2013.6.4.559

Kanu, I. (2014a). *African philosophy: Between literality and orality* (pp. 2–4). Paper presented at the Literati Philosophia International Conference, Anambra State University, Igbariam Campus, Nigeria.

Kanu, I. A. (2014b). The meaning and nature of African philosophy in a globalising world. *International Journal of Humanities Social Sciences and Education, 1*(7), 86–94.

Kanu, I. A. (2017). Igwebuike and the logic (nka) of African philosophy. *IGWEBUIKE: An African Journal of Arts and Humanities, 3*(1), 9–18.

Lévy-Bruhl, L. (1975). *The notebooks on primitive mentality*. Blackwell.

Lloyd, G. (1984). *The man of reason: 'male' and 'female' in Western philosophy*. Methuen.

Masaka, D. (2018). African philosophy and the challenge from hegemonic philosophy. *Education as Change, 22*(3), 1–22. https://doi.org/10.25159/1947-9417/2918

Mbembe, A. (2001). *On the postcolony*. University of California Press. https://www.jstor.org/stable/10.1525/j.ctt1ppkxs

Mignolo, W. D. (2010). Introduction: Coloniality of power and de-colonial thinking. In W. D. Mignolo & A. Escobar (Eds.), *Globalization and the decolonial option* (pp. 1–93). Routledge. https://doi.org/10.4324/9781315868448

Moulton, J. (1983). A paradigm of philosophy: The adversary method. In S. Harding & M. B. Hintikka (Eds.), *Discovering reality: Feminist perspectives on epistemology, metaphysics, methodology, and philosophy of science* (pp. 149–164). Kluwer Academic Publishers.

Mungwini, P., Creller, A., Monahan, M. J., & Murdock, E. G. (2019). Why epistemic decolonization? *Journal of World Philosophies, 4*(2), 70–105.

Nye, A. (1990). *Words of power*. Routledge.

Oruka, H. O. (1991). Sagacity in African philosophy. In T. Serequeberhan (Ed.), *African philosophy: The essential readings* (pp. 47–62). Paragon House. https://doi.org/10.5840/ipq198323448

Perelman, C., & Olbrechts-Tyteca, L. (1969). *The new rhetoric*. University of Notre Dame Press.

Quijano, A. (2007). Coloniality and modernity/rationality. *Cultural Studies, 21*(2–3), 168–178. https://doi.org/10.1080/09502380601164353

Ramose, M. B. (2002). The struggle for reason. In P. H. Coetzee & A. P. J. Roux (Eds.), *The African philosophy reader* (pp. 1–9). Routledge.

Rico, A. R. (2016). Seeking balance: African autobiography as philosophy in Malidoma Patrice Somé's of water and the spirit: Ritual, magic and initiation in the life of an African shaman. *Research in African Literatures, 47*(1), 76–94. https://doi.org/10.2979/reseafrilite.47.1.76

Rooney, P. (1991). Gendered reason: Sex metaphor and conceptions of reason. *Hypatia, 6*(2), 77–103. https://doi.org/10.1111/j.1527-2001.1991.tb01394.x

Senanayake, S. G. J. N. (2006). Indigenous knowledge as a key to sustainable development. *Journal of Agricultural Sciences, 2*(1), 87–94. https://doi.org/10.4038/jas.v2i1.8117

Shahjahan, R. A. (2005). Mapping the field of anti-colonial discourse to understand issues of indigenous knowledges: Decolonizing praxis. *McGill Journal of Education/Revue des sciences de l'éducation de McGill, 40*(2), 213–240.

Sium, A., & Ritskes, E. (2013). Speaking truth to power: Indigenous storytelling as an act of living resistance. *Decolonization: Indigeneity, Education & Society, 2*(1), 1–10.

Toulmin, S. E. (1958). *The uses of argument*. Cambridge University Press.

Van Eemeren, F. H., Grootendorst, R., Johnson, R. H., Plantin, C., & Willard, C. A. (2009). *Fundamentals of argumentation theory: A handbook of historical backgrounds and contemporary developments*. Routledge.

Walsh, C. (2007). Shifting the geopolitics of critical knowledge: Decolonial thought and cultural studies 'others' in the Andes. *Cultural Studies, 21*(2–3), 224–239.

Wilson, W. A. (2004). Introduction: Indigenous knowledge recovery is indigenous empowerment. *American Indian Quarterly, 28*(3/4), 359–372. https://doi.org/10.1353/aiq.2004.0111

Khameiel Al Tamimi is an independent scholar living in Windsor, Ontario, Canada. She holds a PhD in philosophy from York University, Toronto. Her areas of expertise include Argumentation Theory, Ethics, and Feminism. In her dissertation, she developed a narrative account of argumentation. She has attended and presented in several international conferences and has published in academic peer reviewed journals. Email: khameiel@gmail.com

Reconstructing Educational Administration and Leadership Language and Concepts for Teaching in the Arabian Gulf: Critical, Hermeneutic and Postcolonial Dimensions of Decolonising Curriculum

Eugenie A. Samier

Abstract This chapter examines the reconstruction of educational administration and leadership language for graduate teaching in the Gulf region. This includes recognizing the large bodies of literature that have formed in all fields and disciplines internationally and cross-culturally. These also have been approached through critical theory, critical hermeneutics and several forms of postcolonial critiques aimed at decolonization of language, meaning and knowledge. The chapter also identifies a number of curricular and pedagogical practices that need to be kept in mind in authentically teaching the field in an Islamic context with the many values and character traits that are respected and that constitute the norms of Gulf cultures.

Keywords Decolonizing administration and leadership · Islamic values · Islamic character · Colonization · Postcolonial critiques · Cultural competence

1 Introduction

An indication of how terms and concepts used in educational administration vary across cultures comes from the internationalisation that has diversified all disciplines and fields over the last few decades, as well as much of the comparative, cross-cultural & postcolonial literature and related critiques. Conceptual diversities demonstrate that values, roles, styles of social interaction and constructions of social institutions differ across a number of dimensions, such as those described by Trompenaars and Hampden-Turner (1997): universalism versus particularism, individualism versus communitarianism, specific versus diffuse, neutral versus

E. A. Samier (✉)
University of Strathclyde, Glasgow, Scotland, UK

© The Author(s), under exclusive license to Springer Nature
Switzerland AG 2023
A. Sahlane, R. Pritchard (eds.), *English as an International Language Education*, English Language Education 33,
https://doi.org/10.1007/978-3-031-34702-3_22

emotional, achievement versus ascription, sequential versus synchronous time, and internal versus outer directed (see also Branine, 2011; Hofstede et al., 2010).

Public administration, which overlaps with educational administration, has also recognised significant differences cross-culturally for many years, including the varying conceptions and use of language that reflect diversities of meaning involving state and governance values and practices, policy systems, and professional roles and responsibilities across Western countries, and the non-Western and Indigenous worlds (Farazmand, 2018; Henderson, 1995; Jriesat, 2011; Raadschelders et al., 2015). Leadership, too, has undergone a significant cross-cultural and international transformation, such as Western and Garcia's (2018) examination of leadership on a global scale including all world regions, presenting many different forms and constructions of leadership reflecting the diversity of societal conditions and traditions.

Conceptions like leadership, administration, and management and the characteristics associated with them vary considerably internationally; the language used in these fields has to be interpreted and understood in their contexts since they are embedded in the societies and cultures from which they arise. The domination of mostly Anglo-American literature and the definitions and meanings used through globalisation and its neoliberal form (Fuchs, 2010) have (re-)colonisation effects on European countries, non-Western countries and Indigenous peoples through a near universalisation of English in publishing and teaching (e.g., Altbach, 2016). One cross-cultural management text that emphasises the importance of language is Lewis' (2006) *When Cultures Collide,* where language is examined in detail for the way it reflects how thought, behaviour, decisions, values and duties are carried in how language is constructed, understood and used. This is evident in how truth is understood, how styles of interaction vary, how contracts and ethics are interpreted, how gossip and silence in organisations are used, resulting in the variability of meaning in language and interpretations of the same word reflecting very different worlds.

While teaching in English in many countries, one has to be cognizant of how the same terms mean very different things depending upon the religion, values and cultural norms of a community, and be aware of differing values placed upon personality and character traits that may be considered positive or appropriate in some Western countries but have a negative association elsewhere as well as the nature of structure of social institutions that vary, governed by many ethical systems that shape the language used (e.g., Chin et al., 2018; Dimmock & Walker, 2005; Kenny & Fraser, 2013). It is partly through differences in language and communication styles that different traditions and systems of leadership are distinguished, including not only verbal language, but also non-verbal, such as body language, tone of voice, dress, and styles of social interaction that communicate leadership roles and qualities (Harris et al., 2004). For example, teaching educational administration and leadership in English in the Arabian Gulf requires an understanding of how concepts will be interpreted within the Emirati and other Gulf worlds in ways that will not reflect the Anglo-American knowledge that has been dominant through globalisation. 'Leadership' will be interpreted within the social structures of extended family and tribes, cultural norms, Islamic values, and government policy. And teaching effectively means using the language in ways that allow graduate students to interpret and apply the terms within their own society, respecting the many ways in which language and culture are connected for authentic use (Sharifian, 2015).

There are a number of problems and issues that have arisen with the widespread use of English and the hegemony of Anglo-American curriculum that will be explored in this chapter as they relate to language and its decolonisation. Hopkyns (2016) has identified a number of these as they apply to the Gulf countries: the dominance of the English language, declining Arabic abilities, and erosion of cultural identities, having a colonising impact on all societal sectors through this form of globalisation. The result is a colonisation of concepts and language that reshape how students in the Gulf region think, what practices are considered appropriate, and even their conceptions of ethics as they relate to professional practice and their own relationship to the state. Perhaps most importantly, language is also a critical part of the foundation of identity, on personal, cultural and national levels, providing the medium in which one's values, religion, social relations, and the interpretation of one's experience take place (Preece, 2016). Colonizing education through the domination of English is more than the taking over of a social institution and its professional practice; it strikes deeply into identity, religion, and culture. However, research into the language used in these fields has not yet been done sufficiently to establish the terms used and the conceptions involved in non-Western countries and cultures where belief systems, values and socio-cultural roles differ significantly. Instead, the most common practice is to adopt Anglo-American vocabulary that has highly disruptive and negative effects on identity, roles, culture, laws, and social institutions.

This chapter approaches the decolonisation of educational administration and leadership curriculum that makes the field more culturally and societally suitable for the Arabian Gulf, including many of the concepts and terms that originate in foundational fields of public administration, management and leadership. This involves recognising culture and social institutional character through cross-cultural concepts and language and the socio-cultural, political and religious contexts that shape them. It also requires that individuals and groups are understood to be embedded in their contexts for the principles and values of professional practice, and in which the language they use has meaning within this context guiding decision-making, conferring agency and contributing to the organisations they work within (Côté & Levine, 2002). Based on this premise, this chapter first identifies the importance of critical, hermeneutic and postcolonial approaches that provide rationales and principles for the reconstruction of a Gulf Islamic educational administration and leadership through a decolonizing process. The second section reconstructs the language of educational administration and leadership for the Gulf region, and Islamic contexts in general, by identifying differences between Anglo-American cultures and those of the Gulf that affect the meaning of terms, the concepts associated with them, and the way in which they affect decision-making and administrative and leadership professional practice. This includes identification of many virtues, values, and characteristics that distinguish an Islamic approach. The chapter concludes with an identification of principles that faculty need to keep in mind when designing curriculum and teaching in the field in order to decolonise and reconstruct culturally appropriate educational administration and leadership at graduate levels.

2   Critical, Hermeneutic and Postcolonial Approaches

An authentic construction of concepts and terms used for educational administration and leadership in any country requires taking into account the context, including the jurisdictional characteristics like the constitution, laws, government structure and practices, the values, social and cultural structures and norms in social institutions, religious beliefs and practices, and family structures (which in some countries involves large extended family and tribal structures and traditions). Also important is the diversity of the population and the degree of multiculturalism one finds. Just as important are historical conditions such as colonisation effects, periods of invasion, war and deep instabilities such as those one finds in parts of the Middle East and Africa, as well as nation-building and modernisation changes that affect all aspects of society, including its fundamental principles, identities, values and belief systems that inform the purpose and role of education and how it is governed and administered (see Samier, 2019, 2021).

This section focusses primarily on critical, hermeneutic and postcolonial principles that guide a conceptual reconstruction, such as critical theory that aims at disrupting colonising forces (e.g., Bourdieu, 1991), critical hermeneutics (Ricoeur, 2016; Simpson, 2021), and postcolonial considerations of a number of dimensions of language use, including the decolonisation literature applied to higher education (e.g., Bhambra et al., 2018; Jansen, 2019). These approaches also have corresponding literatures in the foundational fields for educational administration such as organisation studies (e.g., Prasad, 2003), management (e.g., Alvesson et al., 2009; Jack & Westwood, 2009), and leadership (e.g., House et al., 2004) that pursue cross-cultural features and diversity from an Arab/Islamic context, for example Branine (2011) and Beekun and Badawi (1999), who provide a foundation from which to rebuild the language and concepts of educational administration and leadership.

There are a number of critical theories that apply to deconstructing power systems in order to reform them (e.g., Habermas, 1989), but for this discussion the critical work of Bourdieu has been selected since he focused early in his career on anthropology in North Africa (Goodman & Silverstein, 2009), and then built a new sociological system informed by differences in conceptual and social constructions (Bourdieu & Wacquant, 1992). His critical perspective was used in a number of studies on education, such as *Language and Symbolic Power* (1991) that investigate how language and concepts become dominant as they are reproduced through the educational process, the one that enables globalised Anglo-American curriculum and pedagogy to permeate the systems of other countries to the detriment of Indigenous culture, beliefs and language. One important critique for decolonising a field's language is Bourdieu and Passeron's (1977) critical theory that exposes the unconscious socialization through hidden curriculum, a critique that can apply directly to many expatriate faculty's curriculum and pedagogy that are imported unchanged in other countries, quite often with the attitude that what they bring is the only knowledge and that locals need to be civilised into primarily Anglo-American curriculum.

Another relevant form of critical theory is that of Foucault, who analyses the concept of governmentality as discourses of knowledge and power that create dominating 'regimes of truth' (Lemke, 2016). His work has been used in educational administration and leadership by Tikly (2003), who applied it to ways of thinking, including philosophies, disciplines, values, ideas, concepts, language and forms of knowledge that are used to construct roles, identities, social relations, thinking and actions in a given context. For Inda (2005), these also form through language the technologies of governmentality – the policies, guidelines, procedures, programs, instruments, assessments and evaluations, professional ethics, as documents and social norms that govern thought, decisions, actions and social relations that can normalize and marginalize or assign deviance in any of these spheres. It is this treatment of language that also contributes to neoliberal regimes grounded in an economic perspective producing values and practices that are at odds with Islamic systems, such as an exclusionary focus on individual self-interest, rational choice practices, and market principles contrary to Islam (Hamann, 2009). These values and practices found in the current neoliberal globalized colonization of education, which in higher education produces the translation of research, curriculum and pedagogy into commodified product form, reshapes academic activities into market-based competitive systems, and eliminates the difference between government and individuals and groups that removes academic freedom through new policy regimes, output measurements, and tying faculty activities to revenue targets (Davies & Bansel, 2010).

Since language use is also the construction and use of meanings, there is a hermeneutic dimension to its study of a discipline or field. Decolonizing the language of educational administration and leadership necessitates an understanding of what terms mean in different contexts. For example, how leadership ethics within a Muslim context may have some similarity to Western models, such as servant leadership; however, the meaning of ethics extends into a number of values and practices that are specific to Islam and the various cultures of societies in the Gulf (ElKaleh & Samier, 2013; Sharifian, 2015). Critical hermeneutics is also necessary in examining language during international periods of dominance like the globalisation of education period we are currently in. For Habermas (1993), it means that one must view language as a function of one's relationship to the world one inhabits, and that language and meaning can be distorted through power relations. In this case, critical hermeneutics is valuable in being able to recognize how meanings of a Gulf culture can be distorted through the use of a globalized Western curriculum.

The largest number of critiques relevant to decolonizing educational administration are postcolonial approaches that emphasize how globalized neoliberal practices can colonize through education. Five of these are examined here for their influence on language and the consequences of foreign language meanings that are imposed: (1) colonization of mind by Thiong'o (1987) that focusses on concept formation and meaning construction; (2) epistemicide – how other knowledge traditions are marginalized or deemed to be of no value or existence; (3) subaltern identity that the colonized assume under colonial masters, relevant to educational roles; and (4) decolonization.

Postcolonial analyses of language and the various experiential and conceptual levels involved, began by the mid-twentieth century with authors like Freire (1954), who examined the colonizing effects of studying and working in a foreign language on psychological, social, cultural and political levels. Fanon (1965), another early postcolonial author, regarded education in a foreign language as an indoctrination that produces a socially conditioned inferiority complex that imposes unconsciously a different ego ideal dissociating people from their own culture. One fundamental level on which language operates colonially is what Thiong'o (1987) called the 'colonisation of mind' that comes from the literature and media of a colonizing language. He regarded its use in education as 'a cultural bomb' that destroys belief in Indigenous names, languages, values, capacities and senses of self. For Thiong'o, a colonized mind will no longer regard as relevant or necessary its own cultural traditions; instead, it will view Western knowledge as the only form that has value. He recommends placing more emphasis on Indigenous literature at the centre of curriculum to correct what the 'neo-colonial establishment' has imposed. Dabashi (2015) has extended this critique of 'mind colonisation' to include the colonizer's negative stereotypes of cultural others as incapable of intellectual thought and therefore of knowledge production, a form of what Said (1978) calls 'orientalism'. Orientalism applies broadly to many Western universities and Western expatriates in the Gulf, whose practices present both constructions of superiority and the denigration of Indigenous knowledge traditions, including conceptions and language.

Related to how a colonization of mind and language affect a field is 'epistemicide' (Hall & Tandon, 2017) or 'epistemic injustice' (e.g., Fricker, 2009; Kidd, 2019) during periods of colonization that devalue or even eliminate educational systems and values. There are a number of issues involved for Muslim contexts: the historical relationship between classical Islamic scholarship that served as a source for many European disciplines and fields; diversity in how administrative and leadership concepts and language are embedded in their contexts; and a form of educational administration and leadership that is consistent with a society' constitution, legal system, religion, and culture to effectively operate within countries involving professionalism and ethics in a supportive and appropriate way.

The subaltern critique of authors like Guha (1982) and Spivak (1988) are important to the field because they expose how language is one of the critical factors in defining roles, responsibilities and duties as colonised people defined by the colonisers. This level of curriculum defines identities, social interaction and organizational structures that are formed out of colonising influences or even direct power in reproducing foreign socio-cultural and educational structures, governance, responsibilities, roles, and practices that create a hierarchically subservient 'subaltern' persona/role and marginalisation. They examine through language how colonisers' discourse socially constructs signifiers reflective of foreign societies that silence other perspectives and experiences and enculturate people into a social/professional language and value system that separates them from their culture, in education defining how one develops curriculum, teaches and, most importantly, exercises the power to devalue or eliminate Indigenous knowledge and values.

On a psychological level, such colonisation reshapes self, identity, and social interaction, producing alienation, shame, sublimation, and a reduced sense of agency producing an idealisation that reorients people into submissive and subjugating positions in colonising structures, analysed existentially and psychoanalytically by Oliver (2004). Another use of language is in social interaction and role construction, and in cultural and social institutions, critiqued by a number of postcolonial authors like Mignolo (2011), Naidoo (2007), and Satterthwaite and Atkinson (2005) as reproductions of foreign structures. This includes educational systems, their governance, leadership and the structures of roles and responsibilities. In this way, education becomes an instrument of colonisation that promotes the coloniser's discourse as signifiers and silences other perspectives, concepts and knowledge traditions, alienating people from their own culture. In this way language also is an instrument for producing the subservient 'subaltern' personae, identities and roles (Gramsci, 1971; Guha, 1982; Spivak, 1988).

Decolonisation of language is part of 'epistemological decolonisation', pursued in order for countries and cultures to recover their sovereignty and protect their political systems, cultures, religions, languages and identities, and social institutions, for which education is a critical causal factor and force for change. This is often carried out in accordance with social justice and the human right to culture and religion such as the International Covenant on Economic, Social and Cultural Rights and Resolution adopted by the Human Rights Council in September 2016 on cultural rights and the protection of cultural heritage that calls upon all states to respect, promote and protect the right of everyone to take part in cultural life, including the ability to access and enjoy cultural heritage (see Hafstein, 2014). Some literature in the field of educational administration and leadership has appeared with a decolonizing focus; among these is Campbell-Stephens (2021), who promotes critical theory and principles of Black liberation to decolonise narratively the labelling assumptions that subordinates through covert racism identities and experiences to a predominantly White and Anglo-American discourse to restructure power relations and what is accepted as 'knowledge' to achieve a diverse, equitable and socially just administration and leadership.

Mignolo and Walsh's (2018) decolonization model of curriculum and research is examined through a critical lens that identifies internationalizing principles in reconstructing a field on foundations that reflect a diversity of Indigenous and non-Western societal institutions, values and identity construction, and knowledge traditions. This requires a much greater and deeper use of contextualization than is often practised in educational administration and leadership, consisting of historical forces, constitutional and legal systems, governance and administration practices, cultural structures and norms, and the way that social institutions are structured differently. Another decolonizing response has come from Eisenstadt (2000) in sociology, whose work on "multiple modernities" recognizes that countries can take their own paths to modernizing instead of replicating the process and structures used in Western countries, an approach that has been influential in general management and leadership literature, but has yet to be developed in educational administration. Decolonization aims to resist the increasing influence of globalization that uncritically promotes the adoption of Western knowledge and language, with little or no consideration of student traditional values, knowledge, history, academic competency, and learning styles.

3 Reconstructing Language and Concepts for the Gulf

A recent approach in foreign language teaching, the contextual-cultural approach (Byram & Grundy, 2003), is most suitable for teaching in a field where speech acts, functions of language in a context, viewing students as 'social actors' operating in socio-political and geopolitical circumstances, and regarding feelings and identities as necessary dimensions of language use are used. Educational administration and leadership in any country or culture consists of all of these factors and dimensions that should be reflected in curricular design. This includes the conceptual metaphors used in constructing language that have meaning only in their cultural contexts, how identity is formed and expressed in social interaction, and should be reflected in curriculum and pedagogy. Even in Western countries, with increasing diversity, language teaching needs to encompass the minority cultures within which people live and work.

The problem of acculturating people, and the language they use, into a dominating language is that they learn predominantly the concepts and terminology that reflect a foreign country, its laws and policies, roles, values and professional responsibilities. In educational administration and leadership, this is evident in the dominating language that is secular, materialist and highly individualistic in conceptions of achievement and success, and reflect an American political culture (Fox et al., 2006). Fox et al. (2006) conducted a comparative values study of the US and Arabian Gulf states that indicate very clearly many of the socio-cultural differences that need to be reflected in educational administration in the region. Where US society prominently values secularity, materialism, individualistic values and the achievement of individual success, efficiency and free enterprise capitalism, the Gulf prioritises values that reflect the dignity and honour of family and religion, providing meaning and morality, loyalty to family and friends, social interaction characterized by hospitality, generosity, sharing, justice, patience, honesty and mercy, compassion for the down-trodden in society, and an orientation that aims for a balance of individual and community responsibility. Central to this value system is a respect for and pride in heritage and tradition. Where Western neoliberal management values legal and technical rational principles, efficiency, and impersonal hierarchies, the Islamic administrative tradition is grounded in Muslim principles, Arab and other non-western cultural norms, with primary values of service to society defining wisdom and judgement, and the quality of personal interactions and family and tribal connections (informed by a high level of trust) (Ahmad & Ogunsola, 2011).

Fundamental cross-cultural and jurisdictional differences shape the language of administration and leadership, even if one uses the English language to teach in, through the way the terms are defined and illustrated, in the Gulf through Islamic principles, values and conceptions. One of these that has to be integrated into one's teaching is a recognition that it is a fundamental religious requirement to seek and acquire knowledge and learn as a life-long pursuit. Other foundational concepts are *adab*, conducting one's life in a culture of courtesy and urbanity that draws from knowledge traditions internationally, and is also in areas like the Gulf region combined with Bedouin virtues of generosity, graciousness and eloquence (Peters, 1973) which also provide continuity with Islamic and Arab social history. This contrasts strongly with current Western emphases on individuality and individual success. Historicity is a fundamental requirement in daily life in Islam: the Prophet Muhammad serves at all times as the embodiment of character and practice through compassion, wisdom and social justice (Hawwa, 1988) and as a measure through the *Sunnah* by which to examine one's conduct and a guide to thought and action in a reflexive process (Adair, 2010; Salahi, 2013) whose personal professional qualities should exemplify kindness, empathy, forgiveness, the use of consultation, and informed decision-making. The Prophet Muhammad has continued to be used in modern administration and management studies as a role model upon which to base good values and practices (e.g., Beekun, 2012). What is important for language decolonization in educational administration and leadership is the explicit use and discussion of the values, ideal characteristics and practices from the fundamental sources of Islam, the Qur'an and the *Sunnah*.

Contrary to so many negative stereotypes of Islam, it is in actuality a fundamental humanistic tradition, that established socio-political and cultural values that should be achieved and maintained: social order for societal stability; principles of justice, fairness, equity and tolerance; the betterment of people's health, welfare and personal development; the development of faiths, that is belief systems that encompass a wholistic vision, in contrast with those with mono-dimensional aims like the material reductionism of neoliberalism; and socio-political accountability (al-Qudsy, 2007). Consequently, character and personality are critical in administration and leadership consisting of the qualities identified above and others that shape the concepts and language one uses in practice: restraint and good manners in public; approaching one's work through brotherhood and the assumption of the equality of mankind; and carrying out one's responsibilities and social interaction with benevolence and the growth of others, that apply to not only one's students, but to staff and colleagues (Kalantari, 1998; Sarayrah, 2004). Part of Islamic professionalism is also a strong work ethic, grounded in honesty, truthfulness, and adherence to human rights and humanistic values understood within an Islamic framework and in different forms of cultural expression that are aimed at achieving justice, safety, the dignity of others, excellence, and self-control (rather than succumbing to destructive emotions), as well as styles of working based upon cooperation and using consultation with others knowledgeable and qualified to advise, assuming responsibility, viewing one's work as a virtue and personal fulfilment, being obedient to legitimate authority and following disciplinary principles (Aldulaimi, 2016). All of these are understood as religious obligations and interpreted within a religious context.

Equally important is the language of social justice, also at the heart of Islamic administration and leadership, governed by the Qur'an and Sunnah, a topic that has grown in recent years along with other literature on Islamic practices (e.g., An-na'im, 2011; Harvey, 2017; Qutb, 2000; Rosen, 2018). Instilling social justice in Islam is a major aim of education, and should inform organizational practices (e.g., Kamali, 2002; Samier, 2016; Shah, 2016; Syed & Ali, 2010), intended to apply equally to women (e.g., Samier & ElKaleh, 2021). In contrast with a number of Western approaches during the neoliberal period that are secular, individualistically-oriented, and materialistic aimed at a profit goal, Islamic justice virtues are defined within a religious framework as religious observances aimed at the fairness, equity and equality for others, in protecting diversity and regarding one's duties and responsibilities as serving the collective good, protecting the weak in society, contributing to harmony and balance in society, advancing consultation in governance, and benefiting society with transparent and meaningful activity. Islamic social justice is also global in perspective, aimed at cultural coexistence and international cooperation, supported by a long tradition of conflict resolution, arbitration, mediation and reconciliation process (Samier, 2018).

Arabic has a large vocabulary of terms for administration and leadership that convey the principles and values of a Muslim context and Arab culture and social mores constructed with Islamic understanding identified by Beekun (2012) through a detailed review of relevant literature in understanding the concepts and language. First are a set of personal characteristics or features of character, *Khuluq,* acquired during growth and development of the individual, of the Prophet Muhammad, that establish the ideal of a good person who has acquired morality, *Fitrah,* and a number of traits that enable them to do the right thing rather than what is convenient or opportunistic: (1) serving as a role model, an *Ouswatoun hasana,* with wisdom, *Hikmah,* in the sense of having sound judgement with an understanding of cause and effect; (2) being truthful, *As-Siddiq,* and being trustworthy and keeping promises, *Amana,* in the sense also of having integrity; (3) conducting one's work and relationships with equity, *'adl,* and with justice, *Qist;* (4) using benevolence, *Ihsan,* to guide one's actions (in organizational terms to avoid much of what is referred to as toxic leadership; (5) conduct one's life with humility, *Altawadue;* (6) exhibit kindness and compassion, *Hanan;* (7) patience in the form of endurance, *Sabr.*

Secondly, there are a number of primary concepts or principles upon which administration and leadership rest: (1) Intention, *Nyat;* (2) awe in one's duty to God, *Taqwa;* (3) gratitude, in the sense of being a sincere servant of God (rather than being arrogant), *Ghibad;* (4) consultation, as in seeking advice that limits power and provides decision-making that reflects the needs and values of others and provides consensus-building, *Shura;* and (5) accountability, aimed at integrity, justice and trustworthiness, *Tabi'a, Masyuwlia, or Almusa'ala.* Beekun (2012) divides the characteristics of good governance and administration into two categories: those that are transforming in nature by contributing to others' development and improvement; and those that are service to others in the performance of one's duties. The former consist of: (1) raising awareness in others of what is right, lawful and just, *Halal*; (2) helping people to look beyond their self-interest and egoism by recognizing human brotherhood, *Ummah*; (3) creating intellectual stimulation necessary to moral development and a just society, through the first word of revelation, read, *Iqra*; (4) having idealized influence or charisma that is ethical rather than lacking a moral compass aimed at self-interest (as well as providing role modelling), *Jadibiyya*; and (5) providing inspiring motivation, understood to mean maintaining focus on higher principles and ethics rather than reacting with vindictiveness. The second set of characteristics focussed on the quality of service to others includes: (1) individual consideration and attention, recognizing the different needs of others; (2) service before self, in doing good for others while forgoing power and wealth as in a leader being a servant of others, *Sayyid al qawn khadimuhum*; (3) listening to others to provide affirmation; (4) creating trust and being trustworthy, *Al-Ameen*; (5) lending a hand to others in the sense of being a good Samaritan for the poor and needy; and (6) focus on what is feasible or possible to accomplish, often gradually over time (pp. 1006–1009).

In addition, there was a long tradition of scholars being 'men of action', often in senior administrative or judicial positions, and senior officials, or 'viziers,' also carrying out a scholarly career throughout their tenure, producing an Islamic humanistic tradition applied to administration that conferred a theoretical and applied validity of praxis that combined higher ideals with practicality. This is evident in the scholar Aḥmad bin Miskawayh (932–1030 CE) whose virtue ethics writings coupled character traits that are valuable in creating useful relationships and fulfilling one's professional duties with the development of a moral character that can also express itself in the highest ideals of government and public service through friendship, piety, cooperation, and the perfection of our identity as human beings. This tradition relies heavily on role modelling and mentoring from those in senior positions (Goodman, 2003).

4   Conclusion

In decolonizing higher education, Tran (2021) promotes the use of the TRAAC model – teaching approach, relationship, activity and assessment, and content – as a way of understanding the complexity of decolonizing a field of study, identifying the benefits of doing so, and responding to various resistances encountered through critical reflection and reflexive conversations, and the inclusion of marginalized knowledges. He demonstrates through critical race theory that education and knowledges are still colonized in UK universities at deep systemic levels where bias in curriculum and teaching still operate to the preference for Western knowledge (despite the fact that most Western knowledge traditions are not originating in the West). Decolonization also, he argues requires a long and complex development process at all levels of curricular development in the coverage of material in class and in the construction of reading lists as well as critically evaluating library collections, pedagogic preparation and delivery for a greater interactive participation that also shifts power structures (see Bourdieu & Passeron, 1977 on reproduction of power through repeated curriculum), and administrative work through policy. Of particular importance for faculty members is unconscious bias that affects how one designs curriculum, relates to students in the classroom and how assessment is done, often coupled with a studied avoidance of learning about one's field in other countries, and how great the diversity of any discipline or field actually is, and in using a hierarchical approach to valuing knowledge traditions.

There are a number of things one must do in acquiring a cross-cultural mindset (Den Dekker, 2016). First, one has to examine one's attitudes, assumptions and parochialism, such as not assuming that students will understand terms in the same way, that because they interpret differently, they don't understand, and that one's own interpretation from a home country is the only truth or are even relevant. Another common assumption is that non-Western countries do not have knowledge worth knowing, or that may even be more valuable than Western knowledge (Aman, 2018). And, one cannot assume that moral and social justice can only be attributed to Western knowledge.

In curriculum design, as noted above in discussion of cross-cultural and internationalized disciplines and fields, readings and topics have to represent international diversity and provide knowledge, standards, techniques and values of the country in which one is teaching. Using only an American or British curriculum both marginalizes and commits to epistemicide other traditions, and in practical professional terms does not prepare students for the countries in which they will serve, such as Gulf students being shaped into ways of understanding, deciding and acting that are culturally inappropriate. These criteria also apply to assessment of student work. These principles need to be applied to all subject areas in educational administration – in policy, ethics, organization studies, administrative studies, leadership and in research methods training. What is important to remember is that the field is an international one, and that embeddedness is critically important for professional preparation in the socio-cultural realities of society and community in which students will work. In the case of the Gulf, it is important to provide either Arabic sources, or sources that include in the text the relevant Arabic terms.

Pedagogy is also an important consideration. Despagne (2020) advocates a post-colonial approach to language teaching of minority students in higher education through the explicit use and comparison of cultural heritages and knowledge traditions in participatory and interpretive activities focussed on exploring decolonization approaches, critiques and research activities, aiming for equity and inclusion. Makoni et al. (2022) present a number of practices for a broad range of non-Western countries to successfully decolonize higher education through the integration of knowledge traditions, explicit use of decolonization topics and techniques of dominating ideologies to achieve this diversity; they include an evaluative approach to language for all fields to address the dominating privileging of Western knowledge. In the language of educational administration and leadership, it is important to understand the teaching culture in which one will operate – how roles are constructed, what social interaction styles are appropriate, and the style of interaction one can use in the classroom and in designing group activities. There are also considerations of presentation, such as more effective uses of powerpoint and graphic work that are consistent with aesthetic culture and stronger oral traditions, as well as embedded Arabic terms in the text being used. In this way, one can encourage students to critique material that isn't appropriate in their countries, and have discussions that define how the terms are used and what value they carry.

In part, what is advocated here in teaching educational administration and leadership in Islamic contexts like the Arabian Gulf draws on the 'cultural turn' in translation studies, but in this case, to 'translate' one meaning in English to that in another cultural context. This draws on Bassnett and Lefevere (1990) who introduced a stronger attention to cultural and social context, part of a functionalist approach in which the value and purpose of the language by users has to be taken into account (Yan & Huang, 2014). In the case of educational administration and leadership, this means translating the terms from their Western meanings that are generally secular, individualistic, and often materialistic into Islamic and Gulf cultural meanings that carry religious and social implications of the countries involved. Particularly important in this field is to embed in administrative and leadership discussions constitutional principles, legal interpretations, governmental and policy regimes, cultural norms and practices, social structures, values and religious beliefs. According to Kramsch (2014) this involves a number of dimensions in the meanings associated with terms. The way that culture is encoded in a linguistic sign, for example 'leadership' connoting a social reality, is often unconsciously constructed (Sapir, 1949), making acculturation a goal of language learning. Just as learning how to thank people for their time can be acquired easily as a phrase in English, what is not carried initially is the concept of time and privacy involved in the particular English language culture it is used in (Lantolf, 1999). 'Leadership', for example, is a term that can be acquired easily with some of its fundamental meanings, but without acculturation it will not convey the values, authority role, style of interaction, and identity. The American meaning of the term will not easily connote what good administration and leadership are in a Muslim context, nor in the cultural context which varies across countries.

Teaching language of educational administration and leadership is not simply providing the terminology and definitions of terms, but as Kim (2020) argues through the nature of cultural-historical activity theory, involves teaching the whole person and the complex situatedness and interactions in life, and what forms it takes in social institutions, how one views one's self and identity and engages all aspects of culture. Understanding how language is used in another culture requires the commitment and openness to participate and become encultured to at least some functional degree. This requires cross-cultural competence, a topic that has been expanding in recent years in many fields and disciplines, and which equally applies to educational administration and leadership in learning not only the meaning of words being used, but also a great deal about the context that language reflects such as values, cultural norms, rituals and ceremonies, styles of social interaction and communication, the roles and expected behaviours and the norms of relationships, including that of teacher and student and often their families which can vary significantly in the Gulf (Berardo & Deardorff, 2012; Carrizales et al., 2016; Lopez-Littleton & Blessett, 2015).

Said (2005) described the political effect of colonization of language in two phases. First, native speakers are required to use the colonizer's language for any significant writing and for formal educational purpose, even to the point of outlawing it in education and administration as happened in Algeria (Nader, 2010), whereas the Indigenous language is relegated to quaint or insignificant uses, and elevating knowledge constructed in the colonizer's language as superior. This chapter focusses on the second phase that consists of various uses of the native language for resistance against colonial power structures, such as appropriating it and transforming it into an instrument of critique and reconstruction (Ashcroft, 2010), although missing many levels of meaning and nuances in the original language.

References

Adair, J. (2010). *The leadership of Muhammad*. Kogan Page.

Ahmad, K., & Ogunsola, O. (2011). An empirical assessment of Islamic leadership principles. *International Journal of Commerce and Management, 21*(3), 291–318. https://doi.org/10.1108/10569211111165325

Aldulaimi, S. (2016). Fundamental Islamic perspective of work ethics. *Journal of Islamic Accounting and Business Research, 7*(1), 59–76. https://doi.org/10.1108/JIABR-02-2014-0006

Al-Qudsy, S. (2007). Values & ethics towards quality public delivery system of Malaysia: An Islamic perspective. *Journal Syariah, 15*(2), 25–43.

Altbach, P. (2016). *Global perspectives on higher education*. Johns Hopkins University Press.

Alvesson, M., Bridgman, T., & Willmott, H. (Eds.). (2009). *The Oxford handbook of critical management studies*. Oxford University Press.

Aman, R. (2018). *Decolonising intercultural education: Colonial differences, the geopolitics of knowledge, and inter-epistemic dialogue*. Routledge.

An-na'im, A. (2011). *Muslims and global justice*. University of Pennsylvania Press.

Ashcroft, B. (2010). Representation and liberation: From orientalism to the Palestinian crisis. In A. Iskandar & H. Rustom (Eds.), *Edward Said: A legacy of emancipation and representation* (pp. 291–303). University of California Press.

Bassnett, S., & Lefevere, A. (1990). *Translation, history and culture*. Printer Publishers.

Beekun, R. (2012). Character centered leadership: Muhammad (p) as an ethical role model for CEOs. *Journal of Management Development, 31*(10), 1003–1020.

Beekun, R., & Badawi, J. (1999). *Leadership: An Islamic perspective*. Amana.

Berardo, K., & Deardorff, D. (Eds.). (2012). *Building cultural competence: Innovative activities and models*. Stylus.

Bhambra, G., Gebrial, D., & Nişancioğlu, K. (Eds.). (2018). *Decolonising the university*. Pluto Press.

Bourdieu, P. (1991). *Language & symbolic power*. Polity Press.

Bourdieu, P., & Passeron, J.-C. (1977). *Reproduction in education, society and culture*. Sage.

Bourdieu, P., & Wacquant, L. (1992). *An introduction to reflexive sociology*. Polity Press.

Branine, M. (2011). *Managing across cultures*. Sage.

Byram, M., & Grundy, P. (2003). Introduction: Context and culture in language teaching and learning. In M. Byram & P. Grundy (Eds.), *Context and culture in language teaching and learning* (pp. 1–3). Multilingual Matters.

Campbell-Stephens, R. (2021). *Educational leadership and the global majority: Decolonising narratives*. Palgrave Macmillan.

Carrizales, T., Zahradnik, A., & Silverio, M. (2016). Organizational advocacy of cultural competency initiatives: Lessons for public administration. *Public Administration Quarterly, 40*(1), 126–155.

Chin, J., Trimble, J., & Garcia, J. (Eds.). (2018). *Global and culturally diverse leaders and leadership: New dimensions and challenges for business, education and society*. Emerald.

Côté, J., & Levine, C. (2002). *Identity formation, agency, and culture: A social psychological synthesis*. Lawrence Erlbaum.

Dabashi, H. (2015). *Can non-Europeans think?* Zed Books.

Davies, B., & Bansel, P. (2010). Governmentality and academic work: Shaping the hearts and minds of academic workers. *Journal of Curriculum Theorizing, 26*(3), 5–20.

Den Dekker, W. (2016). *Global mindset and cross-cultural behavior: Improving leadership effectiveness*. Palgrave Macmillan.

Despagne, C. (2020). *Decolonizing language learning, decolonizing research: A critical ethnography study in a Mexican university*. Routledge.

Dimmock, C., & Walker, A. (2005). *Educational leadership: Culture and diversity*. Sage.

Eisenstadt, S. (2000). Multiple modernities. *Daedalus, 129*(1), 1–29.

ElKaleh, E., & Samier, E. A. (2013). The ethics of Islamic leadership: A cross-cultural approach for public administration. *Administrative Culture, 14*(2), 188–211.

Fanon, F. (1965). *The wretched of the earth*. McGibbon & Kee.

Farazmand, A. (2018). *Global encyclopedia of public administration, public policy, and governance*. Springer.

Fox, J., Mourtada-Sabbah, N., & al-Mutawa, M. (2006). *Globalization and the Gulf*. Routledge.

Freire, P. (1954). *Pedagogy of the oppressed*. Herder and Herder.

Fricker, M. (2009). *Epistemic injustice: Power and the ethics of knowing*. Oxford University Press.

Fuchs, C. (2010). Critical globalization studies and the new imperialism. *Critical Sociology, 36*(6), 839–867. https://doi.org/10.1177/0896920510379441

Goodman, L. (2003). *Islamic humanism*. Oxford University Press.

Goodman, J., & Silverstein, P. (Eds.). (2009). *Bourdieu in Algeria: Colonial politics, ethnographic practices, theoretical developments*. University of Nebraska Press.

Gramsci, A. (1971). *Selections from the prison notebooks*. International Publishers.

Guha, R. (1982). *Subaltern studies I*. Oxford University Press.

Habermas, J. (1989). *The theory of communicative action: The lifeworld and system* (R. McCarthy, Trans.). Beacon Press.

Habermas, J. (1993). Remarks on the development of Horkheimer's work. In S. Benhabib, W. Bonß, & J. McCole (Eds.), *On Max Horkheimer*. MIT Press.

Hafstein, V. T. (2014). Protection as dispossession: Government in the vernacular. In D. Kapchan (Ed.), *Cultural heritage in transit: Intangible rights as human rights* (pp. 25–57). University of Pennsylvania Press. https://doi.org/10.9783/9780812209464.25

Hall, B., & Tandon, R. (2017). Decolonization of knowledge, epistemicide, participatory research and higher education. *Research for All, 1*(1), 6–19. https://doi.org/10.18546/RFA.01.1.02

Hamann, T. (2009). Neoliberalism, governmentality, and ethics. *Foucault Studies, 6*, 37–59. https://doi.org/10.22439/fs.v0i0.2471

Harris, P., Moran, R., & Moran, S. (2004). *Managing cultural differences* (6th ed.). Elsevier Butterworth-Heinemann.

Harvey, R. (2017). *The Qur'an and the just society*. Edinburgh University Press.

Hawwa, S. (1988). *Fusool fi Al-Emarah Wa Al-Amir* [Sections on commanding and commander]. Dar Ammar.

Henderson, K. (1995). Reinventing comparative public administration: Indigenous models of study and application. *International Journal of Public Sector Management, 8*(4), 17–25. https://doi.org/10.1108/09513559510096246

Hofstede, G., Hofstede, G. J., & Minkov, M. (2010). *Cultures and organizations: Software of the mind*. McGraw-Hill.

Hopkyns, S. (2016). Emirati cultural identity in the age of 'englishisation': Voices from an Abu Dhabi university. In L. Buckingham (Ed.), *Language, identity and education on the Arabian peninsula: Bilingual policies in a multilingual context* (pp. 87–115). De Gruyter.

House, R., Hanges, P., Javidan, M., Dorfman, P., & Gupta, V. (Eds.). (2004). *Culture, leadership, and organizations: The GLOBE study of 62 societies*. Sage.

Inda, J. X. (2005). Analytics of the modern: An introduction. In J. X. Inda (Ed.), *Anthropologies of modernity: Foucault, governmentality, and life policies* (pp. 1–21). Blackwell.

Jack, G., & Westwood, R. (2009). *International and cross-cultural management studies: A postcolonial reading*. Palgrave Macmillan.

Jansen, J. (Ed.). (2019). *Decolonisation in universities: The politics of knowledge*. Wits University Press.

Jriesat, J. (2011). *Globalism and comparative administration*. CRC Press.

Kalantari, B. (1998). In search of a public administration paradigm: Is there anything to be learned from Islamic public administration? *International Journal of Public Administration, 12*(12), 1821–1861. https://doi.org/10.1080/01900699808525370

Kamali, M. (2002). *Freedom, equality and justice in Islam*. Islamic Texts Society.

Kenny, C., & Fraser, T. (2013). *Living indigenous leadership: Native narratives on building strong communities*. University of British Columbia Press.

Kidd, I. (Ed.). (2019). *The Routledge handbook of epistemic injustice*. Routledge.

Kim, D. (2020). Learning language, learning culture: Teaching language to the whole student. *ECNU Review of Education, 3*(3), 519–541. https://doi.org/10.1177/2096531112093669

Kramsch, C. (2014). *Language and culture. AILA Review, 27*, 30–55. https://doi.org/10.1075/aila.27.02kra

Lantolf, J. (1999). Second culture acquisition: Cognitive considerations. In E. Hinkel (Ed.), *Culture in second language teaching and learning* (pp. 28–46). Cambridge University Press.

Lemke, T. (2016). *Foucault, governmentality and critique*. Routledge.

Lewis, R. (2006). *When cultures collide: Leading across cultures*. Nicholas Brealey.

Lopez-Littleton, V., & Blessett, B. (2015). A framework for integrating cultural competency into the curriculum of public administration programs. *Journal of Public Affairs Education, 21*(4), 557–574. https://doi.org/10.1080/15236803.2015.12002220

Makoni, S., Severo, C., Abdelhay, A., & Kaiper-Marquez, A. (Eds.). (2022). *The languaging of higher education in the global south: De-colonizing the language of scholarship and pedagogy*. Routledge.

Mignolo, W. (2011). *The darker side of Western modernity: Global futures, decolonial options*. Duke University Press.

Mignolo, W., & Walsh, C. (2018). On decoloniality: Concepts, analytics, praxis. *Duke University Press*. https://doi.org/10.2307/j.ctv11g9616

Nader, L. (2010). Side by side: The other is not mute. In A. Iskandar & H. Rustom (Eds.), *Edward Said: A legacy of emancipation and representation* (pp. 72–85). University of California Press.

Naidoo, R. (2007). *Higher education as a global commodity*. Report for the Observatory on Borderless Higher Education.

Oliver, K. (2004). *The colonization of psychic space: A psychoanalytic social theory of oppression*. University of Minnesota Press.

Peters, F. (1973). *Allah's commonwealth: A history of Islam in the near east, 600–1100 A.D.* Simon & Schuster.

Prasad, A. (2003). *Postcolonial theory and organizational analysis: A critical engagement*. Palgrave Macmillan.

Preece, S. (2016). Introduction: Language and identity in applied linguistics. In S. Preece (Ed.), *The Routledge handbook of language and identity* (pp. 1–16). Routledge.

Qutb, S. (2000). *Social justice in Islam*. Islamic Publications International.

Raadschelders, J., Vigoda-Gadot, E., & Kisner, M. (2015). *Dimensions of public administration and governance: A comparative voyage*. John Wiley & Sons.

Ricoeur, P. (2016). *Hermeneutics and the human sciences: Essays on language, action and interpretation*. Cambridge University Press.

Rosen, L. (2018). *Islam and the rule of justice*. University of Chicago Press.

Said, E. (1978). *Orientalism*. Vintage.

Said, E. (2005). *Power, politics and culture*. Bloomsbury.

Salahi, A. (2013). *Muhammad: His character and conduct*. The Islamic Foundation.

Samier, E. A. (2016). Fairness, equity and social cooperation: A moderate Islamic social justice leadership model for higher education. In L. Shultz & M. Viczko (Eds.), *Assembling and governing the higher education institution: Democracy, social justice and leadership in global higher education* (pp. 35–64). Palgrave Macmillan.

Samier, E. A. (2018). The philosophical and historical origins & genesis of Islamic global governance. In L. Pal & M. Tok (Eds.), *Global governance: Muslim perspectives, contributions and challenges* (pp. 83–104). Palgrave Macmillan.

Samier, E. A. (2019). The politics of educational change in the Middle East: Nation-building, postcolonial reconstruction, destabilized states, societal disintegration, and the dispossessed. In A. Means & K. Saltman (Eds.), *Handbook of global education reform* (pp. 173–197). Wiley-Blackwell.

Samier, E. A. (2021). Educational leadership challenges in destabilised and disintegrating states: The intersectionality of violence, culture, ideology, class/status group and postcoloniality in the Middle East. In K. Arar, D. Örücü, & J. Wilkinson (Eds.), *Neoliberalism and education systems in conflict: Exploring challenges across the globe* (pp. 135–150). Routledge.

Samier, E. A., & ElKaleh, E. (2021). Towards a model of Muslim women's management empowerment: Philosophical and historical evidence and critical approaches. *Administrative Sciences, 11.* https://doi.org/10.3390/admsci11020047

Sapir, E. (1949). In D. Mandelbaum (Ed.), *Selected writings in language, culture and personality*. University of California Press.

Sarayrah, Y. (2004). Servant leadership in the Bedouin-Arab culture. *Global Virtue Ethics Review, 5*(3), 58–79.

Satterthwaite, J., & Atkinson, E. (2005). *Discourses of education in the age of imperialism*. Trentham Books.

Shah, S. (2016). *Education, leadership and Islam*. Routledge.

Sharifian, F. (2015). Language and culture: Overview. In F. Sharifian (Ed.), *The Routledge handbook of language and culture* (pp. 3–17). Routledge.

Simpson, L. (2021). *Hermeneutics as critique: Science, politics, race, and culture*. Columbia University Press.

Spivak, G. (1988). Can the subaltern speak? In C. Nelson & L. Grossberg (Eds.), *Marxism and the interpretation of culture* (pp. 271–313). University of Illinois Press.

Syed, J., & Ali, A. (2010). Principles of employment relations in Islam: A normative view. *Employee Relations, 32*(5), 454–469. https://doi.org/10.1108/01425451011061630

Thiong'o, N. (1987). *Decolonising the mind*. Zimbabwe Publishing House.

Tikly, L. (2003). Governmentality and the study of education policy in South Africa. *Journal of Education Policy, 18*(2), 161–174. https://doi.org/10.1080/0268093022000043074

Tran, D. (2021). *Decolonizing university teaching and learning: An entry model for grappling with complexities*. Bloomsbury.

Trompenaars, F., & Hampden-Turner, C. (1997). *Riding the waves of culture*. Nicholas Brealey.

Western, S., & Garcia, É.-J. (2018). *Global Leadership perspectives: Insights and analysis*. Sage.

Yan, C., & Huang, J. (2014). The culture turn in translation studies. *Open Journal of Modern Linguistics, 4*, 487–494. https://doi.org/10.4236/ojml.2014.44041

Eugenie A. Samier is a Reader at the University of Strathclyde. She has been a guest researcher and lecturer at universities in the US, Germany, Estonia, Russia, the UK, Norway, Lithuania, Finland, Bahrain, Qatar and the UAE and serves on the boards of several journals. Her publications include book chapters and articles on organisational culture and values, the New Public Management, history and biography in educational administration, the role of humanities and aesthetics in administration, Weberian foundations of administration, passive evil, toxic leadership, identity, and Islamic administration and leadership. She is editor and co-editor of 14 books and author of *Secrecy and Tradecraft in Educational Administration*. She also worked as a management consultant to the public sector for a number of years on a broad variety of projects including legislation development, organisational reviews, board development, and government department restructuring and redesign. Email: eugenie.samier@gmail.com

"She Is Not a Normal Teacher of English": Photovoice as a Decolonial Method to Study Queer Teacher Identity in Vietnam's English Language Teaching

Giang Nguyen Hoang Le, Ha Bich Dong, Vuong Tran, and Long Hoang Vu

Abstract In this chapter, we utilize Photovoice as a decolonizing approach to gain an in-depth understanding of the teaching and learning experiences of a transgender teacher of English and a group of English LGBTIQ+ youth learners in Vietnam. Looking at ELT teacher identity theory and the concept of intersectionality, we investigate the role of queer teacher identity in framing LGBTIQ+ youth learners' learning experience. Findings include a sense of inclusiveness and belonging in ELT class. Students' perception of teacher as professional and confident is constructed by the teacher's and students' non-normative gender and sexual identities. Queer teacher identity positively impacts students' language attainment and learning purposes, in which students feel inspired to not only embrace their real identity but also become more passionate about their English study.

Keywords ELT · Vietnamese transgender · Teacher identity construction · Intersectionality · Photovoice

G. N. H. Le (✉)
Faculty of Social Sciences & Humanities, Van Lang University, Ho Chi Minh City, Vietnam
e-mail: giang.lnh@vlu.edu.vn

H. B. Dong
University of Manitoba, Winnipeg, MB, Canada
e-mail: dongc4@myumanitoba.ca

V. Tran
Nipissing University, North Bay, ON, Canada

L. H. Vu
Vietnam National University, Hanoi, Vietnam
e-mail: vuhoanglong@ussh.edu.vn

© The Author(s), under exclusive license to Springer Nature Switzerland AG 2023
A. Sahlane, R. Pritchard (eds.), *English as an International Language Education*, English Language Education 33,
https://doi.org/10.1007/978-3-031-34702-3_23

443

1 Introduction

In recent decades, educators and educational researchers have sought to promote equity and inclusion across global education contexts (Freire, 2004; Johnson, 2018; Le, 2019). Relevant studies indicate a critical need to look into populations who are situated on the periphery of education systems (Altbach, 2004; Phan, 2018). These people include the LGBTIQ+ (lesbian, gay, bisexual, transgender, intersex, queer, and more) community, often seen as a marginalised group of learners and teachers in some educational contexts such as Vietnam (Le et al., 2021). Many educational researchers and English language teaching (ELT) practitioners have designed specific methods to help promote an optimal context for critical discussions on the teaching of English to gender minority and sexual identity learners, such as those from Vietnamese LGBTIQ+ communities. Likewise, we offer a decolonising method and a critical lens to investigate the ELT queer teacher identity in Vietnam.

We study a group of English youth learners who identify as lesbian and gay. Key to our study is an English teacher who is a Vietnamese transgender. We employ photovoice as a decolonising methodology for LGBTIQ+ people (Kessi, 2018). Photovoice is a participatory approach engaging people who are often labelled as peripheral communities in studies that instigate and inspire social change (Wang & Burris, 1997). This approach helps the researcher explore people's inner world and bring forth their voices through photographs (Le et al., 2020a, b). Through the visuality of the photovoice method, we can emancipate the mode of doing research on this marginalised community in education contexts including ELT.

From visual data, consisting of photos taken by participants, we aim to examine queer teacher identity through the perspective of intersectionality. This critical focus allows us to look at language teacher identity constructs (Pennington & Richards, 2016; Richards, 2012) that the transgender teacher of English in our study presents. We use intersectionality to analyse the photograph data. Intersectionality, rooted in feminist theory, refers to the interactivity of social identity structures (e.g., race, class, and gender), in fostering life experiences of those encountering privilege and oppression (Crenshaw, 1994). This concept is used to examine how gender could be intertwined with other identity structures, such as being a teacher of English, to shape the language teacher identity construction of the transgender teacher in this study. The purpose of this chapter is to explore queer teacher identity in the framework of ELT teacher identity constructs (Pennington & Richards, 2016). Given the fact that data, including interviews and photos, were taken by students as research participants, we look at data from the viewpoint of students about the image and the role of their English teacher in forming an ELT gender inclusive environment.

2 Literature Review

2.1 Language Teacher Identity Construction

The present chapter approaches identity from an anti-essentialist viewpoint which rejects the idea that identity is an established and ahistorical classification (Taylor, 2015, p. 1). Similarly, teacher identity is less a fixed classification than a socially constructed category that is shaped through experience and the sense that is made of it (Pennington & Richards, 2016; Sachs, 2005). This approach reveals how language teacher identity is formulated in different locations and situations such as in the classroom and with different groups of students.

According to Pennington and Richards (2016, p. 2), identity is not only the reflection of the context in which a person is situated, but also the sense a person has of the self as an individual (e.g., self-image and self-awareness in front of others). Individual agency is the creation of one's identity and positionality within different cultures, social groups, and contexts for the use of language (Taylor, 2015, p. 2). What identifies the teachers' characteristics are their positions and roles, as well as how they negotiate and interpret meanings embedded in the classroom (Pennington & Richards, 2016, p. 3). As the relationship in the classroom between teachers and students is vital for any educational endeavour, teachers tend to reflect on their teaching in a way that better serves the varied needs of the learners (Pennington & Richards, 2016, p. 11). Zimmerman (1998) calls teachers' reflection "situated identity" (p. 90) which encourages new teachers to position themselves as if they were students and to practise their methods on these younger versions of themselves. The imagined power hierarchy between novice teachers and their learners may make such teacher-student relationship problematic. Developing a good awareness about learners ("student knowledge") is also conducive to effective learning facilitation in that students engage actively with learning content that suits their diverse needs and that boosts their self-esteem (Pennington & Richards, 2016, p. 15). This alternative teacher identity construction, "transposable identity" (Zimmerman, 1998), reflects a more "relationship-centered and learner-centered teacher identity" (p. 91). Nonetheless, for lecturers who have not yet mastered pedagogical skills, the "informal, personal, and authentic" identity construction can be hard to accomplish (Richards, 2006, p. 60).

In the field of language teaching, Richards (2012) lists ten areas that are positioned at the core of teacher identity construction. These areas can be separated into two main groups: foundational competencies and advanced competencies of language teacher identity (Pennington & Richards, 2016, p. 17). Four out of these ten fields as follows stand out as relevant to our research: (1) Contextual knowledge; (2) Learner-focused teaching; (3) Theorizing from practice; (4) Membership in a community of practice. While contextual knowledge and learner-focused teaching belong to foundational competencies, the latter two belong to advanced competencies.

In terms of elemental capacities, to acquire *contextual knowledge*, first, language teachers are not only required to have an explicit understanding of the language they teach, but they also need to develop effective interpersonal skills to be able to communicate with the students who have limited capacity in that language (Pennington & Richards, 2016, p. 7). Second, according to Pennington (2015), a "disciplinary identity," produced through formal education, is required for language teaching. Disciplinary identity helps to draw connections between diverse academic disciplines, which are related to each lesson's content (Pennington, 2015, p. 7). Third, teachers should have a clear idea about the teaching environment in which they will operate (e.g., class size, facilities, teaching resources, etc.) to be in a position to set the right atmosphere in class (Richards, 2012). The practice of *learner-focused teaching*, which results in the ability to facilitate learning practices (Borg, 2006), can be fulfilled by teachers' self-awareness and self-knowledge, that is, being aware of one's strengths and weaknesses to enhance one's teaching practice (Pennington, 1989). Furthermore, since teachers and students are in a mutually interactive relationship in which their thoughts and actions affect each other, teacher identity is constantly being negotiated with student identity (Pennington, 1992).

In terms of advanced competencies, as the teaching act is a 'performative' one, teachers are required to have a degree of flexibility to customise their courses as needed. The teacher identity is expected to integrate knowledge "in all phases of instruction – from planning to performing and then assessing teaching acts" (Pennington & Richards, 2016, p. 13). The whole process from developing a course to transferring knowledge to students is regarded as a mechanism of internalization in which teachers build their own bank of techniques (Pennington & Richards, 2016, p. 14). Moreover, as Borg (2006) concludes from a variety of teaching strategies, experiences, and encounters, the formation of teacher identity is the process of *theorizing corporeal practices into knowledge*. Finally, besides synthesising knowledge, teachers have to nurture a *sense of belonging in a community of practice* for their students (Pennington & Richards, 2016, p. 7). Cummins (2011) emphasizes the linkage of identities of teachers and students; particularly if students are from marginalised social groups, they will immerse with education practices if such engagement affirms their identities.

2.2   Intersectionality

The concept of intersectionality was introduced by Crenshaw in 1989, and it meant the interactivity of social identity structures—such as race, class, and gender—in perpetuating a broad-scale system of domination of Black women in the United States. Today, intersectionality has been widely used by scholars from diverse fields of studies: gender studies, ethnic studies, and education as an analytical tool to investigate the social identity structures of those encountering privilege and oppression across the world (Hill & Bilge, 2016). For example, Hulko and Hovanes (2017) use intersectionality to investigate the diverse ways in which LGBTIQ+ youth find communities and build a sense of belonging in western Canadian small cities and rural areas. In the field of education, Grant and Zwier (2011) utilise an intersectional framework to build a holistic understanding of the multiple forms of discrimination faced by students and its negative impact (i.e., discrimination) on their well-being. Harris and Watson-Vandiver's study (2020) utilises decolonial intersectionality as a theoretical framework to centre around the potential for social sciences curricula to provide students with a greater sense of justice and healing in post-colonial societies such as the United States. Bracho and Hayes (2020) explore the interconnected relationship between gender, sexuality, and race among queer teachers of colour in Western educational contexts.

Lawrence and Nagashima's research (2020) is among the few studies that discuss queer ELT teacher identity in Japan. Their research points out how gender and sexuality impact day-to-day classroom interactions between ELT teachers and students, and thus create unique learning environments wherein teachers may incorporate their lived experiences and queer identity into their English lessons as a way to open up discussions regarding gender equity and social justice, when they feel safe to do so. Findings of Lawrence and Nagashima's (2020, p. 52) study indicate that ELT teachers who have experiences or knowledge of gender and sexual non-conformity, including those with gender and sexual minority identities (e.g., LGBTIQ+ identities), may have an intention to bring in gender and sexuality topics to discuss with their students since they seek to raise students' awareness of gender minorities and sexual identity diversity (Lawrence & Nagashima, 2020, p. 49). This research opens up opportunities for future research to explore how non-normative gender performances in English teachers can potentially enrich the classroom environment and teaching practices by connecting (foreign) language education with social issues outside of the class.

The present chapter is an attempt to fill the literature gap by using intersectionality as a means of examining how the framing of teacher identity in English language education in a post-colonial educational context such as Vietnam can be decolonised. With a focus on teachers with non-normative gender and sexuality identities, we work with *Lien*, a transgender English teacher in Vietnam, and LGBTIQ+ students in her class to investigate how the intertwinement of gender and sexuality shapes her classroom, professional identity, and teaching performance. In particular, our study seeks to understand the influence of a language educator's gender and sexuality on the perceptions that students have of their teaching competence. From an intersectional perspective, the study explores how the English language classroom can be a safe environment for queer students, and how they are empowered to express themselves and address LGBTIQ+ issues and other social problems in the classroom. Overall, the use of an intersectional framework enables us to examine queer teacher identity while also learning to do research on this marginalised community in a way that challenges colonial concepts of gender binarism.

2.3 Decolonization of English Language Teaching Education in Vietnam

The linkage between teaching foreign languages and colonialism is clear-cut. Postcolonial theorists argue that the learning of colonial languages such as English and French in the era of colonialism was a tool to exclude the natives' languages, cultures, and ways of life (DeGraff, 2019). As a former colony, the educational landscape in Vietnam is determined by globalization and international inequality (Nguyen & Zeichner, 2021). As English is being taught globally, inequality in accessing English education should be seen as a great concern, especially in non-English speaking societies (Nguyen & Zeichner, 2021, p. 657). Previous reports have shown that a significant number of English teachers in Vietnamese public schools do not meet the government's standards to teach English (Toan, 2013). Conversely, foreign language programs in private schools tend to be more advanced and are better equipped (i.e., with up-to-date textbook materials, technology for teaching, etc.) (Nguyen, 2011; Nguyen et al., 2014).

Despite the status quo of social inequality caused by the English domination in various fields of society, many English teachers in Vietnam wish to use the English teaching platform to educate students about social justice (Nguyen & Zeichner, 2021). By adopting a decolonial pedagogy in the teaching of foreign language, language users' human rights as well as cultural sovereignty are brought to the fore. Hence, it is clear that ELT profession and the construction of teacher identity involve political agency (Nguyen & Zeichner, 2021; Tran-Thanh, 2020). The Boston College (BC) model of socially just teaching and teacher education (Cochran-Smith et al., 2009), which is adopted in the context of Vietnam, has three components: (1) A multi-dimensional view of learning that goes beyond academic training to include students' social, emotional and civic development; (2) The use of teaching skills that include teachers' ethical beliefs, their knowledge of subject matter and their knowledge of their students' learning styles, backgrounds and cultures; (3) The realisation of the connection between all teachers' actions in the classroom and the larger social and political context that defines students' lives (Nguyen & Zeichner, 2021, p. 660). As such, the aim of social justice education in foreign language teaching is not only to provide learners with appropriate language and communication skills, but also to connect teaching content to students' cultural and linguistic backgrounds.

The inequality that gender minorities have to endure is also a topic that has been addressed in social justice oriented foreign language education (Tran-Thanh, 2020, p. 3). Tran-Thanh (2020) writes:

> The exclusion can, therefore, possibly push queer learners, who might remain silent or passive when the classroom discourse comes to topics related to sexual identity or regular topics being implicitly heteronormative, even further beyond the margins. (p. 3)

As a proposal for the advocacy of queer representations and queer voices, pedagogic values of queer theory must be evaluated from an internationally, multiculturally, and linguistically diverse perspective (Nelson, 2002). Semi-structured interview research conducted by Tran-Thanh (2020) indicated a positive attitude from all participants when they recognised that LGBTQ+ issues should be included in the English classroom. There are three main reasons for participants to promote this issue: (1) Students must be aware of this important social issue; (2) English class is suitable for discussing this topic due to the progressive nature of Western societies; (3) The class can be an educational space where LGBTIQ+ students can be encouraged to negotiate their gender identities and express their value perspectives on difference (Tran-Thanh, 2020).

3 Methodology

3.1 Research Questions

This research aims to answer three main questions: How did students view the image and role of their English teacher in building a gender inclusive classroom where they, as non-normative gender and sexual identity English learners, felt safe and respected? How did the English teacher with a non-normative gender and sexual identity as a transgender person influence her students' learning of English? And how did she use her identities as a transgender and an English teacher to promote a good educational environment for her students?

3.2 Photovoice as a Decolonial Research Method

In this study, we chose to use photovoice as an overarching methodology. Photovoice is a creative form of participatory-action research that involves photography as a visual approach to examine social justice issues, such as education inequity that is experienced by minoritised and gendered others The purpose of using photovoice is to see the world through the viewpoint of people who are leading different lives. Key to this visual method is to allow participants to record and reflect on their community's strengths and concerns, to promote critical dialogue and knowledge about important community issues via photographs that are taken by themselves, and ultimately to reach out to policymakers (Wang & Burris, 1994). Photovoice is deployed as an anti-oppressive and decolonising approach that contests assimilationist colonialist ideologies by empowering gendered others to have authentic voice through visual counter-storytelling. Such images tell stories that serve to expose oppression and inequities within marginalised communities by contesting power imbalance and cultural hegemony (Le et al., 2020c).

According to Le et al. (2020b, p. 4203), through photovoice, voices of participants are amplified, and their stories are told and presented via their photos. Hence, the photovoice research values lived experiences of grassroot communities and is intended to address challenges faced by marginalised people in an oppressive society. For example, Suarez et al. (2020) used photovoice to understand LGBTIQ+ students' grief after an LGBTIQ+ nightclub shooting in the United States. Nguyen et al. (2015) explored the politics of inclusion and exclusion of Vietnamese girls with disabilities through photovoice. Similarly, Le et al.'s study (2020b) used photovoice to examine the personal narratives of three Asian teacher educators about inequities in education toward vulnerable children and youth, such as gay boys in Vietnam, financially disadvantaged children in rural Taiwan, and girls with disabilities in South Korea. In these studies, photovoice showed its ability to facilitate the expression of thoughts and feelings of participants who might find difficulty in telling their stories and sharing thoughts verbally, so photovoice involving photography allows them to do so through images.

3.3 The Context and Participants

In our study, we used photovoice to explore the impact of a teacher's non-normative identity on the learning and perceptions of English learners regarding a sense of belonging and inclusiveness in a private English classroom. We conducted this study at the time that COVID-19 had just expanded to Vietnam in 2020, with a few cases of infection. Under the influence of COVID-19, Vietnamese education experienced considerable disruptions, including nationwide school closures and a move to virtual teaching and learning at all levels of education (Tran et al., 2022). It is important to note that in the scope of this study, we had already planned to carry out our research before the global explosion of the pandemic, so our research purpose is not to investigate its effects on English language education. Rather, we focused on teacher identity from the perspective of learners with non-conforming gender and sexual orientations.

The class of English in this study was led by a transgender English teacher, who did not receive formal ELT training, but she was an influencer in the Vietnamese LGBTIQ+ community through her presentations in media, for example in beauty contests for Vietnamese transgender people. Her English proficiency was showcased in media via TV shows (e.g., Sharktank Vietnam–a reality show for Vietnamese startups and Miss Tiffany Vietnam 2018–a beauty pageant for Vietnamese transgender people). She had learned English by herself and by means of her experience as a homestay business owner for years before her current role as an English tutor. She offered English classes for LGBTIQ+ young adults in her private house in the city of Ho Chi Minh. The class chosen for our study was one of her classes. *Lien* was the tutor and her students who volunteered to engage in this study were four LGBTIQ+ young people: *Xuan, An, Kien,* and *Nien* (pseudonyms). They all were living in the city of Ho Chi Minh for their study or work. They reported that they had been learning English with *Lien* for almost 2 years and they knew her from her engagement in several TV shows as a transgender celebrity influencer. On television, *Lien* was confident and impressed the audience with her English fluency. Thus, students admired her excellent ability to use English. Participants' demographic information are given in Table 1.

Table 1 Background information of the respondents

Name[a]	Lien	Xuan	An	Kien	Nien
Age	28	24	30	20	22
Gender identity	Transgirl	Gay	Transgay	Gay	Transgirl
Occupation	English teacher	Journalist	Salesman	University student	University student
Years of learning English	7	5	12	11	13
Qualification	University	University	College diploma	High school certificate	High school certificate
Hometown	Tuy Phuoc, Binh Dinh	Tri Ton, An Giang	The city of Ho Chi Minh	Bac Lieu	Chau Doc, An Giang

[a]Note: To maintain confidentiality, respondents' names are pseudonyms

3.4 Methods

At the beginning, we ran an information session to introduce our project to participants. The purpose was to familiarise participants with the project's details, including the research purpose; we provided the team with contact information, essential requirements to participate, research activities, steps, and methods to be used. We explained the photovoice method and what they were expected to do in terms of photo production and description. Key participants were four students in *Lien*'s class: *Xuan, An, Kien,* and *Nien.* Even though *Lien* played a crucial role in connecting us to these participants, *Lien* was not required to take photos. *Lien* was the focal point for her students to observe and photograph. Hence, *Lien* in this study is key as we study her teacher identity from the perspective of her students. We asked participants to take photos of their class during their learning of English with *Lien* and send those photos to us every week. We emphasised to them that photos should be related to how *Lien* created a relaxed and stress-free atmosphere in her class in a way that permitted them to freely and safely express their real identities during their English classes. The photos also could depict how they viewed *Lien* as a teacher, whose identity was different from other English teachers who were straight and how *Lien*'s non-conformist transgender identity impacted their learning. We asked for one photo per person with a short description of what they photographed. We created an email address for participants to send their photos and information about their artwork. In this introductory session, we also delivered and collected their consent forms indicating that they were well informed about the project and agreed to participate voluntarily.

    We collected photos from participants for 2 months. After this first data collection, we moved to the second stage in which we went through all photos with a description attached to each photo to identify photos that resonated with us the most in terms of what incidents they described and the meanings/stories they tried to deliver or tell. We selected 10 photos for a focus group discussion. We contacted only those participants who had taken those 10 photos for a discussion. We brought up these photos in our discussion with participants on the hidden meanings of the photos. Participants were invited to draw links between the photos. They recalled what happened when they had taken the photos and what it meant to them. The description given for each photo helped them recount the context of the photo. In this discussion, photos and the meanings of the photos constituted the data which were co-analysed by participants and researchers (Nguyen et al., 2015; Le et al., 2020a, c). This collaboration between participants and researchers makes photovoice a participatory research method (Walton et al., 2012). The research received ethics approval from University of Manitoba, Canada.

4   Findings and Discussion

Findings emerge from our discussions with participants in which we co-analysed data and findings presented through different themes (Creswell, 2013). Findings are supported by photos which demonstrate participants' key ideas about how *Lien*'s special ELT teacher identity has influenced their learning of English. Three key findings are inclusiveness and sense of belonging, students' perception of their teacher, and the teacher's influence. We analysed the findings based on insights from ELT decolonial pedagogy in relation to teacher identity (Pennington & Richards, 2016).

4.1   *Inclusiveness and Sense of Belonging*

Figure 1 captured regular moments in *Lien*'s classroom. On the left side, a boy in a long-sleeve orange t-shirt leaned his head on another student's shoulder happily. Likewise, on the right side, another boy in a grey t-shirt seemed to freely hold another student from his back. The student who took these photos claimed that he wanted to employ the photo to present undisputed closeness and connectedness

Fig. 1   An LGBTIQ+ inclusive class

among group members in this special classroom. He revealed that they felt constantly connected, accepted, and included in all activities in this class, and free to be and act out as themselves, unlike in most traditional educational settings. Some, such as *Nien*, expressed an exclusion from 'mainstream' learning activities at her university, which demonstrates the invisibility of LGBTIQ+ young adult learners, as Tran-Thanh (2020) indicated. *Kien*, a transgender person, reinforced *Nien's* painful experience as facing discrimination and isolation at school and a few English language centres, due to his sexual orientation. He was bullied and excluded from extracurricular activities because a LGBTIQ+ member was not allowed to participate in those activities with heteronormative people (Le et al., 2021). *An* said that "everyone should feel free to be themselves anywhere, but, clearly, LGBT people often do not."

Two gay researchers in this study can understand these students' narratives and experiences because they were themselves excluded, and even harassed at school due to their sexual orientation. It is discrimination that many marginalised LGBTIQ+ populations can relate to without hesitation (Le et al., 2020a, c; Trinh et al., 2022). In the context of Vietnam, Tran et al. (2022) point out the injustice a gay teacher may encounter when he would like to bring sexuality and gender knowledge to mainstream education. Savage and Harley (2009) argue that school curriculum and extracurricular activities reinforce negative thoughts and stereotypes of any sexual orientation other than heterosexual. The exclusion that LGBTIQ+ students and teachers must suffer is structurally widespread in that the presence of their stories, topics, and knowledge is completely ignored in ELT teaching activities in Vietnam (Tran-Thanh, 2020). The ignorance and inequity will exacerbate the oppression the LGBTIQ+ students have suffered for such a long time and that prevents them from attaining their full potential (Trinh et al., 2022). The inclusion and visibility of the LGBTIQ+ people are always critical for this community of identity. Educational equity should involve the promotion of a learning environment, wherein LGBTIQ+ students can feel more accepted and valued by making them more confident in their gender identity to be able to attain their potential academic performance. The visibility of the LGBTIQ+ students is also a crucial contribution to potentially creating an environment where homophobic, biphobic and transphobic discrimination can be problematised.

In this study's learning environment, the visibility of LGBTIQ+ people, an essential tenet of the teaching and learning of English for LGBTIQ+ people (Leal & Grooks, 2018; Moore, 2016), made the teacher and the students feel embraced. Feeling free to unmask their identity shows a sign of social justice in the classroom (Le et al., 2020a, c), which in turn can positively affect their study goals and performance. *Nien* felt "very safe and happy" when learning with those who shared the same identity. *Xuan* posited that the similarity and encouragement of the teacher and other students in uncovering their identity and sexuality played a critical role in helping them to be connected with other peers and understand more about the LGBTIQ+ community.

When having a discussion (see Fig. 1), *Kien* and *Xuan* further pointed out that learning with *Lien* in the last two years usually made them "feel so warm". These students appreciated that *Lien* cared about their feelings, and particularly encouraged them to be themselves and expose their real identities. In other words, instead of only focusing on lesson content and procedures in language teaching, *Lien* attempted to switch her focus to her students and interactions in the classroom, a very important characteristic of a skilled language teacher (Pennington & Richards, 2016), to help them meet their goals in improving their English skills. Her caring created a sense of belonging and inclusiveness: the class becomes their "second home", as *Xuan* and *Kien* said, in that they feel they are part of a "community of practice" (Richards, 2012, p. 46). In this case, *Lien* who faced extreme vulnerability and oppression due to her gender identity understood the realistic needs of her students, who always wanted to find a place where they could feel a sense of belonging. *Lien* also shared their anxiety, stress or crisis caused by social denial or unfair judgment towards their gender identity (Pennington & Richards, 2016; Tran et al., 2022). *Lien* managed to create a community wherein LGBTIQ+ students could have their own place to satisfy their passion and expectation for learning and practising English without facing any possible risks of discrimination. *Nien* indicated that *Lien*'s LGBTIQ+ teacher identity helped the students feel more welcomed, "more communicative," and most importantly, made it "much easier [for them] to acquire knowledge". The participants anticipated that the unique linkage and interconnectedness of the identities of a teacher and their students, members of "marginalised social groups", have made a positive impact on their English skill improvement.

The gender identity solidarity seems to help recognise a teacher's "contextually enacted way of being" (van Lier, 2008, p. 163) that shapes their pedagogical practices to empower themselves and their students in a gender-inclusive classroom (Leal & Crookes, 2018). However, some might argue that Lien's classes are not representative of multilingual/multicultural classes in our globalising world, and hence they would not meet the diverse needs of students with diverse gender identities and sexual orientations. Yet, it remains fair to state that *Lien's* class is a mere fragmentation of real classrooms, and as such she managed to create a gender-inclusive environment, wherein marginalised LGBTIQ+ students are recognised, celebrated and accommodated, unlike in mainstream traditional educational and societal spaces.

4.2   Perception of Teacher

During our conversations with participants about the pictures, we realised that in addition to the particular connection developed between Lien and her students, they were also inspired by *Lien's* self-confidence, her English fluency and overall professional competence. Pennington and Richards (2016) posit that language proficiency and the personality of a teacher in language teaching play a crucial role in educating students who have limited skills to succeed. *Lien* embodied her ability to become an English teacher through her confidence and determination. Talking about *Lien's* ability, *An* stated, "She's so professional." *Kien* added, "I feel that she works very determined. With her confidence and ability, I think she can do it and will be successful." *Xuân* supported her classmates' opinions by revealing that *Lien* is "very professional and confident" in teaching them how to master English skills.

Figure 2 features *Lien* as a 'professional' teacher from her students' perspective of a teacher of English, who needed to be confident and caring. Students asserted that *Lien's* English proficiency through her experience of self-study was inspiring. With her own stories and experience of learning and teaching, values, beliefs, and concepts as a student before and a teacher now, *Lien* built a personal, gender-related understanding of teaching (Borg, 2006). Hence, she integrated her funds of knowledge into her lessons by relating them to "individual classroom actions and decision-making" goals (Pennington & Richards, 2016, p. 15).

Lien also seemed to understand the importance of contextual knowledge in the construction of language teaching identity (Pennington & Richards, 2016; Richards, 2012) and the "contextual factors outside of the teachers themselves" (Miller, 2009, p.175). In the Vietnamese educational context, being gay or lesbian could be perceived as a disease and can face punishment by family and teachers; therefore, exclusion from many social activities, discrimination, bullying, and harassment of LGBTIQ+ students is a big issue faced by a significant proportion of LGBTIQ+ students at school and at home (Human Rights Watch, 2020; Le et al., 2021). LGBTIQ+ students totally disappear in the curriculum building process, causing more injustice for this vulnerable community (Human Rights Watch, 2020). The presence of stories, or the visibility of relevant experiences of LGBTIQ+ students

Fig. 2 Lien as a 'professional' teacher

are rarely seen in the ELT curriculum and daily lessons (Tran-Thanh, 2020). LGBTIQ+ teachers and students in ELT classes can encounter countless "disfavouring conditions – negative influences or inhibiting factors that constrain teaching and learning" (Pennington & Richards, 2016, p.10). However, as *Kien* stressed, *Lien's* students felt "very comfortable and sociable with other peers" because *Lien*, aware of those facets of exploitation, fostered a very welcoming environment in her classroom. *Kien* explained that *Lien's* efforts were very "good and helpful" in the learning process for all the students. "Happy" was the common word often repeated when these students talked about the class atmosphere and the way *Lien* dealt with their feelings during the last 2 years.

From the lens of intersectionality, *Lien* held dual social identities as a teacher and as a transgender that offered her privileges in inspiring students with non-normative gender and sexuality identities. Because of her unique teacher identity, *Lien* contextualised her ELT knowledge and skills (Richards, 2012), including the ability to incorporate gender and sexuality information into her teaching, in a way that helped to create an inclusive environment for LGBTIQ+ youth learners. *Nien* said, "I come to her class to listen to stories of other people who look like me [...] *Lien* also teaches us about safe sex guides for people like us." *Lien* transgressed her role as an English teacher. She did not receive formal training to become a qualified ELT teacher, so she understood her weakness of not being well trained to serve as a professional ELT teacher. The perception and image of Lien as a professional ELT teacher came from her students when they described her as dedicated and caring with regard to making her classes gender inclusive. Such a gender inclusive environment is what made a big difference for her students (Nguyen et al., 2022). Lien's awareness of the importance of her role in creating a gender inclusive classroom refers to "self-knowledge as an element of the competence of a language teacher" (Pennington & Richards, 2016, p. 11). *Lien* theorised her teaching from practice. She had accumulated past experience as a homestay owner through which she interacted with foreigners; she then translated that into her actions of teaching as an English teacher. She had also excelled in using English in TV shows (e.g., Miss Tiffany 2018, a Vietnamese beauty pageant for transgender women); she translated this into her actions of teaching English speaking with confidence. These experiences take *Lien's* language teacher identity beyond training (Richards, 2012) to a higher level of reflection that boosts her ELT competence.

4.3   *Teacher's Influence*

From the students' perspectives about *Lien*, we have recognised the influence of queer teacher identity on students' language attainment and learning purposes. *Lien*, in her students' eyes, first and foremost, is a very beautiful lady who always proudly showed her gender identity. Talking about Fig. 3 below, the students claimed that *Lien* was not afraid of exposing her real identity and fashion taste which she was always fond of, wearing high heel shoes (on the left side) and *ao dai* (on the right

Fig. 3 The Elegant Lien

side) which is a traditional Vietnamese dress; she wore this on some special occasions to show her femininity in front of other people. *An* revealed that *"Lien* rất điệu" in Vietnamese (or "Lien is so stylish and girly" in English) to talk about *Lien's* hobby of wearing high-heel shoes and *ao dai* often. The students loved this side of her authenticity which made them feel more connected and braver in expressing their real identities in this class. *Lien's* students clarified that *Lien's* awareness of her female image and beauty was the first thing to attract students' attention. However, another more important reason that made them decide to study English with her was that they admired her talents and English skills. Although *Lien* did not receive professional training qualifications, she has intelligence, wisdom, positive energy, English competence, impressive confidence in public speaking, and especially the courage of self-expression. These elements, in combination, have built her impactful queer teacher identity for LGBTIQ+ English learners and become a source of inspiration for these students and other LGBTIQ+ populations in Vietnam. *An* argued that "I joined this class because the person I admire the most is my teacher *(Lien)* when I saw her on several TV shows." Likewise, *Xuan* stated that "Admiring Ms. *Lien* is another reason why I enrolled in the class. I have learned a lot from her." *An* also demonstrated her tribute for *Lien* by confessing that "Her *(Lien's)* charisma is amazing, she is smart, funny and so talented." *Kien* added, "I look up to *Lien* because she is so smart, brilliantly talented, and always learning new things. She proved that she was excellent in the top 5 Miss Tiffany 2018."

Figure 3 describes *Lien's* personality as a transgender teacher and an influencer, who promoted the importance of a positive personality and good attitude (Richards, 1996), and legitimised her queer teacher identity in language education (van Lier, 2008) in a way that transcends the confines of mainstream traditional teaching contexts. Her non-formal teacher education background and her impactful media presence have made of her an inspirational educational actor, with exceptional teacher qualities. Her students strongly expressed their wish to continue studying with her in the future. *Kien* said, "I will learn a lot from her who has much knowledge." Similarly, *Xuan* expressed her belief in *Lien's* talent as a teacher. Hence, students showed their support and appreciation for all the activities *Lien* has done for the LGBTIQ+ community in Vietnam. She managed to bring diversity, equity, and inclusiveness to the fore in foreign language education in the Vietnamese context by stressing the urgent need to recognise the marginalised people's needs in curriculum design, to celebrate teacher agency and identity, and to decolonise pedagogical methods, educational administration, and leadership (Banks & Banks, 2019). By fostering a safe and inclusive environment for queer students in our English language teaching classrooms, relevant educational stakeholders will help to empower LGBTIQ+ 'communities of identity' to attain their learning potential.

5 Conclusion

This chapter explores a Vietnamese queer teacher identity and its influence on a group of gender-non-conforming young learners of English. Photovoice is the overarching methodology for this study, which entails a combination of data, including focus group discussions and photos taken by participants. *Lien* is an English teacher who is a transgender influencer in Vietnam, and the participants are her students, whose gender and sexuality identities are lesbian, gay, and transgender. Drawing on Pennington and Richards' (2016) framework of ELT teacher identity and the concept of intersectionality (Crenshaw, 1994), we decolonise the context of ELT in Vietnam, where LGBTIQ+ teachers and students of English are invisible (Nguyen et al., forthcoming). The marginalization of this stigmatised learner population in ELT studies results in less gender-inclusive learning and teaching environments, especially in the non-Western contexts in which 'queerness' is still socially denigrated. Tran-Thanh (2020), Le et al. (2021), and Tran et al. (2022) assert that in Vietnam, gender and sexuality are still sensitive topics, and the underrepresentation of non-normative gender and sexual identity people is a considerable social justice issue across fields of research, including ELT. There seems to be a systematic erasure of gender and sexual minorities and the imposition of regimes of compulsory heterosexuality in Vietnamese upper-secondary ELT textbooks (Nguyen et al., 2022).

Although the limitations of our research (small group of participants and focus on one queer teacher) restrict the study's generalisability, it has important pedagogical implications that are worth sharing. Lien's unique identity as both a teacher and a transgender person gives her insights into how to build a welcoming and caring classroom environment for marginalised LGBTIQ+ students. She transgressed her formal teaching responsibility by not simply training students in English skills, but also by inspiring them to accept, value and express their gender and sexuality identities without fearing societal reproach or resentment. As a result, her students ceased to feel 'out of place' in her class. From the students' perspective, *Lien* appeared confident and professional. Professionalism in their eyes was demonstrated in *Lien's* ability to understand and accommodate the learners' diverse needs. Her students were striving for a sense of belonging and this was realised through the nurturing of communities of identity and practice within the ELT educational space. *Lien*'s identity as a confident and proud transgender teacher influenced her students' performance and perception. They aspired to become as confident and successful as *Lien* in learning English as an additional language. Our study paves the way for further decolonising ELT studies, in relation to LGBTIQ+ research and ELT pedagogy in the Global South.

References

Altbach, P. G. (2004). Globalization and the university: Myths and realities in an unequal world. *Tertiary Education & Management, 10*(1), 3–25. https://doi.org/10.1023/B:TEAM.00000122 39.55136.4b

Banks, J. A., & Banks, C. A. M. (2019). *Multicultural education: Issues and perspectives*. Wiley.

Borg, S. (2006). *Teacher cognition and language education: Research and practice*. Continuum.

Bracho, C. A., & Hayes, C. (2020). Gay voices without intersectionality is white supremacy: Narratives of gay and lesbian teachers of color on teaching and learning. *International Journal of Qualitative Studies in Education, 33*(6), 583–592. https://doi.org/10.1080/0951839 8.2020.1751897

Cochran-Smith, M., Shakman, K., Jong, C., Terrell, D. G., Barnatt, J., & McQuillan, P. (2009). Good and just teaching: The case for social justice in teacher education. *American Journal of Education, 115*, 347–377.

Crenshaw, K. (1994). Mapping the margins: Intersectionality, identity politics, and violence against women of colour. In M. A. Fineman & R. Mykitiul (Eds.), *The public nature of private violence* (pp. 93–120). Routledge.

Creswell, J. W. (2013). *Qualitative inquiry and research design: Choosing among five approaches* (3rd ed.). Sage.

Cummins, J. (2011). Identity matters: From evidence-free to evidence-based policies for promoting achievement among students from marginalized social groups. *Writing & Pedagogy, 3*(2), 189–216. https://doi.org/10.1558/wap.v3i2.189

DeGraff, M. (2019). Against apartheid in education and linguistics: The case of Haitian creole in neo-colonial Haiti. In D. Macedo (Ed.), *Decolonizing foreign language education* (pp. ix–xxxii). Routledge.

Freire, P. (2004). *Pedagogy of indignation*. Paradigm Publishers.

Grant, C. A., & Zwier, E. (2011). Intersectionality and student outcomes: Sharpening the struggle against racism, sexism, classism, ableism, heterosexism, nationalism, and linguistic, religious, and geographical discrimination in teaching and learning. *Multicultural Perspectives, 13*(4), 181–188. https://doi.org/10.1080/15210960.2011.616813

Harris, L., & Watson-Vandiver, M. J. (2020). Decolonizing race and gender intersectionality in education: A collaborative critical autoethnography of hope, healing and justice. *Journal of Cultural Analysis and Social Change, 5*(2), 1–16. https://doi.org/10.20897/jcasc/9321

Hill, C. P., & Bilge, S. (2016). *Intersectionality*. Policy Press.

Hulko, W., & Hovanes, J. (2017). Intersectionality in the lives of LGBTQ youth: Identifying as LGBTQ and finding community in small cities and rural towns. *Journal of Homosexuality, 65*(4), 427–455. https://doi.org/10.1080/00918369.2017.1320169

Human Rights Watch. (2020). *"My teacher said I had a disease": Barriers to the right to education for LGBT youth in Vietnam*. Human Rights Watch. https://www.hrw.org/report/2020/02/12/my-teacher-said-i-had-disease/barriers-right-education-lgbt-youth-vietnam

Johnson, A. (2018). *Privilege, power, difference*. Routledge.

Kessi, S. (2018). Photovoice as a narrative tool for decolonization: Black women and LGBT student experiences at UCT. *South African Journal of Higher Education, 32*(3), 101–117. https://doi.org/10.20853/32-3-2519

Lawrence, L., & Nagashima, Y. (2020). The intersectionality of gender, sexuality, race, and native-speakerness: Investigating ELT teacher identity through duoethnography. *Journal of Language, Identity, and Education, 19*(1), 42–55. https://doi.org/10.1080/15348458.2019.1672173

Le, N. H. G. (2019). Reflection on education equity in Vietnam: Teachers' and students' voices in an English tourism programme. *Transitions: Journal of Transient Migration, 3*(2), 145–155. https://doi.org/10.1386/tjtm_00004_1

Le, G., Blaikie, F., & Tran, V. (2020a). To know, to love and to heal: PhotoStory and duoethnography as approaches to enhancing social justice and self-actualization in high school classrooms. *CSSE-CACS 2020 Proceedings/Actes de la SCÉÉ-ACÉC 2020, 18*(1), 53–55.

Le, N. H. G., Hsiao, C. T., & Heo, Y. (2020b). Trans-cultural journeys of east-Asian educators: The impact of the three teachings. *International Journal for Cross-Disciplinary Subjects in Education, 11*(1), 4201–4210. https://doi.org/10.20533/ijcdse.2042.6364.2020.0513

Le, T., Tran, V., & Le, G. (2020c). Pride and prejudice: An intersectional look at graduate employability to transgender and queer international students. *Journal of Comparative and International Higher Education, 12*(6S1), 153–160.

Le, N. H. G., Tran, V. H., & Le, T. L. (2021). Combining photography and duoethnography for creating a trioethnography approach to reflect upon educational issues amidst the COVID-19 global pandemic. *International Journal of Qualitative Methods*, 1–12. https://doi.org/10.1177/16094069211031127

Leal, P., & Crookes, G. V. (2018). Most of my students kept saying, 'I never met a gay person': A queer English language teacher's agency for social justice. *System, 79*, 38–48. https://doi.org/10.1016/j.system.2018.06.005

Miller, J. (2009). Teacher identity. In: A. Burns & J. Richards (Eds.), *The Cambridge guide to second language teacher education* (pp. 172–181). Cambridge University Press.

Moore, A. R. (2016). Inclusion and exclusion: A case study of an English class for LGBT learners. *TESOL Quarterly, 50*(1), 86–108. https://doi.org/10.1002/tesq.208

Nelson, C. D. (2002). Why queer theory is useful in teaching: A perspective from English as a second language teaching. *Journal of Gay and Lesbian Social Services, 14*(2), 43–53. https://doi.org/10.1300/J041v14n02_04

Nguyen, T. M. H. (2011). Primary English language education policy in Vietnam: Insights from implementation. *Current Issues in Language Planning, 12*(2), 225–249. https://doi.org/10.1080/14664208.2011.597048

Nguyen, C. D., & Zeichner, K. (2021). Second language teachers learn to teach for social justice through community field experiences. *Language Teaching Research, 25*(4), 656–678. https://doi.org/10.1177/1362168819868739

Nguyen, D. C., Le, T. L., Tran, H. Q., & Nguyen, T. H. (2014). Inequality of access to English language learning in primary education in Vietnam: A case study. In H. Zhang, P. W. K. Chan, & C. Boyle (Eds.), *Equality in education* (pp. 139–153). Sense Publishers. https://doi.org/10.1007/978-94-6209-692-9_11

Nguyen, X. T., Mitchell, C., De Lange, N., & Fritsch, K. (2015). Engaging girls with disabilities in Vietnam: Making their voices count. *Disability & Society, 30*(5), 773–787. https://doi.org/10.1080/09687599.2015.1051515

Pennington, M. C. (1989). Faculty development for language programs. In R. K. Johnson (Ed.), *The second language curriculum* (pp. 91–110). Cambridge University Press.

Pennington, M. C. (1992). Reflecting on teaching and learning: A developmental focus for the second language classroom. In J. Flowerdew, M. N. Brock, & S. Hsia (Eds.), *Perspectives on second language teacher education* (pp. 47–65). City Polytechnic of Hong Kong.

Pennington, M. C. (2015). Teacher identity in TESOL: A frames perspective. In Y. L. Cheung, S. B. Said, & K. Park (Eds.), *Teacher identity and development in applied linguistics: Current trends and perspectives* (pp. 16–30). Routledge.

Pennington, M. C., & Richards, J. C. (2016). Teacher identity in language teaching: Integrating personal, contextual, and professional factors. *RELC Journal, 47*(1), 5–23. https://doi.org/10.1177/0033688216631219

Phan, L. H. (2018). Higher education, English, and the idea of 'the west': Globalizing and encountering a global south regional university. *Discourse: Studies in the Cultural Politics of Education, 39*(5), 782–797. https://doi.org/10.1080/01596306.2018.1448704

Richards, K. (2006). Being the teacher: Identity and classroom conversation. *Applied Linguistics, 27*(1), 51–77. https://doi.org/10.1093/applin/ami041

Richards, J. C. (2012). Competence and performance in language teaching. In A. Burns & J. C. Richards (Eds.), *The Cambridge guide to pedagogy and practice in second language teaching* (pp. 45–59). Cambridge University Press.

Sachs, J. (2005). Teacher education and the development of professional identity: Learning to be a teacher. In M. Kompf & P. Denicolo (Eds.), *Connecting policy and practice: Challenges for teaching and learning in schools and universities* (pp. 5–21). Routledge.

Savage, T. A., & Harley, D. A. (2009). A place at the blackboard: LGBTIQ. *Multicultural Education, 50*(4), 2–7.

Taylor, S. (2015). Identity construction. In K. Tracy (Ed.), *International encyclopedia of language and social interaction* (pp. 1–9). Wiley.

Toan, V. (2013). *English teaching in Vietnam: Teacher 're-education.'* Tuoitrenews. http://tuoitrenews.vn/education/8231/print?undefined

Tran, V., Le, G., & Le, T. (2022). Impacts of international education shifts through transnational stories of three Vietnamese doctoral students. In A. W. Wiseman (Ed.), *Annual review of comparative and international education 2021 (International perspectives on education and society)* (Vol. 42A). Emerald Publishing Limited.

Tran-Thanh, V. (2020). Queer identity inclusion in the EFL classroom: Vietnamese teachers' perspectives. *TESOL Journal, 11*(3), 1–16. Portico. https://doi.org/10.1002/tesj.512

Trinh, E., Le, G., Dong, H. B., Tran, T., & Tran, V. (2022). Memory writing as a method of inquiry: When returning becomes collective healing. *Qualitative Report, 27*(3), 824–841. https://doi.org/10.46743/2160-3715/2022.5245

van Lier, L. (2008). Agency in the classroom. In J. P. Lantolf & M. E. Poehner (Eds.), *Sociocultural theory and the teaching of second languages* (pp. 163–186). Equinox.

Walton, G., Schleien, S. J., Brake, L. R., Trovato, C., & Oakes, T. (2012). Photovoice: A collaborative methodology giving voice to underserved populations seeking community inclusion. *Therapeutic Recreation Journal, 46*(3), 168–178.

Wang, C., & Burris, M. A. (1997). Photovoice: Concept, methodology, and use for participatory needs assessment. *Health Education & Behavior, 24*(3), 369–387. https://journals.sagepub.com. https://doi.org/10.1177/109019819702400309

Zimmerman, D. H. (1998). Identity, context and interaction. In C. Antaki & S. Widdicombe (Eds.), *Identities in talk* (pp. 87–106). Sage.

Giang Nguyen Hoang Le is a lecturer at Faculty of Foreign Languages (Van Lang University, Vietnam). He is also a Ph.D. Candidate in Educational Studies, Brock University, Canada. His research covers gender and sexuality in schooling across cultural contexts and the use of Photovoice as a decolonising method. He is using multimodal visual autoethnography to self-study his lived experiences as a gay boy in multiple Vietnamese settings, such as at home, and in school places and spaces. He has published in international journals: *International Journal of Qualitative Methods, APA Journal of Traumatology,* as well as chapters in books with Routledge and Brill/Sense. Email: gianglee89@gmail.com/ giang.lnh@vlu.edu.vn

Ha Bich Dong (she/her) is a graduate student in the Joint M.A. program in Peace and Conflict Studies at the University of Manitoba, Canada. Her research is concerned with healing and reconciliation, strategic peacebuilding, and decolonization in peacebuilding and education. Email: dongc4@myumanitoba.ca

Vuong Tran is a Ph.D. student in Educational Studies, Nipissing University, Canada. He is doing research in financial literacy for LGBTIQ+ people and education equity in the Global South. He is a lecturer in Business and Finance at Ho Chi Minh University of Technology, Vietnam. He has published in the *International Journal of Qualitative Methods* and presented at international conferences, such as *The American Educational Research Association* and *The Canadian Society for the Study of Education*. Email: thv1802@gmail.com

Long Hoang Vu is currently a Master's student in Journalism and Communication Studies at Vietnam National University, Hanoi. Vu-Hoang's research interests encompass education, ethnography, media, and cultural studies. Email: longvu.teamx@gmail.com

Teaching EIL as a Tool of Social and Ideological Manipulation in South Korea: Does School and Student Socioeconomic Status Matter?

Youngeun Jee and Guofang Li

Abstract Framed within a critical perspective on English as an International Language (EIL), the study examined two teachers' classroom instructions and reflections of their instruction related to teaching EIL in different school districts with contrasting socioeconomic statuses (SES) in Korea. Thematic analyses of the teachers' interviews and their instructional practices suggest that the two teachers demonstrated different ideologies towards the EIL paradigm, and that their students' SES backgrounds and English proficiency influenced their incorporation of the EIL perspectives in instruction. The findings suggests that teaching EIL has been a tool of social and ideological manipulation in local school contexts in South Korea.

Keywords English as an international language · Student socioeconomic status · English · Education in Korea

1 Introduction

In the last few decades, with an increasing number of people crossing borders all over the world, English as an international language (EIL) is used in more diverse and dynamic settings by people from different backgrounds within and across countries. However, in many countries, the ability to speak standardized English, particularly that of the U.S. and U.K., is still perceived as a desirable goal by many English learners. In Korea, it is believed that standardized English increases one's competitive edge, brings social and economic benefits (Ra, 2019) and enhances people's social class by providing political, financial, and academic advantages to those with high English proficiency (Nam, 2012). As a result, the legitimacy of local

Y. Jee (✉) · G. Li
Department of Language and Literacy Education, University of British Columbia,
Vancouver, BC, Canada
e-mail: yjee@student.ubc.ca; guofang.li@ubc.ca

© The Author(s), under exclusive license to Springer Nature
Switzerland AG 2023
A. Sahlane, R. Pritchard (eds.), *English as an International Language
Education*, English Language Education 33,
https://doi.org/10.1007/978-3-031-34702-3_24

463

English varieties has been questioned more than ever before (Bhatt, 2001; Canagarajah, 2006; Galloway, 2017; Li, 2017). Korean society's deference to the current superior status of standardized English over different English varieties suggests "the existence of a transnational standard linked to the power of the United States and United Kingdom in particular areas of communication…" (Bolton, 2006, p. 306). This native-English-speakerism ideology, related to societal desires for standardized English, has also been embedded in and reinforced by education systems and schools. Therefore, it is not surprising that the "native-English-speakerism model" that favours standardized English and native-English-speakers has been evident in the field of English education, including instructional materials and assessments (Galloway & Numajiri, 2020).

This adoption of American or British standardized English as a desirable instructional model in English education without careful consideration of local English-speaking contexts in non-English dominant countries can be very detrimental to learners and their local languages on many levels (Canagarajah, 2012; Friedrich, 2012; Jee & Li, 2021; Li, 2017; Matsuda & Friedrich, 2012; Ra, 2019). The pitfall of English learners' strong preference for the native-English-speaker model can be "self-deprecation" (Park, 2009, p. 26), leading to learners' negative attitudes toward other varieties of English (e.g., Ahn, 2014, 2017; Lee, 2010; Yoon, 2007), and low confidence in communicating with various English speakers (e.g., Shim, 2015), due to a lack of exposure to other Englishes or communication strategies (e.g., paraphrasing, asking for clarification to convey speakers' intended meaning, etc.). Thus, Matsuda and Friedrich (2012) assert the necessity of increasing students' awareness and exposure to English varieties through teaching materials, or interaction with English users from different linguistic and cultural contexts, and such effort is "not only a matter of different pronunciation features, but rather a much more encompassing manifestation of cultural, linguistic and other values" (p. 24). McKay (2018) further argues that "all pedagogical decisions regarding standards and curriculum should be made in reference to local language needs and local, social and educational factors" (p. 11).

Despite the strong advocacy for teaching EIL to encompass linguistic, social, and cultural aspects of language use in different varieties of English for international communication, discrepancies have been observed in English teachers' beliefs and teaching practices in non-English dominant countries. For instance, Korean English teachers (Shim, 2015) and pre-service teachers (Sung, 2019) were found to display a positive attitude toward different English varieties and argued for inclusion of English used in diverse English-speaking contexts in school. However, in their instruction, these teachers showed a strong tendency to favour native-English-speakerism. In another study, Ahn (2017) investigated Korean and non-Korean English teachers' attitudes toward 8 different English varieties at the secondary school level and the college level. The results revealed teachers' conflicted responses in terms of their level of resistance toward, or acceptance of these English varieties and pedagogical implementation.

These studies suggest that more research is needed to understand how English teachers apply their understandings of and knowledge about EIL to their classrooms and what contextual factors may influence teachers' EIL teaching practices. In Korea, students' educational gaps exist between schools in wealthy communities and schools in low-income communities. However, little is known about how these school contexts might influence teachers' EIL beliefs and teaching practices. Therefore, this study aims to fill this gap by examining two teachers' classroom instructions and reflections related to their teaching practices in different school districts with contrasting socio-economic status (SES). A teacher called Soojin (pseudonym) taught students from low-income families in a rural area, whereas the other teacher called Minho (pseudonym) worked in a top-tier private boarding school in Korea. Accordingly, this study examines how these two diverse contexts influenced their incorporation of the EIL perspectives in instruction.

2 A Critical Perspective on English Dominance and EIL

In this chapter, we examine the two Korean English teachers' views and practices of EIL from a critical perspective to language ideology. Language ideologies are one of the perspectives through which the relationship between language and society is viewed as "any sets of beliefs about language articulated by the users as a rationalization or justification of perceived language structure and use" (Silverstein, 1979, p. 193). Piller (2015) viewed language ideologies as "beliefs, feelings, and conceptions about language that are socially shared and relate language and society in a dialectical fashion" (p. 4). People's language ideologies reflect their linguistic beliefs that are often linked to the broader social and cultural systems to which they belong. In addition to the structural influences, one's beliefs and assumptions about a language, conscious or unconscious, are also shaped by their social, educational, and cultural experience as well as the contexts in which they live or work (Tollefson, 2000).

Adopting a critical perspective to language ideology, Phillipson (1992, 2010) argued that English dominance in the world is the legacy of European colonialism, and linguistic imperialism related to the global expansion of English and aligned with the interest of British- and American-based professions, including TESOL, distance education, and business. Phillipson (1992) used the metaphor of "core-periphery" to illustrate English dominance and European colonialism. Core-English speaking countries include dominant English-speaking countries (e.g., U.S. or U.K.), whereas periphery-English speaking countries are "countries which require English as an international link language" (e.g., Scandinavia, Japan), and countries on which English was imposed in colonial times, and where the English has been successfully transplanted and still serves a range of international purposes (e.g., India, Nigeria)" (Phillipson, 1992, p. 17).

From a critical view of English dominance, the higher status of standardized English is seen as influenced by political and economic power of dominant English-speaking countries. This view is in line with Bolton's (2006) argument that "partly as the result of the economic and political power of the USA... [standardized American] English has also become the mostly widely taught foreign language in the school systems of Expanding Circle regions and countries such as Europe, China, and Japan" (p. 299). The high status of standardized English reflects unequal power and social order in the world in that periphery countries, such as Korea, remain in a dependent situation.

Similarly, researchers in the EIL paradigm (e.g., Matsuda & Matsuda, 2018) view linguistic hierarchy between standardized and local English varieties from the perspective of language ideology, arguing that these were not neutral but reflected social order and unequal power relationships among different languages and varieties in the world. According to Sharifian (2009), EIL rejects "the idea of any variety being selected as a lingua franca for international communication", arguing that "English, with its many varieties, is a language of international, and therefore intercultural, communication" (p. 2). In other words, EIL recognizes all Englishes used by speakers from different linguistic, cultural, and national backgrounds and accepts heterogeneous perspectives of English. To teach English from an EIL paradigm, Matsuda and Matsuda (2018) noted that the goals are to train students to (1) possess awareness of different English varieties by providing ample exposure to multiple varieties of English, (2) become competent users of EIL, (3) be able to effectively use communication strategies, (4) be exposed to cultural materials from diverse English-speaking contexts (pp. 66–68).

3   Methods

The study employed a qualitative case study approach (Yin, 2003) to provide in-depth descriptions of Korean secondary English teachers' perspectives on EIL and their teaching practices in a Korean educational context. A case study allowed the researchers to explore what the teachers believed about EIL, how those beliefs were formed, and in what ways those beliefs affected the teachers' instruction through "detailed, in-depth data collection involving multiple sources of information" (Merriam & Tisdell, 2016, p. 97).

In this study, two Korean teachers of English from schools with contrasting socioeconomic status were cases of investigation. We conducted 6 one-on-one semi-structured interviews (3 with each teacher) and 10 h of classroom observations in total with the two teachers; short interviews before/during/after each observation were conducted to allow the teachers to check, revise, and build upon what they said in previous interviews or classroom instruction. The first semi-structured interview focused on teachers' backgrounds, English learning experience, exposure to diversity of English uses, EIL users, and EIL teaching experiences. The second and third interviews elicited teachers' reflection on and clarification of their instruction, and future plans for EIL integration as well as their views on the challenges, strategies, and suggestions for teaching EIL in the classroom. Yin (2014) posited that a researcher can gain some insightful ideas from interview data, as it offers "explanation as well as personal views (e.g., perceptions, attitudes, and meanings)" (p. 106). Therefore, data gained from interviews were important for this study to better understand teachers' views and experiences with the issue under scrutiny and ratio-nales behind their teaching practices. All interviews were conducted in Korean; they were audio-recorded and later transcribed and translated into English for further analysis.

Classroom observations and video recordings of two teachers took place at least once a week over a span of 8 weeks for one semester, beginning in May 2019. When classroom observations were not possible at a given time during data collection, teachers video-recorded their lessons and shared it with the researchers. Teaching materials such as lesson plans and presentation materials were also collected as evidence to support our findings. The video-recorded lessons were also transcribed and translated for analysis.

4   Participants and Contexts

Two teachers, Soojin and Minho, were recruited from two different school districts (see Table 1). Soojin was in her early 40s, and she had been teaching English in secondary schools for 10 years. At the time of the study, she was teaching second- and third-year middle school students in Jeollanam-do in Mokpo, a small rural com-munity of about 240,000 people where the gross regional domestic product (GRDP) in 2019 was KR on 76,948,280, which was relatively low, compared to other cities in Korea (Statistics Korea, 2019). Minho was in his mid-30 s, and had been teaching English since 2011 at a private, elite boarding school, called an "autonomous pri-vate school" established in 2009, in Seoul Metropolitan City (GRDP was KRW 435,927,212 in 2019).

In Korea, except for some specialized schools such as foreign language schools, science high school, or autonomous private high schools which are known as elite schools, general schools including both public and private schools provide equiva-lent education programs in terms of curriculum, standards for the assessment, and tuition rate. Soojin's school was one of these general schools established in 1941 by a private endowment, and students were assigned to the school by their home address, rather than by competitive examination. In 2019, it had about 500 students and 38 educational personnel. Though the school was not designed for low-income

Table 1 Teacher demographics[a]

Name	Age	School district	Teaching level	SES	THD	TE	SAE	OE
Soojin	Early 40 s	Mokpo (rural city of Jeolla-do)	General middle school (by allocation)	Low SES	Graduate (master level)	10 years	No	Yes
Minho	Mid 30 s	Metropolitan Seoul	Top-tier private high school (by selection)	High SES	Undergraduate	9 years	No	Yes

[a]*SES* Students' standard of living; *THD* Teachers' highest degree; *TE* Teaching experience; *SAE* Study abroad experience; *OE* Overseas experience

students, it was located in the old town of Mokpo. Therefore, many of Soojin's students were likely to come from low SES communities.

Minho had taught all three levels (freshmen, sophomore, and senior) in the elite high school; and as of 2019, he was in charge of teaching the freshmen a weekly 2-hour-long course called "general English". In 2019, the school had 600 students and 67 teachers. Admission to this school was competitive, so only those who performed well in middle schools could apply and get accepted to it. In addition, the educational expenses, including the tuition rate and extra school activities, were high. Therefore, most students at the school came from high SES groups who paid considerably more monthly private education expenditures per student than those in rural areas such as Mokpo (Statistics Korea, 2020).

5   Data Analysis

Each teacher was a "unit of analysis" (Stake, 2005) in this study due to the fact that they had different beliefs about and ways of incorporating EIL in their respective instruction. Thematic analysis, suggested by Braun and Clarke (2013) and Miles et al. (2014), was employed. Four codes (i.e., (a) teachers' beliefs about EIL, (b) English learning experiences, (c) exposures to different English varieties and EIL users, and (d) conflicts or challenges for EIL instruction) were generated to understand teachers' perspectives on EIL. Three initial codes (i.e., (a) teaching practices, (b) students' socio-economic status (SES), and (c) conflicts or challenges in EIL instruction) were used to identify teachers' actual instruction related to EIL. Sub codes related to teaching practices in EIL such as different English varieties, communication strategies, cultural materials reflecting different English-speaking contexts were then used to further segment the data. These codes and subcodes were entered for each case first and were then categorized into larger themes. Patterns in teachers' beliefs and teaching practices were then compared for cross-case analysis (Miles et al., 2014).

The data gained from the class observations were used to corroborate the interview findings as the direct observations provided "immediacy" and "contextualization" when researchers observed the interviewee's actions within the immediate context of teaching practice (Yin, 2014, p. 106). Similar codes based on the EIL perspective were applied to examine the transcripts of class observations.

Specifically, all teachers' utterances during the class and all audio-visual materials used for instruction were coded based on three major themes: beliefs about EIL, exposures to EIL, as well as school districts' and students' SES. When teachers' utterance about or content of audio-visual materials explicitly dealt with the definition of EIL or importance of raising awareness of EIL, these were coded under the categorization of "beliefs about EIL". Teachers' instructions, involving teachers' utterances, textbook and audio-visual materials, were coded as "exposures to EIL" when these included information related to different English varieties, English users in a global society, communication strategies among English users, and cultural materials reflecting diverse English-speaking contexts. To compare teachers' inclusion of EIL according to students' circumstances, information such as students' prior knowledge about English-speaking contexts, students' English proficiency, and their opportunities to learn about various English uses from school curriculum were collected from the teacher interviews and these were also coded and analyzed. Altogether, the findings of the study were "based on the convergence of information from difference sources" (Yin, 2014, p.114).

6   Teachers' Beliefs and EIL Practices

6.1   English is "the Language of Powerful Nations": Soojin's Conflicted Beliefs about EIL

Soojin regarded English as "a tool of communication among people with diverse cultures, which is for all people." She believed that other languages did not hold the same status as English in a global society. She described her views in detail:

> …if you want to communicate in Korean (in a global community), Korea should become a powerful nation like the United States. Korea is a small country, with a small population. We lack resources, too. Thus, we have been affected by other, more powerful countries, for a long time. Thus, we couldn't help but use English, which is the language of powerful nations. (Excerpts from interview 2:329)

Soojin believed that learning American standardized English was important for her students who "rarely had a chance to interact with English speakers or use English materials out of the school" and "only a few students had experience going abroad…". She also preferred native-English-speaking teachers (NESTs) from Inner circle countries as her co-instructors, because she was concerned that her students may consider local English varieties, such as 'Mexican English' as a standard if they only meet a Mexican English teacher at school. According to Soojin, parents of students and teachers in her school also favoured NESTs who came from specific countries such as the United States or the United Kingdom.

Soojin believed that English is derived from countries where it is used as a first language, therefore, it was "nearly impossible" for ESL/EFL learners to acquire the same English proficiency as people who were born and raised in English-speaking contexts. However, she also acknowledged the existence of English varieties and English users with different backgrounds. For a successful communication, she told her students that "not all people whom you will meet speak in British or American standardized English. So, you should open your mind toward them, try hard to listen to them and practice so that you can understand and communicate when you meet them" (Excerpts from the interview 1:114).

Soojin was mostly exposed to American standardized English first in her middle school in an English conversation class taught by NESTs from the United States and later in English classes in college and in a private English academy taught by instructors from the United States. A pivotal point that gave her an EIL perspective was when she went to Japan as an exchange student in the 11th grade, when she was first exposed to speakers of other languages and Englishes. She remembered she had somewhat negative feeling about Japanese friends' English accents at first and faced some practical challenges in communication.

> I had a Japanese friend when I did my homestay. But it was really hard to understand her English pronunciation. For example, she pronounced the word 'dream' as [dri:mu]. She kept asking me "Whatsu your drea-mu drea-mu" and it made me confused, as I wasn't able to understand her question. (Excerpts from interview 1:108)

As time passed, Soojin became familiar with Japanese English accent and she also learned that some Japanese had difficulty pronouncing a consonant which was placed after a vowel. Later when Soojin and her husband visited Cebu, the Philippines, for their honeymoon, Soojin could understand local Filipino's English; however, the Filipinos could not understand her English accent. Based on her experiences with non-Korean English speakers, Soojin noticed that there existed more than one English variety around the world, "Now I am an adult and have gone abroad a lot. Thus, I met those people around the world and I realized that there are some people who speak with different English pronunciations" (Excerpts from interview 1:114). She emphasized to students that different English accents were not a matter of right or wrong, but "differences." She elaborated,

> In an era of globalization, we do not necessarily follow American or British standardized English. There is no specific rule for this. People should be able to understand each other when they speak English in the way they learned it in Korea. In order to do so, we should be exposed to others. Once we get used to this, we can better understand them. (Excerpts from class observation on June 13)

While she emphasized having an open mind toward different English accents and varieties, Soojin hoped to acquire English fluency like a native-English-speaker. She noted that if she could turn back time, she would want to "go back to her elementary school days and go abroad [to learn to speak like a native-English-speaker]." She came to this conclusion by witnessing her classmates in college who had excellent English pronunciations due to their study abroad experiences. She also believed that ability in standardized English was an "essential requirement" to enhance one's competitive edge in the global society, and no other languages can be substituted for English. She explained, "there are so many times we need to use English in our society. English is also required for the Test of English for International Communication (TOEIC) and employment exams. However, students do not realize why they need to learn English, now" (Excerpt from interview 2:330).

6.2 Minimum Incorporation of EIL in Instruction: Soojin's Practices in Mokpo

Soojin's conflicted views about EIL were reflected in her teaching. She was well aware of her students' needs in a low-SES neighbourhood where "only a few students have gone outside of Mokpo". Like many other students living in rural areas of Korea, her students were facing difficult situations such as low-income family, single-parent homes, and so forth. Thus, not many students had experiences venturing out of their hometown, let alone going abroad. According to her, "the school is in the old downtown and many students don't even have a single English workbook. For some of them, what they learn at school is all they can learn" (Excerpts from interview 1:15). She made an effort to visit students' homes to see "if there are some students who are in need or any of them cannot talk about their personal situation. After I visited their homes, I could better understand students' background and their life" (Excerpts from interview 3:37). Soojin learned from her home visits that many students "did not have an exercise book, nor could they afford private tutoring [in English]" outside school; and unlike many affluent students in bigger cities, her students did not have opportunities to study abroad either.

Since Soojin's students did not receive extracurricular tutoring from their home, Soojin adapted the school curriculum to make up for students' lack of basic English skills. Based on her assessment of students' English level, she decided that her students needed more focus on "vocabulary learning and reading comprehension" using a government approved English textbook written by Chunjae (private publisher) based on national standards. This book was based on American English and included only a few cultural aspects of countries other than the United States. She only occasionally introduced different English varieties, intercultural communication strategies, or cultural materials that reflected different English-speaking contexts when she was able to.

Typically, Soojin began her class with a greeting in English, followed by students exchanging greetings with her in English; and they continued to carry out small talk about the weather, their feelings, and so forth. It was the only occasion on which they communicated in English during the class, except when asking or answering display questions related to reading texts or when singing pop-songs. Overall, Soojin's utterances did not exceed two sentences in English, and students' responses consisted of one or two words. According to Soojin, she could not continue speaking in English during the class because her students could not understand and therefore, she did not implement English-medium instruction. She explained, "these students have little experience receiving private tutoring in English, and they were not exposed to English since when they were young. Some students started booing when I spoke English at the beginning of the class" (Excerpts from interview 1:253).

Soojin also spent considerable class hours on students' vocabulary learning. In each unit, she provided a workbook that included a list of English words and their meanings in Korean. She also utilized a computer application called "Class Card" for students' individualized learning of vocabularies. Using tablets provided by the school or their own smartphones, students could join the virtual class through the App hosted by Soojin, or practise the words on their own, through listening to the sounds of words, playing word-meaning matching games, or filling out the words in a sentence.

For the reading part, she conducted group work or student-led activities, rather than teacher-led lectures, because "quite a few" of her students, esp. the weaker ones, "could not handle it". To ensure students were fully involved in the classroom, Soojin often divided the text into several parts, and assigned the parts to different discussion groups. Each group then shared their discussion with others. In some reading activities, she assigned students "who were good at English" to take the lead in explaining the texts "to those who were not". Since "many students were not well prepared for the exams", Soojin and the other English teachers prepared test-prep worksheets for students before the midterm and final exams to check their reading comprehension.

Due to Soojin's focus on helping students get motivated to study English and be engaged in the class activities, teaching English from an EIL paradigm was rarely observed in her classes and when the question on non-standardized English came up, it was often compared with the standardized American English. An example was her class on June 13, 2019 when she played the audio-recording of a story in the textbook about the main character, Mario, a boy who came to Korea from Peru. After listening to Mario's voice on the recording, Soojin talked to her class about Peruvian English but by comparing it with the recording's American accent.

> Soojin: What was Mario's voice like?
> Student 1: It was a boy.
> Soojin: It was a boy. How was his pronunciation?
> Student 2: He seemed to be shy.
> Student 3: A little bit.
> Soojin: (Did he sound) like an American? He spoke English like a native speaker, like an American. By the way, if Peruvians speak English, would a Peruvian be likely to have this English pronunciation?
> S 4: No.
> A: Have you heard of English that Peruvians speak?
> Student 5: Do Peruvians speak in English?
> (Excerpts from recorded class observation on June 13, 2019)

After this short conversation comparing American and Peruvian English pronunciations, Soojin showed a 5-min YouTube video clip of an interview about Peruvian traditional musical instruments, food, and tourist attractions conducted in English between a Peruvian and a Korean with bilingual subtitles. In the follow-up interview, she explained that she decided to show this clip because the textbook talked about Mario coming from Peru, but did not provide any information about Mario's previous life in Peru or Peruvian's culture, "if (the textbook) includes cultural content that Koreans need to be cautious about in Peru or what we shouldn't do in Peru, it will be interesting to students" (Excerpts from interview 2:262).

Soojin also included some listening tests with various English pronunciations (e.g., Australian English) in her teaching besides American standardized English. She noted that students at first laughed at these English accents; however, she told them to have an open mind toward local English varieties and to avoid showing discomfort when listening to different English varieties and stated that "Korean students' English accents might sound awkward to other English speakers, too" (Excerpts from interview 1:118). However, she felt that her limited experiences with different English varieties hindered her ability to further teach from an EIL perspective. During the interview after the first observed lesson, she noted that, "I would be able to give many examples if I had many experiences, but it was difficult due to my limited experience" (Excerpts from the interview 1:227).

Even though most of her class activities were not specifically designed for building intercultural understanding and communication skills, which are key components of EIL, Soojin did, however, attend to her students' intercultural communication skills by using several instructional methods such as 'speed quiz' that required students to explain a secret word in English through using body language or 'Q & A' tasks with a native-English-speaking teacher in their school. She believed that one's non-verbal gestures, willingness to communicate, and actual communication experience with a NEST were also important for international communication. She encouraged students to give presentations about different cultures such as Peru and Mongol that covered each country's location, language, cultures, and lifestyles. Given students' low proficiency level in English, she allowed the students to present in Korean (with English PowerPoint). The other way that Soojin tried to expose students to other cultures was through encouraging them to introduce a singer from the U.S. and the U.K. including cultural background of the singer, lyrics, and key expressions used in the lyrics.

In sum, Soojin held conflicted views about EIL— believing in the power of standardized English on the one hand but having an awareness of the importance of English varieties and accents on the other hand. Her perception of her students' low English proficiency and lack of economic resources outside school also motivated her to focus on teaching standardized English following the official textbook with only minimum incorporation of EIL in instruction.

6.3   Minho's Firm Beliefs about EIL: "English as a Means of Communication"

Minho defined EIL as "a means of communication that enables people to communicate regardless of their English pronunciation and the way they work". Like Soojin, Minho was also exclusively exposed to American standardized English in his elementary and secondary education, and he tried hard to achieve a desirable American standardized English accent by watching Hollywood movies and listening to American pop songs "all the time" to immerse himself in the American culture. His view was changed in college where he enrolled in double majors in English education and international studies, which offered him various opportunities to use English as a means, not an end, to communicate with speakers of different English varieties. As a student in the Department of International Studies, which offered only English-medium courses, he studied with classmates from non-English speaking countries. Most of his professors were Koreans, and their English pronunciation was not like native-English-speakers from the Inner circle countries, but "they were fluent in English, and they were good enough to convey their content knowledge in English" (Excerpts from interview 1:38).

In addition, he had a chance to watch a TV series called 'Lost' in college; and he realized that there existed more than one English variety in the United States, too. He noted that,

> One of its characters was Korean. I mean, they were Korean Americans, an Iraqi, and a Latin American. I had never seen people with different English accents communicating in one drama before then. I was in college when I watched it and it was then that I first realized that people living in the States spoke with various accents, but they were able to communicate with each other in this way without any difficulties. (Excerpts from the interview 2:40)

These experiences enabled him to have an open mind toward English speakers of other languages, including Korean English speakers. Therefore, for Minho, English was not just a language he was interested in, but also an opportunity to communicate with people of diverse backgrounds in the world.

6.4   Embracing EIL in English Teaching: Minho's Instructional Practices

Minho fully embraced EIL in his teaching in the school. All the students were selected through a highly competitive admission process, through which applicants were evaluated in academic records (which required As in all subjects), personal statements, interviews, and entrance examinations. Most of Minho's students had overseas studying or living experience or graduated from international schools in Korea, and therefore had very high proficiency in English. One of his students even "published an English storybook on Amazon" and others scored "100, 110, or 120 on TOEFL (Test of English as a Foreign Language) during middle school" (Excerpts from interview 1:13). Since his students already gained high proficiency in standardized English, he wanted to broaden their knowledge and experiences in relation to EIL. In his view, having more EIL speakers "would be good for students to communicate not only with people who use English as their mother language, but also those who have different English pronunciations" (Excerpts from the interview 1:78).

According to Minho, students in the school had many opportunities to communicate with English speakers of other languages as there was a student exchange program between a Japanese school and this school; and many international students and teachers from other countries (e.g., Thailand or Bulgaria) occasionally visited this school. The school also held an annual international symposium each summer which typically attracted hundreds of international students and teachers from many different countries (such as China, Japan and others) and offered current students in the school opportunities to volunteer as moderators, presenters and coordinators. These school activities exposed students to different English varieties and offered students opportunities to engage in intercultural communication.

Being very aware of his students' diverse learning opportunities through the school curriculum, Minho's typical class instruction aimed to connect students with real-world issues. Minho chose a philosophy book written in English as a textbook that included "main questions in each chapter; the content is an (imagined) response that philosophers are likely to utter, in regard to the main questions" (Excerpts from interview 1:91). Although the types of tasks varied, according to the content of the chapters, in general, Minho required students to (1) search for the meaning of English words and idioms, as well as the grammar points within the texts (e.g., shady demeanour, unencumbered); (2) respond to reading comprehension questions; and (3) read additional English materials related to social, political, and economic issues covered in the textbook. The assignments included the links to articles or YouTube videos that described actual cases related to social, political, and economic issues that they dealt with in the textbook. Then, students needed to summarize what they read, and give presentations about their main argument, supporting ideas, and examples in English.

In addition to these real-world connections, Minho also aligned the teaching of linguistic knowledge and communication skills with issues he anticipated might emerge in students' intercultural communication with EIL speakers in school events. He taught students "etiquette and manners" and "English expressions" that they could use if they did not understand foreign friends' English pronunciations, such as their Japanese or Chinese names. Each year in preparation for the annual symposium, Minho showed a recorded video of the event from a previous year, to expose students to different English varieties.

He noticed that there were some cases in which the students had the stereotypical thinking that "all foreigners are open-minded" which he thought "was not a matter of English language (by itself)". He believed that "historically, there were still some sensitive issues that were interrelated…" and "Regardless of whether it (i.e., yellow dust from China) was scientifically correct or wrong, it could cause some trouble." (Excerpts from interview 1:118).

To connect students to the real world, he decided to show students a movie called "Crash", "because it not only dealt with social and moral issues such as prejudice and discrimination, but also linguistic aspects". Through the movie, Minho exposed students to the different English accents spoken by African Americans, Latino Americans, Arab Americans, and Asian Americans while discussing the issue of discrimination in America. Minho engaged the students in discussions of specific scenes or characters, with regard to how each group of people was depicted in the movie, for example, "the blacks are criminals", "they didn't tip well", "I'm gonna call the immigration officer" (Asian women threatening a Latino American), and so forth. He posited that students should be aware of the existence of different English varieties and prejudices against English speakers who had different ethnic, linguistic, and cultural backgrounds as "some people experienced unfair treatment due to (racial) prejudice, or others suffered as people had prejudice toward them" (Excerpts from the interview 2:38).

Minho noted that during their last study-abroad trip to Singapore, both he and his students experienced difficulties in understanding Singaporean English. To further help students understand different English varieties and gain intercultural communication strategies, Minho used several teaching materials that reflected EIL communications in various English-speaking contexts. Specifically, he used the YouTube videos and the book, *Born a Crime*, by Trevor Noah, a comedian from South Africa. He explained his choice of these materials for teaching from EIL perspective.

> Under the policy of apartheid in South Africa, it was a crime for white people to marry black people. But his father was white, and his mother was black. So, (the book) described the discrimination he experienced. By the way, he is a stand-up comedian, and he is great at imitating others…He is specialized in (imitating other) "languages". I mean, he is really good at imitating German English accents, French or Russian English accents, as well as African English accents…I thought it would be good to explain about (different English varieties). Thus, I showed the video and explained why these people pronounce English words this way. (Excerpts from interview 1:106)

However, it is also important to note that even though Minho fully embraced EIL in his teaching, the examples he provided were mostly associated with the United States. When asked about the reason, Minho explained,

> I guess that it is a limitation of my knowledge. I used to explain to students something that I was familiar with… I was not interested in the United Kingdom (before), nor did I have living experience there. So, without having any experience, I studied (English) through books. I was also mostly exposed to American (culture), and more interested in (American) politics and cultures. (Excerpts from the interview 3:32)

7 Discussion

Soojin and Minho's stories of (not) teaching EIL in two distinct school contexts suggest that both the teachers' own personal and professional experiences with EIL as well as their students' SES and proficiency levels in English affected the extent of their EIL understanding and adoption in instruction. In both cases, the teachers' understandings of EIL were limited. Soojin's awareness of the importance of EIL mostly stemmed from her small exposure to different speakers of English (e.g., those from Japan) in her K-12 education and later to Filipino English as an adult. Minho, on the other hand, had extensive exposure to different English varieties through his college educational experiences as well as in his current school with different exchange programs and speaker events from non-English speaking countries. However, educated in the Korean context where the native-English-speakerism has been prevalent, both teachers' understandings and instructions were still aligned with this dominant English language ideology.

Soojin tried to support her low-SES students with low English proficiency to master standardized English by using a standardized textbook with only incidental inclusion of EIL in her teaching. Minho actively addressed EIL in his teaching of high-SES students with advanced English proficiency using materials about linguistic and cultural diversity in the U.S. Soojin's decision not to include EIL in her teaching was influenced by her perceptions of her low-SES students' need to prioritize standardized English while Minho's frequent inclusion of EIL in his teaching was aligned with his consideration of his high-SES students' frequent engagement in intercultural communication through school activities and events.

The two teachers' beliefs and understandings of EIL were shaped by their previous English learning experiences in which they had limited access to non-Inner Circle varieties. However, their first-hand experiences with non-English speakers in different contexts raised their awareness of alternative varieties of English used in real-life outer and expanding circle contexts (Kachru, 1985). Their experience and attitude accorded with the fact that many Asian countries usually follow the norms and standards of native-English-speaking countries, and support a biased view that NESTs are ideal and competent teachers and speakers, while non-NESTs are not (e.g., Jee & Li, 2021; Piller & Cho, 2013; Wang & Fang, 2020; Yphantides, 2013).

It is also important to note that the teachers' beliefs and experiences have influenced their teaching practices. Soojin was conflicted about EIL; and therefore, she only included EIL when she was able to. On the other hand, Minho had much acute awareness of EIL and was proactive when he applied EIL paradigms in his English classroom by introducing different English varieties and communication strategies that can be useful for intercultural communication, and by leading discussions related to social issues and languages. The two teachers' practices suggest the importance of individual teachers' experiences in relation to EIL. Not only direct interaction with EIL users, but also relevant exposure to EIL can raise teachers' awareness of different English varieties and related issues (Matsuda & Friedrich, 2012).

Lastly, an analysis of Soojin and Minho's teaching practices revealed that their instruction and inclusion of EIL was highly influenced by students' socioeconomic status and English proficiency which created another social disparity between the students in the two schools as well as in the field of Korean English education (Lee, 2016). Soojin took a more exam-oriented approach to English teaching in her classroom and set an idealized native-English-speakerism model for her low-SES students who had limited educational resources and support from home. Therefore, during the class, Soojin gave priority to bridging the perceived opportunity gaps for her students by teaching basic English skills with a focus on American standardized English which was the basis of the official English examinations in the Korean K-12 education system. Although she agreed that having EIL perspectives was important, she believed that teaching of EIL was beyond the scope of her instruction. Rather, she placed an emphasis on teaching the key components of the textbook when preparing students for their examinations. Thus, there existed little space for her to teach EIL perspectives, and her incorporation of EIL was limited.

On the other hand, Minho worked for an elite high school in which the curriculum and courses were flexible. Minho's students acquired high English proficiency; therefore, Minho could choose the topics with regard to language and social issues and address prejudices or stereotypes toward English users from non-Inner Circle countries. In addition, he actively taught EIL so that his students could better communicate with speakers of other languages through school activities.

As such, students' SES status and English proficiency affected the teachers' decisions about whether they needed to focus on the content of the textbook or use various resources to address the perceived needs and expectations of their students. As a consequence, Soojin's students' English learning experiences and opportunities to learn about EIL were restricted while Minho's students not only gained standardized English but also EIL perspectives that allowed them to become better global communicators. This educational gap yielded another layer of social disparity among students who came from low- and high-income families (Cho, 2017). In this sense, EIL teaching has become a tool of teachers' social and ideological manipulation in local school contexts in South Korea.

8 Pedagogical Implications

Our study suggests that the teachers' direct contact with and exposure to different English varieties had helped them gain an awareness of English use in the globalized world. However, the teachers' deep-rooted preferences for American standardized English and their desire to have native-English fluency had impacted their willingness and ability to include educational resources and instruction in EIL, which in turn has a profound influence on their students' experiences about EIL. The uneven coverage of EIL in different classrooms and school contexts suggests a need for systematic changes in the field of Korean ELT from a native-English-speakerism model to an EIL paradigm. Such changes must address important aspects of EIL in the school curriculum, including local English varieties, intercultural communication strategies, and cultural materials reflecting different non-native English-speaking contexts.

In addition, students' SES and English fluency affected teachers' instruction whether they focused on the content of the textbook or used various resources to satisfy students' needs and expectations. Not including EIL – inspired pedagogies further widens the educational inequity between high- and low-SES students. Professional development must be provided to teachers to equip them with a critical perspective in understanding how EIL and SES are interconnected and how they serve to widen the social and achievement gaps (Li, 2017; Li & Sah, 2020). Teacher preparation programs can systemically incorporate critical pedagogy into their curriculum to mitigate these opportunity gaps caused by socioeconomic and sociocultural factors in students' lives.

References

Ahn, H. (2014). Teachers' attitudes towards Korean English in South Korea. *World Englishes, 33*(2), 195–222. https://doi.org/10.1111/weng.12081

Ahn, H. (2017). *Attitudes to world Englishes: Implications for teaching in South Korea*. Routledge. https://doi.org/10.4324/9781315394305

Bhatt, R. M. (2001). World Englishes. *Annual Review of Anthropology, 30*, 527–550. https://doi.org/10.1146/annurev.anthro.30.1.527

Bolton, K. (2006). Varieties of World Englishes. In B. B. Kachru, Y. Kachru, & C. L. Nelson (Eds.), *The Handbook of world Englishes* (pp. 289–312). Wiley-Blackwell. https://doi.org/10.1002/9780470757598.ch17

Braun, V., & Clarke, V. (2013). *Successful qualitative research: A practical guide for beginners*. Sage.

Canagarajah, A. S. (2006). Changing communicative needs, revised assessment objectives: Testing English as an international language. *Language Assessment Quarterly, 3*(3), 229–242. https://doi.org/10.1207/s15434311laq0303_1

Canagarajah, A. S. (2012). Teacher development in a global profession: An autoethnography. *TESOL Quarterly, 46*(2), 258–279. https://doi.org/10.1002/tesq.18

Cho, J. (2017). *English language ideologies in Korea*. Springer. https://doi.org/10.1007/978-3-319-59018-9

Friedrich, P. (2012). EFL, intercultural communication and the strategic aspect of communicative competence. In A. Matsuda (Ed.), *Principles and practices of teaching English as an international language* (pp. 44–54). Multilingual Matters. https://doi.org/10.21832/9781847697042-005

Galloway, N. (2017). *Global Englishes and change in English language teaching: Attitudes and impact*. Routledge. https://doi.org/10.4324/9781315158983

Galloway, N., & Numajiri, T. (2020). Global Englishes language teaching: Bottom-up curriculum implementation. *TESOL Quarterly, 54*(1), 118–145. https://doi.org/10.1002/tesq.547

Jee, Y., & Li, G. (2021). The ideologies of English as foreign language (EFL) educational policies in Korea: The case of teacher recruitment and teacher education. In K. Raza, C. Coombe, & D. Reynolds (Eds.), *Policy development in TESOL and multilingualism: Past, present and the way forward* (pp. 119–133). Springer. https://doi.org/10.1007/978-981-16-3603-5_10

Kachru, B. (1985). Standards, codification and sociolinguistic realism: English language in the outer circle. In R. Quirk & H. Widdowson (Eds.), *English in the world: Teaching and learning the language and literatures* (pp. 11–36). Cambridge University Press.

Lee, C. H. (2016). *Language ideological approaches to English education in Korea: A sociolinguistic perspective*. (Dissertation, The University of Arizona). Retrieved May 20, 2020, from https://arizona.openrepository.com/handle/10150/612585

Lee, J. A. (2010). Korean elementary school teachers' attitudes toward the English language. *English Language Teaching, 22*(4), 25–51. https://doi.org/10.17936/PKELT.2010.22.4.002

Li, G. (2017). Preparing culturally and linguistically competent teachers for EIL education. *TESOL Journal, 8*(2), 250–276. https://doi.org/10.1002/tesj.322

Li, G., & Sah, P. (2020). Critical pedagogy for preservice teacher education: An agenda for a plurilingual reality. In S. Steinberg et al. (Eds.), *Handbook of critical pedagogy* (pp. 884–898). Sage. https://doi.org/10.4135/9781526486455

Matsuda, A., & Friedrich, P. (2012). Selecting an instructional variety for an EIL curriculum. In A. Matsuda (Ed.), *Principles and practices of teaching English as an international language* (pp. 17–27). Multilingual Matters. https://doi.org/10.21832/9781847697042-003

Matsuda, A., & Matsuda, P. (2018). Teaching English as an international language: A WE-informed paradigm for English language teaching. In E. L. Low & A. Pakir (Eds.), *World Englishes: Re-thinking paradigms* (pp. 66–74). Routledge. https://doi.org/10.4324/9781315562155

McKay, S. L. (2018). English as an international language: What it is and what it means for pedagogy. *RELC Journal, 49*(1), 9–23. https://doi.org/10.1177/0033688217738817

Merriam, S. B., & Tisdell, E. J. (2016). *Qualitative research: A guide to design and implementation* (4th ed.). Jossey Bass.

Miles, M. B., Huberman, A. M., & Saldana, J. (2014). *Qualitative data analysis: A methods source book*. Sage.

Nam, T. (2012). *Youngeo gyegeubsahoe*영어 계급 사회 [English as a class marker]. Spring of May.

Park, J. S.-Y. (2009). *The local construction of a global language: Ideologies of English in South Korea*. Mouton de Gruyter. https://doi.org/10.1515/9783110214079

Phillipson, R. (1992). *Linguistic imperialism*. Oxford University Press.

Phillipson, R. (2010). *Linguistic imperialism continued*. Routledge. https://doi.org/10.4324/9780203857175

Piller, I. (2015). Language ideologies. In K. Tracy, C. Ilie, & T. Sandel (Eds.), *The international encyclopedia of language and social interaction* (Vol. 2, pp. 918–927). Wiley. https://doi.org/10.1002/9781118611463.wbielsi140

Piller, I., & Cho, J. (2013). Neoliberalism as language policy. *Language in Society, 42*(1), 23–44. https://doi.org/10.1017/s0047404512000887

Ra, J. (2019). Exploring the spread of English language learning in South Korea and reflections of the diversifying sociolinguistic context for future English language teaching practices. *Asian Englishes, 21*(3), 305–319. https://doi.org/10.1080/13488678.2019.1581713

Sharifian, F. (2009). English as an international language: An overview. In F. Sharifian (Ed.), *English as an international language: Perspectives and pedagogical issues* (pp. 1–18). Multilingual Matters. https://doi.org/10.21832/9781847691231-004

Shim, Y. (2015). Korean EFL teachers' perceptions of world Englishes. *Korean Journal of Applied Linguistics, 31*(1), 149–172. https://doi.org/10.17154/kjal.2015.03.31.1.149

Silverstein, M. (1979). Language structure and linguistic ideology. In R. Clyn, W. Hanks, & C. Hofauer (Eds.), *The elements: A parasession on linguistic units and levels* (pp. 193–247). Chicago Linguistic Society.

Stake, R. E. (2005). Qualitative case studies. In N. K. Denzin & Y. S. Lincoln (Eds.), *The sage handbook of qualitative research* (4th ed., pp. 445–466). Sage.

Statistics Korea. (2019). 시도별 지역내총생산 *Sidobyul Jiyeoknae Chongsaengsan* [Gross regional domestic product]. Retrieved October 20, 2022 from https://kosis.kr/statHtml/statHtml.do?orgId=101&tblId=DT_1C81&checkFlag=N

Statistics Korea. (2020). 학교급별 사교육비 총액 *Hakgyogeuppyeol sakyukbi chongaek* [Sum of private education expenses according to school level]. Retrieved October 20, 2022 from https://kosis.kr/statHtml/statHtml.do?orgId=101&tblId=DT_1PE003&vw_cd=MT_ZTITLE&list_id=O15_7&seqNo=&lang_mode=ko&language=kor&obj_var_id=&itm_id=&conn_path=MT_ZTITLE

Sung, K. (2019). Korean elementary pre-service teachers' experiences of learning and using English and attitudes toward world Englishes. *The Journal of Asia TEFL, 16*(1), 67–90. https://doi.org/10.18823/asiatefl.2019.16.1.5.67

Tollefson, J. W. (2000). Language ideology and language education. In J. Shaw, D. Lubelska, & M. Noullet (Eds.), *Partnership and interaction: Proceedings of the fourth international conference on language and development* (pp. 43–52) Asian Institute of Technology.

Wang, L., & Fang, F. (2020). Native-speakerism policy in English language teaching revisited: Chinese university teachers' and students' attitudes towards native and non-native English-speaking teachers. *Cogent Education, 7*(1778374), 1–22. https://doi.org/10.1080/2331186X.2020.1778374

Yin, R. (2003). *Case study research: Design and methods* (3rd ed.). Sage.

Yin, R. (2014). *Case study research: Design and methods* (5th ed.). Sage.

Yoon, H. (2007). Pre-service teachers' perceptions of world Englishes: Implications for teacher training. *Studies in English Language and Literature, 49*(1), 171–190. https://doi.org/10.18853/JJELL.2007.49.1.010

Yphantides, J. (2013). Native-speakerism through English-only policies: Teachers, students and the changing face of Japan. In S. A. Houghton & D. J. Rivers (Eds.), *Native-speakerism in Japan: Intergroup dynamics in foreign language education* (pp. 207–216). Multilingual Matters. https://doi.org/10.21832/9781847698704-019

Youngeun Jee is a Ph.D. candidate in the Department of Language and Literacy Education at the University of British Columbia in Canada. Her research interests include critical pedagogies and second language teacher education. Email: yejee0508@gmail.com

Guofang Li is a Professor and Tier 1 Canada Research Chair in Transnational/Global Perspectives of Language and Literacy Education of Children and Youth at the University of British Columbia, Canada. Her program of research focuses on bilingualism and biliteracy development, pre- and in-service teacher education, and language & educational policies & practices in globalised contexts. Email: guofang.li@ubc.ca

Intercultural Competence – A Never-Ending Journey

Zarina Subhan

Abstract This chapter provides a conceptual framework of the journey of English from a language of colonial imperialism to one of a lingua franca (ELF) used by individuals as a tool for transcultural communication. Distinctions are drawn between the use of English as a neo-colonial medium of transmission of an assumed Eurocentric culture and the reality of many non-native speakers of English. The author argues that for intercultural competence to occur, a critical and an intersectional approach is required to equip students and teachers with the necessary skills for the use of English as a lingua franca. The aim is also to highlight how the colonial origins of ELF gave English a power that is now shared with the global majority user, yet the cultural content does not meet their needs. Hence, the main argument is that a more inclusive and deeper cultural representation approach is essential for the promotion of effective teaching and the fostering of a more equitable intercultural competence in ELT textbooks, using a kind of 'lingua culture'. A disruptive process of usualisation of culture and a more balanced and less stereotypical representation of otherness is vital and necessary to help educate students into becoming responsible global citizens who can empathise with one another on real-world issues.

Keywords Imperialism · Lingua franca · Eurocentric · Intercultural competence · Lingua culture · Usualisation · Otherness

1 Introduction

As a descendant of Indian immigrants, growing up in 70s and 80s Britain, I often found myself feeling embarrassed. Alagiah (2003, p. 36) describes it as "the tug of war between heritage and assimilation", which I felt for example over my mother's idea of party food or decision to wear a sari when out and about. Britain, at that

Z. Subhan (✉)
Independent Scholar, San José, Costa Rica

© The Author(s), under exclusive license to Springer Nature Switzerland AG 2023
A. Sahlane, R. Pritchard (eds.), *English as an International Language Education*, English Language Education 33,
https://doi.org/10.1007/978-3-031-34702-3_25

time, had no space for being who you are because assimilation was about becoming invisible. Today, my mother's ability to create the perfect pakora and scones would be equally celebrated on a cooking TV series or in UK primary schools and gives me great pride. To many this illustrates multiculturalism in Britain, as does the existence of the first British-Indian Prime Minister of the UK. However, 'exotic' foods are perhaps more accepted than the people who introduced them to British shores. For example, in the aftermath of the Euro 2020 final match, the English footballers, Marcus Rashford, Jadon Sancho, and Bukayo Saka experienced extreme hate and racist abuse for missing their penalties. It would seem that while being different is very much part of British twenty-first century life, making mistakes is not yet acceptable for a person of colour.

Riz Ahmed has made his name as an actor despite the reality that films with primary and secondary Muslim characters are portrayed as immigrants, or refugees, who speak little or no English. He stated that,

> In the top 200 films over the last few years, Muslims have only 1.6 % of speaking roles .... What makes it worse is that over 90 % of films don't have any Muslim characters whatsoever. But when you do have Muslim characters, a tiny number of them, three quarters of the time, are portrayed as either perpetrators of or victims of violence. (Ahmed, 2021, YouTube video, 11:19)

After decades of textbooks having been Eurocentric, they now have more representation of different cultures, but the manner in which they are represented may be as misleading as Muslim characters are depicted in some Hollywood films.

This chapter aims to illustrate why having intercultural competence should not only entail knowledge of other ways of being, but also needs to embody the skills of how to interact respectfully across cultures, while removing colonial aspects of power relations. It will support the idea that fixed cultures being taught to English language students is outdated and that the idea of a "lingua culture" is more useful to users of English as a lingua franca (ELF) in today's globalised context (Taylor, 2021, p. 227). It will also promote, as Adib (2021) suggests, that instead of a focus on a culture of a nation, a broader focus could produce citizens of the world, which would allow the integration of culture with real-world relevance in topics such as climate change and other social inequalities.

2 Language of Power

Colonialisation brought about an imbalance of power and economic wealth that is still very much in existence today through the consequent power relations it has established. The colonisers created the social inequalities that allowed them easy access to the resources they required throughout their empires. This oppression allowed them to superimpose their language onto those colonised, especially those considered worthy of learning the language due to their higher class and perceived ability to work in the civil service. Such colonial policies not only aided the discrimination between the elite classes native to the country and those of a lower working class, but also devalued local languages. In his Minute on Indian Education Macaulay said:

> All parties seem to be agreed on one point, that the dialects commonly spoken among the natives of this part of India contain neither literary nor scientific information, and are moreover so poor and rude that, until they are enriched from some other quarter, it will not be easy to translate any valuable work into them. It seems to be admitted on all sides, that the intellectual improvement of those classes of the people who have the means of pursuing higher studies can at present be affected only by means of some language not vernacular amongst them. (1935, Clause 8)

The colonisers saw it as a duty to educate their subordinates to lift them out of ignorance, which their own languages were not considered capable of doing. In many ways, it became a self-fulfilling prophecy because those who learnt English had access to higher education in English, which raised their potential further for increasing their earning capacity and their access to the colonial rulers. This Indian upper class became known as the 'brown sahibs', mimicking the white colonisers and filling the elite vacuum once the colonisers had left India. A secondary influence on the education of those colonised by the British was through the religious scholars, who preached in English to the subjugated populations. As Curtis explained, the links between the established church and education were often strong. For example, "most Hong Kong universities were founded by Christian missionaries" (2019, p. 15).

Today there are 22 state languages in India, which include Hindi but not English in the count because it is not a language of any single state. However, Hindi and English remain the official languages being used in Parliament, for communications between the central and state governments, and in the high and supreme courts. Due to India's diversity and the politically delicate nature of language policy, a single language is not considered representative of the historical, socio-political, and cultural aspects of the country as a whole. Therefore, India to date does not have an assigned national language (Kalia, 2021).

In Uganda, 30% of its people speak Swahili in comparison to 100% of neighbouring Kenyans. This is also a political decision because the Ugandan dictator Idi Amin reportedly distrusted any official educated in England who spoke better English than himself. Consequently, Amin had such officials removed from government offices as well as insisting that all official duties were conducted in Swahili. Due to Swahili being associated with the dictatorship, Ugandans chose English over Swahili as their official language while continuing to speak their personal tribal languages (Ellams, 2016). English, therefore, became a useful and safe alternative that helped to avert the power struggles between languages in some of the ex-colonies. English also offered great employment and social mobility opportunities for those who could afford quality higher education, both in the UK and in the post-colonial peripheries.

3   Language and Culture

Because India chose English as one of its official languages, (Article 343 of the Indian Constitution- Official Language of the Union) it now has the highest number of English speakers in the world, when one includes primary English and ELF users. According to worldpopulationreview.com, this translated to 1,393,409,038 users and was twenty times the number of English speakers in Britain in 2021. The fact that English has become such a successful lingua franca means there are more countries using ELF than there are countries using English as a primary language. Moreover, given the fact that the majority of the students of English in the world speak English as a second or additional language and due to the global widespread use of ELF, most learners of English in non-Anglophone countries may only require English to communicate with other non-native speakers (NNSs), both nationally and internationally. As stated in a British Council report, "non-native speakers now far outnumber native speakers – already at an estimated ration of 4:1, which can only grow. Our own forecast is for double digit growth in the demand for English" (2013, p. 4.)

The culture traditionally associated with English was that of a traditional Britain with its typical red post and telephone boxes. Through learning the language, one could access the culture, which in turn enabled one to communicate better with the native, primary user of English. Or so the thinking went. However, if English language learners are more likely to communicate with those from a variety of cultures and other NNSs, it must be questioned whether the focus should remain on cultural traditions of the English-only speaking countries.

Due to the idea of World Englishes, there is no longer a single 'correct' model of English. Similarly, there should not be a single cultural model either. Yet when 'other' cultures are explored in English language teaching books they sometimes skim the surface of practices in 'other' parts of the world. In subtle ways a Eurocentric image of English speakers is portrayed as being central, with anything else being treated as different and distinct. This could be viewed as 'normal' and 'abnormal', or 'us' and 'them', which can (indirectly) project a desirable lifestyle or one to emulate. Matsumoto (2006) points out that ELT materials simultaneously present culture "in very simplistic, stereotypic ways, as if to promote an ideology of differences" (p. 42).

4   The Power of 'Othering'

Being social animals, we use language essentially as a communicative tool to help manage relationships in different spheres of social exchanges. The ease with which we move from sphere to sphere depends on our ability to convey messages about who we are, our intentions, needs, attitudes, values, and key beliefs. Based on this information we gauge with which groups of people we are most likely to have affinity and with whom to form stronger or closer ties. Affirming such social ties requires more than the ability to simply learn patterns of language, thus successful communication requires a careful calculation of not only the choice of words, but also the nuances, gestures, levels of politeness, and status.

This recognition of the crossover of societal norms and language is what gave birth to sociolinguistics, which looks closely at how people manage their interactions, depending on the group they belong to. It delves into language policies, effects of nationalism, ethnicity, gender, occupations, level of education, race, and the social groups one spends time in. Here we will consider this interaction of such differing areas as differing cultures and therefore consider the intersectionality that exists in the use of ELF.

Unlike ELF, Teaching English to Speakers of Other Languages (TESOL) comes from the perspective of users of English as a primary 'native' language and considers all languages apart from English as 'other'. As Liddicoat and Scarino state, "It is a positioning in terms of what the learner is not" (2013, p. 52). Decades after the idea of World Englishes was first mooted, ELT textbooks still seem to lack an acceptance of alternative worlds of English-speaking cultures. This may have its origins in the world of UK English language schools, whose students benefit from considerable cultural input about life in the UK because it provides them with the necessary skills to negotiate their temporary stay there.

Initially, the kind of students who would have been able to travel to experience English language in its home country were those from other parts of Europe. Tomalin and Stempleski (1993) believed the rise in economic wealth of countries outside of Europe to be one of the factors that brought about a greater need to explore and explain cultural differences in detail. One reason why they claimed the study of cross-cultural interaction became more important was that countries which are outside of Europe had the economic power to study in the 'ELT heartlands'. "Countries such as Japan, Korea, Malaysia, Taiwan, and Thailand have very different traditions and cultural behaviours from the traditional ELT heartlands of Europe and North America" (Tomalin & Stempleski, 1993, p. 5). Hence with more students from 'different' cultural traditions having the economic power to study in Anglophone countries, the need to explain and 'teach' about the cultural differences became greater.

It can, therefore, be argued that it was the market created by the language learners visiting the UK from other parts of Europe that originally gave rise to the ELT publishers' focus on European culture in their books, with a substantial layer of British culture built in. However, as Tomalin and Stempleski (1993) reported, those visiting the UK for language study have become ever more international, and yet there is still a tendency to focus on the culture of the "host" country (p. 6).

Despite this functioning beneficially for the language schools that 'host' visiting students to the UK, Ireland, North America, Australia, and New Zealand, it cannot be defined as 'cross-cultural' awareness. It is very much a one-way cultural direction that assumes the onus for becoming more culturally aware is only on the students learning English as an additional language. A further criticism of this type of cross-cultural teaching is that culture should not be tied only to countries or nationalities, because "they simplify and fixate individual categories that are expected to determinate behaviour" (Dervin & Jacobsson, 2021, p. 19).

According to Treaty 018, European Cultural Convention (1954), the Council of Europe (CoE) created criteria in their language frameworks that were designed for all European countries, to encourage their people to be curious and learn about each other's cultures, traditions, and languages. The treaty was created to promote tolerance, understanding, harmony in Europe, and prevent any return to the horrors of war and hatred between its people. Simultaneously, ex-British colonies around the world were clamouring for or dealing with independence and the legacy of the British administration systems, all of which had been in the coloniser's language of English. As discussed, for a variety of reasons, many post-colonial countries like India and Uganda decided to continue to use the language of their colonisers. The newly independent ex-colonies therefore had English in use, often as an official language or a lingua franca, in bilingual or multilingual settings, as well as in the state and private education systems. Therefore, ELT was part of the norm in the general schooling system, either through EMI or as a subject (Migge & Léglise, 2007).

There were British subjects who decided to remain in the former colonies, some of them working in education or in the church, so primary users of English were not uncommon to find after independence. Unlike in the European settings, where travel to the UK provided more probable contact with British English speakers and their language, the ex-British colonial countries had real use of English outside the teaching of the language as a subject. As a result, English in the outer circle countries has evolved into indigenised varieties of English, which are now recognised as World Englishes. "World English has emerged because its users have changed the language as they have spread it" (Brutt-Griffler, 2002, pp. vii–viii).

With the ever-increasing number of people using ELF, it is imperative that publishers carefully consider if the target users still need an emphasis on British culture or if it is time to have a less Eurocentric outlook. However, it appears as if the fact is being ignored that English has become a world language and is being used by millions without any association to an Anglo-American and Western culture. For example, getting students to think about foreign holiday destinations can be, at the very least, embarrassing and at the most insensitive when faced with students who do not have the disposable income, or whose families do not have working conditions for such pleasures. Many people do not earn sufficient money to exchange into a currency that would afford them a holiday abroad. Even those with the economic capacity may not necessarily have the ease of travel due to visa, passport, and entry restrictions. There are also differing ideas of travel which may not equate with pleasure or rest, besides the economic and political barriers to the possibility of travel, that may reduce the likelihood of having such experiences. Some topics can also contribute to an assumption that Eurocentric practices are the 'norm', that they should be emulated, or that everyone has the same kind of life experiences.

5   Equity in an Unequal World

In any kind of teaching, language or otherwise, we cannot assume that all students share the same life experiences and context, or learn the exact same thing at the exact same time simply because it has been taught. If students are only exposed to images and ideas that they cannot associate with, then it is going to interfere with the extent to which they can engage with the material. Therefore, it is a disservice if all language students of English are offered the same kind of material that is primarily aimed at white, European audiences (Victoria & Sangiamchit, 2021).

Major ELT publications are commonly revised to suite cultural and religious tastes in the Middle East, which illustrates that it is not an impossible task. These are not textbooks designed for specific needs of a state school curriculum, but rather well-known publications in the ELT world such as (New) Headway or Q Skills by OUP and Life Series by National Geographic. Although it may seem a perfectly sensible approach to respectfully consider certain traditions, situations, while avoiding sensitivities, an ELT author contended that restrictions on topics made ELT bland. "All we're left with is the environment as a topic, or eating in a restaurant – but then you could never have a wine bottle on the table" (Flood, 2015). A British right-wing tabloid newspaper reported how a Conservative Party member of parliament (MP), who is known for being anti-woke and anti-feminist, complained that making such changes to textbooks was nonsensical and blamed it on political correctness.

The author's viewpoint of 'restrictions', and the MP's argument about 'political correctness' illustrate very clearly a privileged perspective of having the right (and power) to be able to promote a way of life that seems 'normal' in the UK to wherever one wishes. It implies that British culture is unconditionally tied to the English language, with the assumption that if one is to use the language, one also needs to know about the culture of English-speaking countries. Such perspectives may be considered as imposing one's culture on all the rest and are termed ethnocentric. In other words, ethnocentrism occurs when someone is unable to visualise things outside of their culture and they describe their world as being organised into 'us' and 'them', "where one's own culture is superior and other cultures are inferior" (Hammer et al., 2003, p. 424). Dervin and Jacobsson (2021) suggest that the 'us' and 'them' duality tends to emphasise the "mysteries of the Other" (p. 27). The Developmental Model of Intercultural Sensitivity (DMIS) visually illustrates how people may interpret cultural differences (see Fig. 1; Hammer et al., 2003, p. 424).

Fig. 1 The developmental model of intercultural sensitivity

The assumption that the only place you could practise speaking 'real' English is in the UK, or in another 'native' speaker country, is one such example of an ethnocentric perspective. It is also a view that supports the acclaimed musician, Nirtin Sawney's description of his schooling in the UK, "I went through school with an uneasy suspicion that I was inferior" (2003, p. 34). According to Hammer et al.'s model, ethnorelativism accepts that a culture is one of many that are all equal and together they form a complex worldview. This is the reality today, where apart from the countries using English as a primary (Inner circle) or an official state language (Outer circle), much of the rest of the world (Expanding circle) requires the study of English language to enter the global market, access engineering, medical, or scientific publications, present their ideas on the global stage, compete in the sporting world, or work in tourism or business. There needs to be a greater acceptance of alternative worldviews, values, and beliefs with a corresponding respectfulness towards such differences. While not denying that we all have essentially the same universal needs and basic values, as enshrined by the UN, it cannot be ignored that different groups have developed in different contexts, and thus have developed a characteristic flavour of culture – rather like differing accents have been formed over time by communities of people that were limited to different regions because of the geographical lay of the land, resulting in distinct accents, but all of them still speaking the same language.

It is perhaps worth questioning if methodologies, images, topics, culture, and attitudes suit the taste of the Global North because it is in control of the ELT market. Nero (2019) highlights the fact that many TESOL graduate programmes, research projects, policy making, and teaching methods and materials emanate from the US and UK. She states that the ELT industry is "run by mostly White professionals, even though English around the world is more widely used by people of color" (p. 28). In the same vein, Kiczkowiak (2022) analysed 28 coursebooks published by Oxford University Press, National Geographic Learning, Macmillan, Pearson, and Cambridge University Press. His research of 'nativeness' and ethnicity revealed how out of 133 authors, "the vast majority of CBAs [Coursebook Authors] (94%) are white 'native speakers' from the UK or the US" (p. 14).

Hence, ethnorelativism means that ELT publishers need to ensure that authors of English language textbooks are more diverse and able to produce teaching materials that are acceptable to all of their audiences, not only to learners from the Anglocentric contexts. Dervin and Jacobsson (2021) believe that an "un-rethink" (p. 7) is necessary when it comes to a critical look at language and interculturality, and an exploration of how varied centres of knowledge can be represented. However, Kiczkowiak (2022) believes that little will change until coursebook editors are less white and Eurocentric. Publishers therefore not only need to ensure that their materials promote ethnorelativism and are less Eurocentric, but also need to ensure their writers and editors are chosen from a more diverse and international pool.

6   Intersectionality in Language Use

Intersectionality is the individual experience on a daily occurrence that is influenced by a number of factors that coexist within society's perception of that individual. As Collins and Bilge (2020) stated, it can be used as an analytical tool in that

> intersectionality views categories of race, class, gender, sexuality, nation, ability, ethnicity, and age – among others – as interrelated and mutually shaping one another. Intersectionality is a way of understanding and explaining complexity in the world, in people, and in human experiences. (p. 2)

Therefore, social inequality does not equally affect women, children, people of colour, those with disabilities, transgendered people, undocumented populations, or Indigenous groups. The complexity of social context (e.g., having brown skin, being a woman, but speaking English fluently) has given me pause for thought on numerous occasions, both in and out of ELT contexts. It is plain to see that certain assumptions are made about me before I speak, be it in multicultural Britain or elsewhere. For example, outside of the UK, I am often asked several times and in different ways where I am originally from because my interlocutor does not consider the UK to be a satisfactory answer. On one occasion, while I was the director of a British Council teacher training project for Peruvian state school English teachers, a visiting colleague from the UK asked me where I had learnt my English because it was very good for a Peruvian! Usually, the act of speaking, depending on whether it is in English or not, can easily reveal my nationality. However, on this occasion it did not. Kubota explains that "English language is traditionally linked to Whiteness due to its origin and spread through settler colonialism. Native speakers of standardized varieties of English are often imagined as White people" (2021, p. 239).

Such experiences highlight how power relations influence social interaction in societies, whether they are diverse or not. Being born in the UK provides me the privilege of being able to use English as a first language, allowing me a profession in ELT that has taken me to several countries, which many non-native ELT professionals might not have the advantage of visiting. Therefore, my presence as a language expert in non-English speaking countries places me in a higher position than local non-native speaker (NNS) professionals due to the variety of English I am able to speak. However, I am often not the expert they have envisaged and when being 'judged' by, or compared to, a White ELT professional abroad my position in the hierarchy is assumed to be below them. It is, therefore, fair to say that the perception of an ELT professional is mostly of a white individual and that perception automatically places me in a lower position of 'nativeness' when it comes to being 'an expert' in the field.

Hence, in the ELT world we can add location, colonial thinking, citizenship, situation, and the contextual environment to the already complex layers of intersectionality. ELF is used by many people who constantly need to navigate such intricacies of intersectionality to try to improve their human experiences and opportunities. Myers describes an Implicit Association Test which was designed to measure people's unconscious bias. It has been completed by millions online and revealed that for most respondents' "default is white. We like white people. We prefer white" (2014, YouTube, 05:51). Just as Aguilar (2012) suggested that systems can oppress peoples' identities and experiences, it can also be argued that ELT publishers can do likewise by the choices made to depict some cultures and exclude others from textbooks. This is something that Sahlane and Pritchard have written about at length in this volume (Chapter "Assessing Perspectives on Culture in Saudi EFL Textbook Discourse"). Thus, it is important to cast a critical eye on the choices and use of topics around or related to culture, for it can be one of few themes that bring diversity into the limelight, regardless of the culture the students are part of.

7   An Alternative Representation of 'Otherness'

It could be argued that the power of white western English language students is exacerbated by limiting race, culture, and traditions to that of holidays, travel, or food. Such representations can exoticize, or worse, denigrate the only depictions of 'other' cultures in ELT publications. A positive development would be for the ELT publishing industries to give more prominence to World Englishes. If the very existence of other varieties of indigenised and localised Englishes were acknowledged in ELT textbooks, it would send the strong message to English language learners that they are part of a global community of English speakers. It would also signal to those who speak a variety of Englishes, that theirs is a valid form of communication in English and that the so-called 'native speaker' (NS) model of English is not the only one to aspire to. To understand the linguistic undertones of the NS concept, one must appreciate their specific linguistic and cultural identity. The same can be argued for World Englishes; to understand one another on a global scale, while using ELF, one needs some understanding of the cultural context of the people with whom one is expected to communicate. Thus, more than merely acknowledging the existence of World Englishes is required; an interest in those who use English around the world also needs to be cultivated and explored in textbooks. As stated by the CoE (2008), the European Court of Human Rights has recognised that pluralism is built on "the genuine recognition of, and respect for, diversity and the dynamics of cultural traditions, ethnic and cultural identities, religious beliefs, artistic, literary and socio-economic ideas and concepts" (p. 13).

Therefore, recognising and placing a focus on cultural traditions, identities, beliefs, ideas, and concepts should not simply be viewed as engaging topics, but as a means of promoting human rights that can help to construct inclusive societies and lessen the tendency to marginalise and exclude some from mainstream society. Consequently, the subconscious 'othering' of people can give way to recognising one another as fellow citizens of a world – which we need in order to strive to make it more equitable. Thus, limiting, or at least questioning, why people are treated differently depending on their assumed social background (Dervin & Jacobsson, 2021) can encourage changes to occur in one's interactions; this may combat discrimination and social injustice.

8 Intercultural Skills and Citizenship

For those who might consider human rights to be the domain of political studies and not ELT, it must be emphasised that some years earlier, climate change was viewed in the same light, yet it is now a common topic found in many textbooks. It is also worth highlighting that when learning a language, qualities such as being open-minded, willing to enter into discussion and dialogue, and carefully listening to others' points of view are all simultaneously important to develop. In addition, if English language students are using ELF, they will find themselves in a range of positions along the scale of power relations. They will manifest either "inferiorization, denigration, marginalization, and exclusion" (Kubota, 2021, p. 239) or else the 'privileged' syndrome of prejudices, stereotypes, bullying, and intolerance.

Hence, English language teachers are in very strategic roles to enable students to become more curious about the wider world; to question cross cultural divides; to unite religious communities; and generally, to become resilient to conflicts by using dialogue to resolve them whilst preparing them with the necessary linguistic skills. In short, ELT can be used to nurture ethnorelativism. In today's world of internet exchanges, students have ample opportunity to engage with different perspectives and worldviews. Thus, their time spent on the internet could be exploited by the ELT teacher by getting them to review the websites they most visit and reflect upon whether their interactions practise open-mindedness and if they value others' comments and opinions, while being willing to respectfully disagree with their interactants. Through using their interactions, not those artificially created by their teacher, students can autonomously develop intercultural skills and citizenship for a real purpose.

As Schleicher (2018) affirms:

> Engaging with different perspectives in world views requires individuals to examine the origins and implications of others and their own assumptions. This, in turn, implies a profound respect for and interest in who the other is, their concept of reality and their perspectives. Recognising another's position or belief is not necessarily to accept that position or belief. (pp. 31–32)

9 The Teaching Materials

If there is to be equity in the teaching materials used in language teaching, then there needs to be a serious review of representation and the narratives given to the differing power relations that exist in societies both in the Global North and in the Southern Peripheries. Seburn (2021) considers the usualisation approach as one possible solution for balancing representation. It is an approach which, at its basic level, makes the images and characters ordinary and nothing special. Thus women, diverse ethnicities and genders do not necessarily have to only be famous leaders, successful, or generally high achievers. In other words, usualisation is a way of normalising the representation of marginalised communities, who are only marginalised by the majority in societies. Outside of the western world where diverse ethnicities are the global majority, students would become accustomed to seeing people like themselves being represented in their ELT textbooks and would feel more included in the world of English language learning. This would allow such students to have exposure to representations of people who, instead of being your regular Joe Bloggs, are your regular Jamila Bibis.

As Seburn (2021) points out, the increased presence of wider groups of otherness increases the narrative and variety of voices, which result in a subsequent broadening of perspectives that students are exposed to. That does not mean we must become politically correct, rather it would mean that students receive a fairer representation of the world and the people that live in it. Teaching materials may go some way toward lessening the probability of having fixed stereotypes about people and countries, and deconstructing "the Eurocentric and oftentimes racist history of our field" (Dervin & Jacobsson, 2021, p. 37). Myers said, "diversity is being asked to the party; but inclusion is being asked to dance" (Women's Leadership Forum, YouTube, 2015, 05:22.)

This illustrates the difference between simply having diverse people's images in textbooks and actually engaging in the topic of diversity, equity, and inclusion (DEI). Simply having a quota for the number of times 'other' faces appear in a textbook does not suffice; how they are characterised is just as important. It is important to represent fairly without feeding existing biases or negative narratives about different groups, while being conscious of the language used. As Adichie underlines,

> If I had not grown up in Nigeria, and if all I knew about Africa were from popular images, I too would think that Africa was a place of beautiful landscapes, beautiful animals, and incomprehensible people, fighting senseless wars, dying of poverty and AIDS, unable to speak for themselves and waiting to be saved by a kind, white foreigner. (TED Global, 2009, 05:56)

If the ELT publishing industry accepts the fact that the majority of English speakers in the world are using the language as a lingua franca, then they need to take on the responsibility for preparing them for use of ELF in the real world. Therefore, it is unsatisfactory to focus on only the images used in teaching resources; textbook designers and publishers also need to reassess cultural dimensions in textbook design, such as the dialogues, scenarios, names used in texts, listening activities, their associated exercises, the assumptions made, and the unconscious biases fed through the focus of topics discussed and explored. Such activities can question what is and is not socially or personally acceptable, as well as encourage reflection and introspection of why those views are held; it can help to address the "fluidity of culture while delinking from Eurocentric structures" (Dervin & Jacobsson, 2021, p. 47).

10   Culture in ELT

As culture and language have always been intertwined, culture is the perfect vessel to provide some reflection about one's own perspectives while learning about those of others. As Adib (2021) reminds us, contact and communication are easier than they have ever been between people with different linguistic and cultural traditions. Subsequently, the increased access to digital technology and social media provides a greater relevance for students to consider their cross-cultural communications. Educators can therefore assist students to reflect on their experiences and online intercultural exchanges in English through the lens of culture (Victoria & Sangiamchit, 2021).

Authors and publishers of ELT books need to ensure that culture is taught in a relevant manner that piques interest so that students truly engage and learn from the content matter. I once, while observing a class, witnessed a teacher in rural Nepal struggle with teaching a lesson about computers. Neither the teacher nor his class had ever seen a computer, as they lived in a region without electricity, yet they were expected to be able to decipher what a cursor, central processing unit, and monitor were. When the teacher reached the part about the 'mouse,' he was completely at a loss, and frustratingly asked a student to look it up in the dictionary. It was 2002 and the dictionary would have been from the 90s at least, so it only defined the furry kind of mouse with a pointed snout and long tail!

The textbook in question was a state secondary school English book that had been written for the Nepali Ministry of Education by a western ELT author. Those who worked in the ministry should clearly have been more aware, but the ministry as well as its employees are based in the capital city of Kathmandu and rural life is almost as unfamiliar to many of its city dwellers as it perhaps was to the writer, who had either been commissioned to write the book or adapt it. However, it illustrates how privilege and bias are not the bastions of white western Europeans, but the intersectionality of urban/rural, gender, religion, class/caste, and consequent economic power go beyond linguistic power relations.

One would suppose, if books or resources are being designed and written for a specific learning group, such as secondary level education in a particular country, it is relatively easier to produce materials that are better suited to one cultural context than an international textbook for various regions of the world. Because of the economics of publishing, the reality is that books and resources are used by the greatest number of students from the greatest number of regions possible. However, instead of books or resources being suited to one culture or another, they should be made appealing to all. It is just as valuable for students in Hungary or Hong Kong to learn about life in the Swat Valley as it might be to learn about life in Silicon Valley. If students had such an awareness they could reflect on and question why life should be so distinct depending on where they are born; they would be able to develop a high level of empathy – an essential human and language skill.

ELF users should not consider their own culture as superior to anyone else's, or other people's culture as being strange. Thus, intercultural sensitivity involves respecting differences and tolerating 'otherness' without assuming any single culture to be one of a 'default setting'. The Organisation for Economic Cooperation and Development (OECD) emphasises the need to include citizenship alongside interculturalism.

> [S]chooling today needs to be much more about ways of thinking … and about the capacity to live in a multi-faceted world as active responsible citizens … as well as individual academic achievement, enabling students both to think for themselves, and to act for and with others. (Schleicher, 2018, p. 31)

Topics such as climate change could be viewed from differing economic perspectives, which would help foster a sense of responsibility and motivation to act on behalf of and in collaboration with others, while using ELF. This would provide a rich set of concepts around responsibilities, rights, and power relations as the backdrop to the language taught, thus producing what Carter (2005) calls 'cultural straddlers' and suggests they are the most successful in intercultural situations. Future ELF users, therefore, need to be global citizens (i.e., be able to manage themselves respectfully in intercultural situations), therefore it is essential to challenge the status quo of textbooks, resources, and teaching materials as they currently stand because, to some extent, they are helping to exaggerate the assumed rights we hold to live life in a certain way. The world is finally becoming aware of the fact that lifestyle choices of a few can have direct consequences on the lives of many in low economy societies who may suffer the devastating effects of climate emergencies. By inaction, we risk perpetuating the existing, lingering powers of colonialism, while simultaneously supporting the current hierarchy that exists and ignoring the intersectionality of power among global societies. Hence, as Kubota argues, "teachers and learners should think beyond linguistic plurality and critically reflect on how English users' race and other identities, such as gender, class and religion, shape particular power relations, which influences the nature of interactions" (2021, p. 241).

The ELT industry has a collective responsibility to ensure that students are curious about other parts of the world, other cultures and traditions, and are ready to establish relationships to get to know people from 'other' cultural backgrounds. As Myers (2014) points out,

> It's the empathy and the compassion that comes out of having relationships with people who are different from you. Something really powerful and beautiful happens … we cease to be bystanders, we become actors, we become advocates, and we become allies. (TED talk, 13:02)

11   A Way Forward

The Covid-19 pandemic has pushed us beyond our comfort zones in the world of education in a short space of time, resulting in a difficult period for many teachers who had to retrain overnight as online teachers. Educators were forced to become accustomed to and proficient in the use of a variety of digital technologies as teaching tools to deliver their classes. Such technological aids used to be viewed as 'good ideas' because few teachers could afford the time to develop the necessary skills, whereas today they have become part of the norms of online teaching. We are now in a world where hybrid classes are the 'new normal', and many institutions have developed some kind of virtual learning platform to manage announcements, distribute information, provide access to learning material, and where students can upload their work. With these platforms have come transparency and better coordination. This improved administrative system of teaching has led to teachers being (not only willing, but also) able to work more innovatively while also being more conscious of their students' economic situations, mental health, and learning needs. During such a period of adjustment, the situation is optimal for other changes to also take place, possibly the kind that Maley (1998) outlined which would provide teachers with the flexibility to choose their teaching materials and the pace at which activities are completed. The idea was to produce materials that could be picked and mixed by teachers, that together would constitute a course – rather more of a manual than a book. This kind of design enables a greater choice of directions that the teacher could take to cover the same topic, thus different teachers might choose different materials to cover the same points on the curriculum, without the fear that something had been omitted.

In today's digital reality, such ideas no longer seem quite so revolutionary because there can be a readily available bank of resources made available to teachers. Once an institution 'invests' in the 'bank' they could also buy the rights to reproduce pages and share digital versions. Schools in the Global South might prefer to produce hard copies of the teaching materials for their students to use, whereas those in the Global North might opt for digital resources. However, both sets of students would be able to cover the same topics, with possible slight variations to meet the demands of differing curricular needs, governmental policies, and cultural sensibilities. Similarly, for students who do not have internet access at home, screenshots of websites and social media interactions can be used to discuss and facilitate ideas and language that would be required to respond in the equivalent imagined digital interaction. With a differentiation of materials, differing teaching needs can be met, while ensuring a uniformity in teaching aims. Likewise, teachers may use differentiated activities to meet diverse learner needs.

If publishers supplied such options for materials, then they could monitor which resources were being used by specific institutions in certain parts of the world and obtain helpful, immediate user behaviour that could help inform them of the regional preferences, and thus assist in future materials design. The schools on different parts of the planet could even be virtually united to work on particular activities together, through digital platforms that the publishers could provide as part of the package of the materials, such as the EU-funded TEACUP Project discussed in this volume (Chapter "Teacher – Culture – Pluri: An International Initiative to Develop Open Educational Resources for Pluralistic Teaching in FL Teacher Education"). What is more, teachers across the world could observe each other and further their professional development through their interactions with each other. Simultaneously held global classes would allow students to have real, purposeful conversations with peers of different cultural backgrounds, using ELF. This would prepare them well for the real world and their future use of English.

12   Conclusion

With the advent of digital technology, it is time to reassess the assumption that 'one size fits all' when it comes to ELT teaching materials and the transition to online teaching. Due to the Covid-19 pandemic, teachers are more willing to accept that digital technology can be of value and welcome online materials that also save paper-based physical resources. They are therefore likely to continue using digital materials at a greater frequency than in pre-pandemic times, so this could be the perfect opportunity to ensure that teaching practices do not revert to those prior to 2020.

Thus, we should work together with publishers who wish to lead the way in the twenty-first century and shape how materials are created, produced, used and exploited, whilst building diversity, equity, and inclusion (DEI) into conversations. English language teachers can use dialogue and respectful exchange of opinions in classrooms and be supported to lessen the effects of intersectionality by raising awareness of its presence. They can also encourage students to question and reflect on the effects of imperialism, rather than ignore its existence. As Kubota (2021) confirms, "Critical antiracist pedagogy is about fostering awareness, knowledge, and attitudes regarding the intricate nature of racial inequities and approaches to challenge them" (p. 243).

When people from different cultures know one another, it is easier to have conversations and comprehend differences that exist without a sense of superiority or inferiority. ELF helps us to form relationships with people we may not normally mix with, so it can help broaden our perspectives. Such dialogue can build strong relationships and understanding, which may help to prevent or mitigate conflicts. Through English, we can get to know each other, and by getting to know each other, we can remove our biases. "Biases are the stories we make up about people before we know who they actually are" (Myers, TED Talk, 2014, 11:06). ELT could, therefore, play a leading role in promoting harmony, understanding, unity, and combatting hate crimes, which requires action at individual, institutional, and governmental levels. ELT publishers have a key role and responsibility to undo the associations that are made, both intentionally and unintentionally, with the colonial past of English. What we must not do, is do nothing.

References

Adib, N. (2021). Teaching global issues for intercultural citizenship in a Tunisian EFL textbook: "Skills for life". In M. Victoria & C. Sangiamchit (Eds.), *Interculturality and the English language classroom*. Palgrave Macmillan.

Adichie, C. N. (2009). *The danger of a single story*. [Video]. TED conferences. https://www.ted.com/talks/chimamanda_ngozi_adichie_the_danger_of_a_single_story?language=en. Accessed 10 June 2022.

Aguilar, D. (2012). From triple jeopardy to intersectionality: The feminist perplex. *Comparative Studies of South Asia, Africa, and the Middle East, 32*, 415–428.

Ahmed, R. (2021). *Riz Ahmed on Mogul Mowgli and the "life and death" matter of Muslim representation* [Video]. YouTube. https://www.youtube.com/watch?v=GtZSlhcUqkE. Accessed 22 July 2022.

Alagiah, G. (2003). Multicultural – on the face of it. In *VSO (2003), The essays: Cultural breakthrough, defining moments*. VSO Campaign.

British Council. (2013). *The English effect*. https://www.britishcouncil.org/research-policy-insight/policy-reports/the-english-effect

Brutt-Griffler, J. (2002). *World English: A study of its development*. Multilingual Matters.

Carter, P. (2005). *Keepin' it real: School success beyond black and white*. Oxford University Press.

Collins, P. H., & Bilge, S. (2020). *Intersectionality*. Polity Press.

CoE. (2008). *White paper on intercultural dialogue: Living together as equals in dignity*. Strasbourg.

Council of Europe. (1954). *The European cultural convention (ETS No. 018)*. CoE. https://www.coe.int/en/web/conventions/full-list?module=treaty-detail&treatynum=018

Curtis, A., & Romney, M. (Eds.). (2019). *Color, race, and English language teaching: Shades of meaning* (Kindle ed.). Routledge. https://www.amazon.com/Color-Race-English-Language-Teaching/dp/0805856609

Dervin, F., & Jacobsson, A. (2021). *Teacher education for critical and reflexive interculturality*. Palgrave Macmillan. https://doi.org/10.1007/978-3-030-66337-7

Ellams, I. (2016). Cutting through (on black barbershops and masculinity). In N. Shukla (Ed.), *The good immigrant*. Unbound.

Flood, A. (2015, January 14). Pigs won't fly in textbooks. *The Guardian*. https://www.theguardian.com/books/2015/jan/14/pigs-textbooks-oup-authors-pork-guidelines#:~:text=Stringent%20guidelines%20from%20educational%20publishers,to%20light%20amid%20widespread%20criticism. Accessed 10 June 2022.

Hammer, M. R., Bennett, M. J., & Wiseman, R. (2003). Measuring intercultural sensitivity: The intercultural development inventory. *International Journal of Intercultural Relations, 27*, 421–443. https://doi.org/10.1016/S0147-1767(03)00032-4. Accessed 21 Sep 2022.

Kalia, S. (2021). Hindi isn't India's national language. *Why does the myth continue?* https://theswaddle.com/hindi-isnt-indias-national-language-why-does-the-myth-continue/. Accessed 30 Aug 2022.

Kiczkowiak, M. (2022). Are most ELT course book writers white 'native speakers'? A survey of 28 general English course books for adults. *Language Teaching Research, 0*(0), 1–18. https://doi.org/10.1177/13621688221123273. Accessed 21 Sep 2022.

Kubota, R. (2021). Critical antiracist pedagogy in ELT. *ELT Journal, 75*(3), 237–246. https://academic.oup.com/eltj/article/75/3/237/6309401. Accessed 11 July 2022

Liddicoat, A. J., & Scarino, A. (2013). *Intercultural language teaching and learning*. Wiley-Blackwell.

Macaulay, T. B. (1935). Minutes on education. From Bureau of education selections from the educational records, part I (1781–1839). In *National Archives of India, 1965* (pp. 107–117). https://wps.pearsoncustom.com/wps/media/objects/2426/2484749/chap_assets/documents/doc25_2.html. Accessed 30 July 2022.

Maley, A. (1998). Squaring the circle – Reconciling materials as constraint with materials as empowerment. In B. Tomlinson (Ed.), *Materials development in language teaching* (pp. 279–294). Cambridge University Press.

Matsumoto, D. (2006). Culture and cultural worldviews: Do verbal descriptions about culture reflect anything other than verbal description of culture? *Culture & Psychology, 12*(1), 33–62. https://doi.org/10.1177/1354067X06061592

Migge, B., & Léglise, I. (2007). Language and colonialism. Applied linguistics in the context of creole communities. In M. Hellinger & A. Pauwels (Eds.), *Language and communication: Diversity and change* (Handbook of Applied Linguistics) (pp. 297–338). Mouton de Gruyter.

Myers, V. (2014). How to overcome our biases? Walk boldly toward them [Video]. *TED Conferences.* https://www.ted.com/talks/verna_myers_how_to_overcome_our_biases_walk_boldly_toward_them?language=en. Accessed 10 June 2022.

Myers, V. (2015). Diversity is being invited to the party; inclusion is being asked to dance [Video]. *Women's leadership forum.* https://www.youtube.com/watch?v=9gS2VPUkB3M. Accessed 31 Aug 2022.

Nero, S. (2019). An exceptional voice: Working as a TESOL professional of color. In A. Curtis & M. Romney (Eds.). *Color, race, and English language teaching: Shades of meaning* (Kindle ed., pp. 23–36). Routledge. https://www.amazon.com/Color-Race-English-Language-Teaching/dp/0805856609

Sawney, N. (2003). Trust and betrayal. In *VSO (2003), the essays: Cultural breakthrough, defining moments* (pp. 34–35). VSO Campaign.

Schleicher, A. (2018). *World class: How to build a 21st-century school system, strong performers and successful reformers in education.* OECD Publishing.

Seburn, T. (2021). How to write inclusive materials. *ELT teacher 2 writer.* https://eltteacher2writer.co.uk/our-books/how-to-write-inclusive-materials/. Accessed 28 Oct 2022.

Taylor, P. (2021). The 'intercultural' and English as a lingua franca in international higher education: Expectations, realities and implications for language teaching. In M. Victoria & C. Sangiamchit (Eds.), *Interculturality and the English language classroom* (pp. 205–232). Palgrave Macmillan.

Tomalin, B., & Stempleski, S. (1993). *Cultural awareness.* Oxford University Press.

Victoria, M., & Sangiamchit, C. (2021). *Interculturality and the English language classroom.* Palgrave Macmillan.

VSO. (2003). *The essays: Cultural breakthrough, defining moments.* VSO Campaign.

World Population Review. (n.d.). *Global-competency-for-an-inclusive-world.* Retrieved July 20, 2022 from www.worldpopulationreview.com

Zarina Subhan Although originally qualified as a scientist, she has been working in the field of ELT for over 30 years. She has taught at all levels, in both private and government institutions, worldwide. She has worked in/with educational institutions, educational policy makers, NGOs, community leaders, local and state governments and in a variety of training contexts. Zarina's time is now spent between delivering training, conference presentations, and writing materials. Having worked in the science, educational and development sectors, her interests are the neurology of learning, CLIL, continuing professional development for teachers, inclusive and sustainable education. Email: zsbsteps@gmail.com

Redefining EIL Through Embracing Transcultural Ways of Knowing: Challenges, Opportunities, and Future Directions

Rosalind Pritchard and Ahmed Sahlane (iD)

Abstract The role of the English language worldwide has often privileged mono-lingualism, the "Queen's English" (sic) and the native speaker/teacher. There has been an inherent assumption that "white is right". This colonial or neo-colonial ideology denigrates varieties of non-standard English, and other indigenised or minoritised languages. It has been associated with neo-liberal educational policies resulting in a hierarchy of knowledge and worldviews. Now, however, the sharp edges of conflict are being mitigated by new thinking focussing on transcultural competence. English is no longer regarded as the property of the Anglophone world. Boundaries in our globalising world are growing more porous, and English has become a language of commerce, of international communication and even of potential ethnic harmonisation in countries such as Singapore. It is pragmatically useful, and if mutual comprehension of local varieties is assured, it reduces translation costs. A paradigm shift has taken place in English pedagogy and assessment. It is acknowledged that the English language is much more than the mastery of linguistic skills. If sensitively associated with culture, it can help to construct identities that are multiple and dynamic; that give agency and voice; that deconstruct cultural biases by developing critical skills. The new de-colonial perspective has a transformative power that contributes to social justice, and militates against racism, sexism and linguicism itself.

Keywords Africa · Coloniality · English · Epistemic justice · Ethnocentrism · European Union · Intercultural competence · Ireland · Lingua franca · Native-speakerism · Whiteness

R. Pritchard
Faculty of Arts, Humanities & Social Sciences, Ulster University, Coleraine, UK
e-mail: R.Pritchard@ulster.ac.uk

A. Sahlane (✉)
English Language Institute, University of Jeddah, Jeddah, Saudi Arabia
e-mail: asahlan1@uj.edu.sa

A. Sahlane, R. Pritchard (eds.), *English as an International Language Education*, English Language Education 33,
https://doi.org/10.1007/978-3-031-34702-3_26

1   The Polemics of English as an International Language

In the era of English as an international language (EIL), debates about the teaching of English have revolved around the issues of ownership, the (re)definition of English language proficiency, and the appropriate teaching pedagogies and assessment methods. While advocates of native speaker (NS) English argue for the colonialist ideologies that consider the "inner circle" language norms as 'superior' (and thus should serve as target norms for the English language learners), proponents of World Englishes assume the irrelevance of NS English varieties in "outer" and "expanding" lingua franca contexts (Kachru, 1985). The taken-for-granted essentialist conceptions of what counts as legitimate knowledge (including language practices) have always been entrenched in complex dynamics of asymmetrical relations of power and structural inequalities. In this sense, coloniality has outlived colonialism. Coloniality is the imposition of hegemonic Eurocentric ways of being, speaking, and knowing as the universal and natural order by invisibilising, pathologising, and delegitimising alternative pluriversal forms of knowledge production.

As late-modern societies have increasingly become globalised, hybrid, and interconnected, linguistic/cultural borders have become porous. Besides, as English has acquired a heterogenous and pluricentric status (i.e., multilingual speakers of English no longer consider NS norms as their ideal target), the need for a paradigm shift in assessment and pedagogy has become a necessary prerequisite for a healthy (re)conceptualisation of the relationship between English varieties. This 'pluralistic' view of English has profound implications for linguistic/cultural norm-setting and language proficiency assessment in that assessment procedures should be more performance/process-oriented, practice-based, and reflective of effective transcultural and multimodal interactive communication competence. In this sense, for postmodern speakers of English, proficiency involves the ability to negotiate the variability of different varieties of English in their specific linguacultural contexts and at different levels of local/regional and global social interactions. Hence, interlocutors are encouraged to prioritise the acquisition of communication strategies and meaning negotiation skills that serve to facilitate the development of a cognitive ability to transit between diverse speech communities in contextually, sociolinguistically, and culturally appropriate ways.

Likewise, arguments about 'coloniality of language' relate to the prevalence of *Anglonormativity* in educational spaces. The hegemonic power of Anglonormative ideologies manifests itself in the privileging of monolingualist attitudes over multilingualism. For example, there is a continuing tendency to project fluency in NS English, a variety aligning with an "ethnolinguistic repertoire of whiteness" (McKinney, 2017, p. 98), as the normal and natural linguistic order in English language education. Hence, one of the damaging effects of linguistic coloniality is manifested in the prestige attached to "'White' ways of speaking English" (p. 84) and the ongoing denigration of minoritised and Indigenous languages. The concept of Anglonormativity is, thus, used to emphasise the intersections of ideologies of language, race and 'normativity' insisting that multilingual learners "should be proficient in [standard] English and are deficient, even deviant, if they are not" (p. 80). Such a perspective is also "linked to the global position of English, global whiteness and neoliberalism" (p. 75). English monolingualism is woven into most neoliberal educational policies that promote the commodification of education, the hierarchisation of knowledges and worldviews, and the exclusionary legitimisation of neocolonialist language policies and assimilationist research perspectives.

However, in our contemporary world, marked by the daily struggle to cope with mass migration (due to forced mobility and displacement, depletion of natural resources in developing countries, interethnic wars, and international (state) terrorism), the perceived prestigious role and social value associated with English increases. English becomes the language of 'hope', 'mobility', 'power' and global communication.[1] Hence, the goal of learning English as an International Language (EIL) should be to nurture intercultural sensitivity and a global mindset amongst citizens of the world. EIL-aware approaches to English language education can promote the already unfolding process of pluralistic 'cultural hybridisation' that is being instituted, characterised by some sort of 'intercultural' blending or an adaptive 're-culturalisation' process, turning English into a multicultural language.

The concept of English as a *lingua franca* (ELF) has challenged the legitimacy of 'native-speakerism' ideology and the hegemonic norms of US-British cultural 'authenticity' in English language teaching (ELT) pedagogy. Acquiring English for the multilingual learner of English involves a complex process of learning to become a cultural 'hybrid' and 'mediator' between self and others ('intercultural speaker'). Hence, educators embracing a critical perspective have a professional obligation to encourage students to celebrate the multiple identities that they bring to their learning by encouraging them to acknowledge and respect diversity and challenge racism and discrimination. They should tailor their teaching to meet the specific needs of their students by resisting 'native-speakerist' ideologies that continue to permeate several aspects of teaching practices in our superdiverse classrooms.

Another important aim of intercultural education is to foster critical 'intercultural literacy' and promote global competency skills needed for world workplaces. English has acquired a new global identity as it has become the "medium of corporate power," and "a medium of literary and other forms of cultural life in (mainly) countries of the former British Empire" (Halliday, 2006, pp. 349–362). English is also the language of international (and even intranational) communication in *lingua franca* contexts. Today globalisation has profoundly affected business and higher education in post-colonial societies in that international companies and universities have adapted their missions to cater for the pressing demands of globalising workplaces. Intercultural awareness has become one of the most required soft skills for managerial positions. With people from a range of national cultural backgrounds now coming together more frequently to conduct business, it has become necessary

---

[1] However, referring to English as a 'global' language is misleading, since "less than half of the world's population have any proficiency in English" (Phillipson, 2023, p. 143). There are numerous contexts where English cannot be used (see Ashraf, this volume, Chapter "Health Communication in Pakistan: Establishing Trust in Networked Multilingualism").

to take into consideration the different degrees of international experience participants bring to the business settings. Hence, attributing behaviour solely based on an interactant's membership in a national culture overlooks other more important idiosyncratic and situational factors.

The aim of twenty-first century education should be to train learners to become 'global citizens' through the promotion of intercultural and digital technology literacies. This can be attained by preparing learners to interact across different cultural borders, developing empathy towards other cultures, and respect for difference and diversity. However, the increasing focus on the promotion of the learners' intercultural communication competence should not ignore the equal importance of providing opportunities for learners to acquire critical thinking skills; these will help them to deconstruct cultural biases permeating sociocultural practices. It seems that

> very few curricula attached similar importance to the ability to acquire and operate new knowledge, to interpret cultural information or to evaluate critically perspectives, practices and products in one's own and foreign cultures … [P]rimary attention is given to the dimensions of knowledge and attitudes rather than skills…or metacognitive strategies to direct students' own learning (Lavrenteva & Orland-Barak, 2015, p. 674).

Likewise, teacher education programs need to respond to rapidly diversifying local communities. As societies worldwide are increasingly becoming more culturally diverse, we should be aware of the educational challenges that come with globalisation, resulting in ethnic, linguistic, religious, and cultural differences and their intersections. Intercultural education should empower educational stakeholders to act for social change by taking a stand against all forms of social injustice, and persisting colonial legacies entrenched in neo-racist and assimilationist discourses of the West as 'civiliser' of the 'deficient' cultural others. Thus, we should challenge the long-standing assumptions related to 'cultural misbelief' and linguistic 'deficiency' embedded in Orientalist logics and Anglicist rhetoric of native-speakerism.

The conception of language as a fixed code shared by a presumably homogeneous and bounded nationality group (speaking the 'same' language) problematises diversity and variation by espousing the ideology of 'one nation, one language', and this leads to the erasure of the dynamic nature of language and the diverse linguistic practices of its speakers. Besides, the equation of speakers of a 'standardised' language with 'nativeness' invisibilises speakers of other non-standardised regional and social varieties ('dialects' and 'sociolects'). Hence, this diversity among native speaker users renders irrelevant the binary native/nonnative dichotomy. The standardisation process merely serves to frame linguistic variation in hierarchical terms that reflect power relations by conferring the status of 'standard language' on certain linguistic practices, and thus granting privileged 'native-speakership' status to the dominant groups associated with the 'standard' variety. Therefore, it is fallacious to claim that the ownership of English is based on the notion of 'nativeness' that excludes speakers of non-standard varieties of English and other indigenised international versions in postcolonial countries. Language use has a 'performative' power: it is constitutive of identity through social interaction; language learners engage in continuous identity construction and negotiation. Individuals vary their language to mark their complex social, geographical, ethnic, or other forms of linguacultural identities according to context.

The monolithic homogenising policies that dominate traditional ELT theory and practice need to be challenged through teacher education programs. For example, even though Canada is linguistically superdiverse, the government continues to promote English (and to a lesser extent French) and suppresses Indigenous and minoritised immigrant languages. While linguistic diversity is on the rise in Canada due to immigration, multilingual newcomers are gradually assimilated into English monolingualism. A healthy shift to a more critical cosmopolitan and multilingual/multicultural approach to ELT should accommodate the diverse and rich cultural/linguistic capitals and knowledge funds of the relevant educational stakeholders. Public schools are privileged educational spaces for intercultural encounters and for learning how to engage with diversity. If pre-service teachers are trained in developing an awareness of English as an international language, they could incorporate such diversity into their teaching, and thus promote more inclusive learning environments in their classrooms. Besides, as identities are inherently 'emotional', dynamically evolving and hybrid, and historically conjunctural and spatiotemporally situated, they are discursively (re)constructed in a way that reflects teachers' dispositions and agentive roles in rationally negotiating difference.

Therefore, as Sahlane (this volume, Chapter "(En)Countering the 'White' Gaze: Native-Speakerist Rhetorics and the Raciolinguistics of Hegemony") points out, identity is a struggle site for voice and epistemic agency, exposing (re)certifying internationally educated Canadian teacher candidates to ideologies that fail to validate their past alternative knowledge frameworks; this may induce a feeling of symbolic 'violence.' The state of being 'out of place' might be rendered perpetual because the struggle to realise one's professional 'becoming' becomes more challenging. However, it could also be an opportunity to seek alternative constellations of identity reconceptualisation beyond the hegemonic models that continue to deny nonnative English-speaking teachers "the legitimacy of lived experience" (Rivers, 2019, p. 381) by condemning them to "live a scripted life" (Weatherall & Ahuja, 2021, p. 419).

The 'Native-speakerism' fallacy (Phillipson, 1992) is heavily impacted by "whiteness as rightness" ideology (Henry, 2021, p. 309). However, though ESL students generally evaluate native English-speaking teachers (NESTs) as more proficient in teaching speaking/listening skills, they tend to consider non-native English-speaking teachers (NNESTs) as more skilled in motivating students, teaching grammar, literacy skills and using effective methodology (Moussu & Llurda, 2008). Therefore, they tend to evaluate the professionalism of their teachers based on overall teaching ability, not based solely on their accents (p. 331). Besides, as Norton and Pavlenko (2019) note,

> while in spoken interactions, opinions of some L2 users may be discounted by others due to their physical appearance or traces of accent in their speech, published texts constitute excellent equalizers and unique arenas where accents are erased and voices imbued with sufficient authority. (p. 712)

However, 'native-speakerism' continues to permeate several aspects of teaching and employment practices to the effect that "[o]nly certain raced and classed bodies are acknowledged as creative producers, while others are de-authorized despite the cultural reality of their knowledge, labor, and expertise" (Sáez, 2018, p. 364). For example, "MFA [Master of Fine Arts] programs came to function as enclaves that privileged a predominantly white, male, and heteronormative literary tradition" (p. 377). Such "chauvinistic" discourses and practices (Holliday & Aboshiha, 2009, p. 671) are based on the fallacious myth of "linguistic purity and cultural authenticity" (Kramsch, 2016, p. 244) which serves as a powerful purveyor of colonial logics assuming that race shapes language. In this sense, "linguicism" is the new form of culturally oriented "neo-racist" ideology (Holliday, 2014) that "blames the victim in more subtle ways than biologically based racism, by colonising consciousness instead of colonising the body" (Skutnabb-Kangas & Phillipson, 1989, p. 456). In other words, 'native-speakerism' turns what is principally a matter of racist institutional power imbalance into an individual problem by representing racialised educators as linguistically 'deficient' and culturally 'inferior' because they are allegedly uncapable of thinking in 'independent' and 'rational' ways as they belong to 'collectivist' cultures (a form of 'cognitive divide' fallacy) (Holliday & Aboshiha, 2009, p. 679).

There is a resurgent interest in the issue of connecting language and culture in a societal context. The growing body of research promotes the adoption of a politically informed approach to English language education theory and pedagogy. The argument is that language is principally a social phenomenon, which is naturally and intimately intertwined with culture. In other words, language functions as a marker of cultural identity and cannot be reducible to a mere mastery of linguistic skills. Hence, learners of English language need to relate to people from the target culture to be competent in communicating across cultural borders. However, although language practitioners regard culture as a crucially important element of successful language learning, it is difficult to translate this belief into curricular practice. Besides, language is regarded as a site of struggle for the legitimation of cultural authenticity.

At the heart of debates about teaching EIL is the selection of teaching methodology, but the most salient mediators of learning are the language teaching materials because textbooks often serve to legitimise what cultural content to pass on to learners. From the EIL perspective, textbooks should train students to become interculturally competent by integrating a diversity of cultural content. However, the appropriateness of the cultural materials that textbooks disseminate is of paramount importance. Not all cultural content can be suitable for different teaching contexts. Thus, the issue remains how we can design glocal English textbooks that serve to link the foreign language to local realities and that can mediate between indigenous communities and the youth's globalising aspirations and cultural lifestyles.

In post-colonial settings, globalisation has made language planning the target of active institutional intervention. For example, the fast spread of English and its increasingly growing symbolic value is promoted by its vital role as the *de facto lingua franca* of globalisation in that it has established itself as the language of modernisation, global finance, social mobility, employability, the media, international relations, popular culture, and scientific scholarship (*lingua academica*) (Phillipson, 2017, p. 318). However, because "American consumerist capitalism is projected as a *cultura nullius* of universal relevance" (p. 320), "the economic, social and political returns are stacked in favor of English and against the mother tongue" (Kumaravadivelu, 2006, p. 18). English global domination is reflected in the "mushrooming of English-medium education" and the "increasing privatisation of education" worldwide. For example, the destruction of Iraqi higher education after the US-led invasion in 2003 has created a multi-billion market opportunity for the US/British publishing industry, educational consultants, and private English-medium education businesses (Phillipson, 2017, pp. 313–321). The result of such a *McDonaldisation* process is the proliferation of English-medium higher education institutions and an increase in the number of international private schools in the Global South. The growing neoliberal educational policies of post-colonial governments are a new form of "transnational integration" (Phillipson, 2023, p. 152) that shirks national responsibilities for public education by delegating the management of education to "private corporations", "venture capitalists", and "educational entrepreneurs".

2   ELT and the Cultural Politics of Neocolonialism

In our late-modern societies, the forces of globalisation are unavoidably interconnected with English as a global language. As Phillipson (1992) convincingly argues, "English, to a much greater extent than any other language, is the language in which the fate of most of the world's millions is decided" (p. 6). The drive to internationalisation is one of the main characteristics of neoliberal practices in higher education worldwide. English-medium instruction (EMI) programs have proliferated in several non-Anglophone universities. This approach most often implies the use of homogeneous instructional, assessment, and management procedures to enact similar curricular and language proficiency goals. This neocolonial desire for homogeneity also imposes the use of English as a medium of instruction and knowledge production in most Global South settings. Moreover, as Western higher education is branded as a desirable commodity in the global knowledge economy market, Anglophone universities have attracted many educational exchange sojourners from non-Western countries. Besides, the growing number of branches of Anglophone universities in the "expanding circle" countries (e.g., the Middle East) and the rapid proliferation of EMI programs in post-colonial peripheries have turned English into a predatory language killer (Phillipson, 1997, p. 243).

For example, Saudi universities have witnessed an unprecedented growth in the teaching of academic subjects (STEM disciplines) through English, and they are competing to obtain international accreditation for their teaching programs. Technical/vocational colleges have also opted for the internationalisation of their programs. There are over 37 international institutes (24 of them are UK-affiliated) operating in Saudi Arabia. Yanbu Industrial College and Jubail Industrial College introduced a joint MBA program in collaboration with Indianapolis University and Troy University, respectively. McGill University runs Jubail Industrial College's Preparatory Year Intensive English program. King Abdullah University of Science and Technology (KAUST), established in 2009, is the first internationalised and mixed-gender university in Saudi Arabia. KAUST has developed academic partnerships with well-known Western universities and academic research centres. Hence, the internationalisation of Saudi higher education is enacted through recruiting foreign staff (the 'native speaker' brand remains a good marketing tool), seeking international accreditation, benchmarking academic programs, and engaging in academic partnerships with Western higher education institutions (Barnawi & Al-Hawsawi, 2017, pp. 211–3).

The adoption of EMI by Saudi educational policy makers is closely related to the need to improve university graduates' proficiency in English as a key to modernisation and economic development. However, the "internationalization of curriculum theoretically extends colonial dominance" (Parson & Weise, 2020, p. 101). For example, such 'linguicist' practice in academia that involves a subtractive (rather than an additive) shift from Arabic to English in several Middle Eastern countries ("linguistic capital dispossession") would have detrimental implications for national languages and cultures. These countries should not succumb to the market forces and corporate pressures. Rational language policy dictates the maintenance of academic literacy in Arabic as a scholarly language while promoting bilingual additive academic proficiency in English ("linguistic capital accumulation") (Phillipson, 2017). In other words, English should be conceived of as an "additional language" or a "'co-language' functioning not against, but in conjunction with, local languages" (House, 2003, p. 574).

Like in some East Asian countries, Global South nations should actively exercise their agency by "work[ing] with not only global benchmarks but also national-cultural models" and avoid "the reproduction of Western supremacy into national higher education systems" (Xu, 2022, p. 45). Multilingual and translingual practices are pivotal in university teaching, research, and socialisation. Although Saudi universities are required to implement an EMI policy, instructors, faced with the foreign language problem, resort to translingual manoeuvring strategies by calling on students' diverse linguistic resources across a range of semiotic modalities to ensure their full grasp of technical knowledge. However, the failure to sustain the use of English-only teaching policy by smuggling local languages into their classrooms nurtures a sense of 'guilt' because monolingualist ideologies still colonise the minds of educational actors and institutional macro-level policy makers.

Constructing a multilingual/multicultural curriculum that considers the epistemic dialogue between the West and the rest is not only desirable, but viable. The need to empower and revitalise indigenous knowledge, incorporate culturally conscious pedagogy and assessment is very crucial for the promotion of tolerance, empathy, and intercultural dialogue. The United Nations declaration of 2019 as the International Year of Indigenous Languages (IYIL) was an attempt to mobilise the international community to the urgent need to preserve, revitalise and promote endangered Indigenous languages. Hence, the chapters in this book are cries against political cultures of exclusion, epistemic injustice, and the intersectional reproduction of social inequities.

Our aim in this book is to shine light on the transformative power of decolonial perspectives, pedagogies and practices that deploy multilingual and multimodal approaches to engage with the challenge of maintaining daily struggles for social justice and equity in contemporary academic and societal spaces. To this end, chapters in this work range from autoethnographic and photovoice multimodal narrative accounts to other more traditional research genres, such as academic writing, discursive representations of cultural others, teachers' linguistic and cultural perceptions and the usefulness of multilingual literacies in times of crisis. As many chapters in this book attest, academics and educators continue to grapple with finding ways to be agents of social justice in contexts of coloniality.

This book aims not simply at celebrating cultural diversity, but rather it seeks to challenge the institutionalisation and rationalisation of dominance, manifested in the covert injuries of race, class, ethnicity, gender, religion, or culture which we must live with on a daily basis. The present academic contributions also seek to prepare the ground for a pedagogy of revolt against all manifestations of hegemonic regimes of knowledge by invoking a multicultural 'third space' for a critical pedagogy to celebrate difference. What drives the sense of global urgency we find in these chapters is the need to recognise that in our globalising world, we are awkwardly placed in "a new planetary space of unprecedented intervisibility and interdependence... Cultural and linguistic diversity are not normative ideals, they are us—our basic existential situation" (Lin & Sequeira, 2017, p. x).

The present volume argues for a decolonial, anti-racist and anti-sexist approach that contests colonial hierarchical power relations. We need to de-/re-construct not just existing Eurocentric knowledge and research paradigms, but also our different ways of seeing our academic missions. Western epistemological tendencies to universalise international academia and pedagogy by imposing Eurocentric knowledge frames onto relevant global academic/cultural others make the crossing of national, linguistic, and cultural borders a daunting task for the diverse non-native, non-white educational stakeholders. Sahlane and Marom argue in this volume that 'White privilege' remains blatantly uncontested within the hallowed halls of academia and in the wider institutionalised public spaces in Canadian society. Anti-racist policies might prove ineffective because white senior administrators resist implementing them by denying the existence of racist practices in their institutions (Dua, 2009, p. 164). Despite the proliferation of equity services in many Canadian universities, the equity mechanisms remain more 'performative' than substantive: the goal is to attract international students, who pay about 40% of all university tuition fees in Canada (i.e., about $4 billion) (Statistics Canada, 2020), because with the current neoliberalist policies, government funding is shrinking. Hence "an equality regime can be an inequality regime given new form, a set of processes that maintain what is supposedly being redressed" (Ahmed, 2012, p. 8). Such structural discriminatory practices "rob the academy and the broader society of a wealth of talent and the invaluable heterogeneity of people, their knowledge, and the perspectives that could make universities more equitable, diverse and excellent" (Henry et al., 2016, p. 12).

There is a growing empirical support for the need to shift from a monocultural English 'native speaker' competence as a goal for English language education to that of an effective 'intercultural communicator'. However, despite attempts to limit the dominance of English by national laws and to promote linguistic and cultural diversity in world education systems, English continues to gain more terrain in the political, cultural, economic, defence, and juridical domains. Ironically, "if you want to resist the exploitative power of English, you have to use English to do it" (Halliday, 2006, p. 362). Therefore, "[r]ather than trying to fight off global English, which at present seems to be rather a quixotic venture, those who seek to resist its baleful impact might do better to concentrate on transforming it, reshaping its meanings, and its meaning potential" (p. 363). There is no dispute about the utility of English as a valuable linguistic resource in contexts where English represents an instance of *linguistic capital accumulation*. However, in many other contexts, where English is replacing Indigenous mother tongues (*linguistic capital dispossession*) its linguicidal aspect is more of a problem than an asset (Phillipson, 2023, p. 154).

3   English as a World Linguistic Resource

From all that has gone before this final section of the book, certain things have become clear; English has become de-territorialised and no longer "belongs" to the English or even the Americans. The normative model of the native speaker, which was once the aspiration, though it was almost always unattainable, has now become one model among others. It is being widely replaced by the notion of the competent intercultural speaker which is endorsed as a policy of the European Union. The link between language and culture certainly still exists, and is strengthened by the global media, but if it becomes a threat to local values, it can be relativised and diluted. If strategically desired, the language-culture link can be deliberately weakened for political or religious reasons — for example by a Ministry of Education or Culture in the choice of textbooks. Just as relexification can result in one language replacing much or all of a language's lexicon, so too can re-acculturation result in 'English' culture being replaced by that of another community or ethos. For example, in Saudi Arabia, English can even be re-purposed as a tool for spreading Islam (see Sahlane & Pritchard, this volume, Chapter "Assessing Perspectives on Culture in Saudi EFL Textbook Discourse"). Teaching languages is a political act, and politics is conducive to manipulation in promotion of the national interest. Cultural protectionism is a fact of life in many countries. Control of the English language within a jurisdiction may prevent linguicide, though families too must play their part in keeping up heritage languages.

Linguicism leads to people being judged by their language. It can be defined as a form of prejudice that involves forming opinions about an individual's social status, education, wealth, character, etc. Normally the direction of disapproval runs socially from the top downwards, which is to say that those uppermost in a hierarchy make negative judgements on those *below* them who become minoritised or stigmatised groups (Skutnabb-Kangas, 1988). However, the direction of disapproval has sometimes been reversed: "someone" very highly placed may be criticised by "someone" *lower* down — this too is a form of negative linguistic judgement. In a case that we wish to present here, the first "someone" was Lord Altrincham, a British Peer, and the person whom he criticised was none other than the Queen of England, Elisabeth II. He accused her of being out of touch with her subjects and published his ideas in his magazine, *The National and English Review*. He complained that the Queen's Court was too upper-class and called her manner of speaking "a pain in the neck"; according to him, she sounded like "a priggish school girl"! This verbal slanging match happened back in 1957 and caused uproar at the time. When he left a TV studio, after an attempt to explain his ideas, Lord Altrincham was punched in the face by an ex-soldier, Philip Kinghorn Burbridge, who was merely fined the sum of £1 for his attack (Whitfield, 2019).

It might be thought that the Queen would become angry and seek to punish Lord Altrincham, but she took his criticism very seriously and changed her speech style. Audio recordings over time demonstrate the change quite clearly: the Queen of England had adopted a more demotic tone of voice. The Queen was sensitive to the erosion of Empire which greatly accelerated during the 1960s; with it declined the colonialism that had caused much pain and suffering to the colonised; and with it came also the decline of deference and a concomitant threat to the monarchy. The Empire was replaced by the Commonwealth. Not just the Queen's language changed, but gradually language 'purity' was replaced by language mixing which became respectable; canons of correctness were often ignored or subverted in the media and public domain. English changed both in Britain and internationally. Boundaries were broken for ever. Intersectionality was used to build a new ethnography of hope and healing.

However, the idea of 'purity', that was once so attractive, is a pervasive and haunting one; antitheses come readily to mind: pure/impure, clean/unclean. Mary Douglas (1966) in her widely-cited book *Purity and Danger* applies such antitheses to cultural anthropology, and realises that they can be extrapolated to many other disciplines, particularly those where boundary maintenance is an issue. The maintenance of boundaries avoids contamination and keeps power structures intact. Such structures are intimately associated with language, both as idiolect and as sociolect. The notion of purity imparts prestige to monolingualism and to the paradigm of the native speaker. Language hybridisation is viewed as transgressive, too often resulting in semilingualism and subtractive bilingualism (Cummins & Swain, 1986) — though both these terms would now be regarded as deficit terminology. There are fears that mixing will lead to new language forms such as pidgins and creoles that are not always intelligible to outsiders; or indeed even amongst various speaker groupings themselves (Romaine, 1988, Ch. 5). This brings us to the role of English in a de-colonised or de-colonising world. Does English need to be demonised in the interests of fairness, justice, and equity for other languages? The question arises whether local languages are to be cultivated to the exclusion of English (or indeed other former colonial languages such as French). If so, this could become a new form of hegemony.

The experience of Ireland is instructive in this respect. English is a high-resource language. Its sheer usefulness cannot be disputed, especially for industry and commerce. O'Toole (2021) notes that the English language has given an immense economic stimulus to the Irish economy — one that it could never have enjoyed if it had Irish as its *only* national, official language. Now Ireland is a valued member of the European Union. Jointly with Switzerland, it has achieved a ranking of *second highest in the world* on the 2019 Human Development Index (HDI). The HDI considers three main dimensions to evaluate the development of a country: for citizens, a long and healthy life, good education, and comfortable standard of living. Although English has certainly helped Ireland to become economically successful, it is not the only factor; Ireland's lead-time to success was quite long and was greatly facilitated by its membership of the European Union (of which English is the most commonly used working language). The practical value of English is indisputable. Crisp (2017) reports that Irish was the most expensive language to translate in the European Parliament which routinely translates papers of the EU as part of its commitment to multilingualism. The average cost of translating a page into Irish was twice as much as the average for other languages and this contributed to an overspend of millions of Euros in 2017.

One may contrast Africa with the case of Ireland. It is estimated that over 1800 languages are spoken on the African continent (though of course one may argue about what constitutes a "language" and what constitutes a "dialect") (Lingalot. com, 2023). Ten countries are ranked at the very lowest level on the HDI scale and all ten of them are in Africa (World Population Review, 2022). Similarly, seven out of the ten countries in the world with the highest Gini indices of *inequality* are in Africa. They include South Africa, which is ranked as the country with the lowest level of income equality in the world. Its Gini coefficient of 63.0 indicates its positionality: the higher the Gini index, the lower the equality level. Sub-Saharan Africa is the worst-performing area on the Transparency Index which relates to sociopolitical honesty. Based on 49 countries in the region, the score was only 32/100 (Transparency International, 2021). In 2019, the Global Corruption Barometer, Africa revealed that over one in four people paid a bribe to access essential public services (e.g., health care) (Transparency International, 2019).

Correlation is not causality. Multilingualism cannot be blamed for the dire statistics that have just been cited; however, it needs to be deployed as a resource for potential good rather than allowed to become a problem, as may sometimes be the case. The causes of Africa's plight are multifarious. Indeed, some derive from ethnic and racial tensions; and English can function as a means of managing these. Tupas in an interview has spoken of the power of English to bond social groups, especially in a society like Singapore. In an interview with him, Lee (2015) presents Tupas' thoughts on the integrative power of English:

> [I]f you're talking about Singapore identity, then how are you going to cut across the different ethnicities and languages? It is, of course, English. And if you look at English on the ground, if you talk about English in the formal sense, that's where you have all of these other languages coming together, and all of these people from different groups actually using each other's words and phrases to cross boundaries.

Singapore deliberately mitigates the powerful influence of English as the sole medium of instruction by teaching *Mother Tongues* (Mandarin, Malay, and Tamil) as 'subjects' in primary and secondary schools. This is viewed as "cultural ballast" to help protect Asian cultural identities and values against Western influence (Vaish, 2008, p. 451). While English dominates in the domains of media, education, and public space, mother tongues are used mainly in informal situations (e.g., religion, family, friendship) (pp. 452–453).

However, English ceases to be useful when speakers of local varieties can no longer understand each other (see Ashraf, this volume, Chapter "Health Communication in Pakistan: Establishing Trust in Networked Multilingualism"); if this happens, its social benefits are lost. The economic benefits of English as a Lingua Franca shrivel up and disappear at the point where language mixing results in mutual incomprehensibility. The difficulty of preserving comprehensibility can be immense. It is revealed, for example, by *A Dictionary of Sri Lankan English* (Meyler, 2008) which contains about 2500 examples of words and expressions characteristic of Sri Lankan English. Nourished as it is by both Sinhalese and Tamil influences, many of the lexical items are inaccessible to international speakers of English — and the Sri Lankan local variety of English contains many grammatical features which would be considered errors by speakers of British English and *also* by educated Sri Lankan English speakers. Yet excellence can be achieved and maintained within local varieties of English. Recently (in 2022) this has been demonstrated by the fact that the Booker Prize for literature was won by Shehan Karunatilaka for his novel *The Seven Moons of Maali Almeida*. The author is Sri Lankan. He struggled to find an international publisher for the novel because most of them found Sri Lankan politics "esoteric and confusing" and many felt "the mythology and worldbuilding was impenetrable, and difficult for Western readers" (Jayasinghe, 2022).

And so we come to the end of the book. English can be a powerful tool for good as well as a threat to other languages and cultures. The trick is in language policy to manage its role productively. The passionate voices in this book resonate with concern about inequality and injustice, whether this be in the realm of language, gender, race, heritage, identity, class or culture. The contributing authors have an eagle eye for detecting inclusivity as "tokenism". Their voices are assuredly "on the side of the angels" in their deep concern to rectify injustice. We sincerely hope that their work — and ours — will contribute to achieving justice.

References

Ahmed, S. (2012). *On being included: Racism and diversity in institutional life*. Duke University Press. https://doi.org/10.2307/j.ctv1131d2g.1

Barnawi, O. Z., & Al-Hawsawi, S. (2017). English education policy in Saudi Arabia: English language education policy in the Kingdom of Saudi Arabia: Current trends, issues and challenges. In R. Kirkpatrick (Ed.), *English language education policy in the Middle East and North Africa* (pp. 199–222). Springer. https://doi.org/10.1007/978-3-319-46778-8_12

Crisp, J. (2017, Aug 30). European Parliament faces overspend of millions on translation budget — with Irish the most expensive. *The Telegraph*. https://www.telegraph.co.uk/news/2017/08/30/european-parliament-faces-overspend-millions-translation-budget/

Cummins, J., & Swain, M. (1986). *Bilingualism in education*. Longman. https://doi.org/10.4324/9781315835877

Douglas, M. (1966). *Purity and danger: An analysis of the concepts of pollution and taboo*. Routledge. https://doi.org/10.4324/9780203361832

Dua, E. (2009). On the effectiveness of anti-racist policies in Canadian universities: Issues of implementation of policies by senior administration. In F. Henry & C. Tator (Eds.), *Racism in the Canadian university: Demanding social justice, inclusion, and equity* (pp. 160–196). University of Toronto Press. https://doi.org/10.3138/9781442688926-007

Halliday, M. A. K. (2006). Written language, standard language, global language. In B. B. Kachru, Y. Kachru, & C. L. Nelson (Eds.), *The handbook of world Englishes* (pp. 349–365). Blackwell. https://doi.org/10.1002/9780470757598.ch20

Henry, W. L. (2021). Who feels it knows it! Alterity, identity and 'epistemological privilege': Challenging white privilege from a black perspective within the academy. In D. S. P. Thomas & J. Arday (Eds.), *Doing equity and diversity for success in higher education: Redressing structural inequalities in the academy* (pp. 299–312). Palgrave Macmillan. https://doi.org/10.1007/978-3-030-65668-3

Henry, F., Dua, E., Kobayashi, A., James, C., Li, P., Ramos, H., & Smith, M. S. (2016). Race, racialization and indigeneity in Canadian universities. *Race Ethnicity & Education, 20*, 1–15. https://doi.org/10.1080/13613324.2016.1260226

Holliday, A. (2014). *Native-speakerism*. https://adrianholliday.com/wp-content/uploads/2014/01/nism-encyc16plain-submitted.pdf. Accessed 2 Jan 2022.

Holliday, A., & Aboshiha, P. (2009). The denial of ideology in perceptions of 'nonnative speaker' teachers. *TESOL Quarterly, 43*(4), 669–689.

House, J. (2003). English as a lingua franca: A threat to multilingualism? *Journal of SocioLinguistics, 7*(4), 556–578. https://doi.org/10.1111/j.1467-9841.2003.00242.x

Jayasinghe, P. (2022, October 18). Shehan Karunatilaka: 'The state will come after the defenceless'. *Frontline*. The Hindu Group. Retrieved December 18, 2022. https://frontline.thehindu.com/books/interview-shehan-karunatilaka-booker-prize-2022-shortlist-the-state-will-come-after-the-defenceless/article65861579.ece

Kachru, B. (1985). Standards, codification and sociolinguistic realism: English language in the outer circle. In R. Quirk & H. Widdowson (Eds.), *English in the world: Teaching and learning the language and literatures* (pp. 11–36). Cambridge University Press.

Kramsch, C. (2016). Native-speakerism in language teaching. In F. Copland, S. Garton, & S. Mann (Eds.), *LETs and NESTs: Voices, views and vignettes* (pp. 246–247). British Council. https://publications.aston.ac.uk/id/eprint/28660/1/pub_BC_Book_VVV_online_screen_res_FINAL.pdf. Accessed 27 Dec 2023

Kumaravadivelu, B. (2006). Dangerous liaison: Globalization, empire and TESOL. In J. Edge (Ed.), *(Re-)locating TESOL in an age of empire* (pp. 1–26). Palgrave Macmillan.

Lavrenteva, E., & Orland-Barak, L. (2015). The treatment of culture in the foreign language curriculum: An analysis of national curriculum documents. *Journal of Curriculum Studies, 47*(5), 653–684. https://doi.org/10.1080/00220272.2015.1056233

Lee, G. C. (2015). Defining 'mother tongue': An interview with Ruanni Tupas. *Unravel*, October 26, 2015. https://unravellingmag.com/dialogue/an-interview-with-ruanni-tupas/. Accessed 8 Oct 2022.

Lin, C.-C., & Sequeira, L. (Eds.). (2017). *Inclusion, diversity, and intercultural dialogue in young people's philosophical inquiry*. Sense Publishers.

Lingalot. (2023). *Is African a language?* https://www.lingalot.com/is-african-a-language/#:~:text=It%E2%80%99s%20super%20interesting%20to%20know%20that. Accessed 27 Jan 2023.

McKinney, C. (2017). *Language and power in post-colonial schooling: Ideologies in practice*. Routledge.

Meyler, M. (2008). In D. Fernando & V. VanderPoorten (Eds.), *A dictionary of Sri Lankan English* (2nd ed.). Michael Meyler. https://doi.org/10.1075/eww.31.3.06bai

Moussu, L., & Llurda, E. (2008). Non-native English-speaking English language teachers: History and research. *Language Teaching, 41*, 315–348. https://doi.org/10.1017/S0261444808005028

Norton, B., & Pavlenko, A. (2019). Imagined communities, identity, and English language learning in a multilingual world. In X. Gao (Ed.), *Second handbook of English language teaching* (pp. 703–718). Springer. https://doi.org/10.1007/978-0-387-46301-8_43

O'Toole, F. (2021). *We don't know ourselves*. Head of Zeus.

Parson, L., & Weise, J. (2020). Postcolonial approach to curriculum design. In L. Parson & C. Ozaki (Eds.), *Teaching and learning for social justice and equity in higher education* (pp. 93–116). Palgrave Macmillan/Springer Nature. https://doi.org/10.1007/978-3-030-44939-1_6

Phillipson, R. (1992). *Linguistic imperialism*. Oxford University Press.

Phillipson, R. (1997). Realities and myths of linguistic imperialism. *Journal of Multilingual and Multicultural Development, 18*(3), 238–248. https://doi.org/10.1080/01434639708666317

Phillipson, R. (2017). Myths and realities of 'global' English. *Language Policy, 16*, 313–331.

Phillipson, R. (2023). Language policy implications of 'global' English for linguistic human rights. In T. Skutnabb-Kangas & R. Phillipson (Eds.), *The handbook of linguistic human rights* (pp. 143–157). Wiley Blackwell. https://doi.org/10.1002/9781119753926.ch9

Rivers, D. J. (2019). Walking on glass: Reconciling experience and expectation within Japan. *Journal of Language, Identity & Education, 18*, 377–388. https://doi.org/10.1080/1534845 8.2019.1674149

Romaine, S. (1988). *Pidgin and creole languages*. Longman.

Sáez, E. M. (2018). Generation MFA: Neoliberalism and the shifting cultural capital of US Latinx writers. *Latino Studies, 16*(3), 361–383. https://doi.org/10.1057/s41276-018-0134-y

Skutnabb-Kangas, T. (1988). Multilingualism and the education of minority children. In T. Skutnabb-Kangas & J. Cummins (Eds.), *Minority education: From shame to struggle* (pp. 9–44). Multilingual Matters. https://doi.org/10.1075/lplp.14.3.15dan

Skutnabb-Kangas, T., & Phillipson, R. (1989). 'Mother tongue': The theoretical and sociopolitical construction of a concept. In U. Ammon (Ed.), *Status and function of languages and language varieties* (pp. 450–477). De Gruyter.

Statistics Canada. (2020, November 25). *International students accounted for all of the growth in postsecondary enrolments in 2018/2019*. https://www150.statcan.gc.ca/n1/daily-quotidien/201125/dq201125e-eng.htm. Accessed 14 Nov 2022.

Transparency International. (2019, July 11). *Global corruption barometer Africa 2019: Citizens' views and experiences of corruption*. https://www.transparency.org/en/publications/gcb-africa-2019%20/. Accessed 17 Dec 2022.

Transparency International. (2021, January 28). *CPI: Sub-Saharan Africa*. https://www.transparency.org/en/news/cpi-2020-sub-saharan-africa%20/. Accessed 17 Dec 2022.

Xu, X. (2022). Epistemic diversity and cross-cultural comparative research: Ontology, challenges, and outcomes. *Globalisation, Societies and Education, 20*(1), 36–48. https://doi.org/10.108 0/14767724.2021.1932438

Vaish, V. (2008). Mother tongues, English, and religion in Singapore. *World Englishes, 27*(3/4), 450–464. https://doi.org/10.1111/j.1467-971X.2008.00579.x

Weatherall, R. & Ahuja, S. (2021). Learning as moments of friction and opportunity: An autoethnography of ECR identities in queer time. *Management Learning, 52*(4), 404–423. https://doi.org/10.1177/1350507620970335

Whitfield, K. (2019, Oct 9). *Queen snub: How one man's furious tirade against the Queen landed him a punch in the face*. https://www.express.co.uk/news/royal/1188497/Queen-Elizabeth-II-news-Lord-Altrincham-the-crown-royal-history-news. Accessed 17 Dec 2022.

World Population Review. (2022). *Human development index by country 2022*. https://worldpopulationreview.com/country-rankings/hdi-by-country. Accessed 17 Dec 2022.

Rosalind Pritchard is Emeritus Professor of Education and Senior Distinguished Research Fellow at Ulster University, where she was Head of the School of Education and Coordinator of Research. Her research interests include higher education and TESOL (especially cross-cultural adaptation and teaching strategies). She is a member of the British Academy of Social Sciences, an Honorary Member of the British Association for International and Comparative Education, Secretary of the European Association for Institutional Research and a Member of the Royal Irish Academy, of which membership is considered the highest academic honour in Ireland. She has held grants from the Leverhulme Trust, the Economic and Social Research Council, the UK Council for International Education, the German Academic Exchange Service and the Higher Education Innovation Fund. Email: R.Pritchard@ulster.ac.uk

Ahmed Sahlane (PhD, University of Ulster, Belfast) is Senior Lecturer in English at University of Jeddah (English Language Institute). He coordinated several EAP/ESP programs at Saudi universities, where he served in a variety of leadership roles such as business English program academic advisor and curriculum designer. He has taught English at all levels (K-12 and tertiary) in Morocco, Oman, Saudi Arabia, and Canada. He was the winner of Top Gun Master Teacher's Award, CDIS, Burnaby, Canada, 2001. His publications focus on the critical analysis of mediated political discourse from the perspective of argumentation theory and critical linguistics. He has published several articles and book chapters about the coverage of the 2003 Iraq War in Western opinion-editorial press. Sahlane's current research interests revolve around the rhetorics of populist discourse and media (mis)representation of cultural otherness. His research interests also include intersectionality and decoloniality studies, social semiotics, and critical pedagogy. Email: asahlan1@uj.edu.sa

Index